Baseball's War Roster

Dedicated to William Andrew Potter (1919–2005)
United States Army Stock Record Clerk
Served in England and France
Discharged at Jefferson Barracks
Rank: Staff Sergeant

Baseball's War Roster

*A Biographical Dictionary
of Major and Negro League Players
Who Served, 1861 to the Present*

BRETT KISER

McFarland & Company, Inc., Publishers
Jefferson, North Carolina, and London

LIBRARY OF CONGRESS CATALOGUING-IN-PUBLICATION DATA

Kiser, Brett.
Baseball's war roster : a biographical dictionary of Major
and Negro League players who served, 1861 to the present / Brett Kiser.
    p.   cm.

Includes bibliographical references and index.

ISBN 978-0-7864-6679-5
softcover : 50# alkaline paper ∞

1. Baseball players — United States — Biography — Dictionaries.
2. African American baseball players — Biography — Dictionaries.
3. Baseball — United States — History — Dictionaries.
4. Negro leagues — History — Dictionaries.
5. United States — Armed Forces — Sports — History.
I. Title.
GV865.A1K54 2012   796.3570922—dc23   [B]   2011043073

BRITISH LIBRARY CATALOGUING DATA ARE AVAILABLE

© 2012 Brett Kiser. All rights reserved

*No part of this book may be reproduced or transmitted in any form
or by any means, electronic or mechanical, including photocopying
or recording, or by any information storage and retrieval system,
without permission in writing from the publisher.*

Front cover: The Company A, 25th Infantry baseball team
(Fort Huachuca Museum); background © 2011 Shutterstock

Manufactured in the United States of America

*McFarland & Company, Inc., Publishers
Box 611, Jefferson, North Carolina 28640
www.mcfarlandpub.com*

Table of Contents

Acknowledgments vi
Introduction 1

Civil War — Spanish-American War 3
World War I 12
World War II 60
Korean War — Vietnam War 218
Calling on Cooperstown 262

Appendix 267
Bibliography 269
Index 271

Acknowledgments

This volume is the result of research conducted by the author, but many people have contributed to the completion of this work. I would like to thank the former ballplayers who lent me their time, as I thoroughly enjoyed interviewing them all. Their willingness to assist me in this endeavor made composing this volume an enjoyable experience.

I would also like to thank the family members of former ballplayers who helped me along the way. Louise Robinson Johnson, widow of Yankees third baseman Billy Johnson, I thank you for sending a copy of your late husband's obituary. Leroy B. Vaughan, son of former Athletics southpaw Porter Vaughan, thank you for sending the information on your father. Judy Travis, niece-in-law of the legendary Senators shortstop Cecil Travis, thank you for sending the printouts on my favorite ballplayer. Cyndie Poole, relative of former Athletics outfielder Ray Poole, thank you for the information on Mr. Poole's military tenure. Aletha Bartley, wife of Boyd Bartley, thank you for relaying your husband's stories. Eileen Fodge, widow of pitcher Gene Fodge, thank you for the information on your husband.

And thanks to Rita Savage, wife of palmball artist Bob Savage, for opening up your home to a weary traveler.

I would also like to thank Lloyd Hittle, Frank Saucier and Steve Nagy for sending me printouts of their Baseball and military careers. The team of librarians at the Baseball Hall of Fame in Cooperstown, New York—I applaud you for your professionalism and assistance. Professor Dana Andrews, thanks for your guidance and for helping me conquer—and I use the term loosely—that vile monster we all know as *Microsoft Word*. Professor "Just Call Me Bill" Church, I thank you for your assistance as well.

I'd like to mention my parents Bill and Barbara Kiser and my brothers Giles and Daniel Kiser. Their support, as well as that of my grandparents James and Dolly Kiser, made this book possible. Pursuing a daunting task—which this volume assuredly was—is made easier by the unwavering support of the people you can trust. Finally, William Andrew Potter, my departed grandfather, a true prince among men—this is for you.

Introduction

As a child, I remember scanning the reverse side of a reprint baseball card of St. Louis Cardinals great Stan Musial, and I noticed that an entire season's worth of stats were missing. Even at that young age — I must have been eight or nine — I was fascinated by batting averages, bases on balls and stolen bases, but these numbers were absent on Musial's card for the 1945 season. In the place of the numerical line where Stan the Man's RBI and slugging average totals should have been was the phrase "military service." I showed the card to my father and asked him why Musial had to miss time to the military while the players I admired then — George Brett, Tony Gwynn, Nolan Ryan and Glenn Davis — were able to play uninterrupted. That's when I learned of the Second World War and that a man's status as a baseball great could not keep him from serving his country.

In the spring of 2006, shortly after I had lost my grandfather, a World War II veteran, I thought of a way to honor his memory. I had always had an obsession for baseball and a passion for writing, so I thought the best way to honor him would be to undertake the endeavor to write this book. My intentions were to retell the stories of military service of men from my grandfather's generation who left the game of baseball to serve their country in the 1940s. However, since many such volumes on the topic already exist, I expanded the scope of my work to include all players, regardless of the military campaign. As a result, within these pages one can read about 1800s pitcher George Zettlein, who served aboard a ship during the Civil War. Arlington Pond, the old Baltimore Orioles pitcher, who fought in the Spanish-American War, is listed herein as well. World War I, the battle that claimed the life of infielder Eddie Grant, is not neglected, and neither are men like J.W. Porter and Darrel Chaney, who served during the Korean War and the Vietnam War, respectively.

This volume lists every known former major league and Negro League player who served in any war that America was engaged in. Displayed in chronological order, the first chapter combines the Civil War and the Spanish-American War since the list of athletes who fought in those campaigns is quite sparse. The two World Wars, where numerous players were inducted into service, have players listed in alphabetical order. If you are looking for Ty Cobb's war record, peruse the section on World War I and locate those players with the last name that begin with the letter "C," and the Georgia Peach shall be listed there. In the same fashion as the Civil War and the Spanish-American War, the Korean War is combined with the Vietnam War. Former Orioles center fielder Al Bumbry, who fought in Vietnam, will be found in this section as well as former Browns slugger Dick Kokos, who served during the Korean War.

There are a handful of players, such as Ted Williams and Charlie Gorin, who served in multiple wars. For these men, there are entries in both sections. Gorin, like many players before and after him, served during the Second World War before he made his major league debut and missed action at the highest level to the Korean War. As his case demonstrates, the inclusion criteria of this volume is expansive; whether a player served before, during or after his major league career, he is listed in these pages.

Within these pages you can also find entries on former Negro League players who, although segregated by law, served in the military just like their white counterparts. The great Cannonball Dick Redding, who blazed his fastball during the Dead Ball Era, can be found within the chapter on World War I. During the Second World War, such notables as Kansas City Monarchs first baseman Buck O'Neil and Hall of Famers Leon Day and Monte Irvin served in the armed forces. Although statistics are sparse concerning the Negro Leagues, with the help of SABR historian Larry Lester, an extensive list of each player's former teams has been annotated in place of the statistical line found for major league players.

While gathering information for this volume, newspaper archives were the greatest source of information, and they make up the bulk of my references. However, the most rewarding method of gathering information came from direct sources. While working on this book, I interviewed a number of former ballplayers who were gracious enough to lend me their time. As a young writer preparing for my first interview, I was nervous despite the fact that the question-and-answer session was to be conducted over the phone. My initial interview was former Washington Senators third baseman Hillis Layne, and his warm, cordial persona quickly quelled my nervousness and put me at ease for the remainder of my interviews. I thoroughly enjoyed every moment that I spoke with the former ballplayers listed in the appendix, as their stories were the highlight of my work.

The history of athletes fighting in war is an interesting research topic. Although I have covered major league baseball players who served in various military conflicts, there are many more athletes, to include minor league baseball players, who served their country during time of war that are not mentioned within these pages. There are several entries for the Civil War in this volume, but the game wasn't organized at the time — baseball became a business in 1871 with the advent of the National Association. Therefore, many amateurs who played the game before baseball became a thriving enterprise have been lost to time. Any research that unearths new details about baseball during the Civil War is exciting as well as informative. Also, there have been some minor league players, such as Schuyler Williamson, Jeff Stockton and Jonathan Johnston, who left the game to serve their country in Iraq. Although these three men didn't reach the majors, they carry on the tradition of baseball fighting men that made players like Bob Feller and Ted Williams American heroes.

In closing, I would like to salute all the men in these pages for their service to their country. It seems today, in these most obtuse of times, that patriotism is passé, a sentiment regarded for older generations. Although words change meaning over time, those who stand for their country, who fight for its liberty and are willing to lay down their life so others can live in freedom, are, and shall forever be, *heroes* in the eyes of those who matter.

Civil War and Spanish-American War

Frank Erwin "Ham" Allen, *Outfield/Shortstop*

Allen played only one year of Organized Baseball, with the Middletown Mansfields in 1872. An outfielder, Ham could also fill-in on the left side of the infield. Allen was an army veteran of the Civil War. Born in Connecticut, Allen joined the 36th Massachusetts Infantry, Company F for service during the war. The 36th was actively engaged in battles at Fredericksburg and Lexington, Kentucky. They marched to Vicksburg and gained ground deep into the South when they fought at Jackson, Mississippi. War records show that Ham's unit lost six officers and more than one hundred enlisted men during the battle.

G	R	H	2B	3B	HR	RBI	BB	SO	SB	AVG	Slug
17	9	19	3	0	0	11	0	1	0	.271	.314

Douglas L. Allison, *Catcher*

One of baseball's greatest catchers after the Civil War, Allison was listed in an article in the *Boston Daily Globe* as "the star catcher of the period." Doug's days in baseball were quite nomadic as he rarely stayed with one team for longer than a season; the longest tenure he spent with any given team came with the Hartford Dark Blues. But he had a reputation for smart, heady play that served him well wherever he played. After his days in baseball he worked in a government print office and later "kept a chair warm" at the National Museum in Boston.

Doug, whose brother, Art, was also a pro player, was distinguished on the diamond by his appearance. In an era when players like Harry Wright kept full beards, Allison was described as "clean shaven as a priest" in an article printed in the *Reno Evening Gazette*. Before Doug played for the Dark Blues, he served briefly in the Civil War, attached to a 100-day unit that didn't see any combat. There were stories that circulated about Allison's poor hearing, reportedly caused by battlefield noise. A story printed in the *Boston Daily Globe* claimed that Doug was stationed at Fort Sumter, but his unit, the 192nd Pennsylvania Infantry, was not engaged in this skirmish. The story is probably inaccurate but it is likely, whether via training exercises or some other form of wartime preparation, Allison suffered damage to his hearing.

G	R	H	2B	3B	HR	RBI	BB	SO	SB	AVG	Slug
318	236	382	44	10	2	139	24	44	5	.271	.321

David Tildon Altizer, *Utilityman*

"Daredevil Dave" Altizer enlisted in the military before he touched a baseball. He grew up in Pike County, Illinois, and left his hometown to enlist in the army after completing school. Altizer hadn't been in khaki long when he was first shipped out. The Illinoisan spent much of his military tenure overseas, where he was introduced to the game of baseball. Although the game was America's pastime, Altizer wasn't accustomed to baseball until army chums taught him how to play. He quickly established himself as a service star. But it wasn't all baseball and barracks for Daredevil Dave in the army. While serving in the Far East, Altizer took part in the Boxer Rebellion (the only known professional baseball player to serve in the campaign) and was a member of the forces that advanced on Yaku and Tien-Psin. His detachment was assigned to the siege of Peking. However, it was in the Philippines where Altizer became a baseball star. On the islands, Altizer played in a service league while attached to H Battery of the 6th Artillery.

When Daredevil Dave was mustered out of the military, he took his newfound talents for the game of baseball to the professional ranks. He established himself as a valuable commodity on the diamond, given his versatility and speed. His first major league trial came with Jake Stahl's Washington Senators in 1906 and he led American League shortstops in stolen bases. The following year, new skipper Joe Cantillon took full advantage of Dave's versatility, employing him at short, first base and the outfield. Altizer finished his major league career with the 1911 Reds.

G	R	H	2B	3B	HR	RBI	BB	SO	SB	AVG	Slug
514	204	433	36	21	4	116	140	n/a	119	.250	.302

Henry C. Austin, *Outfield*

Little is known about Austin, who had a brief career in baseball. During the Civil War, he enlisted in the 38th New York Volunteer Infantry and served under the command of Captain Charles E. Barbour in Company I. Barbour led his troops in several battles, the most notable being Bull Run, where Austin was engaged in the war.

G	R	H	2B	3B	HR	RBI	BB	SO	SB	AVG	Slug
23	10	25	3	3	0	11	0	5	1	.248	.337

Alfred L. Barker, *Outfield*

Barker's career in Organized Baseball was minuscule, but he was a commissioned officer during the Civil War. Alfred enlisted in the spring of 1861 but transferred to a new regiment, the 74th Illinois Infantry, in the fall of 1862. A 2nd Lieutenant with the 74th, Barker led troops in pursuit of Bragg into the Kentucky countryside and was engaged in battle at Perryville. From there they marched onward and crossed into Tennessee where they saw combat action at both Nashville and Murfreesboro. One of the last campaigns Lt. Barker was engaged in during the war was a battle at Stone's River.

G	R	H	2B	3B	HR	RBI	BB	SO	SB	AVG	Slug
1	0	1	0	0	0	2	1	0	0	.250	.250

Nathan Berkenstock, *Outfield*

When baseball was organized in 1871, Berkenstock was already a grand old man of the game. His days as a useful player were well behind him, but he was used in one contest during that opening year with the Philadelphia Athletics. At the age of 40, Nate was easily the oldest player in baseball's first year of operation as an organized circuit. Like his major league career, Berkenstock's military tenure was brief. He served for less than a month in a Pennsylvanian infantry regiment.

G	R	H	2B	3B	HR	RBI	BB	SO	SB	AVG	Slug
1	0	0	0	0	0	0	0	0	0	.000	.000

Thomas Haney Berry, *Outfield*

Berry enjoyed a blink-and-you-missed-it career in major league baseball. Employed in one game with the Philadelphia Athletics in 1871, Berry had a little longer stint in the military during the Civil War. A commissioned officer in the Pennsylvania volunteer infantry, Lieutenant Berry served with the 197th Pennsylvania Infantry, Company A. One of the many 100-day regiments activated in the heart of the war, the 197th was nicknamed the "Third Coal Exchange" regiment and was organized at Camp Cadwalader under Colonel John R. Haslett. Under Colonel Haslett, Lieutenant Berry's assignment was to guard a POW camp at Rock Island, Illinois.

G	R	H	2B	3B	HR	RBI	BB	SO	SB	AVG	Slug
1	0	1	0	0	0	0	0	0	0	.250	.250

Harry W. Berthrong, *Outfield*

Few people have led a fuller, more interesting life than Harry Berthrong. A ballplayer, soldier, artist and elbow-rubber of the elite, Berthrong lived life to the fullest. Some of the stories concerning his life seem more like folklore than fact—such as his chance meeting with Abraham Lincoln—but for all we know the accounts are true. A professional baseball player one year for the Washington Olympics, Harry had a stint with the army during the Civil War that came before his ball diamond days.

During the Civil War Berthrong joined the 140th New York Volunteer Infantry regiment, Company E, and served in the frontlines in battle. He saw more action on battlefields when he was attached to the 5th Corps Army of the Potomac. He was engaged in every battle that outfit fought until he was mustered out at the end of the war on July 12, 1865. In between battles, Harry had a chance encounter with an American president that spurred him on to a unique career in his later years.

As the story goes, Harry was traveling home on furlough when he stopped in Washington, D.C. He sat down on the grass and began to sketch a drawing of the White House when none other than Abraham Lincoln ventured by and spoke to him. Since Berthrong was wearing his soldier's uniform, Lincoln took a keen interest in what the young soldier was doing. When he spotted the sketch Berthrong was working on, Lincoln is supposed to have been in awe of the work and gave Harry an extra week of leave time. Grateful, Harry gave the sketch to the president as a souvenir. Given Lincoln's admiration for his work, Harry became a famous portrait artist for politicians that worked in Washington after his baseball days.

G	R	H	2B	3B	HR	RBI	BB	SO	SB	AVG	Slug
17	17	17	1	1	0	8	4	2	3	.233	.274

Oscar Bielaski, *Outfield*

A decent outfielder who toiled for five years after baseball became organized in 1871, Bielaski played for a different club each year. Before he embarked on his baseball career, young Oscar did a little story-telling during the Civil War. Like many eager young boys during the war, Oscar enlisted in the military when he had yet to come of age. Bielaski was discharged a month after his enlistment when his actual age was learned. The outfielder did, however, serve briefly during the Civil War and later enlisted in the armed forces during peacetime.

G	R	H	2B	3B	HR	RBI	BB	SO	SB	AVG	Slug
174	117	179	7	2	0	52	10	18	9	.240	.255

David Solomon Birdsall, *Outfield*

Birdsall was an outfielder for the Boston Red Stockings in the game's early years. A nifty flychaser, Dave was also used occasionally behind the dish when needed. Regarded as a swell chap with a fondness for the nightlife, Birdsall was a billiard parlor hound who built quite a reputation as a shark around Boston. But before "The Bird" caught his first flyball with the Red Stockings, he tried to avoid catching bullets during the Civil War.

Birdsall served with the 87th New York Volunteer Infantry, Company C, during the war. Under the command of Colonel Stephen A. Dodge, the 87th was engaged in some heavy fighting. Birdsall's unit fought in battles at Yorktown and Williamsburg before they took part in one of their bloodiest conflicts. Engaged in battle with Southern troops at Fair Oaks, 76 men from Birdsall's regiment were killed in action. Mustered out in 1865, Dave made his way to baseball and played under Hall of Fame pioneer Harry Wright.

G	R	H	2B	3B	HR	RBI	BB	SO	SB	AVG	Slug
48	66	63	6	3	0	39	7	4	7	.264	.314

George Gates Bristow, *Outfield*

Little was known about the enigmatic George Bristow until researcher Peter Morris uncovered some details about his life and shared them with the Society of American Baseball Research in an essay titled "George Bristow Found." It is believed that George Bristow was an alias of George Howlett, who used the false moniker while playing one season with the old Cleveland Spiders. The *Cleveland Plain Dealer* listed Bristow as enlisted in the army with the 1st Arkansas Infantry during the Spanish-American War.

G	R	H	2B	3B	HR	RBI	BB	SO	SB	AVG	Slug
3	0	1	1	0	0	0	0	n/a	0	.125	.250

Benjamin Thomas Caffyn, *Outfield*

Caffyn served in both the Spanish-American War and the First World War. Still a teenager during the Spanish-American War, Caffyn took to baseball after his discharge. He was a star in the minor leagues, and a writer for the *Des Moines Daily News* claimed Ben was "the best outfielder the Western League ever had." However, the major leagues had its share of stars, too, and Caffyn, who was called up to Cleveland in 1906, served as a replacement for .300 hitters Elmer Flick and Bunk Congalton and the swift Harry Bay. The 1906 season was Caffyn's only action in the majors.

G	R	H	2B	3B	HR	RBI	BB	SO	SB	AVG	Slug
30	16	20	4	0	0	3	12	n/a	2	.194	.233

Thomas John Carey, *Shortstop*

One of early baseball's best shortstops, Carey spent three years with the Hartford Dark Blues. Like many players of the era, he had a nomadic career. Tom once toured the country with Cap Anson on a baseball showcase to build support for America's great game. Although Carey had a life in the military both during and after the Civil War, there appear to be some discrepancies that need to be cleared up. Lying about one's age in the 1800s was an easier affair than it is today, but a person has to look the part. Oscar Bielaski lied about his age to enlist during the Civil War and was accepted, but not too long after his real age was discovered he was issued his walking papers. Tom Carey is supposed to have enlisted in the 17th New York Infantry during the Civil War, but this seems highly unlikely. The 17th wasn't engaged in battle for the duration of the war. This regiment was mustered out on June 2, 1863, when Tom would have been all of 16 years of age — if his birth records are accurate. Although there is a likelihood that Carey served with this regiment while under age, it seems more probable that Tom joined soldiers formerly of the 17th Infantry that caught on with another regiment. In fact, many of the 17th Infantry soldiers that stayed on during the war joined the 146th New York Volunteers, and this regiment, not the 17th, is perhaps the one that Carey served in.

However, after the war, Carey traveled out west and soldiered in California during peacetime. He was stationed at Presidio, where he is buried, and also played ball there. But the itch to get back and face top-grade competition got to Carey, and he returned to the East and played for the Dark Blues a few seasons, as well as with other clubs. After he was done as a player, Carey returned to California and fell ill. At the time of his death, he was indigent and nearly blind.

G	R	H	2B	3B	HR	RBI	BB	SO	SB	AVG	Slug
536	405	646	77	14	5		270	16	61	27	.270	.320

Edmund C. Clark, *Pitcher*

One of a handful of former major leaguers buried at Arlington National Cemetery, Ed Clark had two brief cups of coffee at the game's top level. He played with the Athletics in 1886 and the Columbus Solons in 1891. The hurler joined the military after his playing days — deserting his wife and children to enlist — and served with the 18th Infantry during the Spanish-American War.

W	L	PCT	G	GS	CG	IP	H	BB	SO	SHO	ERA
0	1	.000	2	1	1	10	12	2	3	0	5.40

Pierce Devon "Percy" Coleman, *Pitcher*

Coleman spent two rocky seasons in the major leagues, coughing up 121 base hits in only 75 innings of work. He pitched for the 1897 Cardinals and briefly for the 1898 Reds before he enlisted in the military during the Spanish-American War. Coleman's military tenure was shorter in duration than his major league career. He returned to the diamond in 1899 and was regarded as the ace of the minor league San Antonio Bronchos mound crew.

W	L	PCT	G	GS	CG	IP	H	BB	SO	SHO	ERA
1	3	.250	14	6	4	75	121	36	12	0	6.69

Dennis H. Coughlin, *Outfield*

Among the men who played baseball after the game was organized in 1871, Coughlin, perhaps, had the most interesting war record. Regarded as the only future major league ballplayer wounded in action during the Civil War, Coughlin's professional baseball career wasn't substantial: he played one year as a utilityman for the Washington Nationals. Although his baseball career was light, Coughlin's military tenure was marked by battles.

Dennis served in the 140th New York Infantry Regiment, the same outfit as Harry Berthrong, another future major leaguer, in Company E. He enlisted as a private but quickly rose in rank. By the time he was discharged, Coughlin had his sergeant's stripes. But there were many battles between the time Private Coughlin became honorably discharged Sergeant Coughlin.

The 140th New York Infantry Regiment fought at Gettysburg where they lost Colonel Patrick O'Rorke. During the famous battle, 37 men of the regiment were killed alongside the colonel. Despite their losses, the 140th were lauded for their fierce fighting abilities and were distinguished by their French uniforms, called Zouaves, which they wore in campaigns. The regiment would then suffer heavy losses at the Wilderness and Cold Harbor, and Coughlin is to have been wounded in battle at Petersburg. But the 140th wasn't done. They would fight for the duration at such locales as Mine Run, Rappahannock Station, White Oak Swamp and Hatcher's Run. When the fighting finally ended, Sergeant Coughlin was discharged and later played baseball. When he died, he was buried at Arlington National Cemetery.

G	R	H	2B	3B	HR	RBI	BB	SO	SB	AVG	Slug
8	5	11	1	0	0	7	0	0	0	.297	.324

William H. Craver, *Second Base*

Craver was one of the most notorious stars of baseball's early days. Long before the Chicago White Sox accepted money to throw the 1919 World Series, gamblers got to Craver and some of his teammates to alter the outcome of a few contests. Craver and teammates George Hall, Al Nichols and staff ace Jim Devlin lined their pockets with dirty money in order to make gamblers a dishonest dollar or two. Craver and his chums were found out when they started dressing flashy with diamond stickpins and expensive rings. The four ballplayers were kicked out of the league and blacklisted.

Craver, a star middle infielder for the Baltimore Canaries, served in the artillery during the Civil War. After he turned eighteen, Bill joined the 13th New York Heavy Artillery Regiment under the command of Colonel Howard. The unit was activated at Riker's Island and was then attached to the Army of the James. Craver would serve with this outfit for the duration until he was mustered out in the summer of 1865. He would go on to some acclaim in baseball before his crooked dealings with gamblers. As a blacklisted, disgraced former ballplayer that couldn't be trusted, Craver's next profession was in the police ranks.

G	R	H	2B	3B	HR	RBI	BB	SO	SB	AVG	Slug
339	330	445	63	33	2	228	27	34	40	.290	.377

Abner Doubleday, *Not Applicable*

Although it is widely accepted that Abner Doubleday had little if anything to do with the advent of baseball, it's only fitting, as a historical note, to include him in these pages. For many years it was accepted that Doubleday invented the game at Cooperstown, New York, but later research proved that the game evolved on its own before men like Harry Wright and Alexander Joy Cartwright began to draft actual rules. Abner Doubleday was simply more of that great old American folklore, but he was a real man and a military hero to boot.

Doubleday graduated from West Point some twenty years before the Civil War. He gained acclaim as an officer in the Civil War but the military professional also served in various other campaigns, such as the Indian Wars and conflicts with Mexico. During the Civil War, the artillery officer was stationed at Fort Sumter when it was attacked and he is reputed to have fired the first blast in defense of the fort. By that time Abner Doubleday was a Brigadier General who served with the 2nd Brigade, 1st Division of the Third Corps. He led his men in battle at Antietam, Fredericksburg and Gettysburg.

Non-playing historical figure

Jacob Dixon Doyle, *Shortstop/Second Base*

Sometimes listed as "Joe" Doyle, Jacob Dixon Doyle is not to be confused with Deadball Era pitcher Slow Joe Doyle. The infielder played in the second year after baseball was organized, in 1872, with the Washington Nationals. He was only sixteen years old at the time and the second youngest player in the circuit. That one season with Washington was the extent of his baseball career. Doyle eventually joined the navy and made the military his career.

After his one season with the Nationals, Doyle entered the military and was a seasoned serviceman by the time the Spanish-American War broke out. Although just a reserve in baseball, Doyle was a high-ranking official in the navy. He ascended to the rank of Lieutenant Commander, and when America entered the fighting during World War I, Doyle rejoined the navy when he was creeping up on senior citizen status. Doyle died in 1941, just a few months before the Japanese bombed Pearl Harbor.

G	R	H	2B	3B	HR	RBI	BB	SO	SB	AVG	Slug
9	6	11	1	0	0	9	0	0	0	.268	.293

Washington Fayette Fulmer, *Outfield*

Although his kid brother, Chick, had a much more distinguished career in baseball, Fulmer was active during the Civil War. He served with the 71st Pennsylvania Infantry Regiment. During the early years of his enlistment, Wash wasn't engaged in fighting but in manual labor. His unit served at the south bank of the Potomac where they were engaged in building fortifications. Afterwards, his unit took part in combat missions and was active at the advance on Munson's Hill. With his stint in the military over at the end of the war, Fulmer tried his hand at baseball. He played one game in the majors with the 1875 Brooklyn Atlantics, and failed to achieve the fame of his brother on the diamond. Chick Fulmer, it must be noted, claimed to have been a drummer boy during the war, but there is little evidence to support this claim.

G	R	H	2B	3B	HR	RBI	BB	SO	SB	AVG	Slug
1	1	2	0	0	0	1	0	0	0	.500	.500

Charles R. Gessner, *Pitcher*

Charlie Gessner's major league tenure consisted of one complete-game start with his hometown Philadelphia Athletics in 1886. His days in the minors were more fruitful. While playing ball in Iowa, Charlie met and fell in love with Annie Bremer of Davenport; the two were married before his stint in the armed forces during the Spanish-American War.

W	L	PCT	G	GS	CG	IP	H	BB	SO	SHO	ERA
0	1	.000	1	1	1	8	13	5	0	0	9.00

John A. Greenig, *Pitcher*

Greenig's major league career consisted of one lackluster start with the 1888 Washington Nationals when he was in his forties. John served in the Indiana Volunteer Infantry's 132nd Regiment for 100 days during the Civil War.

W	L	PCT	G	GS	CG	IP	H	BB	SO	SHO	ERA
0	1	.000	1	1	1	9	17	4	2	0	11.00

John Thomas Grimes, *Pitcher*

When perusing the baseball record books, the name John Grimes will jump off the page. His offerings had a tendency to jump and strike players as well. Grimes set a record with the 1897 Cardinals when he hit six batters in a nine-inning contest — his claim to fame. Although Grimes struggled in his short major league stint, his service in Uncle Sam's khaki was more controlled. After his time with the Redbirds, Grimes joined the army and was commissioned an officer. During the Spanish-American War, Grimes wasn't an erratic hurler but Captain Grimes.

Grimes spent more than thirty years in the army and was a participant in the Spanish-American War, the Sioux Indian Campaign and World War I. The old military officer lived a long, fruitful life, dying in his mid 90s.

W	L	PCT	G	GS	CG	IP	H	BB	SO	SHO	ERA
0	2	.000	3	1	1	20	24	8	4	0	5.95

Winfield Scott Hastings, *Catcher*

A catcher/outfielder during his baseball days, Hastings played professional ball during the first years of its organized stature. Nomadic as a player, Hastings was also quite nomadic as an individual. After his playing days, Scott moved to the West Coast and worked for the Electric Light Company in California. A veteran of the Civil War, Hastings served in one of the many 100-day units during the middle of the war. He was attached to the 145th Illinois Infantry and served under the command of Captain Edward C. Dew.

G	R	H	2B	3B	HR	RBI	BB	SO	SB	AVG	Slug
294	264	371	44	8	0	139	31	43	43	.279	.325

Otto C. Hess, *Pitcher*

The only major leaguer to have been born in Switzerland, Otto Hess tossed fastballs and curves for Uncle Sam before he ever threw one in the big leagues. During the Spanish-American War, Hess saw action on the Philippine Islands and became versed in a few choice phrases in both Filipino and Spanish. When the Cleveland Indians acquired Otto's services for the 1902 season, veteran Strawberry Bill Bernhard had some advice for the young Hess. A story in the *San Antonio Gazette* stated, "Otto Hess says that he picked up quite a few Spanish and Filipino expressions while fighting for Uncle Sam in the islands, and Bill Bernhard advises him to use a few this summer when the umpires and he do not agree."

Otto Hess became a solid southpaw in the majors, first with Cleveland and later with the Boston Braves. He was a 20-game winner for Cleveland in 1906, but a leg injury kept him out of action for pieces of 1907 and 1908. He was a member of George Stallings' Miracle Braves in 1914 that swept the highly favored Athletics of Connie Mack in the World Series. His major league career ended in 1915, but when Uncle Sam needed him in 1918, Hess answered the called and served during World War I.

W	L	PCT	G	GS	CG	IP	H	BB	SO	SHO	ERA
71	88	.447	198	165	129	1,418	1,355	448	580	18	2.98

Nathan Woodhull Hicks, *Catcher*

One of baseball's first stars, Hicks was a top-flight catcher in the game's early years. Regarded as revolutionizing the art of catching, as far as positioning is concerned, Hicks took a beating behind the dish that cemented his status as a tough ballplayer. An article in the *New York Times* read, "He caught behind the bat close under the batsman and forced the other old line catchers to follow his example." Catching in baseball's early days was a chore because pitchers were closer than the sixty feet, six inches from the plate they are today. And the gear, or lack thereof, was crude, requiring only the toughest of the tough to catch.

Nat Hicks is regarded by several sources as having served in the Civil War, but there hasn't been any definite proof of his tenure. After his death, there were pseudo obituaries that made reference to tenure in the Civil War but it is unclear what regiment Hicks served in. After the war, however, he became a catching sensation and later an umpire in the 1880s. His status as one of the toughest men to play baseball was secure when he was remembered in a *Washington Post* article that spotlighted his days in early baseball. The article described Hicks after a game, which read, "His face was a bleeding mass as a result of being hit by foul tips. His fingers were split and broken, but he never faltered and caught game after game."

G	R	H	2B	3B	HR	RBI	BB	SO	SB	AVG	Slug
257	172	301	35	6	1	116	25	23	9	.264	.307

Nathan W. Jewett, *Catcher*

Jewett had a brief career in the major leagues. In 1872, he caught two games for the Brooklyn Eckfords—the extent of his professional service. During the Civil War, Nat served in the same Pennsylvania infantry regiment as Washington Fulmer. They spent some time engaged in building fortifications along the banks of the Potomac.

G	R	H	2B	3B	HR	RBI	BB	SO	SB	AVG	Slug
2	1	1	0	0	0	0	0	0	0	.125	.125

Caleb Clark Johnson, *Second Base/Outfield*

Johnson, who had a brief major league career, enlisted in the Illinois Volunteer Infantry during the Civil War. Initially assigned to the 140th Infantry Regiment, a 100-day outfit, Caleb joined the 69th Infantry after the 140th was mustered out of service.

G	R	H	2B	3B	HR	RBI	BB	SO	SB	AVG	Slug
16	10	15	1	0	0	7	0	1	0	.224	.239

Clarence Veasey "Slats" Jordan, *First Base/Outfield*

Slats Jordan may have played in two seasons at the major league level but he only appeared in one game each year. The Baltimore native played under fiery manager John McGraw for his hometown Orioles. Jordan played one game at first base in 1901 and one game in the pasture in 1902. Before his brief stint in the majors, Slats served in the armed forces during the Spanish-American War.

G	R	H	2B	3B	HR	RBI	BB	SO	SB	AVG	Slug
2	0	0	0	0	0	0	0	n/a	0	.000	.000

Joseph Leggett, *Catcher*

One of baseball's first great stars, Leggett was the top catcher in the baseball ranks before the game was organized. Famous as the battery mate of baseball's first legend, Jim Creighton, the two stars had no equal as far as pitcher/catcher tandems were concerned. Leggett was the player/captain of the old Brooklyn Excelsiors that dominated baseball before the advent of the National Association in 1871. Although Leggett was a star player during the Civil War, that didn't stop him from enlisting at the beginning of the conflict.

Leggett joined Colonel Isaac F. Quinby's 13th Regiment in 1861—the first year of the war. The 13th was ordered to Fort Corcoran where it was employed in construction work. After their manual labor duties were complete, Quinby's troops joined forces with the 3rd Brigade, 1st Division of the Army of Northeastern Virginia. Leggett's 13th was attached to the 3rd Brigade while they were active at Bull Run. But the war took a less strenuous turn for Leggett and his battle buddies when they were assigned to picket and guard duty along the Potomac banks.

They left their guard posts and reentered the fray shortly thereafter. Leggett and the 13th were engaged in the siege at Yorktown and after that campaign their forces joined that of General Pope's. Attached to Pope's fighting forces, the 13th marched into battle at Fredericksburg and sustained heavy losses. That battle was their last major conflict before they were mustered out of service. Joseph Leggett is not known to modern fans, nor his teammate, the great Jim Creighton, because they were done as players before the National Association came to life in 1871. But Leggett was a giant of his time.

Joseph Leggett's Career Stats: Incomplete

Fergus G. Malone, *Catcher*

One of the greatest players in baseball's early years, Malone was a top catcher in the game's infancy. Fergie teamed with Dick

McBride, widely regarded as the top pitcher in the nation after the death of Jim Creighton, and together they formed what the *New York Times* called the "best battery in the nation." The two men had a connection that went beyond baseball as they served in the same regiment during the Civil War.

In the war's latter years, Malone and McBride joined one of the many 100-day outfits that were activated to lend a hand to the regular soldiers. Fergy and Dick may have had it easy in the 196th Pennsylvania Infantry since their commanding officer was Dick's brother, Francis McBride. Their 100-day regiment was commanded by Captain Francis McBride and First Sergeant Theodore C. Rose. After their stint in the military, the two men returned to their famous positions on the baseball diamond and Fergy was still active in 1871 when baseball became organized.

G	R	H	2B	3B	HR	RBI	BB	SO	SB	AVG	Slug
220	200	288	32	7	1	157	32	19	21	.274	.320

Alphonse Case "Phonney" Martin, *Outfield/Pitcher*

A two-way player during the game's early years, Phonney Martin was equally skilled in the batter's box as he was on the pitching rubber. Martin, a Civil War veteran, wasn't one of the many ballplayers that locked on with a 100-day service outfit. Rather, Martin enlisted in the 9th New York Infantry and saw combat action across the fields of eastern America. Phonney enlisted early in the war and served under the respected Colonel Rush Hawkins at Newport News.

The 9th New York Infantry, under the command of Hawkins, were one of the few Zouaves elements in the Union Army. The Zouaves were fighting forces outfitted in French uniforms that were distinguished as the better fighting forces the North had at its disposal. Under the leadership of Colonel Hawkins, Martin and the 9th marched into battle at Roanoke and were engaged in one of their bloodiest affairs at South Mills. In the latter battle, the 9th lost 75 soldiers in action. Phonney also would be engaged in the battle at Antietam before he was mustered out of the military in 1863.

G	R	H	2B	3B	HR	RBI	BB	SO	SB	AVG	Slug
74	52	82	4	2	0	37	2	8	4	.243	.267

John Dickson "Dick" McBride, *Pitcher*

After the Civil War and before baseball became a more organized affair in 1871, Dick McBride was a well-known ballplayer. Regarded as the top pitcher in America at the time, McBride may not have had the legend of Jim Creighton but he was respected by men in the game nonetheless. He and battery mate Fergy Malone were considered the best pitcher/catcher duo in the game, and the two men joined the military during the Civil War. Dick and Fergy were able to serve in a 100-day outfit commanded by Dick's brother, Francis. After the war, the two men returned to baseball. In 1871, when baseball started as an enterprise, McBride was still handling the pitching duties but his best years were behind him. After his retirement from baseball, he worked as a postal clerk.

W	L	PCT	G	GS	CG	IP	H	BB	SO	SHO	ERA
149	78	.656	237	237	227	2,082	2,420	174	150	10	2.71

Otto W. Parisen, *Early Pioneer*

A star player before the Civil War whose career in baseball was over by the time the game was organized in 1871, Parisen saw combat during the war. Otto enlisted in the 9th New York Infantry, Company C, which was a unit attached to Colonel Rush Hawkins' forces. They initially served at Hatteras, North Carolina, before they were engaged in the battles at Roanoke and South Mills. Parisen served in these campaigns and was active when the 9th was attached to the Army of the Potomac.

The Army of the Potomac suffered heavy losses at the battle at Antietam, where 233 members of the attachment were killed in action. Shortly after that fatal battle, the 9th was mustered out of service and Parisen, unattached in the military, opted to join up with the 122nd Infantry Regiment, Company F. Under the command of Colonel Horace H. Walpole, Parisen and his new 122nd battle buddies saw combat action at Gettysburg where they fought with the 12th Corps. From there, they were engaged in battles at Rappahannock Station and Mine Run before they ventured off to Johnson's Island near Lake Erie.

The heaviest fighting that the 122nd was engaged in was the deadly conflict at the Wilderness. The regiment lost 119 men who were killed in action, wounded in action or missing in action. But the regiment would regroup and march on, and they fought until the end. They were active during the Appomattox campaign and the final push at Petersburg.

Otto Parisen's Career Stats: Incomplete

William Robert Parks, *Pitcher*

Printed obituaries have stated that Parks served with the 196th Pennsylvania Infantry Regiment, but he would have been fifteen years old at the time the regiment was mustered out of the army. It's unlikely that Parks served, but young men were known to have lied about their age to enter service, and Bill could have been one of them. As a baseball player, Parks was a modest pitcher who could also play in the outfield when needed.

W	L	PCT	G	GS	CG	IP	H	BB	SO	SHO	ERA
4	8	.333	16	11	9	112	157	6	3	0	3.54

Thomas W. H. Patterson, *Outfield*

Very little is known about Thomas W. H. Patterson because there isn't any surviving birth record for the former ballplayer. Some sources list Patterson as having served in the army during the Civil War, but newspaper columns can hardly be taken as legitimate confirmation of a man's military service. Although his exact birth isn't known, it is felt that he might have been too young to have enlisted or passed himself off as of age to enlist.

G	R	H	2B	3B	HR	RBI	BB	SO	SB	AVG	Slug
57	42	52	3	0	0	22	1	2	3	.210	.222

Edwin B. Pinkham, *Third Base*

One of the few ballplayers in the game's early years who knew that an on-base percentage could be elevated by drawing a walk, Pinkham was way ahead of his time. Most batters of the game's formative years were swing-happy and had on-base percentages just a hair above their batting averages. Pinkham seemed to be the only man in the game that knew a walk had some value. His baseball career was short, perhaps because no one knew just what he was doing. During the Civil War, Ed served for a few months in the 47th New York Infantry Regiment. During his stint with the group, they were not engaged in battle but were stationed at Edisto Island.

G	R	H	2B	3B	HR	RBI	BB	SO	SB	AVG	Slug
24	27	25	5	5	1	17	18	3	5	.263	.453

Erasmus Arlington "Arlie" Pond, *Pitcher*

A unique player during the game's early days, Arlie Pond was an educated man during a period when baseball was populated with rowdy scrappers. The man from Saugus, Massachusetts, played for the club that embodied rowdyism: Ned Hanlon's Baltimore Orioles. Pond's notable teammates on the Baltimore roster were John McGraw, Dirty Jack Doyle, Hughie Jennings, Wee Willie Keeler, Joe Kelley and Steve Brodie. Their motto was simple: win by any means necessary.

While playing for the rough-and-tumble Orioles, Pond spent his leisure time away from the field in studies. The common ballplayer had the image of a hard-living, rowdy man with an aversion to books, but Erasmus Arlington Pond broke that stereotype. Arlie Pond worked diligently at his education and earned a degree in medicine while he was playing ball for Baltimore. His degree didn't come in handy on the ball diamond but proved quite beneficial after his days in the majors came to a close.

Pond left baseball and enlisted in the Army Medical Corps during the Spanish-American War. He was shipped overseas and spent his service time on the Philippine Islands. The former Oriole enjoyed the islands so much that he opted to stay there. In 1902, the *Fort Wayne News* ran an article about Arlie, which stated that he was pitching for a service ball club on the Philippine Islands. But baseball by that time was simply a leisure pursuit. Doctor Pond was in the process of establishing a leper colony on Cebu Island, part of the Visayan Islands chain in the Philippines. Arlie Pond was able to accumulate a vast wealth on the island, courtesy his medical endeavors as well as his substantial grove of coconut trees. When he died in 1930, the Associated Press ran an article that claimed, "Ex-Oriole Star Leaves Fortune in Philippines."

W	L	PCT	G	GS	CG	IP	H	BB	SO	SHO	ERA
35	19	.648	69	57	46	496	517	150	156	3	3.45

Albert G. Pratt, *Pitcher*

The former major league pitcher lived a long, fruitful life, dying just short of his 90th birthday. Proud of his military accomplishments, Pratt's dying wish was that he be buried in his Grand Army of the Republic uniform. Late in life, Pratt would often boast about being a member of the forces that pushed General Robert E. Lee to surrender. And the war records support the claims made by Pratt, who served with the famous 61st Infantry Regiment that was engaged in the final assault. Through the war, Pratt is said to have learned how to play baseball while at army camps.

Like many ballplayers, Pratt enlisted in one of the 100-day regiments but found military life to his liking. When his 100-day unit was mustered out, Pratt joined up with the 61st Infantry Regiment, Company I, and took part in the battles that outfit fought in. Pratt was with the 61st when they marched into the Shenandoah Valley and participated in the campaign in that region. From there, they encamped and fought at Cedar Creek and then took part in the final assault at Petersburg. At Petersburg, the 61st held the line at Squirrel Level Road and pushed General Lee's forces out of the region.

With General Lee on the run, Pratt's 61st stayed on his heels. They chased General Lee's rear guard, Longsreet's Corps, to Sailor's Creek, where the last shot was fired. Shortly thereafter, the surrender of General Lee at the Appomattox Court House was the final move in the battle. Al Pratt was there and witnessed the last days of the war, having chased the rebels to the very end. After his discharge, Pratt discovered a love for the game he learned in army camps and eventually worked his way through the professional ranks.

W	L	PCT	G	GS	CG	IP	H	BB	SO	SHO	ERA
12	26	.316	43	40	30	330	446	61	41	0	4.41

Robert Reach, *Shortstop*

The brother of famous ballplayer Al Reach, Bob played briefly in the professional ranks after the Civil War. He enlisted in the latter stages of the war with the 5th New York Heavy Artillery Regiment, Company B, in the spring of 1864. Commanded by Colonel Samuel Graham, Reach was in the field for about a month before the unit was ordered to Harper's Ferry.

G	R	H	2B	3B	HR	RBI	BB	SO	SB	AVG	Slug
3	2	3	0	0	0	0	0	0	0	.231	.231

George Henry "Admiral" Schlei, *Catcher*

Nicknames can lead people astray. Although George Schlei served in the military during the Spanish-American War, he was not an admiral. His alias was given to him during his baseball days because there was a famous Spanish-American war hero, Admiral Schley, whose name sounded like that of the backstop. The catcher got a late start in the majors thanks to his military hitch and was a 26-year-old rookie for the 1904 Reds. A catcher who also caught for John McGraw's Giants, Admiral Schlei was an astute game-caller and judge of talent. Of the fabled Chicago Cubs in-field of Steinfeldt, Tinker, Evers and Chance, Schlei once quipped, "Now there's an infield that has about eight brains and sixteen hands."

G	R	H	2B	3B	HR	RBI	BB	SO	SB	AVG	Slug
636	195	455	52	21	6	209	172	n/a	38	.237	.296

William E. Stearns, *Pitcher*

Bill Stearns is best known as the youngest player in the league during the National Association's first year of operation. The righthander pitched a few years at the major league level but had a nomadic career — he was with a different club every season. Stearns played for some of the most hapless teams during baseball's early years and his abysmal .169 career winning percentage will attest to that. Bill Stearns was already in his 40s when he served during the Spanish-American War. He died during the year of the war, but not from wounds sustained in combat action. Some sources also list Stearns as having served in the Civil War, but he had yet to enter his teens, making it highly unlikely.

W	L	PCT	G	GS	CG	IP	H	BB	SO	SHO	ERA
13	64	.169	84	79	73	700	1,167	46	24	0	4.28

Samuel Strang "Sammy Strang" Nicklin, *Utilityman*

An affluent family in Tennessee, the Nicklin clan disapproved of young Samuel's love for the game of baseball. The Nicklins were a well-to-do family in Chattanooga, consisting of scholars and poets, and Samuel's passion for a boy's game was something his family members turned up their noses to. Ever the good son, Sammy enrolled at the University of Tennessee and graduated but couldn't discard the siren's song of athletics. While not studying, Samuel would be on either the baseball diamond or the gridiron, quenching his thirst for sport. When he began playing professional baseball, Samuel, to appease his family, dropped his surname and played simply as "Sammy Strang."

Strang, nicknamed "The Dixie Thrush," played briefly for the old Louisville Colonels of the National League in 1896 before he left baseball for the military. Commissioned a second lieutenant during the Spanish-American War, Strang served overseas during the conflict. He returned home and decided to stay in the military another year before receiving his discharge in 1899 at Anniston, Alabama. From there, his baseball career took off.

Rarely a starter, Sammy was regarded as a valuable reserve. He was swift afoot and versatile, willing and able to take the extra base when the more conservative runner would have held up. Many reports credit Strang with inventing the delayed steal, but his crooning voice received more mileage in the papers. A *Baltimore Sun* writer once quipped, "Strang has always been conceded to be one of the best voiced players that ever sang a lullaby to an umpire." The scribes' fascination with Sammy's vocal dexterity got to his head and he quit baseball to travel to France to study voice lessons with aspirations to join the opera. When the opera failed to materialize, Sammy returned to the States and coached baseball at West Point. At his death, he was the owner of the minor league ballclub in Chattanooga.

G	R	H	2B	3B	HR	RBI	BB	SO	SB	AVG	Slug
901	479	787	112	28	16	253	464	n/a	219	.269	.343

Charles Evard "Gabby" Street, *Catcher*

Just a young buck during the Spanish-American War, Street served in the military before he took to the baseball diamond. Nicknamed "Old Sarge" during his playing days because of his military background, Street was the stereotypical, squatty backstop with a wagging jaw. An all-field, no-hit catcher, Street was the favorite target for legendary pitcher Walter Johnson when the two played together with the Washington Senators.

A master of the publicity stunt, Gabby Street is best remembered today for agreeing to catch balls dropped from the top of the Washington Monument. But Gabby was outdone in the publicity stunt department by one of his players with the St. Louis Cardinals: Dizzy Dean. However, before Street managed the aloof Mr. Dean, he served his country in a second military campaign, the First World War. Although he didn't see action during World War I, Street was preparing for aerial combat at Kelly Field, Texas. A soldier at Kelly Field remarked, "Street has made good as a flyer and has been transferred to a camp somewhere in the east. He is as peppery and noisy in the air as when he caught Walter Johnson in the Majors."

G	R	H	2B	3B	HR	RBI	BB	SO	SB	AVG	Slug
503	98	312	44	11	2	105	119	n/a	17	.208	.256

Seymour L. "Seem" Studley, *Outfield*

Seem Studley's career in baseball amounted to very little since he was a seldom-used reserve with a woeful batting average. He had a brief stint in the majors and a brief stint in the military during the Civil War as well. Seem served with the 54th New York Infantry Regiment, Company C, for a few months late in 1864. During that time, his unit was attached to Schimmelpfenning's Division. He died at a Soldier's and Sailor's Home in Nebraska the same year the American League was established as a major league.

G	R	H	2B	3B	HR	RBI	BB	SO	SB	AVG	Slug
5	3	2	0	0	0	2	0	1	0	.095	.095

Charles Isham Taylor, *Second Base*

Although Negro League executive John W. Connors served in the Spanish-American War, C.I. Taylor is the only known former player from black baseball to have served during that conflict. A second baseman during his playing days, Taylor never was regarded as a top-flight ballplayer. Instead, C.I. made his mark as a manager. He made the Indianapolis ABCs of the Deadball Era a powerhouse with his leadership. He was the skipper of the ABCs during World War I, and the patriotic Taylor would take his players that had been drafted to Washington, D.C., and introduce them to the monuments and show them how things worked in the nation's capital.

(1904–1922): Birmingham Giants, West Baden Sprudels and Indianapolis ABCs

John Franklin Titus, *Outfield*

Had John Titus begun in baseball before for his service hitch, he'd be a rather strong Hall of Fame candidate. One of the top outfielders of the Deadball Era, Titus was an expert batsman who posted solid on-base skills and hit for authority. But he was a 27-year-old rookie in 1903 due to his military service. John served in the army during the Spanish-American War but was never shipped overseas. Although he didn't take part in the fighting, his origins in baseball were pushed back because of his tenure with Uncle Sam.

Before the American League raided the rosters of the National League, the Philadelphia Phillies clearly had the best outfield in the business. They had two Hall of Famers at the corners in Elmer Flick and Ed Delahanty and the greatest on-base machine of the Deadball Era, Roy Thomas, patrolling center. But Flick and Delahanty both left for the newly established American League and the Phillies brought in an old soldier named John Titus to replace Delahanty in left field. By 1904, the Phillies outfield was sensational again, with Thomas remaining in center and Titus and Sherwood Magee flanking him. Titus, who sported a handlebar mustache when they were out of vogue, was regarded as one of the rowdiest ballplayers of the Deadball Era.

G	R	H	2B	3B	HR	RBI	BB	SO	SB	AVG	Slug
1,402	738	1,401	253	72	38	561	620	n/a	140	.282	.385

George B. Treadway, *Outfield*

George Treadway was one of baseball's best outfielders before the turn of the century ... at least for one season. The star player of the 1894 Brooklyn Bridegrooms (who became the Dodgers), George hit a robust .330 in that exceptional season. But he mysteriously dropped off in 1895 and was out of the majors shortly thereafter. The reason for Treadway's quick fall from stardom stems from allegations made on his heritage. It was believed that Treadway had some African blood in his family tree, so opposing players and fans rode the man mercilessly. Once a ranking star, Treadway was run out of the game and has since been forgotten.

During that one magical season, Treadway was among the top players in the game. The great center fielder Jimmy Ryan, when discussing how to play the outfield, said, "The only fellow I ever met who was able to turn the same tricks [as me] was George Treadway." But Treadway, despite his prowess on the diamond, couldn't silence the verbal attacks and his talents suffered because of it. Hall of Fame skipper Ned Hanlon once said, "The worst slip I ever made was when I took George Treadway in preference to Bill Lange." In retrospect, with due respect to the talents of the great Bill Lange, Hanlon probably made a wise choice. Treadway was so highly regarded that he was once traded for two Hall of Famers—Big Dan Brouthers and Wee Willie Keeler—but his skills quickly vanished courtesy of the taunts of others. Several years after his days in the majors, Treadway joined the army and served during the Spanish-American War.

G	R	H	2B	3B	HR	RBI	BB	SO	SB	AVG	Slug
328	259	368	58	46	13	227	165	115	60	.285	.432

William Warren White, *Third Base*

Often mistaken for the great pitcher Will White, Warren White was a third baseman during his time in baseball. Some sources have listed Warren as the brother to star catcher/third baseman Deacon White. Truth is, Deacon and Will White were brothers and legendary players, while Warren White, a modest player at best, wasn't related to the stars. During the Civil War, Warren served with the 14th New York Heavy Artillery, Company F, in the summer of 1863 through the duration of the war. Under the command of Colonel Elisha G. Marshall, the 14th was ordered for duty at New York Harbor. The following year they would be attached to the Army of the Potomac.

G	R	H	2B	3B	HR	RBI	BB	SO	SB	AVG	Slug
168	96	184	13	4	0	64	2	6	8	.254	.284

George Zettlein, *Pitcher*

Nicknamed "The Charmer," Zettlein was a solid pitcher during the game's early years. During the Civil War, Charmer was active on land and on sea. He initially enlisted in the Union Army at the beginning of the war but opted to switch to sea duties in 1863. Zettlein became a sailor in 1863 and served on Admiral Farragut's flagship. An article in the *Logansport Reporter* said that George "was with the admiral on his great battles."

W	L	PCT	G	GS	CG	IP	H	BB	SO	SHO	ERA
129	112	.535	250	244	228	2,177	2,678	145	143	13	2.55

World War I

Edward Wilbur Ainsmith, *Catcher*

The stereotypical image of a catcher is a stocky man with a jaw that never ceases to wag. Eddie Ainsmith, who enjoyed a fifteen-year career in the major leagues, fits that description well. Often referred to as "chatty," Eddie was usually the first player to return his signed contract to management. Although Eddie was eager to play, he was also eager to do his part in the war. The backstop enlisted in the army at Kelly Field, Texas, with aviation aspirations. After missing a portion of the 1918 season to military service, Ainsmith returned to the diamond but was no longer a Senator. He had been shipped to Detroit to play with Ty Cobb and catch Howard Ehmke.

The 1918 season was a rough one for Ainsmith. Although he wanted to do his bit for the war, he had an ailing wife at home and some associates urged him to seek a deferment from military service because he earned more as a baseball player than he would as a soldier. Persuaded to challenge his draft board's order for him to work in defense or enlist, Eddie took the matter to court. He lost his case, as the ruling of the court said, "The scope of the draft's provisions should be so enlarged as to include other classes of persons whose professional occupation is solely that of entertaining." This ruling struck loudly, especially with the vaudeville circuit, but Ainsmith was glad the fiasco was over and he enlisted in the military. However, Eddie lost his wife to illness in the midst of the hearing and was rushed off to the military a widower.

G	R	H	2B	3B	HR	RBI	BB	SO	SB	AVG	Slug
1,068	299	707	108	54	22	317	263	n/a	86	.232	.324

Victor Eddington Aldridge, *Pitcher*

Aldridge's career spanned from 1917 to 1928, as he played his entire career in the National League with three different organizations. After showing promise as a 23-year-old rookie in 1917, Aldridge appeared in just three games for the NL Champion Cubs due to being drafted into the navy. Employing odd mechanics, which were described as "a halting, milk wagon-like delivery," Vic did not appear in another major league game until 1922. He posted consecutive 16-win seasons for the Cubs in 1922 and 1923. In his first season away from the Windy City, Vic won a world championship with the Pirates in 1925 — he and Ray Kremer won two games apiece in the Fall Classic.

W	L	PCT	G	GS	CG	IP	H	BB	SO	SHO	ERA
97	80	.548	248	205	102	1,601	1,671	512	526	8	3.76

Grover Cleveland "Pete" Alexander, *Pitcher*

Legendary pitcher Grover Cleveland Alexander was the ace of the Philadelphia Phillies' staff before the war. Afraid their star would soon be drafted, the Phillies dealt Pete to the Cubs. He appeared in three games in 1918 before Uncle Sam called his number, and he was shipped overseas with the 89th Infantry Regiment. While serving on the frontlines, Pete lost hearing in one of his ears and began experiencing the initial symptoms of epilepsy. To combat his illness and war injuries, Alexander found solace in alcohol. His alcoholism became front-page material during the 1926 World Series when Pete won Games 2 and 6 and celebrated heavily after his victory in the sixth contest. When the Yankees mounted a comeback in Game 7, Alexander was summoned from the bullpen, nursing a hangover, and proceeded to sit down the mighty Yanks for a World Series championship.

Among the ballplayers that saw combat action during the First World War, the Hall of Famer Alexander is the most recognizable. One of the game's top pitchers, Alex had to settle for the meager thirty dollars a month given a soldier during the war. Attached to the 89th Infantry with the 342nd Field Artillery, Grover was on the frontlines during the war. He witnessed some of the most intense fighting. In November of 1918, he wrote a letter home to his wife informing her that he was on the frontlines. He returned home a hero on the same ship as lesser-known players Mike Menosky and Joe Jenkins. When asked how he kept his arm in shape, Alex replied, "Partly by pitching shells at the boche during seven weeks of action near St. Mihiel."

After Alexander's wife received the letter from her husband that informed her about his duty on the frontlines, she told the Cubs brass how deep in the fighting their staff ace was. Chicago executives were sitting on pins and needles, worried that their star pitcher — the man they were placing their hopes on for 1919 — may not make it home. But Grover came home, with more troubles and worries than before he left. He combated those demons by playing baseball, and when the game failed to be therapeutic, he sought alcohol. But Alexander was a legend of his time. He was so widely admired for his baseball and wartime heroics that none other than General Pershing himself sent a wire stateside informing the nation of Grover's expected return home from the war.

W	L	PCT	G	GS	CG	IP	H	BB	SO	SHO	ERA
373	208	.642	696	600	439	5,190	4,868	951	2,199	90	2.56

Artemus Ward "Nick" Allen, *Catcher*

The Federal League was the beginning locale of a handful of decent ballplayers, and Allen made his debut with the Buffalo entry.

A lifelong reserve catcher, Allen played for the Cubs and the Reds during his time in the major leagues. Nick appeared in 37 games with Christy Mathewson's Reds in 1918, as Ivy Wingo's backup, before he left for the armed forces.

G	R	H	2B	3B	HR	RBI	BB	SO	SB	AVG	Slug
216	41	116	13	5	0	36	33	n/a	8	.232	.278

Toussaint L'Ouvertre "Tom" Allen, *First Base*

A slick-fielding first baseman for the Hilldale Daisies, Allen enjoyed a decent career in the Negro Leagues. Unable to stick with a team before the First World War, Tom caught on with the Daisies the year after his discharge and played six years for the team. During World War I, Allen served overseas with the army and was attached to the French Army's 349th Battalion.

(1916–1926): Havana Red Sox, Philadelphia Giants, Hilldale Daisies, Wilmington Potomacs and Newark Stars

John Fred Anderson, *Pitcher*

Nicknamed "Spitball" for obvious reasons, Anderson was the ace pitcher for the Buffalo team in the Federal League. After the Federal League's collapse, Spitball joined John McGraw's Giants. His 1.44 ERA paced the New York team in 1917 and he was instrumental in New York's pennant-winning season that year. At the age of 32, Anderson was inducted into the army and served in their dental corps. A graduate of Oak Ridge Military Institute, Anderson became a full-time dentist after his retirement from baseball.

W	L	PCT	G	GS	CG	IP	H	BB	SO	SHO	ERA
53	57	.482	178	114	62	986	912	247	514	11	2.86

Walter Carl Anderson, *Pitcher*

Anderson's major league career consisted of only seventeen games. The tall and lanky left-hander made the majority of his appearances in 1917 and the remainder in 1919. He missed the entire 1918 season to service in the armed forces. Anderson enlisted in the navy shortly after the close of the 1917 baseball season and was assigned to the Great Lakes Naval Station. He had this to say about his enlistment: "I have no dependents and I don't see why I shouldn't serve."

W	L	PCT	G	GS	CG	IP	H	BB	SO	SHO	ERA
1	0	1.000	17	2	0	53	45	29	20	0	3.23

Frederick Middleton Bailey, *Outfield*

Bailey was placed in the Class I division and served in the Aviation Branch during the war. Nicknamed "Penny," Bailey only played in parts of three seasons in the major leagues, all as a member of the Braves. He went 1-for-4 in 1918 before he lost time to the war effort.

G	R	H	2B	3B	HR	RBI	BB	SO	SB	AVG	Slug
60	10	23	2	1	1	6	9	29	5	.185	.242

Arthur Eugene Bailey, *Outfield*

Bailey made his major league debut in 1917 with the basement-dwelling Athletics, and appeared in only five games. The following year, he missed the entire baseball season to service in the armed forces. When Bailey returned to the major leagues, Connie Mack had shipped him to the Braves where he played briefly under the aloof George Stallings. He was sent to the bushes shortly thereafter and was recalled to the big time in 1923, the only year he played regularly, for the Brooklyn Dodgers.

G	R	H	2B	3B	HR	RBI	BB	SO	SB	AVG	Slug
213	95	156	16	7	2	52	63	61	13	.246	.303

Abraham Lincoln "Sweetbreads" Bailey, *Pitcher*

With one of the strangest nicknames in baseball history, Abraham Lincoln "Sweetbreads" Bailey was signed by the Chicago Cubs as a walk-on in 1917. World War I was already in full swing when Bailey inked his name on the dotted line with the Baby Bears, and he joined the armed forces shortly after signing his first professional contract. Sweetbreads was sent overseas to France and clashed in a pitcher's duel against Hall of Famer Pete Alexander. The contest attracted plenty of attention since both men were named after presidents— Alexander's full name was Grover Cleveland Alexander. When the unknown Bailey beat the star Alexander, he was widely regarded as a phenom. After the war, Bailey returned to baseball and played two and a half years with the Cubs, not quite living up to the boasts made after he beat Pete.

W	L	PCT	G	GS	CG	IP	H	BB	SO	SHO	ERA
4	7	.364	52	6	0	137	154	40	35	0	4.59

Albert Wells Baird, *Second Base*

Baird attended LSU before he began his baseball career and played parts of two seasons for John McGraw's Giants. He was a reserve with the 1917 NL Champion Giants but missed the entire 1918 campaign to military service. He enlisted in the Naval Reserve at Shreveport, as McGraw lost a young player he called a "promising rookie." Baird played every infield position but first base in 1919, his last season in the major leagues.

G	R	H	2B	3B	HR	RBI	BB	SO	SB	AVG	Slug
48	9	27	1	0	0	9	7	11	3	.252	.262

Howard Douglas Baird, *Third Base*

A newlywed at the time of the war, Baird was classified Class 4 for the draft due to some smart jaw-wagging on his part. The nomadic infielder was summoned by his draft board to review his case and maintained that he was engaged, which would allow for a deferment, before the draft law went into effect. The following humorous tale was printed in the *Lincoln Daily Star* concerning Baird's account of his meeting.

"Your marriage came too late for exemption," he was told by the members of his draft board.

"Yes, but I was engaged before the draft law went into effect," maintained Baird.

The Board Examiner asked, "How can you prove it?"

"I can prove it this way," Baird began. "It all happened because of a home run I made in a game in Pittsburgh last April. I ought to be sure of the date. I met the girl I married on the morning before the game and made an engagement to see her that evening. We had been friends for a long time and I had asked her to marry me several times and that morning she said she would agree to it if I knocked a home run that afternoon. That afternoon I hit the bull sign and won a prize of fifty dollars, and when I went out to the house that night, I told her she had to make good and she said 'yes.' That's enough to fix it in anybody's mind, isn't it?"

The draft board was so impressed with his story that Doug was given deferred classification. Baird's yarn bought him some time, enough to lead the Redbirds in stolen bases, but he was summoned for duty near the middle of the season.

G	R	H	2B	3B	HR	RBI	BB	SO	SB	AVG	Slug
617	230	492	86	45	6	191	157	295	118	.234	.326

Delmer David "Del" Baker, *Catcher*

Best known for guiding the 1940 Detroit Tigers to the World Series as a manager, Del Baker was a back-up catcher for a few years with Detroit during the Deadball Era. At the time of the war, Baker had been sent back to the minors and was playing for the San Francisco Seals. Baker joined the navy and tried to get Detroit's young hitter deluxe, Harry Heilmann, to enlist and serve with him. After the signing of the armistice, Baker never made it back to the majors as a player.

G	R	H	2B	3B	HR	RBI	BB	SO	SB	AVG	Slug
172	27	63	9	4	0	22	32	32	5	.209	.265

Jesse Lawrence Barnes, *Pitcher*

Jesse, whose brother, Virgil, also enjoyed a respectable baseball career, was an infantryman during the First World War. Barnes saw action in a French battlefield, which limited the Giants ace to nine games for the 1918 squad. In Barnes' first year back from the war he paced the National League with 25 victories and netted 20 more the following season. He won two games and led all Giant hurlers with 18 strikeouts in their 1921 World Series championship over the Yankees. After his playing days were over, "Nubby" became a police captain.

W	L	PCT	G	GS	CG	IP	H	BB	SO	SHO	ERA
153	149	.507	422	312	180	2,570	2,686	515	653	26	3.22

John Joseph "Jack" Barry, *Shortstop*

Barry is the least-remembered man of Connie Mack's fabled $100,000 Infield as he teamed with stellar first baseman Stuffy McInnis and Hall of Famers Homerun Baker and Eddie Collins. In 1917, Barry was named player/manager of the Red Sox, and led them to a second-place finish in his only season at the helm. He missed all of the 1918 season to the war, managing a navy yard team. While he was gone, Ed Barrow replaced him as the manager of the Sox. Despite a remarkable .592 winning percentage as a skipper, Jack Barry was never again asked to manage at the major league level.

During Barry's stint in the navy, he served as player/manager of the Boston navy yard team. At the navy yard, Jack didn't have proper training facilities for his team so he was forced to look elsewhere to get the necessary practice for his sailors after their duty hours. He turned to some old baseball connections. He knew Hugh Duffy, the diminutive Hall of Fame outfielder, coached baseball at nearby Harvard University and he paid Mr. Duffy a visit. He asked Hugh if he could bring his sailors to campus and practice when the field was open, and Duffy obliged his request. Jack was honorably discharged in December 1918 from the Officer's Material School at Harvard.

G	R	H	2B	3B	HR	RBI	BB	SO	SB	AVG	Slug
1,222	533	1,009	142	38	10	429	396	n/a	153	.243	.303

Raymond Bates, *Third Base*

Bates, whose career consisted of slightly more than 500 at-bats, had a three-year hiatus between his rookie season and his sophomore campaign. The third baseman finished second on the Athletics in RBIs during the 1917 season and then missed all of 1918 to service in the military, which took Ray overseas to France. When he returned to the States, he never again appeared in another major league game.

G	R	H	2B	3B	HR	RBI	BB	SO	SB	AVG	Slug
147	51	120	20	9	2	70	24	48	15	.233	.318

Charles S. Becker, *Pitcher*

One of the few former major leaguers buried at Arlington National Cemetery, Charlie Becker played in pieces of two seasons with the Senators. The southpaw completed every game he started at the major league level. His last big league action came in 1912, and he served in the military during the war in 1918.

W	L	PCT	G	GS	CG	IP	H	BB	SO	SHO	ERA
3	5	.375	15	5	5	80	88	29	36	1	3.94

Joseph Rosenblum Bennett, *Reserve*

Bennett appeared in one major league game and did not record a single big league at-bat. He instead made the military a career and spent many years in the Quartermasters Corps in the United States Army. Joe served in both World Wars as well as the Korean War and retired from the army with the rank of lieutenant colonel.

G	R	H	2B	3B	HR	RBI	BB	SO	SB	AVG	Slug
1	0	0	0	0	0	0	0	0	0	—	—

John Needles "Jack" Bentley, *Pitcher*

Big and husky, Jack Bentley was compared to Babe Ruth because of his physique and his two-way ability on the diamond. Bentley was a terrific southpaw pitcher who helped John McGraw's Giants reach the World Series in 1923 and 1924, but Needles could also hurt the opposition with his lumber. The brawny lefty hit .291 during his career.

Big Jack got his start with the Senators in 1913 and pitched for Washington a few years but didn't quite make good. He was returned to the minors where his two-way ability began to impress. His career was interrupted by World War I as he entered the military. Commissioned an officer, Bentley saw combat action in France and returned home a war hero. However, despite his status as a military star, there were no certainties in the game of baseball. While training for the 1919 season, Bentley didn't have the stuff to stick. J.V. Fitzgerald wrote, "A baseball player has to be something more than a war hero to hold his job in the big leagues, if the case of Jack Bentley can be taken as a criterion. He received two decorations for bravery in action, but they are not going to do him any good in holding down a big league job." Bentley eventually made good at the major league level under John McGraw—five years after the war.

W	L	PCT	G	GS	CG	IP	H	BB	SO	SHO	ERA
46	34	.575	138	89	39	714	761	263	259	4	4.01

John Clebon "Rube" Benton, *Pitcher*

A left-handed pitcher who was quite underhanded off the diamond, Benton was blacklisted by major league baseball for falsely accusing a teammate of accepting money for tossing a game in 1922. He was later reinstated and played three seasons with the Redlegs. Rube left the Giants early in 1918, as the southpaw enlisted at Fort Jackson.

W	L	PCT	G	GS	CG	IP	H	BB	SO	SHO	ERA
156	145	.518	437	311	145	2,518	2,472	712	950	23	3.09

Walter Jacob Bernhardt, *Pitcher*

A star at the University of Pennsylvania, Walter Bernhardt made only one mound appearance at the major league level. Bernhardt tossed one inning for the 1918 Yankees before he entered the armed forces as a dentist.

W	L	PCT	G	GS	CG	IP	H	BB	SO	SHO	ERA
0	0	—	1	0	0	1	0	0	0	0	0.00

John Augustus "Josh" Billings, *Catcher*

Set to compete with Steve O'Neill for the Indians' starting backstop job in 1918, Billings was delayed en route to spring training due to two car accidents. His luck didn't change. He was labeled 1-A by his draft board and was called to the colors after appearing in just two games for the Tribe. Billings entered the navy and while he served his country, he was swapped to the St. Louis Browns, where he was Hank Severeid's backup for five years upon his return to the major leagues.

G	R	H	2B	3B	HR	RBI	BB	SO	SB	AVG	Slug
240	44	106	12	5	0	29	23	73	5	.217	.262

Frederick William Blackwell, *Catcher*

Blackwell's major league career was rather brief. He saw action for portions of three seasons with the Pirates: 1917 through 1919. Fred appeared in eight games for the Pirates in 1918, but his ambition to join the army's aviation branch carried him away from the diamond early in the season. Even though the reserve catcher failed his physical exam, his desire to serve his country was not quelled. He had two operations performed to fit his body for military duty but was still rejected and missed the majority of the baseball season because of his sense of duty. He played one final major league season with Hugo Bezdek's squad in 1919 as a back-up catcher.

G	R	H	2B	3B	HR	RBI	BB	SO	SB	AVG	Slug
35	5	18	3	0	0	10	6	16	0	.205	.239

Luzerne Atwell "Lu" Blue, *First Base*

One of the greatest on-base machines in baseball history, Blue was a star first baseman for the Detroit Tigers in the 1920s. Before he made his major league debut, Blue served in the military during World War I at Camp Lee, Virginia. From the first time he set foot on a major league diamond, the switch-hitting Lu Blue was a heady ballplayer with an exceptional batting eye. Always a headache for hurlers to pitch to, Blue's ability prompted umpire Billy Evans to say that "trying to pull strategy against Blue, who hits equally well from either side of the plate, is a tough proposition."

G	R	H	2B	3B	HR	RBI	BB	SO	SB	AVG	Slug
1,615	1,151	1,696	319	109	44	692	1,092	436	150	.287	.401

Norman Doxie "Tony" Boeckel, *Third Base*

The first active baseball player to die in an auto accident, Boeckel served in the navy during his stint in the military. With no baseball experience as a youth, Boeckel was an uncommon professional since he began playing the game just before his twentieth birthday. Boeckel died tragically when a car driven by a Hollywood personality struck another truck. Boeckel, who was riding in the Hollywood man's car with Yankee star Bob Meusel, was injured in the crash while Meusel and their companion received minor scratches. Boeckel later died as a result of the injuries sustained in the accident.

G	R	H	2B	3B	HR	RBI	BB	SO	SB	AVG	Slug
777	372	813	130	36	27	337	237	218	90	.282	.381

Raymond C. Boyd, *Pitcher*

Boyd had two cups of coffee at the major league level, first with the 1910 Browns and then with the 1911 Reds. Boyd joined the armed forces during the First World War and contracted Spanish flu, a deadly epidemic that swept the nation during the war. Unable to recover from the disease, Boyd died on his birthday in 1920.

W	L	PCT	G	GS	CG	IP	H	BB	SO	SHO	ERA
3	4	.429	10	6	4	58	50	24	26	0	3.10

Cornelius Joseph Brady, *Pitcher*

Sporadic might be the best term to use when describing Brady's major league career. He first saw action with the Yankees in 1915 and then again in 1917 after spending 1916 on the farm. He lost the entire 1918 season to service in the military and didn't resurface in the major leagues until the Redlegs summoned him in 1925, his last season at the highest level.

W	L	PCT	G	GS	CG	IP	H	BB	SO	SHO	ERA
2	3	.400	24	5	2	82	88	32	22	0	4.17

Raymond Bloom "Rube" Bressler, *Pitcher*

One of baseball's finest all-around talents, Bressler began his career as a pitcher and then switched to the outfield when his arm went south. Over the course of his career, Rube hit .302 and also posted a 3.40 ERA. The southpaw was strictly a pitcher for the Reds in 1918 when he left the club for the army on June 24. While serving his country, Rube participated in an Army-Navy Championship game that was held at the Polo Grounds.

W	L	PCT	G	GS	CG	IP	H	BB	SO	SHO	ERA
26	31	.456	107	52	27	540	511	242	229	3	3.40

Otto Briggs, *Outfield*

Nicknamed "The Mirror," Briggs had a long tenure with the Hilldale Daisies as their regular right fielder during the early years of the Lively Ball Era. The speedy outfielder from Kings Mountain, North Carolina, was an exceptional leadoff man. The diminutive right fielder was known for his ability to get on base by any means necessary, including acting—pretending he was hit by a pitched ball when he wasn't. Before Otto became a star with Hilldale, he served in the infantry during World War I, and spent time in France with the 92nd Division.

The Hilldale Daisies were stationed in Philadelphia and Briggs was one of their biggest stars. The Phillies of the major leagues had the great Cy Williams in their outfield. Although Otto didn't have Williams' power, he was just as popular with black fans as Cy was with white fans. Briggs would marry into wealth and remained in Philadelphia after his baseball days. In his book, *The Complete History of the Negro Leagues*, Mark Ribowsky writes, "Briggs would become so entrenched in Philadelphia that he was eventually hired as circulation manager at the *Tribune*."

(1915–1934): Hilldale Daisies, Indianapolis ABCs, Dayton Marcos and Atlantic City Bacharach Giants

Anton Christian "Tony" Brottem, *Catcher*

Tony Brottem's major league career was rather brief. He played pieces of three seasons with three different clubs. His first look came in 1916 with the Cardinals, and he didn't resurface again until 1918. He only appeared in a handful of games before he was drafted into the armed forces, where he served five months in a radio training detachment at Lincoln, Nebraska.

G	R	H	2B	3B	HR	RBI	BB	SO	SB	AVG	Slug
62	10	29	3	0	0	13	9	22	1	.215	.237

Alexander Thompson Burr, *Reserve*

Burr played in one game with the 1914 Yankees without recording an official at-bat. Although Burr's career is just a speck on the map of major league action, the Chicagoan's tenure with Uncle Sam's outfit was heroic. The solidly built who stood 6'3" man witnessed heavy combat action, the type most men did not return home from. In just a few short weeks before the signing of the armistice, Burr was killed in action at France.

G	R	H	2B	3B	HR	RBI	BB	SO	SB	AVG	Slug
1	0	0	0	0	0	0	0	0	0	—	—

Maurice Lennon "Dick" Burrus, *First Base*

As a young man, Burrus matriculated at the Oak Ridge Military Academy. With military service on his mind, Burrus joined the armed forces during the First World War before he made his major league debut. The first baseman was stationed at Camp Gordon. After his discharge, Burrus made his big league debut with Connie Mack's 1920 Athletics. His better seasons came later with the Braves.

G	R	H	2B	3B	HR	RBI	BB	SO	SB	AVG	Slug
560	206	513	87	12	11	211	138	95	18	.291	.373

Willis Everett "Kid" Butler, *Utility Infielder*

Butler had a cup of coffee with Jimmy McAleer's 1907 St. Louis Browns. The thin infielder backed up Hall of Famer Bobby Wallace and second baseman Harry Niles. During the First World War, Kid served in the army.

G	R	H	2B	3B	HR	RBI	BB	SO	SB	AVG	Slug
20	4	13	2	0	0	6	2	n/a	1	.220	.254

Leon Joseph Cadore, *Pitcher*

Cadore is famous for marrying the boss' daughter. He wed Charlie Ebbetts' daughter, Mae. As well as marrying into wealth, Cadore is also remembered as one of the hurlers who took part in the longest game in major league baseball history when he squared off against Joe Oeschger for a 26-inning affair. Both Cadore and Oeschger went the distance for their clubs; Leon stated he couldn't comb his hair for three days after the game.

During World War I Cadore entered the army as a private but was discharged a lieutenant. He was the commander of a battalion of black soldiers in battles at France and the Argonne Offensive. His troops were a combination of colored soldiers from the 92nd Division and the 15th National Guard Regiment of New York. On duty in the St. Die Sector, Lt. Cadore and his men captured more than 1,000 enemy soldiers, to include the Bois Frehaut in the face of heavy machine gun fire. Leon claimed the Germans were deathly afraid of his black troops because they thought they were cannibals from Morocco. The war was an arduous affair for Cadore, but he had luck on his side. He said, "I was knocked down by two high explosive shells and a hand grenade fell beside me in a trench, but failed to explode. Not wounded once. Hope I'll have luck like that in the pinches next summer."

W	L	PCT	G	GS	CG	IP	H	BB	SO	SHO	ERA
68	72	.486	192	147	83	1,257	1,273	289	445	10	3.14

Benjamin Thomas Caffyn, *Outfield*

Caffyn served in both the Spanish-American War and the First World War. Still a teenager during the Spanish-American War, Caffyn took to baseball after his discharge. Caffyn was a star in the minor leagues, and a writer for the *Des Moines Daily News* claimed Ben was "the best outfielder the Western League ever had." However, the major leagues had its share of stars too, and Caffyn, who was called up to Cleveland in 1906, served as a replacement for .300 hitters Elmer Flick and Bunk Congalton and the swift Harry Bay. The 1906 season was Caffyn's only action in the majors.

G	R	H	2B	3B	HR	RBI	BB	SO	SB	AVG	Slug
30	16	20	4	0	0	3	12	n/a	2	.194	.233

Howard Lee Camp, *Outfield*

Howie Camp made his debut in 1917 and was lost to the war effort in 1918. He spent the entire season in service to his country with action overseas and never returned to the major leagues upon his military discharge.

G	R	H	2B	3B	HR	RBI	BB	SO	SB	AVG	Slug
5	3	6	1	0	0	0	1	2	0	.286	.333

Hugh Edward Canavan, *Pitcher*

The southpaw attended school at the Staunton Military Academy in Virginia prior to his professional baseball career. His only major league action came in 1918, which was abbreviated due to service as an electrician at the Newport Naval Station.

W	L	PCT	G	GS	CG	IP	H	BB	SO	SHO	ERA
0	4	.000	11	3	3	47	70	15	18	0	6.32

Harold Gust Carlson, *Pitcher*

Carlson is one of a handful of players to have died while still active, as the right-hander passed away early in the 1930 season of an intestinal hemorrhage. Carlson got his first taste of the major leagues in 1917 and was third on the club in wins. He appeared in just three games in 1918 before he left for the military, where he saw combat action in France after a stint at Camp Grant. Carlson's service time did not affect his game as Hal posted a 2.23 ERA in 141 innings of work upon his return. He pitched for the Pirates until 1923 when he joined the Phillies and finished his career, and life, with the Chicago Cubs in 1930.

W	L	PCT	G	GS	CG	IP	H	BB	SO	SHO	ERA
114	120	.487	377	235	121	2,002	2,256	498	590	17	3.97

James Howard "Buster" Caton, *Shortstop*

Caton was a diminutive middle infielder, and sportswriters of the time enjoyed poking fun at his small stature. When Caton was an active player, he was the smallest man in baseball, and papers often referred to Buster as "Midget." He enlisted in the army late in the 1918 baseball season, as local newspaper headlines read "Small, But Enlists." An Associated Press writer had this quip to describe how he envisioned Caton's battlefield adventures: "When Buster gets to France he won't have to dig a trench very deep to shield him from the fire of the enemy."

G	R	H	2B	3B	HR	RBI	BB	SO	SB	AVG	Slug
231	85	184	18	16	0	53	83	52	18	.226	.287

Bert Edgar Chaplin, *Catcher*

Before Bert Chaplin made his major league debut, he served with the United States Army during World War I. The left-handed-hitting backstop spent the bulk of his major league career as star catcher Muddy Ruel's backup. Not much with the stick, Chaplin's arm was once lauded by writer Melville Webb Jr.

G	R	H	2B	3B	HR	RBI	BB	SO	SB	AVG	Slug
35	10	14	2	1	0	7	13	11	2	.184	.237

Harry E. Chapman, *Catcher*

A journeyman catcher who saw the bulk of his playing time in the Federal League, Harry Chapman's last major league action came with the 1916 Browns. Chapman joined the armed forces during World War I and would never again see home. He died after contracting Spanish flu, a serious epidemic that was the cause of 17,000 reported deaths throughout army bases.

G	R	H	2B	3B	HR	RBI	BB	SO	SB	AVG	Slug
147	38	80	8	5	1	44	37	n/a	7	.198	.250

LaVerne Ashford "Larry" Chappell, *Outfield*

The lofty expectations placed on a gifted young athlete can be a heavy burden. When White Sox owner Charles Comiskey drained the bank to acquire Larry Chappell, a can't-miss outfielder from Illinois, writers across the sphere of baseball proclaimed the new Pale Hose recruit as another Ty Cobb. The White Sox owner paid the highest price ever for an amateur outfielder when he bought Chappell's contract. He arrived in Chicago in 1913 to plenty of fanfare and had a modest rookie season. Given Chick Mattick's atrocious season, it looked like Chappell was primed to take the outfielder's starting assignment in 1914. Instead, Larry failed to impress, and by 1916 he was with a new organization. He was on the Boston Braves roster when World War I broke out.

After Chappell failed to make the grade at the major league level, he entered the armed forces. Larry enlisted in the United States Navy at San Francisco. With Chappell still in his late 20s, a return to the majors and eventually making good on his early promise wasn't out of the realm of possibility. But it was an option that Chappell wouldn't be dealt. While serving in the navy, Chappell, like so many servicemen, contracted Spanish flu and died in November.

G	R	H	2B	3B	HR	RBI	BB	SO	SB	AVG	Slug
109	27	69	9	2	0	26	25	42	9	.226	.266

Oscar McKinley Charleston, *Outfield*

Charleston is what modern scouts would refer to as a five-tool talent. The former Negro League legend had all the tools for stardom, and he achieved greatness in black baseball. Widely regarded as the best outfielder in Negro League history, Oscar covered more ground than his peers and could hit for both average and power. The well-traveled Charleston actually began his journeys before he started out in black baseball. Oscar left home at the age of fifteen and joined the army. A soldier during peacetime, he was shipped overseas and played some service ball on the Philippines.

Born and raised in Indianapolis, Oscar returned home after his stint with the 24th Infantry and caught on with the Indianapolis ABCs. The young outfielder perfected his game while he served at Manila with his infantry regiment. Oscar quickly established himself as a star in black baseball but also gained a reputation for his mean streak. Early in his career with the ABCs, he was once arrested for assaulting an umpire. During World War I, the legendary Negro Leaguer spent the bulk of his time playing baseball and working a defense job. He later returned to the military and spent some time under Uncle Sam during World War I.

(1915–1941): Indianapolis ABCs, Pittsburgh Crawfords, Homestead Grays, Harrisburg Giants, New York Lincoln Stars, Chicago American Giants, St. Louis Giants, Hilldale Daisies, Philadelphia Stars and Indianapolis Clowns

Verne James Clemons, *Catcher*

Nicknamed "Stinger," the husky Clemons was a good line-drive hitter who played for both St. Louis entries—the Cardinals and the Browns. He made his debut with the Browns in 1916 but didn't stick. It was back to the bushes for Stinger in 1917 and then on to the military. Verne joined the navy and married the former Gail Whinery just before he was transferred to the Great Lakes

Naval Training station. Timing was on Stinger's side when he was discharged at Newport. Days after he was mustered out of the navy, the branch discontinued discharges. Verne would join the Redbirds and play with them through 1924.

G	R	H	2B	3B	HR	RBI	BB	SO	SB	AVG	Slug
474	78	364	56	11	5	140	119	62	6	.286	.380

Joseph Stanley Cobb, *Pinch Hitter*

In a Moonlight Graham-type career, Cobb, whose real last name was Serafin, walked in his only major league game. He served in the military for the better part of the 1918 season, and when he returned from the armed forces, he never again reached the major league level. Cobb died on Christmas Eve in 1947 due to exposure to the cold.

G	R	H	2B	3B	HR	RBI	BB	SO	SB	AVG	Slug
1	0	0	0	0	0	0	1	0	0	—	—

Tyrus Raymond Cobb, *Outfield*

The common picture of Cobb is a demon in baseball dress, snarling and cursing with his steel spikes used as a weapon to inflict pain rather than a tool of his trade. I am of firm belief that the majority of the stories concerning Cobb's volatile ways are merely the works of sportswriters whose desire to construct fables has created the All-American villain through a troubled Southern man.

Cobb served with the legendary Christy Mathewson, as well as Branch Rickey, with the Chemical Warfare Service in 1918. As an instructor, Cobb would lead soldiers into a gas chamber where lethal chemical gas was released. During one exercise, in which Cobb and Mathewson were in the chamber with a group of soldiers, both baseball greats inhaled a dose of the deadly vapors. Cobb had a colorless discharge drain from his chest for several weeks and suffered from a hacking cough. He would fully recover, but Mathewson inhaled enough gas to slowly destroy his lungs.

After the gas chamber ordeal, Cobb stated that the war presented no further hazards for him, although a shell fragment came close to removing one of his eyes. He returned to the Tigers early in 1919 and led the American League with a .384 batting average.

G	R	H	2B	3B	HR	RBI	BB	SO	SB	AVG	Slug
3,034	2,246	4,189	723	298	117	1,939	1,249	n/a	892	.366	.512

Edward Trowbridge Collins Sr., *Second Base*

Arguably the greatest second baseman of all-time, Hall of Famer Eddie Collins is best known as the cleanest of the 1919 Black Sox. A baseball man to the core, Collins served as a player, manager and executive in his long affiliation with our great game. Although he was a tremendous player, Collins is also remembered for signing two future Hall of Famers in one West Coast trip: Ted Williams and Bobby Doerr. The White Sox, who won the pennant in 1917, finished sixth in 1918, due in large part to the loss of Collins and the holdout of Shoeless Joe Jackson. During the war, Collins served in the U.S. Marine Corps.

G	R	H	2B	3B	HR	RBI	BB	SO	SB	AVG	Slug
2,826	1,821	3,315	438	187	47	1,300	1,503	n/a	743	.333	.429

John Bertrand "Jocko" Conlan, *Outfield*

Although Jocko Conlan never quite made the grade as a player, his career in the game was longer than usual. The little outfielder began as a batboy before working his way up as a player. About fifteen years before he reached the majors, the Chicagoan served in the military during the First World War. Conlan then got the call he'd been waiting for when his hometown White Sox brought him up to Chicago in the mid 1930s. However, Jocko lasted just two years as a player before he embarked on a storied career as an umpire. It was his work as an on-field arbiter that ushered Jocko into the Baseball Hall of Fame.

G	R	H	2B	3B	HR	RBI	BB	SO	SB	AVG	Slug
128	55	96	18	4	0	31	33	13	5	.263	.334

Richard Daniel "Rip" Conway, *Second Base*

Conway appeared in fourteen games for the Boston Braves before he received his draft notice in 1918. Those fourteen games would be the only major league contests that Rip would see. During the war, Conway served at Camp Devens, Massachusetts, and Camp Lee, Virginia. An avid horseshoe thrower, Conway was rather small, standing at 5'6" tall.

G	R	H	2B	3B	HR	RBI	BB	SO	SB	AVG	Slug
14	4	4	0	0	0	2	2	4	1	.167	.167

Rollin Edward Cook, *Pitcher*

Cook had a cup of coffee with Branch Rickey's Browns of 1915. He worked in just over a dozen major league innings before "The Mahatma" was finished with him. After his major league sojourn, Rollin joined the armed forces for World War I. The former Brownie right-hander returned to the colors in the 1940s to lend a hand during the Second World War as well.

W	L	PCT	G	GS	CG	IP	H	BB	SO	SHO	ERA
0	0	—	5	0	0	14	16	9	7	0	7.07

James Edward Cooney, *Shortstop*

Cooney, whose claim to fame is recording an unassisted triple play, was stationed at Fort Devens with the 12th Infantry. He was commissioned a lieutenant and missed the entire 1918 baseball season to service in the military. The Cranston, Rhode Island, native was a well-traveled player. He spent time with six different organizations in his seven-year major league career.

G	R	H	2B	3B	HR	RBI	BB	SO	SB	AVG	Slug
448	181	413	64	16	2	150	76	58	30	.262	.327

Claude William Cooper, *Outfield*

A gritty outfielder who was often compared to Benny Kauff, Cooper never quite reached his potential. He broke in with the 1913 Giants but the following year he had joined the upstart Federal League (the same locale as Kauff) and was the Brooklyn franchise's regular left fielder for the two years of the circuit's existence. When the Federal League folded, Claude joined the Phillies and spent two years as a weak-hitting reserve outfielder. He missed all of the 1918 season to military service. When the war concluded, Cooper never reached the major leagues again.

G	R	H	2B	3B	HR	RBI	BB	SO	SB	AVG	Slug
373	156	283	47	23	4	104	119	n/a	6	.260	.356

John Daniel Couch, *Pitcher*

A "Gentleman Scholar," Couch made his major league debut with the Tigers in 1917. He missed the entire 1918 campaign to service in the army where he fought in Europe as a lieutenant in the infantry. His big league career did not resume until 1922 when the Cincinnati Reds brought him up from the bushes. He was a sixteen-game winner his first year with the Reds but was never again an effective hurler. After his playing days were over, Couch became a California highway patrolman.

W	L	PCT	G	GS	CG	IP	H	BB	SO	SHO	ERA
29	34	.460	147	62	26	642	785	171	112	3	4.64

Clarence Calvert "Sam" Covington, *First Base*

Covington's major league career spanned three seasons, first with the 1913 St. Louis Browns as an eighteen-year-old and then with the Braves of 1917 and 1918. He saw the majority of his big league action as a teenager because he was used sparingly by the Braves in his two seasons with that club. Sam missed the majority of the 1918 season to the war effort, and after the signing of the armistice, never again returned to the major leagues.

G	R	H	2B	3B	HR	RBI	BB	SO	SB	AVG	Slug
40	11	23	2	1	1	14	9	11	4	.178	.233

Maurice Montague "Molly" Craft, *Pitcher*

Craft toiled for parts of four seasons with the Washington Senators and never could attain a major league victory. He made 29 appearances with that ominous "W" stenciled upon his cap and couldn't quite achieve that elusive win. Molly appeared in three games for the 1918 Senators, posting a 1.29 ERA in the process, before he left the diamond for the army. He returned in 1919, at which time he fashioned a 0–3 mark in his last taste of the major leagues.

W	L	PCT	G	GS	CG	IP	H	BB	SO	SHO	ERA
0	4	.000	29	3	1	81	93	33	33	0	3.56

Walton Edwin Cruise, *Outfield*

As the sole provider for his parents and sister, Cruise was initially classified Class 3. However, with a manpower need in the army, Walton was switched to Class 1 and drafted. He appealed this decision, but after 70 games for the Redbirds, Cruise was lost to the war effort. Cruise teamed with Rogers Hornsby to give St. Louis a solid offensive punch in 1917 but was dealt after a rough start to the 1919 season.

G	R	H	2B	3B	HR	RBI	BB	SO	SB	AVG	Slug
736	293	644	83	39	30	272	238	250	49	.277	.386

Eugene Holmes Curtis, *Outfield*

Curtis had the pleasure and misfortune of playing with the Pittsburgh Pirates after the turn of the century. The Bucs were the best team in the National League with the finest roster; therefore, Gene played with winners but wasn't used often. He was stuck behind Hall of Famer Fred Clarke and stars Ginger Beaumont and Jimmy Sebring. During World War I Gene served with the armed forces but was one of 17,000 servicemen to succumb to the Spanish flu epidemic.

G	R	H	2B	3B	HR	RBI	BB	SO	SB	AVG	Slug
5	2	8	1	0	0	3	1	n/a	0	.421	.474

Frank Talmadge "Dixie" Davis, *Pitcher*

With a nickname like "Dixie," you know this fellow hailed from the South. Davis is one of the few pitchers who couldn't latch on in the Deadball Era but flourished after the livelier ball was introduced and the spitball deemed illegal. Dixie made his major league debut in 1912 with the Cincinnati Reds but didn't stick in the show until the Browns acquired him in 1920. He made 17 appearances with the Phillies in 1918 before he was lost to the military and didn't resurface in the majors until the Browns gave him a look. Dixie won 18 games in 1920, 16 in 1921 and 12 in 1925 — his last good season in the majors.

W	L	PCT	G	GS	CG	IP	H	BB	SO	SHO	ERA
75	71	.514	239	164	77	1,317	1,311	688	460	10	3.97

Ralph Fenton "Joe" Dawson, *Pitcher*

Before Dawson made his major league debut, he served with the navy during World War I. Joe enlisted in the navy's aviation wing and became a licensed pilot at the San Diego Naval Airbase. He would use his pilot's license to his benefit during his playing career. While he played for the Pirates in the late 1920s, Joe earned the nickname "Aviator" because he often flew his plane on road trips while his teammates stowed away in the locomotives.

W	L	PCT	G	GS	CG	IP	H	BB	SO	SHO	ERA
11	17	.393	59	18	5	239	233	112	62	0	4.14

James Alvin "Yank" Deas, *Catcher*

A mite catcher, little Yank Deas is best associated with the Atlantic City Bacharach Giants. Yank was a solid defender with limited offensive capabilities who often platooned behind the dish. During World War I, Yank remained stateside and played some service ball at Fort Dix.

(1916–1923): Atlantic City Bacharach Giants, New York Lincolns and Hilldale Daisies

John Herman "Hank" DeBerry, *Catcher*

In the wide-open catching race for the Indians, DeBerry had a chance to win the role going into the 1918 season. DeBerry was only 22 years old and was due to compete with a pair of 25-year-olds who couldn't hit .200 in 1917. However, with the war raging overseas, DeBerry had the desire to the join the U.S. Marine Corps and do his part. He missed the entire 1918 baseball season but was rejected by the Marines on account of a physical disability. Hank went on to enjoy a lengthy career with the Brooklyn Dodgers throughout the 1920s as a mainstay on Wilbert Robinson's Daffiness Boys.

G	R	H	2B	3B	HR	RBI	BB	SO	SB	AVG	Slug
648	170	494	81	16	11	234	148	119	13	.267	.346

Adam Joseph Debus, *Utility Infielder*

Adam's only major league action came in 1917, as he spelled Chuck Ward and Tony Boeckel on the left side of the infield. Unlike most ballplayers, Debus missed two entire years, 1918 and 1919, to service in the armed forces.

G	R	H	2B	3B	HR	RBI	BB	SO	SB	AVG	Slug
38	9	30	5	4	0	7	7	14	2	.229	.328

Joshua M. Devore, *Outfield*

An ideal lead-off man, Devore was both swift and adept at judging pitched balls. With the feet of Mercury and the eye of an eagle, Josh was a favorite of scrappy skipper John McGraw. When he joined the Giants in 1908, McGraw's outfield trio of Mike Donlin, Cy Seymour and Spike Shannon were all at least thirty years of age. Youth was in order in 1909 but Devore missed most of the season to illness. He won the left field job in 1910 and swiped 43 bases while also scoring 92 runs—a high total for the Deadball Era. Josh was a key ingredient in McGraw's NL flag-capturing teams of 1911 and 1912. He led the team in walks and steals in 1911 and had a good showing in the 1912 World Series.

After McGraw was done with Josh, he played some with the Reds and Phillies before he caught on with the Braves. His last major league action was with the world champion Braves of 1914. Four years later Devore entered the army and served at Camp Sherman. Legendary writer Harry Grayson remembered Devore's vice with playing cards. Grayson described Josh as "a gambler on and off the field. He always ended the season flat broke. He loved to gamble but wasn't lucky at it. He was only lucky as a ballplayer with bunts and bases on balls."

G	R	H	2B	3B	HR	RBI	BB	SO	SB	AVG	Slug
601	331	520	58	31	11	149	222	n/a	160	.272	.359

George Clark Dickerson, *Pitcher*

This Texas native's major league career consisted of one perfect inning for the 1917 Indians. Before his major league debut Clark attended military school, which served him well during his stint in the armed forces. After Clark joined Uncle Sam he quickly ascended to the rank of corporal and before he knew it, he was promoted to sergeant. With his background, Dickerson decided to seek a commission and he became a lieutenant before the war was over. After his discharge he didn't return to the majors.

W	L	PCT	G	GS	CG	IP	H	BB	SO	SHO	ERA
0	0	—	1	0	0	1	0	0	0	0	0.00

William Martin "Pickles" Dillhoefer, *Catcher*

A fan favorite for his hustling style of play, the diminutive Pickles (5'7" and 154 pounds) died while still an active player of typhoid fever. Shortly after Dillhoefer's marriage, he was hospitalized with the disease and his new bride stayed by his bedside until his final days. His playing career was less than stellar, as he hit .223 over 600 at-bats, but his gritty appeal endeared him to fans. Pickles missed the majority of the 1918 season to military service where he was stationed at Camp Merritt, New Jersey, in the Quartermasters Corps. Upon his discharge, Dillhoefer had reached the rank of sergeant.

G	R	H	2B	3B	HR	RBI	BB	SO	SB	AVG	Slug
247	59	134	16	10	0	48	35	30	12	.223	.283

William "Dizzy" Dismukes, *Pitcher*

Kansas City Monarchs legend Buck O'Neil credited Dismukes with teaching him the managerial and business sides of baseball. Dizzy was the traveling secretary of the Monarchs while O'Neil managed the team, and the two men were inseparable friends. Although Dismukes was regarded by Buck as a smart front office man, Dizzy was a fine pitcher before he took to the executive ranks. An exceptional man to have on your payroll, Leslie A. Heaphy described Dizzy as "smart and mentally tough which made him a dream player for every manager."

A journeyed ballplayer who pitched all over the country, Dismukes enjoyed a nomadic career. He may be best associated as a player with C.I. Taylor's Indianapolis ABCs even though he had a long tenure with the Monarchs in the front office. A submarine-style pitcher, Dizzy would work for the ABCs in the 1910s with an interruption to military service during World War I. He served with the 803rd Pioneer Infantry, and after his discharge took his first managerial role with the Dayton Marcos. Dismukes pitched into 1930 when he left the playing field for the manager's office. A man of many hats, Dizzy Dismukes played, managed and served as an executive in the Negro Leagues, and once the color line was knocked down, he scouted for the New York Yankees.

(1910–1930): Indianapolis ABCs, West Baden Sprudels, St. Louis Giants, Brooklyn Royal Giants, Lincoln Stars, Chicago American Giants, Dayton Marcos, Pittsburgh Keystones, Birmingham Black Barons, Memphis Red Sox, St. Louis Stars and Kansas City Monarchs

John Wesley Donaldson, *Pitcher*

A pitching star of the Deadball Era, Donaldson suffers from the quality stigma that hinders many Negro League ballplayers. John played ball for an integrated ballclub in the 1910s operated by white businessman J.L. Wilkinson, which would barnstorm throughout the country. They would play any team, any time, of any quality, which resulted in some bloated statistics on the players' part. Donaldson and other Negro League stars could pad their stats by playing teams of marginal caliber, such as steel mill and factory clubs. Wilkinson's All Nations team, which John pitched for, was a barnstorming outfit that played teams minor league clubs could easily beat.

Despite the quality stigma, Donaldson is a better known early star of the Negro Leagues. The left-hander had a sweeping curve and his drop was considered his "out-pitch." A native of Glasgow, Missouri, Donaldson pitched predominately with the All Nations team before World War I. During the war, John was inducted into the army and spent time in France with the infantry. Upon his stateside return, John kicked around baseball for two years before reuniting with Wilkinson when he established the Kansas City Monarchs. Although he was passed his prime, John worked a few seasons with the Monarchs but spent most of the 1920s playing in lesser semipro leagues. In her book, *The Kansas City Monarchs*, Janet Bruce wrote that Donaldson was once offered a hefty sum of money to move to Cuba, change his name, and return stateside and play ball in the white ranks as a Cuban.

(1913–1934): Kansas City Monarchs, All Nations, Chicago Giants, Indianapolis ABCs, Brooklyn Royal Giants, Lincoln Giants and Detroit Stars

McKinley "Bunny" Downs, *Second Base*

Downs was regarded as a fine glove man who left more than a little to be desired as a batter. He was often used in the number two slot to sacrifice the lead-off man into scoring position. Like white baseball's Ty Cobb, Downs served in the military during World War I at the end of the baseball season and missed little time on the diamond.

(1916–1928): Hilldale Daisies, Brooklyn Royal Giants, St. Louis Giants, Indianapolis ABCs, Atlantic City Bacharach Giants, Lincoln Giants and Philadelphia Tigers

John Leo "Paddy" Driscoll, *Utility Infielder*

Driscoll's career was rather brief. He appeared in only 13 games for the 1917 Cubs. However, Paddy is a member of the Hall of Fame ... the Football Hall of Fame, that is. Driscoll saw action at every infield position for the 1917 Cubs except first base. During World War I, Paddy served in the navy and was stationed at the Great Lakes.

G	R	H	2B	3B	HR	RBI	BB	SO	SB	AVG	Slug
13	2	3	1	0	0	3	2	6	2	.107	.143

Louis Baird "Pat" Duncan, *Outfield*

A noted hothead, Duncan was the first player to swat a homerun over the deep left-field fence at Crosley Field in Cincinnati. He constantly gave Cincinnati management fits with his behavior. Duncan once refused to sign his contract because the organization would not pay for his wife's hotel bill while she visited him during training. His disputes with Reds president August Herrmann were kept in the organization, but he found himself on the hot seat when he accosted umpire E.C. Quigley during a game. Quigley reported Duncan to Commissioner Landis, with a note that read he had "never been so grossly insulted in all [his] life." He missed the entire 1918 season to the war effort as well as the majority of the Reds' 1919 championship season. He returned in time for the Fall Classic and led all participants with eight runs batted in.

G	R	H	2B	3B	HR	RBI	BB	SO	SB	AVG	Slug
727	361	827	137	50	23	374	184	164	55	.307	.420

Benjamin Franklin Dyer, *Utilityman*

Capable of playing anywhere on the field, Dyer was regarded by writer Sam Crane as a "brilliant fielder." Dyer began his career under John McGraw in 1914 with the New York Giants but found a new home with the Tigers in 1916. Never a regular player, Ben only appeared in 13 games—he even tossed two shutout innings—before he was summoned for military duty in 1918.

G	R	H	2B	3B	HR	RBI	BB	SO	SB	AVG	Slug
105	27	49	10	1	0	18	15	47	4	.237	.295

James Joseph Dykes, *Third Base*

An argument could be made for Jimmy Dykes as the greatest manager in baseball history. Unlike men such as Stengel and Torre, Jimmy never had much talent but he always got the best out of what was given him. An outspoken, genial man, Dykes was a well-respected manager who was adept at handling different personalities. The aloof Jimmy Piersall raved about Dykes, and the legendary Connie Mack handpicked Dykes to replace him at the helm of the Athletics when he stepped down after fifty years as skipper.

Jimmy was a rookie during the 1918 season, the year that was interrupted by military duty during the First World War. The Mackmen were a last-place team and Connie was using Dykes at second base his freshman season. Jimmy was inducted into the army and spent a few months of service at Camp Greenleaf, Georgia. He joined the Athletics midway through the season and hit below .200 as a rookie. He would eventually make a name for himself in the game as a steady third baseman and stellar field general.

G	R	H	2B	3B	HR	RBI	BB	SO	SB	AVG	Slug
2,282	1,108	2,256	453	90	108	1,071	955	849	70	.280	.399

Harry Josiah Eccles, *Pitcher*

A tall strikeout pitcher, Eccles had a cup of coffee with Connie Mack's 1915 Athletics. Harry appeared in five games for the Mackmen, losing his only decision. He spent the 1918 season in the armed forces.

W	L	PCT	G	GS	CG	IP	H	BB	SO	SHO	ERA
0	1	.000	5	1	0	21	18	6	13	0	6.86

Macajah Marchand "Mack" Eggleston, *Catcher*

Mack had just started his career in Negro League baseball when he was drafted for service in the military during World War I. During the war, "Egg" remained stateside and served at a camp in Ohio. He returned to baseball and even though his career spanned into the 1930s, he isn't associated with any one team because of his nomadic nature. After his playing days, Mack entered the clergy and became a high-ranking official in the church.

(1919–1936): Baltimore Black Sox, Dayton Marcos, Detroit Stars, Columbus Buckeyes, Indianapolis ABCs, Washington Potomacs, Hilldale Daisies, Harrisburg Giants, Atlantic City Bacharach Giants, New York Black Yankees, Washington Pilots, Nashville Elite Giants and Homestead Grays

Howard Jonathan Ehmke, *Pitcher*

Ehmke began his career in the Federal League, which threatened the American and National leagues in 1914 and 1915. The tall right-hander became a reliable hurler for the Tigers when they acquired him after the Federal League folded. He won 17 games in both 1919 and 1922 and became a 20-game winner his first year with the Boston Red Sox. The Red Sox as a team in 1923 won just 61 games, with Ehmke posting 20 for a club with a .401 winning percentage.

Ehmke missed the entire 1918 season to service in the navy where he was stationed at the submarine base in San Pedro. Able to play baseball at San Pedro, Howard played with Chicago White Sox shortstop Swede Risberg, who would be banished for his role in the 1919 World Series. During his stint in the military, Howard pitched a benefit game that was held by the Red Cross. His return to the Tigers helped to turn the franchise around, as his 17 wins assisted the club in their 25-game improvement over the 1918 campaign.

W	L	PCT	G	GS	CG	IP	H	BB	SO	SHO	ERA
166	166	.500	427	338	199	2,822	2,873	1,042	1,030	19	3.75

Welton Claude "Rube" Ehrhardt, *Pitcher*

The stout right-hander was a 29-year-old rookie with Wilbert Robinson's 1924 Dodgers. Used primarily as a relief pitcher during his stint in the major leagues, Rube served in the armed forces during the First World War, which interrupted his minor league seasoning.

W	L	PCT	G	GS	CG	IP	H	BB	SO	SHO	ERA
22	34	.393	193	41	22	588	633	200	128	3	4.15

Henry Knox "Heinie" Elder, *Pitcher*

Elder appeared in one game for the 1913 Tigers, managed by Hall of Famer Hughie Jennings. The big southpaw gave up the diamond chores for a career in the military. Heinie served in both World Wars, and retired from the military with the rank of lieutenant colonel.

W	L	PCT	G	GS	CG	IP	H	BB	SO	SHO	ERA
0	0	—	1	0	0	3	4	5	0	0	9.00

Harold Bell "Rowdy" Elliott, *Catcher*

Rowdy saw his first major league action as a 19-year-old for Fred Lake's Boston Braves in 1910 when he appeared in three games. The light-hitting catcher waited six years before he saw big league duty again — with the Cubs. Elliott went 0-for-10 in 1918 before he lost the season to service as a firefighter in the navy.

G	R	H	2B	3B	HR	RBI	BB	SO	SB	AVG	Slug
157	36	97	15	5	1	44	19	23	5	.241	.311

Herbert Spencer Ellison, *Utilityman*

Ellison was the prototypical all-field and no-hit player. His chief asset was his versatility, as the Arkansas native was capable of playing almost anywhere on the field. He got into seven games for Hughie Jennings' Tigers in 1918 before he was summoned for the war effort. He was inducted into the armed forces on April 26, 1918, and missed the remainder of the baseball campaign. He served close to his home at Camp Pike.

G	R	H	2B	3B	HR	RBI	BB	SO	SB	AVG	Slug
135	32	75	13	4	1	39	30	55	9	.216	.284

Russell Elwood Ennis, *Catcher*

Ennis appeared in one game for the 1926 Senators when the club had star backstops Muddy Ruel and Hank Severeid on the roster. The backstop served in the armed forces during World War I before his major league debut and returned to the service after his playing days to participate in the Second World War.

G	R	H	2B	3B	HR	RBI	BB	SO	SB	AVG	Slug
1	0	0	0	0	0	0	0	0	0	—	—

Eric George Adolph Erickson, *Pitcher*

Much like Ty Cobb, Erickson was able to play a decent amount of the baseball season before he was lost to the military. His 2.49 ERA at the time of his departure was tops among Bengal hurlers. Erickson claimed to have ties to the Civil War, boasting that he was a descendent of the man who invented the monitor. During World War I, Erickson served in the United States Army and spent his time stationed at Fort Dix.

W	L	PCT	G	GS	CG	IP	H	BB	SO	SHO	ERA
34	56	.378	145	94	42	822	805	379	367	3	3.85

William James Evans, *Pitcher*

Not to be confused with the Hall of Fame umpire of the same name, the pitcher Evans spent pieces of three years in the major leagues with an interruption courtesy of World War I. The only club Evans pitched for was the Pirates, with whom he enjoyed his finest year in 1916 — his rookie campaign. He missed a portion of the 1917 season due to an undisclosed illness and the entire 1918 season to the war.

W	L	PCT	G	GS	CG	IP	H	BB	SO	SHO	ERA
2	13	.133	28	12	6	127	122	48	41	0	3.83

Joseph Patton Evans, *Third Base*

The light-hitting Evans, who swatted only three home runs in more than seven hundred games played, was the Indians primary third baseman when he was called for military service. Upon his return to the diamond, he found himself supplanted by veteran Larry Gardner. Evans was drafted into the army and trained at Little Rock, Arkansas. After his baseball career was over, he became a physician and surgeon.

G	R	H	2B	3B	HR	RBI	BB	SO	SB	AVG	Slug
733	306	529	71	31	3	210	212	152	64	.259	.328

Urban Clarence "Red" Faber, *Pitcher*

Baseball Hall of Fame right-hander Red Faber is considered a key ingredient to the 1919 Black Sox Scandal. Although Faber was no Eddie Cicotte, many think that had the injured spit-baller been healthy enough to take his turn in the World Series rotation, the scandal never would have happened. The redheaded Faber missed the majority of the 1918 season to service in the navy, which cut short a season in which he posted a 1.22 ERA over eleven games. While serving in the navy, Red was able to play a little baseball for the Great Lakes squad.

W	L	PCT	G	GS	CG	IP	H	BB	SO	SHO	ERA
254	212	.545	669	483	275	4,087	4,106	1,213	1,471	29	3.15

James Lamar "Rags" Faircloth, *Pitcher*

Before Faircloth took his turn on a major league pitching mound, he tossed some innings for Uncle Sam. Rags played service ball with the Great Lakes Naval Station team in 1918 and saw his only major league action the following season with the Phillies. Rags' arm didn't hold up as he blew out his wing in 1920 and went to work for Westinghouse Electric Company as a sales engineer.

W	L	PCT	G	GS	CG	IP	H	BB	SO	SHO	ERA
0	0	—	2	0	0	2	5	0	0	0	9.00

James Alexander Ferguson, *Pitcher*

Ferguson appeared in just one game in 1918, his major league debut, before he departed for the army. During his military tenure, Ferguson served at Fort Meade. He wouldn't get another look in the big leagues until 1921, again with the Yankees, but his career didn't take off until he was sent to the Red Sox. After posting an ERA near six with the Bronx Bombers, Alex posted a respectable 4.32 mark in his first year with Boston.

W	L	PCT	G	GS	CG	IP	H	BB	SO	SHO	ERA
61	85	.418	257	166	62	1,242	1,455	482	397	2	4.93

Wilson Lloyd "Chick" Fewster, *Utilityman*

Best known as one of the men on base when Babe Herman tripled into a double play, Fewster played briefly for the Yankees in 1918 before he joined the military. A scrappy, versatile ballplayer, Chick's baseball career was a painful one. After his military discharge, he was nearly killed by a pitched ball from the hand of Jeff Pfeffer. With his skull fractured, a steel plate was placed in Fewster's head that allowed him to return to the game. Had the accident occurred before his military induction, Uncle Sam would have assuredly rejected him on medical grounds.

G	R	H	2B	3B	HR	RBI	BB	SO	SB	AVG	Slug
644	282	506	91	12	6	167	240	264	57	.258	.326

Dana Fillingim, *Pitcher*

Although Fillingim was a decent major league pitcher with a misleading win-loss record, he enjoyed his greatest success on the mound while serving in the navy. Dana served with a naval reserve unit based out of Newport and posted twenty wins while hurling for the military. He spent five years playing for the Braves and saw action with the two Philadelphia clubs between his stint in Beantown. His bread-and-butter pitch was the spitball, which allowed him to post a 3.56 ERA in his career.

W	L	PCT	G	GS	CG	IP	H	BB	SO	SHO	ERA
47	72	.395	200	114	59	1,076	1,170	313	270	10	3.56

Ray Lyle Fisher, *Pitcher*

Fisher had been a reliable starting pitcher for the Yankees, leading the club with a 2.19 ERA in 1917, the year before he left the game for the military. As a 30-year-old, Fisher was stationed at Fort Slocum where he served as an assistant physical director. When he returned to the game, Fisher was no longer a Yankee. He had been sent to the Cincinnati Reds and proceeded to win a world championship in the infamous 1919 World Series.

W	L	PCT	G	GS	CG	IP	H	BB	SO	SHO	ERA
98	95	.508	279	207	110	1,755	1,667	481	680	20	2.82

Edward Henry Fitzpatrick, *Second Base*

When Fitzpatrick reached the major leagues in 1915, he was groomed to replace veteran second baseman Johnny Evers, who was constantly battling nagging injuries. He played 71 games at second in 1915 and 46 the following year. When Evers was dealt, Fitzpatrick wasn't given the second base role but platooned with Johnny Rawlings and Mike Massey. Ed missed the entire 1918 season to service in the armed forces and gave up baseball upon his return because he made more money working on his family farm.

G	R	H	2B	3B	HR	RBI	BB	SO	SB	AVG	Slug
251	91	158	35	7	1	59	70	84	22	.227	.301

Ira James Flagstead, *Outfield*

Flagstead was an amateur boxer with aspirations of making a career out of pugilism until a fight forced him to change his mind. Billed to fight an unknown boxer, Flagstead showed up in the ring and, much to his dismay, was forced to spar with a man forty pounds heavier. After the bout, Flagstead gave up boxing and took to the baseball diamond. Noted as an exceptional but reckless defender, Flagstead was an original "wallbanger" who saw action in Europe during the war.

G	R	H	2B	3B	HR	RBI	BB	SO	SB	AVG	Slug
1,218	644	1,201	261	49	40	450	467	288	71	.290	.460

John Edmond Frill, *Pitcher*

A sturdy southpaw who pitched for three teams in two major league seasons, John Frill saw his last big league action with the 1912 Reds. When the war broke out, Frill's major league career was over but his military career was just beginning. However, his time in khaki didn't last long. The Spanish flu, an epidemic that bombarded army posts during the war and claimed 17,000 servicemen's lives, took the life of John Edmond Frill in September of 1918.

W	L	PCT	G	GS	CG	IP	H	BB	SO	SHO	ERA
3	2	.600	16	10	3	67	90	7	33	1	5.91

Dellos Clinton Gainer, *First Base*

Gainer was a reserve first baseman with the Detroit Tigers when he was dealt to the Red Sox in 1914 to back up Dick Hoblitzell. He offered a solid bat off the bench. Gainer missed the entire 1918 season when he enlisted as a yeoman at Boston Yard where he played some service ball with Jack Barry. Gainer also saw some action on the Great Lakes baseball club during his stint in the military.

G	R	H	2B	3B	HR	RBI	BB	SO	SB	AVG	Slug
546	218	438	75	36	14	185	149	n/a	54	.272	.390

Frederick Jacob Gaiser, *Pitcher*

The German-born Fred Gaiser appeared in one game for the 1908 Cardinals of John McCloskey. Ten years after his major league debut Fred was doing his part during the First World War when he contracted Spanish flu, a deadly epidemic that killed 17,000 servicemen, one of which was Gaiser.

W	L	PCT	G	GS	CG	IP	H	BB	SO	SHO	ERA
0	0	—	1	0	0	2	4	3	2	0	9.00

Lawrence Kirby "Gil" Gallagher, *Shortstop*

A little switch-hitting shortstop, Gallagher's major league career consisted of seven games with Fred Mitchell's last-place 1922 Braves. The Braves that year were the only major league team to lose 100 games. Gil played more ball in the service during World War I than he played in the show.

G	R	H	2B	3B	HR	RBI	BB	SO	SB	AVG	Slug
7	1	1	1	0	0	2	1	7	0	.045	.091

James Cato "Bad News" Galloway, *Second Base*

James Cato Galloway owns one of the strangest nicknames in baseball history. His moniker originated from some exercises in cunning on his part. While playing in the minors, Galloway knew he could make more money playing a pickup game with an amateur team that would give him a cut of the gate receipts. As a result, he would often wire the team that owned his contract and inform his skipper that he was too ill to play in order to take the field with the amateur squad. His wires always relayed "bad news."

Bad News played for the 1912 St. Louis Cardinals — his only major league action — and missed a season in the bushes to service in the armed forces during the First World War. After his playing days concluded, Galloway took his bad news routine and applied it to umpiring in the low minors.

G	R	H	2B	3B	HR	RBI	BB	SO	SB	AVG	Slug
21	4	10	2	0	0	4	5	8	2	.185	.222

Robert Edward "Jude" Gans, *Outfield*

A Deadball Era star who spent a number of seasons with the Chicago American Giants, Gans would often jump the team to play ball in the East but usually returned to the Windy City. During the First World War, Jude entered the military and was commissioned an officer. He served some time overseas with the 59th French Division.

(1911–1927): New York Lincoln Giants, Chicago American Giants, Cuban Giants

Robert Norton Geary, *Pitcher*

Nicknamed "Speed," Bob Geary spent parts of three seasons in the major leagues — two with Philadelphia and one with the Cincinnati Reds. Speed was in the midst of a solid season in 1918 (two shutouts in just seven starts) when he was summoned by his Cincinnati draft board for service in the United States Army. When Geary returned to the major leagues, he was no longer effective, as his ERA skyrocketed to 4.78 in 1919.

W	L	PCT	G	GS	CG	IP	H	BB	SO	SHO	ERA
4	9	.308	35	10	7	148	164	51	41	2	3.47

Joseph Edward Genewich, *Pitcher*

Genewich had a nine-year career at the major league level, spent predominately with the Boston Braves after World War I. Joe was in his early twenties when he joined the navy during the First World War. He was able to play some service ball while stationed at the Great Lakes. He made his major league debut after his discharge, pitched with the Braves and Giants, and later returned to the military to help out during World War II.

W	L	PCT	G	GS	CG	IP	H	BB	SO	SHO	ERA
73	92	.442	272	166	71	1,401	1,610	402	316	8	4.29

Walter Gerber, *Shortstop*

One of the finest shortstops of the 1920s, Gerber manned the position for the Browns from 1917 to 1928. "Spooks" lost the majority of the 1918 season when he reported for military duty at Camp Sherman in Chillicothe, Ohio. A broken leg sustained in 1925 hindered Gerber's game, as he accumulated only eight extra-base hits in 131 games during the 1926 campaign. Gerber followed a legacy at the position for the Browns (who are now the Baltimore Orioles), which began with Bobby Wallace and saw Vern Stephens, slick-fielding Mark Belanger and "Iron Man" Cal Ripken Jr. succeed Spooks.

G	R	H	2B	3B	HR	RBI	BB	SO	SB	AVG	Slug
1,522	558	1,309	172	46	7	476	465	357	41	.257	.313

Edward James Gill, *Pitcher*

The year before Gill made his major league debut he served in the armed forces during World War I. After his discharge he joined Clark Griffith's Senators and won one game while losing his only other decision. In the mid 1990s, the former teammate of such notables as Walter Johnson, Sam Rice, Joe Judge and Clyde Milan was one of the oldest living former ballplayers. He died two months after his 100th birthday.

W	L	PCT	G	GS	CG	IP	H	BB	SO	SHO	ERA
1	1	.500	16	2	0	37	38	21	7	0	4.86

William Patrick Gleason, *Second Base*

Not related to the star St. Louis Browns player of the late 1800s of the same name, the younger Gleason had three cups of coffee at the major league level. Originally called up by the Pirates in 1916, Billy was used sparingly by the Bucs that year and again in 1917. He spent the 1918 season in the military and didn't return to the majors until 1921 — with the Browns.

G	R	H	2B	3B	HR	RBI	BB	SO	SB	AVG	Slug
40	9	26	1	1	0	8	11	11	1	.220	.246

Frank Elmer Gleich, *Outfielder*

Gleich joined the Yankees in 1919 — the year after his military hitch — and played with them through the 1920 season. The Bronx Bombers had already brought in Red Sox star Duffy Lewis by 1919, and when they bought another Bosox outfielder named Babe Ruth, Gleich's chances of cracking the Yankees outfield were nil. Shortly after he left the Yankees, Frank worked for the railroad and played semi-pro ball with his locomotive outfit.

G	R	H	2B	3B	HR	RBI	BB	SO	SB	AVG	Slug
29	6	6	0	0	0	4	7	10	0	.133	.133

Harry Melville Glenn, *Catcher*

Husky Harry Glenn made his major league debut with the 1915 Cardinals of Miller Huggins. That year the Redbirds had behind the dish ironman receiver Frank Snyder, who led major league catchers with 144 games caught. Glenn was farmed out by St. Louis and remained on the plantation until World War I requested his services. While training in the army as a mechanic, Husky contracted pneumonia and died at an army training facility.

G	R	H	2B	3B	HR	RBI	BB	SO	SB	AVG	Slug
6	1	5	0	0	0	1	3	0	0	.313	.313

Clyde Samuel Goodwin, *Pitcher*

Goodwin's career consisted of four games with the 1906 Senators of Jake Stahl. The 19-year-old kid from Shade, Ohio, lost his only two major league decisions. Twelve years after his major league debut, Clyde served with the U.S. Navy during the First World War.

W	L	PCT	G	GS	CG	IP	H	BB	SO	SHO	ERA
0	2	.000	4	3	1	22	20	13	9	0	4.50

Marvin Mardo Goodwin, *Pitcher*

Goodwin was a people's hero during the First World War. He enlisted in the Air Corps, surrendering a promising ball diamond career to serve his country. He was quickly establishing himself as one of the Cardinals' best pitchers as he paced the club with a 2.22 ERA in 1917. However, Goodwin's loyalty to his country came first and he left the diamond to lend his services to the armed forces.

Goodwin initially attended ground school in San Antonio, which would prepare him for a stint in the Air Corps Reserves. While wearing military fatigues, Goodwin was commissioned as a lieutenant and served as a flying instructor. He returned to the ball diamond in 1919 to post the lowest ERA on the Redbirds staff with a 2.51 mark. After the conclusion of the 1925 season, Goodwin, then a member of the Cincinnati Reds, suffered severe injuries due to a plane crash. The injuries would later claim his life.

W	L	PCT	G	GS	CG	IP	H	BB	SO	SHO	ERA
21	25	.457	102	48	19	447	467	100	121	3	3.30

Theodore Lee Goulait, *Pitcher*

Ted Goulait's major league career consisted of one start for the 1912 Giants. In 1918, with the war in full swing, Goulait joined the armed forces and was sent overseas to France. Although the conditions weren't ideal, Ted was able to visit his ancestral lands during the war. After his big league career, Mr. Goulait served in politics in his native Michigan. In 1933, he saved the state capitol building at Lansing when he spotted a fire and rounded up folks to fight it.

W	L	PCT	G	GS	CG	IP	H	BB	SO	SHO	ERA
0	0	—	1	1	0	7	11	4	6	0	6.43

Henry Morgan Gowdy, *Catcher*

A patriot in every sense of the word, Hank Gowdy saw action during World War I with the 166th Infantry Regiment in France. Gowdy left baseball early in 1917 to enlist in the military (one of only four major league players to do so), which created a void at the catcher position that forced the Braves to fall from a .586 winning percentage in 1916 to .471 percentage without his services.

Gowdy owned the respect of baseball fans before he joined the armed forces, as the good-natured man could often be found playing sandlot ball with the kids of Boston while serving as a member of the Braves. However, as the war raged overseas, America embraced Hank wholeheartedly. He was the first major league player to leave the ball diamond and enlist in the army, initially as a private in the Ohio National Guard. Eager to go overseas and do his duty, Gowdy was part of the first American attack during the war. He witnessed firsthand some of the hardest fighting. In letters he sent back to teammates Art Nehf and Ed Reulbach, he informed his old chums about going "over the top" six separate times and never receiving a single scratch.

The army was well aware of Gowdy's strength as a leader and quickly promoted him to the rank of sergeant. He had other plans and sought out a commission as well as a change in military vocation. Gowdy was transferred to the gas division and was awarded his commission as a lieutenant. Always one to offer baseball analogies, he stated that wearing a gas mask was less comfortable than donning a catcher's mask. Newspapers across the country kept strict tabs on Hank, baseball's first true hero, and his actions overseas. A common headline in the papers was "Hank Gowdy Over There is Busy Gassing Boches."

During the holiday season, Gowdy was busy fighting for his country but took time out to write a letter home. Hank wrote, "It would be great to wake up in old Boston Christmas morning and get out in Copley Square and wish everyone a Merry Christmas, whether I know him or not." But the season's greetings were interrupted by some inaccurate journalism. The hearts of Americans skipped a beat when it was falsely reported that he was killed in the Argonne Forest. In the midst of enjoying a meal overseas, Gowdy read the story of his death in a mess hall and immediately became concerned with his mother's well-being, worried that her health would slip after reading the false reports of his battlefield demise.

When Hank returned to America, he was warmly received like no other athlete had ever been. Writer Jack Keene regarded Hank as the game's "biggest idol" for the upcoming 1919 baseball campaign. A lifelong supporter and promoter for the YMCA, Gowdy returned to service for World War II as a 53-year-old man to organize athletics for the army, serving in two separate conflicts. Although his playing career was modest at best, Hank Gowdy's legacy stretches beyond the foul lines, to a place where men of uncommon valor reside.

G	R	H	2B	3B	HR	RBI	BB	SO	SB	AVG	Slug
1,050	270	738	122	27	21	322	311	247	59	.270	.327

Edward Leslie Grant, *Utility Infielder*

One of the more academically distinguished men to play professional baseball, Eddie Grant was a Harvard graduate. A valuable reserve infielder during his playing days, "Harvard Eddie" could fill in anywhere on the infield. The swift man from Massachusetts wasn't of the same caliber as Honus Wagner or Bill Dahlen — infield stars of the Deadball Era — but possessed value courtesy of his versatility. Grant broke in with the Indians in 1905 but didn't stick. He made good with the 1907 Phillies and remained at the major league level through 1915. After the 1915 season, Grant quit John McGraw's Giants to return to college with law school aspirations.

Grant put the books aside when America entered the war. With his heart set on acquiring a commission in the army, Grant left the college campus and attended officer's training at Plattsburg. From Plattsburg, the officer went to Camp Upton before he eventually was shipped overseas. With the 307th Infantry Regiment, Harvard Eddie witnessed heavy combat action. His outfit was designated with the unenviable assignment of finding and bringing back the Lost Battalion, trapped behind enemy lines somewhere in the Argonne Forest. The Lost Battalion, under the leadership of Major Charles Whittlesey, waited for their rescue, pinned down by enemy fire.

Captain Grant led his troops into the Argonne Forest to locate the Lost Battalion but it would be his final mission. On October 21, 1918, while trudging through the thick Argonne Forest, Captain Grant was felled by an enemy shell. Killed in action, Grant was the first such casualty in the annals of major league baseball.

Eddie Grant's close friend, Captain Harry McCormick, suggested that the New York Giants recognize Grant's sacrifice by offering some form of tribute for the fallen hero. Given that Grant's last seasons were played at the Polo Grounds under John McGraw, McCormick went to the Giants brass with his request. The Giants were accommodating and erected a monument in Captain Grant's honor within the walls of the Polo Grounds. Eddie Grant may not have been as good as the Wagners and Cobbs on the ball diamond, but he had the stuff that heroes are made of. Of Grant, Alex Sullivan wrote, "He was lacking in aggressiveness on the diamond, although he could always be depended on to fight till the last ditch for victory. He was the sort of chap that never gave up, no matter how big the odds were against his side."

G	R	H	2B	3B	HR	RBI	BB	SO	SB	AVG	Slug
990	399	844	79	30	5	277	233	n/a	153	.249	.295

Leroy Grant, *First Base*

A hulking first baseman, Grant had a long association with the Chicago American Giants that began in the Deadball Era and continued through the Lively Ball Era. Men as large as Grant weren't common in the Deadball Era, but when bashing the ball became popular, fellows like Grant were in demand. With abilities akin to that of old Washington Senators first baseman Zeke Bonura, Leroy was a rather immobile, stationary first baseman who played because of his bat. Able to play most of the 1918 baseball season, Grant was inducted into the military late in the war effort.

(1911–1924): Chicago American Giants, New York Lincoln Giants, Indianapolis ABCs and Cleveland Browns

Howard Watterson Gregory, *Pitcher*

Gregory had a cup of coffee with the 1911 St. Louis Browns and appeared in just three contests. Although his major league service time was brief, Gregory had a long life in baseball. After his playing days, Howie spent many years managing in the minor Western League. He served in the military during World War I and also pitched briefly for a shipyard team.

W	L	PCT	G	GS	CG	IP	H	BB	SO	SHO	ERA
0	1	.000	3	1	0	7	11	4	1	0	5.14

Burleigh Arland Grimes, *Pitcher*

One of the last legal spitballers during his playing days, Grimes was nicknamed "Ol' Stubblebeard" because he wouldn't shave the morning of his scheduled starts. In 1918, Grimes was a youngster who had just started a career on the diamond that would carry him to Cooperstown. Unlike many players who served during the war, Burleigh played the 1918 season out to its entirety. One of the few bright spots for Brooklyn that year, he led the staff with 19 wins. After the close of the baseball season, he and fellow Brooklyn moundsman Rube Marquard enlisted in the navy. Grimes reported to the Great Lakes.

W	L	PCT	G	GS	CG	IP	H	BB	SO	SHO	ERA
270	212	.560	615	497	314	4,178	4,406	1,295	1,512	35	3.52

John Thomas Grimes, *Pitcher*

When perusing the baseball record books, the name John Grimes will jump off the page. His offerings had a tendency to strike persons as well. Grimes set a record with the 1897 Cardinals when he hit six batters in a nine-inning contest — his claim to fame. Although Grimes struggled in his short major league tenure, his service in Uncle Sam's khaki was more controlled. After his stint with the Redbirds, Grimes joined the army and was commissioned an officer. During the Spanish-American War, Grimes wasn't an erratic hurler but Captain Grimes.

Grimes spent more than thirty years in the army and was a participant in the Spanish-American War, the Sioux Indian Campaign and World War I. The old military officer lived a long, fruitful life, dying in his mid 90s.

W	L	PCT	G	GS	CG	IP	H	BB	SO	SHO	ERA
0	2	.000	3	1	1	20	24	8	4	0	5.95

Louis Joseph Guisto, *First Base*

One of the four major league players to enlist during the 1917 season, Guisto served in the navy. He didn't see major league action again until 1921 as a reserve. Guisto's name is familiar to residents near St. Mary's College in California; their baseball diamond is named after him.

G	R	H	2B	3B	HR	RBI	BB	SO	SB	AVG	Slug
156	35	88	19	3	0	59	46	44	5	.196	.252

Bruno Philip Haas, *Pitcher*

Arguably the worst pitcher in the history of the major leagues, Bruno couldn't buy a strike at the major league level. He only tossed 14 innings at the highest level but they were 14 of the ugliest frames ever worked. Haas averaged two walks per inning, for a grand total of 28 free passes. Haas, a well-built athlete, would eventually give up baseball for the gridiron. However, before Bruno took to the pigskin, he served in the navy during World War I.

Like a number of White Sox players, Bruno was listed as ineligible by the Pale Hose for quitting the team and working for a shipyard. The bosses of the White Sox had it wrong. Haas did leave the Chisox but not for the shipyards: he enlisted in the naval aviation wing in November 1917. Bruno took his ground school at Boston and was commissioned an ensign. He proved such a natural at flying that the navy sent him to the Pensacola Flying School to work as an instructor. He spent the war helping aviation cadets learn to fly.

W	L	PCT	G	GS	CG	IP	H	BB	SO	SHO	ERA
0	2	.000	6	2	1	14	23	28	7	0	12.21

George Stanley Halas, *Outfield*

A gifted natural athlete, many people thought Halas would excel at baseball if only he would give up the gridiron. His arm was likened to that of Duffy Lewis—one of the top defensive outfielders of the Deadball Era. But George gave up on baseball after an unsuccessful trial with the 1919 Yankees, and New York gave his outfield job to some kid they obtained from the Red Sox named Babe Ruth. During the First World War Halas played service ball with the navy at the Great Lakes and was instrumental in the team's success on the football field. After his discharge he tried his hand at baseball but gave it up for football. It was a wise choice on his part; he was a charter member of the Pro Football Hall of Fame.

G	R	H	2B	3B	HR	RBI	BB	SO	SB	AVG	Slug
12	0	2	0	0	0	0	0	8	0	.091	.091

Raymond Timothy "Pat" Haley, *Catcher*

Unlike most players, Haley missed two full seasons to the war effort as he served in the army through 1919. Usually a third- and sometimes even a fourth-string catcher, Haley caught Babe Ruth while he played for the Red Sox in 1915. A trade to Connie Mack's Athletics gave Haley a better chance for playing time but he never was a regular receiver.

G	R	H	2B	3B	HR	RBI	BB	SO	SB	AVG	Slug
81	17	53	8	1	0	15	11	32	2	.248	.294

Newton Schurz Halliday, *Pinch Hitter*

Halliday had one at-bat at the major league level. With the 1916 Pirates, Newt struck out in his only plate appearance. Newt was eager to get another chance to show his stuff at the highest level but the war interceded, forcing him to wait. He enlisted in the navy and was stationed at the Great Lakes. At the Great Lakes, he contracted pneumonia and died.

G	R	H	2B	3B	HR	RBI	BB	SO	SB	AVG	Slug
1	0	0	0	0	0	0	0	1	0	.000	.000

Earl Andrew Hamilton, *Pitcher*

Hamilton was a typical hard-luck pitcher. He spent his best years toiling for the poor St. Louis Browns. During his stint with the Browns, the club posted team winning percentages of .344 in 1912, .373 in 1913 and .409 in 1915. His luck changed when he was dealt to the Pirates prior to the 1918 season. Hamilton shot out of the gate as well as any pitcher could hope for in 1918, as he appeared in six games and tossed a complete-game victory in all of those contests with a 0.83 ERA. However, the day after his sixth consecutive complete-game victory, Hamilton enlisted in the navy and missed the remainder of the season.

W	L	PCT	G	GS	CG	IP	H	BB	SO	SHO	ERA
117	147	.443	410	262	140	2,342	2,319	773	790	17	3.16

Earl Sylvester Hanson, *Pitcher*

Sometimes listed as "Ollie" Hanson, Earl made two starts with the 1921 Cubs. Those two appearances both resulted in losses and were the extent of his major league career. Before his Chicago sojourn, Hanson served with distinction in the United States Army. He saw action on the French battlefields and returned home to play ball in the minors. During spring training in 1921, Earl impressed skipper Johnny Evers and made two starts before he was shipped back to the minors. Although he never made good at the highest level, Earl had a fine minor league career.

W	L	PCT	G	GS	CG	IP	H	BB	SO	SHO	ERA
0	2	.000	2	2	1	9	9	6	2	0	7.00

Harry Francis Hanson, *Reserve*

Hanson was a 17-year-old kid when he made his major league debut with Frank Chance's 1913 Yankees. The youngest player on the squad, Harry appeared in only one game—the extent of his major league career. He beat around the minors for a few years until the United States entered the war. Hanson enlisted in the armed forces and decided to make the military a career. Rather than return to the diamond, Harry stayed with Uncle Sam and was still active in the military when World War II began.

G	R	H	2B	3B	HR	RBI	BB	SO	SB	AVG	Slug
1	0	0	0	0	0	0	0	0	0	.000	.000

William Henry "Pat" Hardgrove, *Pinch Hitter*

Hardgrove's major league career consisted of two at-bats. Short and slender, he was unable to wrest command of any position for the powerhouse White Sox. His two at-bats came in 1918, the same season he left the diamond to serve in the United States Army.

G	R	H	2B	3B	HR	RBI	BB	SO	SB	AVG	Slug
2	0	0	0	0	0	0	0	0	0	.000	.000

Joseph Harris, *First Base*

Harris served in the 80th Division of the 320th Infantry during his time in the military. He saw action on the frontlines, where he suffered a fractured skull (this is the widely accepted story, but more on that later), which affected his play throughout the remainder of his career. Before Harris left for the war, he was Cleveland's second-best hitter, behind Hall of Famer Tris Speaker. He was declared ineligible in 1920 for playing in an outlaw league but was reinstated in 1922. While playing with the Red Sox in 1922, he paced the club with a .316 batting average.

Harris wasn't one of the lads that spent the war idle. He was an enlisted fighting man in the infantry and combat was the route for him during the war. When he was about to get sent overseas, he learned that two Cleveland teammates, pitchers Ed Klepfer and Red Torkelson, had both been commissioned lieutenants. Joe said,

"It doesn't seem right for a .300 hitter to salute his own pitchers—wonder if I'll have to keep it up after we get back?" But Harris didn't have to worry about saluting pitchers when he was shipped overseas with the 320th Infantry Regiment. Sent to the frontlines, Sergeant Harris saw plenty of combat action and feared he'd never make it home.

In a letter Joe wrote home to friend and sportswriter Henry P. Edwards, he said, "I have seen some wonderful sights and had some terrible experiences. Was up to the line for fifteen days and bid ol' Cleveland goodbye more than once, as I thought there was not much chance. Got caught between our barrage and the Jerrys one morning and thought I would have to face Old Nick before the morning was over but I guess God was with me." Harris would later suffer a fractured skull that was initially listed as gravely serious by writers. Many thought he was horribly wounded in battle by shrapnel tearing through his scalp, but Joe was actually involved in a motor vehicle accident that left him in poor condition. Shortly after news came across the seas that Sergeant Harris was on his deathbed in France, Cleveland skipper Lee Fohl received a wire from Joe that read, "Arrived in New York today. Will be ready to play in two weeks."

Joe did sustain some rather serious wounds in the accident—his skull was fractured and he broke several ribs—but he never conceded that he was ever gravely injured. When he returned stateside, he was still under the care of a surgeon but was determined to play baseball in short time. In 1919, he showed that his wounds didn't hinder his play when he hit .375 in 62 games. Unjustly blacklisted shortly thereafter for playing in an outlaw league, Harris was simply trying to get more at-bats under his belt for the time he missed while on the frontlines in Europe. His reinstatement was an obvious course of action.

G	R	H	2B	3B	HR	RBI	BB	SO	SB	AVG	Slug
970	461	963	201	64	47	517	418	188	35	.317	.472

Lemuel Hawkins, *First Base*

Like white baseball's Blackie Schwamb, Negro Leaguer Hawkins was an ominous cloud that hung over the game. Although a ballplayer, Hawkins was essentially a career criminal who was shot and killed during a failed robbery attempt after his playing days. Killed by his own partner in the heist, Lemuel was shot through the brain. During World War I, Hawkins was spotted by John McGraw and Casey Stengel when he was playing service ball at Fort Huachuca, and Stengel recommended him to Kansas City Monarchs owner J.L. Wilkinson. Wilkinson promptly bought Hawkins and a number of his Fort Huachuca teammates, which included Hall of Famer Bullet Rogan, on McGraw and Stengel's testimonies.

(1921–1928): Kansas City Monarchs and Chicago American Giants

Edmund Hearn, *Pinch Hitter*

Hearn had two at-bats with the 1910 Red Sox—the extent of his major league career. The California native enlisted in the army during World War I and served with B Battery of the 144th Field Artillery.

G	R	H	2B	3B	HR	RBI	BB	SO	SB	AVG	Slug
2	0	0	0	0	0	0	0	0	n/a	.000	.000

Harry Edwin Heilmann, *Outfield*

A pupil of the great Ty Cobb, Heilmann became an overnight hitting success due in part to the tutelage given by the Georgia Peach. He took what Cobb taught him and applied it, thus garnering four batting titles, which gave teacher and student fifteen such titles between them. Harry was a raw youngster when World War I broke out, rotating between first base and the outfield. The Hall of Famer was able to play in 79 games for the Tigers in 1918 before he was summoned by Uncle Sam. As an older man, during the Second World War, Heilmann entertained troops at various ballparks.

G	R	H	2B	3B	HR	RBI	BB	SO	SB	AVG	Slug
2,146	1,291	2,660	542	151	183	1,537	856	550	112	.342	.520

Harry Anton Heitmann, *Pitcher*

Not to be confused with Detroit's Hall of Fame Slugger Harry Heilmann, Heitmann appeared in only one major league game. The right-hander received his look in 1918 before he was whisked away into the navy.

W	L	PCT	G	GS	CG	IP	H	BB	SO	SHO	ERA
0	1	.000	1	1	0	1	4	0	0	0	108.00

Otto C. Hess, *Pitcher*

Otto Hess was a solid southpaw in the majors, first with Cleveland and later with the Boston Braves. He was a 20-game winner for Cleveland in 1906, but a leg injury kept him out of action for pieces of 1907 and 1908. He was a member of George Stallings' Miracle Braves in 1914 that swept the highly favored Athletics of Connie Mack in the World Series. His major league career ended in 1915, but when Uncle Sam needed him in 1918, Hess answered the called and served during World War I.

W	L	PCT	G	GS	CG	IP	H	BB	SO	SHO	ERA
71	88	.447	198	165	129	1,418	1,355	448	580	18	2.98

George Edward Hesselbacher, *Pitcher*

Connie Mack didn't have to travel far to find Hesselbacher. The manager of the Athletics looked to his backyard and signed the Philadelphia native after he had lost such star hurlers as Eddie Plank and Chief Bender. The American League's doormat at the time George joined them, the A's finished 36–117 in 1916, George's only season with the club. Hesselbacher gave the game up for life in the armed forces. The ex-ballplayer served as a commissioned officer during the war.

W	L	PCT	G	GS	CG	IP	H	BB	SO	SHO	ERA
0	4	.000	6	4	2	26	37	22	6	0	7.27

David James Hickman, *Outfield*

Hickman attended the Bingham Military Academy prior to his baseball career, which gave him a taste of what he would endure during the 1918 season. A former Federal League player, Hickman joined Hall of Famer Wilbert Robinson's Dodgers after the Federal League folded. He spent one year as a regular in the Dodger lineup, hitting the worst among regulars with a .219 batting average. He was able to play in 53 games before he was lost to the military in

1918. During the war, he served in the navy and took part in an Army-Navy Championship game.

G	R	H	2B	3B	HR	RBI	BB	SO	SB	AVG	Slug
253	84	158	26	13	8	70	37	114	27	.217	.322

Andrew Aird High, *Third Base/Second Base*

Handy Andy was a capable, versatile defender throughout his baseball career. The little infielder could fill in almost anywhere and had a gifted batting eye. High was one of baseball's toughest strikeout victims, and his ability to make contact was sensational. Before Handy Andy played his first major league baseball game, he served his country during the First World War. During the battle, High was a member of the United States Navy. He would later become baseball's top scout.

G	R	H	2B	3B	HR	RBI	BB	SO	SB	AVG	Slug
1,314	618	1,250	195	65	44	482	425	130	33	.284	.388

Bruce Smith Hitt, *Pitcher*

Bruce Hitt appeared in two major league games, both in 1917 with the Cardinals. The Texan spent the entire 1918 season off the ball diamond and in the employ of the United States Navy.

W	L	PCT	G	GS	CG	IP	H	BB	SO	SHO	ERA
0	0	—	2	0	0	4	7	1	1	0	9.00

William Lee Hobbs, *Reserve*

Hobbs had two cups of coffee with the Reds during the Deadball Era and Cincinnati finished in seventh place each season. His last major league action came with the 1916 Reds of Christy Mathewson. During World War I, Hobbs served with the United States Army.

G	R	H	2B	3B	HR	RBI	BB	SO	SB	AVG	Slug
10	1	2	1	0	0	1	2	3	1	.133	.200

Richard Carleton Hoblitzell, *First Base*

Hoblitzell came from a family of practicing dentists and joined the Army Dental Corps in 1918. It was a chore on his part simply to enter the service since he was initially refused by the army on medical grounds. After Dick had surgery to cure his deficiencies, he was accepted for duty. He was stationed at Nitrate Plant #1 in Sheffield, Alabama, and remained in the army while other ballplayers returned to the diamond. Hoblitzell missed the entire 1919 and 1920 seasons to military service and never played another game of major league baseball upon his discharge.

G	R	H	2B	3B	HR	RBI	BB	SO	SB	AVG	Slug
1,314	591	1,310	194	88	27	593	407	n/a	173	.278	.374

Edward Francis Hock, *Outfield*

A minor league sensation who never made the grade in the majors, the man from Franklin Furnace, Ohio, was only given ten at-bats in three major league trials. Before Hock broke in with the 1920 Cardinals, he served in the armed forces during the First World War. Eddie enlisted in the army and missed a season of minor league action to the war effort.

G	R	H	2B	3B	HR	RBI	BB	SO	SB	AVG	Slug
19	7	1	0	0	0	0	0	2	0	.100	.100

William Booth Hopper, *Pitcher*

Nicknamed "Bird Dog" because he trained canines in the art of retrieving fallen birds before he became a pro ballplayer, Hopper spent two years with the Cardinals and one with the Senators. The right-hander from Tennessee was never able to get that elusive victory at the major league level in three seasons of play. His last big league action came with the 1915 Senators, a team that featured the best pitcher of the era in Walter Johnson. During the First World War, Bird Dog served with the United States Army.

W	L	PCT	G	GS	CG	IP	H	BB	SO	SHO	ERA
0	4	.000	19	3	2	60	65	29	12	0	4.20

Oscar Theodore Horstmann, *Pitcher*

A pitcher from the rural town of Alma, Missouri, Oscar Horstmann served as a grain inspector after his days in baseball. As far as his baseball career is concerned, Horstmann played in pieces of three seasons for the St. Louis Cardinals. He went 9–4 in his rookie season, 1917, and never again won a game at the major league level. A right-handed pitcher who constantly battled control problems, Oscar appeared in nine games for the Redbirds in 1918 before he left for the armed forces.

W	L	PCT	G	GS	CG	IP	H	BB	SO	SHO	ERA
9	7	.563	50	15	4	176	154	80	61	1	3.68

Roland Boatner Howell, *Pitcher*

Robust Roland Howell appeared in three games with the 1912 Cardinals of Roger Bresnahan. The big right-hander had trouble finding the strike zone in this short trial, and when he did find the zone, he was punished. Howell left the majors and never resurfaced in the bigs again. He spent 1918 in the armed forces.

W	L	PCT	G	GS	CG	IP	H	BB	SO	SHO	ERA
0	0	—	3	0	0	2	5	5	0	0	22.50

Waite Charles Hoyt, *Pitcher*

The "Schoolboy" sensation, Waite Hoyt was a Hall of Fame pitcher for Babe Ruth's Yankees and a terrific broadcaster with the Cincinnati Reds. However, before he was ushered into Cooperstown and long before he sat behind the golden microphone, Hoyt was a young buck eager to help his country. When Hoyt went to enlist in the army during World War I, he was rejected by the military because he was too young. Hoyt bided his time and signed to play baseball with John McGraw's Giants. The Schoolboy pitched one inning for McGraw's squad and fanned a pair of batters without allowing a runner to reach base. But Waite wasn't satisfied.

Shortly after his major league debut, John McGraw's young flinger was inducted into service. Hoyt wanted to serve with distinction so he sought a commission and was sent to Middlebury, Vermont, for reserve officer's training late in 1918. While there the war ended and Hoyt returned to the diamond. However, McGraw had cashed in on the schoolboy sensation headlines and sent Waite to the Red Sox. Hoyt struggled to make good in Beantown before he was dealt to the Yankees and immediately became a winner with the Bronx Bombers.

W	L	PCT	G	GS	CG	IP	H	BB	SO	SHO	ERA
237	182	.566	674	424	226	3,762	4,037	1,003	1,206	25	3.59

Jess James Hubbard, *Pitcher*

Hubbard, who came from an interracial couple — one black parent and another Native American — had a light complexion that almost allowed him to play in the major leagues. A big right-hander from Texas, Hubbard learned how to pitch after he dropped out of school and played amateur ball for the sawmill that he worked for. He broke into the Negro Leagues in 1917 but spent the next year in the army stationed at Fort Dix during World War I. He pitched for the Brooklyn Royal Giants after the war and was thus in the shadow of black baseball's two greatest pitchers of the time: Smokey Joe Williams and Cannonball Dick Redding.

(1917–1935): Brooklyn Royal Giants, Hilldale Daisies, New York Lincoln Giants, Atlantic City Bacharach Giants, Baltimore Black Sox, Homestead Grays and New York Black Yankees

Clarence Bill Huber, *Third Base*

An adequate hot corner custodian, Huber was the Phillies' regular third baseman for two years in the 1920s. He broke in with the Tigers in 1920 after service in the military during World War I but was blocked by Bobby Jones. He caught on with the Phillies in 1925 and played regularly with the club through 1926. The Phillies were a poor club, given that they had the only staff earned run average above 5.00 both years Clarence was there.

G	R	H	2B	3B	HR	RBI	BB	SO	SB	AVG	Slug
254	95	225	47	13	6	93	59	67	12	.263	.370

Albert Alfred Huenke, *Pitcher*

Huenke's major league career consisted of one game with the 1914 Giants. The pitching staff was made up of legends Christy Mathewson, Rube Marquard, Jeff Tesreau and Hooks Wiltse. With all that pitching talent at McGraw's disposal, a youngster like Al wasn't needed. He left baseball and joined the military during World War I. After his days in the military and baseball, Huenke embarked on a career in politics and was named the commissioner of his town during World War II.

W	L	PCT	G	GS	CG	IP	H	BB	SO	SHO	ERA
0	0	—	1	0	0	2	2	0	2	0	4.50

Harry Joseph Hulihan, *Pitcher*

This slim southpaw from Vermont spent one year at the major league level with the 1922 Braves. Harry, despite just six starts, was the second-winningest southpaw on the staff behind Hall of Famer Rube Marquard. Before his major league debut, Hulihan, while still a teenager, served in the armed forces during World War I.

W	L	PCT	G	GS	CG	IP	H	BB	SO	SHO	ERA
2	3	.400	7	6	2	40	40	26	16	0	3.15

Herbert Harrison Hunter, *Utilityman*

A journeyman ballplayer, Hunter was referred to by a writer for the *Oakland Tribune* as "the most erratic infielder the big leagues has ever tried." The man who gave Hunter his first trial was none other than John McGraw. But McGraw sent Herb to the Cubs in the midst of his rookie season. Used infrequently by the Cubs the following year, 1917, Hunter made plans to enlist at the U.S. Submarine base at San Pedro before the 1918 ball season. While stationed at San Pedro, Herb was able to play some ball with the San Francisco Seals on furlough before he was transferred east.

G	R	H	2B	3B	HR	RBI	BB	SO	SB	AVG	Slug
39	8	8	0	0	1	4	2	6	0	.163	.224

Walter Kingsley Irwin, *Pinch Runner*

The fleet-footed Irwin was used in only four major league games. Nicknamed "Lightning," Walt had his cup of coffee with the 1921 Redbirds. Irwin served in the armed forces during the First World War.

G	R	H	2B	3B	HR	RBI	BB	SO	SB	AVG	Slug
4	1	0	0	0	0	0	0	1	0	.000	.000

Charles Herbert Jackson, *Outfield*

Jackson appeared in 41 games as a 23-year-old for the Pittsburgh Pirates in 1917, which would be his only major league action. He missed the entire 1918 campaign to service in the army.

G	R	H	2B	3B	HR	RBI	BB	SO	SB	AVG	Slug
42	7	29	3	2	0	1	10	23	4	.238	.295

William Chester "Baby Doll" Jacobson, *Outfield*

The oddly named Baby Doll came about his unusual moniker after hitting a game-winning home run in the minor leagues. A band began to play a popular tune that used the term "baby doll" in its lyrics, and the nickname stuck with Jacobson throughout his career. One of the finest outfielders of his time, the underrated Baby Doll served in the navy during World War I. Because of the war, he missed the entire 1918 baseball campaign. As well as being a solid hitter, Jacobson held 13 different fielding records at the time of his retirement.

G	R	H	2B	3B	HR	RBI	BB	SO	SB	AVG	Slug
1,472	787	1,714	328	94	83	819	355	410	86	.311	.450

William Henry James, *Pitcher*

Standing at 6'4", Big Bill James earned his nickname. Nowadays, we expect our hurlers to be men of large height, but in the early 1900s, men like James were rare. He was able to spend the majority of the 1918 season with the Tigers, with 18 starts, but he lost the end of the season to military service. His last year in the major leagues, 1919, was a nomadic one for Big Bill, who began with Detroit and was then shipped off to the Red Sox. He ended the year with the American League champion White Sox and threw his last game with the crooked Black Sox in the World Series. His claim to fame is being the pitcher who replaced Lefty Williams in the final Fall Classic contest after the southpaw had already buried the team in a sizable deficit.

W	L	PCT	G	GS	CG	IP	H	BB	SO	SHO	ERA
65	70	.481	203	147	67	1,180	1,108	576	408	9	3.21

William Lawrence James, *Pitcher*

Nicknamed "Seattle Bill" to distinguish him from another pitcher with the same name, James missed three and a half consecutive years of baseball. He lost a portion of the 1915 season to a shoulder injury that sidelined him through his military callup in 1918, at which time he served as a drill instructor. He returned to pitch in just one more game in 1919, his last major league action. As a young hurler, James ran afoul of Hall of Fame second baseman Johnny Evers when Seattle Bill thought Evers was playing out of position. James motioned for Evers to move into a better spot, which infuriated The Crab, but James proved to possess superior knowledge as the batter stroked a base hit precisely where Seattle Bill wanted Evers to dwell.

W	L	PCT	G	GS	CG	IP	H	BB	SO	SHO	ERA
37	21	.638	84	60	44	541	469	199	253	5	2.28

Harold Chandler Janvrin, *Utility Infielder*

Janvrin was a lieutenant in the army during World War I, stationed at Camp Bowie. Under his command were 408 soldiers, as the renowned marksman gave up his baseball uniform for officer's bars. Hal's tour in the army was a nomadic one. Initially stationed at Camp Devens, Janvrin was a commanding officer at Camp Bowie and was mustered out at Camp Lee. He returned to the military in the 1940s during World War II, at which time Janvrin served in the Department of Civil Defense in Boston.

G	R	H	2B	3B	HR	RBI	BB	SO	SB	AVG	Slug
756	250	515	68	18	6	210	171	n/a	79	.232	.287

Joseph Daniel Jenkins, *Catcher*

In a nondescript career, Jenkins strolled to the plate only sixty times. A graduate from Vanderbilt University, he missed the entire 1918 season to service in the army. Not an idle soldier, Jenkins was shipped to the European Theatre where he was engaged in combat action. He returned to the States on the same vessel with the much more publicized Grover Alexander. A member of the White Sox infamous 1919 clan that purposely lost the World Series to the Reds, Joe didn't see any action in the Fall Classic.

G	R	H	2B	3B	HR	RBI	BB	SO	SB	AVG	Slug
40	0	8	2	1	0	3	2	17	3	.133	.200

William H. Johnson, *Catcher*

A soldier during peacetime, Johnson enlisted in the army before World War I. Still active in Uncle Sam's fighting forces during the war, Bill was stationed at Schofield Barracks, Hawaii. After four-plus years in the armed forces, the Sparta, Georgia, native entered the Negro Leagues.

(1920–1929): Homestead Grays, Dayton Marcos, Washington Potomacs, Harrisburg Giants, Hilldale Daisies, Philadelphia Tigers and Brooklyn Royal Giants

Frederick Edward Johnson, *Pitcher*

Cactus Fred Johnson had yet to make his major league debut when he joined the military during World War I. The right-hander from Texas made his debut with John McGraw's Giants in 1922. They won the World Series that year and returned to the Fall Classic with Cactus in tow during the 1923 season. Fred didn't pitch in either World Series. Used in a limited capacity by McGraw, the majority of Johnson's major league innings didn't come until 1938 with the Browns.

W	L	PCT	G	GS	CG	IP	H	BB	SO	SHO	ERA
5	10	.333	27	12	6	118	145	44	39	0	5.26

Oscar "Heavy" Johnson, *Outfield/Catcher*

Johnson came by his nickname for obvious reasons. A robust fellow, Heavy was generously listed at 250 pounds but many felt he weighed more than that amount. Despite his rotund build, Johnson was a noted longball threat in the Negro Leagues during the 1920s. Before he signed with the Kansas City Monarchs, and when he was a bit trimmer, Heavy served in the army during World War I. Assigned to the 25th Infantry, Uncle Sam used Johnson as a catcher when he played in the service. Johnson enlisted several years before the war and was thus a peacetime soldier. During the fighting in Europe, Heavy was stationed at Hawaii where he remained even after the war ended.

(1922–1933): Memphis Red Sox, Kansas City Monarchs, Baltimore Black Sox, Harrisburg Giants and Cleveland Tigers

Russell Conwell "Jing" Johnson, *Pitcher*

One of baseball's more intelligent players, Johnson became a chemist after his playing days were over. His desire for money drove him from the game, as he believed that he could earn a better living outside of baseball. When the Athletics refused to meet his salary demands, he pursued the lucrative life outside of the game. However, manager Connie Mack kept sending Jing contracts over the course of seven years after his salary dispute, which made him an uncommon seven-year holdout. Johnson, a veteran of World War I, became a training officer at Philadelphia's naval yard during World War II.

W	L	PCT	G	GS	CG	IP	H	BB	SO	SHO	ERA
24	38	.387	101	64	36	548	559	179	171	0	3.33

Paul Oscar Johnson, *Outfielder*

One of the players Connie Mack brought in after his Federal League-inspired fire sale, Johnson played two years in Mr. Mack's pasture. Paul served in the military in 1918 and made his debut with the Athletics in 1920. His last major league action came with the Mackmen in 1921.

G	R	H	2B	3B	HR	RBI	BB	SO	SB	AVG	Slug
67	23	55	6	2	1	15	13	25	2	.276	.342

Thomas Johnson, *Pitcher*

Nicknamed "Schoolboy" because he attended Morris Brown College before his baseball days, Johnson spent the bulk of his career with the Chicago American Giants. During the war, the college man was commissioned a lieutenant in the infantry and played some service ball at Camp Grant before he was shipped overseas. Tom served with the 365th Infantry in France. After his playing days, he became an umpire in the Negro Leagues.

(1914–1923): Chicago American Giants, Indianapolis ABCs and Pittsburgh Keystones

Ellis Walter "Walt" Johnson, *Pitcher*

Although he bore the same name as the greatest pitcher of his day, Ellis Walter Johnson was a poor substitute for Walter "Big Train" Johnson. Walt had three cups of coffee at the major league level: his first with the 1912 White Sox; his second with the Pale Hose again in 1915; and his last with the A's in 1917. Walt missed the 1918 season to service in the military and didn't make a return to the majors after the war.

W	L	PCT	G	GS	CG	IP	H	BB	SO	SHO	ERA
0	2	.000	9	2	0	30	29	15	19	0	5.40

Percy Lee Jones, *Pitcher*

A decent major league southpaw, Percy Jones had an adequate career with the Cubs in the 1920s. While still a teenager, Jones served with the U.S. Navy during the First World War. After he was mustered out of the service, Percy received his first big league trial with the 1920 Cubs. He became skipper Joe McCarthy's go-to southpaw during the late 1920s, but the year after he left Chicago, the Cubs finally made the World Series while Percy went 7–15 for the last-place Braves.

W	L	PCT	G	GS	CG	IP	H	BB	SO	SHO	ERA
53	57	.482	251	114	49	1,026	1,137	494	381	8	4.34

Theodore Charles Jourdan, *First Base*

A native of New Orleans, Jourdan saw limited major league action with the White Sox over the course of four years. The majority of his playing time came in 1920 after Chick Gandil refused to report to the Sox because of the Black Sox Scandal. He platooned with Shano Collins that year and hit .240 in the process. Ted tallied ten plate appearances in 1918 before he was summoned into the armed forces.

G	R	H	2B	3B	HR	RBI	BB	SO	SB	AVG	Slug
75	19	42	6	2	0	11	19	21	5	.214	.265

Herbert Victor Juul, *Pitcher*

The son of a famous Illinois politician named Niels Juul, Herb appeared in one game with the 1911 Reds. His brother, Herold, a Federal League pitcher, served in the United States Army Air Force during the war. Both of the Juul boys had extreme difficulties throwing strikes.

W	L	PCT	G	GS	CG	IP	H	BB	SO	SHO	ERA
0	0	—	1	0	0	4	3	4	2	0	4.50

Francis Thomas Kane, *Outfield*

Kane had two cups of coffee at the major league level. His first trial came with the 1915 Brooklyn Feds. He then spent time in the bushes before he was inducted into the army in 1918. After his discharge, Frank had one pinch-hitting appearance with the 1919 Yankees.

G	R	H	2B	3B	HR	RBI	BB	SO	SB	AVG	Slug
4	2	2	0	1	0	2	0	n/a	0	.182	.364

Benjamin Joyce Karr, *Pitcher*

Due to the thinning hair atop his head, Benn Karr was given the nickname "Baldy" by his peers. The southern right-hander was inducted into the armed forces before he made his major league debut. After his discharge, Karr made his way to Boston after the Red Sox sold Babe Ruth to the Yankees.

W	L	PCT	G	GS	CG	IP	H	BB	SO	SHO	ERA
35	48	.422	177	58	29	781	921	260	180	1	4.60

Benjamin Michael Kauff, *Outfield*

The short-lived Federal League's answer to Ty Cobb, Kauff enjoyed a solid and controversial career. Benny, who was dubbed "The Ty Cobb of the Feds," is one of a handful of players that Commissioner Kennesaw Mountain Landis banished from organized baseball for life. Caught up in an auto theft case during 1920, Kauff was acquitted in May of 1921 but was subsequently barred from the game by Landis. The high-profile star, who enjoyed dressing in excessive style and employing a fancy walking cane, served in the army at Camp Sherman during World War I.

G	R	H	2B	3B	HR	RBI	BB	SO	SB	AVG	Slug
859	521	961	169	57	49	454	367	n/a	234	.311	.450

Charles Hugh Kavanagh, *Pinch Hitter*

Charlie had five plate appearances with the 1914 White Sox when the Federal League was in its first year of operation. The hometown boy slapped out one base hit at the major league level. He served in the military during World War I.

G	R	H	2B	3B	HR	RBI	BB	SO	SB	AVG	Slug
5	0	1	0	0	0	0	0	2	0	.200	.200

David Edwin Keefe, *Pitcher*

Much like Three Finger Brown, Keefe pitched with a mangled hand and possessed unusual motion on his offerings. He is credited with inventing the forkball although he threw it naturally due to his missing finger. As well as inventing a pitch, Keefe also fanned Babe Ruth three times in one contest. After showing promise in his first season, a 1.80 ERA in three outings, Keefe lost the 1918 season to service in the armed forces. He appeared in only one game for the Athletics in 1919 but led the club with a 2.97 ERA in 1920.

W	L	PCT	G	GS	CG	IP	H	BB	SO	SHO	ERA
9	17	.346	97	27	12	353	403	113	126	1	4.16

John Patrick Kelleher, *Utility Infielder*

Kelleher enjoyed an intermittent career at the major league level. Before the war he was given a trial with the Cardinals in 1912 and later with the Dodgers in 1916. He failed to impress in either stint and was toiling in the minors when he was summoned for military service for the First World War. After his discharge, John landed with the Cubs and spent three years with Chicago as a backup infielder.

G	R	H	2B	3B	HR	RBI	BB	SO	SB	AVG	Slug
235	81	206	29	8	10	89	45	42	9	.293	.400

George Lange Kelly, *First Base*

Hall of Fame first baseman George Kelly was a versatile infielder, capable of playing numerous positions in a pinch. Prior to the war, Kelly gave no indication of being a future Hall of Famer, as he hit a miniscule .158 in 1916. However, with the advent of a new "livelier" ball, Kelly posted some solid-single season numbers. Kelly served at Kelly Field, Texas, in the U.S. Army Air Corps during the war. As an old man, standing at the podium in Cooperstown giving his induction speech, Kelly stated, "The finest thing that life can send is a gift of one who can call a friend."

G	R	H	2B	3B	HR	RBI	BB	SO	SB	AVG	Slug
1,622	819	1,778	337	76	148	1,020	386	694	65	.297	.452

Joseph Henry Kelly, *Outfield*

The Braves were the first team in the major leagues to lose their entire set of starting outfielders to the military. With Wally Rehg and Ray Powell, Kelly enlisted into the navy with his garden chums. Of the trio, Kelly was the least missed as the speedster struggled to hit major league pitching throughout his career. He was able to get into 47 games for George Stallings' boys before he left for the navy.

G	R	H	2B	3B	HR	RBI	BB	SO	SB	AVG	Slug
376	131	300	38	22	6	117	80	143	66	.224	.298

Edward Aloysius Kenna, *Catcher*

Nicknamed "Scrap Iron," Ed Kenna was a tough little West Coast backstop who spent one year at the major league level. Kenna was a 30-year-old rookie with the 1928 Senators. That year he served as Muddy Ruel's backup and hit a nifty .297. Scrap Iron, who used to carry bats for members of the San Francisco PCL team when he was a kid, spent a year in the armed forces during the First World War.

G	R	H	2B	3B	HR	RBI	BB	SO	SB	AVG	Slug
41	14	35	4	2	1	20	14	8	1	.297	.390

John Wesley "Happy Jack" Kibble, *Reserve*

Kibble had a cup of coffee with Cleveland in 1912 and never again appeared in a major league contest. He established himself as a minor league star in Montana and was so revered in Billings and the surrounding area that he made it his home after the war.

G	R	H	2B	3B	HR	RBI	BB	SO	SB	AVG	Slug
8	1	0	0	0	0	0	0	n/a	0	.000	.000

Joseph William Kiefer, *Pitcher*

"Harlem Joe" served in the United States Army before he donned a major league uniform. The right-hander had issues with accuracy that he never did address at the highest level. He pitched for the White Sox after the infamous Black Sox Scandal and later tossed two seasons with the Boston Red Sox.

W	L	PCT	G	GS	CG	IP	H	BB	SO	SHO	ERA
0	5	.000	15	4	0	50	56	30	9	0	6.12

Peter John Kilduff, *Second Base*

Dealt by the Giants to the Cubs in his rookie season, Kilduff paced the Chicago team in batting average during his initial campaign. The following year he appeared in only 30 games due to being drafted into the navy. When he returned to the game, Pete was sent to the Brooklyn Dodgers where his .301 batting average was second to Hy Myers on the club. He finally earned an everyday assignment in 1920 as he played an instrumental part in Brooklyn's ascension from fifth to first place. He played one final season, when he hit an astounding .388 in 1921.

Kilduff played thirty games for the Cubs in 1918 before the navy beckoned his services; he thus missed out on their National League championship of that year. When he returned to the game, Kilduff inquired with the Cubs president about whether he could be awarded a percentage of the World Series money that his teammates made since he played a portion of the season with the club. He was denied his share of the World Series purse because the president didn't feel that he should pay a player for a half-a-season worth of play.

Upon his return from the navy, Kilduff had a story that he enjoyed reciting regarding the hectic life of a star baseball player aboard a battleship. He felt that some naval officers had too keen a sense of comedy. While serving on a battleship, Kilduff had this conversation with an officer who halted him.

"Young man!" said the officer. "You are Kilduff the noted ballplayer of the Chicago Cubs, are you not?"

"Aye, aye sir!" saluted Kilduff.

The officer continued, "You were, I believe, so highly regarded by the management that they made you the clean-up man?"

"Aye, aye sir," responded Kilduff.

"Then," said the officer, "you are just the man I'm looking for. Take this pail and clean up this deck!"

G	R	H	2B	3B	HR	RBI	BB	SO	SB	AVG	Slug
428	163	374	62	28	4	159	134	132	28	.270	.364

William Lavier Killefer, *Catcher*

An all-field, no-hit backstop, "Reindeer Bill" was regarded as the catcher deluxe in the National League at the time of the First World War. Killefer, who made his big league debut in 1909, was a seasoned veteran when the war broke out. He spent a number of years catching for the Phillies before the Cubs acquired his services just before the war. Bill played in the 1918 season and even participated in that year's World Series, but after the Fall Classic it was army time for the reindeer.

Killefer came from a long line of military veterans. His father was a decorated veteran of the Civil War, so the soldier's life wasn't a foreign lifestyle to the Killefer clan. Killefer was inducted into the army and served at Camp Custer with the rank of sergeant. He enjoyed the military training, saying, "I'll admit that the army has done wonders for me. Last year I had little ailments that I never had in a season before. But after I got to the army camp and began going to bed early and arising early and eating regularly and doing the outdoor work, all those ailments disappeared."

Bill spent his military tenure stateside, working in an office and assisting soldiers who were being discharged from service by handling their paperwork. Killefer described his army duties by saying, "My work at present is connected with the mustering out of soldiers. All I have to do is push a pen from morning to night." Eager to leave the mundane work behind, Killefer applied for a commission and was slated to attend officer's training when the war ended. Killefer said, "Of course I wanted to be an officer if the war had gone on. But perhaps it's nicer to be able to come back and catch for the Cubs."

G	R	H	2B	3B	HR	RBI	BB	SO	SB	AVG	Slug
1,035	237	751	86	21	4	240	113	n/a	39	.238	.283

Arthur Kimbro, *Third Base*

A hot corner custodian for the New York Lincoln Giants before World War I, Kimbro would not return to the game after the war. While stationed at Fort Dix, Arthur contracted Spanish flu, a deadly epidemic that swept through the nation during the war years, and died shortly after his discharge.

(1915–1918): New York Lincoln Giants and Hilldale Daisies

Wally Lyons Kimmick, *Utility Infielder*

Before Kimmick played his first major league game, he served in the United States Army during World War I. The service hitch cut into Wally's seasoning, but when he reported for training with the Redbirds in 1919, he impressed the club. Umpire Billy Evans saw Wally play and proclaimed, "I rate him a pretty good little infielder."

G	R	H	2B	3B	HR	RBI	BB	SO	SB	AVG	Slug
163	39	90	9	5	1	31	34	61	4	.261	.325

William Kindle, *Utility Infielder*

A graduate from Fiske University, Kindle was a solid defender who could fill in anywhere on the diamond. A natural second baseman, however, Bill fit into the mold of the all-field, no-hit middle infielder. Kindle, who played sporadically with the Brooklyn Royal Giants throughout the Deadball Era, missed the 1918 season to military service. During World War I, Bill played service ball at Fort Dix.

(1911–1925): Brooklyn Royal Giants, West Baden Sprudels, New York Lincoln Giants, Chicago American Giants and Indianapolis ABCs

Edward Lee King, *Outfield*

King became the Pirates regular right fielder in 1917 and finished second on the club in the doubles department. The next year he appeared in 36 games before he was summoned into the armed forces. King returned to the diamond in 1919 as a member of John McGraw's Giants and proceeded to hit .100 in twenty at-bats. Despite that awful showing, McGraw gave King the center field job in 1920 and he raised his average 176 points from the previous year. By 1922, he was out of the major leagues.

G	R	H	2B	3B	HR	RBI	BB	SO	SB	AVG	Slug
411	134	294	60	18	15	144	82	175	16	.247	.366

Henry Lees "Harry" Kingman, *First Base*

Credit the Yankees with signing the first player born in China. Although Kingman wasn't of Chinese ancestry, he was born of American parents on Chinese soil. He enjoyed a blink-and-you-missed-it trial at the major league level with the 1914 Bronx Bombers. During the First World War Harry joined the army and served at Fort Lewis, Washington.

G	R	H	2B	3B	HR	RBI	BB	SO	SB	AVG	Slug
4	0	0	0	0	0	0	1	2	0	.000	.000

LaRue Kirby, *Outfield/Pitcher*

A gifted two-way athlete, Kirby's introduction to Organized Baseball makes for an amusing yarn. Giants skipper John McGraw sent his lieutenant Wilbert Robinson to Michigan to evaluate young LaRue Kirby during a game. However, when a storm impeded play and led to the cancellation of the game, Kirby persuaded Robinson to catch some of his pitches in the rain. Determined to not miss his chance at the big time, Kirby worked out in a downpour while Uncle Robby caught his offerings. After a few pitches, Wilbert called it quits and took LaRue to a diner at Traverse City where they ate dinner in silence without a word regarding Kirby's future. LaRue saw Robby off at the train station and before the locomotive pulled off, he told the young Michigan native that he'd made good. Robinson likened Kirby's curveball to that of Hall of Famer Mordecai Brown.

LaRue Kirby is best known as a case study for the Federal League. When the Feds were trying to establish their circuit as a major league in 1914, they showed the two older leagues they meant business when they outbid other clubs for Kirby's services. LaRue pitched briefly for McGraw's Giants in 1912 but needed more seasoning in the minors. When he was deemed ready for the majors, the Federal League loosed their purse strings and persuaded Kirby to join their ranks. Due to the signing of LaRue Kirby, many critics saw the Federal League as a legitimate threat to the American and National leagues.

Kirby played for the St. Louis entry in the Federal League during its two years of operation and never again returned to the majors when the Feds closed up shop. During the First World War, Kirby's services were in demand again when Hall of Famer Johnny Evers assembled a military all-star team and recruited LaRue to play.

G	R	H	2B	3B	HR	RBI	BB	SO	SB	AVG	Slug
116	37	87	14	5	2	34	31	n/a	8	.230	.310

Theodore Otto Kleinhans, *Pitcher*

Kleinhans was an old man when he broke into the major leagues. Born in 1899, Ted was 35 years old when the Phillies gave him his first trial in 1934. His rookie season was split between the Phillies and Reds and he would later play with the Yankees. He served in the armed forces during both World Wars. Ted, who coached college ball at Syracuse University, was a captain stationed in England as a mess officer during World War II.

W	L	PCT	G	GS	CG	IP	H	BB	SO	SHO	ERA
4	9	.308	56	12	1	143	185	76	48	0	5.29

Edward Lloyd Klepfer, *Pitcher*

Klepfer posted a remarkable record of 14–4 in 1917 for the Indians and would lose the entire 1918 season to military service. He was drafted into the United States Army on February 6, 1918, as a 30-year-old. Klepfer was shipped overseas and saw combat action in France. While in transit on a ship, he wrote Smoky Joe Wood telling his old friend that he had to dodge U-Boats while en route to France. After his discharge from the army, Klepfer only tossed seven more innings of big league baseball.

W	L	PCT	G	GS	CG	IP	H	BB	SO	SHO	ERA
22	18	.550	98	50	16	448	457	137	165	2	2.81

Henry Antone "Cotton" Knaupp, *Shortstop*

Knaupp had the misfortune of coming up with the Indians when they had such notable infielders as Hall of Famer Nap Lajoie, the superb fielder Terry Turner, and "Everyday" Ivy Olson. Cotton had little opportunity to play. A minor league veteran, Knaupp played ball in the bushes with his three brothers and is the only known player in Southern League history to have recorded an unassisted triple play. He missed minor league action due to the war but was instrumental in developing Joe Sewell into a Hall of Fame shortstop.

G	R	H	2B	3B	HR	RBI	BB	SO	SB	AVG	Slug
31	5	18	4	1	0	11	8	n/a	4	.184	.245

Ernest Gerald Koob, *Pitcher*

Koob, who missed the entire 1918 baseball campaign to tenure in the Air Service, is one of the lesser-known pitchers to have tossed a no-hitter in the major leagues. His no-hitter, one of only 24 victories in his major league career, is one that is shrouded in scandal. The official scorer arrived to the game late and inquired as to whether or not Koob's opposition, the Chicago White Sox, had recorded a hit and was met with varying viewpoints. The scorer accepted the testimony of a trusted friend who told him that the White Sox hadn't tallied a base hit as of yet and that a play in question should be scored as a defensive miscue rather than a hit charged to Koob. The forkball artist tossed the rest of game without yielding a base hit and the rest is history.

During the war, Koob served with the Air Service, attached to the 380th Aero Squadron at Selfridge Aviation Field. Koob's military duties were in the Signal Corps of the Aviation Division at a school for mechanics. The southpaw spent the bulk of his military tenure overseas in London, but before he was shipped out, he had a taste of no-hit success against the baseball nine at the University of Minnesota. During that contest, Ernie fanned 22 batters as a precursor to his no-hit gem that he would throw in the major leagues.

W	L	PCT	G	GS	CG	IP	H	BB	SO	SHO	ERA
24	31	.436	125	55	19	501	488	186	121	3	3.13

Walter Henry Kopf, *Third Base*

The brother of Reds star shortstop Larry Kopf, Wally had a cup of coffee with John McGraw's champion Giants of 1921. Blocked by Hall of Famer Frankie Frisch, Wally appeared in only a couple games. He missed some minor league action to service in the armed forces.

G	R	H	2B	3B	HR	RBI	BB	SO	SB	AVG	Slug
2	0	1	0	0	0	0	1	1	0	.333	.333

Merlin Henry Kopp, *Outfield*

In a deadlocked contest on May 21, 1918, Kopp became an unlikely hero in the 14th inning. With the game tied and Kopp on third base, Merlin broke for home and stole the plate, thus ending an extra-inning affair with a dramatic theft. Shortly thereafter, on June 29, Kopp was summoned by his draft board and missed the remainder of the season to military service. The switch-hitter played one final season with Connie Mack's Athletics, as he posted more triples than home runs and doubles combined.

G	R	H	2B	3B	HR	RBI	BB	SO	SB	AVG	Slug
187	96	146	9	11	1	30	89	105	39	.232	.286

Floyd Myron Kroh, *Pitcher*

Often referred to as "Rube" Kroh, he was anything but a hayseed. Players of the Deadball Era nicknamed "Rube" were usually uneducated bumpkins with poor social skills, but Floyd Kroh was regarded as a heady pitcher. During a training game, he is purported to have picked off Ty Cobb four times. An article in the *Wichita Daily Times* claimed that Floyd was "a hurler who pitched with his noodle as well as his arm." Clearly, the handle of "Rube" was a misnomer.

The name Rube Kroh is famous today for the role he played in the infamous Merkle Boner. Fred Merkle, a green Giants youngster, failed to touch second base when Al Bridwell slapped what appeared to be a walk-off game-winning hit in a nail-biting Cubs-Giants clash. Merkle instead ran from his station at first base to the clubhouse while the field was besieged with fans. Chicago Cubs second baseman Johnny Evers spotted Merkle's mistake and had Kroh fetch the ball Bridwell hit. He is supposed to have found the ball, which he wrestled from a fan, and tossed it to Evers, who forced Merkle out at second by touching the base Fred neglected to reach. The umpire ruled with Evers and Kroh and called Merkle out. The play has gone done in history as "The Merkle Boner," and the Cubs, who won the World Series thanks to Evers and Kroh's quick play, haven't won a World Series since.

When World War I broke out, Kroh's days as a major leaguer were already behind him. The old southpaw last pitched in a major league contest with the 1912 Boston Braves of Johnny Kling, an old Cubs teammate. Kroh enlisted in the army and saw combat action overseas. While fighting the enemy, Kroh sustained a wound in battle and was shipped home. The heady left-hander recovered from his injuries and lived until the Second World War, when he died as a civilian in 1944.

W	L	PCT	G	GS	CG	IP	H	BB	SO	SHO	ERA
13	9	.591	36	25	13	215	182	67	92	3	2.30

Ernest George Krueger, *Catcher*

Krueger was a professor of mathematics who missed all but 30 games to military service in 1918. He was acquired by the Dodgers midway through the 1917 season to serve as Bill Fischer's backup. He and Otto Miller platooned behind the plate for the next three years in Brooklyn. During the war, Ernie was able to play some baseball for a service team based at Norfolk. He took to teaching after his playing days concluded.

G	R	H	2B	3B	HR	RBI	BB	SO	SB	AVG	Slug
318	87	220	33	14	11	93	64	85	12	.263	.376

Walter Charles "Red" Kuhn, *Catcher*

When White Sox legendary receiver Billy Sullivan was at the end of his rope in 1912, the Pale Hose needed a young replacement for the aging star. That man appeared to be Red Kuhn. The Fresno native started more games behind the plate than any other man on the Chicago roster in 1912, but things didn't go according to plan for Kuhn. The White Sox called up a young backstop named Ray Schalk and he, not Kuhn, became the heir apparent to Billy Sullivan.

With the iron man Hall of Famer Ray Schalk on the club, Kuhn's services weren't needed and he was sent back to the bushes. Red left the White Sox in 1914 and never again played at the major league level. But the story of Walter "Red" Kuhn doesn't end there. He enlisted in the army during World War I and suffered a freak accident that permanently killed his chances of returning to baseball. While stationed at Camp Travis, Kuhn and some battle buddies were killing time in the barracks with a little roughhousing and horseplay. One of Kuhn's pals snapped a bath towel at Red, but his aim was too high and the edge of the towel struck Kuhn in the right eye. An army surgeon looked over Kuhn's eye and determined that the pupil was severely damaged and the eye could not be saved. The injury led to a medical discharge from the army and an end to his days as a professional athlete. Rather than take up the ball and bat after his discharge, Red joined the Dallas police department.

G	R	H	2B	3B	HR	RBI	BB	SO	SB	AVG	Slug
118	25	55	9	0	0	15	41	n/a	8	.205	.239

Edward Francis Lafitte, *Pitcher*

Edward Lafitte was an educated man who had the stigma of placing more importance on his studies than his play. While he was playing with the Tigers of Cobb and Crawford, Lafitte attended dental school. The New Orleans native debuted with the AL champion Tigers of 1909 but wasn't used in the World Series. He won eleven games for the Bengals in 1911—his finest season—before struggling mightily in 1912. When the Federal League opened for business in 1914, Lafitte jumped the Tigers and signed on with the Brooklyn entry of the upstart league. Ed would win 18 games his first year in the Federal League but just eight the next—his last in the majors.

Lafitte's background in dentistry earned him a commission in the United States Army and introduced him to the horrors that young men faced in battle. Although Dr. Lafitte didn't witness any combat action firsthand, he saw the effects the war had on boys. During the war, Lafitte was assigned to a reconstruction hospital in St. Louis, Missouri, where he had to perform surgeries on the shattered jaws of returning war casualties.

W	L	PCT	G	GS	CG	IP	H	BB	SO	SHO	ERA
37	35	.514	106	75	47	647	668	262	262	0	3.34

William Harmong Lamar, *Outfield*

"Good Time" Bill Lamar served his country in both World Wars. He missed a large portion of the 1918 season as a 21-year-old rookie outfielder. Good Time Bill was a prototypical contact hitter—not drawing many walks and not striking out often. The bulk of his major league playing time came in the mid 1920s with Connie Mack's Philadelphia Athletics. Lamar's high-water season came in 1925 when he hit .356 as Mr. Mack's regular left fielder.

G	R	H	2B	3B	HR	RBI	BB	SO	SB	AVG	Slug
550	303	633	114	23	19	245	86	78	25	.310	.417

Otis Samuel Lambeth, *Pitcher*

Lambeth's major league career was rather brief—he saw action in only three seasons. With the loss of Ed Klepfer to the military, Cleveland needed Lambeth to assume Big Ed's role. However, Otis followed Klepfer into the service after only five appearances for the Tribe in 1918. Although his diamond career was lackluster, Lambeth's career in khaki was just the opposite.

After Lambeth had received his stateside training, the right-hander prepared for service overseas. Shipped out to Europe, Otis' time in the old country wasn't spent idle. In constant tangle with the Germans, Lambeth's life was in constant danger. In a letter he wrote home to writer Henry P. Edwards, Lambeth penned, "Fritz has tried to shell me, to gas me, to bomb me and I presume he is lying awake nights now thinking other means to obliterate me from this earth of ours. So far I have been spared and he has wasted a lot of powder trying to get me. And all the time we have been sending him a little better than he has handed us."

Otis Lambeth served in a field artillery unit that saw action in Europe. The sergeant was one of many men who crossed the great Rhine River in pursuit of combat. For his wartime heroics, the sturdy right-handed hurler was awarded a medal for bravery in combat. Lambeth felt combat action had a positive impact on his nerves, stating, "There's one thing about this war: it takes a fellow's nervousness away. I don't care how the Red Sox and Tigers try to ride me anymore. And I won't be afraid of getting beaned in the future." Despite his heroics abroad, Lambeth was unable to reclaim a spot on Cleveland's roster for the 1919 season and never tossed another pitch in the major leagues.

W	L	PCT	G	GS	CG	IP	H	BB	SO	SHO	ERA
10	9	.526	43	19	5	178	176	74	58	0	3.19

Frederick Arthur Lamline, *Pitcher*

Dutch had two cups of coffee at the major league level, first with the 1912 White Sox and then with the 1915 Cardinals. In five major league games, the Great Lakes native didn't factor in a decision. Lamline missed minor league service time to the armed forces during World War I.

W	L	PCT	G	GS	CG	IP	H	BB	SO	SHO	ERA
0	0	—	5	0	0	21	28	5	12	0	5.57

Robert Eugene "Bobby" Lamotte, *Utility Infielder*

The Senators brass raved about their military find in Bobby Lamotte. Clark Griffith, the Washington club president, said that

Lamotte was "a good mechanical player with baseball brains." A solid infielder with a rifle arm, Bobby served the better part of two years in the army during the First World War and saw action in Europe. After the war the Senators brought Lamotte to Washington and he played three years in D.C.

G	R	H	2B	3B	HR	RBI	BB	SO	SB	AVG	Slug
221	99	175	34	9	3	85	66	50	11	.253	.341

Grover Cleveland Land, Catcher

From 1908 to 1913, Land played the shuttle routine, as the Indians would call him up every other year for a brief trial. Grover never could stick with the Tribe. When Cleveland debuted a young Steve O'Neill in 1912, Land knew he'd never get a chance to play with the Indians. Good fortune came Grover's way when the Federal League began play in 1914. He jumped the Indians and cast his lot with the Tip-Tops of Brooklyn. Grover was Brooklyn's regular receiver in both of the Federal League's years of operation. When the Federal League folded, Land's days as a major leaguer were over.

Grover Land was a gabby wisecracker and the life of the party wherever the festivities may be. Fans adored his antics and felt he was a natural for the stage. With the suggestions of acquaintances pushing him towards vaudeville, Grover relented and tried his hat on the stage. But it wasn't meant to be. Stage fright gripped Grover and he wasn't comfortable in the theater until a crude act by a patron relaxed his nerves. A theatergoer, perturbed by Grover's performance, hurled a cabbage at Land on stage. Immediately, the lights and props no longer intimidated Land and he felt right at home. The scrappy ex-backstop proclaimed to the folks of the theater, "If the benighted, bat-headed descendent of an iridescent hyena who threw this cabbage will come up here on this stage, I'll kick the excelsior stuffing out of him right now!"

Since vaudeville wasn't meant to be for Grover Land, he took to the military during the First World War. He enlisted in the coast artillery in February of 1918 and was assigned to an artillery unit outside St. Louis, Missouri. While Grover served his country in the armed forces, his wife did her bit with the Red Cross in Washington. In August of 1918 Grover left the St. Louis base and was shipped overseas to France to help in the war effort. Shortly thereafter the armistice was signed and Land worked his way back home.

G	R	H	2B	3B	HR	RBI	BB	SO	SB	AVG	Slug
292	62	219	26	5	2	79	27	n/a	14	.242	.288

Peter Nelson Lapan, Catcher

Little Pete Lapan was a reserve catcher for two years at the major league level with the Senators. Although he owned a lifetime batting average above .300, Lapan wasn't given regular duty by Washington. Before his major league debut, Lapan served in the United States Army during World War I with C Company of the 14th Infantry.

G	R	H	2B	3B	HR	RBI	BB	SO	SB	AVG	Slug
13	7	11	1	0	1	6	3	4	1	.306	.417

Edward Francis Larkin, Catcher

Larkin had a cup of coffee with the 1909 Athletics when Connie Mack's team was still a powerhouse. Ed was simply the fourth-string catcher and appeared in only two games. During World War I, Larkin served with the United States Army Air Corps.

G	R	H	2B	3B	HR	RBI	BB	SO	SB	AVG	Slug
2	0	1	0	0	0	1	1	n/a	0	.167	.167

Walter Arlington "Arlie" Latham, Third Base

One of the greatest third basemen of the 1800s, Arlie Latham was born when the nation was preparing for the Civil War. His last year as a regular ballplayer was 1896, but he was such a drawing card, given his lively, entertaining antics, he stuck around the game until his death in the 1950s. Nicknamed "The Freshest Man on Earth," Latham stole close to 800 career bases and wouldn't make for a poor Hall of Fame selection should he be so honored.

At the time of World War I, Arlie was pushing sixty years of age but no one would have known it. The little legend was as spry as ever and still famous among baseball men. So highly regarded was Latham, he toured England during the war and instructed British troops on America's grand ol' game. Latham, who dabbled in acting, became a favorite of King George. When the king was asked to throw out the first pitch at a service game held on the Fourth of July, he summoned Arlie to his side to teach him how to grip a baseball.

G	R	H	2B	3B	HR	RBI	BB	SO	SB	AVG	Slug
1,621	1,470	1,851	249	86	27	641	589	n/a	791	.272	.345

Charles T. E. "Chick" Lathers, Utility Infielder

Chick played two years with his hometown Tigers but couldn't crack Detroit's sound infield of O'Leary, Bush and Moriarty. After two seasons of riding the pine, Lathers gave up on the game and became an auto salesman. Out of baseball at the time of the war, Chick spent a year in Uncle Sam's outfit.

G	R	H	2B	3B	HR	RBI	BB	SO	SB	AVG	Slug
70	9	29	3	0	0	7	13	n/a	0	.228	.252

John Leonard "Doc" Lavan, Shortstop

Lavan was the Senators regular shortstop in 1918, his only season with the club. Before he joined the Senators, Doc was a mainstay with the Browns despite his modest hitting. Aware that a man's life in baseball was limited, Lavan studied medicine at the University of Michigan. Due to his medical training, Lavan enlisted in the navy after the 1918 baseball season and served in the medical corps as a lieutenant. Doc Lavan was assigned to the *USS Mississippi* that saw action in the Atlantic.

After the war Lavan returned to baseball but to a new team: the St. Louis Cardinals. With the advent of the Lively Ball Era in 1920, batting averages across America began to spike. Lavan, never much of a hitter before, saw his batting mark rise to .289 in 1920 but he was the only member of the Redbirds infield that failed to hit .300. His average fell below .260 in 1921 while his infield mates, Rogers Hornsby, Jack Fournier and Milt Stock, all easily eclipsed the .300 mark again. He lost his job to Specs Toporcer in 1922 and was done as a major leaguer by 1924. Doc wasn't done with the Navy, however, as he rejoined them during World War II. During the Second World War Lavan served as the senior medical officer at the Toledo Training Station.

G	R	H	2B	3B	HR	RBI	BB	SO	SB	AVG	Slug
1,162	338	954	134	45	7	377	209	376	71	.245	.308

Otis Carrol Lawry, *Second Base*

One of the few players to miss two full seasons to World War I, Lawry was groomed by Connie Mack to succeed Hall of Fame second baseman Nap Lajoie when he left for the army. The two years he missed hindered his development and Jimmy Dykes became Lajoie's replacement instead. Lawry served in the army during the war but was initially rejected for service because he failed his physical exam, even though he was regarded as a remarkable sprinter.

G	R	H	2B	3B	HR	RBI	BB	SO	SB	AVG	Slug
71	17	34	1	0	0	5	11	30	5	.191	.197

Robert Baker Lawson, *Pitcher*

Professor Lawson's tenure at the highest level came at the turn of the century when the American League had just established itself as a major circuit. He pitched the 1901 season with the Braves and then left Boston to join the Baltimore Orioles in 1902 — the team's last year in existence before the Orioles became the New York Highlanders (now the Yankees).

At the time World War I broke out, Lawson was already in his early 40s and had used his baseball earnings to put himself through college. Bob used his education when Uncle Sam needed him as he joined the Army Medical Corps during the war. After the war, Lawson became a professor.

W	L	PCT	G	GS	CG	IP	H	BB	SO	SHO	ERA
2	4	.333	9	6	5	59	66	31	17	0	3.66

Eugene Francis Layden, *Reserve*

Layden's major league career consisted of three games with the 1915 Yankees. Highly regarded for his defense, Layden's bat was viewed as a weakness but he did go 2-for-7 in his limited trial. He spent the 1918 season in the armed forces.

G	R	H	2B	3B	HR	RBI	BB	SO	SB	AVG	Slug
3	2	2	0	0	0	0	0	1	0	.286	.286

Frederick Francis Lear, *First Base*

It didn't take too much ingenuity for folks to tab Fred with the nickname of "King," but that was his handle in the papers at times. A headstrong fellow around the time of the First World War, Lear wrote a letter to Cubs management during the 1917–1918 off-season that offered the Chicago brass some advice. Lear's suggestion was simple: trade star first baseman Fred Merkle because his shoes could be capably filled by one Fred "King" Lear. The note was discarded and the suggestion fell on deaf ears. Merkle finished second on the club in games played while Lear only appeared in two contests. He spent the bulk of the season in the bushes and ended the year in the United States Navy.

G	R	H	2B	3B	HR	RBI	BB	SO	SB	AVG	Slug
75	20	39	3	2	2	18	17	28	2	.235	.313

John Louis Leary, *First Base*

Leary played two years at the major league level and was the Browns regular first baseman both seasons. He made his debut in 1914 and hit a respectable .265. His numbers dropped off in 1915, and St. Louis had a kid named Sisler waiting his turn. Leary lost his job to Gorgeous George and never played another game at the major league level. During World War I, John played service ball in the navy for a team managed by former Athletics star shortstop Jack Barry.

G	R	H	2B	3B	HR	RBI	BB	SO	SB	AVG	Slug
219	54	196	38	7	0	60	15	107	11	.258	.326

DeWitt Wiley "Bevo" LeBourveau, *Outfield*

A former minor league batting champ, Bevo played ball at Seattle before he was inducted into the armed forces in 1918. After his discharge, LeBourveau, who was nicknamed "The Flying Frenchman," made his major league debut with the 1919 Phillies. When Leo Callahan lost his right field job in 1920, Bevo was there for the taking, but he was beat out by Casey Stengel for the assignment. With Casey injured in 1921, Bevo played regularly and hit .295 in his only year as a starter.

G	R	H	2B	3B	HR	RBI	BB	SO	SB	AVG	Slug
280	100	217	27	11	11	70	79	125	15	.275	.379

William Joseph Lee, *Outfield*

Billy played two years with the Browns, 1915 and 1916, and couldn't crack their starting lineup. He had to fight for playing time with such solid outfielders as Tilly Walker, Burt Shotton, Baby Doll Jacobson, Windy Ward Miller and Jack Tobin. With such competition, Lee failed to make the grade. When America entered the war, Lee was in the bushes. He joined up and served a year in the army.

G	R	H	2B	3B	HR	RBI	BB	SO	SB	AVG	Slug
25	3	13	1	0	0	4	7	6	1	.186	.200

Holsey Scranton Scriptus "Scrip" Lee, *Pitcher*

A submarine pitcher born in Washington D.C., Lee pitched predominately with the Hilldale Daisies during the 1920s. Scrip is perhaps the most decorated veteran of World War I to play in the Negro Leagues. After school, he enlisted in the National Guard and helped General Pershing quell an uprising near the Mexican border instigated by Pancho Villa. Two years later, during World War I, Scrip was shipped overseas where he fought in combat on the frontlines. Scrip, an infantryman, was attached to the 157th French Brigade and was awarded the Purple Heart and two Battle Stars for his heroics. After his years in baseball, Lee worked for the Veterans Administration for three decades.

(1922–1934): Hilldale Daisies, Baltimore Black Sox, Atlantic City Bacharach Giants, Cleveland Red Sox and Philadelphia Stars

Wade Hampton Lefler, *Outfield*

A Duke grad, Lefler had a cup of coffee one year in the majors whose tab was picked up by two clubs. He had one at-bat with the

Braves before he was traded to the Senators in 1924. The Senators of that season were baseball's world champions, as Wade had a terrific five-game trial. He went 5-for-8 with three doubles and six RBIs. But with an outfield of Goslin, Rice and Leibold, and with Earl McNeely and Wid Matthews on the bench, there wasn't room for Wade. During the First World War, Lefler served in the army.

G	R	H	2B	3B	HR	RBI	BB	SO	SB	AVG	Slug
6	0	5	3	0	0	6	0	1	0	.556	.889

Hubert Benjamin "Dutch" Leonard, *Pitcher*

Dutch Leonard is now remembered as the charlatan who accused two legends of Baseball, Ty Cobb and Tris Speaker, of throwing a game. It was later revealed that Leonard harbored a grudge against the two player-managers for not offering him a roster spot when he was let go by his previous organization. Despite the dark cloud hanging over the memory of Leonard, he spent the majority of the 1918 season working for various shipyards.

W	L	PCT	G	GS	CG	IP	H	BB	SO	SHO	ERA
138	111	.554	330	272	152	2,190	2,019	661	1,158	33	2.77

Joseph Howard Leonard, *Utilityman*

Joe Leonard's life was cut short at the beginning of the 1920 season when he died due to a ruptured appendix in May. He was only 25 years old. During the war, Joe served in the navy and was stationed at the Great Lakes Naval Training Station.

G	R	H	2B	3B	HR	RBI	BB	SO	SB	AVG	Slug
269	94	179	23	12	2	61	99	113	17	.226	.293

Walter Fred Leverenz, *Pitcher*

"Tiny" had a long career as a player in professional baseball but spent only three seasons at the highest level. He pitched for the Browns during the Federal League uprising, and when that little revolution was quelled, Walt went back to the bushes. Still in the minors when the war broke out, Walt had a short service hitch before he returned to the minor leagues.

W	L	PCT	G	GS	CG	IP	H	BB	SO	SHO	ERA
8	31	.205	62	44	19	323	277	160	131	2	3.15

George Edward "Duffy" Lewis, *Outfield*

The first man to master left field in Boston, Lewis was a mainstay in the pasture for the Red Sox until owner Harry Frazee sent him to the Yankees. The following year, Frazee (always looking for money to finance his plays) sold another Boston outfielder, Babe Ruth to New York in the same fashion. Lewis served as a petty officer in the navy, stationed at Mare Island. While at Mare Island, Duffy was in charge of the baseball program. He had quite a cast of characters, including catcher Rowdy Elliott and two of the infamous 1919 Black Sox players: Swede Risberg and Fred McMullin.

G	R	H	2B	3B	HR	RBI	BB	SO	SB	AVG	Slug
1,459	612	1,518	289	68	38	793	352	n/a	113	.284	.384

Charles Edward Loudenslager, *Second Base*

Charlie played one game at the major league level with the 1904 Dodgers. The Baltimore native was summoned for military duty in 1918.

G	R	H	2B	3B	HR	RBI	BB	SO	SB	AVG	Slug
1	0	0	0	0	0	0	0	0	n/a	.000	.000

Louis Bailey Lowdermilk, *Pitcher*

Of the Lowdermilk boys, Lou's brother, Grover, had the better career. Lou played two seasons at the highest level with the Cardinals, managed by Hall of Fame catcher Roger Bresnahan. His major league career was over by the time he was summoned for duty during World War I. Lou served in the army at Camp Shelby, Mississippi, and played some service ball on the installation.

W	L	PCT	G	GS	CG	IP	H	BB	SO	SHO	ERA
4	5	.444	20	4	4	80	86	38	22	0	3.38

James Lyons, *Outfield*

A swift left fielder who mastered the Deadball Era style of play, Lyons was a great bunter who excelled at beating out infield hits. Lyons spent several years with the St. Louis Giants and Indianapolis ABCs before his stint in the military during World War I. The ABCs of the World War I era had a terrific outfield of Lyons, Hall of Famer Oscar Charleston and George Shively. It was broken up when Jimmie entered the army. Shipped overseas to France, he was able to play some ball in the Allied Expeditionary Force League.

After his discharge from the war, Negro League pioneer Rube Foster broke up the league and realigned some of its players to create more for parity. With powerhouse teams like the ABCs running away with titles, Foster sought more balance and removed Lyons from the Indianapolis roster and placed him on the Detroit Stars. But Foster's best-laid plans didn't work. The Negro Leagues was characterized by contract jumping and nomadic play and any attempt to designate players was a failure from the outset. Jimmie jumped the Stars early in the 1920 season and joined the Bacharach Giants of Atlantic City. He then spent the next few seasons in Chicago with the American Giants. A gritty, rough-styled ballplayer, Jimmie fit the Ty Cobb "baseball is war" mold who was reputed, like Cobb, to have sharpened his spikes and cut players without mercy.

(1910–1925): Chicago American Giants, St. Louis Giants, New York Lincoln Giants, Brooklyn Royal Giants, Indianapolis ABCs, Detroit Stars, Atlantic City Bacharach Giants, Washington Potomacs and Cleveland Browns

Edmund Burke "Stubby" Magner, *Utility Infielder*

Magner, whose stature led to the nickname "Stubby," played briefly with the 1911 Yankees as a backup middle infielder. During the First World War word spread that Edmund Magner was killed in action, but it wasn't the Magner who played on the diamond. The Edmund Magner who was killed while serving his country was a yeoman on the *USS Salem* while Edmund "Stubby" Magner was a lieutenant.

G	R	H	2B	3B	HR	RBI	BB	SO	SB	AVG	Slug
13	3	7	0	0	0	4	4	n/a	1	.212	.212

Anthony Mahoney, *Pitcher*

The left-handed pitcher suffered much the same fate as New York Giants legend Christy Mathewson. While overseas during World War I, Mahoney was gassed and never fully recovered. He pitched briefly in the Negro Leagues after the war but with his health in decline, he quit the game and was later admitted to Walter Reed Army Hospital. He died at the hospital in the fall of 1924.

(1920–1923): Brooklyn Royal Giants, Indianapolis ABCs and Baltimore Black Sox

John Walter "Duster" Mails, *Pitcher*

Baseball has known its fair share of colorful players, with the likes of Dizzy Dean, Casey Stengel and Mickey Rivers. Mails falls into this subgenre of aloof ball diamond performers. John Walter Mails, who playfully referred to himself as "The Great" Duster Mails, was said to have possessed as much natural ability as the legendary Rube Waddell — a colorful critter in his own rite. Before a game in which he was slated to start against the mighty White Sox of Collins, Jackson and Weaver, Duster boasted, "Those birds are made to order for me."

Never lacking in confidence in his own abilities, Duster Mails had a tendency to back up his self-assured boasts with magnificent play. In his return trip to the major leagues after the war, he posted a perfect 7–0 record with a microscopic 1.85 ERA. He topped off that magical 1920 campaign by twirling 15⅔ scoreless innings during the World Series. Despite his obvious skill on the pitcher's mound, he was one of only four major league ballplayers to enlist before the 1917 baseball season. His outspoken desire to join the military cost the great left-hander two full seasons of major league service and only after a stint in the Pacific Coast League was he able to return to the majors for his World Series appearance in 1920.

W	L	PCT	G	GS	CG	IP	H	BB	SO	SHO	ERA
32	25	.561	104	61	29	515	554	220	232	5	4.11

David Julius Malarcher, *Third Base*

"Gentleman Dave," as Malarcher was known, could play ball in the rough and rowdy style that characterized the Deadball Era, but he was always polite off the field and led a clean life. A switch-hitter, Dave learned the game under two of black baseball's greatest teachers: Rube Foster and C.I. Taylor. Malarcher broke in with Taylor's ABCs before World War I and had yet to establish himself before he was inducted into service. Dave served overseas in France and played some service ball in Le Mans.

After the war Malarcher caught on with the Chicago American Giants and was schooled by Foster. The third baseman on Foster's strong Chicago teams, Malarcher was an apt pupil, and Foster made the switch-hitter from Louisiana his team captain. After Foster was institutionalized with a mental disorder, Dave took over in Chicago. Never a terrific hitter, Dave was more of a situational player with a solid glove who got by on baseball brains. After his stint in baseball, Malarcher established a real estate business and published some poetry.

(1916–1934): Chicago American Giants, Indianapolis ABCs, Detroit Stars and Chicago Columbia Giants

Lewis Aloysius Malone, *Third Base*

Malone was only 18 years old when he made his major league debut in 1915 with Connie Mack's Athletics. The holdout of Frank "Homerun" Baker caused Mack to juggle his daily lineup, as catcher Wally Schang was forced into a platoon role with the teenage Malone at the hot corner. He became a member of the Dodgers by 1917 and spent the entire 1918 campaign in the military. During the war, Lew served at an aviation field in Rockford, Illinois. He played one final year in the majors with the 1919 Dodgers, employed in Wilbert Robinson's hot corner carousel.

G	R	H	2B	3B	HR	RBI	BB	SO	SB	AVG	Slug
133	28	74	11	7	1	28	28	60	8	.202	.278

Albert Leon Mamaux, *Pitcher*

Al ran afoul of Dodger owner Charlie Ebbets during the 1918 campaign. The owner accused the player of deserting the team. Mamaux left the club and took a job at Four Rivers Shipbuilding Plant — doing his bit for the war — and acquired the wrath of Ebbets for his actions. It was widely speculated that Al ventured off to the shipyards to avoid military duty, but the pitcher denied such claims. Never one to be on the best of terms with owners, Mamaux earlier upset Pirates owner Barney Dreyfuss, which facilitated his trade to Brooklyn.

W	L	PCT	G	GS	CG	IP	H	BB	SO	SHO	ERA
76	67	.531	254	138	78	1,294	1,138	511	625	15	2.89

Walter James Vincent "Rabbit" Maranville, *Shortstop*

The diminutive and eccentric Maranville, a member of the Baseball Hall of Fame, is the smallest twentieth century player enshrined. His legacy is based off his acrobatic style of play as well as his bizarre antics — one of which is reported as eating raw goldfish. Given his diminutive size, Rabbit was forced to play "small ball" because his stature wasn't conducive to long ball swatting. A long-time Brave, Maranville made several stops in his major league career but always seemed to go back to Boston. During the war, Rabbit served in the navy and played service ball at the Great Lakes Naval Training Station.

G	R	H	2B	3B	HR	RBI	BB	SO	SB	AVG	Slug
2,670	1,255	2,605	380	177	28	884	839	756	291	.258	.340

Clifford Monroe Markle, *Pitcher*

Cliff Markle's name made its rounds during the First World War. Before the war, Cliff showed some promise with the New York Yankees in 1915 but struggled in 1916 and was sent back to the bushes for further seasoning. When the war broke out, Markle's name wasn't attached to any roster in affiliated ball, and it was assumed that he had joined the colors. Cliff was reported as missing in action in the French forest in May 1918 and then labeled as killed in action the following month. When June turned into July, Markle's name made the war papers again when he was listed as a prisoner of war, held captive at Limbourg. The baseball world bemoaned the plight of Cliff Markle and championed him a great American hero until he walked into the offices of his hometown paper to set the record straight.

The Cliff Markle who gained renown on the battlefields was not the ex-Yankees pitcher but a man by the same name. The *Warren Evening Times* put the baseball populace in the know with its story on Cliff. Markle wasn't on any team's roster in 1918, not because he was serving in the military but because he was taking the year off to nurse a dead arm. When he read reports of his battlefield demise in the paper, Cliff decided to march to the nearest print shop and clue the boys in. Shortly thereafter, the pitcher followed the war hero into the service.

W	L	PCT	G	GS	CG	IP	H	BB	SO	SHO	ERA
12	17	.414	56	21	12	235	235	110	90	2	4.10

Richard William "Rube" Marquard, *Pitcher*

A Hall of Fame southpaw, Marquard had already gained renown as a member of John McGraw's Giants by 1918. He gave McGraw one of the greatest righty-lefty tandems in baseball history by joining Christy Mathewson for a number of years in New York. The duo combined for fifty wins in 1911—Matty had 26 and Rube chipped in 24. In 1912, they won a combined 49, with Rube notching 26 and Matty 23. This great duo pitched the Giants to three straight World Series appearances from 1911 to 1913. When the Giants reached rock bottom in 1915, McGraw broke up the duo by sending Matty to the Reds to manage that ballclub and Rube to Brooklyn. He helped pitch the Dodgers to the World Series his first year there.

When World War I broke out, Rube was still a solid major league pitcher. He went 19–12 for Brooklyn in 1917 but struggled with poor run support in 1918. The war invaded rosters in 1918 but Marquard spent the entire season with the Dodgers. Brooklyn had no offense outside of veteran stars Zach Wheat and Jake Daubert and Rube led the league with 18 losses. After the season, he and teammate Burleigh Grimes enlisted in the navy. The two Hall of Fame hurlers reported to the Great Lakes Naval Training Station. Marquard, who chirped about gaining fifteen pounds of muscle in the navy, served briefly with a mine-sweeping unit.

W	L	PCT	G	GS	CG	IP	H	BB	SO	SHO	ERA
201	177	.532	536	406	197	3,307	3,233	858	1,593	30	3.08

William Earl Marriott, *Utilityman*

Marriott made his major league debut in 1917 and missed the entire 1918 campaign to service in the armed forces. He didn't return to the majors until 1920, when he appeared in 14 games for the Cubs. In 1925, he settled in as a third baseman with the Boston Braves and finished out his career two years later with the Brooklyn Dodgers.

G	R	H	2B	3B	HR	RBI	BB	SO	SB	AVG	Slug
264	86	220	27	14	4	95	57	55	16	.266	.347

Christopher Mathewson, *Pitcher*

"I saw Christy Mathewson doomed to die," Ty Cobb mentioned in his biography. Mathewson and Cobb, as well as many other famous sports figures of the time, served in the Chemical Warfare Service in 1918. Mathewson and his athletic peers were assigned as instructors to oversee and train rejects from the various branches of service. The theory behind their assignment was that problem soldiers would listen to star athletes.

The instructors would march soldiers into a gas chamber to test their protective masks. With the lone warning of the release of the gas nothing more than a hand signal, the soldiers were trained to be alert and quick. On one given day, the signal was missed. When the gas was released, men clamored to be set free from the chamber: many inhaled a dose of the poison, Mathewson and Cobb included. Eight soldiers died on the spot. As for Mathewson, the trail of suffering had just begun.

Christy Mathewson inhaled just enough chemical gas to weaken his lungs. In a matter of time, he contracted tuberculosis in both of his lungs, and later possessed only the use of his fingers and forearms. To keep his mind off his ailment, Mathewson delved into baseball strategy, analyzing plays and devising the best way to attack a situation on the field. Before his death, he served as president and part-owner of the Boston Braves. Ty Cobb said of Christy Mathewson, "He was truly magnificent in every way ... no other phrase fits."

W	L	PCT	G	GS	CG	IP	H	BB	SO	SHO	ERA
374	188	.665	635	551	434	4,780	4,218	844	2,502	79	2.13

Frank Spruiell "Jakie" May, *Pitcher*

Jakie began his career in 1917 with the St. Louis Cardinals. He appeared in fifteen games, all but one in relief. May was able to spend the majority of the 1918 season on the ball diamond and served briefly in the armed forces. When he returned to the diamond, he struggled mightily with his control, pacing the National League in walks despite tossing just 126 innings. The short southpaw spent the majority of his major league career with the Cincinnati Reds and retired in 1932.

W	L	PCT	G	GS	CG	IP	H	BB	SO	SHO	ERA
72	95	.431	410	160	70	1,563	1,645	617	765	7	3.88

Walter A. Mayer, *Catcher*

Mayer played sporadically in the major leagues and never received much of an opportunity to play on a regular basis. He made his major league debut with Hugh Duffy's White Sox in 1911. The most action he saw in four years with the Pale Hose was 39 games in 1914. During the 1918 baseball season, Wally platooned briefly with Sam Agnew before he was lost to the war effort.

G	R	H	2B	3B	HR	RBI	BB	SO	SB	AVG	Slug
129	22	53	14	3	0	20	42	n/a	1	.193	.266

Mark Andrew "Patsy" McGaffigan, *Second Base*

The diminutive second sacker played only two years in the major leagues, one of which was cut short by World War I. During the war, Patsy served in the army and even played in the Army-Navy Championship game. After his discharge, McGaffigan was never again summoned to play in the majors.

G	R	H	2B	3B	HR	RBI	BB	SO	SB	AVG	Slug
73	22	49	4	2	1	14	16	30	4	.194	.238

Robert Emmett McGraw, *Pitcher*

The 1918 season began on rocky terrain for Bob McGraw as he made one start and didn't record a single out. In fact, he walked the four batters he faced before a reliever was called upon to take his place. McGraw was unable to redeem himself after such a horrendous start to the season because he was summoned into the colors and served his country on foreign soil. McGraw saw combat action on the frontlines but returned home unscathed. He enjoyed a nine-year career in the major leagues, with five different clubs. The majority of his time was spent as a relief hurler.

W	L	PCT	G	GS	CG	IP	H	BB	SO	SHO	ERA
26	38	.406	168	47	17	591	677	265	164	1	4.89

Thomas Patrick McGuire, *Pitcher*

Tom saw most of his major league action in 1914 with Joe Tinker's Chicago Federal League outfit. He spent the next few seasons in the bushes before he received another look in the majors with the White Sox in 1918. However, with the war raging overseas, McGuire entered the armed forces and missed the entire season while serving as the Regimental Sergeant Major of Divisional Trains at Camp Grant. In the infamous 1919 season, Tom appeared in just one game for Kid Gleason's boys and tossed three innings of relief.

W	L	PCT	G	GS	CG	IP	H	BB	SO	SHO	ERA
5	6	.455	25	12	7	134	148	60	37	0	3.83

John Phalen "Stuffy" McInnis, *First Base*

One of the greatest players not enshrined in the Baseball Hall of Fame, McInnis is famous for being the first baseman on Connie Mack's $100,000 Infield with Jack Barry and Hall of Famers Homerun Baker and Eddie Collins. After the 1917 season, Connie Mack, known for selling off his talent, sent McInnis to Boston where he teamed briefly with Jack Barry once again. He played in 117 games for the Red Sox in 1918, missing a small amount of major league action to service time.

G	R	H	2B	3B	HR	RBI	BB	SO	SB	AVG	Slug
2,128	872	2,406	312	101	20	1,060	380	n/a	172	.308	.381

Fred Drury McMullin, *Third Base*

Banished from baseball for his role in the 1919 World Series, McMullin was a reserve infielder on the Black Sox AL champion squad. Although Fred was a backup, he was wise to the fix and was kicked out of baseball by Judge Landis. Good chums with White Sox shortstop Swede Risberg, the two left the White Sox for the military in 1918 and served on the West Coast. They played service ball for a team managed by Red Sox star left fielder Duffy Lewis.

G	R	H	2B	3B	HR	RBI	BB	SO	SB	AVG	Slug
304	120	234	21	9	1	70	91	105	30	.256	.302

Michael Joseph McNally, *Utility Infielder*

McNally was eager to join the navy as he stated that he would be perfectly happy if he could "bag a German submarine." The utilityman missed the entire 1918 baseball season to service in the navy. After playing regularly for the Red Sox in 1920, McNally was sent to the Yankees where he platooned at third base with Homerun Baker and then Joe Dugan.

G	R	H	2B	3B	HR	RBI	BB	SO	SB	AVG	Slug
492	169	257	16	6	1	85	92	97	39	.238	.267

George Earl McNeely, *Outfield*

McNeely started in the professional ranks after his military discharge. The Sacramento lad was a rookie sensation in 1924 when he slapped the game-winning hit that scored Muddy Ruel in the 1924 World Series. Earl, who was regarded by writer Jay Sehorn as a "quiet, deep-thinking" individual, returned home after his playing days and served as the owner and president of the minor league Sacramento Senators.

G	R	H	2B	3B	HR	RBI	BB	SO	SB	AVG	Slug
683	369	614	107	33	4	213	183	187	68	.272	.354

Michael William Menosky, *Outfield*

Leaping Mike Menosky made his major league debut with the upstart Federal League's Pittsburgh franchise, playing sparingly as a youngster. However, the Senators saw enough potential in the outfielder to acquire his services after the Federal League folded in 1915. He worked his way into the regular lineup in 1917 but missed the entire 1918 campaign to the military. Menosky was initially stationed at Camp Custer in the army but was later shipped out overseas. Attached to Uncle Sam's fighting forces, Mike saw combat action on the frontlines. He returned to the Senators in 1919, with new found power, as he socked twice as many homers as the runner-up on the club. Despite his bulky hitting, the Senators sent Leaping Mike to the Red Sox to fill the void created in the Bosox lineup when Babe Ruth was sold to New York. Although he played well for the Red Sox, he was unable to make any Boston fan forget the Sultan of Swat.

G	R	H	2B	3B	HR	RBI	BB	SO	SB	AVG	Slug
809	382	685	98	38	18	250	295	260	90	.278	.370

John Wayne Middleton, *Pitcher*

Middleton appeared in only two games at the major league level with the 1922 Indians of Tris Speaker. A fresh-faced teen during the First World War, Middleton also leant his services to his country as a 40-year-old during World War II.

W	L	PCT	G	GS	CG	IP	H	BB	SO	SHO	ERA
0	1	.000	2	1	0	7	8	6	2	0	7.71

Horace Robert Milan, *Outfield*

The younger brother of star Senator center fielder Clyde Milan, Horace appeared in only 42 major league games but hit an astounding .320. On Christmas Eve of 1917, Horace Milan enlisted in the army and missed the entire 1918 season to military service. Horace served overseas where he was engaged in combat action with the enemy. He never again played in a major league game.

G	R	H	2B	3B	HR	RBI	BB	SO	SB	AVG	Slug
42	14	32	4	2	0	16	12	16	6	.320	.400

John Kenneth Miljus, *Pitcher*

A staunch patriot with an eagerness to fight that is unrivalled, Miljus may be the most celebrated soldier to ever wear a baseball uniform. On the diamond, Miljus (who was known as "Big Serb") had a forgettable career as he appeared in 127 games, mostly in relief. However, it was in another uniform that Miljus earned his status as a hero.

Big Serb served in the army as a member of the 320th Infantry. His military travails took him to France with his army bunkmate, Joe Harris, a solid major league ballplayer. He saw action in the Argonne Offensive and was wounded during the conflict when an enemy bayonet found his body. His injury was severe enough that he was slated to return to the States, but while in an army hospital waiting to be shipped back home, Big Serb snuck out of the infirmary to rejoin his unit and continue fighting. He was engaged in battle to the very end of the war and was wounded in the campaign's final skirmish. He returned to the ball diamond in 1920 with the Dodgers and helped take Brooklyn to the World Series.

W	L	PCT	G	GS	CG	IP	H	BB	SO	SHO	ERA
29	26	.527	127	45	15	457	526	173	166	2	3.92

John Barney "Dots" Miller, *Utility Infielder*

Dots broke into the major leagues in 1909 with the Pittsburgh Pirates. He appeared in 151 games as a rookie, where he served as Honus Wagner's double-play partner, and collected seven hits in that year's World Series. He suffered with a slight case of the sophomore jinx but righted himself in 1911. At the beginning of the 1912 campaign, Miller was shifted to first base and remained there into 1913, at which time he was second in the NL with 20 triples. Dots was sent to the Cardinals for the 1914 season and rotated between first base and shortstop while pacing the Redbirds with 88 RBIs. His versatility was an asset for Miller Huggins during his tenure in St. Louis, as he placed Dots at every station on the infield.

At the age of 31, Dots missed the entire baseball season to service during the war. He didn't spend his time under Uncle Sam idle, as Dots was eager to see action. When he learned the military wanted him to remain stateside and play baseball, Dots was dejected but let everyone know of his intentions. Dots had this to say about what he wanted out of the military: "Gee, I don't want to be drafted and play ball. I want to fight — that's why I joined this outfit. And now they want me to play ball. Can you beat such luck?"

During his stateside training, Dots served at Parris Island where he was an expert marksman. He established the monthly shooting record at the island with a score of 289 out of a possible 300 points. However, given his desire to fight, Dots was shipped out to France with the 83rd. Miller served with the U.S. Marines and took part in combat action. Dots was able to play a pickup baseball game in Flanders between battle lines. He spent nearly a year and a half with the Marines and returned to America on the cruiser *Charleston*.

A true patriot with a zealous mindset toward fighting, Dots made it known early that he had no intention of working a factory job while the war raged overseas. The scrappy and versatile ballplayer showed his eagerness to fight by stating that he didn't want to "make a run for the shipyards and grab a handful of rivets."

G	R	H	2B	3B	HR	RBI	BB	SO	SB	AVG	Slug
1,589	711	1,526	232	108	32	715	319	n/a	177	.263	.357

Hugh Stanley Miller, *First Base*

Miller made his major league debut with the 1911 Phillies of Red Dooin and appeared in just one game. It took the intrusion of the Federal League for Miller to make good at the highest level. He played for his hometown St. Louis team in the upstart league, as the regular first sacker in 1914 and as a reserve in 1915. When the Federal League folded, Miller's professional career was all but over.

Although Miller's baseball days were in his rearview mirror, his moment of glory rested ahead of him. Shortly after the United States entered fighting in the First World War, Hughie enlisted in the U.S. Marine Corps. Unlike other ballplayers that stayed stateside and hit the horsehide sphere, Miller went overseas and participated in heavy combat action. The former first baseman was wounded three times in action. He was initially wounded at Bellaeu Wood, but after he was bandaged up he returned to the frontlines, only to be wounded again in Vierzy. The afflictions didn't hinder Hughie's desire to fight as he entered fighting for the third time. His third battlefield endeavor resulted in "severe wounds" that signaled an end to his fighting.

General Pershing awarded Miller the Distinguished Service Cross for his actions in the European Theatre. Even though Hughie's baseball career was all but over when he enlisted, it was officially complete courtesy his battlefield wounds. Yankees owner T.L. Huston, who served overseas with the 16th Engineers, said of Hughie, "Baseball should do something for Hugh Miller and other baseball men who have been wounded. I am sure that the league will make some provision for those who have become incapacitated." But Miller didn't regard himself as incapacitated — he desired to run for the post of alderman in his hometown after his discharge.

G	R	H	2B	3B	HR	RBI	BB	SO	SB	AVG	Slug
140	51	112	21	5	0	49	27	n/a	4	.226	.288

Raymond Peter Miller, *First Base*

Miller's only major league service came in 1917. He began that year with Lee Fohl's Cleveland Indians, where he served as war hero Joe Harris' backup, but was later dealt to Pittsburgh and played sparingly. He missed the entire 1918 campaign to service in the armed forces.

G	R	H	2B	3B	HR	RBI	BB	SO	SB	AVG	Slug
25	2	8	2	0	0	2	10	6	0	.167	.208

Clarence Elmer Mitchell, *Pitcher*

A solid hitting pitcher, Mitchell enjoyed a rather lengthy major league career. He made his debut in 1911 and retired in 1932. Clarence's time in the military wasn't spent idle, as the southpaw saw action in the same field artillery unit that Dodger teammate Chuck Ward was assigned to. He served overseas in Europe where he saw combat action and returned to the Dodgers in time to take part in the 1919 season. During Brooklyn's championship run in 1920, Clarence was used sparingly but was the only hurler to pitch in the Fall Classic for the Dodgers who didn't surrender an earned run. After suffering an ankle injury, he was shipped off to the Phillies in 1923 and played with them through 1928. He retired as a member of the Giants in 1932.

W	L	PCT	G	GS	CG	IP	H	BB	SO	SHO	ERA
125	139	.473	390	278	145	2,217	2,613	624	543	12	4.12

William Mitchell, *Pitcher*

A solid left-handed pitcher for a handful of years, Mitchell enjoyed his breakout campaign in 1913 with the Indians, posting 141 strikeouts to go along with a microscopic 1.74 ERA. He finished second with 179 strikeouts in 1914 and was sent to Detroit after initially struggling in 1916. He was never quite the same pitcher with the Tigers, as he made just one start in 1918 before he joined the military. Willie played service ball at Camp Pike, Arkansas, with fellow Tiger Bert Ellison. But it wasn't all baseball in the army for Willie. Shipped overseas, he saw action in the European Theatre. Mitchell returned to the diamond in 1919 to make three final major league appearances.

W	L	PCT	G	GS	CG	IP	H	BB	SO	SHO	ERA
84	92	.477	275	190	94	1,632	1,464	605	921	16	2.86

Edward Oliver Monroe, *Pitcher*

In a brief major league career, Monroe didn't help his cause by jumping the Yankees after making just one appearance for them in 1918. He bolted out of pinstripes to work in a shipyard but was drafted into the armed forces shortly after bidding adieu to the Bronx Bombers.

W	L	PCT	G	GS	CG	IP	H	BB	SO	SHO	ERA
1	0	1.000	10	1	1	31	36	8	13	0	3.48

Walter "Dobie" Moore, *Shortstop*

Moore can credit his start in baseball to his stint in the military during World War I. Dobie played service ball at Fort Huachuca with the 25th Infantry and impressed Casey Stengel and John McGraw of the major leagues. Stengel tipped off J.L. Wilkinson, a white owner in the Negro Leagues, recording a handful of good players at Fort Huachuca, and he signed Moore along with future Hall of Famer Bullet Rogan from the army ranks for his Kansas City Monarchs. An exceptional all-round player, Moore's career was cut short due a shooting involving a scorned brothel owner he was having an affair with.

(1920–1926): Kansas City Monarchs

William Allen "Scrappy" Moore, *Reserve*

The last player signed by Branch Rickey for the Browns before the general manager left the club, Scrappy had a cup of coffee with his hometown team in 1917. A Vanderbilt star, Moore never made good at the major league level. He missed the 1918 season to military service and did not return to the majors after his discharge.

G	R	H	2B	3B	HR	RBI	BB	SO	SB	AVG	Slug
4	1	1	0	0	0	1	0	0		.125	.125

Guy Morton Sr., *Pitcher*

Morton posted a 10–10 record in 1917 and appeared primed to assist aces Stan Coveleski and Jim Bagby Sr. in the upcoming campaign. He spent the majority of the season with the Tribe, pacing the club in strikeouts (good for fourth in the league), but was lost to the war effort near the close of the campaign. The "Alabama Blossom" was an officer candidate in the armed forces but was able to return to Cleveland in 1919 without missing any action. During his stint in the army, Morton was stationed at Camp Pike where military training beefed the pitcher up. He wrote a letter to skipper Lee Fohl that read, "It's hard work, this Army life, but it's filling me out to beat the band and I'm stronger and harder than ever. I weigh ten pounds more than when the season opened."

W	L	PCT	G	GS	CG	IP	H	BB	SO	SHO	ERA
97	86	.535	316	184	80	1,629	1,520	583	830	19	3.13

Paul Musser, *Pitcher*

Musser was a highly sought after commodity in the minor leagues as he was tutored by former star ballplayer Frank Isbell in the Western League. His major league career never took off like many had hoped. However, when he seemed to be in top form, he entered the military in 1918. Musser missed the entire baseball season that year and was stationed at Des Moines.

W	L	PCT	G	GS	CG	IP	H	BB	SO	SHO	ERA
1	2	.333	12	6	1	41	42	24	24	0	3.29

Elmer Glenn Myers, *Pitcher*

Few players make an immediate splash in the fashion of Elmer Myers. As a 21-year-old, Myers made one appearance for the Athletics in 1915. He pitched the entire nine innings and struck out twelve batters in a shutout. Given that performance, manager Connie Mack surely had high hopes for the kid. Myers failed to live up to that early promise, as he paced major league baseball with 168 walks the following year. Myers missed only a brief time to the war effort: he was able to make fifteen starts for the Athletics in 1918 and averaged merely a single strikeout per game.

W	L	PCT	G	GS	CG	IP	H	BB	SO	SHO	ERA
55	72	.433	185	127	78	1,102	1,148	440	428	8	4.06

Roleine Cecil Naylor, *Pitcher*

Naylor's poor career winning percentage has a great deal to do with the fact that he languished on a very poor Philadelphia ballclub for seven years. For the first four years of his major league career, Naylor's Athletics were the last-place team in the American League. His teammates didn't give the Texan much of a chance to nail down victories. He was out of the major leagues after 1924, at which time Connie Mack was beginning to assemble his next dynasty. Rollie missed the entire 1918 baseball season to military service and saw action in the French battlefields.

W	L	PCT	G	GS	CG	IP	H	BB	SO	SHO	ERA
42	83	.336	181	136	67	1,010	1,174	346	282	2	3.94

Fred Nicholson, *Outfield*

The pride of Honey Grove, Texas, Nicholson retired with a respectable career batting average but was never able to grasp a full-time job at the major league level. Fred missed the entire 1918 season to service in the armed forces, and when he returned to the majors, he had become a member of Hugo Bezdek's Pittsburgh Pirates. Despite his .360 batting average in 247 at-bats (the Pirates as a team hit just .257 in 1920), Fred served as a reserve behind more established veteran players. He spent the following two years as a reserve with the Braves and was out of the major leagues by 1922.

G	R	H	2B	3B	HR	RBI	BB	SO	SB	AVG	Slug
303	112	247	34	21	12	105	65	97	21	.311	.452

Louis Alexander North, *Pitcher*

North saw his first major league action with the 1913 Detroit Tigers—the worst pitching team in the American League. He made one start and all he had to show for it was an unflattering ERA of 15.00. It would take Lou another four years before he made his return to the highest level, as he got into five games for the Cardinals in 1917. As a 27-year-old, North missed the entire 1918 season to the war and returned to the majors in 1920. He spent five more years in the majors and finished his time with the Braves.

W	L	PCT	G	GS	CG	IP	H	BB	SO	SHO	ERA
21	16	.568	172	25	8	463	509	200	199	0	4.43

Winfield Charles Noyes, *Pitcher*

Noyes was another in the long line of spitball artists during the Dead Ball Era. Win saw his first major league action as a 24-year-old with the 1913 Boston Braves and then didn't see big league time again until Connie Mack summoned him in 1917. His future seemed bright, as he was second on the Athletics' staff in wins in 1917, but he missed all of 1918 to military service. After his return from France, where he was engaged in heavy combat action on the frontlines, Noyes posted a 1–5, 5.69 record for Philadelphia. That facilitated a trade to the White Sox where his ERA swelled to 7.50. The moistballer never again saw action in the major leagues after the Pale Hose cut him loose.

W	L	PCT	G	GS	CG	IP	H	BB	SO	SHO	ERA
11	15	.423	49	29	14	247	254	98	93	1	3.75

Leslie Grant Nunamaker, *Catcher*

A veteran catcher by the time World War I started, Nunamaker had played at the major league level since 1911. Les played on the same Boston Red Sox team as Tris Speaker from 1911 to 1914, and the two men struck up a friendship. After the 1918 baseball season, when Les was with the Browns and Speaker with the Indians, the two pals enlisted in the navy and attended the Massachusetts Technical Naval Aviators School. Shortly after graduation, the war ended, but even if it hadn't, Nunamaker may not have given Uncle Sam much. After Les completed the aviation training, he was involved in a traffic accident that nearly claimed his life. He would recover in time to participate in the 1919 baseball season.

G	R	H	2B	3B	HR	RBI	BB	SO	SB	AVG	Slug
715	194	533	75	30	2	215	176	n/a	36	.268	.339

Delmar Harold Paddock, *Third Base*

A graduate of Dubuque University, Paddock split his only season in the majors between the White Sox and Yankees. The portside-swinging hot corner custodian saw his only major league action during the 1912 campaign. One of the few South Dakota residents to make the majors, Paddock served in the armed forces during the First World War.

G	R	H	2B	3B	HR	RBI	BB	SO	SB	AVG	Slug
46	26	45	5	3	1	14	23	n/a	9	.287	.376

George Washington Payne, *Pitcher*

A minor league legend, Payne appeared in more than 900 games in the bushes. His longevity was courtesy of his employ of the easy motion of the knuckleball, which he fluttered for one season at the major league level. While the White Sox were engaged in the infamous World Series scandal, owner Charlie Comiskey gave Payne his only trial at the highest level in 1920. Payne earned the nickname "Old Sergeant" in the minors due to his tenure with Uncle Sam during the First World War.

W	L	PCT	G	GS	CG	IP	H	BB	SO	SHO	ERA
1	1	.500	12	0	0	30	39	9	7	0	5.40

Herbert Jefferis Pennock, *Pitcher*

Another player that was shipped off to the Bronx by the Red Sox, Pennock enjoyed success in the Big Apple (thanks largely to run support), which carried him to Cooperstown. The Hall of Famer served in the navy during World War I and once disembarked a ship at Liverpool to pitch a game against a team of army all-stars.

W	L	PCT	G	GS	CG	IP	H	BB	SO	SHO	ERA
241	161	.600	617	419	247	3,572	3,900	916	1,227	35	3.60

Jesse Lee Petty, *Pitcher*

An above-average pitcher during the Lively Ball Era, Petty had terrific control and kept his ERA down in an age when earned run averages were swollen. The southpaw served with Uncle Sam's outfit before he tried on his first major league duds. Petty served with the United States Army as a dispatch rider during the war. After his discharge, Jesse was able to focus wholeheartedly on his ball diamond aspirations. He made good with Wilbert Robinson's Dodgers in the mid 1920s where he teamed with Hall of Famer Dazzy Vance in the Brooklyn rotation.

W	L	PCT	G	GS	CG	IP	H	BB	SO	SHO	ERA
67	78	.462	207	153	76	1,209	1,286	296	407	6	3.68

Edward Joseph "Jeff" Pfeffer, *Pitcher*

A longtime Brooklyn hurler, Pfeffer spent 1913 through 1921 twirling the apple for the Dodgers. He enjoyed his breakout year in 1914 when he posted a 23–12 record as one of the Dodgers few decent arms. Jeff was able to post 19 wins in 1915 and 25 in 1916—he guided the Dodgers to a pennant in the latter season. The Dodgers sank in 1917. Pfeffer posted a misleading 11–15 record, as his 2.23 ERA was tops on the team. In 1918, Jeff made one start, tossing a complete-game shutout in the process, before he left for the war effort. He enlisted in the Naval Reserve and played on a navy championship team in the service.

The return to the diamond offered Jeff no problems, as he paced the club in wins and innings pitched. His solid season in 1920 was instrumental in Brooklyn copping another NL crown, although the Dodgers lost the World Series to Tris Speaker's Indians, a team of destiny. Early in 1921, Jeff was shipped off to the Cardinals where he enjoyed one final good year in 1922, when he led the Redbirds with 19 victories.

W	L	PCT	G	GS	CG	IP	H	BB	SO	SHO	ERA
158	112	.585	347	279	194	2,407	2,320	592	836	28	2.77

Valentine John Picinich, *Catcher*

Picinich caught in 47 games for the Senators in 1918 before he was lost to the war effort. During World War I, Val served in the United States Navy and returned to bat .274 in 1919. He spent the remainder of his career as a platoon catcher and retired in 1933 with the Pittsburgh Pirates.

G	R	H	2B	3B	HR	RBI	BB	SO	SB	AVG	Slug
1,037	298	743	166	25	27	298	314	382	31	.258	.361

Walter Clement Pipp, *First Base*

Some baseball players are forever linked with one of their former teammates. Wally Pipp is such a player. If it weren't for Lou Gehrig, Wally Pipp would be just another name in the annals of baseball history. However, players today still refer to Wally Pipp, with traceable trepidation in their voices. Pipp was the man who decided to take a day off, allowing the Iron Horse a chance to showcase his skills. One day on the mend cost Pipp his job, as the Yankee brass realized he could not hold down the first base position any longer with a far more talented Gehrig on the roster.

The story of Wally Pipp's baseball career ends in Cincinnati where he was shipped off for more playing time. While playing in the Big Apple, Pipp took part in three consecutive American League pennant championships; he never again saw action in a Fall Classic after the transaction that sent him out of New York. A solid first baseman, Pipp missed a portion of the 1918 season to service in the Naval Aviation wing. While away from the diamond, Wally spent three months at the Massachusetts Institute of Technology and was attending ground school at Pensacola, Florida, when the war ended.

G	R	H	2B	3B	HR	RBI	BB	SO	SB	AVG	Slug
1,872	974	1,941	311	148	90	996	596	551	125	.281	.408

Spottswood Poles, *Outfield*

One of the greatest stars in black baseball during the Deadball Era, Poles was a short, stocky fellow built along the lines of Hall of Famer Billy Hamilton. Like Sliding Billy, Spot was unusually swift for his build and a terrific defensive outfielder. A switch-hitting center fielder from Winchester, Virginia, Poles was often referred to as a "black Ty Cobb." He began his career in the Negro Leagues about the same time Cobb had become a star in Detroit. Both men were fast and hit for batting averages well above the league norm. Once, in a game against Hall of Famer Grover Alexander, Spot had three base hits.

Poles was already a star in the Negro Leagues when World War I broke out. He had established himself with the New York Lincoln Giants by 1911. Two years later he had his fine showing in an exhibition game against Alexander. Tied to Alexander again in 1918, Poles joined the military and served on the frontlines in battle. Much like white baseball's Hall of Fame pitcher, Poles was a decorated war hero who earned the Purple Heart and five Battle Stars. An infantryman in the army, Spot was attached to the French Army with the 369th. When he returned home from the war, he was at the end of his baseball career. He played a few more years in New York before retiring and operating a taxi fleet. Poles is buried at Arlington National Cemetery.

(1909–1923): New York Lincoln Giants, Philadelphia Giants, Brooklyn Royal Giants, Hilldale Daisies and Atlantic City Bacharach Giants

Charles Elmer Ponder, *Pitcher*

Ponder showed promise in 1917 when he tossed 21 innings and only allowed 12 hits in his first major league action. Despite his promise on the ball diamond, Ponder was a dedicated soldier who missed more time than most baseball players during World War I. The 1918 season was lost to Ponder as well as the majority of the 1919 campaign. During the war, Ponder served in France as an army lieutenant.

During the war, Ponder was the first ballplayer to be awarded the French War Cross for valor. A distinguished pilot, he earned the designation of "ace" prior to the signing of the armistice. A war hero of high caliber, Elmer returned to the Pirates in early July of 1919 as the idol of thousands. But his return was rocky from a performance standpoint. He finished the 1919 season with an unflattering 0–5 record with as many walks as strikeouts.

W	L	PCT	G	GS	CG	IP	H	BB	SO	SHO	ERA
17	27	.386	69	42	20	378	395	72	113	3	3.21

Raymond Reath Powell, *Outfield*

The Boston Braves lost their entire starting outfield in one day when Powell and teammates Wally Rehg and Joe Kelly enlisted together in the navy. Manager George Stallings had to scramble to find their replacements, calling on numerous ballplayers to fill the void. Powell established himself in Boston during the 1917 campaign while leading the team in home runs. A heavy hitter with a tendency to strikeout (he paced the NL with 79 strikeouts in 1919), Powell played for the Braves from 1917 through 1924.

G	R	H	2B	3B	HR	RBI	BB	SO	SB	AVG	Slug
875	467	890	117	67	35	276	321	461	51	.268	.375

O'Neal Pullen, *Catcher*

A chunky catcher, Pullen served in the army before he started his baseball career. During World War I, the Texas native served overseas in France. After his discharge, Pullen played some ball with the Baltimore Black Sox of the Negro Leagues and other teams but his weight problem forced him out of the game.

(1920–1927): Baltimore Black Sox, Brooklyn Royal Giants, Hilldale Daisies, Kansas City Monarchs and New York Lincoln Giants

Thomas Finners Quinlan, *Outfield*

The story of Finners Quinlan could easily be described as a tragic tale, but the man who lived it would beg to differ. Before the war, Finners was an outfield prospect who had yet to make good at the major league level. The Cardinals gave him a trial in 1913 and the White Sox did the same in 1915. Each time the lefty struggled to hit major league pitching. Trying to fight his way back to the majors by toiling in the minors, Quinlan put his dream of a return trip to the show on hold when the war broke out.

Quinlan trained stateside and was shipped overseas where he saw heavy combat action. The Scranton native was wounded in action but felt it his duty to return to the frontlines and continue fighting. He rejoined his outfit in the Argonne Forest near the end of the war, but neither he nor the enemy knew the war was in its final stages. Just 40 hours before the signing of the armistice, Finners Quinlan was struck by a German shell in the forest. The injuries were substantial. Finners lost his left eye, but the orb was only a fraction of the terrible affliction his body suffered. The shell also dislodged from his person his left arm.

Taken from the frontlines, Quinlan was rushed to a field hospital and then was sent to American Red Cross Military Hospital Number 2 in Paris. Quinlan's life was saved, but his aspirations for a return to baseball were snuffed. His wounds were enough to destroy the countenance of any man, but Finners refused to allow his tragic fate on the battlefield to level his pride. With an outlook worthy of praise, Quinlan said, "I'll be all right before long. An artificial arm will take the place of the old southpaw and I'll have a glass eye. The doctors and nurses are taking good care of me, and the Red Cross is keeping me supplied with everything I want. So they needn't worry about me at home."

Finners Quinlan would live a happy, healthy life despite never again taking up the game of baseball. He became active in local politics after he left the military and never used his wartime injuries as an excuse to falter in the game of life.

G	*R*	*H*	*2B*	*3B*	*HR*	*RBI*	*BB*	*SO*	*SB*	*AVG*	*Slug*
55	12	30	3	0	0	8	5	20	3	.183	.201

Morris Charles Rath, *Second Base*

Jackson, Weaver and Cicotte tend to be the names most often associated with the infamous 1919 World Series, but Rath's name has been passed down through generations with the crooked men as well. Leading off in the first game of the Fall Classic, Rath was the batter who Cicotte hit with a pitch to supposedly signal the gamblers that the fix was on. Rath possessed an exceptional batting eye, which made him an obvious selection as the lead-off hitter for Pat Moran's Reds. He paced the Reds with 64 walks in 1919. During World War I, Rath, who was 31 years old, missed the entire baseball campaign to service in the navy.

G	*R*	*H*	*2B*	*3B*	*HR*	*RBI*	*BB*	*SO*	*SB*	*AVG*	*Slug*
563	291	521	36	7	4	92	258	n/a	82	.254	.285

Richard "Cannonball Dick" Redding, *Pitcher*

Arguably the best pitcher that black baseball had to offer during the Deadball Era, Redding's main rival for that title is Hall of Famer Smokey Joe Williams—an occasional teammate. He earned the nickname "Cannonball" for his speed and is credited in some circles as having thrown 30 no-hit games against all levels of competition. Cannonball was paired with Smokey Joe on the New York Lincoln Giants in 1912 and they mowed away all their competition. It was because of talent stockpiling that Rube Foster broke teams apart around World War I for the sake of parity.

Many black sportswriters compared Redding to white baseball's greatest pitcher, Senators legend Walter Johnson. Redding had the heat of Big Train Johnson but also had the support of Smokey Joe Williams, so Cannonball was often on winning teams while Johnson toiled for the lowly Senators. During World War I, Redding left the diamond and joined the army where he saw combat action in France. He returned to the States and pitched in Atlantic City until he caught on for a long run with the Brooklyn Royal Giants. After his first year in Brooklyn, the Royal Giants brought in Smokey Joe Williams, and Cannonball was regarded as the number two pitcher—a designation that didn't sit well with him. A feud began between the two ace pitchers, and they would often refuse to shake hands or have photographs taken together.

If Cannonball was considered a lesser pitcher than the great Smokey Joe Williams, it was by the most meager of margins. When old Negro Leaguers would discuss their all-time teams, Williams and Redding were often mentioned as the top pitchers. There were many who believed that Satchel Paige wasn't the best pitcher that black baseball ever boasted. They would tell folks to look a little further back in history. Hall of Fame executive Cum Posey once said, "We never considered Paige as good a player as Smokey Joe Williams or Dick Redding." A special committee on the Negro Leagues elected close to twenty former players and executives for the Baseball Hall of Fame a few years back, but there were a few glaring omissions. Cannonball Redding was probably their most apparent oversight.

(1911–1932): Brooklyn Royal Giants, New York Lincoln Giants, Indianapolis ABCs, Chicago American Giants and Atlantic City Bacharach Giants

William Wright Regan, *Second Base*

Regan was a youngster during World War I when he served his country in his late teens. After his military discharge, Regan began to work towards a career in baseball. He eventually made the majors with Boston in 1926 and served as the team's regular second baseman through 1930.

G	*R*	*H*	*2B*	*3B*	*HR*	*RBI*	*BB*	*SO*	*SB*	*AVG*	*Slug*
641	236	632	158	36	18	292	122	245	38	.267	.387

Antone "Tony" Rego, *Catcher*

Since Rego was a slight 5'5" he was dubbed "Mighty Midget" by his peers. The Hawaiian native served his country during the First World War, before his major league debut. A longtime minor league player and manager, Rego also possessed a sharp sense of humor. After the slightly built catcher caught the offerings of tall right-hander Long Tom Hughes during a game, Rego quipped, "Now I know how Gabby Street felt when he caught the balls dropped from the Washington Monument."

G	*R*	*H*	*2B*	*3B*	*HR*	*RBI*	*BB*	*SO*	*SB*	*AVG*	*Slug*
44	10	26	3	1	0	8	4	5	0	.286	.341

Walter Phillip Rehg, *Outfield*

Rehg patrolled the outer garden with Joe Kelly and Ray Powell in 1918 as manager George Stallings' regulars, but he and his mates enlisted in the navy on the same day. The entire starting outfield was taken away in a single swath. Wally played with four different major league clubs over the course of his career and was rarely used as a regular. He ended his career by playing in five games for the National League champion Cincinnati Reds of 1919.

G	R	H	2B	3B	HR	RBI	BB	SO	SB	AVG	Slug
258	85	188	24	11	2	66	52	66	26	.250	.319

Edgar Charles "Sam" Rice, *Outfield*

Baseball became Edgar Rice's sanctuary after a tornado claimed the life of his wife, two children and both of his parents. He traveled the country, taking odd jobs as they came, until he enlisted in the navy. After he was signed out of the navy in 1914, the unassuming Rice was introduced by Senators owner Clark Griffith as "Sam" Rice rather than his given name Edgar. Not wanting to correct his boss in the face of the media, Rice played out his entire career under the name of Sam. Rice made a plea to finish out the 1918 season before entering the military. His plea fell on deaf ears, as Rice appeared in only seven contests with the Senators before he left the team for the military. Had Rice, a Hall of Famer, not missed the majority of the 1918 season, he would certainly be a member of the 3,000 Hit Club.

G	R	H	2B	3B	HR	RBI	BB	SO	SB	AVG	Slug
2,404	1,514	2,987	497	184	34	1,078	709	275	351	.322	.427

Wesley Branch Rickey, *Catcher*

"The Mahatma's" playing career was long behind him when World War I broke out. Rickey played for the Browns and Yankees before the calendar displayed 1910. By 1913, he was managing the Browns. Dismissed by the Browns in 1915, Rickey joined the crosstown Cardinals and began to build that squad through a revolutionary system called the farm chain. But before Rickey was churning out prospects for the Redbirds at a record clip, he joined the armed forces during the war.

Branch Rickey was commissioned a major with the United States Army Chemical Warfare Branch. Under his leadership were such ball diamond luminaries as Ty Cobb and Christy Mathewson. The baseball legends served overseas, training soldiers on how to protect themselves during a chemical attack. While Rickey was wearing Uncle Sam's khaki, sportswriters stateside were championing the Mahatma as the next president of the National League — a post he did not accept.

G	R	H	2B	3B	HR	RBI	BB	SO	SB	AVG	Slug
119	38	82	9	6	3	39	27	n/a	8	.239	.327

Arthur Ramon Rico, *Catcher*

Appendicitis claimed the life of Arthur Rico shortly after his discharge from the navy. The young catcher, who appeared in only seventeen major league games, played briefly for the Braves in 1916 and 1917. He lost the entire 1918 season to the war and died before he was able to resume his baseball career. During the war, Rico saw action in foreign waters as he served on the *USS Georgia*.

G	R	H	2B	3B	HR	RBI	BB	SO	SB	AVG	Slug
17	1	4	1	0	0	2	0	2	0	.222	.278

Charles August "Swede" Risberg, *Shortstop*

The only regular of the eight banished White Sox players of 1919 to serve in the military during World War I, Risberg's name will forever be tarnished due to the scandal. Fellow banished Black Sox player Shoeless Joe Jackson spent the season at work for the government while Risberg played out the season in military fatigues. Swede, who served as a quartermaster in the military, further enhanced his status as a disgraced player when after his banishment he accused several White Sox players on the 1917 roster of bribing Detroit Tigers players to throw a series of games in their favor.

G	R	H	2B	3B	HR	RBI	BB	SO	SB	AVG	Slug
476	196	394	72	27	6	175	148	180	52	.243	.332

Eppa Rixey, *Pitcher*

A tall southpaw, Rixey came from a wealthy Virginia family and was a student at the University of Virginia, majoring in chemistry. The Rixey clan had a long line of soldiers in its family tree. He had ancestors that fought on the Potomac. The Hall of Famer missed the entire 1918 baseball season while serving in an Army Chemical Warfare unit. An article in the *Racine Journal* listed Eppa's military duties, which claimed, "The former pitcher belongs to the defensive division of chemical warfare service. On his shoulders falls the work of setting off screen clouds to obscure artillery and the movement of troops."

Rixey had yet to establish himself as a star before the war. With the 1917 Phillies, he had a 20-loss season and played second fiddle to Grover Alexander. When the Phillies sold Alex to the Cubs, Eppa was expected to carry the Phillies pitching staff but Uncle Sam had other plans. Rixey joined the military and understood the importance of his task. He said, "The Army is the place for me. It's hard work, but it is pleasing to know that one is engaged in the big task of the world. I knew there was only one thing for me to do, and that was to join, so here I am."

W	L	PCT	G	GS	CG	IP	H	BB	SO	SHO	ERA
266	251	.515	692	553	290	4,495	4,633	1,082	1,350	38	3.15

Leroy Roberts, *Pitcher*

An adequate pitcher in the Negro Leagues, "Everready" Roberts served in the U.S. Army during World War I at the beginning of his career in baseball. Roy served his military hitch at Fort Dix where he was able to play plenty of service ball. After his discharge, the pitcher spent the bulk of his career with the Atlantic City Bacharach Giants.

(1916–1934): Atlantic City Bacharach Giants, Hilldale Daisies, Brooklyn Royals Giants, Columbus Buckeyes, New York Lincoln Giants and Cleveland Red Sox

Charles Culbertson Robertson, *Pitcher*

One of the lesser-known pitchers to have tossed a perfect game at the major league level, Robertson served with the U.S. Army during World War I. After his military discharge, Charlie pitched briefly for the White Sox in 1919, but the American League champs had stars Eddie Cicotte and Lefty Williams chewing up the innings. When those two stalwarts were kicked out of baseball after the 1920 season, Robertson was given a second chance and delivered with his perfecto on April 30, 1922.

W	L	PCT	G	GS	CG	IP	H	BB	SO	SHO	ERA
49	80	.380	166	141	60	1,004	1,149	377	310	6	4.45

Wilbur "Bullet" Rogan, *Pitcher/Outfield*

Perhaps the greatest two-way player in the history of the Negro Leagues, Hall of Famer Bullet Rogan was an exceptional pitcher and a terrific hitter. The Oklahoma City native could have made the Hall of Fame as either a pitcher or an outfielder. But Rogan was fortunate to have made the Negro Leagues at all. An unknown commodity at the time of World War I, Rogan was spotted by John McGraw and Casey Stengel while he played service ball at Fort Huachuca. Stengel tipped off J.L Wilkinson, a white owner in the Negro Leagues, and Wilkinson signed Rogan for his Kansas City Monarchs. Unlike most Negro League players, Rogan's loyalty to the Monarchs was unwavering and he played for them his entire career.

(1920–1938): Kansas City Monarchs

Herold Dominic "Muddy" Ruel, *Catcher*

During Ruel's prime he was one of the best catchers in the game. He caught the legendary Walter Johnson when the Senators won the World Series in 1924 and carried them to another Fall Classic the following year, which the Senators lost in seven games. Muddy was drafted into the army on June 21, 1918, as a 22-year-old. At the time the armistice was signed, Muddy had just earned his aviator's license. He returned to the Yankees the following year and took the starting backstop duties from incumbent Truck Hannah. During his playing career, Ruel earned a law degree and later practiced before the Supreme Court after his baseball career was over.

G	R	H	2B	3B	HR	RBI	BB	SO	SB	AVG	Slug
1,470	494	1,242	187	29	4	532	606	238	61	.275	.332

Walter Henry "Dutch" Ruether, *Pitcher*

Ruether, a hero of the 1919 World Series, socked two triples in the Fall Classic and batted a robust .667 with four RBIs. Although he was a sensational hitting pitcher throughout his career with a lifetime .258 batting average, historians use Dutch's solid offensive showing as a case study to indicate that the White Sox pitchers were not bearing down. Ruether left the Reds after 1920 and pitched with Brooklyn and Washington before he ended his career with the Yankees. During the war, Dutch served in the United States Army at Fort Lewis.

An amusing yarn, printed in the *Fort Wayne Journal*, concerning Ruether's pitching as a private in the military, circulated during the war. While engaged in a service ball game, Dutch's teammate, Tigers backstop Del Baker, was ejected from the contest. Ruether felt than Baker wasn't given a square deal and refused to pitch until his catcher was reinstated. Private Ruether on the hill had little sway over the official, a captain serving as umpire. The umpire hollered at Dutch, "Private Ruether, you have just thirty seconds to get in the box and pitch or you go back to Camp Lewis under guard!" Ruether gave the captain a salute and took his place on the mound.

W	L	PCT	G	GS	CG	IP	H	BB	SO	SHO	ERA
137	95	.591	309	272	154	2,124	2,244	739	708	17	3.50

William George Rumler, *Outfield*

Bill Rumler's major league career was relatively brief, but he was no stranger to adversity. One of the many players often accused of throwing games in the pastime's early era, Rumler was banished from the game and played the majority of his career in outlaw leagues. He missed the entire 1918 season after his draft into the army where he broke his leg, which kept him from returning to the Browns in 1919. After his playing days were over, he became a police chief.

G	R	H	2B	3B	HR	RBI	BB	SO	SB	AVG	Slug
138	15	43	7	4	1	32	14	28	4	.251	.357

Branch L. Russell, *Outfield*

A left-handed hitter and right-handed thrower, Russell spent the bulk of his career in the Negro Leagues with the St. Louis Stars. Able to fill in at second base, Branch was predominately a right fielder. A late arrival to the baseball ranks, Russell was a soldier before World War I and served in peacetime. Before the war, he helped secure the border with Mexico. Russell spent the better part of a decade in the army, attached to the 25th Infantry, and signed his first pro contract after his discharge.

(1922–1932): St. Louis Stars, Kansas City Monarchs and Cleveland Cubs

John Albert Russell, *Pitcher*

Russell's major league career wasn't very distinguished, as he won two games and posted an unflattering ERA of 5.40. The southpaw spent his first two major league seasons with the Brooklyn Dodgers and ended with two years on the White Sox roster. He appeared in just one game in 1918. He spent the majority of the baseball season in the military.

W	L	PCT	G	GS	CG	IP	H	BB	SO	SHO	ERA
2	7	.222	21	10	5	90	103	46	19	0	5.40

Louis Santop, *Catcher*

A recent Hall of Fame inductee, the massive catcher from Texas was nicknamed "Big Bertha" after the Germans' famous long-range artillery devices. Already a star player in New York and Brooklyn, Santop joined the navy during World War I. When he returned, he built a legend in black baseball as its first real home run threat. This distinction earned him the title of "the black Babe Ruth," one that is often associated with the legendary Josh Gibson.

As black baseball's greatest long ball threat before the years of Gibson, Santop would be a more accurate contemporary to Ruth. The Babe and Santop were both stars by World War I, even though Ruth was regarded as a pitcher then, while Josh wasn't even ten years old. Like Ruth, Santop swung the bat left-handed while Josh Gibson was a right-handed swinger. Santop made his debut several years before Babe Ruth, but when the Babe reshaped the landscape of baseball with his home run blasting, Lou was doing the same in the Negro Leagues. Ed Bolden, Santop's owner, would often schedule games for his Hilldale Daisies when the Yankees were slated to be in town so fans could compare the two heavy hitters.

(1909–1926): Brooklyn Royal Giants, Hilldale Daisies, NY Lincoln Giants, Philadelphia Giants and Chicago American Giants

Alexander Schacht, *Pitcher*

A ho-hum pitcher for the Senators after the war, Al Schacht was anything but a yawn-inducing bore off the pitcher's mound. Al, a classic entertainer, became famous as "The Clown Prince of Baseball." Schacht would perform his one-man comedy act across the major league circuit when not coaching for the Senators. Known for employing a glove the size of a trampoline in his skits, Schacht was also a true-blue patriot who served his country when needed. A soldier during the First World War, Schacht took his comedy act overseas during the Second World War and entertained troops at various military installations.

W	L	PCT	G	GS	CG	IP	H	BB	SO	SHO	ERA
14	10	.583	53	18	8	197	254	61	38	1	4.48

Maurice Francis Schick, *Outfield*

Morrie's major league career was rather brief—he appeared in just fourteen games for his hometown Cubs in 1917. The entire 1918 baseball season was lost to Schick when he left for the military. He was unable to make a return to the major leagues.

G	R	H	2B	3B	HR	RBI	BB	SO	SB	AVG	Slug
14	3	5	0	0	0	3	3	10	0	.147	.147

Raymond Henry Schmandt, *Second Base*

A rather tall second baseman, Schmandt made his major league debut with the St. Louis Browns in 1915. The next two years he played in the bushes and made his return to the highest level in 1918 with Brooklyn. He was able to appear in 34 games that season before he was summoned by Uncle Sam. When the demobilization order went through, Ray was serving at Camp Pike. He played four more years in the major leagues—all with Brooklyn—as a first baseman in his latter years.

G	R	H	2B	3B	HR	RBI	BB	SO	SB	AVG	Slug
317	122	284	36	13	3	122	46	75	11	.269	.337

Henry Walter Schreiber, *Third Base*

Abbreviated and sporadic are the two more appropriate words to use when describing the major league career of Hank Schreiber. He was initially summoned to the major leagues by the White Sox in 1914 and then spent the next two years in the bushes. He resurfaced in 1917 with the Braves and was touted as a top prospect but the war interrupted and Hank served with a regiment based in Ohio. In 1919, he was a member of the National League champion Reds but didn't see any action in the World Series. The 1920 season was spent in the bushes and he returned to the NL in 1921 with the Giants; he only played in four games for John McGraw. He spent 1922 through 1925 in the minors and saw his last major league action in 1926 with Joe McCarthy's Cubs.

Schreiber had some tough luck around the time of his military induction. Before he was accepted for military duty, Hank mangled his hand in an accident involving heavy machinery. This incident pushed his induction date back a spell but he still missed the entire 1918 season to the war effort. While serving in the military, Schreiber was pulling sentry duty in freezing conditions and wasn't properly outfitted for the task. He suffered from frostbite on the same hand that he had mangled the year prior.

G	R	H	2B	3B	HR	RBI	BB	SO	SB	AVG	Slug
36	10	18	5	0	0	6	1	16	0	.198	.253

John Clement Schulte, *Catcher*

A journeyman catcher with decent power and an exceptional batting eye, Schulte never could stick with a club. Given his robust on-base percentage, it seems unusual that Johnny was a constant castoff, but the receiver never played two consecutive seasons at any major league stop. Before his major league debut with the 1923 Browns, Johnny served in the armed forces during World War I.

G	R	H	2B	3B	HR	RBI	BB	SO	SB	AVG	Slug
192	59	98	15	4	14	64	76	49	1	.262	.436

James "Death Valley Jim" Scott, *Pitcher*

Scott was the first major league pitcher to leave the game to enlist in the army. A prototypical "hard luck" pitcher, Death Valley Jim finished his career with a losing record despite posting the ninth-best career ERA in the history of the game (among hurlers with at least 1,500 innings under their belt). Although he recorded a 1.87 ERA in 1917 before he left for the military, Scott never again took the hill in a major league game.

Scott spent his tour in the military instructing recruits in the art of grenade pitching at Fort Lewis. A renowned curveball wizard, Death Valley Jim served in the infantry. He applied for officer's training at Leon Springs, Texas, and became the first ballplayer to obtain a commission of high rank in the army after he passed officer's training at Presidio. A magnificent pitcher in his day, Scott, who became teammate Buck Weaver's brother-in-law, was discharged from the army after he attained the rank of captain.

W	L	PCT	G	GS	CG	IP	H	BB	SO	SHO	ERA
109	113	.491	317	225	125	1,871	1,624	609	945	26	2.32

Harry "Socks" Seibold, *Pitcher*

Not to be confused with Dead Ball Era Slugger Ralph "Socks" Seybold, the twirler Seibold missed all of the 1918 season to service in France. Seibold was off to a promising career as a 21-year-old pitcher when he lost the 1918 baseball campaign to the war. Like other players, he returned from the war a lesser performer than when he left. His ERA, which had been below 4.00 in 1917, had climbed to 5.28 in 1919. Banished to the minors after the 1919 season, it would take Socks ten years before he was given another chance at the major league level.

W	L	PCT	G	GS	CG	IP	H	BB	SO	SHO	ERA
48	86	.358	191	135	64	1,065	1,179	405	296	8	4.42

Henry Levai Severeid, *Catcher*

A highly intelligent catcher who was nicknamed "The Detective of the Diamond," Severeid drew comparisons with Hall of Fame backstop Ray Schalk. Hank, who holds the distinction of catching two successive no-hitters (although one is open for debate, as the official scorer didn't arrive to the park until the third inning), enlisted in the Tank Service during the 1918 baseball season. One of the finest receivers of his time, Severeid was an extremely difficult strikeout victim, only fanning a total of 169 times in a 15-year career.

Before Hank was inducted into the military, he wrote a personal letter to American League president Ban Johnson, asking Johnson how he could enter the officer's reserve corps. Johnson was taken with Hank's desire to serve his country and was willing to assist the receiver in any capacity. During the war, Severeid was sent to France where he saw combat action.

G	R	H	2B	3B	HR	RBI	BB	SO	SB	AVG	Slug
1,390	408	1,245	204	42	17	539	331	169	35	.289	.367

Joseph Wheeler Sewell, *Shortstop*

Sewell, a Hall of Famer, served in the armed forces before his major league debut. His debut was of the front-page variety as he took over the Indians shortstop post after the great Ray Chapman was struck and killed by a pitched ball. Without Chapman, Cleveland's chances were perceived as weak, but Sewell filled Ray's shoes nicely and led Cleveland to a World Series title. Joe's claim to fame is as the most difficult player to strikeout in baseball history. In more than 1,900 games, Joe whiffed only 114 times—most modern day power hitters fan that often by the All-Star break.

G	R	H	2B	3B	HR	RBI	BB	SO	SB	AVG	Slug
1,903	1,141	2,226	436	68	49	1,051	844	114	74	.312	.413

Ralph Edward Sharman, *Outfield*

The story of Ralph Sharman is a tragic tale of untapped potential. As a young minor leaguer, Ralph tore up the Ohio State League, which attracted the eye of Giants skipper John McGraw. McGraw, ever the astute judge of talent, referred to Sharman as "one of the best looking prospects I've seen in years." The Giants skipper quickly signed Ralph to a contract and farmed him out. But McGraw's Giants, typically an NL powerhouse, had a strong outfield at the time, and it looked as if Ralph was doomed to stagnate in the Giants chain. But Connie Mack, manager of the Athletics, opened his wallet and bought Ralph's contract. Mack brought Ralph up at the end of the 1917 season and he showed great promise by hitting .297 in thirteen games.

The great promise Ralph displayed that season would go unfulfilled. A gifted athlete who modern day scouts would call a "five-tool player," Sharman enlisted in the army's Field Artillery branch before spring training. Connie Mack said farewell to his talented young prospect, eager to watch the young man grow into a ranking star upon his return. But Ralph Sharman would not return to baseball. While training with the army at Camp Sheridan, Ralph drowned in the Alabama River. Once looked upon as a successor to stellar center fielders like Ty Cobb and Tris Speaker, Ralph Sharman wasn't given the chance to make good on his wealth of promise.

G	R	H	2B	3B	HR	RBI	BB	SO	SB	AVG	Slug
13	2	11	2	1	0	2	3	2	1	.297	.405

Benjamin Nathaniel Shaw, *First Base*

Ben Shaw's major league career didn't amount to much, as he only appeared in 23 games over two seasons with the Bucs. The stocky first baseman saw the majority of his major league action in 1918, prior to being called to arms.

G	R	H	2B	3B	HR	RBI	BB	SO	SB	AVG	Slug
23	5	7	1	0	0	2	2	2	0	.184	.211

James Robert Shawkey, *Pitcher*

The first great Yankee pitcher, Shawkey was obtained by the Bronx Bombers from the Philadelphia Athletics during the 1915 season. To this day, Shawkey ranks sixth all-time in Yankees history in career wins, ahead of such notable hurlers as Mel Stottlemyre and Hall of Famers Herb Pennock and Waite Hoyt. He enlisted in the navy in 1918, limited to just three games for the club that year, and returned to post his second 20-win season for the Yankees in 1919. Shawkey would win 110 games over a six-year period for New York before injuries began to take their toll.

During the war, the Yankee ace served at a Philadelphia naval yard before his assignment to the *USS Arkansas*. Shawkey served as a chief yeoman when his ship entered hostile waters. He and his shipmates constantly had to dodge torpedoes shot from Hun submarines. His ship was a troop convoy vessel that the enemy desperately wanted to sink but never managed to connect with its torpedoes. While serving on the *USS Arkansas*, he was able to witness firsthand the surrender of the German fleet. Upon his return to the States, Bob was presented with a wrist watch and a mini gold baseball as gifts from a navy yard for his wartime service.

W	L	PCT	G	GS	CG	IP	H	BB	SO	SHO	ERA
198	150	.569	488	331	194	2,938	2,722	1,018	1,360	32	3.09

Eugene Anthony "Red" Sheridan, *Second Base*

Red netted one base hit in his major league career, which spanned two brief service calls to Brooklyn. He was first summoned to Ebbett Field in 1918 but missed time to the war effort in the process. Red played in just three games for Wilbert Robinson's boys in 1920.

G	R	H	2B	3B	HR	RBI	BB	SO	SB	AVG	Slug
5	0	1	0	0	0	0	1	1	1	.167	.167

Urban James Shocker, *Pitcher*

One of baseball's tragic figures, Shocker contracted pneumonia during the 1928 season and died in early September of that year. A master of the spitball, Urban Shocker saw action in France during World War I, which interrupted a remarkable season he was having on the mound for the Browns: a 1.80 ERA in 95 innings. A brilliant pitcher and borderline Hall of Fame candidate, Shocker paced the American League with 27 wins in 1921 and posted four consecutive seasons of 20 wins or more. The fact that he achieved this feat while twirling for a middling club like the Browns enhances the grandeur of the accomplishment.

When Shocker returned stateside after the war, the star pitcher, who had seen combat action, confided to relatives the horrors he had endured in battle. He told his relatives that he had survived a "narrow escape" in the European battlefields. During a brief hand-to-hand skirmish, in which Shocker thrust his own bayonet through a German soldier to save his own life, he sustained a bayonet wound to the head. Urban was able to live through the ordeal and venture back to the diamond where he ruled over the American League for another ten years.

W	L	PCT	G	GS	CG	IP	H	BB	SO	SHO	ERA
188	117	.616	412	319	202	2,681	2,709	657	983	28	3.17

Ernest Grady Shore, *Pitcher*

Joining the Yankees prior to the 1918 season from the Red Sox, skipper Miller Huggins had to wait an entire season before Shore put on a Yankee uniform. He lost the entire 1918 season when he enlisted in the navy and entered a school for ensigns at Cambridge. Shore was no longer the same pitcher when he returned to the diamond as his ERA, which usually hovered close to 2.00, had climbed up to 4.17 in 1919 and 4.90 in 1920, his final major league season.

W	L	PCT	G	GS	CG	IP	H	BB	SO	SHO	ERA
65	42	.607	161	120	55	982	906	271	310	9	2.47

Charles Henry "Chick" Shorten, *Outfield*

Shorten was a contact hitting reserve outfielder when he enlisted in the navy in 1918. Before he left for the colors, Chick was the Red Sox main reserve outfielder as he played behind the likes of Hall of Famer Harry Hooper and star Duffy Lewis. He played for the Great Lakes ballclub in the navy and returned to the majors in 1919 as a member of the Detroit Tigers. There, Shorten's job was to backup two better outfielders in Ty Cobb and Bobby Veach.

G	R	H	2B	3B	HR	RBI	BB	SO	SB	AVG	Slug
527	161	370	51	20	3	134	110	68	12	.275	.349

Edward Joseph Sicking, *Utility Infielder*

With an aging infield in 1918, John McGraw worked the young Eddie Sicking into the mix as much as possible. However, McGraw lost the versatile infielder when he was summoned for duty in the United States Army. Sicking served with teammate Benny Kauff at Camp Sherman during the war. When he returned to baseball, he started the 1919 campaign with McGraw's Giants but was dealt early in the season to the hapless Phillies. He received his last look at the major league level in 1927 with the Pirates after six seasons in the bushes.

G	R	H	2B	3B	HR	RBI	BB	SO	SB	AVG	Slug
203	51	135	13	2	0	59	39	43	14	.226	.255

Daniel James Silva, *Third Base*

Silva played one game with the Senators in 1919 after his stint with Uncle Sam. The Massachusetts native returned to the armed forces in the 1940s to lend a hand during the Second World War.

G	R	H	2B	3B	HR	RBI	BB	SO	SB	AVG	Slug
4	0	1	0	0	0	0	0	0	0	.250	.250

George Harold Sisler, *First Base*

One of the greatest players in baseball history, Sisler was already a star by the time World War I broke out. He hit .353 in 1917, and during the 1918 season he hit .341. But that 1918 season was met with hostility from some writers. Given that George was a famous athlete, he was an easy target for writers holding a grudge. When it was learned that Sisler had turned down an assignment with the Chemical Warfare Division — an assignment that Branch Rickey lined up for him — writers took shots at Sisler, claiming he refused the assignment because he didn't want to pay for his military uniforms.

The negative publicity got to Sisler and he ended up enrolling in Rickey's Chemical Warfare Division with the likes of Ty Cobb and Christy Mathewson. George's military tenure was brief as he returned to the Browns in 1919 to hit .352 in 132 games. After the war, Sisler established himself as one of the greatest hitters in the game when he hit .407 with a record 257 base hits in 1920. His record stood until 2004 when Seattle's Ichiro Suzuki broke it with 260 safeties.

G	R	H	2B	3B	HR	RBI	BB	SO	SB	AVG	Slug
2,055	1,284	2,812	425	164	102	1,175	472	327	375	.340	.468

Yale Yeastman "Tod" Sloan, *Outfield*

Good chums with Baby Doll Jacobson, he and the star center fielder enlisted in the navy on the same day. Although Sloan possessed lesser playing ability, his devotion to his country mirrored that of his ball diamond pal. He and Baby Doll enlisted near the close of the 1917 baseball season and missed the entire 1918 campaign to service in the navy.

G	R	H	2B	3B	HR	RBI	BB	SO	SB	AVG	Slug
143	43	94	8	5	2	33	41	46	9	.234	.294

Walter Clayton Smallwood, *Pitcher*

Smallwood appeared in parts of two seasons in the major leagues, all with the Yankees. The tall native of Dayton, Maryland, missed the entire 1918 campaign to service in the United States Army. Walt served overseas in the European Theatre of Operations and was engaged in combat missions.

W	L	PCT	G	GS	CG	IP	H	BB	SO	SHO	ERA
0	0	—	8	0	0	24	21	10	7	0	4.50

Earl Sutton Smith, *Catcher*

A member of John McGraw's back-to-back world champion teams of 1921 and 1922, Earl Smith was a high-average hitter who often platooned behind the dish. Earl, a lifetime .303 hitter, made his major league debut after he served in Uncle Sam's outfit.

G	R	H	2B	3B	HR	RBI	BB	SO	SB	AVG	Slug
860	225	686	115	19	46	355	247	106	18	.303	.432

Elmer John Smith, *Outfield*

Smith paced the Indians with 23 doubles in 1916 but was dealt the following year to the Senators. After the deal, Cleveland reacquired Smith during the 1917 season. He lost the entire 1918 season to service in the army but returned to post three times as many home runs as his runner-up on the Cleveland squad in 1919.

G	R	H	2B	3B	HR	RBI	BB	SO	SB	AVG	Slug
1,012	469	881	181	62	70	540	319	359	54	.276	.437

John "Jack" Smith, *Outfield*

A longtime Redbird, the fleet-footed Smith played from 1915 through 1926 with the Cardinals. Smith became St Louis' regular center fielder in 1916 and tied Bob Bescher and Rogers Hornsby for the home run title on the club. As a 23-year-old, Jack was able to appear in 42 games for the Cards in 1918 before he was drafted into the army. He returned in 1919 to pace the Redbirds in steals. During the 1926 season, Smith was dealt to the Braves and finished out his career there in 1929.

G	R	H	2B	3B	HR	RBI	BB	SO	SB	AVG	Slug
1,406	783	1,301	182	71	40	382	334	348	228	.287	.385

Sherrod Malone Smith, *Pitcher*

Smith served in the United States Army during World War I and held down the post of a military police officer. His military travails took him abroad to Paris. He lost time at Ebbets Field to time in Uncle Sam's unit. The southern southpaw made his major league debut in 1911 with the Pirates. After sparse action in two seasons with Pittsburgh, it was back to the bushes for Sherry. He returned in 1915 with the Dodgers and posted the second best winning percentage on the club.

Smith missed the entire 1918 season to the war. When the armistice was signed, Smith was overseas but showed an eagerness to get back to the States. When Smith was preparing for his return home, he said, "I feel so good to think that we are going back that I'd be willing to workout this winter in Charlie Ebbets' cold storage plant. Charles may be a tough old bird but he's a whole lot better than the boches." When Sherry returned, he had newfound, pinpoint control: he walked just 29 batters in 173 innings. He retired after the 1927 season as a lifelong serviceable hurler who was always in the shadows cast by his fellow pitchers.

W	L	PCT	G	GS	CG	IP	H	BB	SO	SHO	ERA
114	118	.491	373	226	142	2,052	2,234	440	428	16	3.32

Frank Elton Snyder, *Catcher*

When Snyder was drafted into the armed forces, a newspaper headline stated that his departure was "a serious blow to the pennant prospects of St. Louis." This was a pretty lofty statement for a club that had finished in the second division for years, but sportswriters have always enjoyed fabricating excuses for the plight of their favored ballclub. He was initially summoned to the majors as a 19-year-old in 1912 and began to platoon with Ivy Wingo by 1914. His high water mark came in 1915, when he paced the Redbirds with a .298 batting average, but the following year he lost time to Mike Gonzalez. He played in 39 games for the Redbirds in 1918 before he was drafted and was traded to the Giants upon his return. Snyder retired after the 1927 season, spending his final year where his career began, back in St. Louis.

G	R	H	2B	3B	HR	RBI	BB	SO	SB	AVG	Slug
1,392	331	1,122	170	44	47	525	281	416	37	.265	.360

Tristram E. Speaker, *Outfield*

Arguably the greatest all-around talent in baseball history, Tris Speaker was without a flaw on the ball diamond. The Grey Eagle could run like the wind, hit for both precision and authority, and was without a peer in outfield defense. Speaker would often play a shallow center field, which enabled him to participate in double plays and infield rundowns, while his speed and exceptional judgment allowed him to track down balls hit over his head. Simply put, Tris Speaker was the perfect five-tool talent.

Speaker was able to play the entire 1918 season with the second-place Indians managed by Lee Fohl. After the close of the baseball campaign, Speaker, who was obsessed with flying, enlisted in the navy with former Red Sox chum Les Nunamaker. The two ballplayers enrolled at the Massachusetts Technical Naval Aviators School after the ball season came to a close. Shortly after Speaker graduated from the school, the war was over and he left the navy and returned to the Indians. During the 1919 season, Speaker became Cleveland's player/manager.

G	R	H	2B	3B	HR	RBI	BB	SO	SB	AVG	Slug
2,789	1,882	3,514	792	223	117	1,527	1,381	n/a	433	.345	.500

Charles Dillon "Casey" Stengel, *Outfield*

Considered by many sources as greatest manager in the history of baseball, Stengel's solid playing career left little to be desired as well. "The Old Professor" began his career for Bill Dahlen's Brooklyn Dodgers in 1912. The following year, Stengel took over as the everyday centerfielder and hit .272. His high point as a player came in the 1923 Fall Classic when he hit the first World Series home run in Yankee Stadium history as a member of the visiting Giants. Stengel, who served in the navy during World War I, would go on to manage the Dodgers (.453 winning percentage), Braves (.432), Yankees (.623) and Mets (.302), in that order.

G	R	H	2B	3B	HR	RBI	BB	SO	SB	AVG	Slug
1,277	575	1,219	182	89	60	535	437	453	131	.284	.410

John Franklin "Stuffy" Stewart, *Second Base*

Stuffy made his major league debut with the 1916 Cardinals. He was carried on the team in 1917 but failed to make the grade and was shipped to Denver for some seasoning. While playing in Denver, Stewart quit the baseball team when his Florida guard unit was activated. He returned to the southern state and served with the quartermaster's department at the rank of sergeant. A wiseacre Associated Press writer claimed, "It will be his duty to see that the beans are properly apportioned."

Stewart returned to baseball when his guard unit was deactivated. He beat around the minors for a short while before he was given another shot in the majors with the 1922 Pirates. Pittsburgh had .345-hitting Cotton Tierney at second, so Stuffy's services weren't needed. He then latched on with the 1923 Dodgers and backed up Jimmy Johnston. The bulk of his major league service came with the Senators in the late 1920s where he served as kid-manager Bucky Harris' reserve.

G	R	H	2B	3B	HR	RBI	BB	SO	SB	AVG	Slug
176	74	63	14	3	1	18	17	32	21	.238	.325

Charles Evard "Gabby" Street, *Catcher*

A master of the publicity stunt, Gabby Street is best remembered today for agreeing to catch balls dropped from the top of the Washington Monument. But Gabby was outdone in the publicity stunt department by one of his players with the St. Louis Cardinals:

Dizzy Dean. However, before Street managed the aloof Dean, he served his country in a second military campaign: the First World War. Although he didn't see action during World War I, Street was preparing for aerial combat at Kelly Field, Texas. A soldier at Kelly Field remarked, "Street has made good as a flyer and has been transferred to a camp somewhere in the east. He is as peppery and noisy in the air as when he caught Walter Johnson in the majors."

G	R	H	2B	3B	HR	RBI	BB	SO	SB	AVG	Slug
503	98	312	44	11	2	105	119	n/a	17	.208	.256

Dennis William Sullivan, *Outfield*

Sullivan's last major league action came with the 1909 Cleveland Indians. Between the time he made his last major league appearance and the outset of the First World War, Sullivan studied medicine and became a doctor. He put his medical training to good use when Uncle Sam gave him the come-hither sign. Dr. Sullivan served in the Army Medical Corps during both World Wars.

G	R	H	2B	3B	HR	RBI	BB	SO	SB	AVG	Slug
254	106	221	25	7	1	51	59	n/a	31	.239	.285

Thomas Augustin Sullivan, *Pitcher*

Sullivan appeared in three games for the 1922 Phillies of Kaiser Wilhelm. The Phillies mound staff that year was led by two twelve-game winners in Lee Meadows and Jimmy Ring. Tom missed minor league action to service in the First World War.

W	L	PCT	G	GS	CG	IP	H	BB	SO	SHO	ERA
0	0	—	3	0	0	8	16	5	2	0	11.25

George Alexander Sweatt, *Outfield*

Although he wasn't a heavy hitter, Sweatt was a valuable player due to his versatility. At home in either the outfield or the infield, George enabled managers some flexibility when penciling their lineups. Before he began in the Negro Leagues, Sweatt served in the military during World War I. He served with the 816th Pioneer Infantry and was shipped out to France. Just two weeks after docking in Europe, the armistice was signed.

(1921–1927): Kansas City Monarchs and Chicago American Giants

Zebulon Alexander Terry, *Shortstop*

Terry made his major league debut in 1916 with the Chicago White Sox, where he served as Eddie Collins' double play partner as a rookie. He appeared in only two games the following year and by 1918 was a member of the Braves. He was enjoying a breakout year that season, hitting the apple at a .305 clip, when he enlisted in the army. During the war, he served in an artillery unit based out of Camp Taylor. The layoff hurt Terry. He returned to the diamond and his once-ascending batting average began to descend as he finished 1919 with a meager .227 average. Terry joined the Cubs in 1920, splitting time between second base and shortstop, and ended his major league career two years later with the same organization.

G	R	H	2B	3B	HR	RBI	BB	SO	SB	AVG	Slug
640	254	605	90	24	2	216	179	133	32	.260	.322

Claude Alfred Thomas, *Pitcher*

Lefty pitched one season at the major league level with the 1916 Senators. Washington had the greatest pitcher in the game with Walter Johnson on the roster, but a punchless offense kept them in the second division. Claude was able to win just one game that year, and it had to be a shutout. Two years later, in July 1918, Claude was mustered into the army at Camp Travis, Texas.

W	L	PCT	G	GS	CG	IP	H	BB	SO	SHO	ERA
1	2	.333	7	4	1	28	27	12	7	1	4.18

Clinton Cyrus Thomas, *Outfield*

A star with the New York Black Yankees in the 1930s, Clint played center field with such ease that he was regarded as "the black Joe DiMaggio." Thomas began in baseball well before the Yankees unveiled DiMaggio, but the two played so much alike that the tag stuck with the veteran Thomas. From Greenup, Kentucky, Thomas served in the military during World War I before he started out in black baseball. After his discharge, a friend recommended him to Negro League legend Pop Lloyd and his career took off. Clint was nicknamed "Hawk" because of his sharp eye at tracking down flyballs as well as selecting pitches to hit in the batter's box. A gifted five-tool athlete, the sketchy records kept by the Negro Leagues credit Thomas with 367 career home runs.

(1920–1938): New York Black Yankees, Hilldale Daisies, Brooklyn Royal Giants, Columbus Buckeyes, Detroit Stars, Atlantic City Bacharach Giants, New York Lincoln Giants, Indianapolis ABCs and Newark Eagles

Frederick Harvey Thomas, *Third Base*

Thomas was another of the many ballplayers to have been cycled through the baseball club at the Great Lakes during his stint in the military. Despite the fact that Thomas only appeared in 44 games for the Red Sox in 1918, he still played more games at third base than any other man on the roster that season. When he took his .257 batting average to the navy, Red Sox skipper Ed Barrow struggled to fill the void his departure caused. The four men he tried to fill the hot corner vacancy all hit below .172.

G	R	H	2B	3B	HR	RBI	BB	SO	SB	AVG	Slug
247	88	193	19	14	4	45	84	90	24	.225	.293

John Dudley "Lee" Thompson, *Pitcher*

Thompson made four forgettable starts with the 1921 White Sox — the year after eight players from their World Series team of 1919 were banished from the game. A southpaw, Lee couldn't fill the shoes of exiled Claude Williams as he lost three games and had one no decision. Although Dudley was a one-season-and-out baseball player, he was more than that for Uncle Sam. He served in the navy during World War I, and during the Second World War the trim Thompson returned to the navy and served with the Seabees.

W	L	PCT	G	GS	CG	IP	H	BB	SO	SHO	ERA
0	3	.000	4	4	0	21	32	6	4	0	8.14

James Arthur "Cotton" Tierney, *Second Base*

A scrappy little infielder, Cotton Tierney was a high-average hitter who didn't set the league afire with his glove. Tierney served in the military prior to his major league callup. He made his debut with the 1920 Pirates, and in his six years at the highest level he played for four different teams.

G	R	H	2B	3B	HR	RBI	BB	SO	SB	AVG	Slug
630	266	681	119	30	31	331	109	187	28	.296	.415

Austin Ben Tincup, *Pitcher*

A stellar hitting pitcher, Tincup was one of the first legitimate relief pitchers in major league history. Before teams looked toward the future, clubs fought for one season and wore down their pitchers with excessive use. Names like Smoky Joe Wood, Orvie Overall and Noodles Hahn, unknown to the common fan, were the best pitchers of their day but are left out of the Baseball Hall of Fame because they failed to pitch the mandatory ten years in the majors. During the Phillies' championship season of 1915, Ben was used exclusively out of the bullpen by skipper Pat Moran — a tactic rarely seen in that day and age.

During the 1918 season, Tincup, a Native American, appeared in eight games before he was summoned into the army. He played in the Army-Navy Championship game while wearing Uncle Sam's khaki and served his tenure at Camp Merritt. When the war ended, Tincup went back to the bushes and waited ten more years before his return to the majors with the 1928 Cubs.

W	L	PCT	G	GS	CG	IP	H	BB	SO	SHO	ERA
7	11	.389	48	18	9	212	229	78	127	3	3.10

Chester LeRoy "Red" Torkelson, *Pitcher*

With an earned run average above seven, it is understandable to assume that Red struggled at the major league level. However, despite his lofty ERA, he posted a career winning percentage above .500. Torkelson's only major league service time came in 1917 as the right-hander missed all of 1918 to service as a commissioned officer in the armed forces. During the war, Red served as a mechanic and was shipped overseas where he saw duty in Europe.

W	L	PCT	G	GS	CG	IP	H	BB	SO	SHO	ERA
2	1	.667	4	3	0	22	33	13	10	0	7.77

Walter Joseph Tragesser, *Catcher*

Tragesser spent several years in the major leagues as a backup catcher. He saw brief action in 1913 with the Braves but was up to stay by 1915, when he served as a third-string receiver behind Hank Gowdy and Moose Whaling. When Gowdy left for the military in the middle of the 1917 season, manager George Stallings gave Walt the regular catching duties. The following year, Tragesser joined Gowdy in the colors.

Catchers of this time, with the crude gear they wore, often sustained numerous injuries that other players weren't as subject to. Walt tried to join the military before the 1918 season but was rejected after his physical evaluation revealed a crippled finger sustained while catching pitched balls. Walt played most of the 1918 season but was accepted by the navy late in the year. Tragesser served as a yeoman at the Newport News Naval Station.

G	R	H	2B	3B	HR	RBI	BB	SO	SB	AVG	Slug
272	54	148	31	3	6	66	35	125	14	.215	.295

Robert Gustave "Bun" Troy, *Pitcher*

Troy's major league career consisted of one start with the 1912 Detroit Tigers. The tall right-hander was born in Germany and raised in the United States. During the First World War, Troy joined the army and took up arms to help the Allies subdue the enemy in France. On October 7, 1918, engaged in combat on a battlefield in France, Bun Troy was wounded at Petit Maujoy. Later that day he would die from his wounds.

W	L	PCT	G	GS	CG	IP	H	BB	SO	SHO	ERA
0	1	.000	1	1	0	7	9	3	1	0	5.14

Frederick Franklin "Clancy" Tyler, *Catcher*

Tyler played just one year at the major league level with the world champion Braves of 1914. His brother, Lefty, was the star southpaw on George Stallings squad who locked horns in an extra-innings pitcher's duel with Bullet Joe Bush in Game 3 of the Fall Classic. Before the 1918 season, when Clancy was property of Worcester, he was drafted by the army. His draft opened the door for yet another Tyler boy, kid brother Bill, who was given a trial to replace Clancy, who left for Fort Devens.

G	R	H	2B	3B	HR	RBI	BB	SO	SB	AVG	Slug
6	2	2	0	0	0	2	1	5	0	.105	.105

Samuel Bruce Vick, *Outfield*

Vick strolled to the plate three times in 1918 before he was whisked away into the armed forces— tallying two base hits in the process. During the war, Sammy served on foreign soil and returned to the Yankees in 1919 as their regular right fielder. His claim to fame is losing his job to the greatest of them all ... Babe Ruth.

G	R	H	2B	3B	HR	RBI	BB	SO	SB	AVG	Slug
213	90	159	28	11	2	50	51	91	12	.248	.335

Alfred Holmes "Fritz" von Kolnitz, *Utilityman*

Baseball was little more than a recreational endeavor for the philosophical von Kolnitz. While he played the game, Fritz was enrolled in college and worked towards a degree in law. A highly versatile ballplayer, Fritz could fill in anywhere on the diamond. He was a valuable player for the Reds in 1914 and 1915 when many players left the National League to join the Federal League. His supreme versatility was a boon for skipper Buck Herzog. After the Reds let Fritz go, he caught on with the White Sox and served as Bucky Weaver's backup.

Fritz's major league career ended in 1916, the year he was able to play with boyhood chum Shoeless Joe Jackson. While Fritz was acquiring his commission in the army at Fort Gordon during World War I, his pal Jackson was working for a shipyard. The sportswriters took nasty shots at Jackson for not joining the military. They felt a healthy, strong ballplayer should fight on the frontlines and not build ships on the homefront. Such journalistic jabs infuriated Major von Kolnitz, and the army officer felt it his duty to stand up for the uneducated Jackson. Fritz said,

"I have known Joe for a long time — long before he was ever

known in major league baseball. I am aware of the dependence upon him of his mother, her two minor children and his wife. He is dependent upon his salary for the support of his family. It has always been a puzzle to me why Joe was picked out of the hundreds of shipyard workers and persecuted. You know and I know the main reason. He was a star in his profession and the small-mindedness of some people makes them delight in blaming anyone high up whom they can criticize."

Able to ascend in rank in the army quickly, von Kolnitz reached the rank of major while stationed at Fort Gordon. He claimed that his law school training assisted him greatly in his rise through the army ladder. He used his rank to support Shoeless Joe and those like him, men at work in the shipyards, diligently building vessels to be used for the war effort. Fritz held no grudge or ill will towards the able-bodied men who opted to work stateside rather than take up arms and fight overseas. Fritz, while supporting Jackson once again, wrote an article for the Associated Press, which proclaimed, "The term 'patriotic American' embraces a multitude of occupations. Because a man chose to do his bit in a shipyard makes him not one wit less patriotic than the doughboy who swings the bayonet."

G	R	H	2B	3B	HR	RBI	BB	SO	SB	AVG	Slug
115	15	48	9	1	0	19	15	33	5	.212	.261

Philip Vance Voyles, *Outfield*

Voyles spent one year in the majors with the last-place Boston Braves in 1929. Phil only had two extra-base hits in his career, both triples. Before he made his major league debut he served in the navy during World War I. When America was involved in the Second World War, Voyles rejoined the navy and worked as an electrician.

G	R	H	2B	3B	HR	RBI	BB	SO	SB	AVG	Slug
20	9	16	0	2	0	4	6	8	0	.235	.294

Thomas Fred Walden, *Reserve*

Fred played in one game with the 1912 Browns without recording a single at-bat. A minor league player, Walden served in the armed forces during World War I.

G	R	H	2B	3B	HR	RBI	BB	SO	SB	AVG	Slug
1	0	0	0	0	0	0	0	0	0	—	—

James Charles Walsh, *Outfield*

Walsh, a native of Ireland, was a favorite of Philadelphia Athletics skipper Connie Mack. After dealing Walsh to New York in 1914, Mack quickly reacquired the versatile player during the season. Jimmy Walsh served in the navy and never returned to the major leagues after his tour in the military.

G	R	H	2B	3B	HR	RBI	BB	SO	SB	AVG	Slug
536	235	409	70	31	6	150	249	n/a	92	.231	.316

William Adolph Wambsganss, *Second Base*

Often listed simply as "Wamby" in the box scores, Bill had a long shelf life in the game of baseball. Wambsganss was a stellar second baseman during the Deadball Era whose career bridged the gap between that and the Lively Ball Era. During the Second World War, when baseball was suffering, Wamby agreed to manage in the All-American Girls Professional Baseball League. But his claim to fame is doing something no other player has yet to duplicate: turn an unassisted triple play in the World Series.

Wambsganss was Cleveland's everyday second baseman in 1918 when he received his draft notice midway through the baseball campaign. He returned to Fort Wayne, where he was registered, and took his pre-induction physical. Bill was able to play in 87 games for the Tribe before he was assigned to Camp Taylor for military training. An intelligent, educated man, Wamby was a college graduate and had attended seminary school in St. Louis before he took to baseball. With his background, he sought a commission and was transferred to Camp Gordon for officer's training, which is where he was located when the war ended.

G	R	H	2B	3B	HR	RBI	BB	SO	SB	AVG	Slug
1,492	710	1,359	215	59	7	519	490	357	142	.259	.327

Aaron Lee Ward, *Utilityman*

A longtime Yankee who was able to share the clubhouse with the likes of Babe Ruth, Homerun Baker and Lou Gehrig, Ward appeared only in 20 games for the Yankees in 1918. He began his career as a Jack-of-all-trades before settling into the second base position early in the 1920s. The emergence of Tony Lazzeri made Ward expendable and he was shipped off to the White Sox. During the First World War, he served in the army and was discharged at Camp Pike.

G	R	H	2B	3B	HR	RBI	BB	SO	SB	AVG	Slug
1,059	457	966	158	54	50	446	339	457	37	.268	.383

Charles William Ward, *Third Base*

Ward saw his first major league action with the 1917 Pirates. He accepted the daunting task of filling in at shortstop for the aging Honus Wagner. He lasted only one year in Pittsburgh and was shipped off to Brooklyn for the 1918 season. Ward played in two games for the Dodgers that year — he drove in three runs — before he was summoned for military duty. Chuck served with a field artillery unit in Europe with the rank of corporeal. He and teammate Clarence Mitchell were in the same unit and witnessed combat together. When he returned stateside, he played for pieces of four more years with Brooklyn.

G	R	H	2B	3B	HR	RBI	BB	SO	SB	AVG	Slug
236	52	175	20	6		72	51	67	7	.228	.269

Hoke Hayden "Hooks" Warner, *Third Base*

Warner appeared in only 67 major league games, collecting five extra-base hits. The portside-swinging third baseman missed the entire 1918 campaign, where he served overseas with the army. Warner saw his last big league action in 1921, when he hit .211 for the lowly Chicago Cubs.

G	R	H	2B	3B	HR	RBI	BB	SO	SB	AVG	Slug
67	16	50	2	1	2	19	11	22	7	.228	.274

Harry Abraham Weaver, *Pitcher*

Legendary skipper Connie Mack beckoned Weaver to the major leagues in 1915. The 23-year-old tossed two complete games with a 3.00 ERA but lost both decisions. Despite missing much of the 1918 season to the war effort, Harry made more appearances in that abbreviated slate than he made in any other campaign.

W	L	PCT	G	GS	CG	IP	H	BB	SO	SHO	ERA
3	6	.333	19	8	4	82	82	31	21	2	3.62

William Joseph Webb, *Utilityman*

Only a few major league careers have been shorter than that of Billy Webb's ball diamond tenure. He appeared in only five games for the Pirates in 1917 and missed the entire 1918 season to service in the military. Upon his discharge, Webb never returned to the major leagues.

G	R	H	2B	3B	HR	RBI	BB	SO	SB	AVG	Slug
5	1	3	0	0	0	0	2	3	0	.200	.200

William "Speck" Webster, *Catcher*

A good catcher for the Brooklyn Royal Giants before World War I, Webster was asked to manage the Fort Dix baseball team during the war. He had some of black baseball's finest young ballplayers at the camp for that one season he was under Uncle Sam.

(1911–1924): Brooklyn Royal Giants, Chicago American Giants, New York Lincoln Giants, Indianapolis ABCs, Hilldale Daisies, Atlantic City Bacharach Giants, Dayton Marcos and Detroit Stars

Charles Evis Whitehouse, *Pitcher*

Whitehouse pitched in the Federal League in its two years of operation and made six appearances with the 1919 Senators after the Feds closed up shop. The slender Illinoisan did his bit in both World Wars.

W	L	PCT	G	GS	CG	IP	H	BB	SO	SHO	ERA
4	3	.571	25	6	3	78	93	28	33	0	4.50

George Bostic "Possum" Whitted, *Outfield*

An eccentric Southern gentleman, Possum Whitted gave the Phillies an enviable outfield trio just before the war with Slugger Gavvy Cravath and flychaser Dode Paskert. He was a member of the Phillies' National League pennant-winning squad of 1915, but in 1918 he surrendered is left field job to Irish Meusel. Possum enlisted in the army early in the 1918 baseball campaign and was stationed at Camp Merritt, New Jersey, for the duration.

When Whitted returned from the war, he was unable to reclaim his left field job from Meusel and the Phillies traded him to the Pirates. Possum found the confines at Pittsburgh to his liking. Former Pirates public address announcer Art McKennan remembered Possum as an avid hunter who would go shooting for birds at the drop of a hat. McKennan said, "We had a player, Possum Whitted, who used to keep his hunting bird dogs in a kennel by the clubhouse."

G	R	H	2B	3B	HR	RBI	BB	SO	SB	AVG	Slug
1,024	440	978	145	60	23	451	215	310	116	.270	.362

Frank Wickware, *Pitcher*

An enigma for historians of black baseball, Wickware was a legend during the Deadball Era, but his career was so nomadic it's quite difficult to get an accurate reading on just how good he was. He once beat Washington Senators legend Walter Johnson, 1–0, which proves he was terrific since he beat the best the major leagues had to offer. Wickware, however, would jump from one team to the next, even during the same season, therefore making his career difficult to track and thus piece together his stats. He also suffers greatly from the quality stigma attached to the Negro Leagues because he'd often accept money to pitch as a ringer against teams of lesser quality — beneath the minor league level — and easily stand them on their ears, inflating his numbers.

Wickware had already established himself as an elite pitcher by World War I with a number of teams, but his personality had turned off more than a few managers. Unreliable and an alcoholic, Frank was not a stable individual to keep on a roster. His team jumping was tolerated to a certain degree, but when he gave way to lazy play before the war, teams began to lose interest in the former great. Near the end of the line by the war, Wickware served in the army and played off and on after his discharge with little of the stuff he had during his heyday.

(1910–1925): Chicago American Giants, Leland Giants, Brooklyn Royal Giants, Louisville White Sox, New York Lincoln Giants, Indianapolis ABCs, Detroit Stars and St. Louis Giants

Wabishaw Spencer "Doc" Wiley, *Catcher*

A longtime catcher for the Lincoln Giants, a team padded with the best talent black baseball had to offer, Wiley graduated from the Howard School of Dentistry, which earned him his nickname. While he caught for Lincoln, Wiley operated a dentist office in East Orange, New Jersey. His career was interrupted by World War I when Wiley enlisted in the Army Dental Corps as a lieutenant. After his discharge, he spent less time on the diamond and more time at his dentist's office.

(1910–1924): New York Lincoln Giants, West Baden Sprudels, Brooklyn Royal Giants, Philadelphia Giants and Atlantic City Bacharach Giants

Irvin Key "Kaiser" Wilhelm, *Pitcher*

With one of the least unique nicknames in baseball history, "Kaiser" Wilhelm was a hard-luck pitcher during the Deadball Era. He posted close to twice as many losses as he had wins over the course of his career. During World War I, Wilhelm was in his 40s and last pitched at the major league level with the upstart Federal League. Despite his advanced age, Wilhelm leant his services to Uncle Sam during the war.

W	L	PCT	G	GS	CG	IP	H	BB	SO	SHO	ERA
58	106	.354	216	158	118	1,432	1,495	418	444	12	3.44

Robert Lawns Williams, *Shortstop*

A diminutive shortstop remindful of Rabbit Maranville, Williams had yet to establish himself in the Negro Leagues before the war. During World War I, Bobby served with the 803rd Pioneer Infantry in France. After his discharge, the scrappy shortstop caught on with the Chicago American Giants of the legendary Rube Foster.

(1918–1934): Chicago American Giants, Indianapolis ABCs, Homestead Grays, Cleveland Tigers, Atlantic City Bacharach Giants, Pittsburgh Crawfords, Columbus Blue Birds and Cleveland Red Sox

Kenneth Roy Williams, *Outfield*

This forgotten Slugger was a star in his day but was overshadowed, just like everyone else, by the legendary Babe Ruth. He didn't establish himself in the major leagues until 1920, as a 30-year-old. He played sparingly with the Redlegs in 1915 and 1916 and appeared in just two games for the Browns in 1918 due to the war. The majority of the 1919 season was lost to injury, but in 1920 he enjoyed his first solid season at the highest level. Teaming with George Sisler, Baby Doll Jacobson and Jack Tobin, Williams and his Browns became an offensive force. He paced the league with 39 home runs in 1922, the only year from 1919 to 1925 that Babe Ruth wasn't atop the leader board.

G	R	H	2B	3B	HR	RBI	BB	SO	SB	AVG	Slug
1,397	860	1,552	285	77	196	914	566	287	154	.319	.531

John Nicodemus Wilson, *Pitcher*

Wilson's major league career consisted of three appearances for Clark Griffith's second-place Senators of 1913. Lefty made all of his appearances out of the bullpen. During the Second World War, John served with the U.S. Navy.

W	L	PCT	G	GS	CG	IP	H	BB	SO	SHO	ERA
0	0	—	3	0	0	4	4	3	1	0	4.50

Ernest Judson "Jud" Wilson, *Third Base/First Base*

Recently inducted into the Baseball Hall of Fame, Jud Wilson was one of black baseball's greatest Sluggers. A sensational hitter for both average and power, he had a reputation, akin to Ted Williams, for an absolute loathing of all pitchers. Although Wilson was a dynamo with the bat, he was a train wreck on the field. Teams tried him out all over the field but his best position was hitter. Predominately a third baseman, Wilson was a hitting sensation for the Baltimore Black Sox during the 1920s and the Philadelphia Stars of the 1930s. However, before Jud embarked on his storied career in black baseball, he served in the armed forces during World War I.

(1922–1945): Baltimore Black Sox, Homestead Grays, Philadelphia Stars and Pittsburgh Crawfords

Samuel Marshall "Mike" Wilson, *Catcher*

Wilson's major league career consisted of four at-bats with the 1921 Pirates. Mike gave up the ball diamond sport for the game on the gridiron and played several years in the NFL. During the First World War, Wilson served with the United States Marine Corps.

G	R	H	2B	3B	HR	RBI	BB	SO	SB	AVG	Slug
5	1	0	0	0	0	0	1	2	0	.000	.000

William Clarence "Mutt" Wilson, *Pitcher*

Mutt's major league career consisted of three games with the 1920 Tigers. The right-hander from North Carolina spent a year with the U.S. Army during World War I before he made his major league debut.

W	L	PCT	G	GS	CG	IP	H	BB	SO	SHO	ERA
1	1	.500	3	2	1	13	12	5	4	0	3.46

Lawton Walter "Whitey" Witt, *Shortstop*

During the war, Witt was stationed at the navy yard in Charleston, which cost him the entire 1918 baseball season. Witt had already become Connie Mack's regular shortstop by 1916, his rookie season, but lost his job to Joe Dugan while he served his country. When Whitey returned to the diamond, Mack molded the youngster into a Jack-of-all-trades. From Philadelphia, he was shipped off to New York where he played with Yankees' AL championship teams of 1922 and 1923.

G	R	H	2B	3B	HR	RBI	BB	SO	SB	AVG	Slug
1,139	632	1,195	144	62	18	302	489	309	78	.287	.364

Frank Russell Woodward, *Pitcher*

Woodward spent a handful of seasons in the major leagues; his debut came in the war-interrupted campaign of 1918. Frank appeared in two games as a reliever before he left the club for the military. He struggled at the outset of 1919 but flourished after he was dealt to the Cardinals, lowering his ERA to 2.63. He saw his last major league action in 1923 with the Chicago White Sox.

W	L	PCT	G	GS	CG	IP	H	BB	SO	SHO	ERA
9	15	.375	42	21	8	194	199	74	55	0	4.22

Earl Hershey Yingling, *Pitcher*

"Chink" made his major league debut in 1911 with Firebrand Stovall's Cleveland Indians. He later saw action with two different teams the following three years and was seemingly out of baseball after 1914. Earl resurfaced with the Senators in 1918, at which time he appeared in five games, before he left the diamond for the army. While wearing khaki, Yingling was stationed at Camp Taylor but left the installation to seek a commission.

W	L	PCT	G	GS	CG	IP	H	BB	SO	SHO	ERA
25	35	.417	94	61	31	568	611	141	192	5	3.22

Albert Clyde "Chief" Youngblood, *Pitcher*

A Native American from Texas, Albert Youngblood made two mound appearances for the 1922 Senators. A large man, Youngblood struggled with command in his major league sojourn and never again played at the highest level after his initial trial. Albert served in the army as a teenager during the First World War and returned to Uncle Sam's outfit for more action during the Second World War.

W	L	PCT	G	GS	CG	IP	H	BB	SO	SHO	ERA
0	0	—	2	0	0	4	9	7	0	0	15.75

Jonathan Thompson
Walton Zachary, *Pitcher*

World War I interrupted Zachary's rookie season, as the 22-year-old appeared in only two games that year, but he would go on to play in 533 over the course of his long career. Although he was able to keep his ERA at respectable marks, he issued more walks than strikeouts and allowed an immense amount of base hits in his career.

W	L	PCT	G	GS	CG	IP	H	BB	SO	SHO	ERA
185	191	.492	533	407	185	3,136	3,580	914	720	23	3.72

World War II

Clifford Alexander Aberson, *Outfield*

A natural athlete, Aberson led his minor league circuit in home runs the year before he was summoned for the war. The strong, raw-boned outfielder served at Keesler Field for a time and played some service football even though he never played the game at the collegiate level. But military life wasn't all fun and games for Aberson. He was attached to L Company of the 314th Infantry and saw combat action in the European Theatre. For his battlefield heroics, Cliff was awarded the Bronze Star and various other medals.

Although Aberson was on the fast track to the major leagues before the war, he had a change of heart after his discharge. One of the men who played service football at Keesler Field with Cliff was Packers veteran Herman Rohrig, who recommended Cliff to the Green Bay brass. Despite his lack of gridiron experience, Aberson played in the NFL in 1946 before he decided to return to baseball. He spent three years as a reserve outfielder, backing up such notables as Andy Pafko, Phil Cavaretta and the war era's greatest power hitter, Bill "Swish" Nicholson.

G	R	H	2B	3B	HR	RBI	BB	SO	SB	AVG	Slug
63	25	45	7	3	5	26	25	44	0	.251	.408

Calvin Ross Abrams, *Outfield*

Best known as a valuable reserve outfielder with the post–World War II powerhouse Brooklyn Dodgers, Cal possessed one of the best batting eyes of his time. The Dodgers had a strong outfield of Snider, Furillo and Pafko, so Abrams wasn't used much in Flatbush outside of a bat off the bench. Once the Dodgers traded him away, he was able to play regularly and had a couple of good years in Pittsburgh and Baltimore. Abrams served in the military with an anti-aircraft outfit in the South Pacific before he made his major league debut.

G	R	H	2B	3B	HR	RBI	BB	SO	SB	AVG	Slug
567	257	433	64	19	32	138	304	290	12	.269	.392

Robert Henry Adams, *Second Base*

Bobby had yet to make his major league debut when he was inducted into the Army Air Corps for World War II but was able to pick the brain of the finest player of his time while wearing Uncle Sam's threads: Joe DiMaggio. He played service ball for the same Santa Ana Airbase team as the Yankee Clipper and the team also boasted the talents of his brother, Dick Adams. After the war, Adams went directly to the majors and platooned at second base on the 1946 Reds with the aging former All-Star Lonny Frey.

G	R	H	2B	3B	HR	RBI	BB	SO	SB	AVG	Slug
1,281	591	1,082	188	49	37	303	414	447	67	.269	.368

Richard Leroy "Dick" Adams, *First Baseman*

Adams spent one year at the major league level with Connie Mack's 1947 Athletics. Dick was used infrequently because Mack had the smooth Ferris Fain, a service all-star, manning first. Before his big league debut, Adams served in the Army Air Corps at the Santa Ana Airbase with his kid brother, Bobby, and the legendary Joe DiMaggio.

G	R	H	2B	3B	HR	RBI	BB	SO	SB	AVG	Slug
37	9	18	2	3	2	11	2	18	0	.202	.360

Robert Gordon Addis, *Outfield*

Just a teenager when the war broke out, Addis came of age when America was engaged in some heavy combat overseas. After high school, Bob joined the U.S. Marines and shortly after boot camp was shipped out to the Pacific Theatre. When Bob returned from the war it took him some time to get acclimated to the pro ranks. He spent several years beating around the minors until he showed promise in spring training of 1950. Cardinals skipper Eddie Dyer liked what he saw in the Braves rookie that year, stating, "I think Addis is a coming star. The kid has looked good to me."

G	R	H	2B	3B	HR	RBI	BB	SO	SB	AVG	Slug
208	70	150	22	2	2	47	37	47	8	.281	.341

William G. Akers, *Utility Infielder*

Akers had a brief major league career. He served as a backup shortstop for Billy Rogell in Detroit before he spent his last season as a reserve infielder with the 1932 Braves. Bill's days as a player in top company were over by the mid 1930s when he left the game to seek employment by other means. The occupation Akers chose was the military. He enlisted in the army before the United States was actively engaged in the Second World War. When Detroit lost Hank Greenberg to the draft in 1941, Bill was asked by the Tigers brass to visit Hank and help prepare him for military life.

After the bombing on Pearl Harbor, Akers was joined by a steady flow of incoming soldiers who were former athletes. The former big league shortstop was pushing his fortieth birthday and served as a pseudo father figure for younger soldiers that had just been mustered into the service. Bill was stationed at a camp in Mississippi before his unit received orders to be shipped out to the Pacific Theatre. He wasn't one of the idle lads who played baseball throughout his service hitch, but a soldier who saw action away from home. Akers was awarded the Presidential Citation for his military heroism, and when the boys returned home after the war, Bill stayed with Uncle Sam and retired as a soldier.

G	R	H	2B	3B	HR	RBI	BB	SO	SB	AVG	Slug
174	64	124	17	9	11	69	63	64	7	.261	.404

Edward John Albosta, *Pitcher*

A wild right-hander, Albosta pitched with the Brooklyn Dodgers before the war and played one season with the Pirates after the fighting had ceased. Ed was inducted into the army in January of 1943 and was stationed at Camp Livingston, Louisiana. He received his discharge in October of 1945 and played for the Pirates in 1946. After his playing career concluded, Albosta managed the Minot Mallards in the early 1950s.

W	L	PCT	G	GS	CG	IP	H	BB	SO	SHO	ERA
0	8	.000	19	8	0	53	52	43	24	0	6.11

Harold John "Jack" Albright, *Shortstop*

A shortstop prospect with the Phillies, Albright fought with Skeeter Newsome for playing time in 1947. Jack, who saw action during World War II with an underwater demolition unit, made it out of the war unscathed but only lasted a few weeks in the majors. He suffered a broken leg in 1947, his rookie season, and never again returned to the majors.

G	R	H	2B	3B	HR	RBI	BB	SO	SB	AVG	Slug
41	9	23	4	0	2	5	10	11	1	.232	.333

Dale Leonard Alderson, *Pitcher*

Dale spent 1945 in the navy's physical training branch, having spent the previous year and a half in the Cubs' bullpen. A remarkable natural athlete, Alderson set an Iowa Conference scoring record in basketball as an amateur.

W	L	PCT	G	GS	CG	IP	H	BB	SO	SHO	ERA
0	1	.000	16	3	0	36	52	12	11	0	6.56

Robert Somerville Alexander, *Pitcher*

Alexander never pitched for the St. Louis Browns and made his debut as a 32-year-old with the Orioles after the franchise had moved from St. Louis. A minor league veteran with only a brief trial in the majors, Bob attended a Navy Pre-Flight School during World War II but was never shipped overseas.

W	L	PCT	G	GS	CG	IP	H	BB	SO	SHO	ERA
1	1	.500	9	0	0	11	18	7	2	0	10.64

Thomas Edison Alston, *First Base*

Alston had the misfortune of playing first base for the Cardinals in the mid 1950s. The legendary Stan Musial was still hitting at a great clip, but due to age was playing more often at first base than the outfield when Tom arrived in St. Louis. With Stan the Man entrenched at first, Alston couldn't crack the lineup and was essentially a reserve player during his major league days. Before he signed his first pro contract, Alston enlisted in the navy after his high school graduation. He served as a landing boat operator on a cargo ship during the final year of the war. After his discharge, Tom enrolled in college and was a bit older than the average young ballplayer when he signed his first contract. He played briefly in the Negro Leagues before catching on with the Cardinals.

G	R	H	2B	3B	HR	RBI	BB	SO	SB	AVG	Slug
91	30	66	15	2	4	36	25	46	3	.244	.358

Wayne Harper Ambler, *Shortstop/Second Base*

Wayne played with the A's after their dynasty days of Foxx, Grove, Cochrane and Simmons. He spent three years at the highest level with Connie Mack's Athletics: 1937 through 1939. The Duke University grad enlisted in the navy during the Second World War and saw combat action overseas. Ambler served in the Pacific Theatre and was awarded a battle star of his military actions.

G	R	H	2B	3B	HR	RBI	BB	SO	SB	AVG	Slug
271	60	175	39	2	0	73	83	64	4	.224	.279

Andy Holm Anderson, *Utility Infielder*

Anderson had a short major league career but it didn't begin until after he had served time in a German prisoner of war camp. A native of the Pacific Northwest, Andy enlisted in the army, took his basic training, and then prepared for action overseas. He was shipped to the European Theatre of Operations and was shortly captured by the Nazis. He spent a few harrowing months behind the wire of Nazi detention areas before the Allied Forces marched through and liberated his camp. When Anderson returned stateside, he found the game of baseball therapeutic. He tried out for the San Antonio Missions in 1946 and won a job. The Browns summoned him in 1948 and he played pieces of two seasons in St. Louis.

G	R	H	2B	3B	HR	RBI	BB	SO	SB	AVG	Slug
122	23	41	8	1	2	17	22	36	0	.184	.256

Ferrell Jack Anderson, *Catcher*

Before the war, Anderson was a star football player at the University of Kansas. He was torn between his two favorite sports, football and baseball, while he played hardball for a semipro outfit in Joplin, Missouri. Ferrell felt that an athlete had a longer shelf life in baseball, so he wrote the Joplin Miners' front office, which was worried he'd give up baseball for the gridiron, and stated, "I've thought it over and baseball gets my vote."

Anderson gave up football and concentrated his efforts on baseball. But his sports career was put on hold when Uncle Sam beckoned him. Ferrell was inducted at Fort Bragg and served with an armored division there. While there, he yearned for the sportsman's paradise of Joplin, where he relocated, and wrote a letter to the Miners' front office that read, "Maybe Roy Foster got a few quail last season since I wasn't there to beat him to the punch." Dreams of bird-hunting aside, Anderson was transferred from Fort Bragg to a base in Oklahoma where he assisted in a reconditioning program for soldiers sent to hospitals. After his discharge, Ferrell made the 1946 Dodgers and platooned with Bruce Edwards behind the dish. Writer Steve Snider made fun of Ferrell's appearance when he wrote, "Anderson is the best cross-eyed rookie in baseball."

G	R	H	2B	3B	HR	RBI	BB	SO	SB	AVG	Slug
97	20	61	12	0	2	15	18	25	1	.261	.338

Arnold Revola "Red" Anderson, *Pitcher*

A big right-hander from Iowa, Anderson spent pieces of three seasons at the major league level with the Senators. He joined the navy in 1942 and never again pitched at the highest level. Anderson served overseas and played some baseball in Hawaii.

W	L	PCT	G	GS	CG	IP	H	BB	SO	SHO	ERA
5	8	.385	36	9	3	137	150	69	40	0	4.35

John Edward Andre, *Pitcher*

Long John Andre spent one year at the major league level, ten years after his military discharge. The Massachusetts native left the sandlots to join the Army Air Corps during World War II. His military travails took him overseas where he served in the South Pacific. Long John returned to the States and kicked around the minors until Stan Hack gave him a trial with the 1955 Cubs. He failed to get a win but he did record a save for Smiling Stan.

W	L	PCT	G	GS	CG	IP	H	BB	SO	SHO	ERA
0	1	.000	22	3	0	45	45	28	19	0	5.80

William Morgan Andrus, *Third Base*

Given two cups of coffee at the major league level, Bill failed to make the grade. Unable to get a safety in nine at-bats, Andrus was deemed a minor league lifer and shipped back to the bushes. Although the tough Texan didn't make the grade in baseball, he reached a pay grade few former athletes attained in the military. He enlisted in the army as a grunt but showed terrific leadership qualities in Uncle Sam's outfit and climbed in rank swiftly. When the dust cleared on his army career, Andrus had reached the rank of first sergeant.

G	R	H	2B	3B	HR	RBI	BB	SO	SB	AVG	Slug
6	0	0	0	0	0	1	0	3	0	.000	.000

William James Antonello, *Outfield*

Just a pup when the war broke out, Antonello came of age when the fighting was hot. The Brooklyn native left the schoolyard for the United States Navy and was shipped to the South Pacific. His military duties were in supply maneuvers and troop transportation while he served on a carrier. After the war Bill went to the minor leagues and was summoned by his hometown Dodgers a few years before they relocated to Los Angeles.

G	R	H	2B	3B	HR	RBI	BB	SO	SB	AVG	Slug
40	9	7	1	1	1	4	2	11	0	.163	.302

Peter William Appleton, *Pitcher*

At the time of World War II, Appleton had already been in the major leagues for many years. He made his debut with the Cincinnati Reds in 1927 and pitched with a number of teams before he joined the Browns in 1942. Pete split the 1942 season with the White Sox and Browns as a 38-year-old veteran. Neglecting his advanced age, Appleton enlisted in the navy and went to the Naval Pre-Flight School held at North Carolina. While in North Carolina, Pete was given lieutenant's bars and was reassigned to Quonset after completing the school. At the Quonset Naval Air Base, Appleton served as the installation's baseball manager. He returned to the majors late in 1945, as a 41-year-old man, and split the season—his last in the major leagues—between St. Louis and Washington.

W	L	PCT	G	GS	CG	IP	H	BB	SO	SHO	ERA
57	66	.463	341	73	34	1,141	1,187	486	420	6	4.30

Lucius Benjamin Appling, *Shortstop*

One of the greatest players in White Sox history, and one of the finest shortstops of all-time, Appling was nicknamed "Old Aches and Pains" on account of his constant nagging injuries and tendency to make those injuries known to passersby. His illustrious career began in 1930 and ended some twenty years later in 1950. As a player, Luke only wore the uniform of the White Sox, but he donned a Kansas City Athletics uniform in 1967 when he was appointed their manager. Appling possessed exceptional plate discipline, posting a career walk-to-strikeout ratio close to 3-to-1.

In 1943, Appling was already 36 years old, and with the likes of Williams, DiMaggio and Travis gone, he was able to cop a batting title that year. The following year, however, Appling joined the three aforementioned stars in the service. Appling took his old aches and pains act to the army where he was stationed at Fort Lee, Virginia. With Father Time hounding him, Luke told troops at Fort Lee that he wasn't going to return to baseball after the war. From Fort Lee, Luke was assigned to the reconditioning service at Lawson General Hospital in Atlanta, where he spent the rest of his military tenure.

Luke's loss to service in 1944 saved the White Sox a sizable amount of money. Appling was regarded as a shrewd batter, slapping foul ball after foul ball in an effort to get his desired pitch. The White Sox management issued a statement after the 1944 season had concluded, stating that they used 120 dozen fewer balls with Appling in the service.

G	R	H	2B	3B	HR	RBI	BB	SO	SB	AVG	Slug
2,422	1,319	2,749	440	102	45	1,118	1,302	528	179	.310	.398

Angel Valdes "Jack" Aragon, *Catcher*

The movie *Field of Dreams* introduced the world to the factual ballplayer known as Archibald "Moonlight" Graham, who played in one major league game but did not record an at-bat. Such was the career of Angel Aragon. Aragon played in a single game with the 1941 Giants and then entered the service after the 1941 season. He spent three years in the navy and was never able to tally a major league at-bat.

G	R	H	2B	3B	HR	RBI	BB	SO	SB	AVG	Slug
1	0	0	0	0	0	0	0	0	0	—	

George Albert Archie, *First Base*

Archie was one of the many men asked to fill the gaping whole at first base in Washington before the great Mickey Vernon arrived. George didn't last long on the job before he was dealt to the Browns. After the 1941 season, George enlisted in the army. During his first year in service, he played baseball with the Dizzy Dean All-Stars—a group of service men selected by the great right-hander to play amateur games. However, Archie's main task with Uncle Sam wasn't a game. He was shipped off to Austria to see action in the European Theatre.

Archie served with the 65th Infantry Division in Austria. Although his military duties came before baseball, George was able to play some ball with fellow former major leaguer Harry "The Hat" Walker. He served as Walker's bench coach, as Harry said, "He's the best assistant manager I ever had." Archie coached engineers in Austria on how to build ball diamonds in his spare time, but his occupational duties concerned reconnaissance. He was the point corporeal on his recon squad as he battled Wehrmachters and Storm Troopers in Austria and Germany. As the point corporeal, Archie's group was the first element to see and make contact with the enemy.

G	R	H	2B	3B	HR	RBI	BB	SO	SB	AVG	Slug
121	49	115	24	4	3	53	37	47	10	.273	.371

Rinaldo Joseph "Rugger" Ardizoia, *Pitcher*

Ardizoia's major league career consisted of a cup of coffee with the world champion 1947 Yankees. The war presented an unusual dilemma for Rugger. Since he was a foreigner, there were speculations that he might be an enemy alien, but the Italian passed the service background checks and was inducted in the Air Corps. While serving on the West Coast in 1943, he participated in a service all-star game with such notables as Red Ruffing, Charlie Gehringer and Walt Judnich. Ardizoia served in the maintenance department and was deployed to the South Pacific. After his discharge, Rugger, a minor league journeyman, caught on with the Yankees for his brief major league trial.

W	L	PCT	G	GS	CG	IP	H	BB	SO	SHO	ERA
0	0	—	1	0	0	2	4	1	0	0	9.00

Henry Irven Arft, *First Base*

Regarded as one of the best defensive first basemen of his time, the smooth-fielding Arft spent his entire five-year major league career with the Browns. In his major league debut, Hank showed he was made of the stuff by swatting a home run and legging out a triple. It wasn't long before he took playing time away from Chuck Stevens. But Arft's bat wasn't of the Mize, Vernon or Fain mold, and he began to lose playing time to such better hitters as Footsie Lenhardt and Jack Graham. But given his sensational fielding — he led first basemen in fielding percentage in 1948 and 1950 — he was often employed when the big bats failed to field cleanly.

Before Hank made his major league debut, the Missouri boy served in the U.S. Navy during the war. Many young ballplayers were able to get assignments in the athletic department and play ball during their tenure, but Arft only saw the diamonds on the occasional idle hour and after the war. Hank was stationed aboard a destroyer in the South Pacific that was engaged in many of the Pacific campaigns. When the bomb was dropped, he was able to go home and lock on shortly with the Great Lakes baseball team managed by Bob Feller while he awaited his discharge.

G	R	H	2B	3B	HR	RBI	BB	SO	SB	AVG	Slug
300	116	229	46	13	13	118	137	133	8	.253	.375

Morris Arnovich, *Outfield*

Regarded as an all-out, hustling style of ballplayer, "Snooker" was a solid all-around talent who missed four complete baseball seasons to World War II. Arnovich platooned with Earl Brown in the Phillies outfield as a rookie in 1937 and he hit .290 in his first full major league season. He became the everyday left fielder in 1938 and paced the lowly Phillies in at-bats and RBIs. He hit .324 in 1939 but after a slow start in 1940, Morrie was dealt to the world champion Reds. He caught on with Bill Terry's Giants in 1941 and then missed the 1942 through 1945 seasons to military service.

Morrie was rejected by the military in 1941 due to dental deficiencies. He said, "I have been wearing partial upper and lower dental plates for the last fifteen years as the result of losing several teeth in basketball." Although he was initially turned down by Uncle Sam, Morrie was given the thumbs up for service in 1942. Arnovich was inducted into the army at Fort Sheridan. Upon his induction Morrie said, "Why shouldn't I be in the army? I'm healthy and glad to serve Uncle Sam. I hope that I will be of some slight assistance in this war for liberty."

His first assignment came at Fort Lewis, Washington, where he suffered a freak injury in the shower. Morrie slipped and plunged his arm through a window glass. His arm was cut badly, especially the forearm where thirteen stitches had to be taken. After he healed from his injury, Morrie was asked to participate in a service all-star game with Bob Feller and Cecil Travis. From Fort Lewis, Morrie was transferred to Camp Beale in April of 1944 where he coached an installation ballclub. He received his promotion to staff sergeant early in 1944 and was then shipped overseas.

While serving overseas, Morrie was stationed at Oro Bay where he ran into Al Schacht, a former major league pitcher, and at the time, the Clown Prince of Baseball. Schacht was entertaining troops when he spotted Arnovich in the crowd. Recognizing Morrie, Schacht invited him up to the stage to poke fun at the ex–major leaguer. In Al's military memoirs, *GI Had Fun*, he writes of awarding Morrie the winner of the nose championship. Schacht wrote, "I put on a stage show at the camp and there was Morrie, a Sergeant. I got him up on the stage with me, dramatically measured his nose with my fingers, and then measured mine and gave him the title. It takes quite a nose to beat me."

Having fun with Schacht's rhubarb, Arnovich plotted revenge on the Clown Prince of Baseball. After Schacht's show, Morrie took Al to Oro Bay's infamous barber, since Al was in need of a haircut. Not knowing of the barber's poor reputation among the service men, Al sat down in the barber's chair to receive his cut. Merrily, Arnovich watched as the barber butchered Schacht's locks.

G	R	H	2B	3B	HR	RBI	BB	SO	SB	AVG	Slug
590	234	577	104	12	22	261	185	139	17	.287	.383

James Curtis Atkins, *Pitcher*

Atkins had two cups of coffee with the Red Sox in the 1950s. A big Southern right-hander, Jim served in the Marine Corps during World War II. After his discharge he kicked around the minors for a few years before the Sox gave him his first trial in 1950.

W	L	PCT	G	GS	CG	IP	H	BB	SO	SHO	ERA
0	1	.000	4	1	0	15	15	11	2	0	3.60

Maurice Dailey "Toby" Atwell, *Catcher*

A rookie sensation for the 1952 Cubs, Toby and Smoky Burgess were the only two catchers in the majors to hit .290 — both Berra and Campanella failed to reach their heights. That solid freshman showing couldn't keep Atwell in Wrigley, and he was traded to Pittsburgh the following season. Atwell spent a few years platooning with Jack Shepard for the Pirates in the 1950s and retired with a modest .260 batting average. During the Second World War, Toby served with the U.S. Army Air Corps.

G	R	H	2B	3B	HR	RBI	BB	SO	SB	AVG	Slug
378	116	290	41	7	9	110	161	84	4	.260	.333

William Franklin Atwood, *Catcher*

A .300 hitter as a rookie in 1936, Bill couldn't keep up the pace throughout his career. His mark fell to .244 the following year when skipper Jimmie Wilson platooned him with Earl Grace. When his batting average fell below .200 in 1938, the Phillies acquired solid-hitting receiver Spud Davis to take his place. Bill was retained by the Phillies through 1940 but he failed to get his batting average above .200 in his final year in the majors.

With his baseball career at the end of the line and America engaged in strained discourse with foreign countries, Atwood prepared for life as a soldier. After Pearl Harbor was bombed, Bill desperately wanted to join the Air Corps as a fighter pilot but his age restricted his desire. An Associated Press article read, "He was eager to become a combat pilot, having already many hours of flying to his credit, but his 31 years was just a step over the age limit for those assigned to combat duty."

With many civilian hours of airtime, Bill was received as a pilot and attended the flight instructor's familiarization course at Tulsa, Oklahoma. Atwood wanted an overseas assignment and got it. Despite his advanced age, Bill was sent to the Pacific Theatre and flew in excess of 200 hours "over the hump." Uncle Sam then sent Bill to a pilot check-out school at India where he assisted in the mustering out of military pilots when the war came to a close.

G	R	H	2B	3B	HR	RBI	BB	SO	SB	AVG	Slug
342	82	220	41	4	7	112	93	89	4	.229	.302

James Epherium "Jay" Avrea, *Pitcher*

Avrea had a cup of coffee with the 1950 Reds managed by Luke Sewell. The right-hander spent time in the United States Navy during World War II.

W	L	PCT	G	GS	CG	IP	H	BB	SO	SHO	ERA
0	0	—	2	0	0	5	6	3	2	0	3.60

Russell Awkard, *Outfield*

An angular center fielder who played for two years before World War II, Awkard served in the military from 1941 to 1945. A quartermaster in the army during the war, Russell was shipped overseas and served in England and France for a time.

(1940–1941): Newark Eagles and New York Cubans

Richard John "Dick" Aylward, *Catcher*

A journeyman catcher in the bushes, Dick enjoyed a lengthy career in the minor leagues but only a four-game trial at the highest level. The Indians gave Aylward his only look in 1953 and he was able to catch some side sessions of legendary pitchers like Bob Feller, Early Wynn, Bob Lemon and Big Bear Garcia. During the Second World War, Dick served with the United States Army and served in the European Theatre.

G	R	H	2B	3B	HR	RBI	BB	SO	SB	AVG	Slug
4	0	0	0	0	0	0	0	1	0	.000	.000

Edson Garfield Bahr, *Pitcher*

The Canadian-born Bahr won a job on the Pirates staff after his discharge from the navy despite his lack of experience. He had never pitched in the majors before the war but impressed skipper Frankie Frisch enough to keep him on the roster. All Edson did was lead the Pirates in ERA and finish third on the team in wins. He was unable to sustain his good luck and last pitched in the majors in 1947.

W	L	PCT	G	GS	CG	IP	H	BB	SO	SHO	ERA
11	11	.500	46	25	8	219	210	95	69	0	3.37

William Presley Baker, *Catcher*

A reserve catcher who seldom struck out, Baker played at the major league level with the Reds, Pirates and Cardinals. Bill was inducted into the navy after the 1943 season. He served at the Great Lakes and played service ball under Hall of Fame catcher Mickey Cochrane.

G	R	H	2B	3B	HR	RBI	BB	SO	SB	AVG	Slug
263	45	145	25	5	2	68	68	30	6	.247	.315

Harold Earl Bamberger, *Reserve*

Hal had a cup of coffee with New York in 1948. The Giants began that year managed by Mel Ott but replaced him midseason with Leo Durocher. Hal appeared only in seven games and slapped out one base hit. During World War II he served with the Marine Corps.

G	R	H	2B	3B	HR	RBI	BB	SO	SB	AVG	Slug
7	0	1	0	0	0	0	1	2	0	.083	.083

Daniel Robert Bankhead, *Pitcher*

The first black pitcher to work in the major leagues, Bankhead came from a baseball family. Dan had four brothers who also played in the Negro Leagues. His brother, Sam, a shortstop, was one of the finest stars of black baseball before World War II. Dan, however, was a pitcher (brothers Garnett and Joseph were also pitchers) who appeared in three Negro League All-Star Games in 1941, 1946 and 1947. Bankhead finished the 1947 season on the Brooklyn Dodgers pitching staff but struggled with his command in ten innings of work.

Jackie Robinson was summoned by Brooklyn in 1947, and when he proved his worth to the fans and the Dodgers brass, he paved the way for Bankhead to join him late in the season. The Dodgers had a decent pitching staff after the war with Ralph Branca, Preacher Roe, Joe Hatten and youngsters Rex Barney and Carl Erskine. With the talent Bankhead had to compete with, he was shipped to the minors for seasoning in 1948 and posted a terrific 20–6 worksheet at Nashua that season. Promoted to St. Paul the following season, Dan had another 20-win season in the bushes before Brooklyn gave him another look. Although he mastered the minors, Dan struggled with his command at the major league level and never established himself with Brooklyn.

An All-Star before and after World War II, Bankhead missed three baseball seasons to the war effort. His stint with Uncle Sam didn't hinder him, indicated by his back-to-back All-Star selections after his discharge. A fine hitting pitcher and a good all-around athlete, Dan left Organized Ball in the mid 1950s and played south of the border in Mexico for a handful of years. He pitched in Mexico into the 1960s and was 45 years old when he threw his last pitch as a professional.

W	L	PCT	G	GS	CG	IP	H	BB	SO	SHO	ERA
9	5	.643	52	13	2	153	161	110	111	1	6.53

Sam Barber, *Pitcher*

A pitcher for the Birmingham Black Barons before the war, Barber missed some action to military service during World War II. After his discharge he pitched a few years with the Cleveland Buckeyes when the Negro Leagues had become strictly a minor circuit after they started losing players to the major leagues.

(1940–1950): Cleveland Buckeyes and Birmingham Black Barons

John Duncan "Red" Barkley, *Shortstop*

Barkley had two brief cups of coffee before the war with the Browns and Braves. His career had stalled out but when major leaguers began leaving for service, Red received another trial with the Dodgers in 1943. He played in 20 games that season as a backup for Hall of Famer Arky Vaughan. But Barkley would leave the majors for the military shortly thereafter. He was a private in the Army Air Corps at Sheppard Field who was transferred to Waco in 1944 where he played service ball under Birdie Tebbetts.

G	R	H	2B	3B	HR	RBI	BB	SO	SB	AVG	Slug
63	16	43	9	0	0	21	19	26	2	.264	.319

William Barnes, *Pitcher*

A right-handed pitcher from Birmingham, Barnes pitched briefly in the Negro Leagues before World War II and even less after it. He spent two years in the military during the war.

(1941–1947): Baltimore Elite Giants, Memphis Red Sox and Indianapolis Clowns

Rex Edward Barney, *Pitcher*

Barney enjoyed a modest career in the 1940s with the Dodgers of Brooklyn. Despite his inability to find the strike zone, he posted a career winning percentage above .500, largely due to playing for an offensive powerhouse. Rex was a raw-boned rookie in 1943, as the 18-year-old walked 41 batters in 45 innings of work. He was then taken into the military, where he threw wild pitches from 1944 to 1945 for Uncle Sam.

Rex was drafted in early January of 1944 and played some stateside service ball in the Western Victory League with Brooklyn teammate Pistol Pete Reiser and Cardinal outfielder Harry "The Hat" Walker. He was then shipped overseas and served in Europe as part of the 65th Infantry Division, which was also the unit of former St. Louis Brown George Archie. Phil Itzoe recalled a story that Rex once told him, regarding a meeting he had with General Patton overseas. Itzoe said, "Rex was on a tank and General Patton came riding over. 'Son, where is the front line?' he asked Rex. 'Right in front of this tank,' Rex said." After his playing days had concluded, Barney became a popular PA announcer for the Baltimore Orioles.

W	L	PCT	G	GS	CG	IP	H	BB	SO	SHO	ERA
35	31	.530	155	81	20	599	474	410	336	6	4.33

Victor Dee Barnhart, *Shortstop*

A war-era ballplayer, the bulk of Barnhart's tenure at the highest level came with the 1945 Pirates. When the war ended, Pittsburgh employed the slick-fielding Billy Cox at short, and Vic was used only sparingly. He served briefly during the war and was with the United States Army at a post in Texas.

G	R	H	2B	3B	HR	RBI	BB	SO	SB	AVG	Slug
74	21	55	7	0	0	19	10	12	2	.270	.304

Richard William Bartell, *Shortstop*

They broke the mold with Rowdy Richard. When any conversation is undertaken regarding the game of baseball's most energetic "pepper-pots," the name of Dick Bartell should head the list — or at least dwell near the top. Bartell was a star shortstop for a number of years, spent primarily with the Giants. Many writers regarded Bartell as a "fiery and temperamental sparkplug."

His major league career began in 1927 with the Pittsburgh Pirates. The Pirates had a 100-RBI shortstop during Rowdy Richard's rookie season in Buckshot Glenn Wright, but an injury to Buckshot in 1928 opened the door for Bartell. He took advantage of the playing time by hitting .305. Dick took over the regular shortstop job in 1929, and led all NL shortstops with a .302 batting average. In 1930, Rowdy Richard hit .320 but was dangled as trade bait during the offseason since the Bucs team ERA was an abysmal 5.24. Bartell packed his bags, joined the Phillies in 1931, and stroked 43 doubles in Philadelphia. After the 1934 season, in which Bartell finished third in the NL in stolen bases, he was dealt to the Giants for the first time. He played with the Giants until 1939 and returned in 1941 after stints with the Cubs and Tigers. As a 35-year-old, Bartell hit .270 in his last baseball season before military induction.

Although he was an aging veteran, Rowdy Richard still had a few years left. Bartell's first military stop was recruit training at Farragut Naval Training Station, where he was given his military haircut. Of the haircut Bartell said, "My head looks like a bare infield!" As far as major league baseball players were concerned, Bartell wasn't alone at Farragut. The man who he had supplanted in the Pirates lineup many years before, Buckshot Glenn Wright, greeted him there as an instructor. Rowdy Richard took his boot camp at Idaho and from there went to Bainbridge for an eight-week course on physical instruction, welfare and recreation. At Bainbridge, Bartell served as a petty officer third class before he received his reassignment to Treasure Island. At Treasure Island it was rumored that he was due to be sent overseas to play in a navy all-star game in Hawaii. Of the rumor, Dick said, "I'm in the Navy now. And you know as much as I do about where I'll go next."

He became a baseball coach at Treasure Island, and while serving there he was honored by the Oakland Boosters, who held a ceremony in his honor. He gave a short speech at the ceremony, saying, "I've been called a holler guy, a fellow who pops off and does a lot of yelling. Well, tonight I'm speechless." When asked about the likelihood of returning to baseball after the war, Dick said, "I doubt very much if I'll go back to playing, for if the war goes another year and a half I'll be 40 and that's a tough age to go back to actual competition. If I'm released by next spring I may be able to play a few more seasons, but if I miss the 1946 season, there's no question about my quitting the field."

Rowdy Richard received his discharge from the navy in October of 1945 and strapped on his spikes for one final season. He appeared in only five games for the Giants in 1946 while his main duties entailed coaching. Bartell coached at the major league level through the 1950s and served as a manager in the minor leagues. A great all-around player, Bartell has Hall of Fame-caliber numbers when compared to his middle infield peers.

G	R	H	2B	3B	HR	RBI	BB	SO	SB	AVG	Slug
2,016	1,130	2,165	442	71	79	710	748	627	109	.284	.391

Boyd Owen Bartley, *Shortstop*

A University of Illinois graduate, Bartley was summoned to the major leagues with haste. Shortly after graduation, he was wearing the uniform of the Brooklyn Dodgers. He did not last long in Brooklyn, however, since he was called to service in the army after he appeared in just nine games for the Dodgers. He attended OCS at Fort Benning, Georgia, and in 1945 Bartley was shipped overseas to the Philippines where he led a rest camp for combat troops. He received his discharge from the army in 1946 but was unable to return to the Dodgers due to an injury he sustained while in the military. Bartley remained in the game as a manager, with the Ponca City, Oklahoma, club from 1947 to 1952, with a brief military recall in 1951. He scouted for the Dodgers until his retirement in 1990.

G	R	H	2B	3B	HR	RBI	BB	SO	SB	AVG	Slug
9	0	1	0	0	0	1	1	3	0	.048	.048

David Robert Bartosch, *Outfield*

A war-era ballplayer, Bartosch spent the 1945 season with the Redbirds. The outfielder had spent the previous summer with Uncle Sam but was mustered out in time to play in the majors during the last year of the war. After the war, when Redbird stars Stan Musial, Enos Slaughter and Terry Moore returned, there was no room for Bartosch.

G	R	H	2B	3B	HR	RBI	BB	SO	SB	AVG	Slug
24	9	12	1	0	0	1	6	3	0	.255	.277

Romanus "Monty" Basgall, *Second Base*

Monty was the Pirates regular second baseman in 1949 before he was supplanted by Danny Murtaugh. He played three years at the major league level with Pittsburgh but had a lengthy career in the game. A close chum with Tommy Lasorda, Basgall spent many years on the Dodgers coaching staff. During World War II, Monty served at the Sioux Falls Army Airfield and played service ball with first baseman Don Bollweg.

G	R	H	2B	3B	HR	RBI	BB	SO	SB	AVG	Slug
200	52	110	15	3	4	41	46	51	1	.215	.279

Matthew Daniel Batts, *Catcher*

A decent backstop, Batts had a ten-year career at the major league level, which began with the Red Sox in 1947 and ended with the 1956 Reds. Matt was a solid-hitting receiver who made an immediate splash at the highest level. The first hit he tallied in the majors was a home run. Before his debut, Batts served in the military during World War II. He played service ball at Randolph Field with fellow Red Sox prospect Boo Ferriss.

G	R	H	2B	3B	HR	RBI	BB	SO	SB	AVG	Slug
546	163	432	95	11	26	219	143	163	6	.269	.391

Henry Albert Bauer, *Outfield*

A mainstay on the Yankees powerhouse teams of the 1950s, Bauer was a solid-hitting outfielder for the Bronx Bombers. Hank made his major league debut with the Yankees in 1948 as the tough scrapper was a virtual unknown during the war. Although Bauer had yet to make good on the ball diamond, it didn't take him long to make the grade in Uncle Sam's outfit.

Bauer enlisted in the Marine Corps in 1942, determined to see combat action. After stateside training, Hank was shipped overseas where he was anything but idle. While many athletes served in the physical instructor's department in their respective branches, Hank was taking on the enemy. He saw combat action at New Georgia, Okinawa and Guam and was awarded two Purple Hearts, two Bronze Stars and eleven other campaign ribbons for his wartime heroics. Ed Nichols wrote, "Hank Bauer was a genuine hero in World War II with the Marines. He fought the Japs. He has the shrapnel marks to prove that he saw combat. He was wounded several times and won many decorations, but he refused to wear them for fear people thought he was showing his ego."

A noted brawler who never backed away from a fight, Bauer was part of the wild nighttime crowd that made the Yankees powerful on the diamond and in the night clubs. A no-nonsense man, Hank had the image of a battle-hardened veteran. Despite his heroics, many thought that athletes were simply coddled when they were taken into service, and a congressman named Hess from Ohio investigated the allegations of preferential treatment. One of the names that were initially on his report was Bauer's, and the congressman learned that not all ballplayers played games while in the armed forces; some fought with great distinction.

G	R	H	2B	3B	HR	RBI	BB	SO	SB	AVG	Slug
1,544	833	1,424	229	57	164	703	521	638	50	.277	.439

Russell Lee Bauers, *Pitcher*

Russ couldn't buy a strike when he walked into Forbes Field in 1936; he walked four batters in his first inning of work. He harnessed his potential under skipper Pie Traynor in 1937 when he finished 13–6 with a 2.87 ERA. Bauers showed remarkable ability at missing bats in 1938, when he allowed 207 hits in nearly 250 innings of work. His arm gave out in 1939 and his career was essentially over, despite hanging on for a couple more seasons. He was inducted into the military and missed the 1944 and 1945 baseball seasons to World War II.

Bauers was initially assigned to Camp Grant, Illinois, but was shipped overseas after a brief stateside assignment. He served with the 90th General Hospital in England as a private. His duties at the hospital entailed assisting wounded soldiers in their rehabilitation. After his discharge, Russ pitched briefly with the 1946 Chicago Cubs and the 1950 St. Louis Browns.

W	L	PCT	G	GS	CG	IP	H	BB	SO	SHO	ERA
31	30	.508	129	71	27	599	562	271	300	5	3.53

Frank Conrad Baumholtz, *Outfield*

A gifted natural athlete, Baumholtz may have been a better basketball player than a baseball player, and he wasn't too shabby on the diamond. Before Frankie turned pro in either sport, he did a stint with Uncle Sam. He enlisted in the navy and was initially sent to the Great Lakes Naval Training Station. While serving there, Frankie was a star on both the hard court and the ball diamond. The skipper of the Great Lakes baseball team, Hall of Fame catcher Mickey Cochrane, was thoroughly impressed with Frankie's abilities in baseball and urged the youngster to stick to the diamond. But in 1943, sports were the furthest thing on young Baumholtz's mind.

After his promotion to ensign in the summer of 1942, Frankie prepared for life overseas. His navy unit was shipped out and Baumholtz witnessed combat action on the high seas. By late January of 1944, a *Stars and Stripes* article detailed the travails of Frankie. He had made ten trips to Murmansk, participated in the North African campaign, and then his ship saw action in the South Pacific. Discharged in 1945, Baumholtz initially discarded Cochrane's championing of baseball and signed to play pro basketball. He played three years in the cage before he turned his attention to the outdoor sport. The Reds brought him up in 1947 and he paced the team in triples that year. A corner outfielder, Frankie's lack of power was his main weakness and he was traded to the Cubs in 1949 where he spent the bulk of his career.

G	R	H	2B	3B	HR	RBI	BB	SO	SB	AVG	Slug
1,019	450	1,101	165	51	25	272	258	258	30	.290	.389

Cramer Theodore "Ted" Beard, *Outfield*

Beard spent a number of years on the bench with the Pirates after the war. Used exclusively as a backup outfielder/pinch-hitter, Beard was good at drawing the occasional walk and had some speed but didn't hit enough to play regularly. Before Ted made his major league debut he served in the military during World War II. Beard wasn't one of the boys carrying a sack of balls from the barracks to the ball field; rather, he carried medical supplies on the battlefield as a combat medic in the Pacific Theatre.

G	R	H	2B	3B	HR	RBI	BB	SO	SB	AVG	Slug
194	80	94	11	6	6	35	78	107	16	.198	.285

Henry Eugene "Gene" Bearden, *Pitcher*

The hero of the 1948 world champion Cleveland Indians, Bearden was atop the baseball scene that season. He led the American League in ERA that year, teamed with Bob Lemon to give the Tribe two 20-game winners, and saved the final game of the World Series when Lemon got in a jam. In that magical Fall Classic, Gene pitched a complete-game shutout against the Braves in Game 3 and then put out Lemon's fire to secure the championship for Cleveland in Game 6. He worked a combined 10.2 innings without allowing a run. Of Bearden's World Series worksheet, skipper Lou Boudreau said, "He was the big guy. Of course, it was a team victory but, well, we wouldn't be where we are today without Gene." But it was a wonder that Bearden made the majors at all.

A decorated World War II veteran, Bearden suffered severe injuries during the war that not only came close to ending his baseball career but nearly claimed his life. While serving in the navy on the *USS Helena*, Bearden's vessel was torpedoed by the Japanese. Aboard the sinking ship, Bearden suffered wounds to his leg and scalp. Shrapnel tore a gash in Bearden's skull that nearly killed him and service doctors debated on whether or not to amputate his wounded leg. Surgery was in store for Gene, who had his leg mended without amputation and an aluminum plate inserted into his skull. It was a miracle that Bearden survived the battle and an unlikely occurrence that he became a World Series hero.

Bearden was property of the Yankees while he was in the service, and New York tried him out after he had recovered from his injuries. They felt the left-handed knuckleballer didn't have the stuff for the majors and cut him loose. Cleveland Indians owner Bill Veeck, a war hero with the Marines who lost a leg in combat, had a soft spot for Bearden and gave him a trial. Signed to a contract with the Indians, Bearden made his debut in 1947, and with an ERA of 81.00, gave no indication of the heights he'd reach in 1948. But success was Bearden's during that magical 1948 season. The war hero was baseball's darling. Grantland Rice, the legendary sportswriter, put it best when he wrote, "His post of honor as a war casualty who came back from the strife to prove that crippling injuries cannot down an athlete who has the will to win is forever secure."

W	L	PCT	G	GS	CG	IP	H	BB	SO	SHO	ERA
45	38	.542	193	84	29	789	791	435	259	7	3.96

John Andrew Beazley, *Pitcher*

Beazley teamed with Mort Cooper to give the Redbirds a devastating one-two punch in their rotation in 1942 and pitched the Cards to the World Series. Johnny went 21–6 with a 2.14 ERA during the season and 2–0 in the Fall Classic. In Game 5 of the 1942 World Series, Beazley outpitched Hall of Famer Red Ruffing to give the Cardinals the title. That game, as dramatic as any he ever pitched, was his last until 1946.

Johnny enlisted in the Army Air Corps after the World Series. He said, "I'll never go back to pitching. Baseball's a thing of the past for me. I'm going to make a career out of the Army." Johnny rose quickly through the military ranks; he received his promotion to corporeal in his first year of service at Fort Oglethorpe. In 1943 he attended Officer's Training School at Miami Beach and married the former Carolyn Frey while stationed in Florida. He was awarded his lieutenant bars in 1943 and was transferred to Berry Field where he was named the physical education director for the Fourth Ferrying Command. He received his promotion to captain in 1945 and was shipped out to Hawaii that year as well. Able to play some service ball on the islands, Johnny tossed a no-hitter in 1945.

Despite being adamant about making a career out of the military when he enlisted, Johnny returned to baseball in 1946. A lights-out pitcher prior to the war, he blew out his arm his first year back to the majors. The Cardinals shipped him out in 1947 and he caught on with the Braves. Johnny tried to soldier through his arm woes, but only managed 29 innings in 1947, sixteen in 1948 and two innings in 1949, his final season at the major league level.

W	L	PCT	G	GS	CG	IP	H	BB	SO	SHO	ERA
31	12	.721	76	46	21	374	349	157	147	3	3.01

Joseph Edward Becker, *Catcher*

A backup catcher for two years in the mid 1930s with Cleveland, Becker served with the U.S. Navy during World War II. With his playing career over after the war, Joe embarked on a long career as a minor league manager.

G	R	H	2B	3B	HR	RBI	BB	SO	SB	AVG	Slug
40	8	20	5	2	1	13	8	8	0	.241	.386

Joseph Stanley Beggs, *Pitcher*

Fluent in five different languages, including Serbian and Slavish, Beggs made a valuable asset to the military. He enjoyed a breakout year as the Reds top relief pitcher in their pennant-winning season of 1940. During the regular season Joe posted a 1.99 ERA while leading the team in saves. Beggs teamed with Clyde Shoun to give the Reds a reliable righty/lefty combo in the bullpen in 1943, but during 1944, Shoun moved to the rotation and Joe was inducted into the armed forces.

Pete Suder, an infielder for Connie Mack's Athletics, was on the same draft board as Joe. Beggs served as a commissioned officer in the navy and managed a service ball team at Camp Shelton with his occupational duties as a gunnery officer. He had 18 months worth of sea duty as a gunnery officer in charge of 42 men on a C2 Troop Transport in the North Atlantic. Beggs said, "I was with the cold meat service. Not much cooking in some of those North Atlantic seas."

After his discharge, Joe played major league ball from 1946 to 1948, enjoying his finest year the season after his discharge. Beggs posted a 12–10 record with a team-best 2.32 ERA in 1946. In 1949, Joe made his way back to the bushes after a season and half with the Giants. Serving as a minor league manager, Joe said, "I have a pre-war and post-war family and I guess I missed out on a boy when I was in the navy." Joe had two daughters, Jo Anne before the war and Elizabeth Jean after the war.

W	L	PCT	G	GS	CG	IP	H	BB	SO	SHO	ERA
48	35	.578	238	41	23	694	687	189	178	4	2.96

Henry Bernard Behrman, *Pitcher*

Behrman had his major league debut pushed back a few years courtesy of the war. On the cusp of reaching the majors before his induction, Hank had to wait his turn while wearing the khaki of Uncle Sam's fighting forces. Discharged in time for the 1946 season, Hank made his debut with his hometown Dodgers and won the ballgame played on his birthday.

W	L	PCT	G	GS	CG	IP	H	BB	SO	SHO	ERA
24	17	.585	174	27	5	430	427	228	189	2	4.40

Julian "Jute" Bell, *Pitcher*

A pitcher of some repute with the Memphis Red Sox, Bell was known for his tight-breaking curveball. By the time of World War II, Bell's career in the Negro Leagues was over. At the age of 41 when Pearl Harbor was bombed, Bell was above the age of service but he was eager to do his part. Jute worked with the USO at Camp Forest.

(1927–1930): Memphis Red Sox and Birmingham Black Barons

Joseph Rosenblum Bennett, *Reserve*

Bennett appeared in one major league game and didn't tally a single big league at-bat. He instead made the military a career and spent many years in the Quartermasters Corps in the United States Army. Joe served in both World Wars as well as the Korean War and retired from the army with the rank of lieutenant colonel.

G	R	H	2B	3B	HR	RBI	BB	SO	SB	AVG	Slug
1	0	0	0	0	0	0	0	0	0	—	—

Vernon Adair Benson, *Outfield*

Benson's major league career spanned five years but he played an average of eleven games a season. He appeared in two games as a teenager with the Athletics before the war. Vern was drafted during the 1943 season and missed all of the 1944 and 1945 campaigns to service in the armed forces. He played briefly at the major league level with the Athletics and Cardinals after the war. In 1977, he managed one game for the Braves, tallying a win in the process.

G	R	H	2B	3B	HR	RBI	BB	SO	SB	AVG	Slug
55	17	21	5	1	3	12	13	22	0	.202	.356

John Alton Benton, *Pitcher*

Benton was an adequate long relief pitcher and spot starter throughout his major league career. The bulk of his tenure came with the Detroit Tigers, as he played in Detroit from 1938 to 1948, with two years lost to the military. Benton served in the United States Navy and was stationed at the Norman Naval Center. He received an early medical discharge due to chronic migraine headaches. He returned to the diamond to pitch four more years with the Tigers before he ended his career with the Red Sox in 1952.

W	L	PCT	G	GS	CG	IP	H	BB	SO	SHO	ERA
98	88	.527	455	167	58	1,689	1,672	733	697	10	3.66

John Berardino, *Second Base*

The allure of Tinseltown beckoned Johnny Berardino away from the game at the latter stages of his career. The former keystone man appeared in numerous television shows, such as *General Hospital* and *Annie Oakley*, while also trying his hand in feature films. Berardino served in the air corps during his stint in the armed forces. Prior to his military induction, Johnny attended a civilian flying course to prepare for Uncle Sam's pre-flight school. He served three years during the war and saw action in the South Pacific.

G	R	H	2B	3B	HR	RBI	BB	SO	SB	AVG	Slug
912	334	755	167	23	36	387	284	268	27	.249	.355

Morris "Moe" Berg, *Catcher/Utility Infielder*

One of the most mysterious characters in American history, Moe Berg was a modest major league ballplayer who possessed a mind many a philosopher would envy. A highly educated man with an enviable intellect, Berg was an honor graduate at Princeton, earned a law degree from Columbia University, and studied at the prestigious Sorbonne. But much to the dismay of his family, Berg's first love wasn't letters, but baseball.

In 1934, when Berg was a backup for the Cleveland Indians, he joined a collection of baseball all-stars on a tour of Japan. Moe wasn't asked along for his ball diamond skills but because he spoke Japanese fluently. No one honestly knew how many languages Moe could speak, but his rowdy teammate and chum Ted Lyons once said that Moe "can speak seven languages but can't hit in any of them." Moe's brother, Dr. Sam Berg, after his brother's death tried to set the record straight on just how many languages Moe knew. Dr. Berg said, "He knew English, Spanish, French, Italian, German and Japanese fluently. That's all, unless you count Greek and Latin. But they aren't useful for conversation. And he had a working knowledge of Russian."

It was on the 1934 tour of Japan when ballplayers noticed something unusual about Berg's tourist behavior. He appeared to go out of his way to take photographs of land features that any normal tourist wouldn't have bothered photographing. These photographs were supposedly used by the army to plan attacks on Japan. This is when Berg's eccentric behavior began to take on a more mysterious tone. Scribe Whitney Martin described Berg by writing that "he speaks very softly out of the corner of his mouth, barely moving his lips, and gives the impression that everything he says is very, very confidential."

By the time World War II was underway, Berg's days as a major leaguer were over. Still a useful man on a ballclub, given his intelligence — which consisted of book smarts and baseball know-how — Berg was a bullpen coach in the majors. With the war raging overseas, Berg lamented to a sportswriter, saying, "Europe is in flames, withering in a fire set by Hitler. All over the continent men and women and children are dying. Soon we, too, will be involved. And what am I doing? I'm sitting in the bullpen, telling jokes to the relief pitchers."

The jokes shortly came to a close as Moe, a close friend to Nelson Rockefeller, was handed a job with the Office of Inter-American Affairs. In that capacity, Rockefeller sent Berg to South America as a goodwill ambassador. But Moe wanted to do more and joined the forerunner of the CIA — the Office of Strategic Services. While working in this classified branch, Berg was sent to Germany as a spy. He is supposed to have been on a mission that required him to sit in on lectures given by famous German scientist Werner Heisenberg, who was working on an atom bomb for the Nazis. It was Moe's assignment to assess Heisenberg and evaluate his ability to perfect the bomb. Berg surmised that Heisenberg was too far along in his work for the Allies to be concerned. However, it is rumored that if Berg felt the German scientist was close to perfecting the bomb, he was expected to assassinate the doctor.

After the war, Moe returned to life in the States, but a life of aimless wandering. A man who once had dinner with Albert Einstein had become somewhat of a leech, bouncing from one friend's home to another, but always keeping up his mysterious persona. Many people felt he was still employed as a spy by the government since he never gave any personal details or shared much of anything regarding his past. Al Schacht, the great Clown Prince of Baseball, described Moe Berg as well as anyone when he said that Berg was "the most mysterious guy in the world. You never know what he's thinking, or what he's going to do, or anything about him."

G	*R*	*H*	*2B*	*3B*	*HR*	*RBI*	*BB*	*SO*	*SB*	*AVG*	*Slug*
663	150	441	71	6	6	206	78	117	11	.243	.299

Lawrence Peter "Yogi" Berra, *Catcher*

Like a film director casting Audrey Totter as a drab, meek housewife in a motion picture, Yogi Berra didn't look the part of a great baseball player — but, boy, was he ever one. The stocky kid from St. Louis swung the bat at everything and more often than not connected. And he often connected with authority. He may have looked more like an ice cream vendor or the washing machine repairman, but Berra was one of the finest catchers in baseball history.

Before Yogi swung at his first shoulder-high fastball at the major league level, he served with Uncle Sam during World War II. A great number of ballplayers were able to play baseball in the service, fielding grounders at the Great Lakes or hitting curveballs at Bainbridge, but Lawrence Berra wasn't so fortunate. He had yet to establish himself in the professional ranks and nearly never had the opportunity to do so. Yogi saw heavy combat action at Normandy as part of the invading Allied Forces trying to take the stretch of land. His combat duties weren't relegated to Normandy. Berra also saw action with the navy in North Africa and Italy.

After the war Berra returned to the States and was the fifth man on the Yankees catching depth chart. The legendary Bill Dickey was aging, but power-hitting Aaron Robinson had a terrific season in 1946 while a couple of solid youngsters named Gus Niarhos and Ken Silvestri saw more action behind the dish than Yogi. When Dickey took Berra under his wing and taught him the subtleties of catching, he took off and wrested the starting catching duties away from Robinson. Although he wouldn't have fit the Hollywood typecast of a brawny, star athlete, Berra showed that typecasts are nullified when one has the drive to succeed.

G	*R*	*H*	*2B*	*3B*	*HR*	*RBI*	*BB*	*SO*	*SB*	*AVG*	*Slug*
2,120	1,175	2,150	321	49	358	1,430	704	414	30	.285	.482

Cornelius John "Neil" Berry, *Shortstop/Second Base*

Berry was a light-hitting reserve infielder at the major league level from 1948 to 1954. A Michigan native, Berry played the bulk of his major league career with the Tigers. Before Neil made his major league debut, he served in the Army Air Corps during World War II.

G	*R*	*H*	*2B*	*3B*	*HR*	*RBI*	*BB*	*SO*	*SB*	*AVG*	*Slug*
442	148	265	28	9	0	74	113	105	11	.244	.286

Herman Besse, *Pitcher*

Besse left for the army the day after he beat the Tigers in July of 1943. That victory was the only win he posted in the 1943 season. Besse was stationed at Fort Leavenworth, Kansas, where he was able to participate in the semi-pro baseball ranks. His two finest seasons came while toiling for Uncle Sam, as Herman was awarded back-to-back MVP awards for his work in the Kansas semi-pro ranks. He returned to the Athletics in 1946 and posted a 0–2 record in his final major league action.

W	L	PCT	G	GS	CG	IP	H	BB	SO	SHO	ERA
5	15	.250	65	25	5	243	298	128	118	0	6.96

Louis Eugene Bevil, *Pitcher*

Lou, who shortened his last name from Bevilacqua, appeared in four games for the 1942 Senators, the extent of his major league career. He served in the army for three years, stationed at Camp Bowie with the 13th Armored Division. Bevil played service ball for the 13th Armored Division, whose team name was the Black Cats. At the time of his discharge, he had reached the rank of sergeant.

W	L	PCT	G	GS	CG	IP	H	BB	SO	SHO	ERA
0	1	.000	4	1	0	10	9	11	2	0	6.30

Vernon Edgell Bickford, *Pitcher*

Although Braves fans had a famous saying "Spahn and Sain and pray for rain," their pitching staff consisted of a little more than the two stars. Bickford was a dynamo rookie right-hander for the 1948 Braves who helped them reach the World Series. His Fall Classic ERA was even lower than Spahn's. Vern won 16 games in 1949 compared to Sain's ten, and he logged an NL-best 312 innings in 1950 with 19 wins. Spahn, Sain and Bickford accounted for 61 of the Braves' wins that season but only Warren and John get any credit for their success.

Before Bickford tossed his first fastball in the major leagues, he served his country during time of war. Plucked from the bushes by Uncle Sam, Vern joined the United States Army. After boot camp, Bickford was shipped overseas and served in the Pacific Theatre of Operations. After his discharge, Vern joined the Braves in 1948 and helped them make the World Series. He tossed a no-hitter in 1950, but after an injury in 1951, his career was essentially over, although he hung on for a few more seasons.

W	L	PCT	G	GS	CG	IP	H	BB	SO	SHO	ERA
66	57	.537	182	149	73	1,077	1,040	467	450	9	3.71

James Melvin Bilbrey, *Pitcher*

Bilbrey served with the United States Navy during World War II. A stout right-hander from Tennessee, Jim was regarded as a promising moundsman for the Browns before the war and was deemed a top prospect after his discharge. Since he spent several years in the service, the Browns farmed Bilbrey out in 1946 and didn't give him a major league trial until 1949. He only worked one inning and walked the bases full in his lone frame.

W	L	PCT	G	GS	CG	IP	H	BB	SO	SHO	ERA
0	0	—	1	0	0	1	1	3	0	0	18.00

Charles Biot, *Outfield*

A tall outfielder from Orange, New Jersey, Biot played three years in the Negro Leagues before World War II. Leslie A. Heaphy, in *The Negro Leagues: 1869–1960*, described Biot "as a player with a strong arm, speed and consistent bat." Charlie was able to play ball in the service, where he was designated as player/manager for the 93rd Division of the 369th Regiment while in the army. After his discharge, Biot didn't return to baseball.

(1939–1941): New York Black Yankees, Newark Eagles and Baltimore Elite Giants

Frank Stephen Biscan, *Pitcher*

Biscan, who was nicknamed "Porky," was a wild relief pitcher for three years with the Browns. His first action came in 1942 with St. Louis when Porky posted a 2.33 ERA before he was plucked by Uncle Sam during the season. He enlisted in the navy and worked out with the Great Lakes Baseball club managed by legendary catcher Mickey Cochrane. Biscan married his wife on a ball diamond and celebrated the union by tossing a shutout.

W	L	PCT	G	GS	CG	IP	H	BB	SO	SHO	ERA
7	9	.438	74	4	1	149	170	104	64	0	5.26

Charles Tuller Bishop, *Pitcher*

Bishop made his major league debut after the war, when Connie Mack had already stepped down as skipper. He was a member of the A's when the franchise relocated to Kansas City. Charlie missed minor league seasoning time when he was drafted for the war.

W	L	PCT	G	GS	CG	IP	H	BB	SO	SHO	ERA
10	22	.313	69	37	6	295	307	168	121	1	5.31

Hiram Gabriel Bithorn, *Pitcher*

The Puerto Rican-born Bithorn spent his entire major league career in the Windy City—three years with the Cubs and a lone season with the Pale Hose. Hi led Cubs pitchers in appearances during his rookie season in 1942 and then became one of the National League's finest pitchers in 1943. Bithorn posted an 18–12 record while leading the league in shutouts and displayed a remarkable ERA of 2.59. Right when Hi was about to become one of the game's elite hurlers, he was inducted into the Puerto Rican Navy. He served at a Naval Air Station in San Juan and managed a service ballclub. He received his discharge in September of 1945 and returned to the Cubs in 1946. Hi, whose career looked bright before the war, was relegated to the Cubs bullpen in 1946. He played in only two games with the White Sox the following year, ending his major league career.

W	L	PCT	G	GS	CG	IP	H	BB	SO	SHO	ERA
34	31	.523	105	53	30	510	517	171	185	8	3.16

Joseph Black, *Pitcher*

Black, a pitcher of some success in the Negro Leagues, graduated from Morgan State College in 1943 and was later drafted into the U.S. Army during World War II. He remained stateside throughout most of the war and was even able to play in some games for the Baltimore Elite Giants while on furlough in 1944 and 1945. After his discharge, he returned to Baltimore and pitched for the club until 1950 when the Brooklyn Dodgers bought his contract. Joe was called up to Brooklyn and had some success as a fireman in the major leagues. He ended his career in the majors with a sparkling .714 winning percentage and 25 saves.

W	L	PCT	G	GS	CG	IP	H	BB	SO	SHO	ERA
30	12	.714	172	16	2	415	391	129	222	0	3.90

James Ray Blackburn, *Pitcher*

Blackburn pitched 18 games at the highest level and never did get that elusive victory. The tall, rangy right-hander from Kentucky had two cups of coffee at the major league level after the war. Although he wasn't as talented on the mound as Ewell Blackwell and Johnny Vander Meer, writers were interested in Jim after he returned home from the war. He may not have had the smoke of Vandy or the whip-like delivery of Ewell, but Jim's military story was one of courage and despair.

Blackburn joined up with the army and served with the 7th Armored Infantry Division. His unit saw heavy combat action at the Battle of the Bulge, where Jim was wounded in action. The 7th AID was sent to assist a unit that requested help during the epic battle. Blackburn described his combat action as "pretty rough." He said, "We were sent up to support a green outfit, which was having a hard time. We found the outfit disorganized and pretty soon the Germans swarmed all over us. I was hit in the leg by a piece of shrapnel and suffered a concussion. We were helpless and had to surrender."

Blackburn and his pals were mustered into a German prisoner-of-war camp. The cold European winters wrecked Jim's body, added with the lack of food they were given by the Nazis. Jim said, "We weren't really mistreated. It was just that the Germans had nowhere to keep us and nothing to feed us. I lost my toenails because my feet were frozen." When a scribe spotted Jim's bare feet after he had returned home, the writer made up a story of his own, spurred on by that blind muse that guides fiction writers, and claimed the Germans tortured Jim by ripping his toenails off with a pair of pliers. The Kentucky right-hander didn't appreciate the bogus reporting. He said, "Those stories don't help me at home. I've got a lot of German friends there."

All counted, Jim spent half a year as a POW in Germany. The conditions behind the Nazi fences were close to unbearable but the strong-willed Blackburn endured the best he could. When his already-slight frame withered to 100 pounds due to a lack of nutrition, he couldn't take it anymore and lost consciousness. Blackburn recalled his POW experience, saying, "My weight dropped to 100 pounds. I froze my feet and finally passed out. They put me in a German hospital, not as a patient, but to work around." Shortly thereafter the camp was liberated by U.S. troops. Of his rescue, Jim said, "The Americans came and I was never so glad to see anyone in my life. They shipped me to a field hospital, then flew me to Paris. For awhile they fed me eight meals a day to fatten me up."

W	L	PCT	G	GS	CG	IP	H	BB	SO	SHO	ERA
0	2	.000	18	0	0	36	46	16	11	0	5.50

Ewell Blackwell, *Pitcher*

Of all the players who had their careers interrupted to World War II, Cecil Travis and Dominic DiMaggio are perhaps the only men who lost more than Blackwell. These three men could have been household names, even Hall of Famers, had their careers not been shortened by a war. Travis was an exceptional hitting shortstop, far superior to Pee Wee Reese or Phil Rizzuto, and Dom DiMaggio was a terrific all-around talent. But Ewell "The Whip" Blackwell was a remarkable pitcher for a handful of years just after the war, and he missed three prime seasons to service under Uncle Sam.

Blackwell threw his first pitch in the majors during the 1942 baseball season. After the season, he entered the United States Army and missed the next three years to the war effort. Ewell was widely regarded as the game's finest pitching prospect when players began entering the service. Despite his lofty billing as a "can't-miss prospect," Blackwell desired to serve his country. His initial plan was to enter the Army Air Corps as a pilot, but with his physical stature — a wiry six feet, six inches — he was unable to enter the flying corps. So Ewell built planes during the winter of 1942 since he was rejected by the Army Air Corps.

Although his beanpole stature kept him from flying planes, the Whip entered the army as an infantryman. He was initially stationed at Fort Benning where he was a two-sport star for the installation, showcasing his talents on the ball diamond as well as the hard court. He was shipped out to the European Theatre with the 17th Division of the 3rd Army and was stationed at Augsburg. In Germany, Ewell became the sensation of service ball. White Sox second baseman Don Kolloway said that Blackwell was one of the best pitchers he had ever seen. Blackwell was enjoying his service ball fame in Germany but still longed for his return home, saying, "I am a mess sergeant but when I finally get home I have a wife who will cook me plenty of roast beef."

The Whip saw combat action with the 3rd Army from March 12 until the German surrender. Of the surrender, Ewell said, "It was one of the happiest days of my life because I knew we could begin playing a little ball and would start home." Even though he had become a legend in the service ranks, Blackwell wasn't convinced it would translate to the major leagues. He said, "I believe I am better than before I entered the army, although maybe my record here just looks good because most service batters try to murder the ball and knock it out of the small parks."

Blackwell sold himself short; he returned to Cincinnati as one of the greatest pitchers in the majors. He paced the National League with six shutouts on a 2.46 ERA for the offensively challenged Reds. He had his breakout year at the major league level in 1947, as a 24-year-old, by leading all pitchers with 22 wins. He also led the NL in complete games and strikeouts, and finished just three whiffs behind Bob Feller for tops in all of baseball. After three years of extensive use in service ball and two spectacular years with the Reds, Blackwell's arm gave out in 1948. He soldiered on with less than his best stuff, enjoying a successful comeback season in 1950; Ewell posted a 17–15 record with 188 strikeouts, just three behind league leader Warren Spahn (in thirty fewer innings of work). He went 16–15 with the inept Reds in 1951, as their team batting average of .248 was easily the worst in the NL. The Whip was dealt to the Yankees in 1952 and pitched remarkable baseball down the stretch: a 0.56 ERA. His arm went limp again in 1953, and he played one final season with the Kansas City Athletics in 1955 before retiring.

The legend of Ewell "The Whip" Blackwell is one for the what-if series. What if the war hadn't interrupted his career? Those three years that he baffled service ballplayers with his sidearm delivery were possibly the finest years his arm ever had. Three years lost to the war and several exceptional years at the major league level with an awful organization have buried the memory of Ewell Blackwell. But to many who saw him throw, he was one of the finest.

W	L	PCT	G	GS	CG	IP	H	BB	SO	SHO	ERA
82	78	.513	236	169	69	1,322	1,150	562	839	16	3.30

Louis Nathan "Buddy" Blair, *Third Base*

Buddy Blair was Connie Mack's everyday third baseman during the 1942 baseball season. Despite his title as a regular in 1942, Blair never again played major league baseball after his service hitch had completed. He missed three years to service in the armed forces, as the portside-swinging hot corner man was stationed at Monroe, Louisiana.

G	R	H	2B	3B	HR	RBI	BB	SO	SB	AVG	Slug
137	48	135	26	8	5	66	30	30	1	.279	.397

Garnett E. Blair, *Pitcher*

Blair joined the Homestead Grays in 1942, and the following year the Pennsylvania native was inducted into the military for service during World War II. Garnett returned to the Grays in 1945 and went 7–1 after two years in the army. Once the color barrier was broken, he played one year in the minor leagues but failed to reach the majors.

(1942–1948): Homestead Grays

Edward James Blake, *Pitcher*

Blake had worn eyeglasses throughout his life and took his spectacles with him when he was inducted into the army. However, Uncle Sam ordered him to shelve the glasses and outfitted him with his first pair of contact lenses. With a new set of eyewear Blake was shipped overseas with his infantry regiment. While fighting during the Philippine Liberation campaign, Blake was wounded in action and awarded the Purple Heart. Ed made his debut with the 1951 Reds and last pitched for the Kansas City A's of 1957.

W	L	PCT	G	GS	CG	IP	H	BB	SO	SHO	ERA
0	0	—	9	0	0	9	15	4	1	0	8.00

John Louis Blatnik, *Outfield*

Like most Native Americans that played baseball, Johnny was often listed as "Chief" Blatnik rather than his given name of John. An infielder as an amateur, Johnny was moved to the pasture by the Phillies while he was toiling in the minors. Just before his induction into the army, Blatnik made a successful transition to the outfield. An article in the *Charleston Daily Mail* read, "Those who know John 'The Chief' Blatnik are sure he'll be just as successful in his change from a ballplayer to a soldier as he was in his switch from third base to center field."

G	R	H	2B	3B	HR	RBI	BB	SO	SB	AVG	Slug
138	59	113	27	8	6	46	40	83	3	.253	.389

Robert Garnett "Buddy" Blattner, *Second Base*

Before he was summoned for military duty, Blattner had a career batting average of .043. During his three-year service stint, he was eager to get back to the majors to elevate that weak mark. During the 1941 and 1942 offseason, Buddy worked a defense job for a small arms plant in St. Louis. He was asked to do more in 1943 when he was inducted into the service. Buddy was shipped overseas and played service ball in the South Pacific in 1945 with a team managed by Mace Brown that put on exhibitions at various posts, including Saipan and Tinian.

Blattner played at the major league level upon his discharge and was able to raise his numbers. However, despite an adequate major league career, Buddy is best known as a play-by-play man. He became a broadcaster for the Angels, and writer Ross Newhan referred to him as "the Angels' answer to Vin Scully." Buddy also had the daunting task of broadcasting the *Game of the Week* with colorful personality Dizzy Dean. Buddy said, "Working with Dean was like taking a pledge to poverty. I'm just glad I'm still alive." He ended his broadcasting career as the original voice of the Kansas City Royals, tutoring 2007 Ford C. Frick Award winner Denny Matthews.

G	R	H	2B	3B	HR	RBI	BB	SO	SB	AVG	Slug
272	112	176	34	8	16	84	102	96	18	.247	.384

Seymour "Cy" Block, *Third Base*

Block played sparingly with the Cubs over the course of three years at the major league level. He saw action with the baby bears in 1942, 1945 and 1946. He missed two and a half years to service in the U.S. Coast Guard.

G	R	H	2B	3B	HR	RBI	BB	SO	SB	AVG	Slug
17	9	16	1	1	0	5	7	3	2	.302	.358

James Henry Bloodworth, *Second Base*

Bloodworth served as a weapons instructor in the United States Army during World War II, which interrupted his ball diamond pursuits. A light-hitting second baseman, Jimmy began his major league career with the 1937 Washington Senators. He platooned with veteran Buddy Myer but took over the regular job in 1940. The Tigers made a deal for Jimmy after the 1941 baseball season and he finished second on the team in home runs behind Rudy York. He was inducted into the army shortly after the conclusion of the 1943 baseball season and was stationed at Fort Leonardwood, Missouri, in the 37th Engineer Training Battalion. He returned to the Tigers after his discharge and finished his career with stops in Pittsburgh, Cincinnati and Philadelphia.

G	R	H	2B	3B	HR	RBI	BB	SO	SB	AVG	Slug
1,002	347	874	160	20	62	451	202	407	19	.248	.358

Milton Francis Bocek, *Outfield*

By the time World War II broke out, Bocek had made the transition to managing. He played for the White Sox in the mid-1930s but by 1940 he was managing in the minors at Gastonia. One of the first ballplayers drafted into service, Milt was taken before Pearl Harbor was bombed. Due to his age, he was released on the "Over 28" basis, but after the catastrophe on the Hawaiian Islands Milt returned to military duty.

Milt was stationed at Camp Custer where he served in the 10th Infantry and managed their baseball club to the division championship. From Custer, Bocek was transferred to Camp McCoy, Wisconsin, an installation known mostly for its cold-weather training. Senators legend Cecil Travis trained there before he was shipped out to Europe. While stationed at Camp McCoy, Milt managed a baseball team while his military duties were in the MP Corps.

G	R	H	2B	3B	HR	RBI	BB	SO	SB	AVG	Slug
30	6	16	2	0	1	6	9	11	0	.267	.350

Joseph Edward "Eddie" Bockman, *Third Base*

Sports kept Bockman from combat action during World War II. He was drafted into the navy and was sent to San Pedro for military training in mine sweeping. After training, Eddie's unit was due to be sent overseas. When they were packing their ship for deployment, Eddie saw a group of troops loading sporting gear into a station wagon. He asked the soldiers what they were up to and was informed they played for an installation basketball team. A natural athlete, Bockman asked if he could join. He was told that if he made good, they'd get him out of his deployment, and that's precisely what happened.

Bockman was transferred from his mine-sweeping unit to the navy's athletic program. He was sent to Bainbridge for physical instructor's school and returned to the West Coast to play service sports at the San Diego Naval Training Center. Eddie was a star on the basketball team as well as the baseball squad. His time in the navy was akin to years in the minors. Bockman said, "We had a lot of major league baseball players on our team those two years. Getting to play with them did a lot for my confidence." After his discharge, Eddie had a brief trial with the 1946 Yankees but the majority of his playing time came later with the Pirates.

G	R	H	2B	3B	HR	RBI	BB	SO	SB	AVG	Slug
249	54	109	16	4	11	56	46	87	5	.230	.350

John Edward Bolling, *First Base*

Jack served as a reserve first baseman with the Phillies in 1939. He spelled Gus Suhr in his only year in Philadelphia. He didn't return to the majors until 1944, when the depleted Dodgers summoned him up to the parent club. Bolling rocketed off to a tremendous start in 1944 but was inducted into the military with a .351 batting average after 56 games.

G	R	H	2B	3B	HR	RBI	BB	SO	SB	AVG	Slug
125	48	107	25	1	4	38	25	14	6	.313	.427

Donald Raymond Bollweg, *First Base*

Known as "Boll Weevil" by Yankees skipper Casey Stengel, Bollweg was an adequate first baseman who never really got his chance at the major league level. The Cardinals, Yankees and Athletics all gave Don a look at the highest level but he failed to register 500 at-bats. Before Don made his major league debut, he served in the Army Air Corps at the Sioux Falls Airfield and played service ball with longtime Dodgers coach Monty Basgall.

G	R	H	2B	3B	HR	RBI	BB	SO	SB	AVG	Slug
195	62	110	22	7	11	53	60	68	2	.243	.396

Anthony Thomas "Nino" Bongiovanni, *Outfield*

Nino played two years at the major league level with the Reds in the late 1930s. His last major league at-bat came in the 1939 World Series when he was used as a pinch-hitter. During the course of his career, Bongiovanni was often joshed about his name. With a surname that was difficult to squeeze in a box score, writers often had fun with Nino. One newspaper headline read, "Baseball writers to petition outfielder to shorten his name." During the war, Nino served with the United States Army Air Corps.

G	R	H	2B	3B	HR	RBI	BB	SO	SB	AVG	Slug
68	17	43	7	0	0	16	9	8	0	.259	.301

Henry John "Zeke" Bonura, *First Base*

Weighing 210 pounds, Bonura was a stout man with the reputation for being an "all-hit, no-field" first baseman. He made his major league debut with the Chicago White Sox in 1934 and played with the Pale Hose through 1937. In his rookie campaign, Big Zeke hit .302 and paced the club with 27 homers, 110 RBIs and 64 walks. His numbers dipped slightly in 1935, but he enjoyed a monster year in 1936. Big Zeke posted a remarkable line of 39 doubles, 12 home runs, 137 RBIs and a .330 batting average that year. In 1937, his batting average reached new heights, as he hit the apple at a .345 clip. Despite his amazing feats with lumber in his grasp, the White Sox dealt him to the Senators the following season and replaced Zeke with a better fielder in Joe Kuhel. From there, his career became nomadic until World War II broke out.

Bonura was one of the first major league players to enlist in the army during the war. At the age of 32, he knew all too well that his baseball career would probably be over when the war concluded. His initial assignment was at Camp Shelby, Mississippi, where he served on the installation's recreational branch. Zeke didn't serve too long, as the good-natured, personable fellow was discharged late in 1941 because the draft age was lowered, allowing the 33-year-old Zeke to return to baseball if he so desired.

Given his autumn discharge, it was too late for Zeke to return for the 1941 baseball season. The game would never again be graced with the presence of Bonura, as the big man decided to re-enter the army in January of 1942. Bonura said, "It will be bullets for the Japanese instead of big league baseball for me." He was recalled to Camp Shelby, where he served briefly before departing overseas.

Bonura was sent to North Africa where he remained in the army's recreation branch. He set up numerous sporting events for soldiers overseas, ranging from baseball and football games to various other athletics. While serving in North Africa, he taught soldiers and citizens of different countries the art of playing baseball. He had a simple answer for world peace, saying, "Teach those people in Europe to play baseball instead of to kill."

As the army's sports director in the Mediterranean Theatre, Zeke stated, "I was the Judge Landis of Europe." He attracted many allied soldiers, and he was informally invited to England to teach baseball after the war when a couple of British officers were impressed by his teaching abilities. Bonura reached the rank of master sergeant by 1944 and was awarded a certificate of merit for promoting athletics in the army. When the war concluded, Bonura was in his late thirties and too old to make a return to the major leagues.

G	R	H	2B	3B	HR	RBI	BB	SO	SB	AVG	Slug
917	600	1,099	232	29	119	703	404	180	19	.307	.487

Raymond Otis Boone, *Shortstop*

Ray, the father of All-Star catcher Bob Boone and the granddad of former big league infielders Aaron and Bret Boone, was a solid power-hitting shortstop at the major league level. Before he made his major league debut, Boone served in the military during World War II. After his discharge, Ray spent two years in the minors before the Indians gave him a look during their championship season of 1948. The Cleveland front office wanted the young Boone to supplant player/manager Lou Boudreau at short, but the fans, who idolized Lou, staged a bit of a revolt when the prospect of some kid replacing their hero arose. The inevitable occurred in 1950 when Ray hit over .300 and Boudreau failed to bat .270. Lou was sent to Boston and Boone took over at short.

G	R	H	2B	3B	HR	RBI	BB	SO	SB	AVG	Slug
1,373	645	1,260	162	46	151	737	608	463	21	.275	.429

Melvin Edward Bosser, *Pitcher*

A war-era pitcher, Bosser was a 31-year-old rookie when he made his debut with the 1945 Reds. Mel, who had spent the previous summer in the Army Air Corps, impressed Reds skipper Bill McKechnie after his discharge. The Hall of Fame manager used Bosser as a starting pitcher in a few contests despite the fact that he never pitched above Class D ball. Nicknamed "The Tennessee Rambler," Mel won his only two decisions but struggled finding the strike zone and wasn't asked back in 1946.

W	L	PCT	G	GS	CG	IP	H	BB	SO	SHO	ERA
2	0	1.000	7	2	0	16	9	17	3	0	3.38

Lyman Wesley Bostock Sr., *First Base/Outfield*

Father of former Minnesota Twins batting star Lyman Bostock Jr., the elder Bostock was there when his son was murdered by his ex-wife in 1978. Lyman Senior was an all-star in the Negro Leagues before the war. After three-plus years in the army, he had added weight and lost much of his mobility. It took him some time to round back into baseball shape, and after the color barrier was broken, he spent several years playing in the minor leagues.

(1938–1949): Birmingham Black Barons, Brooklyn Royal Giants, Chicago American Giants and New York Cubans

John Charles Bottarini, *Catcher*

A minor league veteran, Bottarini was summoned by the Cubs for a cup of coffee in 1937, his only major league action. The Cubs had Gabby Hartnett, who hit .354, behind the dish that year and his chief substitute, Ken O'Dea, was also a .300 hitter. John's presence was needed only to warm up pitchers. After his sojourn in the Windy City, John returned to the bushes where he would remain throughout his playing days.

Bottarini looked at basic training in the army as something he had to do. He said that boot camp "is just like a baseball camp only you can't hold out against coming here." The aging catcher liked to keep his fellow soldiers engaged in the usual aspects of life while they trained. He said of basic training, "One meets all kinds of fellows here and from all walks of life. We bunk seven in a room and have our powwows and singing nights."

After boot camp, Bottarini was stationed at Fort Bliss, Texas. In the fall of 1943 he was promoted to corporal and the following year he was reassigned to Miami Beach. At the sunny Florida locale, John attended non-commissioned officer's school. After his graduation from Miami Beach, John was sent to Kirtland Field, New Mexico. While stationed in the southwestern state, John's wife gave birth to twin sons. Later in life, at Jemez Springs, New Mexico, he and a son were fishing on vacation when their boat capsized and both men drowned.

G	R	H	2B	3B	HR	RBI	BB	SO	SB	AVG	Slug
26	3	11	3	0	1	7	5	10	0	.275	.425

Grover Bill Bowers, *Outfield*

Bowers had a cup of coffee with the 1949 White Sox. The club had a modest outfield at best, but they also had a young Slugging recruit named Gus Zernial who was well ahead of Billy on the depth chart. Bowers only saw action in that one season and was sent back to the bushes. He missed minor league seasoning time to service during World War II.

G	R	H	2B	3B	HR	RBI	BB	SO	SB	AVG	Slug
26	5	15	2	1	0	6	4	5	1	.192	.244

Stewart Cole Bowers, *Pitcher*

Although "Doc" was kept on the Red Sox roster for three years in the mid–1930s, he only appeared in 15 major league games. Stew, who was a graduate of Gettysburg College, last pitched at the highest level in 1937. When the war broke out, his major league career was behind him. He served in the armed forces during World War II.

W	L	PCT	G	GS	CG	IP	H	BB	SO	SHO	ERA
2	1	.667	15	2	1	30	36	19	5	0	4.50

Charles James Bowles, *Pitcher*

Charlie Bowles was inducted into the Army Air Corps after he made two complete-game starts for Connie Mack in 1943. He missed the entire 1944 season to service in the armed forces and returned late in the 1945 campaign. He posted an 0–3 record for the 1945 Athletics, his last stint at the highest level.

W	L	PCT	G	GS	CG	IP	H	BB	SO	SHO	ERA
1	4	.200	10	6	3	51	52	27	17	0	4.41

Cloyd Victor Boyer, *Pitcher*

Cloyd, whose brothers Ken and Clete were All-Star third basemen, was just a pup when World War II broke out. Major league baseball was a chaotic enterprise during the war and teams lifted rocks to find talent wherever possible. Cloyd was just 16 years old when the Cardinals signed him to a contract. A schoolboy pitcher, Boyer gave up the mound work late in the war when he joined the navy after high school graduation. His service time was brief given the latter stages of the war when he came of age. Cloyd made his major league debut in 1949.

W	L	PCT	G	GS	CG	IP	H	BB	SO	SHO	ERA
20	23	.465	112	48	13	394	393	218	198	3	4.75

Herbert "Doc" Bracken, *Pitcher*

It's not known why Bracken was nicknamed "Doc," but the tall right-hander from St. Louis had some success in the Negro

Leagues. He pitched for the St. Louis Stars before he was inducted into the U.S. Navy in 1944 during the Second World War. Doc served at the Great Lakes Naval Training Station his first year in the navy and lost a tough 1–0 contest to Hall of Famer Mickey Cochrane's club. Shipped overseas to Hawaii, Doc played service ball on the islands before he returned to the States and pitched two seasons with the Cleveland Buckeyes.

(1940–1947): Cleveland Buckeyes and St. Louis Stars

William D. Bradford, *Pitcher*

Bradford served with the United States Navy during the war. He had yet to make his major league debut by the time he left for the service and it would take him many years after his discharge before he took the hill in a major league game. The A's had relocated to Kansas City by the time Bill was summoned, and he appeared in one game for Lou Boudreau's 1956 Athletics.

W	L	PCT	G	GS	CG	IP	H	BB	SO	SHO	ERA
0	0	.000	1	0	0	2	2	1	0	0	9.00

Henry Victor Bradford, *Outfield*

A University of Alabama football star, Bradford gave up the gridiron for a shot at major league baseball. Vic's baseball career consisted of six games with the 1943 Giants. The natural athlete missed the next three years to service in the United States Navy.

G	R	H	2B	3B	HR	RBI	BB	SO	SB	AVG	Slug
6	1	1	0	0	0	1	1	1	0	.200	.200

George Washington Bradley, *Reserve*

Named after America's first president, Bradley had a cup of coffee with the Browns in 1946. The 32-year-old rookie spent the previous summers in the military at ages when he would have been in his prime.

G	R	H	2B	3B	HR	RBI	BB	SO	SB	AVG	Slug
4	2	2	1	0	0	3	0	1	0	.167	.250

George Thomas Bradshaw, *Reserve*

Bradshaw served with the United States Marine Corps during World War II. The North Carolina native didn't begin his pro career in the game until after his military discharge. His only big league action came with the 1952 Senators.

G	R	H	2B	3B	HR	RBI	BB	SO	SB	AVG	Slug
10	3	5	2	0	0	6	1	2	0	.217	.304

Robert Randall Bragan, *Utilityman*

Doc Prothro, skipper of the 1940 Philadelphia Phillies, used Bragan as the everyday shortstop in 1940 and 1941. With a young Danny Murtaugh looking for playing time in 1942, Bobby began shuffling between positions that season. Showing supreme versatility, Bragan even caught twenty-two games in 1942. The Dodgers picked up Bragan for the 1943 season and used him primarily as a backstop. He played out the entire 1944 year but was summoned for his induction physical after the season. Bobby requested service in the navy and spent one year in the colors. He received his discharge in time to participate in 1946 spring training.

G	R	H	2B	3B	HR	RBI	BB	SO	SB	AVG	Slug
597	136	456	62	12	15	172	110	117	12	.240	.309

Albert Brancato, *Shortstop*

A scrappy little infielder, Brancato signed his first contract while he was still in high school. When his high school chums were walking the floor during their graduation, Brancato was off training with the Athletics. After Al was farmed out to the minors for experience, Mack summoned him to the big leagues in 1939 for his first taste of the major leagues. He and Bill Lillard shared the shortstop job in 1940 but the position was all his in 1941. Only Hall of Famers Lou Boudreau and Luke Appling started more games at short in the American League that year than Brancato. When his career looked on the proper track, he was inducted into the military for service during World War II.

One of the first Athletics inducted into the service, Brancato joined the navy just a month after Pearl Harbor was bombed. He went to a recruiting station where Connie Mack saw him off, but it would be awhile before Al left the States. He worked at the recruiting station as a storekeeper second class, signing up young sailors for the navy until the *USS Boston* was ready for duty. Assigned aboard the *USS Boston*, Brancato was shipped overseas to the Pacific Theatre and made a stop at Hawaii that changed his military duties. He said, "One day I got off the ship in Hawaii just to go ashore and I ran into Walt Masterson. Next thing I knew, I was off the ship. Masterson told his commander at the sub base about me and he made a few calls that got me off the *Boston*."

Able to play some service ball with Masterson on the Hawaiian Islands, Brancato's navy duties were that of a storekeeper second class—same as the recruiting station. In between duties with the navy, Al played baseball on the islands. He participated in an Army-Navy World Series played at Hawaii and had an unexpected meeting with two soldiers he knew from back home. Brancato said, "I met my two brothers going into Hawaii. One was with a submarine unit while the other was with the Seabees. So the three of us met in Hawaii and had our picture taken, which went all over the country."

After he said goodbye to his brothers, Brancato went on a baseball exhibition tour with Johnny Mize around the South Pacific. They put on games for the soldiers at various islands until Brancato was assigned to a base at Tinian. He remained there for the duration. When he was sent back home, he had a layover in Hawaii in the late summer of 1945 and was asked to stay on the islands and play baseball, but Al declined the offer because he had been away from home since 1942. He came back at the end of the 1945 season and couldn't do much to help the woeful A's, who finished dead last thirty-five games out of first place.

G	R	H	2B	3B	HR	RBI	BB	SO	SB	AVG	Slug
282	117	199	37	11	4	80	96	92	5	.214	.290

Norman Downs Branch, *Pitcher*

Branch pitched for two years at the major league level with the Yankees, seldom finding the strike zone. The Spokane native missed three full years to service in the U.S. Coast Guard, and upon his discharge never returned to the Major Leagues.

W	L	PCT	G	GS	CG	IP	H	BB	SO	SHO	ERA
5	2	.714	37	0	0	63	55	42	41	0	3.71

William George Brandt, *Pitcher*

Little Bill Brandt pitched three years with the Pirates before the war and didn't pitch a single inning after it. A serviceable long arm out of the bullpen, Brandt served with the United States Navy and played service ball with Mickey Cochrane's powerhouse Great Lakes squad.

W	L	PCT	G	GS	CG	IP	H	BB	SO	SHO	ERA
5	3	.625	34	7	1	80	85	27	21	0	3.60

Alpha Eugene Brazle, *Pitcher*

A fixture in the Cardinals pitching staff of the late 1940s and early 1950s, "Cotton" pitched in only thirteen games prior to the war. He showed immense promise in those thirteen games, however, with a remarkable 1.53 ERA. Shortly after the close of the 1943 baseball season, Cotton was inducted into the armed forces at Jefferson Barracks with fellow Redbird Harry Walker. Unlike many pitchers, Brazle came back from the war just fine. He fashioned a 3.29 ERA in 1946 and led the club in ERA during the 1947 season.

W	L	PCT	G	GS	CG	IP	H	BB	SO	SHO	ERA
97	64	.602	441	117	47	1,375	1,387	492	554	7	3.31

William Robertson Breckinridge, *Pitcher*

A Dartmouth law school student, Breckinridge made it clear to A's skipper Connie Mack that baseball was rather low on his to-do list. Bill wanted to work in court but Mack thought he had enough talent to stick in the majors. Bill did throw a no-hitter while at Dartmouth and looked decent in his debut. Bill said about his first major league game: "It was like pitching in a World Series to me." But the law school student valued his education more than his ball diamond work and became a bit of a target for his teammates.

Breckinridge's only big league action came with the 1929 Athletics of Foxx, Simmons, Grove, Dykes and Cochrane that won the World Series. Connie Mack was known to be partial to college kids and he gave Bill a hefty $5,000 bonus to sign. After the World Series, A's catcher Mickey Cochrane handed Bill what he called "the bench-warming prize" for the highest-paid dead weight on a roster. Bill signed a $5,000 contract for the season, and when added to his $5,000 bonus, his season's take rose even higher when he was given a $5,600 cut of the World Series money. Bill only pitched ten innings and had an 8.10 ERA. He quit the game and finished his education. During World War II, Bill served in the armed forces as a commission officer.

W	L	PCT	G	GS	CG	IP	H	BB	SO	SHO	ERA
0	0	—	3	1	0	10	10	16	2	0	8.10

James Ehrenfeld Brideweser, *Utility Infielder*

A natural shortstop, Brideweser was a journeyed major leaguer who backed up Phil Rizzuto, Chico Carrasquel and Harvey Kuenn. Just a teenager during the war, Jim served at the end of the war following his high school graduation. He was able to attend college on the GI Bill where he was noticed by scouts.

G	R	H	2B	3B	HR	RBI	BB	SO	SB	AVG	Slug
329	79	156	22	6	1	50	63	77	6	.252	.311

Thomas Jefferson Davis Bridges, *Pitcher*

One of the greatest pitchers not in the Hall of Fame, Bridges was arguably the best American League pitcher of his day. He is widely regarded as possessing the greatest curveball of his time and may have snapped off the best breaking balls ever thrown by any pitcher, regardless the era. A slight hurler, standing at 5'10" and weighing just over 150 pounds, Tommy didn't quite resemble the bulky hurlers of modern times. However, he was a durable star for Detroit, guiding the club to the 1934 World Series with 22 wins and posting 21 victories in 1935 and a league-best 23 in 1936. Tommy also paced the American League in strikeouts in both 1935 and 1936.

Bridges was 36 years old when he was drafted into the army after the 1943 baseball season. He was inducted at Fort Sheridan and took his basic training with Pittsburgh Pirates outfielder Maurice Van Robays. After basic training, Tommy was stationed at Camp Crowder. During an army furlough, he attended the 1944 World Series, which pitted the two St. Louis franchises against one another. While in the stands, dressed in his army duds, Tommy caught a foul ball to the applause of his fellow spectators. He received his discharge late in the 1945 baseball season, when he collected his second-to-last win and appeared in that season's World Series.

W	L	PCT	G	GS	CG	IP	H	BB	SO	SHO	ERA
194	138	.584	424	362	200	2,827	2,675	1,192	1,674	32	3.57

Leland Victor "Lou" Brissie, *Pitcher*

One of the most distinguished war heroes to have played in the major leagues, Lou Brissie overcame extraordinary odds to make the grade as a professional athlete. The severe wounds he suffered in battle would have been enough for most men to lie down and resign themselves to the uncompromising whims of fate, but not Brissie. He refused to view himself as handicapped and fought to reach his dream. With a leg encased by a nine-pound brace to protect his wounds, Brissie made the grade and pitched in the majors for seven seasons. The great Ted Williams once said, "If he had two good legs, he would have been against the law."

Brissie had yet to reach the major leagues when he was inducted into service for World War II. After basic training, Brissie went to airborne school and became a paratrooper with the 88th Infantry Regiment. As a member of one of Uncle Sam's finest fighting forces, Brissie was destined to be shipped overseas. He received orders for assignment to the European Theatre and combat was just around the corner. Brissie jumped into the Appenine Mountain regions of Italy in late 1944 and was severely wounded in action. On December 7, 1944, the Germans wiped out Lou's entire patrol—excluding the southpaw, who was wounded with extensive damage done to his legs. A shell went off near Lou's feet and he was forced to drag himself to a creek to wait for help.

Once Lou was rescued, the lengthy process of mending his tattered body began. Dr. Wilbur K. Brubaker operated on Lou's legs in Naples after Brissie demanded that doctors not amputate. During consultations with physicians, Lou was told he'd never be the same, that if his legs remained, he'd forever walk with a limp. But he also knew that without his legs, his dreams of playing major league baseball would be obsolete. So Dr. Brubaker began the surgeries. All the muscle and tendons in Lou's left leg were gone and fractured bones had to be knitted back together. After his first series of operations, Brissie wrote a letter home to writer Scoop Latimer detailing his injuries. Brissie wrote that he had been struck in twenty places by shell fragments, had a broken left leg, two broken feet, and suffered wounds to both arms and shoulders. But he ended the note to Latimer by writing, "I'll play ball again, but it will be quite a while. I want to play ball. If God lets me, I'll play it too. That's my ambition."

The road to ambition was a rocky one for Brissie. His aching, broken body could not be shrugged off. But never was a man more determined to do anything than Lou was to make the majors. After he returned home, it would take more months of recovery before he could walk to a pitcher's mound. With his bulky leg brace, Lou had to completely rework his mechanics. Lou said, "I used to rear back and push off my leg. Now I have to pivot off it."

With many hours of practice while relearning how to pitch, Brissie decided he'd give Connie Mack a look at his progress. He had a showcase in training camp for Mack in 1947. The great gentleman of baseball said, "If determination can do it, I know he'll make good. I'll never forget how he looked last summer. He had just undergone an operation and was about to undergo another. He was on crutches and I thought, 'Poor boy, he'll never be able to pitch again.' But crutches and all, he could not stay away from baseball." Brissie was determined to make it, not only to prove something to himself, but to fulfill a wish of his departed father. While fighting his way back, Lou said, "It was my father's greatest wish that I pitch in the big leagues — and for Connie Mack. I can't let him down."

One of the greatest human interest stories in America during 1947, Brissie was able to make it back to baseball. Connie Mack, who remained loyal to the young lad, farmed him out to the minors to get experience against live competition. While pitching in the Sally League, Lou struck out 17 batters in a game. With that small sample of success, Brissie wasn't overjoyed. He'd get that way only after he reached the majors. The call came late that season when Mack brought him up to Philadelphia. Mack did everything he could to support Brissie, even comparing him to Lefty Grove, which would help the confidence of any young pitcher. He started one game for the A's in 1947 and the next season he won 14, followed by 16 in 1949. Lou Brissie had overcome the greatest odds and made his dreams come true despite staggering obstacles. He remains a hero for all ages.

W	L	PCT	G	GS	CG	IP	H	BB	SO	SHO	ERA
44	48	.478	234	93	45	898	867	451	436	2	4.07

John Albert Brittin, *Pitcher*

Before Brittin made his debut with the National League champion 1950 Phillies, he served in the U.S. Navy during World War II. A right-handed pitcher who battled control issues his entire career, John took his wild right arm to Uncle Sam for combat duty. Shipped overseas to the Pacific Theatre, Ensign Brittin was engaged in LST duty for ten months in the Okinawa Campaign. The battle veteran was discharged in 1945, and after a long stretch without watching a baseball game, no less playing in one, Brittin tried to do too much when he returned to the game. He said, "I had a bad arm. After I got out of the navy I tried to pitch too soon and pulled a shoulder tendon."

W	L	PCT	G	GS	CG	IP	H	BB	SO	SHO	ERA
0	0	—	6	0	0	8	7	9	6	0	6.75

Sigmund Theodore Broskie, *Catcher*

One of the many catchers employed by the Braves in 1940, Sig Broskie had his only major league stint that season. During World War II, the stocky catcher joined the U.S. Navy. Broskie regarded as a warm, genial, easy-to-like type of guy, leading Dick Hudson to describe him by writing, "Sig called almost everybody 'Chopper' for some unexplained reason. He was the life of the party with a never-ending flow of stories and experiences. He never met anyone who was a stranger for more than five minutes."

G	R	H	2B	3B	HR	RBI	BB	SO	SB	AVG	Slug
11	1	6	1	0	0	4	1	2	0	.273	.318

Joseph John Brovia, *Reserve*

Brovia had a long playing career in the professional ranks but only an 18-at-bat trial at the major league level. A native of California, Joe opted to stay out on the West Coast and play in the PCL, where he starred for 16 years. Regarded as a good fielder but weak hitter, Brovia's military duties during World War II were in the coast artillery.

G	R	H	2B	3B	HR	RBI	BB	SO	SB	AVG	Slug
21	0	2	0	0	0	4	1	6	0	.111	.111

Alton Leo Brown, *Pitcher*

Alton "The Deacon" Brown played baseball only as a recreational diversion before the war. While he served in the United States Army and played service ball against some pro ballplayers, Brown got the idea that he could do this for a living. Following his army discharge, he signed his first pro contract and eventually made the majors with the 1951 Senators.

W	L	PCT	G	GS	CG	IP	H	BB	SO	SHO	ERA
0	0	—	7	0	0	12	14	12	7	0	9.00

Barney Brown, *Pitcher*

Considered one of the top southpaws in the Negro Leagues in the years before World War II, Brown was noted for his expert control of the screwball. A four-time All-Star, Barney had a fine pitching career in black baseball but was a legend in Mexico. He won 19 games south of the border in 1941 before he returned stateside in 1942. Brown was summoned for military service in 1943 but was only on limited service and pitched throughout most of the war with the Philadelphia Stars. He returned to Mexico in the 1950s and then tried his luck in the minors in 1952 and 1953 with solid results, but his age prevented him from making the majors.

(1931–1953): Philadelphia Stars, New York Black Yankees and Cuban Stars

Hector Harold "Hal" Brown, *Pitcher*

A solid pitcher at the major league level who spent the bulk of his career with the Baltimore Orioles, Brown served in the Army Air Corps before he signed his first pro contract. After he was discharged, Hal, who played some service ball, signed on the dotted line and embarked on a successful career in baseball.

W	L	PCT	G	GS	CG	IP	H	BB	SO	SHO	ERA
85	92	.480	358	211	47	1,680	1,677	389	710	13	3.81

James Roberson Brown, *Utility Infielder*

Brown became Leo Durocher's double-play partner in his rookie season of 1937 and hit 73 points higher than his teammate. He played with the Cardinals through 1943, rarely striking out each season. In 1938, for instance, Jimmy fanned only nine times all year. He led the NL in at-bats during the 1939 season and only whiffed eighteen times in 645 trips to the plate. Brown was in his early thirties and on the downward slope of his career when he left for the military. He played for and managed the Memphis Ferrying Command's baseball club while in the service.

G	R	H	2B	3B	HR	RBI	BB	SO	SB	AVG	Slug
890	465	980	146	42	9	319	231	110	39	.279	.352

Mace Stanley Brown, *Pitcher*

Brown began his major league career with the 1935 Pittsburgh Pirates and became one of the game's first stellar relief pitchers. He paced the National League in saves during the 1937 season and appeared in more games than any other NL pitcher in 1938. Manager Pie Traynor experimented with Mace in the rotation during the 1939 season and again in 1940. Early in the 1941 season, Mace was dealt to the Dodgers where he suffered an ankle injury. Brooklyn soured on Mace and sent him to the Red Sox for the 1942 season. Boston skipper Joe Cronin used Brown exclusively out of the bullpen for two years—leading the American League in games pitched in 1943—before he was summoned by Uncle Sam.

When Mace Brown joined the colors, he was already 35 years old. Given his age, it seemed highly unlikely that he would be able to make a return to baseball after his discharge. Brown was commissioned a lieutenant and served in the Pacific Theatre, where he arranged sporting events for the navy. After his naval discharge, Mace spent one final year in the major leagues. He appeared in eighteen games for the AL champion Red Sox of 1946. He stayed in the Red Sox organization and served as a scout, with his most notable sign being Jim Rice.

W	L	PCT	G	GS	CG	IP	H	BB	SO	SHO	ERA
76	57	.571	387	55	18	1,075	1,125	388	435	3	3.47

Norman Ladelle Brown, *Pitcher*

Brown's major league career consisted of five games for the Athletics, dispersed over the course of two seasons in Philadelphia. He missed two full seasons to service in the armed forces and returned to pitch sparingly for the 1946 Athletics.

W	L	PCT	G	GS	CG	IP	H	BB	SO	SHO	ERA
0	1	.000	5	1	0	14	13	6	4	0	3.21

Willard Jessie Brown, *Outfield*

Recently inducted into the Baseball Hall of Fame, Brown was part of the large class of former Negro League players and executives elected a few years ago. His election was one of the more suspect. Brown had a trial in the major leagues with the 1947 Browns and his swing-happy approach was greatly exploited by pitchers. With his absence of plate discipline, Willard got by on raw power and an enhanced tools set, but many historians of black baseball believe he never fulfilled his potential. He was a fine defender, when he wanted to be, ran the bases well when it concerned him, and hit prodigious home runs, when he made contact.

Regarded as the Negro Leagues' top power hitter during the 1940s, Willard took the place of Josh Gibson when the legend began to slow down due to age and illness. Although Willard had sensational power, he was too raw and too often played the game in a lackadaisical manner. James A. Riley wrote that Willard "considered anything that left the pitcher's hand a strike." With that mindset, he swung at everything and had a modest on-base percentage. A member of the Kansas City Monarchs, Brown took his booming bat to the army during World War II. In the quartermaster's corps, Willard assisted in the Normandy Invasion, hauling ammunition and supplies to the troops on the frontlines. He was also tasked in guarding prisoners captured in battle.

After the fighting, Willard played some service ball and participated in the GI World Series where he had success against Reds star pitching prospect Ewell Blackwell. Mustered out of the service, Willard returned to the Monarchs and played with them in 1946 until the St. Louis Browns bought his contract. Major league pitchers took full advantage of Brown's swing-at-anything approach and he struggled mightily in his only stint in the majors. After the Browns cut him loose, he returned to Buck O'Neil's Monarchs and played with them into the 1950s. He would later have some success in the Texas League, but Willard's undoing was his carefree play. Often accused of playing only for large crowds, Brown's legacy is that of untapped potential.

(1935–1956): Kansas City Monarchs and St. Louis Browns (AL)

Earle Francis Brucker Jr., *Reserve*

Like his father, Earle played for the Philadelphia A's under legendary skipper Connie Mack. Brucker the elder had a much more substantial career, as Junior played in only two major league games. During the war, Brucker Jr. served in the U.S. Navy.

G	R	H	2B	3B	HR	RBI	BB	SO	SB	AVG	Slug
2	0	1	1	0	0	0	1	1	0	.167	.333

Walter Roy Bruner, *Pitcher*

Bruner's three years at the major league level were spent with a last-place team. Despite his less-than-stellar career numbers, he probably would have notched a victory had he played elsewhere. Roy was inducted into the service during the 1941 baseball season, the second Phillies player to follow Hugh Mulcahy into the service. Unlike his major league career, Bruner spent his military career with two different organizations, the Army Air Corps and the navy.

W	L	PCT	G	GS	CG	IP	H	BB	SO	SHO	ERA
0	7	.000	19	5	2	62	80	44	28	0	5.81

William Haron Bruton, *Outfield*

After the war the stolen base had become a lost art form. Men like George Case and Bill Werber tried to keep it alive but brawny bashing was the order of the day. When the Braves debuted speedy Bill Bruton, he played the game like Case and Werber and brought speed back to the diamond. The swift outfielder was late signing his first pro contract because he served in the military during World War II.

G	R	H	2B	3B	HR	RBI	BB	SO	SB	AVG	Slug
1,610	937	1,651	241	102	94	545	482	793	207	.273	.393

Allen "Lefty" Bryant Jr., *Pitcher*

Bryant grew up in Kansas City and played pro ball for his hometown Monarchs. The southpaw was regarded as a soft-tosser who got by on mixing speeds and throwing in a knuckleball. He left the Monarchs during World War II and served a few years in the U.S. Army.

(1937–1947): Kansas City Monarchs and Memphis Red Sox

John George Bucha, *Catcher*

Pitchers liked throwing to Johnny because his squatty body made for an ideal target behind the plate. Bucha had a brief career in the majors with the Tigers and Cardinals. During the war, Johnny served with the U.S. Navy, which interrupted his minor league career.

G	R	H	2B	3B	HR	RBI	BB	SO	SB	AVG	Slug
84	18	40	10	0	1	15	25	21	1	.205	.272

Nelson Edward Burbrink, *Catcher*

A well-respected man in baseball, Burbrink was a player/manager in his twenties while he played minor league ball before he made his major league debut. When Nels finally made the majors in 1955, he served as Bill Sarni's chief backup. Burbrink served in the U.S. Navy during the war. After his playing career, he was the chief scout of the New York Mets.

G	R	H	2B	3B	HR	RBI	BB	SO	SB	AVG	Slug
58	11	47	8	1	0	15	14	13	1	.276	.335

Selva Lewis "Lew" Burdette, *Pitcher*

Burdette was originally signed by the Yankees, but the Bronx Bombers gave up on Lew after a two-game trial in 1950. He never forgave the Yankees for quitting on him so soon and got a measure of revenge against them in the 1957 World Series. The hero of that affair, Burdette stood the great Yankee batters on their ears, winning three games and keeping his ERA below one. Before his major league heroics, Burdette, a borderline Hall of Famer, served in the armed forces during World War II. Just a young lad, he joined up after high school and served in the Air Force Cadet Program. The war would end before the young man from Nitro, West Virginia, would have to be shipped out.

W	L	PCT	G	GS	CG	IP	H	BB	SO	SHO	ERA
203	144	.585	626	373	158	3,068	3,186	628	1,074	33	3.66

Forrest Harrill "Smoky" Burgess, *Catcher*

The most underrated catcher of the 1950s, Burgess was a quality backstop for the Phillies, Reds and Pirates. In later years, Smoky would become an acclaimed bat off the bench and set numerous records for pinch-hitters. But before the chunky receiver from Caroleen, North Carolina, made his major league debut, he served in the armed forces during World War II. Just a teenager throughout the war, Smoky signed up after graduation and spent a year in the army at the end of the campaign.

G	R	H	2B	3B	HR	RBI	BB	SO	SB	AVG	Slug
1,691	485	1,318	230	33	126	673	477	270	13	.295	.446

William Max Burich, *Shortstop*

Burich lost three years to World War II and saw action with the Phillies in the two years before and after his induction. Bill hit .288 with the Phillies in 1942. He saw action at short and third base, and returned to Philadelphia in 1946 to play in a handful of games.

G	R	H	2B	3B	HR	RBI	BB	SO	SB	AVG	Slug
27	4	23	1	0	0	7	6	13	2	.284	.296

George Harvie Burpo, *Pitcher*

Burpo had a cup of coffee with the Reds right after the war. Never one to put too much stock in accuracy, George issued five walks in his two major league innings. The southpaw from Kentucky served in the U.S. Navy during the war and was stationed in Oklahoma as a seaman second class. Before he was shipped overseas, George was engaged to the former Nancy Jane Riddell. After combat action away from American soil, Burpo returned to the States and to baseball. Writer Hank Squire remembered Burpo as "the chap who used to run up amazing strings of strikeouts. He also kept the fans jittery on many occasions with his lack of control."

W	L	PCT	G	GS	CG	IP	H	BB	SO	SHO	ERA
0	0	—	2	0	0	2	4	5	1	0	18.00

Paul Robert Burris, *Catcher*

Burris spent pieces of four seasons in the majors with the Braves. He had to contend with some pretty fair catchers in Walker Cooper and Del Crandall for playing time and more often than not it wasn't forthcoming. Before his stint at the highest level, Burris served in the armed forces during World War II.

G	R	H	2B	3B	HR	RBI	BB	SO	SB	AVG	Slug
69	15	43	5	0	2	24	8	21	0	.219	.276

Edward Frank "Moe" Burtschy, *Pitcher*

A big, strong right-handed pitcher from Cincinnati, Moe was a wild, live-armed hurler for the A's during the 1950s. He was a member of the Philadelphia A's and was still with the team when they relocated to Kansas City. Before he made his major league debut, Burtschy enlisted in the U.S. Navy during World War II. During the war, Moe served on the battleship *USS Ticonderoga*.

W	L	PCT	G	GS	CG	IP	H	BB	SO	SHO	ERA
10	6	.625	90	1	0	185	178	126	97	0	4.72

James Franklin Busby, *Outfield*

A teenager throughout the war, Busby served with the army for a year at the end of the great conflict. After his discharge, Jim made a name for himself as a collegiate football star. However, he opted to give up football and concentrated on baseball. A good fly-chaser throughout his career, Busby was a nomadic outfielder who played for six teams.

G	R	H	2B	3B	HR	RBI	BB	SO	SB	AVG	Slug
1,352	541	1,113	162	35	48	438	310	439	97	.262	.350

Wilburn Rue "Bill" Butland, *Pitcher*

Tall and slender, Butland's major league career spanned four separate seasons, all of which were served with the Red Sox. His finest year came in 1942, the year before he was drafted, when he went 7–1 with a 2.51 ERA. That year, Bill tied a record for most putouts in a game by a pitcher. During his stint in the army, Bill played service ball at Fort Gordon with Hugh Mulcahy. He returned to pitch portions of two more years in the majors with Boston. After his playing days were over, he and his wife were recipients of a thief's wrath in 1969; as they were robbed and locked in the trunk of his car for four hours before they were rescued.

W	L	PCT	G	GS	CG	IP	H	BB	SO	SHO	ERA
9	3	.750	32	15	7	150	138	56	62	2	3.90

Thomas Joseph Byrne, *Pitcher*

Byrne possessed a gifted arm, but along with his golden wing came a lack of accuracy. He walked more than 1,000 batters in just over 1,300 innings of work, averaging nearly a free pass an inning. The southpaw made his debut with the 1942 Yankees; he walked 35 batters in 32 innings. He missed the next two years to service in the navy. When Tommy returned to the major leagues, he pitched sparingly until 1948, at which time he posted more than 100 innings pitched for the first time. His personal nemesis was Johnny Lipon, who broke up two no-hit bids Tommy made in his career. Control was always an issue throughout Byrne's career, which also saw him pitch for the Browns, White Sox and Senators.

W	L	PCT	G	GS	CG	IP	H	BB	SO	SHO	ERA
85	69	.552	281	170	65	1,363	1,138	1,037	766	12	4.11

Robert Max Cain, *Pitcher*

Best known as the only major league pitcher to have pitched to a midget, Cain was on the hill when little Eddie Gaedel stepped up to the plate in place of injured Frank Saucier. Unable to keep his composure, Cain, in between bouts of laughter, issued four balls to Gaedel. Before his misfires to Gaedel, "Sugar" served in the armed forces during World War II.

W	L	PCT	G	GS	CG	IP	H	BB	SO	SHO	ERA
37	44	.457	140	89	27	629	618	316	249	3	4.49

Frederick John Caligiuri, *Pitcher*

Fred was one of the Athletics hurlers who faced Ted Williams on the final day of the 1941 baseball season. The Splendid Splinter proceeded to smack the Athletics' onion offerings all over Shibe Park to end the season with a .406 batting average. After a good showing in 1941, Fred struggled through the 1942 season — his last in the majors — with an ERA of 6.33. He would miss the next four years to service in the military.

Many major leaguers who entered the military were able to play baseball as their primary military occupation; Fred wasn't one of the lucky ones. He served with the Amphibious Forces in the army and saw action in both the European and Pacific Theatres of operation. He did play a little baseball prior to being shipped out, as he played with Ducky Detweiler and Pat Mullin for the Army Reception Center club at New Cumberland.

W	L	PCT	G	GS	CG	IP	H	BB	SO	SHO	ERA
2	5	.286	18	7	4	80	90	32	27	0	4.50

Alexander Sebastian Campanis, *Second Base*

Born in the same vicinity as Hippocrates on the Greek isle of Kos, Campanis appeared in seven major league games during his brief career. In his only season at the highest level, Al served as Hall of Famer Billy Herman's backup. Campanis lost two years to service in the military and never made another plate appearance at the major league level after his discharge.

G	R	H	2B	3B	HR	RBI	BB	SO	SB	AVG	Slug
7	3	2	0	0	0	0	4	5	0	.100	.100

Bruce Douglas Campbell, *Outfield*

Campbell was a veteran ballplayer who was nearing the final stages of his career when he was summoned for military duty. He had hit fifteen home runs with 93 RBIs for the Tigers in 1941, and was hitting a solid .278 in 1942 when Uncle Sam took him from the Senators late in the season. However, he was 32 years old when he joined the army and missed out on his golden years on the diamond. When the war concluded, Campbell was 36 years old and did not attempt a major league comeback.

When Campbell left the Senators late in 1942, he joined Cecil Travis and Buddy Lewis as offensive stars of Washington who had made their way to the military. The Senators were hit the hardest at the beginning of the draft, as three main cogs to their offense had been taken away without reimbursement. Bruce hooked up with an elite service ballclub at the Waco Army Air Field. Birdie Tebbetts, the great major league catcher and manager, served as his army skipper. He also played with Sid Hudson, Buster Mills and Hoot Evers, all major league ballplayers.

G	R	H	2B	3B	HR	RBI	BB	SO	SB	AVG	Slug
1,360	759	1,382	295	87	106	766	548	584	53	.290	.455

Paul McLaughlin Campbell, *First Base*

Paul Campbell had yet to establish himself at the major league level when he was called to arms. The timing couldn't have been much worse for the young first baseman. Jimmie Foxx, the Bosox regular first baseman, had just been shipped off to Wrigley Field and a replacement was needed. Instead of taking over for Double X, Campbell joined the Air Force and served at a physical training center in Morris Field, North Carolina. He was later shipped overseas to Europe where he played some baseball for a squad that toured British air bases.

G	R	H	2B	3B	HR	RBI	BB	SO	SB	AVG	Slug
204	61	97	17	5	4	41	28	54	4	.255	.358

Clarence "Soup" Campbell, *Outfield*

An extremely intelligent man, Campbell used to teach mathematics and history during the offseason. Soup's major league career lasted two years; he played briefly for the Indians prior to World War II and didn't return after the war had concluded. Campbell served in the United States Army and once played a service game against a navy outfit. Lining up opposite Soup for that contest was a common face during his days with the Tribe: his roommate, Bob Feller. Campbell served at the Grand Island Army Air Field in Nebraska, where he received his promotion to captain. Soup spent five years in the army and was discharged with the rank of major late in 1946.

G	R	H	2B	3B	HR	RBI	BB	SO	SB	AVG	Slug
139	44	96	11	4	3	37	38	33	1	.248	.318

Milo Cain Candini, *Pitcher*

An adequate relief pitcher for Washington during the 1940s, Milo missed one year to military service during the war. He served in the United States Army at Camp Beale during his lone year in khaki. Candini returned to the Senators and pitched sparingly for skipper Ossie Bluege in 1946. His accuracy deserted him in 1948 and new skipper Joe Kuhel used him only three times in 1949. However, in 1949, Milo was assigned the duty of protecting President Truman from foul balls during the home opener.

W	L	PCT	G	GS	CG	IP	H	BB	SO	SHO	ERA
26	21	.553	174	37	13	538	530	250	183	5	3.91

Thomas Francis Aloysius Carey, *Utility Infielder*

A versatile ballplayer who was already 32 years old when Uncle Sam gave him the come-hither sign, Carey was the recipient of a jest from an unknown Boston sportswriter of his day. The newspaper caption read on the day that Carey was drafted: "Highest Priced Hitter Gets His Call From Army." Now, one must note that Tom Carey was far from the highest-paid player in baseball, but he strolled to the plate once in 1942 and collected a base hit in that lone at-bat. His salary for the season was $5,000, which spurred the writer to claim Carey the game's highest-priced Slugger — slapping one base hit all year for a whopping five grand.

G	R	H	2B	3B	HR	RBI	BB	SO	SB	AVG	Slug
466	169	418	79	13	2	169	66	75	3	.275	.348

James Arthur Carlin, *Outfield*

Carlin had a brief trial at the major league level but lost four years to military service when he could have fought for playing time. Jim was inducted into the navy and played in a service all-star game with Cleveland great Bob Feller. Carlin served overseas in the South Pacific and played some service ball in Hawaii.

G	R	H	2B	3B	HR	RBI	BB	SO	SB	AVG	Slug
16	2	3	1	0	1	2	3	4	0	.143	.333

Matthew "Lick" Carlisle, *Second Base*

The longtime second baseman for the powerhouse Homestead Grays of the late 1930s and on into the war years, Lick was a hustling ballplayer who batted in the number two slot ahead of legends Josh Gibson and Buck Leonard. Merely an average player, Carlisle ran well but was simply serviceable in other departments. During the war Lick was near the end of the line as a ballplayer and he spent just one year, the final 1945 season, in the military.

(1931–1946): Homestead Grays, Birmingham Black Barons, Montgomery Grey Sox and Memphis Red Sox

Donald Herbert Carlsen, *Pitcher*

Carlsen was a teenager before the war with major league dreams. His aspirations of reaching the bigs were almost extinguished during the war. While in the South Pacific, Carlsen's ship was attacked and he fell into the ocean and nearly died. Don was rescued and sent to an army hospital in India where he was nursed back to health. After his discharge, Don took to baseball and received his promotion to the Cubs in 1948. He pitched three years at the highest level, with the Cubs and Pirates, but when he failed to make the grade he quit the game and became a teacher.

W	L	PCT	G	GS	CG	IP	H	BB	SO	SHO	ERA
2	4	.333	13	7	2	54	75	21	23	0	6.00

Edwin Elliott Carnett, *Outfield*

Carnett learned to play the game in Ponca City, Oklahoma, and became a solid left-handed pitching recruit. The Yankees acquired him and he played in the minors with Phil Rizzuto and Jerry Priddy. Although he was a fine southpaw pitcher, Eddie could swing a mean stick as well, and when the war began to take players from major league rosters, the White Sox acquired Carnett, a family man, and made him their regular left fielder in 1944. He hit a solid .276 as a rookie that year. As a married father, Carnett was initially deferred by his draft board, but that didn't stop some from taunting him and his teammates. He said, "The year before I was drafted we went to Fort Dix and some guys in the bleachers would call us draft-dodgers, but the guys in the service didn't mind. They took care of us and didn't let the people in the bleachers talk to us like that, but some of them were pretty crude."

In 1945, Carnett began the season with the Indians as a two-way player, but then it was his turn to be inducted into service. To get acclimated to military life, Carnett and a group of Cleveland players visited a military hospital where soldiers who had been wounded at Omaha Beach were convalescing. Joining Carnett on the trip was Indians Slugging first baseman Hal Trosky, who met a big, strapping soldier who had his eyes shot out at Omaha Beach. With Trosky in the room, the soldier, a great admirer of the Slugger, stood up and mimicked Troksy's swing. Hal, who had been in a slump, saw a mechanical flaw in his swing through this wounded soldier and remained by his new friend's side the rest of the trip.

Inducted into the navy, Carnett was an older man with a wife and child back home while most of his new battle buddies were kids fresh from high school. Carnett said, "I was thirty years old. Stationed with all these kids in boot camp, I was their dad, you know. They'd come to me with a sad story, crying, and I'd sit them down and tell them it wasn't all that bad." Issued his sailor's gear in basic training, Carnett found that the issuing process was more take-it-or-leave-it than getting measured for a suit at a men's department store. He said, "They issued me boots in the navy that were so big I had to wash them in hot water three or four times before they fit me. And my hat went clear down over my head, so I had to wash it too."

Carnett spent a little under a year in the navy and after his discharge he found the going tough in baseball. He was a 30-year-old ex-sailor in training camp with young kids fresh out of college, high school or the service, all determined to prove they had the stuff to make the majors. As a veteran ballplayer, the post-war experience wasn't as rosy as the kid just starting out. Eddie said about his first postwar training camp, "All of a sudden you look up and all these kids who were just as good a ballplayer as I was—some of them better and I was better than some—but who do you think a club is going to pick, a thirty-year-old with a couple seasons left or the twenty-year-old with twelve?" Unable to latch on in the majors after the war, Carnett returned to the bushes and had success at Seattle and Wichita Falls before calling it a career.

G	R	H	2B	3B	HR	RBI	BB	SO	SB	AVG	Slug
158	56	142	25	8	1	67	28	44	5	.268	.351

Robert Louis Carpenter, *Pitcher*

Carpenter posted a perfect 1.000 winning percentage his rookie season in 1940 with the Giants and then finished second on the team in victories the following year. He had become a reliable starting pitcher by 1942 but was inducted into the army and missed three years to military service. When he returned to the diamond in 1946, Bob suffered an injury and was ineffective when used. His last year was 1947, a season split between the Giants and Cubs.

W	L	PCT	G	GS	CG	IP	H	BB	SO	SHO	ERA
25	20	.556	80	54	23	400	411	132	134	4	3.60

Frank Willis Carswell, *Outfield*

When "Tex" made his major league debut, his military hitch was long behind him. He was a 33-year-old rookie with the 1953 Tigers, eight years after his military discharge. Carswell, who also played professional basketball, had a cup of coffee at the major league level but was a stockholder in the coffee business in the bushes. He managed in the minors for a number of years.

G	R	H	2B	3B	HR	RBI	BB	SO	SB	AVG	Slug
16	2	4	0	0	0	2	3	1	0	.267	.267

Marlin Theodore Carter, *Utility Infielder*

A fine ballplayer from Texas who could play anywhere on the infield, Carter's usual assignment was the hot corner. He spent the bulk of his career in the Negro Leagues with the Memphis Red Sox. Usually a lead-off or number two hitter, Marlin was a fine table-setter for his Memphis squads. An All-Star during the 1942 season, Carter was drafted into the military during World War II and spent three years in the U.S. Coast Guard.

(1933–1948): Memphis Red Sox, Cincinnati Tigers and Chicago American Giants

Hugh Thomas Casey, *Pitcher*

One of baseball's first great relief specialists, Casey had a brilliant major league career in the 1940s. He moved between the rotation and bullpen in 1939 under skipper Leo Durocher, and he finished second on the team with fifteen wins and a 2.93 ERA. Casey became a full-fledged reliever in 1942, when he paced the National League in saves and posted a 2.25 ERA. Right when Hugh had come into his own at the major league level, he was inducted into the armed forces.

In 1943, his first year in the service, Casey pitched for the Norfolk Naval Air Station ballclub. He was later shipped out to Hawaii and participated in the Hawaiian Service League, playing for a navy team based out of Honolulu. While there, the big relief pitcher got into a scrape with major leaguer Barney McCosky during a game, proving that even in service baseball the passion to win persisted. Hugh broke his ankle in a service game and said, "I had enough points to get out, was just marking time waiting for a ship." Casey was discharged from the navy with the rank of chief specialist.

W	L	PCT	G	GS	CG	IP	H	BB	SO	SHO	ERA
75	42	.641	343	56	24	940	935	321	349	3	3.45

Jack Dempsey Cassini, *Pinch Runner*

Cassini played eight games at the major league level, scored three runs but never had an at-bat. Employed as a pinch runner by skipper Billy Meyer, Jack was used only for his speed. He missed minor league action due to the war and after his playing days were over, Jack had a lengthy career as a minor league skipper.

G	R	H	2B	3B	HR	RBI	BB	SO	SB	AVG	Slug
8	3	0	0	0	0	0	0	0	0	—	—

James Vincent Castiglia, *Catcher*

Castiglia's baseball career was rather brief, as Connie Mack initially signed the gridiron star as a bullpen catcher. He showed Mack enough promise to give him a spot on the roster in 1942. Jim responded with a .389 batting average in a handful of games. He quit baseball and returned to football, and saw action in the NFL from 1945 to 1948.

Castiglia was sworn into the army on July 7, 1942, as a private. Jim played service baseball for the Greensboro ORD Tech-Hawks. Later, Castiglia was shipped overseas where he managed the Overseas Replacement Depot baseball team. He also didn't neglect the gridiron, as he was the quarterback for the Personnel Distribution Command football squad.

G	R	H	2B	3B	HR	RBI	BB	SO	SB	AVG	Slug
16	2	7	0	0	0	2	1	3	0	.389	.389

Peter Paul Castiglione, *Third Base*

A third baseman by trade who could start anywhere around the infield, Castiglione spent a number of years with the Pirates. Pete didn't receive his first big league start until after the war, at which time he served in the U.S. Navy. The sailor was discharged in time to participate in the 1946 spring training but didn't make his debut until the following year.

G	R	H	2B	3B	HR	RBI	BB	SO	SB	AVG	Slug
545	205	426	62	11	24	150	103	126	10	.255	.349

Hardin Abner Cathey, *Pitcher*

A star at the minor league level, Cathey once tossed a no-hitter in the bushes, but his success didn't translate to the majors. Hardin had a cup of coffee with the 1942 Senators and was hit quite easily. Sent back to Chattanooga, Cathey was on the Lookouts' war list during the Second World War.

W	L	PCT	G	GS	CG	IP	H	BB	SO	SHO	ERA
1	1	.500	12	2	0	30	44	16	8	0	7.50

Marvin Earl "Pete" Center, *Pitcher*

The Indians used Center out of the bullpen for four years, as the right-hander — who was built like a mountain — missed a year and a half to service in the United States Army. Pete was inducted into the armed forces after he made 24 appearances for the Tribe in 1943. He was stationed at Daniel Field, Georgia, where he ran across fellow major league players Burgess Whitehead and Cleveland teammate Chubby Dean.

W	L	PCT	G	GS	CG	IP	H	BB	SO	SHO	ERA
7	7	.500	77	9	2	160	154	70	50	0	4.11

Clifford Day Chambers, *Pitcher*

Bob Feller, Allie Reynolds and Chambers were the only three pitchers to toss a no-hitter in 1951. Cliff, a big southpaw, tossed his no-no as a member of the Pirates, which made him the first Pittsburgh pitcher since Nick Maddox in 1907 to fire a no-hitter. He served in the armed forces before he made his major league debut, which came with the 1948 Cubs.

W	L	PCT	G	GS	CG	IP	H	BB	SO	SHO	ERA
48	53	.475	189	113	37	897	924	361	374	6	4.29

Spurgeon Ferdinand "Spud" Chandler, *Pitcher*

Regarding pitchers with at least 100 career wins, Spud Chandler ranks first all-time in career winning percentage. This Southern right-hander did benefit greatly from pitching for the Yankees, but he was a great pitcher on his own laurels. Spud began his major league career with the Yankees in 1937 and never saw action in any other uniform at the time of his retirement. He made only one start with the Yankees in 1944 before he received his draft notice from Uncle Sam. He was inducted into the army at the age of 36 and performed rehabilitation work with wounded soldiers at a hospital in Asheville, North Carolina. Spud returned to the Yankees near the close of the 1945 baseball season and ended his career in 1947.

W	L	PCT	G	GS	CG	IP	H	BB	SO	SHO	ERA
109	43	.717	211	184	109	1,485	1,327	463	614	26	2.84

Samuel Blake Chapman, *Outfield*

A gifted natural athlete, Chapman was a star football player at the collegiate level. He passed up a profession on the gridiron to ply his trade on the ball diamond. Connie Mack signed Sam off the college campus and brought him up to Philadelphia with haste. He stepped into the regular lineup from day one, as a left fielder in 1938, and finished second on the club in home runs his rookie season. He shifted to center field the following year and enjoyed his breakout campaign in 1940. Sam finished the season with an offensive line that consisted of a .276 batting average with 27 homers and 75 RBIs. In his last year before the war, Chapman hit .322 and was a 100-RBI man for the first time. However, with the war raging overseas, Sam enlisted in the armed forces after season.

Sam Chapman enlisted in the navy after the close of the 1941 baseball season under the Tunney Program as a chief petty officer. However, Chapman's heart lied in flying and he accepted a demotion in rank in order to qualify for pilot training. Concerning his desire to enter flight school, Sam said, "I want to get out where there's some action!"

He was transferred to an aviation base at Washington D.C. to begin his flight training. Chapman later became an ensign in the Naval Air Corps specializing in torpedo bombing. After his training, Sam was assigned to the Naval Air Station in Corpus Christi, Texas, just in time to participate in the post's football season in late 1942. While serving in the navy, Sam met and wed the former Mary Jo Frey.

His discharge papers came late in the summer of 1945 and Sam was able to play in nine games at the tail end of the baseball season. He became the lone dynamic offensive presence in Connie Mack's lineup in 1946, with Sam posting four times as many long balls as his runner-up on the Philadelphia club. Of Sam, Joe DiMaggio once said, "We moved back to the fence when Sam came up and no one took any chances with his arm."

G	R	H	2B	3B	HR	RBI	BB	SO	SB	AVG	Slug
1,368	754	1,329	210	52	180	773	562	682	41	.266	.438

Robert Vincent Chesnes, *Pitcher*

As a rookie with the 1948 Pirates, Bob led the team in wins. He took his regular turn in the rotation in 1949 but was done after a short 1950 season. Chesnes missed minor league seasoning time when he was inducted into the armed forces during World War II.

W	L	PCT	G	GS	CG	IP	H	BB	SO	SHO	ERA
24	22	.522	61	55	25	378	377	189	130	1	4.67

Emory Nicholas "Bubba" Church, *Pitcher*

A Southern pitching star, Church had yet to make his major league debut when he joined the service during World War II. Bubba enlisted in the United States Army and after some stateside training, he received his orders to be shipped out. The Birmingham native spent time in the South Pacific and was stationed at India. It took Bubba five years to make the majors after his discharge.

W	L	PCT	G	GS	CG	IP	H	BB	SO	SHO	ERA
36	37	.493	147	95	32	713	738	277	274	7	4.10

Theodore Walter Cieslak, *Third Base*

A war-era ballplayer, Cieslak's only major league action came with the war-depleted 1944 Phillies. Ted was a 31-year-old rookie who got by on grit and hustle. Scribe Sam Davis claimed that "Cieslak looks like Pepper Martin at third base. Like the Wild Hoss, his baseball knickers barely cover the knees, and he everlastingly is kicking and picking up dirt." Ted served in the army at Fort Dix, which interrupted his all-too-brief trial in the majors.

G	R	H	2B	3B	HR	RBI	BB	SO	SB	AVG	Slug
85	18	54	10	0	2	11	21	17	1	.245	.318

Albert Joseph Cihocki, *Utility Infielder*

A war-era ballplayer, Cihocki spent the 1945 season as a backup infielder for Lou Boudreau's Indians. Al had baseball in his veins at an early age. His father gave him a bat and ball at the age of four, and Al said, "I went out in the yard, found another kid, and we started to play in mid-winter. I've had baseball in my blood ever since." Cihocki, who played amateur ball on a town team in Nanticoke with one-armed sensation Pete Gray, served with the U.S. Coast Guard during the war. Given a medical discharge early in 1945, Al was able to attend spring training with the Indians that year and was on the roster all season — his only year at the highest level.

G	R	H	2B	3B	HR	RBI	BB	SO	SB	AVG	Slug
92	21	60	9	3	0	24	11	48	2	.212	.265

Louis Alexander Ciola, *Pitcher*

The 1943 season was the only year in which Lou Ciola played at the major league level. This small right-hander from Norfolk notched one career win before entering the navy. Lou spent two years in the United States Navy and was stationed at Honolulu, Hawaii.

W	L	PCT	G	GS	CG	IP	H	BB	SO	SHO	ERA
1	3	.250	12	3	2	44	48	22	7	0	5.52

George Joseph Cisar, *Outfield*

A fleet-footed outfielder, Cisar's major league tenure consisted of a cup of coffee with the 1937 Dodgers. He stole three bases in his brief stay at Brooklyn late in the season. When World War II broke out, Cisar was finished as a major league ballplayer but he was able to play for Uncle Sam. Stationed at Fort Sill, Cisar was able to play some service ball before he was shipped overseas. Deployed to the European Theatre, George saw action in England and France.

G	R	H	2B	3B	HR	RBI	BB	SO	SB	AVG	Slug
20	8	6	0	0	0	4	2	6	3	.207	.207

Alfred Aloysius Clark, *Outfield*

One of the few players to have won back-to-back World Series championships with two different clubs, Clark won his first ring with the 1947 Yankees and his second with the Indians the following year. Before he tried on his first Yankees uniform, Clark served in the armed forces during World War II.

G	R	H	2B	3B	HR	RBI	BB	SO	SB	AVG	Slug
358	131	267	48	4	32	149	72	70	2	.262	.410

Melvin Earl Clark, *Outfield*

Clark made his debut with the Phillies the year after their improbable NL pennant-winning season of 1950. He spent five years as a fourth outfielder, stuck behind such notables as Hall of Famer Richie Ashburn and RBI-machine Del Ennis. Before Mel made his first Opening Day roster, he served with distinction in the Pacific Theatre during World War II. He was stationed on a destroyer that patrolled the waters in the Pacific. Mel stepped off his ship at such locales as Iwo Jima and the Philippine Islands.

G	R	H	2B	3B	HR	RBI	BB	SO	SB	AVG	Slug
215	82	182	29	15	3	63	37	61	3	.277	.381

Michael John Clark, *Pitcher*

A big New Jersey native, Mike has a perfect 3–0 record at the major league level but his peripheral stats wouldn't suggest perfection. He struggled with his control and was quite easy to hit, but three wins and no losses is a perfect record. Mike spent two years with the Cardinals in the early 1950s, and during the war he served in the navy and was shipped out to the Pacific Theatre.

W	L	PCT	G	GS	CG	IP	H	BB	SO	SHO	ERA
3	0	1.000	35	6	0	61	78	35	27	0	5.31

William Stuart "Stu" Clarke, *Utility Infielder*

Stu played two years with the Pirates when they had an enviable infield of Gus Suhr, George Grantham, Dick Bartell and Pie Traynor. All these players were stars in their day, which meant Stu had little opportunity to crack the lineup. When the war broke out, Stu was in his upper thirties but that didn't stop him from serving his country. He joined the navy and was nearing his fortieth birthday when he was mustered out of the service.

G	R	H	2B	3B	HR	RBI	BB	SO	SB	AVG	Slug
61	22	51	5	8	2	23	20	21	3	.273	.417

James Buster "Bus" Clarkson, *Shortstop*

Like Vern Stephens in the major leagues, Clarkson helped redefine the shortstop position. Little fellows like Reese and Rizzuto were considered the ideal shortstop for their agility and nimble work around the keystone sack, but Bus showed that teams could also get quality run production out of the position. A terrific power hitter, Clarkson was once walked with the bases loaded by the great Satchel Paige. When asked why he walked Clarkson with the bases full, Paige remarked, "I'd rather give up one run instead of four."

A native of South Carolina, Bus was a dead-red pull hitter with above average power. Before he starred in the Negro Leagues, Clarkson was a two-sport athlete at Wilberforce University in baseball and football. With baseball in the blood, Bus gave up football and played hardball year round. When the Negro League schedule was over, Bus would hop a flight to the Caribbean or catch a ride to Mexico and play south of the border. He caught on with the Philadelphia Stars just before the war. Bus was inducted into the army and spent three years in the service. After his discharge, he returned to the Stars and played in the Negro Leagues until the color line was broken. The Braves signed Bus, but by that time he was no longer able to play shortstop and was moved to third base. With future Hall of Famer Eddie Mathews on the Braves roster, Clarkson wasn't needed and he spent his time after integration as a minor leaguer.

(1937–1956): Philadelphia Stars, Pittsburgh Crawfords, Toledo Crawfords, Newark Eagles, Baltimore Elite Giants and Boston Braves (NL)

Spurgeon Chester Clemens, *Outfield*

A war-era ballplayer, Clemens played briefly with the Braves in 1939 but didn't show enough skill to stick. With World War II taking many of the game's finest stars, minor leaguers were needed to fill out the major league rosters. Chet returned to the majors in 1944 but received his draft notice late in the year. Clemens spent the 1945 and 1946 baseball seasons in the armed forces and wasn't called back to the majors after his discharge.

G	R	H	2B	3B	HR	RBI	BB	SO	SB	AVG	Slug
28	9	8	1	1	0	3	3	5	1	.200	.275

William Melville Clemensen, *Pitcher*

Clemensen pitched in pieces of three seasons with the Pirates and missed four years to service in the armed forces during World War II. After his four-year layoff, Bill returned to the Pirates and pitched two innings of perfect relief.

W	L	PCT	G	GS	CG	IP	H	BB	SO	SHO	ERA
1	1	.500	15	2	1	42	39	27	19	0	5.57

Thomas Knox Clyde, *Pitcher*

Clyde appeared in four major league games as a nineteen-year-old with the 1943 Athletics, his only stint at the highest level. The right-hander missed the 1944 and 1945 seasons to service in the armed forces.

W	L	PCT	G	GS	CG	IP	H	BB	SO	SHO	ERA
0	0	—	4	0	0	6	7	4	0	0	9.00

David Lamar Coble, *Reserve*

Coble had a cup of coffee with Doc Prothro's 1939 Phillies, the extent of his major league service. Aware that his baseball career had stagnated, Dave took a job with the U.S. Engineers in 1942 and worked on a barge prior to his enlistment in the army. Coble was sent to Randolph Field where he played for and managed a service ballclub on the installation. By 1945, Dave had become Lieutenant Coble when he was transferred from Randolph Field. After his military days were over, Coble embarked on a lengthy career as a minor league skipper.

G	R	H	2B	3B	HR	RBI	BB	SO	SB	AVG	Slug
15	2	7	1	0	0	0	0	3	0	.280	.320

Gordon Stanley "Mickey" Cochrane, *Catcher*

Perhaps the greatest catcher in baseball history, Cochrane was the backbone of Connie Mack's last Athletic dynasty. Mack had such stars as the surly Lefty Grove, the foul-mouthed Al Simmons and the laid-back Jimmie Foxx, but it was Mickey who kept the team going. A natural behind the dish, Cochrane was also a gifted hitter and not the automatic out such great catch-and-throw backstops were. But Mickey's stardom came to a sudden halt when he was beaned by Bump Hadley and was forced to retire. Unable to leave the game, Mickey became a bench manager, officially hanging up his catcher's gear in 1937. Doctors warned him that another blow to the head would be fatal.

After Pearl Harbor was bombed, Mickey felt it was his duty to serve his country and assist in any way possible. Given that his severe ball diamond injury forced him to an early retirement, he was aware the military would reject him as unfit physically to serve. But Mickey was able to secure a job with the navy as baseball manager of their Great Lakes Naval Training Station nine. The two-time MVP was commissioned an officer and began his tour with Uncle Sam.

Cochrane spent the bulk of his military time at the Great Lakes, tutoring young soldiers. He was asked on several occasions to form military all-star teams, which he would manage, but his duties always brought him back to the young sailors at the Great Lakes. One such young athlete was a fireballer from Alabama named Virgil Trucks. Property of the Tigers, Cochrane took the young Trucks under his wing and made a pitcher out of him. Trucks said, "I didn't know anything about pitching until I met him."

The patriotism that coursed through Mickey Cochrane's veins was passed along to his son, Mickey Cochrane Jr. The younger Cochrane enlisted in the armed forces and was shipped out to the European Theatre. The father and son would never see one another again. While serving in the ETO, Cochrane Jr. was killed in action in February 1945. Cochrane Sr. went on a tour in the Pacific before he was transferred to the Iowa Pre-Flight School where he was mustered out.

G	R	H	2B	3B	HR	RBI	BB	SO	SB	AVG	Slug
1,482	1,041	1,652	333	64	119	832	857	217	64	.320	.478

James Clarence Cohen, *Pitcher*

As a kid, Jim never played baseball. He was introduced to the game only after taking a job in the coal mines when he left school. Cohen played for his coal mine team until he was drafted into the service, where he was able to refine his pitching. Jim served at Camp Lee's Replacement Center and played baseball throughout his military hitch. After his army discharge, Cohen caught on in the Negro Leagues with the Indianapolis Clowns. He played with them on into the 1950s when Negro League baseball was no longer of high caliber due to integration.

(1946–1952): Indianapolis Clowns

Richard Roy "Dick" Cole, *Utility Infielder*

Cole was a teenager when he served in the military during World War II. After his discharge he was able to devote his attention to the game of baseball. He made his big league debut with the 1951 Cardinals but was traded to the Pirates during the season. The versatile infielder ended his major league career on the 1957 world champion Braves.

G	R	H	2B	3B	HR	RBI	BB	SO	SB	AVG	Slug
456	106	303	50	10	2	107	132	124	2	.249	.312

Gerald Francis "Jerry" Coleman, *Second Base*

A fine second baseman for the New York Yankees during the 1950s, Coleman was unable to play baseball without interruptions. Before he made his major league debut, the young San Jose native served in the military during World War II. When the war was over Jerry returned to baseball and made his debut in 1949. But the infielder was also a pilot, and when Uncle Sam needed flying men for the Korean War, Coleman answered the call again. For more on Coleman, see his listing in the section on the Korean War.

G	R	H	2B	3B	HR	RBI	BB	SO	SB	AVG	Slug
723	267	558	77	18	16	217	235	218	22	.263	.339

Joseph Patrick Coleman, *Pitcher*

An adequate pitcher, Coleman's career record would be much better had he not toiled for the lowly Philadelphia Athletics. He pitched for Connie Mack's aggregation the majority of his career. Joe spent 1942 through 1953 with the White Elephants. Coleman, who later pitched with the Tigers and Orioles, had a son named Joe Coleman Jr., who followed his father to the major leagues.

The elder Coleman appeared in one game with the Athletics prior to World War II, with the teenager tossing six innings of solid relief. He joined the Navy Air Corps and took his pre-flight training with the likes of Ted Williams, Johnny Pesky, Buddy Gremp and Johnny Sain. He missed out on three full baseball campaigns while he served his country and returned to a cellar-dwelling Philadelphia club in 1946.

W	L	PCT	G	GS	CG	IP	H	BB	SO	SHO	ERA
52	76	.406	223	140	60	1,133	1,172	566	444	11	4.38

Raymond Leroy Coleman, *Outfield*

A decent role player throughout his career, Ray was adept at legging out three-baggers. Before his major league debut, Ray served in the United States Navy and was aboard a ship that traversed waters in the Pacific Theatre. After his discharge, he made his way to the majors with the 1947 Browns. Ray enjoyed a pinball career at the major league level that always seemed to send him back to St. Louis. The Browns dealt him in 1948 but reacquired his services on two other occasions.

G	R	H	2B	3B	HR	RBI	BB	SO	SB	AVG	Slug
559	208	446	74	33	20	199	148	158	19	.258	.374

Edward Trowbridge Collins Jr., *Outfield*

Although many men follow in the footsteps of their father, by seeking the same profession as his old man Edward Trowbridge Collins Jr. had an awful lot to live up to. The son of a Hall of Fame second baseman, Collins Jr. made it to the major leagues in 1939 and was done by 1942. However, World War II took Junior from the game in 1943, the beginning of his three years under Uncle Sam. Collins, who attended Yale University, served in the navy. He was inducted as an ensign at Arlington and assigned to the Bureau of Navigation in Washington. During his stint in the navy, he and his wife—the daughter of Hall of Fame pitcher Herb Pennock—gave birth to Edward Trowbridge Collins III.

G	R	H	2B	3B	HR	RBI	BB	SO	SB	AVG	Slug
132	41	66	9	3	0	16	24	29	4	.241	.296

Joseph Edward Collins, *First Base*

Collins played ten years at the major league level, all with the Yankees. He began with the Bronx Bombers during the post-war hoorah of Joe DiMaggio and was still on the club when the young double-play duo of Bobby Richardson and Tony Kubek was unveiled. He was a member of eight New York pennant winners. Before he embarked on his rewarding major league career, Collins served in the navy during World War II. The first baseman was assigned to the Naval Air Corps.

G	R	H	2B	3B	HR	RBI	BB	SO	SB	AVG	Slug
908	404	596	79	24	86	329	338	263	27	.256	.421

Jack Dean Collum, *Pitcher*

Just a teenager when World War II broke out, Collum joined the colors at the end of the war. Mustered out before his twentieth birthday, the young southpaw worked his way through the bushes until the Redbirds gave him a call in 1951. A journeyman long reliever and spot starter, Collum played for six teams in his nine-year major league career.

W	L	PCT	G	GS	CG	IP	H	BB	SO	SHO	ERA
32	28	.533	171	37	11	464	480	173	171	2	4.15

Jim Colzie, *Pitcher*

Colzie's career as a soldier lasted twice as long as his career in the Negro Leagues. Jim pitched two seasons with the Indianapolis Clowns after a four-year hitch with Uncle Sam during the war. Jim's son was a star safety in the NFL during the late 1970s and early 1980s.

(1946–1947): Indianapolis Clowns

Merrill Russell Combs, *Shortstop*

Although Combs played five years at the major league level, his career statistical line appears to be for a season's worth of play. A portside-swinging infielder, Combs served with the United States Army before he made his big league debut. After his playing days, Combs had a successful career as a baseball scout.

G	R	H	2B	3B	HR	RBI	BB	SO	SB	AVG	Slug
140	45	73	6	1	2	25	57	43	0	.202	.241

Richard Conger, *Pitcher*

Conger spent three years at the major league level with three different teams: the Detroit Tigers, Philadelphia Phillies and Pittsburgh Pirates. Dick was inducted into the U.S. Marines after the 1943 season and served three years in the service. After his discharge, Dick did not return to the majors.

W	L	PCT	G	GS	CG	IP	H	BB	SO	SHO	ERA
3	7	.300	19	12	2	70	86	35	24	0	5.14

Mervin Thomas "Bud" Connolly, *Shortstop*

The type of man who always comported himself with an air of humble dignity, Connolly was one of baseball's premier gentlemen. Although his playing career lasted one single season, Bud was a well-respected man in the game. His lone trial at the major league level came with the basement-dwelling 1925 Red Sox. When World War II broke out, Connolly's days as a player were well behind him. Still in the game, however, Bud was the manager of the Madison Blues, a minor league squad, when he answered the call to arms as a 40-year-old man.

Connolly left the dugout of the Blues and joined the navy. Although he was advanced in years, Bud kept his rather small frame in fine physical condition. Henry J. McCormick wrote that Bud was "the kind of man who knows how to handle young players." He took his expert managing skills and applied them in the military where he served with the Seabees.

G	R	H	2B	3B	HR	RBI	BB	SO	SB	AVG	Slug
43	12	28	7	1	0	21	23	9	0	.262	.346

Edward Joseph Connolly Sr., *Catcher*

A light-hitting catcher, Connolly was followed to the major leagues by his son Edward Junior. The elder Connolly made his debut with the Red Sox in 1929. It was certainly a trick for him to hit above .200 in an era when many good players could hit .300 with relative ease. His major league career was over by the time World War II broke out but the aging Connolly joined the navy despite his advanced age.

G	R	H	2B	3B	HR	RBI	BB	SO	SB	AVG	Slug
149	13	66	11	4	0	31	29	50	0	.178	.229

Mervin James Connors, *Third Base/First Base*

The Babe Ruth of the minor leagues, Merv Connors was one of the most fearsome hitters the bushes ever boasted. The brawny slugger blasted more than 400 home runs in the minors but only tallied eight in the big show. He was given a brief trial with the White Sox in the late 1930s but his game was centered on his offense. Jimmy Dykes, skipper of the Pale Hose, already had an all-hit, no-field first baseman in Big Zeke Bonura, so Merv wasn't needed. When Dykes grew tired of Bonura's terrible defense and traded him away, he acquired slick-fielding, modest-hitting Joe Kuhel to play first, and the Slugging Connors backed up the better defender his last year in the majors.

A sensation in the minors, Connors was more than a terrific long ball threat — he was also quite an entertainer. Together, with the great Charlie Grimm and teammates Prince Oana and Joe Berry, the four men sang in a barbershop quartet while in the minors. But when the war broke out, Connors hung up his spikes for the duration and put on hold his crooning voice as well. Before he was inducted, however, he had a run-in with his bosses on the Fort Worth club who felt that Merv had withheld his draft status from the team. Commissioner Landis was asked to look into the affair, and the judge said, "We found that his statement that he was in Class 3-A when he signed was true as far as he knew, for he received no notice of any change in his classification until April 1."

Switched from 3-A Classification, which meant he was deferred, to Class 1-A, Connors was inducted into the United States Army. His induction couldn't have come at a worse time, for many baseball men felt that Merv was on the cusp of returning to the majors. Hall of Fame third baseman Pie Traynor, who was employed as a scout at the time, saw Merv play just before his induction and gushed, "Why, if Larry MacPhail had seen him the night he hit two home runs against Beaumont, he would have bought Connors right there." But Merv had to forego thoughts of a major league return because Uncle Sam needed him.

Connors was inducted into the army and trained as a paratrooper in the infantry. The big blaster from Berkeley was shipped overseas and saw heavy combat action as a member of Uncle Sam's airborne troops. Connors opened his chute in many hostile areas, including North Africa, the Ardennes and the ETO. For his wartime gallantry, Merv was awarded many medals and citations that include the Bronze Arrowhead. After serving a few years as a fighting man from the skies, Connors returned to baseball but never did get that return call to the majors.

G	R	H	2B	3B	HR	RBI	BB	SO	SB	AVG	Slug
52	26	46	8	1	8	25	23	36	2	.279	.485

William Gordon Conroy, *Catcher*

Bill Conroy spent his major league career as a back-up catcher. When he came up to the bigs in 1935, he served as a fourth-string catcher with the Philadelphia Athletics and ascended to third string by 1937. However, Bill spent the next four seasons in the bushes before returning to the majors in 1942 with the Red Sox. The majority of his major league service time came as a war-era player, as he played for Joe Cronin through 1944. He was inducted into the navy after the 1944 season and never played at the highest level again.

G	R	H	2B	3B	HR	RBI	BB	SO	SB	AVG	Slug
169	45	90	13	3	5	33	77	85	3	.199	.274

Jack Clements Conway, *Utility Infielder*

Conway served four years in the United States Navy but was initially released due to an eye ailment. Undeterred, Conway returned to the navy intent to serve, and they took the versatile ballplayer back. Jack made his debut in 1941 with the Indians—playing briefly—and then was in the employ of Uncle Sam the next four years. In 1946, he saw action at every infield post except first base. He ended his career with the 1948 Giants, playing thirteen games at second, six at short and three at third base.

G	R	H	2B	3B	HR	RBI	BB	SO	SB	AVG	Slug
128	35	80	10	3	1	27	28	54	2	.223	.276

Herbert Leroy Conyers, *First Base*

Like Reds pitcher Ewell Blackwell, Conyers was a taller-than-average man with aspirations of combat flying during World War II. Uncle Sam didn't like his pilots to be very tall because the larger men couldn't eject properly when forced to abandon the plane. Blackwell was rejected by the Army Air Corps because of his beanpole build while Conyers' dimensions were deemed suitable for cockpit employment. Herb went through flight school and learned the art of aerial combat. When his training was completed, he was shipped overseas.

Conyers was able to participate in combat missions, with the tall first baseman flying his aircraft in the Pacific Theatre of operations. When the war came to a close, Conyers was returned stateside and Uncle Sam helped him get back into the swing of things. Sent to Ellington Air Force Base, Herb assisted the installation's club in capturing the South Coast Victory League's championship. After he was mustered out, Conyers became a champion in both the Interstate League and Texas League where he won batting titles. Despite his Slugging at the minor league level, Conyers only had a brief trial with the 1950 Indians.

G	R	H	2B	3B	HR	RBI	BB	SO	SB	AVG	Slug
7	2	3	0	0	1	1	1	2	1	.333	.667

Rollin Edward Cook, *Pitcher*

Cook had a cup of coffee with Branch Rickey's Browns of 1915. He worked in just over a dozen major league innings before "The Mahatma" was finished with him. After his major league sojourn, Rollin joined the armed forces for World War I. The former Brownie right-hander returned to the colors in the 1940s to lend a hand during the Second World War as well.

W	L	PCT	G	GS	CG	IP	H	BB	SO	SHO	ERA
0	0	—	5	0	0	14	16	9	7	0	7.07

Allen Lindsey "Dusty" Cooke, *Outfield*

A good role player throughout his career, Cooke was usually a fourth outfielder and spot starter. The husky lad from North Carolina had some of his better years with the Red Sox but ended his playing days with the 1938 Reds. Dusty, who had an interest in medicine, was inducted into the navy and served as a PhMSc during the war. With his background in healing, the Phillies gave Dusty a job after his naval discharge as the team's trainer.

G	R	H	2B	3B	HR	RBI	BB	SO	SB	AVG	Slug
608	324	488	109	28	24	229	290	276	32	.280	.415

Robert Daniel Cooney, *Pitcher*

Cooney pitched two years at the Major League level in the early 1930s with the Browns. He had limited success and proved rather easy to hit. The right-hander joined the military ten years after he threw his final pitch in the bigs and served in the South Pacific.

W	L	PCT	G	GS	CG	IP	H	BB	SO	SHO	ERA
1	5	.167	28	7	2	110	140	56	36	0	5.97

William T. Cooper, *Utilityman*

A weak hitter but a swift runner with terrific versatility, Cooper was a former college football standout. A gritty, hard-nosed ballplayer, Bill was nicknamed "Dr. Jekyll" because his off-field personality was in stark contrast to his take-no-prisoners style on the diamond. Cooper missed three years to the military during World War II and played only one season with the New York Black Yankees after his discharge.

(1938–1946): Philadelphia Stars, New York Black Yankees and Atlanta Black Crackers

Calvin Asa Cooper, *Pitcher*

Cooper had a rather forgettable debut at the major league level. In one inning, he coughed up five hits and posted an ERA of 45.00. His debut, unfortunately, was his only appearance at the highest level. During the war Cooper served with the United States Navy.

W	L	PCT	G	GS	CG	IP	H	BB	SO	SHO	ERA
0	0	—	1	0	0	1	5	1	0	0	45.00

William Walker Cooper, *Catcher*

The best catcher in baseball during the war years, Cooper was able to play throughout the war with just a minor interruption. Early in the 1945 season he was called to service and spent less than a year in the military. Walker, who formed a terrific sibling battery with his brother, Mort, had his contract sold to the Giants while he was in the navy. Although an All-Star in St. Louis, Cooper's best year came in New York. With the 1947 Giants he swatted 35 home runs and drove in 122 runs.

G	R	H	2B	3B	HR	RBI	BB	SO	SB	AVG	Slug
1,473	573	1,341	240	40	173	812	309	357	19	.285	.464

Claude Elliott Corbitt, *Utility Infielder*

A scrappy infielder from North Carolina, Corbitt played for two Hall of Fame skippers in his brief major league trial: the shady Leo Durocher and the respectable Bill McKechnie. Corbitt, who attended Duke University before his service hitch, was inducted into the Army Air Corps. The infielder remained stateside throughout the war and was stationed at Maxwell Field, Alabama. Discharged before the end of the war, Claude made his major league debut with the 1945 Brooklyn Dodgers.

G	R	H	2B	3B	HR	RBI	BB	SO	SB	AVG	Slug
215	60	153	22	1	1	37	47	30	8	.243	.286

Edward Christopher Cotter, *Third Base/Shortstop*

Cotter hit the apple well in his cup of coffee with the 1926 Phillies but failed to stick. The Hartford man was pushing forty years of age when he entered service during World War II with the United States Navy.

G	R	H	2B	3B	HR	RBI	BB	SO	SB	AVG	Slug
17	3	8	0	1	0	1	4	1	.308	.385

Clinton Dawson Courtney, *Catcher*

Courtney, who was nicknamed "Scrap Iron," played briefly with the Yankees in 1951. With a man named Berra in the fold, Clint wasn't needed and was shipped to the Browns. With the 1952 Browns, Scrappy won the AL Rookie of the Year Award. Before he earned the hardware, Courtney served in the United States Army briefly after his high school graduation.

G	R	H	2B	3B	HR	RBI	BB	SO	SB	AVG	Slug
946	260	750	126	17	38	313	265	143	3	.268	.367

William Donald Cox, *Pitcher*

Not to be confused with the slick-fielding third baseman of the same name, the pitcher Cox played with both St. Louis entries as well as the White Sox during his major league career. A wild pitcher, Bill's last pitch at the highest level came in 1940 with the Browns. He left the game, joined the United States Army and was shipped overseas to Germany during World War II.

W	L	PCT	G	GS	CG	IP	H	BB	SO	SHO	ERA
2	9	.182	50	12	3	117	137	74	45	0	6.54

William Richard Cox, *Shortstop*

Regarded by many who saw him play as the greatest defensive third baseman ever, Cox initially came up with the Pirates as a shortstop. Billy served as Hall of Famer Arky Vaughan's backup during his rookie season in 1941. The next four years were lost to the war, as Cox served in the army. He became the Pirates' everyday shortstop after his discharge and led all NL shortstops with a .290 batting average. As well as being a dynamo with the leather, Billy was also a very difficult strikeout victim — he fanned just fifteen times in 411 at-bats in 1946. It wasn't until his trade to Brooklyn when Billy settled in at the hot corner. Former teammate and Orioles PA announcer Rex Barney said, "Billy Cox was the best third baseman I ever saw."

G	R	H	2B	3B	HR	RBI	BB	SO	SB	AVG	Slug
1,058	470	974	174	32	66	351	298	218	42	.262	.380

Harry Francis Craft, *Outfield*

Harry announced his presence at the major league level with authority in 1938 but never could duplicate the numbers he posted in his rookie season. He played in the 1939 World Series and managed a .091 batting average against the Yankees. Craft's numbers declined steadily over the course of his career until he was summoned for military duty. Craft, who would go on to manage the Kansas City Athletics, served in the navy and played service ball at Chapel Hill.

Craft trained at Chapel Hill and was awarded the rank of ensign. His training was in the physical instructor branch, which tested the agility and durability of the former big leaguer. Of the training, Craft said, "I liked it fine in the navy, but it was one tough thirty days at Chapel Hill. I am telling you that you have to be in condition to go through that. They keep you on the jump from 5:30 A.M. to 10:30 P.M. and you have absolutely no idle moments on your hands." From Chapel Hill, Craft was transferred to the physical instructor's wing at Del Monte Navy Pre-Flight School.

G	R	H	2B	3B	HR	RBI	BB	SO	SB	AVG	Slug
566	237	533	85	25	44	267	110	203	14	.253	.380

Howard Oliver Craghead, *Pitcher*

A notorious hothead, Craghead could have generated more mileage from his talents had he applied himself. An educated man, "Judge" was far more interested in his academic pursuits than anything baseball had to offer. When he was toiling in the minors, he was considered one of the best-educated men in baseball, but all his education couldn't guide him along in the game. He once refused to pitch in the final game of the season because he intended to quit baseball and further build upon his education.

The Judge pitched for the Indians briefly in the early 1930s, and given his less-than-lofty ambitions on the diamond, didn't fare well in Cleveland. He was farmed out after the 1933 season and was never heard from again at the major league level. Ten years later, Craghead joined the United States Navy and was able to play a little service ball in the colors. But Craghead didn't join the service to play a game he had little use for when he was in its professional ranks. The Judge was a leader of soldiers with the rank of lieutenant commander.

W	L	PCT	G	GS	CG	IP	H	BB	SO	SHO	ERA
0	0	—	15	0	0	23	27	12	4	0	6.26

Patrick Francis Creeden, *Reserve*

Creeden had a cup of coffee with the 1931 Red Sox managed by Shano Collins. The Massachusetts native was a star athlete at Boston College but failed to make the grade in the professional ranks. During the war, the college graduate had a knack for foreign languages and was sent to the University of Pennsylvania to study Japanese just before the war ended.

G	R	H	2B	3B	HR	RBI	BB	SO	SB	AVG	Slug
5	0	0	0	0	0	0	1	3	0	.000	.000

Robert Anthony Cremins, *Pitcher*

A talented man, "Crooked Arm" Cremins was a noted artist who became a cartoonist with the *Philadelphia Evening Bulletin* after his baseball career. His tenure at the major league level was brief. He pitched for the 1927 Red Sox and would often in his latter years tell folks that the first batter he ever faced in the bigs was none other than Babe Ruth, who he retired on a ground out. During the Second World War, Cremins served on an air-sea rescue vehicle.

W	L	PCT	G	GS	CG	IP	H	BB	SO	SHO	ERA
0	0	—	4	0	0	5	5	3	0	0	5.40

Frank Angelo Joseph "Creepy" Crespi, *Second Base*

Crespi was a hard-nosed second baseman for the Cardinals in the late 1930s and early 1940s. His baseball tenure came to an end while serving in the military, as an injury sustained while playing service ball ruined his career. Creepy worked for Emerson Electric Company prior to his military induction, and the scrappy infielder was ordered to report for his military induction at Jefferson Barracks on February 20, 1943. Crespi was stationed at Fort Riley where he played on the same service team as Dodger great Pistol Pete Reiser.

It was during a game at Fort Riley when Creepy suffered his career-ending injury. He broke his leg during the game and doctors would later perform 22 separate operations on his leg. A brace was fixed to the shattered shin bone but the screws on the brace worked through Crespi's flesh and caused an infection. Skin and bone grafts were made to repair the damage, and with his leg encased in a cast, he was confined to a wheelchair. When the war had ended and all the ballplayers had returned to their respective teams, Creepy was stranded in the army, unable to receive his discharge while he was healing in hospitals. Former teammate Johnny Hopp described

Creepy's plight by saying, "Frank has dropped out of our lives and from all I can learn, he's out for good. Why, a piece of bone had to be taken from his leg this big (holds thumb and forefinger about two and one-half inches apart), but that's no reason for us to forget he's alive. He's had an awful bad break but if I know Crespi, he'll beat it yet."

Creepy Crespi finally received his discharge from the army in the fall of 1946. With the discharge came aspirations of renewing his baseball career. After his discharge, Creepy said, "I've got just that one operation left for the leg I broke in an army game with a semi-pro outfit. Sometimes a guy is up and around three weeks after the job, but I figure it will take me another six weeks to work into shape." Despite his unmatched work ethic and desire to resume his career, Crespi was unable to work his leg back into condition and had to forego his dream of returning to the majors.

G	R	H	2B	3B	HR	RBI	BB	SO	SB	AVG	Slug
264	125	240	32	4	4	88	90	102	8	.263	.321

John Melvin "Jack" Crimian, *Pitcher*

A teenager during the war, Crimian joined Uncle Sam's outfit shortly after his high school graduation. Jack served a year with the 82nd Airborne Division at Fort Bragg, North Carolina, before he made his major league debut. His initial game at the highest level didn't come until 1951 when he joined Marty Marion's Redbirds. He would later pitch with the Kansas City Athletics and the Detroit Tigers.

W	L	PCT	G	GS	CG	IP	H	BB	SO	SHO	ERA
5	9	.357	74	7	0	160	177	65	69	0	6.35

Joffre James Cross, *Shortstop*

A back-up shortstop, Cross hit just two points over his weight during his major league career. He played with the Redbirds in 1942 and then missed the next three seasons to service in the armed forces. Jeff returned to the Cardinals in 1946 and played sparingly with them until he was dealt to the Cubs during the 1948 season, his last in the majors.

G	R	H	2B	3B	HR	RBI	BB	SO	SB	AVG	Slug
119	22	23	4	0	0	10	20	18	4	.162	.190

Frank Donald Croucher, *Second Base*

Croucher supplanted the aging Billy Rogell as the Tigers' starting shortstop in 1939 and hit .269 in his rookie season. Despite his decent showing, Detroit obtained the fiery star Dick Bartell for the 1940 season and Frank became a reserve infielder. He retained his starting job in 1941 but was the only Detroit regular who struck out more than he walked. Looking for some infield help after losing Cecil Travis and Buddy Lewis, the Senators obtained Croucher for the 1942 season, but he was sidelined with a sore arm most of the year. The following season, Croucher was inducted into the United States Army.

Croucher, who had a history of injuring himself on the ball diamond, was stationed at Fort Sam Houston. Bucky Harris had just converted Frank into a second baseman as the former major leaguer took his new-found versatility to the military. He played service ball with Cardinal pitcher Howie Pollet at the San Antonio Aviation Cadet Center. After his military tour had concluded, Croucher never again played at the major league level.

G	R	H	2B	3B	HR	RBI	BB	SO	SB	AVG	Slug
296	94	235	37	5	7	86	56	128	4	.251	.324

Arthur Elliott "Buddy" Crump, *Outfield*

Crump played one game at the major league level. He started in center field in a contest for John McGraw's 1924 Giants and failed to get a hit. But his two errors in the field sealed his fate. He was banished from the Giants and never returned to the majors. In his forties during the war, Crump served with the United States Army.

G	R	H	2B	3B	HR	RBI	BB	SO	SB	AVG	Slug
1	0	0	0	0	0	1	0	1	0	.000	.000

John William "Jimmie" Crutchfield, *Outfield*

A lean center fielder from Moberly, Missouri, Crutchfield was a fine all-around player with good speed and a nice line-drive stroke. Because he hit liners and not home runs, writers likened him to white baseball's Lloyd Waner. A star with the Pittsburgh Crawfords during the 1930s, Jimmie's greatest attribute was his glove. A gifted ballhawk and a bit of a showman, he would sometimes catch flyballs behind his back if the game had stalled. Jimmie missed a short stretch to the war effort during World War II, but his baseball career was practically over by that time.

(1930–1945): Pittsburgh Crawfords, Newark Eagles, Chicago American Giants, Birmingham Black Barons, Indianapolis ABCs, Philadelphia Stars and Cleveland Buckeyes

Benjamin Baldy Culp, *Catcher*

Culp spent two and a half years at the major league level. He received very little playing time as a third- or fourth-string catcher. Benny, who was the father of five children during his playing days, took his pre-induction physical in late May of 1944. Shortly thereafter, early in the 1944 baseball season, Culp was inducted into the navy.

G	R	H	2B	3B	HR	RBI	BB	SO	SB	AVG	Slug
15	5	5	1	0	0	2	3	3	0	.192	.231

Vernon Eugene Curtis, *Pitcher*

Curtis pitched briefly at the major league level. He was drafted into the armed forces early in the 1944 baseball season. Curtis missed the better part of two years to service in the United States Navy and returned to the Senators to pitch in 1946, his last action at the highest level.

W	L	PCT	G	GS	CG	IP	H	BB	SO	SHO	ERA
0	1	.000	16	1	0	30	30	19	10	0	5.70

Nicholas Dominic Dallessandro, *Outfield*

Except for a brief stint with the 1937 Boston Red Sox, Dom spent his entire major league career with the Cubs. A short outfielder, Dom became the Cubs' starting left fielder in 1941. The diminutive Dom led the team with 36 doubles that year and then made the move to center field in 1942. The use of eyeglasses saved his career in its early stages. He was able to play ball through the majority of the war but was drafted into the army in 1945. Dom spent one year in the army, stationed at Fort Lewis.

G	R	H	2B	3B	HR	RBI	BB	SO	SB	AVG	Slug
746	242	520	110	23	22	303	310	150	16	.267	.381

Harry Danning, *Catcher*

Nicknamed "Harry the Horse," Danning caught for the Giants from 1933 to 1942. When he first came up, the Giants already boasted a remarkable catcher in Gus Mancuso, as the Horse served as Mancuso's backup until 1937, when an injury to Mancuso opened the door for Harry. Danning, who was a free-swinger at the plate, hit the apple at a .288 clip in 1937. Skipper Bill Terry saw enough in Danning to name him the regular catcher over Mancuso in 1938. The Horse responded by hitting .306 with 60 RBIs. Harry enjoyed his finest year in 1939, when he hit .313 with 16 home runs and 74 RBIs. He drove in 91 runs the following year, but the Giants had steadily been sinking in the standings after Terry replaced Mancuso with Harry in 1937.

Danning was initially granted a deferment by his draft board because he and his wife were expecting a child. His deferment allowed him to work for a Los Angeles film studio after the 1942 baseball season, but since his job was not instrumental to the war effort, he was inducted into the army in early 1943. Upon his induction, Danning said, "I'm through with baseball. From now on I'm going to be in there pitching instead of catching."

The Horse served with the Long Beach Air Ferry Command and played some service ball in his spare time. Due to aching knees, Harry converted himself into a pitcher while playing for Uncle Sam. He received a medical discharge from the army in 1945 due to arthritic conditions in both of his knees. Because of the injury, Harry wrote a letter of retirement to the Giants' president, stating, "The army doctors warned me not to play any more ball."

G	R	H	2B	3B	HR	RBI	BB	SO	SB	AVG	Slug
890	363	847	162	26	57	397	187	217	13	.285	.415

Clifford Roland Dapper, *Catcher*

Dapper, a catcher who had his remarkable 1942 season cut short, was drafted into the Navy with a .471 batting average. He played ball on the same service club with Billy Herman, Bob Lemon and Whitey Platt at Pearl Harbor. He was attached to a squadron that was en route to land on Tokyo Bay when President Truman dropped the bomb on Hiroshima, an action he credits for saving his life.

G	R	H	2B	3B	HR	RBI	BB	SO	SB	AVG	Slug
8	2	8	1	0	1	9	2	2	0	.471	.706

Alvin Ralph Dark, *Shortstop*

A gifted natural athlete, Dark was a football sensation at the college level during the war. A gridiron standout in 1943 and 1944, Dark appeared poised for a long career in the pro ranks of football but he left the campus for the Marine Corps near the close of the war. Dark was commissioned a lieutenant in the Marines and served a year in the colors near the end of the fighting. After he received his discharge, Dark signed to play baseball and won the 1948 NL Rookie of the Year Award.

G	R	H	2B	3B	HR	RBI	BB	SO	SB	AVG	Slug
1,828	1,064	2,089	358	72	126	757	430	534	59	.289	.411

Lawrence Columbus "Crash" Davis, *Utility Infielder*

Crash's name was used in the classic film *Bull Durham*. Much like the character in the film, Crash Davis' major league career was quite brief. He strode to the plate 444 times in three years with the Athletics. He served as a backup for infielders Benny McCoy and Pete Suder. Crash left for the navy after the conclusion of the 1942 baseball season and played service ball for the Norfolk Naval Air Station. His occupational duties centered on physical training.

G	R	H	2B	3B	HR	RBI	BB	SO	SB	AVG	Slug
148	43	102	12	2	2	43	35	56	2	.230	.279

John Humphrey Davis, *Third Base*

Davis played one year at the major league level as he served as Dick Bartell's backup. John was inducted into the U.S. Army Air Corps after the 1941 season and spent four years in the armed forces. Upon his discharge, Davis never made it back to the majors.

G	R	H	2B	3B	HR	RBI	BB	SO	SB	AVG	Slug
21	8	15	3	0	0	5	8	12	0	.214	.257

Ross Davis, *Pitcher*

A right-handed pitcher with a brief career in the Negro Leagues, Davis missed the 1944 and 1945 seasons to military service during World War II.

(1940–1947): Cleveland Buckeyes, Baltimore Elite Giants and Boston Blues

Thomas Oscar "Tod" Davis, *Utility Infielder*

Davis played with the first Philadelphia A's team ever managed by a man not named Connie Mack. Tod had a trial with the A's in 1949 when Mack was still at the helm but last played for the club in 1951 after Jimmy Dykes replaced the veteran skipper. Davis missed some minor league action to military service.

G	R	H	2B	3B	HR	RBI	BB	SO	SB	AVG	Slug
42	7	21	0	1	1	6	10	19	0	.233	.289

Leon Day, *Pitcher*

One of black baseball's finest pitchers in the years before World War II, Day was elected to the Baseball Hall of Fame just prior to his death. An outstanding pitcher who hit exceptionally well, Day could be likened to white baseball's Wes Ferrell. A member of the Newark Eagles before the war, Day was clearly the staff ace and regarded as the best talent on the team. Near the top of his game, Leon was drafted into the military during World War II. Attached to an amphibious unit, Leon was active in the Utah Beach Invasion.

Although Day only missed two years to the war, they were prime years and perhaps the best seasons of baseball he could have had. After his discharge, he pitched an Opening Day no-hitter in 1946. He led the Eagles to a World Series victory over the Kansas City Monarchs that season. Since Day was in his thirties after Jackie Robinson broke the color barrier, teams passed on him. Author Mark Ribowsky wrote, "Day was a great team leader and arguably the most consistent pitcher in the Negro Leagues in the 1940s." He last pitched in the Negro Leagues in 1950 and signed to play some minor league ball during the 1950s but was no longer a star pitcher and couldn't work his way to the majors.

(1934–1954): Newark Eagles, Baltimore Elite Giants and Baltimore Black Sox

Alfred Lovill "Chubby" Dean, *Pitcher*

Dean could have easily made a name for himself on the basketball court, as he was described as a "cage luminary" during his collegiate days at Duke University. A southpaw with a deceptive delivery, he received praise from White Sox star Taffy Wright, who claimed Chubby was the best pitcher he ever faced. An all-around gifted athlete, Dean hit at a .274 clip during his stay in the major leagues.

Connie Mack gave Dean his first trial in 1937 with his Philadelphia Athletics, and the portsider won his only decision that year. He led the Athletics in saves during the 1939 campaign and suffered through a horrendous 1940 season, which saw his ERA skyrocket to 6.62. After picking up where he left off the following year, Dean was dealt to the Indians, where he lowered his ERA to 3.60 in 1942. Chubby posted a 5–5 record in 1943 before he was drafted into the army late in the season. He was inducted into the army at his hometown of Mount Airy, North Carolina, and was assigned to Daniel Field where he teamed with Cleveland chum Pete Center.

A U.S. Marine ballclub came to Daniel Field to take on Dean's Fliers. One of the players on this Marine outfit was Cleveland catcher Gene Desautels. The two players knew one another well, serving as battery mates in the major leagues. When the game reached the ninth inning, Desautels was due to face Dean in a pivotal moment in the game. The Marine manager ordered Gene back to the dugout and sent in a soldier named McNamara, who had no Organized Baseball experience. The skipper told McNamara that Dean was well aware of Desautels' weaknesses, so he decided to send in an unknown commodity to face the professional southpaw. The skipper said, "Dean knows Desautels but he doesn't know a thing about you. Go up there and win the game."

Chubby Dean proceeded to strikeout McNamara on three straight pitches. The soldier strolled back to the dugout with his bat on his shoulder, upset for having lost the game. He glared at his manager and said, "Dean may not have known anything about me, but it didn't take him long to learn."

After Chubby Dean was discharged, the Indians told him they had no use for him. The lefty tried to catch on with any interested party but found his only taker in a Class D league, based in his hometown of Mount Airy.

W	L	PCT	G	GS	CG	IP	H	BB	SO	SHO	ERA
30	46	.395	162	68	23	686	781	232	195	1	5.08

William Alexander Deitrick, *Outfield/Shortstop*

Deitrick made his major league debut in the late 1920s with the Phillies. In only his second year at the highest level, Bill sustained a broken leg that all but ended his days as a professional ballplayer. However, he was a highly educated man and had options to pursue outside of baseball. With a degree in law, Bill took to the courts and argued cases before judges and juries.

His baseball career was halted by a broken leg, and when Pearl Harbor was bombed, Bill's law career was put on hold for military employment. Deitrick joined the United States Navy as a commissioned officer, but not the type that sat behind a desk and pushed papers. Lieutenant Commander Deitrick was in combat action with his troops and built a distinguished service record while participating in battles at Iwo Jima and Okinawa. He returned home a decorated war hero. But while he was able to escape death on the battlefield, Bill's life was claimed a few months after he returned to America.

G	R	H	2B	3B	HR	RBI	BB	SO	SB	AVG	Slug
57	14	21	6	0	0	7	17	10	1	.198	.255

Mike Dan Dejan, *Outfield*

Dejan had a cup of coffee with the 1940 world champion Reds. That championship season was the extent of Mike's major league career. Although his career on the ball diamond was brief and undistinguished, his tenure under Uncle Sam was the opposite. Dejan enlisted in the army and served in the Tank Battalion. Shipped overseas, Sergeant Dejan witnessed heavy combat action in his armored vehicle unit. Wounded in action on the French battlefields, Dejan received a Silver Star among other medals for his war-time gallantry.

G	R	H	2B	3B	HR	RBI	BB	SO	SB	AVG	Slug
12	1	3	0	1	0	2	3	0	0	.188	.313

Garton Orville Del Savio, *Shortstop*

A war-era ballplayer, Del Savio had a cup of coffee with the 1943 Phillies. He had voluntarily retired in 1942 to work a war-time plant job but returned to ball with the Syracuse club in 1943. In need of some infield depth, the Phillies purchased Garton's contract and used him in a few games in the 1943 season. Del Savio, a proficient oil painter, then left baseball and joined the United States Coast Guard where he served for the duration.

G	R	H	2B	3B	HR	RBI	BB	SO	SB	AVG	Slug
4	0	1	0	0	0	0	1	0	0	.091	.091

James Henry Delsing, *Outfield*

A decent little outfielder with a good batting eye and some surprise power, Delsing served in the military prior to his major league debut. The portside swinger spent some time with the Pale Hose and Yankees before he was finally able to play regularly with the Browns in the early 1950s.

G	R	H	2B	3B	HR	RBI	BB	SO	SB	AVG	Slug
822	322	627	112	21	40	286	299	251	15	.255	.366

William Lester DeMars, *Shortstop*

Best known as the longtime hitting coach for the Philadelphia Phillies, DeMars served with the U.S. Navy during World War II before his major league debut. In the navy DeMars was able to hone his baseball skills with some pretty fair company while not engaged in his military duties. While recollecting on his time in the navy, DeMars said, "I was able to play baseball in the navy. I played shortstop and my double play partner was a second baseman named Charlie Gehringer, who was one of the best. The left fielder on that service club was Ted Williams. So we had a pretty good team."

DeMars served in the radio branch while in the navy. The kid from Brooklyn received his discharge and was sent to Nashua, a Dodgers farm club, after the war. On that team were three future Brooklyn legends: Walter Alston, Roy Campanella and Don Newcombe. But after the season his career made a sharp turn when the Athletics took him in the Rule V Draft. Kept on the roster the entire year before he was ready for the majors, he was used sparingly, which didn't have a positive impact on his development. He would later play with the Browns for a time before a stint as a minor league manager and then major league batting coach.

G	R	H	2B	3B	HR	RBI	BB	SO	SB	AVG	Slug
80	29	50	5	1	0	14	28	16	0	.237	.270

Cornelius Francis "Con" Dempsey, *Pitcher*

Dempsey had a cup of coffee with Billy Meyer's 1951 Pirates and was roughed up in his brief trial. The right-hander from San Francisco missed minor league time while he served in the armed forces during World War II.

W	L	PCT	G	GS	CG	IP	H	BB	SO	SHO	ERA
0	2	.000	3	2	0	7	11	4	3	0	9.00

Samuel Joseph Dente, *Shortstop*

Dente served in the armed forces before he made his major league debut. The scrappy infielder played briefly for the Braves but didn't become a regular until the Senators acquired him in the late 1940s. Sam, who is the grandfather of current Tigers pitcher Rick Porcello, handled the bat nicely and was very difficult to strike out.

G	R	H	2B	3B	HR	RBI	BB	SO	SB	AVG	Slug
745	205	585	78	16	4	214	167	96	9	.252	.305

Eugene Abraham Desautels, *Catcher*

A lightweight catcher, Gene spent the majority of his major league career in platoon situations. His first major league assignment was sharing backstop duties with Ray Hayworth and Pinky Hargrave in Detroit. He then caught on with the Red Sox and platooned with Moe Berg, a famous spy during World War II after his playing days had concluded, and Johnny Peacock. His last assignment came with the Indians, where he split time with Rollie Hemsley and a young Jim Hegan. Gene only missed one full baseball season to the war effort, as he served at Parris Island in the Marine Corps. He received his discharge in late July 1945 and played one final year with the Tribe.

G	R	H	2B	3B	HR	RBI	BB	SO	SB	AVG	Slug
712	211	469	71	11	3	186	233	167	12	.233	.285

Robert Sterling "Ducky" Detweiler, *Third Base*

With a career batting average over .300, it may come as a shock to some that Ducky wasn't given much of a chance to stick in the major leagues. He had brief trials with the Braves in 1942 and 1946, with the years in between lost to military service. A great minor league player, Detweiler hit in 40 consecutive games in the Three-I League. During his stint in the military, Ducky served at the New Cumberland Reception Center where he played on a service ballclub with Philadelphia Athletics wallbanger Elmer Valo.

G	R	H	2B	3B	HR	RBI	BB	SO	SB	AVG	Slug
13	3	14	2	1	0	5	2	7	0	.311	.400

William Malcolm Dickey, *Catcher*

Hall of Fame catcher Bill Dickey is now best known for "learning Yogi Berra all of his experiences." An adept teacher, Dickey was also a student of the game, regarded by more than one analyst as the best catcher in baseball history. In the same manner as teammate Red Ruffing, Bill was at the end of his major league career when Uncle Sam requested his presence. In 1943, his last year before his military stint, Bill had already begun platooning behind the plate with Rollie Hemsley, as his days were obviously coming to a close. Despite his impending end as a baseball player, Dickey was still able to manage a .351 batting average for the 1943 season.

Bill missed the 1944 and 1945 seasons to service in the United States Navy. In his upper thirties, he was asked to organize recreational activities for soldiers in the Pacific. The Yankees backstop was stationed at a naval hospital on the islands. He was able to travel the Pacific with a group of baseball players, putting on exhibition games for the morale of the soldiers. His final year in the majors was served as a player/manager with the 1946 Yankees, when he was asked to succeed the legendary Joe McCarthy.

G	R	H	2B	3B	HR	RBI	BB	SO	SB	AVG	Slug
1,789	930	1,969	343	72	202	1,209	678	289	36	.313	.486

George Willard Dickey, *Catcher*

Dickey, brother of Yankees Hall of Fame catcher Bill, served in the navy during World War II, missing out on three baseball campaigns. The switch-hitting receiver began his career with the Red Sox in 1935 and ended it with the White Sox in 1947.

G	R	H	2B	3B	HR	RBI	BB	SO	SB	AVG	Slug
226	36	101	12	0	4	54	63	62	4	.204	.253

George Emerson Dickman, *Pitcher*

Dickman was one of many major league ballplayers summoned for duty during World War II who was unable to regain his status as a major leaguer upon his military discharge. Never a solid pitcher, Dickman began the 1941 baseball campaign with the Red Sox but was the first Boston player to leave for the military. He enlisted in the Naval Reserve and was shipped to Hawaii, where he served at a Merchant Marine Academy. He married a former Powers model near the time of his military hitch.

W	L	PCT	G	GS	CG	IP	H	BB	SO	SHO	ERA
22	16	.595	125	24	6	350	403	153	126	1	5.32

Murry Monroe Dickson, *Pitcher*

A lot of innings were logged out of little Murry Dickson's right arm. Despite losing two full years to military service, Murry still tossed in the excess of 3,000 major league innings. Dickson made his debut in 1939 but didn't stick with the Redbirds until 1942. He was inducted into the military at Fort Leavenworth late in the 1943 baseball season. His time in the military wasn't spent instructing soldiers in physical fitness but dodging enemy bullets. Hugh Fullerton Jr. wrote, "Murry Dickson and Howie Krist, former Cardinal hurlers, met recently in a foxhole somewhere in France — and those weren't base hits whistling overhead, either."

Although the war offered hazardous duty for Murry, he was able to take time out to pitch on occasion. He pitched and won the first American baseball game held in Germany during the war. In the contest, Murry took the hill for the 15th Army's 35th Division as he led them to victory over the 106th Division. He returned to baseball in 1946 a much better pitcher than when he left. Murry led the Cardinals to the 1946 World Series with a 15–6 record. His .716 winning percentage was tops in the NL, and he was named the starting pitcher of Game 7.

W	L	PCT	G	GS	CG	IP	H	BB	SO	SHO	ERA
172	181	.487	625	338	149	3,053	3,029	1,058	1,281	27	3.66

Charles Edward Allen Diering, *Outfield*

Diering had to wait his turn at the major league level. When he made his debut, the Redbirds had an enviable outfield of Stan Musial, Terry Moore and Enos Slaughter, so Chuck was used as a pinch-hitter. When Moore retired, the door was opened for Chuck. Throughout his baseball career, Diering showcased a selective batting eye. Before he made his major league debut, he served in the armed forces during World War II.

G	R	H	2B	3B	HR	RBI	BB	SO	SB	AVG	Slug
752	217	411	76	14	14	141	237	250	16	.249	.338

Lloyd Arthur "Dutch" Dietz, *Pitcher*

On the Dodgers' war roster, Dutch never appeared in a major league game with Brooklyn. He was an off-season acquisition from the Phillies after the 1943 season. Used primarily as a relief pitcher during his career, Dietz spent two years in the service and never pitched in the majors again after the war.

W	L	PCT	G	GS	CG	IP	H	BB	SO	SHO	ERA
14	16	.467	106	21	7	294	303	113	79	1	3.89

Robert Bernard Dillinger, *Third Base*

Military service actually benefited some young ballplayers. The bespectacled Dillinger was a virtual unknown before the war, but while playing service ball he became a top prospect that every team wanted. A throwback-type of ballplayer, Bob was a speedy third baseman who almost single-handedly brought back the stolen base. The age in which Dillinger played was characterized more for its Slugging and less for its speed, but Bob's game was based on speed.

Dillinger joined the Army Air Corps when he was still playing minor league ball. His tenure in Uncle Sam's outfit may have pushed back his major league debut, but it also set a stage for Bob to showcase his talents. In the service, Bob was shipped overseas to the Pacific Theatre of operations. On foreign grounds, Bob was able to play some service ball with Browns star center fielder Walt Judnich and another post-war sensation named Ferris Fain. After his discharge from the AAF, Dillinger made the Browns roster. By 1947, he copped his first stolen base crown — he was the only player in the majors to eclipse 30 steals that season.

G	R	H	2B	3B	HR	RBI	BB	SO	SB	AVG	Slug
753	401	888	123	47	10	213	251	203	106	.306	.391

Dominic Paul DiMaggio, *Outfield*

If it weren't for his brother, Dominic DiMaggio would have been the top center fielder of his time. The bespectacled Bosox outfielder was a gifted natural athlete who could hawk flyballs with the best of them, run with the fleetest stars of his day, and hit for average with modest power. He patrolled the Boston outfield for a number of years alongside the legendary Ted Williams, and the two men built a lasting friendship that remained until Williams' death.

When Dom was called up to the major leagues, he didn't have the typical rookie reception. All his life he was compared to Joe and had to overcome more scrutiny than most kid ballplayers. While DiMaggio played in San Francisco as a minor leaguer with the Seals, sportswriters chastised Seals management for signing Dominic, claiming they were just milking the player's last name. Dom's ambition was to show the writers that he could play this game, and when he made the majors — and made it well — he forced those West Coast writers to eat their words. A .300 hitter as a rookie in 1940, Dom followed that up with 117 runs scored in 1941. An on-base machine, he knew his job was to get on so Williams, Doerr or Foxx could drive him in. But right when the Red Sox had their team assembled for a World Series push, World War II intervened.

With poor eyesight he'd had since childhood, Dom was destined for a deferment from his draft board. When he took his induction physical, he was refused for service because his eyesight was below military standards. This piece of news may have been a blessing to some, but it was a charge against DiMaggio's fitness as a man, and he fought it. DiMaggio said, "I had to fight my way into the navy. I enlisted and at first they refused me, claiming my eyesight disqualified me. We talked and talked and talked, and I practically begged the optometrist to clear me." His pleads worked, as the doctors informed him that he could join the navy only if the War Department countersigned his request for duty, which they did.

Inducted into the navy, DiMaggio played some service ball with Benny McCoy and Don Padgett before he was reassigned to the West Coast. His military assignment during the war enabled him to remain close to home. DiMaggio said, "I was in the shore patrol and they gave me a stripped down PT boat. I was inducted at Treasure Island, in San Francisco Bay. They gave me the boat and I did errands. I knew San Francisco Bay like the back of my hand, so it was easygoing for me. People used to spot me across the Bay and say, 'There goes Dom!'"

After his discharge, DiMaggio returned to the Red Sox with their other star athletes that missed time to the war. Denied their American League championships from 1943 to 1945, Boston captured the AL flag handily — twelve games ahead of the second-place Tigers — and went to the World Series. Boston fans may have missed out on the greatest dynasty the team ever had, courtesy of a war, but Dominic DiMaggio had no regrets. He was in his baseball prime when inducted for military service, and the Red Sox had finally put all the pieces together, but something far more important was at hand and Dom was eager to help out. DiMaggio said, "I would never have stayed out of the military, no matter what. I wanted in. And I don't regret or resent any part of it. I just enjoyed that I could serve. I wasn't about to play the war on the baseball field."

G	R	H	2B	3B	HR	RBI	BB	SO	SB	AVG	Slug
1,399	1,046	1,680	308	57	87	618	750	571	100	.298	.419

Joseph Paul DiMaggio, *Outfield*

Joe DiMaggio had a reputation of being abrasive toward the media, but he had every reason to be. Joltin' Joe was a great baseball player — cited by many as the greatest of all-time — and with the war raging overseas, baseball players were expected to do their bit as well. The Yankee Clipper had played in the 1941 and 1942 Fall Classics and was preparing for a life in the military early in 1943, but all the newspapers seemed to care about were the reports concerning his marital problems. The Knaves of the Newspapers constantly infiltrated his personal affairs, neglecting to write about his baseball exploits or his desire to enlist in the army. Scandal was their concern, and DiMaggio, who cherished privacy, was portrayed as an abrasive swell-head because he didn't give the reporters full disclosure.

Joe DiMaggio voluntarily enlisted in the army despite his 3-A classification, thus surrendering a $43,750 salary for $50 a month under Uncle Sam. DiMaggio said at his enlistment, "I'm glad this business has been settled. I'll try my best to make a good soldier and I think I'll be able to hit this new kind of pitching." The Yankee Clipper took his basic training at the AAF West Coast Training Center in Santa Ana, California. Despite the fact that many ballplayers who had been serving in the armed forces were able to play baseball, Joe decided not to bring his diamond gear with him to Santa Ana.

At Santa Ana, Joe served as a physical instructor. He was in charge of running troops, as he'd take a group of cadets into the countryside and run one or two miles with them. After that run, Joe would take another group out and then another; he often ran eight to ten miles a day in the army. He thoroughly enjoyed life in the army, far away from the ball diamond and the social stardom that came with it. Joe said, "In the army I lead the sweet, pure life. I weigh 198 pounds now — and that's right on the button."

A promotion to sergeant came in his first year in the army. Sergeant Joltin' Joe said, "Sometimes I go to bed as early as 7:30 or 8 o'clock at night. I get up at 5 o'clock every morning, too." He was shipped overseas and spent six months with the 7th Air Force in Hawaii. While in Hawaii, Joe played some baseball, did radio work and visited convalescent hospitals.

After DiMaggio received his discharge, he displayed an eagerness to return to the game, saying, "It will take a lot of overtime for me to regain my coordination ... but of course I've got my heart set on coming back. I miss the game." Joe hit .290 his first year back in pinstripes, and finished behind Charlie Keller for second on the club in home runs and RBIs. After a third-place finish in 1946, Joltin' Joe guided the Yankees to an American League championship in 1947, when he paced the club in hits, home runs, RBIs and batting average. Although he had been back for two years, he enjoyed his finest season since 1941 when he led the AL with 39 home runs and 155 RBIs in 1948. When his numbers began to slip in 1951, the ever graceful and dignified DiMaggio hung up his spikes when he was no longer able to play like the Joltin' Joe of old.

G	R	H	2B	3B	HR	RBI	BB	SO	SB	AVG	Slug
1,736	1,390	2,214	389	131	361	1,537	790	369	30	.325	.579

Robert Louis Paul DiPietro, *Reserve*

Just a youngster during World War II, Bob joined the service after high school and served in the latter stages of the war. Bob had a cup of coffee with the 1951 Red Sox, his only major league action.

G	R	H	2B	3B	HR	RBI	BB	SO	SB	AVG	Slug
4	0	1	0	0	0	0	1	1	0	.091	.091

John Craig "Sonny" Dixon, *Pitcher*

A switch-hitting pitcher from North Carolina, Dixon spent the bulk of his career as a long arm out of the bullpen. Originally with the Senators, Dixon moved on to the Philadelphia A's and was with the club when they relocated to Kansas City. He ended his major league career with the 1956 world champion Yankees. Before he threw his first pitch at the major league level, Sonny served in the navy and was stationed in the Pacific Theatre.

W	L	PCT	G	GS	CG	IP	H	BB	SO	SHO	ERA
11	18	.379	102	12	4	263	296	75	90	0	4.17

Raymond Joseph Dobens, *Pitcher*

Dobens had a cup of coffee with the last-place Red Sox of 1929. Before he took the mound at Fenway, Ray pitched at the college level under World War I veteran Jack Barry at Holy Cross. When the Second World War broke out, Dobens was pushing forty but he joined the navy to lend his hand in the battle. He served in the Pacific Theatre and was stationed in China for a time. After his discharge, Dobens coached high school athletics and then operated an insurance company in his hometown of Nashua until his death.

W	L	PCT	G	GS	CG	IP	H	BB	SO	SHO	ERA
0	0	—	11	1	0	28	32	9	4	0	3.86

Joseph Gordon Dobson, *Pitcher*

Nicknamed "Burrhead," the Oklahoma native was the most successful hurler the Red Sox used in the 1946 World Series. In that season's Fall Classic, Dobson tossed 12 innings and surrendered just four hits while posting a 0.00 ERA.

Dobson made his debut with the 1939 Cleveland Indians and pitched with pronounced wildness out of Ossie Vitt's bullpen. He was dealt to the Red Sox in 1941 and posted a solid 12–5 record for Boston. He spent the next year as the team's number three starter (behind Tex Hughson and Charlie Wagner) and was summoned for military duty after the conclusion of the 1943 baseball season. He was inducted into the army on December 22, 1943, and was stationed at Camp Wheeler, Georgia. During a visit to Fenway Park while on furlough, Joe met with team secretary Phil Troy to talk about his army training. Dobson said to Troy, "Ask me some names of gun parts. I know lots of guns and I know how to pull 'em apart.

I can assemble 'em too, without having any parts left — big or small."

W	L	PCT	G	GS	CG	IP	H	BB	SO	SHO	ERA
137	103	.571	414	273	112	2,172	2,048	851	992	22	3.62

Lawrence Eugene Doby, *Second Base*

Before Larry Doby was an All-Star outfielder with the Cleveland Indians, he was a second baseman with the Negro Leagues' Newark Eagles. A Hall of Famer, Doby had just started his career in the Negro Leagues when he was inducted into the armed forces for service during World War II. He served two years in the navy before he returned to the Eagles and helped them to a title in 1946. Signed by the Cleveland Indians, Larry was the first black player in the American League.

Although Larry received less press than Jackie Robinson, he was subjected to the same pressures and abuse as the first black ballplayer in the American League. Many sportswriters didn't deem it necessary to write the same stories about Doby since they covered the ground earlier with Robinson. Granted, he came along after Jackie, but Doby's trail was no less arduous. In his book, *A Complete History of the Negro Leagues,* Mark Ribowsky contrasted Larry with Jackie. He wrote, "Doby, who has none of Robinson's white-hot inner fire, was an eerily quiet and timid man, and was prone to accept things as they came."

G	R	H	2B	3B	HR	RBI	BB	SO	SB	AVG	Slug
1,533	960	1,515	243	52	253	970	871	1,011	47	.283	.490

Robert Pershing Doerr, *Second Base*

The premier second baseman in baseball during the 1940s, Doerr took over the role vacated when Charlie Gehringer's career was at its end. A star in the Pacific Coast League before he made the majors, Doerr was signed by the Red Sox on the same scouting trip that also netted the team Ted Williams. Boston received two Hall of Famers for the price of one California ticket. By the time World War II broke out, Doerr was already established as an elite major league second baseman. He enjoyed a 100-RBI season in 1940 and had his second such campaign in 1942. The Red Sox were on their way up but the war intervened and Doerr was about all Boston had left.

Doerr was still active on the Red Sox roster in 1944 after they had lost Williams, DiMaggio, Pesky and Harris. With such star power gone, Doerr had little support on the Red Sox roster, and Boston never made a run during the war years. Late in the 1944 season, it was Bobby's turn to join his chums in the military. Of his stint in the army, Doerr said, "I was in the infantry stationed at Camp Roberts, California, and I remained there for the duration. After I went through basic training, I helped train soldiers. It was a pretty strenuous thing, you know, it was wartime so it was all serious business. You got up early every morning and a lot of times you were out late at night on missions."

At Camp Roberts, Doerr was well aware of what the Red Sox were missing out on. They had built their powerhouse club after years of finishing behind the Yankees, Athletics and Tigers, but the war tarnished their plans. However, the Red Sox players had a sense of duty and harbored no ill feelings for their time in the service. They knew that once they all came back, the American League was theirs for the taking. Doerr said, "We came back pretty good, really, the Red Sox. Most of the guys like Williams, Pesky and DiMaggio came back and we all had pretty good seasons. Of course, we won the pennant that year in '46 after everyone came back."

G	R	H	2B	3B	HR	RBI	BB	SO	SB	AVG	Slug
1,865	1,094	2,042	381	89	223	1,247	809	608	54	.288	.461

Willard Earl "Bill" Donovan, *Pitcher*

Before they were taken away for the war effort, the Braves touted Donovan and Warren Spahn as the future cornerstones of their pitching staff. The jury was out regarding who would make the better major leaguer. Donovan posted a 3.44 ERA in 1942 while Spahn's was 5.63. The two southpaws left for the military in 1943, but only one would return to the Braves. Donovan was unable to regain his form after the war and never broke off another breaking ball at the major league level.

W	L	PCT	G	GS	CG	IP	H	BB	SO	SHO	ERA
4	6	.400	38	10	2	104	114	41	24	1	3.20

Harry Dorish, *Pitcher*

A stout right-handed pitcher, Dorish had a fine major league career as a fireman after the war. Harry served with the U.S. Army before he made his major league debut. He received his first big league assignment with the defending American League champion Red Sox in 1947. Harry would flourish in the 1950s as a valuable relief pitcher in Paul Richards' White Sox bullpen.

W	L	PCT	G	GS	CG	IP	H	BB	SO	SHO	ERA
45	43	.511	323	40	13	835	850	301	332	2	3.83

Calvin Leavelle Dorsett, *Pitcher*

Many major league ballplayers were able to serve in physical training detachments: Cal Dorsett wasn't so fortunate. Although Dorsett wasn't considered a solid major league ballplayer when drafted, he did have two years of service in the bigs. Cal, who was affectionately known as "Preacher," served with the U.S. Marine Corps and his initial task was to instruct soldiers on the proper technique of hurling grenades. As a corporeal, Dorsett used his knowledge as a pitcher to teach soldiers at Camp Elliott, California, how to toss grenades like a big leaguer.

From Camp Elliott, Preacher was sent overseas where he saw action on foreign soil. The day after D-Day, he was in charge of hauling supplies from the beaches to the frontlines. Preacher would lose four years to World War II and wasn't given another look at the major league level after he received his discharge from the Marines.

W	L	PCT	G	GS	CG	IP	H	BB	SO	SHO	ERA
0	1	.000	8	2	0	13	25	13	6	0	12.46

Howard James "Danny" Doyle, *Catcher*

Doyle's major league career was rather brief, with appearances in thirteen games for the 1943 Red Sox as his lone duty. The standout basketball star of Oklahoma University lost the 1944 and 1945 seasons to service in the armed forces. After his discharge, Doyle never again suited up at the major league level.

G	R	H	2B	3B	HR	RBI	BB	SO	SB	AVG	Slug
13	2	9	1	0	0	6	7	9	0	.209	.233

Clemens Johann Dreiseward, *Pitcher*

A southpaw from Old Monroe, Missouri, "Steamboat" made his debut in the majors during the war years. Clem made seven starts with the 1944 Red Sox, and the following year was only able to make a pair of starts before he was inducted into the service. Dreiseward spent less than a year in the military at the end of the war.

W	L	PCT	G	GS	CG	IP	H	BB	SO	SHO	ERA
6	8	.429	46	10	3	141	160	39	39	0	4.53

Walter Dropo, *First Base*

A rookie sensation with the Red Sox in 1950, few freshmen have had a better debut than "Moose." Dropo hit .322, stroked 34 homers and tied teammate Vern Stephens for the American League lead in RBIs with 144. The Sox had an amazing lineup of Dropo, Stephens, Bobby Doerr, Dom DiMaggio and Ted Williams that year but finished four games behind the Yankees. The sophomore jinx bit Dropo in a big way the following year as his production was trimmed by more than half. Before his debut, Walt played some service ball at the Fort Devens Reception Center during World War II.

G	R	H	2B	3B	HR	RBI	BB	SO	SB	AVG	Slug
1,288	478	1,113	168	22	152	704	328	582	5	.270	.432

John Joseph Dudra, *Utility Infielder*

Much like teammate Ducky Detweiler, Dudra played sparingly and posted an amazing career batting average. John's only major league duty came in 1941. He hit .360 and saw action at every station on the infield. However, he entered the armed forces after the season and spent four years under Uncle Sam. Dudra earned five Battle Stars in the European Theatre.

G	R	H	2B	3B	HR	RBI	BB	SO	SB	AVG	Slug
14	3	9	3	1	0	3	3	4	0	.360	.560

Frank Duncan Jr., *Catcher*

Sometimes listed as Frank Duncan Sr., the tough, heady catcher was really a junior but he had a son, also named Frank, who played in the Negro Leagues who was usually called Frank Duncan, Jr. even though he was really Duncan the third. The elder Duncan was a fine defensive catcher for the Kansas City Monarchs of the 1920s, although he was a clear liability offensively. Baseball of the 1920s was characterized by high averages and power numbers, but Duncan usually hit around .230. He remained employed due to his leadership skills, which served him well as the team's manager.

A borderline Hall of Fame candidate as a manager, Duncan helped make the Monarchs a Negro League powerhouse. Duncan, who was born in Kansas City, became the face of the Monarchs franchise with Bullet Rogan, Newt Allen and Buck O'Neil. Near the end of his career, Frank would sometimes employ himself as a catcher or pinch-hitter to wild ovations by the Kansas City crowd. But by the 1940s, he was essentially done as a player. Despite his age, he was drafted for service during World War II and served as a sergeant in the 371st Infantry Regiment. When the age requirements were lowered, Duncan was honorably discharged after a few months of service.

(1920–1947): Kansas City Monarchs, New York Cubans, Chicago American Giants, Homestead Grays, Pittsburgh Crawfords and New York Black Yankees.

Frank Duncan III, *Pitcher*

Although he was really Frank Duncan III, Duncan was listed as "Junior" because he shared the same name as his father and manager of the Kansas City Monarchs. Junior was a pitcher and part-time outfielder of modest skills who formed an unusual father/son battery with the kid doing the pitching and the old man the receiving. Junior spent two years in the military in the early years of the war before his discharge. Afterwards, he left the Monarchs and played in Baltimore for the Elite Giants.

(1940–1947): Baltimore Elite Giants and Kansas City Monarchs

Grant Lester Dunlap, *Pinch Hitter*

Dunlap, a star at Occidental College, had a cup of coffee with Eddie Stanky's 1953 Cardinals. Despite his terrific numbers as a pinch-hitter, Dunlap was pushing thirty and wasn't called back to St. Louis after the season. During the war, Dunlap served with the U.S. Marine Corps. He joined the Marines in 1942 and remained until 1946 after most men had returned home. Dunlap was a 2nd lieutenant in the infantry before he was promoted to captain. He served overseas in the Pacific Theatre and was stationed in China. While in China, Dunlap served with future star shortstop Alvin Dark on a service basketball team that won the Southern Pacific Championship.

G	R	H	2B	3B	HR	RBI	BB	SO	SB	AVG	Slug
16	2	6	0	1	1	3	0	2	0	.353	.647

Joseph "Jake" Dunn, *Shortstop*

A versatile ballplayer that could play just about anywhere, Dunn served as a player/manager in Philadelphia. An adequate player for the Philadelphia Stars, Dunn would often rotate around the diamond to open up playing time for his younger players. After the bombing of Pearl Harbor, Jake was one of the first Negro League players to join the military. After his military discharge, he never played pro baseball again.

(1930–1941): Philadelphia Stars, Washington Pilots, Nashville Elite Giants and Baltimore Black Sox

Elmer Cable "Red" Durrett, *Outfield*

The tale of Red Durrett is a tragedy of unfulfilled potential. Before the United States became active participants in the war, Durrett was a top-level prospect in the Dodgers chain. A big, strong Texan, Red had the hitting ability to crush balls as far as Johnny Mize and the pitch recognition talents of Charlie Keller. Brooklyn held hopes of Red's power bat leading their club into the 1940s and beyond. But Brooklyn's best-laid plans did not elapse as hoped as the Japanese bombed Pearl Harbor in 1941 and Durrett quickly enlisted in the U.S. Marine Corps.

Red trained with the Marines and was one of the first fighting forces to be actively engaged in the war. Shipped overseas, Durrett and his Marines entered heavy combat action at Guadalcanal. The fighting was intense. Durrett was engaged in battle for twelve months. The tropical environment, as well as the opposing forces, took their toll on the Slugger from Sherman, Texas. During his time at Guadalcanal, Red would suffer from dysentery, malaria and a foot infection while receiving wounds and developing shell shock.

His wounds took him from the battlefield to the military hospital beds. Durrett suffered immensely from his sicknesses and wounds, so much that once in complete agony and despair he begged the doctors to end his misery. But the wounds healed and the diseases passed away, but the shell shock remained. Given an honorable discharge and a Purple Heart for his heroics, Durrett was mustered out of the Marine Corps. A completely different man, Durrett, who was once the classic physical specimen of a gifted power hitter, was a gaunt, frail-looking young man when discharged. But Red was eager to return to the ball diamond. He said, "I only wish those fellows in France were thinking about hitting a curveball now instead of thinking what they're thinking."

When Red returned to the Dodgers for spring training in 1944, the Brooklyn brass was shocked at his appearance. Their once promising, strong-as-an-ox outfielder was now in need of conditioning. The Dodgers fed Durrett well in order to get his weight up, but their choice of a training locale for 1944 was a poor selection that only exacerbated Durrett's condition. With the war underway and gasoline rationed, the Dodgers couldn't venture south for spring training and stayed up north and held their camp at West Point. Scribe Oscar Fraley described Red's first spring training back from the war, capturing the despair of the Texan by writing, "His movements were wooden and mechanical; the baseball flannels hung slackly on that once robust frame and twice, when cadet guns roared in target practice, Red hit the dirt with automatic fear."

Unable to shake the horrors of war, Durrett had a poor showing that spring and was farmed out by the Dodgers. The young man battled in the minor leagues and made his major league debut in 1944. He was given another brief trial by the Dodgers in 1945, but by 1947 the once promising prospect couldn't reach his pre-war level. That year, while toiling in the minors, Fraley wrote, "Durrett seems further away than ever today from the dream he cherished as a promising rookie. And his hopes lay in recovering that elusive something he left on the island called Guadalcanal."

G	R	H	2B	3B	HR	RBI	BB	SO	SB	AVG	Slug
19	5	7	1	0	1	1	10	13	0	.146	.229

Ervin Frank Dusak, *Outfield*

A gifted natural athlete, "Four Sack" Erv Dusak played predominantly as an outfielder but also saw time in the infield and even pitched 54 innings. During his time in the service, Erv showcased his talents on the basketball court as well as the ball diamond. He was the star player on the Fort Sheridan basketball squad. Four Sack also served with the Second Army at Memphis with former Phillies hurler Hugh Mulcahy. He was shipped overseas in 1945 and played service ball at Manila.

G	R	H	2B	3B	HR	RBI	BB	SO	SB	AVG	Slug
413	168	251	32	6	24	106	142	188	12	.243	.355

James Robert Dyck, *Third Base/Outfield*

A spot starter who could fill-in at the hot corner and in the outfield, Dyck's major league debut was pushed back courtesy of the war. Close to thirty by the time he reached the majors, Dyck showed adequate power at the highest level but was more of a role player than a regular. He missed valuable minor league time to service in the armed forces during World War II.

G	R	H	2B	3B	HR	RBI	BB	SO	SB	AVG	Slug
330	139	242	52	5	26	114	131	140	4	.246	.389

Thomas Francis Aloysius Earley, *Pitcher*

Many baseball executives feared their players would gain too much muscle mass from military training, thus hindering their mobility. General managers were worried about how athletic their ballplayers would be when they returned from a prolonged stay in the military. In 1945, Tom Earley returned to the Braves from a two-year hitch in the navy. He became a valuable case study for Braves farm director Bob Quinn.

Quinn said, "One year, maybe, but three, four and even five years [of military training] they will have developed a new set of muscles that are necessary for war but lack the skillful coordination so vital for a big leaguer." When Earley participated in Boston's spring training in 1945, it was written that he "shot put" the ball because of a stiff back and shoulder muscles. Of Tom's predicament, Quinn said, "Tom is only 27 and he ought to be able to come around. But he's a good example. He hasn't thrown a ball for over a year and you see what happens."

During Earley's stint in the navy, he served at the Norfolk Naval Training Station. While at Norfolk, Tom was able to participate occasionally on the installation's ball team. After he received his discharge, the Braves organization spurned the youngster who had served his country for two years, as they informed Tom to "wait and see" regarding a contract for the 1945 season.

W	L	PCT	G	GS	CG	IP	H	BB	SO	SHO	ERA
18	24	.429	91	37	15	360	349	143	104	2	3.78

Jacob Willard Early, *Catcher*

A gabby catcher who prided himself on disrupting opposing batters through verbal discourse, Early spent one season with the Browns and the remainder of his career with Washington. Early joined the Senators in 1939 and spent his first two years in a platoon with Rick Ferrell. Skipper Bucky Harris gave Early the starting chores in 1941 and he responded by leading the team in home runs. He drove in sixty runs in 1943 for the second-place Senators and then missed the next two years to service in the armed forces.

Jake, who was nicknamed "The Plumber" by his teammates, packed up his rifle arm and joined the army after he passed his physical exam early in 1944. His glaring deficiency on the ball diamond was his inability to read foul pop flies. To cure his ailment, Benny Bengough, a Washington coach, would hit pop-ups to him by the hour. The fiery ballplayer returned to the Senators in 1946 where Hall of Famer Harry Heilmann dubbed him "Scrap Iron Jake Whattaman."

G	R	H	2B	3B	HR	RBI	BB	SO	SB	AVG	Slug
747	216	532	98	23	32	264	281	259	7	.241	.350

George Livingston "Moose" Earnshaw, *Pitcher*

Earnshaw's brilliant career was already in the books by the

time World War II broke out. As a young lad, Moose pitched for Connie Mack's Athletics dynasty, where he formed the best righty-lefty tandem in the game with Hall of Famer Lefty Grove. Earnshaw was the hero of the 1930 World Series when he won two games, posted a 0.72 ERA and fanned 19 batters. But those ball diamond heroics were long in the past when the Japanese bombed Pearl Harbor. Despite his advanced age, the 40-year-old Earnshaw joined the navy.

In 1942, Moose had become Lieutenant Earnshaw of the United States Navy. The former pitching great was stationed at the Jacksonville Naval Air Station. By 1944, Moose was still stateside and had attained the rank of lieutenant commander before he was shipped out. Sent to the South Pacific, Earnshaw served as a gunnery officer aboard a navy aircraft carrier. It was on this massive vessel that Moose earned his wartime medals. Admiral Chester W. Nimitz awarded Moose a special citation when he saved his carrier from enemy fire at Truk. The citation read:

For meritorious conduct in the performance of outstanding service as gunnery officer of a US aircraft carrier during operations against the enemy at Truk April 29, 1944. With exceptional ability and judgment and commendable calmness, he controlled and directed effective anti-aircraft fire against three fast low-flying enemy torpedo planes and contributed directly in saving his ship from serious damage.

W	L	PCT	G	GS	CG	IP	H	BB	SO	SHO	ERA
127	93	.577	319	249	114	1,916	1,981	809	1,002	17	4.38

Gordon Hugh East, *Pitcher*

Hugh East had a forgettable major league career, which spanned three years with the Giants. He issued a ton of walks but when he did find the strike zone, batters hit him handily. East left the Giants for the navy during the 1943 season and didn't return to the Polo Grounds after his military discharge.

W	L	PCT	G	GS	CG	IP	H	BB	SO	SHO	ERA
2	6	.250	19	8	1	63	85	41	27	0	5.43

Howard Easterling, *Third Base*

The Homestead Grays' third baseman through most of the 1940s, Howard was a fixture at third in the Negro League All-Star Games. A switch-hitter from Mount Olive, Mississippi, Easterling was always overshadowed on the Grays team that featured Josh Gibson and Buck Leonard. Had he played on another team, he probably would have batted in the three of four slots the two Hall of Famers owned. During the winter of 1943–1944, knowing he was going to be drafted into the military, Howard swindled owner Cum Posey by requesting advance money for the upcoming season. After his military discharge, he returned to the Grays and apparently all was forgiven.

(1936–1949): Homestead Grays, Cincinnati Tigers, Chicago American Giants and New York Cubans

Charles Bruce Edwards, *Catcher*

The Dodgers' regular catcher in the years just after the war, Bruce did an adequate job of holding down the fort until a guy named Campanella came along. Edwards was a decent hitter with above-average power, and the Dodgers tried to get Bruce's bat in the lineup by experimenting with him at third base and the outfield. But he was a natural catcher and didn't take to the new positions. Edwards lost some minor league time to service in the armed forces during the war.

G	R	H	2B	3B	HR	RBI	BB	SO	SB	AVG	Slug
591	191	429	67	20	39	241	190	179	9	.256	.309

Foster Hamilton Edwards, *Pitcher*

A tall, lanky right-hander, Foster pitched four years with the Braves and two games with the Yankees. All of his major league action came before the war. More than ten years after he threw his last pitch at the highest level, Edwards joined Uncle Sam and served in the armed forces during World War II.

W	L	PCT	G	GS	CG	IP	H	BB	SO	SHO	ERA
6	9	.400	56	17	4	170	193	84	60	0	4.76

Henry Albert Edwards, *Outfield*

Edwards played with the Tribe from 1941 to 1949 — with two years lost to military service — and then played for five different clubs in his last four years. He came up in 1941 and served as a reserve outfielder until 1943, when his season was cut short due to a broken collarbone. After he had healed, Hank was drafted into the army and missed the 1944 and 1945 seasons to service under Uncle Sam. He played some service ball in Hawaii with Eddie Erautt. His return to the diamond in 1946 was prosperous, as Hank paced the American League with 16 triples.

G	R	H	2B	3B	HR	RBI	BB	SO	SB	AVG	Slug
735	285	613	116	41	51	276	208	264	9	.280	.440

Jacob Henry Eisenhardt, *Pitcher*

A war-era pitcher, Eisenhardt pitched only one-third of an inning with the war-ravaged 1944 Reds. The southpaw from Pennsylvania spent one year in the army during World War II.

W	L	PCT	G	GS	CG	IP	H	BB	SO	SHO	ERA
0	0	—	1	0	0	0.1	0	1	0	0	0.00

Harry Eisenstat, *Pitcher*

With pinpoint control, Eisenstat enjoyed a decent major league career, which spanned from 1935 through 1942. A marksman with a baseball, Harry served his country for four years and did not return to the diamond upon his military discharge. Although Harry had an important off-season job as head of production at the Weatherhead Company, he was summoned by his Brooklyn draft board after the 1942 baseball season. He attained the rank of lieutenant upon his discharge at Camp Beale.

W	L	PCT	G	GS	CG	IP	H	BB	SO	SHO	ERA
25	27	.481	165	33	11	479	550	114	157	1	3.83

Henry Knox "Heinie" Elder, *Pitcher*

Elder appeared in one game for the 1913 Tigers, managed by Hall of Famer Hughie Jennings. The big southpaw gave up the diamond chores for a career in the military. Heinie served in both World Wars and retired from the military with the rank of lieutenant colonel.

W	L	PCT	G	GS	CG	IP	H	BB	SO	SHO	ERA
0	0	—	1	0	0	3	4	5	0	0	9.00

Charles Willard "Red" Embree, *Pitcher*

The day after Red tossed a shutout against the Tigers in June of 1945, he left the team for the military. Red missed half of the 1945 as well as half of the 1946 season to service during the war.

W	L	PCT	G	GS	CG	IP	H	BB	SO	SHO	ERA
31	48	.392	141	90	29	707	653	330	286	1	3.72

Delmer Ennis, *Outfield*

One of the greatest RBI men in the decade directly after the Second World War, Ennis was the muscle of the Phillies legendary Whiz Kids brigade. But before Ennis was the run-producing monster the Phillies needed, he was just a kid in the navy—albeit one with tremendous skill. After his high school graduation, Ennis joined up with the navy in 1943. Del took his boot camp at Sampson Naval Training Station. He was shipped out to the South Pacific and served in the same outfit as major leaguers Johnny Vander Meer and Billy Herman. The exposure to star baseball players was an asset for Del, as he said, "They were a great help to me. I owe much to Herman. He showed me a lot about hitting and gave me other valuable advice."

Although he was just a teenager with little experience, Ennis' legend began to grow in the service ranks. The kid Slugger was the talk of Pacific Theatre baseball circles as he was often compared to Hall of Fame swatter Jimmie Foxx. Both men were powerfully built and could sock the sphere immense distances. Although his stardom was limited to the service ranks, the folks back home heard about him when former major league pitcher Johnny Rigney returned from service. Rigney sang young Ennis' praises, claiming the kid "hits a longer ball than Johnny Mize."

After Del's navy discharge, the Phillies were eager to see just how much talent their hometown boy had. Brought to spring training directly from the crude baseball diamonds of the South Pacific, Ennis wowed the Phillies brass and won the left-field assignment in 1946. Del gushed, "I'm the luckiest guy alive. I never thought I'd be playing in the majors so soon. It was a big thrill to me when Ben Chapman put me in left field when I came out of the navy in April, just after the season opened." Del Ennis had a terrific rookie season in 1946 and was named to his first All-Star team. He would go on to enjoy a very good career as an elite run-producer.

G	R	H	2B	3B	HR	RBI	BB	SO	SB	AVG	Slug
1,903	985	2,063	358	69	288	1,284	597	719	45	.284	.472

Russell Elwood Ennis, *Catcher*

Ennis appeared in one game for the 1926 Senators when the club had star backstops Muddy Ruel and Hank Severeid on the roster. The backstop served in the armed forces during World War I before his major league debut and returned to the service after his playing days to participate in the Second World War.

G	R	H	2B	3B	HR	RBI	BB	SO	SB	AVG	Slug
1	0	0	0	0	0	0	0	0	0	—	—

Albert Paul Epperly, *Pitcher*

A native of Glidden, Iowa, Epperly made his major league debut in 1938 with the Cubs. In an unusual course of events, "Pard" wouldn't return to the majors until after the war when the 1950 Dodgers gave him another trial. During the war, the journeyed right-hander served with the U.S. Army.

W	L	PCT	G	GS	CG	IP	H	BB	SO	SHO	ERA
2	0	1.000	14	4	1	36	42	20	13	0	4.00

Harold Franklin Epps, *Outfield*

Epps was a triples machine in his brief stay at the major league level. One sportswriter wrote that Hal ran "like a jackrabbit." He spent time at the major league level with both St. Louis organizations and saw his last action at the highest level in 1944 with Connie Mack's Athletics. Hal spent the 1945 and 1946 seasons in the armed forces. He served his time in the South Pacific with the United States Army.

G	R	H	2B	3B	HR	RBI	BB	SO	SB	AVG	Slug
125	58	99	13	9	1	21	37	43	5	.253	.340

Edward Lorenz Sebastian Erautt, *Pitcher*

Erautt enjoyed a six-year major league career, spent mostly with the Reds. Eddie, whose brother Joe also played in the majors, is listed in the *Baseball Encyclopedia* as having passed away in 1976, but this was his brother's date of death: Eddie Erautt is still very much alive. A right-handed pitcher who looked quite sharp in the Pacific Coast League before the war, Eddie pitched a three-hitter for Hollywood in his last start before boot camp. He served in the training division of the U.S. Army and played some service ball with Hank Edwards.

Shipped out to the Pacific Theatre, Erautt played service ball on the Hawaiian Islands during the war. After the war, he returned stateside and back to the PCL. He was regarded as a "sensational young fast ball pitcher" in an article published in the *Oakland Tribune*. The Reds took a flier on the hard-throwing kid when the great Lon Warneke gave Eddie his stamp of approval. "The Arkansas Hummingbird" said of Erautt, "He's got the pitches to win anywhere right now." Cincinnati called Eddie up in 1947, three years before his older brother, Joe, made the majors. He pitched at the highest level until 1953.

W	L	PCT	G	GS	CG	IP	H	BB	SO	SHO	ERA
15	23	.395	264	22	4	379	434	179	157	0	4.87

Joseph Michael Erautt, *Catcher*

A catcher for parts of two seasons at the major league level with the White Sox, Joe was the older brother of Reds pitcher Eddie Erautt. Joe had yet to make the majors when he was summoned by Uncle Sam for duty during World War II. The former catcher made a terrific soldier and quickly ascended in rank. When he was shipped out to the European Theatre, Joe served as a staff sergeant who saw action in Italy.

G	R	H	2B	3B	HR	RBI	BB	SO	SB	AVG	Slug
32	3	8	1	0	1	4	5	0	.186	.209	

Calvin Coolidge Ermer, *Second Base*

Ermer's major league playing career consisted of one game with the 1947 Senators. Although his time in the majors was brief,

Cal was a baseball lifer. He managed in the minors for five decades and had a brief trial in the majors as the Twins skipper in the late 1960s. He missed some minor league action to military service during the war.

G	R	H	2B	3B	HR	RBI	BB	SO	SB	AVG	Slug
1	0	0	0	0	0	0	0	0	0	.000	.000

Carl Daniel Erskine, *Pitcher*

One of the better pitchers in Brooklyn Dodgers history, "Oisk" retired with a healthy career winning percentage. He was still with the organization when the Dodgers relocated to Los Angeles in the late 1950s. During World War II, Carl was a high school student until the war had reached its latter stages. After high school graduation, Erskine joined the navy and spent a year at the Boston Navy Yard.

W	L	PCT	G	GS	CG	IP	H	BB	SO	SHO	ERA
122	78	.610	335	216	71	1,719	1,637	646	981	14	4.00

Alfred Hubert Evans, *Catcher*

A longtime Washington backstop, Evans wore the threads of the Senators for eleven years, with one year missed to the war. He spent a great deal of his career in platoon situations with the likes of Hall of Famer Rick Ferrell, Jake Early and Mickey Grasso. Evans was inducted into the navy just before the 1943 season began and returned near the end of the 1944 campaign. Al, who attended the Oak Ridge Military Academy, was stationed at the Norfolk Naval Training Station with Brooklyn Dodgers Hall of Famer Pee Wee Reese.

G	R	H	2B	3B	HR	RBI	BB	SO	SB	AVG	Slug
704	188	514	70	23	13	211	243	206	14	.250	.326

William Lawrence Evans, *Pitcher*

Evans had two brief trials at the major league level. His first action came with the 1949 White Sox and his last cup of coffee was with the 1951 Red Sox. Bill, not to be confused with the umpire of the same name, struggled with his accuracy throughout his career. During the war, Evans served in the U.S. Army and was shipped to the European Theatre.

W	L	PCT	G	GS	CG	IP	H	BB	SO	SHO	ERA
0	1	.000	13	0	0	21	21	16	4	0	5.14

Walter Arthur "Hoot" Evers, *Outfield*

A soft-spoken ballplayer in the same mold as teammate Charlie Gehringer, Hoot was referred to as an introvert by many sportswriters of his day. As far as baseball was concerned, Hoot was rather green at the time World War II broke out. He played briefly with the Tigers in 1941 and then lost the 1943 through 1945 seasons to service in the Army Air Corps. While serving under Uncle Sam, Evers was able to play service ball for Detroit teammate Birdie Tebbetts. With Birdie, Sid Hudson, Buster Mills and Bruce Campbell, Hoot lent his talents to a powerful service ballclub at the Waco Army Airfield.

Hoot returned to the Tigers in 1946, but suffered a broken ankle during the season and was able to appear in just 81 games. His breakout year came in 1947, as Hoot pounded the onion at a .292 clip with ten home runs as the Tigers' everyday center fielder. He followed up that stellar campaign with a better one by pacing the Tigers with 103 RBIs, 33 doubles and a .313 batting average in 1948. The 1950 season was his finest year, and a good one for the Tigers, who finished second in the American League despite a lofty .617 winning percentage. Hoot paced the AL with eleven triples while smacking 21 home runs and driving in 103 runs. His .323 batting average was second on the club behind batting champ George Kell. He finished his career in nomadic fashion, playing for the Red Sox, Giants, Tigers, Indians and Orioles in his last three years.

G	R	H	2B	3B	HR	RBI	BB	SO	SB	AVG	Slug
1,142	556	1,055	187	41	98	565	415	420	45	.278	.426

George Lincoln Eyrich, *Pitcher*

Eyrich was an eighteen-year-old pitching wonder from Reading, Pennsylvania, who as an amateur was touted as the next Bob Feller. The Phillies outbid other clubs for his service and he joined the major league club shortly after signing. He made nine appearances as an eighteen-year-old with the 1943 Phillies but was inducted into the navy before the season concluded. George, who had two brothers also in the service, pitched a no-hitter for the Naval Armed Guard of Treasure Island against a team of Marines in May of 1944. He never lived up to his billing as the next Rapid Robert, as his arm gave out before he rejoined the Phillies.

W	L	PCT	G	GS	CG	IP	H	BB	SO	SHO	ERA
0	0	—	9	0	0	19	27	9	5	0	3.32

Everett Joseph Fagan, *Pitcher*

A Jersey native, Fagan played for pieces of two seasons at the major league level. After posting a poor 2–6 record in 1943, Everett was drafted into the armed forces before the close of that season. He returned to the Athletics in the middle of the 1946 baseball campaign. Fagan was one of a handful of players to have two baseball seasons split by Uncle Sam.

W	L	PCT	G	GS	CG	IP	H	BB	SO	SHO	ERA
2	7	.222	38	2	0	82	88	38	21	0	5.49

Ferris Roy Fain, *First Base*

One of baseball's greatest selective hitters, routinely Fain walked 120 times a season with only 30 strikeouts. A two-time batting champion, Fain was a gifted hitter who could hit for average with an extraordinary on-base percentage. Although he lacked the pop of Ted Kluszewski, Fain was an elite batsman after the war years. But before the war, no one knew exactly who Ferris Fain was. He had yet to make his major league debut, but when he hit service pitching with gusto, players under Uncle Sam's employ began to rave about the gifted youngster.

The talk of the service baseball ranks, Fain was a soldier with the 7th Air Force. While stateside he began to show his expert abilities with the lumber, but it was on a tour of the South Pacific that Fain caught eyes. After he played in the Hawaiian Service League, Fain embarked on a baseball tour with such notables as Enos Slaughter, Joe Gordon and Stan Rojek. Their tour took them across the Pacific to such locales as Guam, Tinian, Saipan and Iwo Jima. At these stations, the men gave baseball exhibitions, and Fain led the tour with a .400 batting average. After his discharge, Fain spent a season in the bushes before he took the aging George McQuinn's job in 1947.

G	R	H	2B	3B	HR	RBI	BB	SO	SB	AVG	Slug
1,151	595	1,139	213	30	48	570	904	261	46	.290	.396

Bibb August Falk, *Outfield*

One of the best hitters few have ever heard of, Bibb was an offensive dynamo for the White Sox of the 1920s. The left fielder hit a robust .352 in 1924, led American League left fielders in RBIs in 1926, and hit over .300 each season he played for the Indians. Bibb was also a noted bench jockey who was rumored to be able to curse for an hour straight without repeating himself. Already forty years of age at the time of World War II, Falk was a non-combatant, but he still served and played baseball at the Randolph Airfield.

G	R	H	2B	3B	HR	RBI	BB	SO	SB	AVG	Slug
1,354	656	1,463	300	59	69	785	412	279	46	.314	.448

Luvern Carl "Vern" Fear, *Pitcher*

A knuckleballer, Fear had a cup of coffee with the 1952 Cubs of player-manager Phil Cavaretta. At the time of the war, Fear was considered the ace of his minor league staff in 1942 but he would give up the diamond pursuits and join the military. Fear spent his time in the navy during the war.

W	L	PCT	G	GS	CG	IP	H	BB	SO	SHO	ERA
0	0	—	4	0	0	8	9	3	4	0	7.88

Alfred Federoff, *Second Base*

The door to regular duty was opened to Federoff in 1952 when Detroit's regular second baseman, the shady Jerry Priddy, broke his leg. Federoff took over at second but failed to impress and never again played another game at the major league level. "Whitey" attended Duquesne University after his military discharge. When his playing days were over, the college grad enjoyed a lengthy career as a minor league skipper.

G	R	H	2B	3B	HR	RBI	BB	SO	SB	AVG	Slug
76	14	56	4	2	0	14	16	13	1	.238	.272

Edward Isadore Feinberg, *Utility Infielder*

Feinberg had a brief career with the Phillies during the late 1930s when the club was the National League's doormat. The Phillies were weak at every position during Eddie's time there but he couldn't claim a job. His last major league action came in 1939. But Feinberg saw more action with Uncle Sam. A combat soldier, Eddie was one of the few former major leaguers who saw combat duty during the Battle of the Bulge.

G	R	H	2B	3B	HR	RBI	BB	SO	SB	AVG	Slug
16	2	7	1	0	0	2	1	0	.184	.211	

Marvin Wilfred Felderman, *Catcher*

Felderman played only three games at the major league level, whiffing four times in six at-bats. The catcher served in the United States Navy at Bainbridge with fellow professional ballplayers Johnny Mize and Barney McCosky. In 1944, Marv was assigned to a ship and served overseas for a year and a half.

G	R	H	2B	3B	HR	RBI	BB	SO	SB	AVG	Slug
3	0	1	0	0	0	0	1	4	0	.167	.167

Robert William Andrew Feller, *Pitcher*

The day after Pearl Harbor was bombed, Feller enlisted in the navy. Rapid Robert initially reported to the Hampton Roads Naval Training Station. He later served as an anti-aircraft gunner on the battleship *Alabama* and earned five campaign ribbons and eight battle stars. At the time of his enlistment, Feller was the most dominant pitcher in the game. He struck out 260 batters in 1941, his last season before he enlisted. Only two other pitchers eclipsed 175 strikeouts that season: Johnny Vander Meer (202) and Whit Wyatt (176). He returned to make nine starts in 1945 and became the first pitcher since Rube Waddell (in 1904) to strikeout more than 340 batters in a season. Had Feller not missed the better part of four years to the war, he would be revered as the greatest pitcher ever. But then again, Feller's legacy is far grander as a war hero than his status as an athlete.

At the top of his game before the war, Feller was in a class by himself as a pitcher. He was without question the most dominating pitcher the game had seen since Walter Johnson several decades before. The farmboy from Iowa had the greatest fastball in the game and was so swift batters would often fake an illness to be removed from the lineup on the day Rapid Robert was scheduled to pitch. But Feller's sense of duty to his country was far more overpowering that any pitch he threw. His selfless actions after the nation's greatest catastrophe were an inspiration to all young men of the country. Shortly after Feller's enlistment, Jack Guenther wrote, "It is a nice thing for the other boys in America to know that one of them who had everything gave everything without thinking of the years of work that lay behind him or the years of fame and fortune which lay ahead." Feller passed his physical exam at the Great Lakes Naval Station and was sworn into the navy by Lieutenant Commander Gene Tunney. When Rapid Robert addressed the press afterwards, he said, "Nobody knows what's going to happen. Maybe I'll see you fellows again and maybe I won't." Feller went through navy boot camp and was later in demand for service baseball games. He pitched some at the Great Lakes and at Norfolk, but Feller didn't enlist in the navy to play a game — he wanted to serve his country in arms, fighting for liberty and the American way of life.

Promoted to chief boatswain mate in 1943, Feller was shipped overseas while his father was dying of brain cancer back home. His family could have benefited greatly from what would have been a sizable contract from the Indians, but doctors told the elder Feller that his case was terminal and there was no hope for survival. His father would die during the war.

While serving in foreign waters, Feller wrote a letter home to good friend and former major leaguer Lew Fonseca. He described his daily routine aboard a navy vessel to the old infielder, writing, "Operations are beyond the scene of athletic activity now. It's quite different to remain in condition, as continuous operations keep us on our toes and sleep is about all we have time for now." The operations that Feller and his unit were engaged in were hostile. He served a little more than two years in the Pacific Theatre, was engaged in the Leyte Invasion, and was awarded numerous citations for his war-time heroics, to include the Gold Star.

W	L	PCT	G	GS	CG	IP	H	BB	SO	SHO	ERA
266	162	.621	570	484	279	3,828	3,271	1,764	2,581	44	3.25

Edward Paul Fernandes, *Catcher*

The 1945 season was spent in the navy for Fernandes, a journeyman minor league catcher who played only two years at the major league level. His first look came with the Pirates in 1940; he didn't receive another trial at the highest level until 1946 with the White Sox.

G	R	H	2B	3B	HR	RBI	BB	SO	SB	AVG	Slug
42	5	12	3	0	0	6	15	13	0	.185	.231

Froilan "Nanny" Fernandez, *Third Base*

Fernandez played one year of major league ball before the war, rotating between third base and the outfield for the 1942 Braves. Nanny led the club with fifteen steals his rookie season and then missed the next three years to service in the armed forces. He was shipped overseas and stationed in Hawaii where he played for a service ballclub at Wheeler. Nanny returned to the Braves in 1946 and recaptured his third-base post. However, he lost his speed, as Nanny only swiped one base all season.

G	R	H	2B	3B	HR	RBI	BB	SO	SB	AVG	Slug
408	139	336	59	5	16	145	109	142	20	.248	.334

William Joseph Ferrazzi, *Pitcher*

Always partial to collegiate players, A's skipper Connie Mack was known for offering college football players baseball contracts. On rare occasions—think Sam Chapman—the signings panned out, but they usually were poor moves on Mack's part. Ferrazzi was an All-American football player at the University of Florida in the early 1930s. Mack persuaded Ferrazzi to sign a baseball contract and he pitched briefly with the Mackmen in 1935. His major league days were long behind him when he served in the military during World War II.

W	L	PCT	G	GS	CG	IP	H	BB	SO	SHO	ERA
1	2	.333	3	2	0	7	7	5	0	0	5.14

Thomas Jerome Ferrick, *Pitcher*

Tom Ferrick best fits the description of a journeyman relief pitcher. The stout right-hander never spent more than two consecutives seasons with any given team. He had two trials each with the Senators and Browns while he missed three full baseball campaigns to World War II. Tom served in the navy and was able to pitch for Mickey Cochrane's military juggernaut, the Great Lakes Naval Training Station nine. After his time spent near the Great Lakes, Ferrick was shipped overseas to the Pacific Theatre. He appeared in a navy all-star game held at Guam while serving in the Pacific.

W	L	PCT	G	GS	CG	IP	H	BB	SO	SHO	ERA
40	40	.500	323	7	4	674	654	227	245	1	3.47

David Meadow "Boo" Ferriss, *Pitcher*

Chances are baseball fans never got to see Boo Ferriss at his best. He was a solid pitcher for the Red Sox in 1945 and was a stud when he led them to the World Series the following year, but his arm gave out shortly thereafter. His best years, perhaps, were spent toiling for Uncle Sam. Scribe Dick Hudson wrote about Boo, "He had size, he had poise, he had sense, he had control, he had youth and he had the arm. But something happened to the arm and those who know Boo Ferriss best consider it one of the major tragedies of baseball."

Like many young men who hadn't established themselves in the pro circuit, Ferriss made the most of his military exposure. Boo became a star hurler in the semi-pro ranks while wearing Uncle Sam's khaki, but something was wrong with Ferriss and he was mustered out of the Army Air Force. The Southern right-hander had asthma and was given a medical discharge in time to join the Red Sox during spring training for the upcoming 1945 season. The rookie from Mississippi led the team in wins his first two years in Boston. Initial success was Boo's as he won his first eight decisions for the 1945 Sox. His terrific debut spurred Jack Hand to write, "If Dave Ferriss is a fair example, the GI athlete with big league ambitions is headed in the right direction."

W	L	PCT	G	GS	CG	IP	H	BB	SO	SHO	ERA
65	30	.684	144	103	67	880	914	314	296	12	3.64

Wilmer Leon "Red" Fields, *Pitcher*

Fields was a solid pitcher for the Homestead Grays in the 1940s who enjoyed some success playing minor league ball in Canada after integration. A gifted two-way player in the minors, Red won several MVP awards in the low minors but never did get a trial in the majors. Red missed a few years to military service during World War II.

(1940–1950): Homestead Grays

Samuel Lawrence File, *Reserve*

File had a cup of coffee with Doc Prothro's last-place Phillies in 1940. He appeared in only seven games—the extent of his major league career. During the war, File left the game of baseball and enlisted in the U.S. Coast Guard.

G	R	H	2B	3B	HR	RBI	BB	SO	SB	AVG	Slug
7	0	1	0	0	0	1	0	2	0	.077	.077

Joe Filmore, *Pitcher*

A big, hard-throwing right-hander from Victoria, Texas, Filmore was nicknamed "Fireball" on account of his speed. Joe was an up-and-coming prospect with the Philadelphia Stars when World War II interrupted his career. In the army, Fireball served with the Special Services and did little but play baseball in the service.

(1940–1952): Philadelphia Stars and Baltimore Grays

Edward Raymond Fitz Gerald, *Catcher*

Fitz Gerald had a long career at the major league level as a back-up catcher. Often in a platoon situation with such catchers as Clint Courtney and Joe Garagiola, Ed was a right-handed complement to the portside swingers. Before he signed his first pro contract, Fitzy served in the United States Army. The backstop saw action in Germany several years before he took his first swing at the major league level.

G	R	H	2B	3B	HR	RBI	BB	SO	SB	AVG	Slug
807	199	542	82	10	19	217	185	235	9	.260	.336

Walter Leonard Flager, *Shortstop*

A war-era player, Flager played at the major league level in 1945 with two teams. Both squads he played for were the bottom-feeding teams of the National League: the seventh-place Reds and the last-place Phillies. Before his major league sojourn, Flager spent time with the army but was discharged early enough to take part in the war-interrupted 1945 campaign.

G	R	H	2B	3B	HR	RBI	BB	SO	SB	AVG	Slug
70	26	53	5	1	2	21	25	20	1	.241	.300

Albert Deli Flair, *First Base*

The 1941 baseball season was the only action Al Flair saw at the major league level. He would go on to lose the next four years to service in the United States Army, missing out on his bid to replace Jimmie Foxx as the Red Sox first baseman. Flair, who was adamant in his fondness for firearms, was stationed at Fort Bragg in the Field Artillery Replacement Center. He was later reassigned to Fort Gordon, where he was able to play some baseball before he received orders to be shipped out to New Guinea. Al was able to tour the South Pacific and played some baseball for a team managed by Phillies pitcher Hugh Mulcahy.

G	R	H	2B	3B	HR	RBI	BB	SO	SB	AVG	Slug
10	3	6	2	1	0	2	1	1	1	.200	.333

Raymond Arthur Flanigan, *Pitcher*

Regarded as a coming star just before the war, Flanigan had all the talent to make the grade in the majors. But the kid from West Virginia came of age at an inopportune time. The war was in full swing and young men were needed to assist in the effort and Ray answered the call. An article in the *Syracuse Herald* described Flanigan's fate, which claimed, "Only one thing be-shadows Flanigan's quick rise to the big show and that one thing is contrarily the very thing which gives him his biggest chance of going to the majors: the war."

Inducted into the armed forces, Flanigan wasn't one of the fortunate souls that was able to play baseball for the duration of the war. The gifted right-hander was with a combat division that was shipped out to the European Theatre. Ray saw combat action in the German battlefields and was a decorated war hero. But all his war-time heroics couldn't make up for the fact that he had missed out on a lot of baseball. When he returned stateside, Ray's talent was still there but he lacked command. The Indians gave him a trial in 1946 but he failed to make the grade and never pitched in the major leagues again.

W	L	PCT	G	GS	CG	IP	H	BB	SO	SHO	ERA
0	1	.000	3	1	0	9	11	8	2	0	11.00

Leslie Fletchard "Bill" Fleming, *Pitcher*

A serviceable big league pitcher, Fleming spent two years with the Red Sox and four with the Cubs. He was one of the few pitchers on the Cubs' 1942 roster who posted fewer hits allowed than innings pitched. He appeared in 39 games for the Cubs in 1944 and then missed the 1945 season to service in the army. After the war, Bill appeared in just fourteen games.

W	L	PCT	G	GS	CG	IP	H	BB	SO	SHO	ERA
16	21	.432	123	40	14	440	443	193	167	3	3.80

Elburt Preston Fletcher, *First Base*

A slick fielding first baseman, Fletcher tutored amateur baseball players in the navy on the fine art of picking at the initial sack while stationed at Bainbridge. Not a fearsome power hitter in the Jimmie Foxx mold, Elbie was a brilliant select hitter who drew a ton of walks. Fletcher served as Buck Jordan's backup in his first trial at the major league level but was handed the first-base job in 1937 when he played for the Braves. Elbie didn't establish himself until he was traded to the Pirates midway through the 1939 season. Despite playing in only 102 games, Elbie led the Pirates in home runs and RBIs. He paced the NL in walks during the 1940 campaign with an astounding total of 119. He drew 118 walks in 1941, again good for the league lead, but finished four shy of Mel Ott in 1942.

Fletcher was inducted into the armed forces after the 1943 baseball season and missed the next two years to service in the navy. He was initially assigned to the Bainbridge Naval Training Station and attended the physical instructor's course held at the installation. He was shipped overseas and played service ball in a sports troupe led by Red Sox pitcher Mace Brown. While serving in the South Pacific, Elbie played against Hall of Famer Johnny Mize on several occasions.

G	R	H	2B	3B	HR	RBI	BB	SO	SB	AVG	Slug
1,415	723	1,323	228	58	79	616	851	495	32	.271	.390

Alfred Vanoide "Van" Fletcher, *Pitcher*

Fletcher had a cup of coffee as a 30-year-old with the 1955 Tigers of Bucky Harris. Van served in the armed forces during World War II before he signed his first pro contract.

W	L	PCT	G	GS	CG	IP	H	BB	SO	SHO	ERA
0	0	—	9	0	0	12	13	2	4	0	3.00

Charles Wesley Flowers, *Pitcher*

Flowers received his first look with the Dodgers in 1940 and then was summoned for the last time during the war year of 1944. The left-hander from Arkansas served briefly in the armed forces during the war.

W	L	PCT	G	GS	CG	IP	H	BB	SO	SHO	ERA
2	2	.500	14	3	0	38	49	23	11	0	5.45

Dee Virgil Fondy, *First Base*

An underrated first baseman during the 1950s, Dee Fondy had yet to sign his first professional contract before the war. The Texan joined the colors and took boot camp shortly after he left school. Fondy was assigned to a combat division that saw heavy action in the battlefields. He was awarded the Purple Heart for his gallantry on the battlefield of Utah Beach where he was wounded in action.

After his discharge, the war hero returned home and took to the game of baseball. A fine all-around ballplayer, Fondy spent several years in the minors before the Cubs gave him his first look in

1951. The only thing standing between Dee and the Cubs' first-base job was film star Chuck Connors, whose position Fondy claimed in 1952. A .300 hitter his first full season with the Cubs, Fondy also showed fine speed by leading the club in stolen bases. In 1952 and 1953, Fondy and Frankie Baumholtz were the only .300 hitters in the Cubs lineup. They received some help in 1954 when a kid named Ernie Banks took over at short. Fondy ended his career with the 1958 Reds.

G	R	H	2B	3B	HR	RBI	BB	SO	SB	AVG	Slug
967	437	1,000	144	47	69	373	203	526	84	.286	.413

Richard John Fowler, *Pitcher*

One of two Canadian-born pitchers on the Athletics who missed time to World War II, Fowler was a thick-bodied man who played with the A's from 1941 to 1952. Fowler joined fellow Canadian Phil Marchildon under Connie Mack in 1941. He was inducted into the Canadian Army after the close of the 1942 baseball season and missed the next two and a half years to military service.

A minor league skipper said of Dick, "I never saw a better fellow on a ball club." An upstanding gentleman off the field, Fowler was stationed at Brantford, Ontario, but was reassigned to Toronto after a squabble ensued for his services. In high demand to pitch in the Canadian Service League, Dick pitched for the Toronto Army District Depot Invaders. He returned to the Athletics late in the 1945 season and recorded a win in seven games. His finest year on the diamond came in 1947, when Dick posted a 12–11 record while pacing the Mackmen in shutouts and ERA.

W	L	PCT	G	GS	CG	IP	H	BB	SO	SHO	ERA
66	79	.455	221	170	75	1,304	1,367	578	382	11	4.11

Charles Francis Fox, *Catcher*

If you blinked in 1942, you missed the major league playing career of Irish Charlie Fox. However, he became the Giants manager after their move west, and helmed the organization from 1970 to 1974. The former catcher served three years in the navy during World War II.

G	R	H	2B	3B	HR	RBI	BB	SO	SB	AVG	Slug
3	1	3	0	0	0	1	1	2	0	.429	.429

Frederick Meloy Frankhouse, *Pitcher*

A fine pitcher throughout the 1930s, Fred's career ended with the 1939 Braves. Able to tally more than 100 career wins, the right-hander from Port Royal was skipper Bill McKechnie's ace during the mid–1930s. Frankhouse was a member of the 1928 NL pennant-winning Cardinals that boasted the likes of Jim Bottomley, Frankie Frisch, Grover Alexander and Jesse Haines. The Redbirds were swept by the Yankees in that year's World Series, and Fred didn't see any Fall Classic action.

After his days as a major league pitcher were over, Fred enlisted in the army after the bombing on Pearl Harbor. He attended the army school for special services at Lexington, Virginia. Stationed at Fort Hamilton, New York, Fred's military duties revolved around the installation's athletic program. Lieutenant Frankhouse was in charge of overseeing the athletics at the army post. While stationed there, Fred suffered a freak accident when he was struck by a vehicle on base. Severe damage was done to his kneecap and he was laid up for a time at the post's hospital.

W	L	PCT	G	GS	CG	IP	H	BB	SO	SHO	ERA
106	97	.522	402	212	81	1,888	2,033	701	622	10	3.92

Murray Asher Franklin, *Shortstop*

Franklin was one of a handful of players barred by Commissioner Happy Chandler for playing ball south of the border. After the war, an influential Mexican businessman began raiding major league rosters, offering higher salaries to play in his league. A few made the jump, Murray included, but returned when they didn't receive the money promised them. Franklin never returned to the major leagues after defecting to Mexico. His major league career spanned two seasons with the Detroit Tigers and another three lost to service in the United States Army during World War II.

G	R	H	2B	3B	HR	RBI	BB	SO	SB	AVG	Slug
61	25	43	8	0	2	16	9	7	0	.262	.348

Herman Louis Franks, *Catcher*

Franks' managerial career lasted longer than his playing career, but the stocky receiver lost four complete baseball seasons to service in the navy. He managed the Giants from 1965 to 1968 and served as the Cubs' skipper from 1977 to 1979. A weak offensive player, Franks was Babe Phelps' backup in Brooklyn before the war. The navy called Herman away from the field in 1942 as he served as an ensign in the Naval Reserve. After he completed a course at Annapolis, he was sent to the Naval Air Station in Pensacola, Florida.

G	R	H	2B	3B	HR	RBI	BB	SO	SB	AVG	Slug
188	35	80	18	2	3	43	57	37	2	.199	.275

Joseph Filmore Frazier, *Outfield*

Cobra Joe served in the armed forces during World War II before he made his major league debut. He was initially called up by the Indians in 1947 but stayed in the bushes for a number of years before the Cardinals gave him a second chance in 1954. Used mainly as a pinch-hitter and back-up outfielder, Frazier managed the New York Mets briefly in the late 1970s.

G	R	H	2B	3B	HR	RBI	BB	SO	SB	AVG	Slug
217	31	68	15	2	10	45	35	46	0	.241	.415

Edwin Charles Freed, *Outfield*

A diminutive outfielder from Pennsylvania, Freed tallied ten major league hits in thirteen games. He played with the Phillies in 1942 and then served the next three years in the armed forces.

G	R	H	2B	3B	HR	RBI	BB	SO	SB	AVG	Slug
13	3	10	3	1	0	4	3	1		.303	.455

Antonio "Tony" Freitas, *Pitcher*

A slightly built southpaw that Jack Dailey described as a "vest pocket portsider," Freitas was a stellar minor league pitcher who pitched a few seasons at the major league level. Tony broke in with Connie Mack's Athletics in 1932 when the dynasty was beginning to crumble. He pitched in Philadelphia for two years before he joined the Reds of the mid–1930s. After his stint in the majors was over, Freitas returned to the West and had a lengthy career in the minors.

Tiny Tony Freitas left the minor league ranks and enlisted in the army during the Second World War. He joined the Army's Air Corps and was stationed at the Ellington Army Airfield. As a corporeal, Tony's military duties centered on safety inspections, as he was in charge of looking over aircraft before the pilot's used them in battle. An Associated Press article described Tony's duties, stating, "During duty hours you'll find Freitas in the inspection division of the Ellington Field production line maintenance hangar for navigation training planes. He is an engine control and accessories man there and gives the planes a final check before take-offs."

W	L	PCT	G	GS	CG	IP	H	BB	SO	SHO	ERA
25	33	.431	107	63	22	518	614	137	135	1	4.48

Lawrence Herbert French, *Pitcher*

A finesse pitcher, French would have easily attained 200 career wins had World War II not interrupted his career. The war came when French had reached the twilight of a remarkable career, spent predominantly with the Chicago Cubs. He was an 18-game winner with the Pirates as a 24-year-old in 1932 and followed that season with an identical 18 victories in 1933. The Pirates fell into the second division in 1934 and Larry was sent to the Cubs during the offseason. His first season in the Windy City, French paced the team in shutouts and guided them to a World Series. They lost the Series in six to a far-superior Tigers club, but Larry posted an ERA of 3.38 for the contest. In 1939, French posted a 15–8 record but was dealt to the Dodgers during the 1941 campaign. In his last year at the major league level, the 34-year-old French paced the NL with a .789 winning percentage on a microscopic 1.82 ERA. Then, Uncle Sam called.

French was commissioned a lieutenant in the United States Navy. When he was sworn into the navy, French said, "My only disappointment is that I probably never will be able to pass the 200-victory mark. Baseball doesn't matter. This deal I'm going into is more important right now." He was stationed at a navy yard in Brooklyn, which gave French hope for the possibility of pitching for the Dodgers on the weekends so he could reach 200 career wins. He put in a request with the navy to be allowed to pitch weekends with the Dodgers; he even made an offer to turn over his Dodgers pay to the Navy Relief Fund. However, despite his willingness to sacrifice his salary, Rear Admiral W.B. Young denied Larry's request.

French was certain baseball would overcome the loss of numerous established players through the war, saying, "Sure baseball will survive during the war and it will be a good class of ball too. Although it has been hit hard by the manpower shortage, it is still the richest sport in the world and will continue to be."

Larry was sent overseas and served in the Navy Amphibious Forces in the European Theatre in 1944. He had the task of landing men and equipment in Normandy on D-Day. Of the famous attack, French wrote Ford Frick saying, "This is going to be a great show, and in years to come I will be proud to say I was there in some capacity or other. This staff I am attached to has the landing craft to be used in this operation, and you may gather from that it will be very interesting. Sorry security stops me from telling you more."

After D-Day, Larry was assigned to the *USS New York* as a supply officer. He wrote a letter to former teammate Augie Galan, sharing his desire for the rest of the southpaws in the major leagues. French wrote, "I'd like to have them all over here and walk them ahead of me to clear out the mines. Then I'd be the only one left. Might be able to go back and win the three games I need to fill out 200 wins in the books." He returned stateside late in 1945 and said, "The American game is being transplanted to foreign soil and eventually may become a global pastime."

French received his discharge from the navy on November 11, 1945, with every intention of resuming his baseball career with the Dodgers. The long layoff, however, had greatly affected the masterful southpaw, as he reconsidered his stance on making a comeback. Just before spring training in 1946, Larry wrote a simple, concise yet heart-breaking letter to Branch Rickey, stating, "I'm 38 now and I guess it's time to quit."

W	L	PCT	G	GS	CG	IP	H	BB	SO	SHO	ERA
197	171	.535	570	383	198	3,152	3,375	819	1,187	40	3.44

Linus Reinhar Frey, *Second Base*

Frey was a stellar middle infielder with a solid eye at the plate. Lonny knew how to draw walks and take an extra base. He began his major league career in 1933 with the Brooklyn Dodgers, where he saw some time at shortstop after the injury to Buckshot Glenn Wright. Originally a switch-hitter when he came up, Frey eventually scrapped batting from the right side and stuck with the left. Not a big man, Frey did lead all Brooklyn batters in every extra-base hit category during the 1935 season. He joined the Reds in 1938 and was inserted into the lineup as their regular second baseman.

Lonny was arguably the best second baseman in the league in 1939 as he guided the Reds to the World Series. However, the Cincinnati bats went cold in the Fall Classic and they were swept by the Yankees. He paced the National League in stolen bases during the 1940 season as part of the world champion Reds of that year. He led all NL second basemen in walks in the 1942 season and was then inducted into the army after setting an NL fielding record for second basemen in 1943. He missed two years to the war effort and returned to the game playing three final years with four different clubs.

G	R	H	2B	3B	HR	RBI	BB	SO	SB	AVG	Slug
1,535	848	1,482	263	69	61	549	752	525	105	.269	.374

Marion John Fricano, *Pitcher*

Fricano spent his entire major league career with the Athletics. He was a member of the final Philadelphia A's team and the original Kansas City Athletics. Before Fricano made his major league debut, he served in the navy during World War II. The right-hander served overseas as a radio operator on an amphibious vehicle.

W	L	PCT	G	GS	CG	IP	H	BB	SO	SHO	ERA
15	23	.395	88	43	14	388	393	164	115	0	4.31

James Riley Fridley, *Outfield*

Big Jim Fridley had a sporadic career at the major league level. He debuted with the 1952 Indians. Sent back to the bushes, he then joined the Baltimore Orioles in their first year after their relocation from St. Louis in 1954. It was back to the bushes for Fridley again and his last stint in the majors didn't come until the Reds called him up in 1958. Before he signed his first pro contract, Big Jim enlisted in the army during World War II.

G	R	H	2B	3B	HR	RBI	BB	SO	SB	AVG	Slug
154	50	105	12	5	8	53	35	83	3	.248	.356

Frederick Ferdinand Frink, *Reserve*

Frink played two games at the major league level without stepping to the plate. He played with Jimmie Wilson's 1934 Phillies, a seventh-place team that had the NL's worst staff ERA. During the Second World War, Frink joined the United States Navy. A commissioned officer, Captain Frink coached athletics at the Jacksonville Naval Air Technical Training Center.

G	R	H	2B	3B	HR	RBI	BB	SO	SB	AVG	Slug
2	0	0	0	0	0	0	0	0	0	—	—

Charles Andrew Frye, *Pitcher*

Although Charlie Frye died in 1945, a war year, his death wasn't a result of injuries sustained on the battlefield. In fact, he died shortly after he was discharged from the army. Frye spent one year in the majors with the 1940 Phillies and fashioned an 0–6 record.

W	L	PCT	G	GS	CG	IP	H	BB	SO	SHO	ERA
0	6	.000	15	5	1	50	58	26	18	0	4.68

Carl Anthony Furillo, *Outfield*

Nicknamed "The Reading Rifle," Furillo was a star right fielder for the powerhouse Brooklyn Dodgers after the war. A borderline Hall of Fame candidate, Carl ended his career with a batting average just below the coveted .300 mark. Before the Reading Rifle embarked on his career in the majors, he served briefly in the armed forces during World War II. After his discharge he went directly to Brooklyn and starred in a stellar outfield with Pete Reiser and Dixie Walker.

G	R	H	2B	3B	HR	RBI	BB	SO	SB	AVG	Slug
1,806	895	1,910	324	56	192	1,058	514	436	48	.299	.458

Frank Howard Gabler, *Pitcher*

Nicknamed "The Great Gabbo," Gabler got plenty of mileage out of his right arm but perhaps extracted more out of his mouth. A noted storyteller, Gabler pitched all over the land and once played some ball in Mexico. While playing south of the border, the Great Gabbo was caught tossing spitballs to which the umpire demanded he stop. Frank raised his arms in protest and said, "Heck, anything goes in Mexico." Frank, who scouted some for the Houston club after his playing days, served in the U.S. Coast Guard during World War II.

W	L	PCT	G	GS	CG	IP	H	BB	SO	SHO	ERA
16	23	.410	113	31	10	377	457	107	109	1	5.25

Kenneth Harlin Gables, *Pitcher*

The husky mop-up pitcher from Walnut Grove, Missouri, had a brief stint in the military during World War II. Ken served in the army in 1943 but was given a medical discharge and returned to baseball. After his playing career, Ken returned to Walnut Grove and worked as a deputy sheriff until his death.

W	L	PCT	G	GS	CG	IP	H	BB	SO	SHO	ERA
13	11	.542	62	23	6	240	255	88	88	0	4.69

Jonas Donald Gaines, *Pitcher*

A little southpaw from New Roads, Louisiana, Gaines was a mainstay with the Baltimore Elite Giants of the late 1930s. He pitched with the team until he was inducted into the military during the Second World War. He returned to Baltimore after the war before he joined the Philadelphia Stars and then integrated ball. After two years in the minor leagues, Jonas was one of the first Americans to play professional ball in Japan.

(1937–1953): Baltimore Elite Giants, Philadelphia Stars, Newark Eagles and Japan

Willard Roland "Nemo" Gaines, *Pitcher*

Gaines had a cup of coffee with George McBride's Senators of 1921. After the season, Nemo quit baseball and enrolled in the Annapolis Naval Academy. The southpaw gave up a career on the ball diamond and made the navy his profession. Still active in the navy twenty years later, Nemo was a high-ranking officer during World War II.

W	L	PCT	G	GS	CG	IP	H	BB	SO	SHO	ERA
0	0	—	4	0	0	5	5	2	1	0	0.00

Dennis Ward Galehouse, *Pitcher*

A solid innings-eater, Galehouse made his major league debut with the 1934 Cleveland Indians. The right-hander from Ohio was a fine-wine pitcher, meaning he got better with age. As a 31-year-old with the 1943 Browns, Denny paced the team in strikeouts and innings pitched, and posted a solid 2.77 ERA. His finest hour may have come during the 1944 World Series, the Browns' lone Fall Classic appearance, as Galehouse beat the cross-town rival Cardinals in Game One. He was drafted into the navy shortly after the World Series had concluded and spent one year in the colors, where he played service ball at the Great Lakes.

W	L	PCT	G	GS	CG	IP	H	BB	SO	SHO	ERA
109	118	.480	375	258	100	2,003	2,148	735	851	17	3.98

Joseph Emmett Gallagher, *Outfield*

A big man, Gallagher's intimidating physique earned him the nickname "Muscles." A solid hitter, Muscles spent two seasons at the major league level with three teams. He split the 1939 season with the Yankees and Browns and then divided 1940 with the Browns and Dodgers. Even though Gallagher never reached his full potential, many scouts believed he was a better prospect than fellow Yankees farmhand Charlie "King Kong" Keller.

Joe was one of the first ballplayers to enlist in the service during World War II, and he missed five full baseball campaigns to the war effort. He enlisted early in 1941 and was hand-picked by Dizzy Dean to play for his all-star team comprised of fellow major leaguers in the service, among them Washington's Cecil Travis.

G	R	H	2B	3B	HR	RBI	BB	SO	SB	AVG	Slug
165	73	133	26	5	16	73	26	76	4	.273	.446

Stanley Joseph Galle, *Third Base*

Galle played briefly in the major leagues for the 1942 Senators. He manned the hot corner in three games for skipper Bucky Harris and spent the next three years in service to his country. Stan spent his military time in the United States Coast Guard.

G	R	H	2B	3B	HR	RBI	BB	SO	SB	AVG	Slug
13	3	2	0	0	0	1	1	0	0	.111	.111

Lee Jesse Gamble, *Outfield*

A favorite pinch-hitter of Hall of Fame skipper Bill McKechnie, Gamble was on the Reds' pennant-winning teams of 1939 and 1940. Lee's last major league action came with the world champion Reds of 1940. Sent back to the minors, Gamble played until 1943, when he quit the game to operate a gas station at his home in Punxsutawney, Pennsylvania. He would operate the service station for many decades with a two-year reprieve during the war. Gamble was stationed at the Greensboro Army Air Force's Overseas Replacement Depot where he played service ball with White Sox star Taft Wright and young third baseman Grady Hatton.

G	R	H	2B	3B	HR	RBI	BB	SO	SB	AVG	Slug
165	51	91	12	3	0	21	10	21	6	.266	.319

Joseph Henry Garagiola, *Catcher*

A schoolyard chum of Hall of Fame catcher Yogi Berra, Garagiola signed his first pro contract as a teen in 1943 with Columbus. He was the youngest player in the league, but shortly thereafter the able-bodied teenager was inducted into the armed forces. Joe served his hitch overseas in the Pacific Theatre. Able to play some service ball on foreign land, Joe was the catcher on Kirby Higbe's Manila Dodgers squad. While playing service ball, Garagiola came to the attention of major league personnel. Chuck Dressen went on a USO tour and saw Joe play. He lauded the youngster from St. Louis, saying, "He's a big fellow. I called him Gargantua from his name. Looks like a good hitter."

After Garagiola's discharge, the Cardinals brought Joe along quickly and called him up in 1946. At just 20 years of age, Joe did the bulk of the Redbirds catching in their championship season of 1946. He held his own against the Red Sox's pitching of Ferriss, Hughson, Harris and Dobson by hitting .316 during the Fall Classic. Joe would play with his hometown Cardinals through 1951 when he was traded to the Pirates. His last major league action came with the 1954 Giants. With a quick wit and a knack for telling stories, Garagiola had a successful career as a broadcaster after his retirement from playing.

G	R	H	2B	3B	HR	RBI	BB	SO	SB	AVG	Slug
676	198	481	82	16	42	255	267	173	5	.257	.385

Edward Miguel "Mike" Garcia, *Pitcher*

A vastly underrated pitcher, "Big Bear" Garcia had the blessing and misfortune of pitching for the post-war Indians. They had the best concentration of pitching in the majors with Feller, Lemon, Wynn and Newhouser — all Hall of Famers. Given that collection of star pitching, it was easy for Big Bear to go unnoticed. In 1951, Feller, Wynn and Garcia all reached 20 wins, and in 1952, Wynn, Lemon and Garcia all exceeded 20 wins. Cleveland was a contender based on its pitching alone but with all those stars in the sky, Garcia was overlooked. Before Big Bear made his major league debut, he served in the armed forces after he was drafted in 1943.

W	L	PCT	G	GS	CG	IP	H	BB	SO	SHO	ERA
142	97	.594	428	281	111	2,175	2,148	719	1,117	27	3.27

Robert Ford Garrison, *Outfield*

A war-era ballplayer, Garrison played for the Red Sox and A's during the fighting. Traded to the Mackmen in 1944, "Snapper" had his only regular job that season as their everyday left fielder. In 1945, early in the baseball season, Garrison was inducted into the military and served for less than a year.

G	R	H	2B	3B	HR	RBI	BB	SO	SB	AVG	Slug
185	80	180	22	3	6	56	37	67	11	.262	.329

Francis Joseph "Hank" Garrity, *Catcher*

Garrity had a cup of coffee with the 1931 White Sox. More than ten years later, Hank would serve in the military during World War II.

G	R	H	2B	3B	HR	RBI	BB	SO	SB	AVG	Slug
8	0	3	1	0	0	2	1	2	0	.214	.286

Ned Franklin Garver, *Pitcher*

Garver was a fine major league pitcher saddled to some rather poor teams. He pitched the bulk of his career with the Browns and the downtrodden Kansas City A's. He is one of the few pitchers in history to have won 20 games for a last-place team. But before Garver ever pitched with a heavy yoke on his shoulders, he served in the armed forces during World War II. In his first year of organized ball, Ned tossed a no-hitter.

W	L	PCT	G	GS	CG	IP	H	BB	SO	SHO	ERA
129	157	.451	402	330	153	2,477	2,471	881	881	18	3.73

Eugene Francis Joseph "Huck" Geary, *Shortstop*

Pittsburgh was never regarded as home to Huck Geary. He quit baseball in 1943 because he didn't enjoy playing in Pittsburgh. Pittsburgh writers poked fun at Huck's expense, referring to him as "Homesick Huck," regarding his lack of desire to play at Forbes Field. Geary deserted the Pirates on numerous occasions, which fueled the writers and gave their nickname perceived truth. Geary said, "I know they call me 'Homesick Huck' but that was just something the writers thought up."

His multiple desertions finally led to his being sold to the Phillies, but the transaction was voided when Geary was inducted into the military. Huck had been working with the maintenance department of the Buffalo Arms Corporation prior to his navy callup. He was inducted into the navy in April of 1945 and received his discharge in December of the following year.

G	R	H	2B	3B	HR	RBI	BB	SO	SB	AVG	Slug
55	20	30	4	0	1	15	20	9	3	.160	.197

Elmer John Gedeon, *Utilityman*

Elmer Gedeon's name lacks the mystique of the great baseball players who served their country during World War II, but the former hurdles champ of the University of Michigan gave his life for his country, earning the title of "hero" that modern athletes could never attain.

As far as playing in the major leagues is concerned, Gedeon's career was anything but noteworthy. He played briefly for the 1939 Washington Senators; he posted only 15 at-bats for his career. Patriotism was a trait that Gedeon possessed like few others, as the natural athlete left for the military in 1941. He was initially stationed at Fort Thomas, Kentucky, before a transfer to Raleigh. While serving at Raleigh, Gedeon had his first brush with death. He was awarded the Soldier's Medal of Heroism as a lieutenant when he rescued an injured crew member of a bomber that crashed in Raleigh. Despite sustaining injuries in the crash — he was badly burned and suffered several broken ribs— Elmer returned to the flaming wreckage and carried his fellow crew member to safety.

Following his heroic deeds in Raleigh, Elmer Gedeon was sent to Ardmore Air Field in Oklahoma where he was promoted to the rank of captain. He was assigned to the 586th Bombardment Squadron as a pilot and operations officer and was thus shipped overseas to Europe.

Gedeon stared death in the eyes once and defeated it, but he wasn't as lucky in his second bout. On April 20, 1944, Gedeon and his fellow crew members were flying a mission over France in which they never returned. They were initially labeled missing in action until wreckage of their plane was found and his unit confirmed that he had died in the plane crash.

G	R	H	2B	3B	HR	RBI	BB	SO	SB	AVG	Slug
5	1	3	0	0	0	1	2	5	0	.200	.200

Charles Leonard Gehringer, *Second Base*

Gehringer always went about his business in a workmanlike fashion, playing hard and lacking a boisterous persona. Charlie, who was referred to as "The Mechanical Man," had always been a player one could look upon with the utmost respect. He was silent, workmanlike and arguably the greatest second baseman that ever lived.

As a member of the Baseball Hall of Fame, Gehringer's name will live on as long as there is Baseball. He got his start with the Tigers, the only team he ever played for, in 1924. Charlie had amassed 2,839 hits before World War II started and was unable to collect another after the fighting stopped. He was beginning to slow down by 1941, and he was a pinch-hitter in 1942, which would serve as proof that he probably would not have reached 3,000 hits had the war not taken three years from him.

Charlie was unable to finish the 1942 baseball season since he was drafted into the navy during the season. He served with the athletic department at the Navy Pre-Flight School held at St. Mary's College in California. At St. Mary's, Charlie served as a coach on the baseball club and was later transferred to Jacksonville from the California-based college. After 43 months of active duty, in which time he had attained the rank of lieutenant commander, Charlie was discharged from Jacksonville Naval Air Station. He officially retired from baseball after his discharge and took an executive post at a Detroit-based manufacturing agency. The game called him back, as Charlie served several years as the Tigers' general manager.

G	R	H	2B	3B	HR	RBI	BB	SO	SB	AVG	Slug
2,323	1,774	2,839	574	146	184	1,427	1,185	372	181	.320	.480

Paul Arthur Gehrman, *Pitcher*

A star pitcher in the Pacific Coast League, Gehrman had a cup of coffee with the last-place 1937 Reds. While still active in the PCL, Paul was inducted into the U.S. Army during World War II. An infantryman, Gehrman served his duty at Camp White with the 383rd Infantry Regiment. While he was stationed there his old PCL battery mate, Harry Land, also served at the camp with the 174th Infantry.

W	L	PCT	G	GS	CG	IP	H	BB	SO	SHO	ERA
0	1	.000	2	1	0	9	11	5	1	0	3.00

Joseph Edward Genewich, *Pitcher*

Genewich had a nine-year career at the major league level, spent predominately with the Boston Braves after WWI. Joe was in his early twenties when he joined the navy during the First World War. He was able to play some service ball while stationed at the Great Lakes. He made his major league debut after his discharge, pitched with the Braves and Giants, and later returned to the military to help out during World War II.

W	L	PCT	G	GS	CG	IP	H	BB	SO	SHO	ERA
73	92	.442	272	166	71	1,401	1,610	402	316	8	4.29

George Michael Genovese, *Reserve*

A longtime minor league manager, Genovese's major league career consisted of a cup of coffee with the 1950 Senators. Used in just three games, George was a good glove man in the minors with a modest stick. During World War II, Genovese saw combat action at Okinawa while he served in the U.S. Army Signal Corps.

G	R	H	2B	3B	HR	RBI	BB	SO	SB	AVG	Slug
3	1	0	0	0	0	0	1	0	0	.000	.000

Samuel Christopher Gentile, *Outfield*

Sam Gentile's only major league hit was a two-bagger, as the outfielder strode to the plate on four separate occasions. His lone major league action came in 1943, as he missed the 1944 and 1945 seasons to military service.

G	R	H	2B	3B	HR	RBI	BB	SO	SB	AVG	Slug
8	1	1	1	0	0	0	1	0	.250	.500

Floyd George Giebell, *Pitcher*

An unknown pitcher in 1940, Giebell made headlines at the end of the year when the Tigers and Indians squared off in a contest to decide the American League pennant. The Indians called the greatest pitcher of his generation, Bob Feller, to the mound while the Tigers countered with Giebell. The start was Floyd's second appearance all season for the big league club, but he tamed the Indians and bested Rapid Robert. One of the most unlikely of heroes, Giebell had little success before that start or after it.

A native of West Virginia, Giebell made his major league debut in 1939, pitched twice in 1940, including his magical victory over Feller, and last pitched in the majors in 1941. Beaten like a drum in 1941, Giebell, the hero of the season before, was cut loose and never heard from in the majors again. Before Floyd was inducted into the military for service during World War II, he suffered a fractured jaw. Sent to a hospital to recover, doctors ordered Giebell to remain in bed. When a nurse checked up on him, all she found was a note in his room. The note Giebell left behind read, "I'm leaving. Give this bed to someone who is really sick."

W	L	PCT	G	GS	CG	IP	H	BB	SO	SHO	ERA
3	1	.750	28	4	2	67	78	42	30	1	4.03

Andrew Gilbert, *Outfield*

Andy Gilbert's major league career consisted of just eight games—six in 1942 and two in 1946. In between his brief trial at the highest level, Gilbert served in the armed forces. He missed three full baseball campaigns to military duty.

G	R	H	2B	3B	HR	RBI	BB	SO	SB	AVG	Slug
8	1	1	0	0	0	1	1	3	0	.083	.083

Charles Mader Gilbert, *Outfield*

Charlie was the son of former major leaguer Larry Gilbert, who played with the Boston Braves in 1914 and 1915. The younger Gilbert served as a reserve outfielder with the Cubs, Dodgers and Phillies over the course of his career. He missed two full years to service in the armed forces.

G	R	H	2B	3B	HR	RBI	BB	SO	SB	AVG	Slug
364	109	195	27	9	5	55	86	82	7	.229	.299

Myron Nathan "Joe" Ginsburg, *Catcher*

Ginsburg appeared at the major league level for three decades. A little catcher, Joe was a teenager during the Second World War. The portside swinger served with the U.S. Army, and at the end of the war he was stationed at the Philippine Islands where he was able to play some service ball. After his discharge, Ginsburg locked on with the Tigers and made his debut in 1948. His last action came with the expansion Mets of 1962.

G	R	H	2B	3B	HR	RBI	BB	SO	SB	AVG	Slug
695	168	414	59	8	20	182	226	125	7	.241	.320

Albert Francis Gionfriddo, *Outfield*

Famous for robbing the great Joe DiMaggio of a sure extra-base hit in the 1947 World Series, Gionfriddo was essentially a war-era player. His only regular duty in the majors came in the war-ravaged 1945 season. A good little flychaser with speed and a solid batting eye, Al served briefly in the military early in the war years and was discharged in time to play some ball in 1944.

G	R	H	2B	3B	HR	RBI	BB	SO	SB	AVG	Slug
228	95	154	22	12	2	58	91	39	15	.266	.355

James Walter Gladd, *Catcher*

Gladd had a brief trial with the New York Giants after the war. The Giants had very little in the way of talent with an aging Mel Ott acting as player-manager. Their talent suffered a huge blow when Johnny Mize, the best Slugger on the club, broke his hand. When Gladd joined the team, the Giants were fighting with the Pirates for the cellar. But just the year before, Gladd was engaged in a more meaningful fight overseas. Attached to the 71st Infantry Division, Jim saw action in the ETO. After the fighting he was able to play some ball in Germany with Reds star prospect Ewell Blackwell.

G	R	H	2B	3B	HR	RBI	BB	SO	SB	AVG	Slug
4	0	1	0	0	0	0	1	4	0	.091	.091

Roland Edouard Gladu, *Third Base/Outfield*

A war-era ballplayer, Gladu made his major league debut at the age of 33 with the war-ravaged Braves. The left-handed-hitting hot corner custodian was French Canadian, and during the war he served in the Canadian Army. His time in the military took him away from home, as Gladu was sent to England. He was shipped back home and discharged in time to participate in 1944 spring training.

G	R	H	2B	3B	HR	RBI	BB	SO	SB	AVG	Slug
21	5	16	2	1	1	7	3	8	0	.242	.348

Thomas Giatano Glaviano, *Third Base*

A great on-base percentage guy, Glaviano owned one of the sharpest batting eyes of his generation. Able to draw plenty of walks, Glaviano was the type of player that made for an ideal tablesetter for the big bats. He made his debut with the 1949 Cardinals. Before his time in the majors, Tommy served with the U.S. Coast Guard during World War II.

G	R	H	2B	3B	HR	RBI	BB	SO	SB	AVG	Slug
389	191	259	55	6	24	108	208	173	11	.257	.395

James Joseph Gleeson, *Outfield*

A serviceable switch-hitting outfielder, Gleeson played for the Reds just before the war. He joined the club right after their back-to-back World Series appearances in 1939 and 1940. After the Reds cut him loose in 1942, Jim made his way to the U.S. Navy. While he served with the navy during World War II, Jim was able to play some service ball at the Norfolk Training Station with Dominic DiMaggio and Benny McCoy.

G	R	H	2B	3B	HR	RBI	BB	SO	SB	AVG	Slug
392	195	336	77	19	16	154	158	147	20	.263	.391

Alban Glossop, *Utilityman*

Never given much of a chance at the major league level, Glossop tried to crack five starting lineups with no success. He first came up with the 1939 Giants and was stuck behind Burgess Whitehead. A trade to the Braves midway through the 1940 season sent Al to Boston where he backed up Bama Rowell. His only stint as a regular came in 1942 with the lowly Phillies, as Al netted 454 at-bats. He joined the Dodgers in 1943, where he served as a reserve for their stellar infield of Billy Herman, Arky Vaughan and Frenchy Bordagaray. His last major league stint came with the 1946 Cubs.

Glossop missed the 1944 and 1945 seasons to World War II. He passed his physical exam in November of 1943 and was sworn into the navy shortly thereafter. Al served at the Great Lakes and played service ball under Hall of Famer Mickey Cochrane. He was shipped out to the South Pacific and spent a portion of his time in the same outfit as Hall of Famer Johnny Mize.

G	R	H	2B	3B	HR	RBI	BB	SO	SB	AVG	Slug
309	99	199	29	2	15	86	89	105	5	.209	.291

Isadore "Izzy" Goldstein, *Pitcher*

Goldstein attended the same New York-based high school as Hall of Famer Hank Greenberg. As young men, both signed contracts with the Detroit Tigers. Izzy joined the Tigers first in 1932, but that would be his only action in the majors. Born in the Ukraine, Goldstein grew up in New York and during World War II he joined the army while in his mid-thirties.

W	L	PCT	G	GS	CG	IP	H	BB	SO	SHO	ERA
3	2	.600	16	6	2	56	63	41	14	0	4.50

Leslie Elmer "Lonnie" Goldstein, *First Base*

Goldstein scratched one base hit in his major league career, which spanned two seasons with the Reds. Lonnie joined the Reds in 1943 and smacked his hit that season. He spent the 1944 campaign in the bushes, and during spring training of 1945, he sent a letter to Reds management that stated he would not attend training since he was preparing for the draft. He was inducted into the army early in 1945 and missed one year to service with Uncle Sam.

G	R	H	2B	3B	HR	RBI	BB	SO	SB	AVG	Slug
11	2	1	0	0	0	0	3	2	0	.100	.100

Stanley Goletz, *Pinch Hitter*

A strong two-way player in the minors, Goletz was called up by the White Sox for a brief trial in 1941. Stan had five at-bats but didn't play the field nor did he take the pitcher's mound. Goletz went 3-for-5 with three singles and two strikeouts in his major league sojourn. His career was interrupted by the war when he joined the military in 1942 and served for the duration. Stan was shipped overseas where he saw action in the Mariana Islands.

G	R	H	2B	3B	HR	RBI	BB	SO	SB	AVG	Slug
5	0	3	0	0	0	0	0	2	0	.600	.600

Joseph Madrid Gonzales, *Pitcher*

Gonzales had a cup of coffee with the 1937 Red Sox. They debuted Bobby Doerr that year but had yet to bring Williams, DiMaggio and Pesky into the fold. Joe appeared in a handful of games that year, his only season at the major league level. In 1943, Joe was commissioned an ensign in the navy. He served as a deck officer on a vessel in foreign waters.

W	L	PCT	G	GS	CG	IP	H	BB	SO	SHO	ERA
1	2	.333	8	2	2	31	37	11	11	0	4.35

William Dale Goodman, *Infield*

An all-hit, limited-field infielder for the Bosox of the 1950s, Goodman was always a threat to cop the batting title throughout his career. After high school he signed to play with the Atlanta Crackers but the teen was inducted into the navy and served a year in the Pacific Theatre near the end of the war. After his discharge he returned to the Crackers before Boston called him up in 1947. A few years later, in 1950, he would win the American League batting title.

G	R	H	2B	3B	HR	RBI	BB	SO	SB	AVG	Slug
1,623	807	1,691	299	44	19	591	669	329	37	.300	.378

Raymond Daniel Goolsby, *Reserve*

The Alabama native actually has his time in the army to thank for his trial in the majors. An unknown before the war, Goolsby served in the navy in the same outfit as Washington Senator Sherry Robertson. The two played a lot of service ball together, and after the war Robertson finagled a contract with the Senators for Goolsby.

G	R	H	2B	3B	HR	RBI	BB	SO	SB	AVG	Slug
3	0	0	0	0	0	0	1	1	0	.000	.000

Joseph Lowell Gordon, *Second Base*

Joe Gordon made his debut in 1938, assuming the vacated second-base post left behind by Tony Lazzeri, and swatted 25 home runs as a rookie, which was handily the highest total of all major league second basemen. He made strides the following year when he cut down on his strikeouts while adding three more homers and eclipsing the 100-RBI plateau. He became a 30-home run man in 1940 and finished third in the league in the stolen base department. He regressed in all of the offensive categories in 1941 but paced the Yankees with a .322 batting average in 1942. However, the strides he made in plate discipline had all but vanished, as he also lead the league in strikeouts. His last year before the war, Gordon had an atrocious season. His batting average fell 73 points from the prior year and he was unable to redeem himself in 1944 because he entered the military. He even quit the game after the 1943 World Series, saying that he was "tired of baseball."

Upon his army induction, Gordon, who possessed a civilian pilot's license, put in a request for duty in the Army Air Transport Service. He was very eager to fly planes for Uncle Sam, and at his induction, Gordon said, "[I'm] happy to be in the service of my country. I desire action duty as soon as possible." Much to his dismay — a lesser man would have been ecstatic — Gordon was informed that his age prevented him from participating in combat flying duty. Many friends and family members stated that this news greatly disappointed him, since Flash wanted nothing more than to do his best for his country.

Flash took up the game of baseball in the service as an alternative to flying planes. He was sent overseas to Hawaii and experimented with batting left-handed on the islands. During one contest, in which Joe batted exclusively from the left side of the plate, he went 4-for-5 with seven RBIs. After he missed two full years to service in the army, Joe returned to the Yankees in 1946 and mustered a poor .210 batting average. He was dealt to the Indians the following year and proved to the league that the Bronx Bombers gave up on him too soon. Joe hit .272 and swatted 29 home runs with 93 RBIs, while his replacement in New York, Snuffy Stirnweiss, hit .256 with five homers and 41 RBIs. His final season in the sun, and possibly his finest year, came in 1948 when he led the Indians to a world championship. He led the team with 32 home runs and 124 RBIs, proving even further that the Yankees should have allowed him to regain his pre-war form.

G	R	H	2B	3B	HR	RBI	BB	SO	SB	AVG	Slug
1,566	914	1,530	264	52	253	975	759	702	89	.268	.466

Sidney Gordon, *Third Base*

One of baseball's lesser known great third basemen, the compact Sid Gordon was a solid force in the Giants' lineup throughout the 1940s. He initially came up as an outfielder with the 1941 Giants and made the transition to the hot corner in 1942. Due to Dick Bartell owning third base, Sid became a Jack of all trades in 1943, the year before his military induction. He lost two years to service in the U.S. Coast Guard and returned to the Giants in 1946 to hit the apple at a .293 clip. His breakout year came in 1948 when he was finally able to stick at one position — third base — for the course of a season. He posted an offensive line of a .299 batting average, 30 home runs and 107 RBIs.

G	R	H	2B	3B	HR	RBI	BB	SO	SB	AVG	Slug
1,475	735	1,415	220	43	202	805	731	356	19	.283	.466

Charles Perry Gorin, *Pitcher*

One of the few ballplayers to have served in two wars, Gorin was a teenager during the Second World War and served at the end of that conflict. After he joined the Navy Reserves in the early 1950s, he was called back to active duty for the Korean War. A little left-handed pitcher, Gorin lost four years to two separate wars but only two seasons of pro ball because he had yet to sign a contract when he enlisted during World War II.

Growing up in Austin, Texas, during the war years, Gorin knew when he came of age there was one thing to do—go lend a hand. Boys were rushing off to war in the mid–1940s and Gorin felt it his duty to do the same. He said, "I've always been proud of my service. You know, back in the 1940s guys would drop out of high school to join. Joining up was the thing to do and we all felt good about it. Some guys needed to join up because it would mature them and make them responsible. I'm glad I went, I can tell you that."

After his high school graduation, Gorin enlisted in the navy in 1945. The war was near its end but no one knew that at the time. He took his boot camp at the San Diego Naval Station and awaited orders from there. He would soon get his orders as the *USS Stevens*, a naval destroyer, came into port for repairs. Gorin said, "The *USS Stevens* had been hit by a kamikaze and they came in for repairs and assigned about thirteen of us younger guys on it. I was on the ship out on the West Coast when they dropped the bomb on Hiroshima, and boy that stopped the war right there."

Gorin remained in the navy through 1946 and helped out at San Diego as a swarm of destroyers came back from the war. When the war ended, Gorin and his *USS Stevens* was one of the many ships that returned stateside. He said, "After the bomb was dropped, all the destroyers came back to San Diego. When we pulled in there I bet I saw 250 destroyers." With the war completed, Gorin assisted in the demobilization of the naval fleet before he was discharged. With the GI Bill, he went off to college. Gorin said, "The military was good to me because it gave me the GI Bill. Without it I wouldn't have made it through school because my folks weren't too well off. The GI Bill was good for the country and very good for a poor Texas boy like me."

After he completed college, Gorin signed with the Boston Braves and embarked on his pro baseball career. When a friend asked him to sign up with the Navy Reserves, Gorin didn't hesitate to put his name on the dotted line. With the war over, he felt secure in his station as a baseball player, but then another war broke out in Korea and Gorin was called back to service. In his second stint in the navy, Gorin was sent to the Pre-Flight School at Pensacola, Florida. About his duties at Pensacola, Gorin said "At the Pre-Flight School I was an instructor in physical fitness, so I had to know about gymnastics and conditioning and the like. Well, there were a lot of boys coming through the school that couldn't swim. I couldn't imagine being a *navy* pilot and not knowing how to swim. So I had to give swimming lessons and I taught deepwater survival, and, of course, we also played baseball."

The Pensacola Pre-Flight School had an admiral that was obsessed with athletics, and his favorite was football. The navy, which takes its sports seriously, had just acquired the services of a star collegiate quarterback who was slated for duty at the Pre-Flight School. But things didn't go as planned for the admiral until he exerted his authority. Gorin tells the story, saying, "At the Pre-Flight School we had every sport. The admiral of the base was really athletic minded. There was this real good quarterback who got sent down to Pensacola who said that he'd come down to Florida to learn how to fly and that he was through with football. So the admiral sent a note down to his unit that read, 'Tell that young man he'd better give me his shoe size if he expects to get anywhere in this man's navy.'"

W	L	PCT	G	GS	CG	IP	H	BB	SO	SHO	ERA
0	1	.000	7	0	0	10	6	9	12	0	3.60

Herbert Allan Gorman, *Pinch Hitter*

Gorman had one at-bat at the major league level with the 1952 Redbirds. While trying to work his way onto the Cardinals' 1953 roster, Gorman collapsed during a game and died that day from a heart attack. Herb missed some minor league action to service in the U.S. Coast Guard during the war.

G	R	H	2B	3B	HR	RBI	BB	SO	SB	AVG	Slug
1	0	0	0	0	0	0	0	0	0	.000	.000

Thomas Aloysius Gorman, *Pitcher*

Not to be confused with the Giants pitcher who also served during the war, Tom A. Gorman pitched for his hometown Yankees after the war. The Yankees won the World Series the first two years Gorman was on the team. He was used in each Fall Classic, but when the Yankees failed to capture the AL pennant in 1954, they shipped Tom off to Kansas City for extra parts. During the war, Tom served in the navy and was sent to the Pacific Theatre.

W	L	PCT	G	GS	CG	IP	H	BB	SO	SHO	ERA
36	36	.500	289	33	5	690	659	239	321	2	3.77

Thomas David Gorman, *Pitcher*

Not to be confused with the other Tom Gorman — also a pitcher — who played with the Yankees and Kansas City A's after the war, Tom D. Gorman had a cup of coffee with the 1939 Giants. Gorman, a rather big man, joined the military during the Second World War and spent time overseas in England. He was a star baseball and basketball player in the service ranks in Britain but never made it back to the mound in the majors after his discharge. Instead, Gorman started to work as an umpire and had a lengthy career as an on-field arbiter.

W	L	PCT	G	GS	CG	IP	H	BB	SO	SHO	ERA
0	0	—	4	0	0	5	7	1	2	0	7.20

Henry Frank Gornicki, *Pitcher*

On the short list of pitchers who have won two games in one day, Gornicki spent his major league days with the Cardinals, Cubs and Pirates. Hank split the 1941 season with the Redbirds and Cubs and joined the Pirates in 1942. He led Pirate pitchers with a 2.57 ERA in 1942 and then paced the team in saves and games pitched in 1943. During the offseason he worked at a defense plant near his hometown in Niagara Falls. It was off to the military in 1944 for Hank, as he was inducted into the army at Camp Upton, New York. After two years of service, Hank returned to the Pirates to pitch his last thirteen innings in the majors.

W	L	PCT	G	GS	CG	IP	H	BB	SO	SHO	ERA
15	19	.441	79	33	12	285	275	107	123	4	3.38

John Joseph Perry Gorsica, *Pitcher*

One of the many major league ballplayers to be cycled through the military baseball juggernaut at the Great Lakes Naval Training Station, Gorsica missed only one full season to military service. Johnny made 20 starts as a rookie and posted a .500 winning percentage. He was never again able to duplicate the success he had in his rookie campaign of 1940, and pitched worse when stars left for the military.

W	L	PCT	G	GS	CG	IP	H	BB	SO	SHO	ERA
31	39	.443	204	64	22	724	778	247	272	4	4.18

Joseph LaVerne Grace, *Outfield*

Grace hit .340 in limited action for the 1938 St. Louis Browns, his first action in the major leagues. He hit .304 the following year, when he served as a platoon player. In 1940, he began to experiment with catching and played in nine games behind the plate in 1941. He enlisted in the army after the baseball campaign of 1941 and missed four years to service. Joe returned to the Browns in 1946 but was dealt to the Senators during the season. He played his last major league game in 1947.

G	R	H	2B	3B	HR	RBI	BB	SO	SB	AVG	Slug
484	225	442	76	18	20	172	179	135	9	.283	.393

Jack Bernard Graham, *Outfield/First Base*

A legend in the minors who blasted close to 400 career dingers, Graham had a trial at the major league level and showcased well-above-average power there as well. His downfall was his low batting average and less-than-stellar defense. Graham served two years in the Army Air Corps and was stationed at Camp Kearns, Utah. While there, the big power hitter was able to play plenty of baseball and when he was discharged, the Dodgers gave him a brief trial in 1946 before they sent him to the Giants.

G	R	H	2B	3B	HR	RBI	BB	SO	SB	AVG	Slug
239	105	179	28	5	38	126	84	99	1	.231	.427

Newton Michael "Mickey" Grasso, *Catcher*

Nicknamed "Mickey" because he resembled the great Mickey Cochrane in appearance, Grasso was a noted loudmouth receiver with a penchant for choice words. During the 1949 season, Grasso is said to have been thrown out of 23 games for excessive arguing and poor word selection in debating with umpires. Although Grasso looked the part of Cochrane, he was hardly the player. Grasso ended his career with a meager .226 batting average while the Hall of Famer Cochrane hit .320.

Before Grasso made his major league debut, he suffered through some horrendous experiences in the war. Mickey, ever the patriot, enlisted in the army shortly after Pearl Harbor was bombed. After boot camp, Grasso was sent to the 34th Infantry Division that was mustered out shortly thereafter. In February of 1943, the 34th was engaged in combat with the Germans in Tunisia when they were overtaken and the survivors were captured. Sent to a Nazi prison camp, Grasso spent a combined 27 months as a prisoner of war.

Not content to be herded behind barbed wire fences, Grasso made several attempts to escape and suffered horrible beatings when he was caught. Despite his failed attempts to escape, Grasso never gave up. While held captive at Stalag III, Grasso tried for the last time to escape from his captors and was finally successful. Taken in by the Allied Forces, Grasso was promptly sent home to recuperate from his terrible ordeal. After his discharge, Mickey caught on with the Giants and found the baseball diamond to offer therapeutic charms. Never a star catcher, Grasso spent the bulk of his career with the Washington Senators in the early 1950s.

G	R	H	2B	3B	HR	RBI	BB	SO	SB	AVG	Slug
322	78	216	23	1	5	87	81	108	2	.226	.268

Milton Marshall Gray, *Catcher*

Gray had a cup of coffee with the 1937 Senators of Bucky Harris. The backstop only appeared in two games for the club. During the war, Gray served in the navy.

G	R	H	2B	3B	HR	RBI	BB	SO	SB	AVG	Slug
2	0	0	0	0	0	0	0	1	0	.000	.000

Ted Glenn Gray, *Pitcher*

Gray made his major league debut with his hometown Tigers after his discharge from the service. While he served in the navy, Ted showed immense potential in service games and was deemed a "can't-miss" prospect. The promising southpaw played with Detroit from 1946 to 1954. In his final year, 1955, he played with four different American League teams.

W	L	PCT	G	GS	CG	IP	H	BB	SO	SHO	ERA
59	74	.444	222	162	50	1,133	1,072	595	687	7	4.37

William Henry Greason, *Pitcher*

Greason was a pitcher in the Negro Leagues during the Second World War. He left the diamond during the great conflict and joined the U.S. Marine Corps. After his discharge, Bill returned to the Negro Leagues and wasn't part of the mass exodus to the major leagues after Jackie Robinson and the Dodgers broke the color barrier. Instead, Bill remained in the Negro Leagues until he was summoned by the Marines again for duty during the Korean War.

W	L	PCT	G	GS	CG	IP	H	BB	SO	SHO	ERA
0	1	.000	3	2	0	4	8	4	2	0	13.50

Henry Benjamin Greenberg, *Outfield/First Base*

Modern players like Barry Bonds and Milton Bradley complain about bad press, but Hank Greenberg was in an entirely different league as far as mudslinging is concerned. Hugh Mulcahy may have been the first major league player drafted for military duty during World War II, but Greenberg was certainly the first superstar taken by Uncle Sam. However, Hank was urged by "friends" to seek a deferment due to his flat feet, which would have been accepted as a legitimate medical deferment. When the press received word that Hammerin' Hank had applied for a deferment, papers across the nation labeled Greenberg as a traitor to his country.

Newspaper captions all across America had headlines like the one in Mason City, Iowa, which read, "Hank Greenberg Center of Draft Storm." Of the ordeal, Hank said, "I'm just sorry the public has been given the wrong impression. I felt a lot better after Ben Shepherd, the chairman of my draft board, came up yesterday and told me that I had done only the things asked of me — that I had asked no special privileges. I'm too smart to think I can gain special consideration because I am Hank Greenberg."

Not only was Hank the recipient of harsh criticism by the writers, but the fans, who devour the words written by the Knaves of the Newspaper, began sending hate mail to Hammerin' Hank. Greenberg said, "People send me clippings and add to their own condemnation of me. They say I am not willing to do my part for my country. Sportswriters I have never met in far distant cities are taking nasty cuts at me. That hurts.... Why couldn't I have been inducted into the army like anyone else? I have never tried to have it any other way."

At the time Hank was drafted, he was the highest-paid player in baseball. His salary called for $55,000, but he had to forfeit that sizable allowance for Uncle Sam's base salary of $21 a month. The day before he left for the army, Hank swatted a pair of home runs to defeat the Yankees. On his induction day, Hank said, "I've asked no favors and I'll accept none now. I'll do my best to be a good soldier."

Before departing for his first military assignment, Hank said, "I am sorry I have to go into the army under a cloud as a result of a lot of unfair and undesired things that have been written about me." Hammerin' Hank's initial assignment was basic training at Fort Custer, which prepared him for a job in the Army Air Corps. Of his army training, Hank stated that it changed his entire outlook on life, remarking, "I'm afraid I was a little bit selfish."

After completing basic training, Hank served in an anti-aircraft outfit and his occupational duties were to assist in development and supervision of the physical training program. Of army life, Hank said, "When I was playing ball I used to squawk if the hotel mattresses weren't thick enough. In the army, I've been sleeping on the ground and learning to like it." Aside from his newfound fondness for a terra firma mattress, Hank was released early by the army due to the passing of a law that allowed soldiers over 28 years of age an honorable discharge. Hank accepted the discharge but rejoined the army voluntarily on January 30, 1942.

Relinquishing the opportunity to be a civilian again, Hank returned to the army and was subsequently sent overseas. He was stationed at a Super Fortress Base in India where an act of heroism eclipsed anything he ever accomplished on a ball diamond. At the base, Hank was engaged in friendly chitchat with Colonel Kenneth Stack when the two men witnessed a B29 crash at the end of the runway on its takeoff. As the two men ran toward the fallen aircraft in an effort to save the crew, half of the B29's bomb load went off when they were 100 yards away. The blast blew Hank and Colonel Stack off their feet. Undaunted, they ran around the plane looking for the crew when the remainder of the bombs went off. Hank and Colonel Stack fell to the ground for cover and when the blasts lessened, they picked themselves up and saw six other men — the members of the crew — taking cover in a nearby rice paddy.

Greenberg returned to the States and the game of baseball in 1945, as the press who blasted him during his trials with the draft board now lauded him as a hero. His heroic status would only ascend as he returned to the game and proceeded to lead the Tigers — seemingly single-handedly — to a World Series title that year. His brilliant return encouraged other players in the military, as many harbored feelings of a lost career, but Hank put those feelings to rest with his triumphant return.

G	R	H	2B	3B	HR	RBI	BB	SO	SB	AVG	Slug
1,394	1,051	1,628	379	71	331	1,276	852	844	58	.313	.605

James Elbert "Joe" Greene, *Catcher*

Few athletes, black or white, were as deeply engaged in World War II as Negro League catcher Joe Greene. At the height of his baseball career, Greene joined the U.S. Army in 1943. He saw combat action attached to the 92nd Division in Italy as a member of an anti-tank outfit. His travails in the European Theatre of Operations took him to Algiers and Milan, where his unit took down the bodies of Benito Mussolini and his mistress, Clara Petacci, who had been executed and strung up by their feet. When the fighting ended, Joe played some service ball overseas and helped his squad win the Mediterranean Theatre of Operations Championship.

Greene returned to the States in 1946 and latched on with the Kansas City Monarchs. They won the pennant that season but were beaten in the World Series. A fine catcher with an exceptional throwing arm, Greene hit for good power but had a weakness for curveballs. Nicknamed "Pea" because he threw peas to second base to nab would-be base stealers, Greene was a fine catcher adept at quelling the opposition's running game.

(1932–1948): Atlanta Black Crackers, Kansas City Monarchs, Homestead Grays and Cleveland Buckeyes

James Raymond Greengrass, *Outfield*

One of the game's top power hitters in the mid 1950s, Greengrass was a productive Slugger for the Reds. Jim gave the Reds an enviable Murderer's Row with Ted Kluszewski, Gus Bell and Wally Post for a time. Before Jim started in baseball, however, he served his country as a teenager at the end of World War II.

G	R	H	2B	3B	HR	RBI	BB	SO	SB	AVG	Slug
504	243	482	82	16	69	282	165	271	6	.269	.448

Louis Edward "Buddy" Gremp, *First Base*

Buddy Gremp was a light-hitting first baseman for the Braves from 1940 to 1942. He made his debut in 1940, as Boston already had a light-hitting first baseman in Buddy Hassett. Gremp's presence forced Hassett to elevate his game, and he raised his batting average 62 points in 1941. When Hassett was dealt to the Yankees in 1942, Gremp began to play regularly at the initial sack but entered the military midway through the 1942 season.

Buddy attended the Navy Pre-Flight School with Red Sox stars Ted Williams and Johnny Pesky, Athletics hurler Joe Coleman and fellow Braves Johnny Sain. He was the second Braves player to enlist in the naval aviation branch, following the lead of Big Johnny Sain. Together, the Braves youngsters trained at Chapel Hill, but Buddy's training was cut short due to an operation he had on his knee.

G	R	H	2B	3B	HR	RBI	BB	SO	SB	AVG	Slug
113	19	65	14	0	3	31	18	24	1	.223	.302

Robert Lee Griffith, *Pitcher*

A mountain of a man, Griffith was 6'5" and tipped the scales at 240 pounds. The big right-hander from Liberty, Tennessee, was a master of the spitball around the World War II era, long after the major leagues outlawed the pitch. A journeyman pitcher, Bob made his rounds in the Negro Leagues and Latin America. During World War II, he served in the European Theatre with the U.S. Army.

(1933–1951): Philadelphia Stars, Baltimore Elite Giants, New York Black Yankees, Kansas City Monarchs and Indianapolis Clowns

Lee Theo Grissom, *Pitcher*

Lee Grissom was a big-bodied southpaw who joined the military in his mid thirties. He was a reliable swing-man at the major league level, beginning in 1934. His finest year came in 1937 as he posted 12 wins for a last-place team and finished ten strikeouts behind league leader Carl Hubbell. However, Lee injured his knee the following year and was never again the dominant pitcher that he showed in 1937. Lee spent just half a season with the Phillies in 1941—his last year in the majors—before he joined the colors after the season.

Grissom was widely regarded as an eccentric southpaw with an unhealthy obsession with the great Lefty Grove. A rumor circulated that Lee had a few teeth pulled, despite them not ailing, because he learned that Grove had the same operation. Of the rumor, Lee said, "Ain't so! I got 'em teeth pulled 'cause they was a hurtin'!" Grissom entered the army after the 1941 baseball season and served as an MP at Camp Tyson, Tennessee. He received his discharge in September of 1945 but didn't grace the game of baseball with his bizarre presence after shaking loose of his army threads.

W	L	PCT	G	GS	CG	IP	H	BB	SO	SHO	ERA
29	48	.377	162	95	23	702	668	305	384	6	3.88

John Grodzicki, *Pitcher*

A dedicated soldier, Grodzicki scoffed at the idea of spending the war as a physical instructor and demanded that he be given an assignment with a paratrooper outfit. With a bevy of good young arms in St. Louis prior to the war, manager Eddie Dyer named Johnny as the best, saying, "[Johnny is] the best pitcher in the minor leagues." Despite the lofty scouting report given by his skipper, Johnny enlisted in the army and went to war as a paratrooper.

Grodzicki was inducted into the army in January of 1942 and was assigned to the 17th Airborne Division. Johnny's two brothers also served in the military, as one brother was in the Medical Corps while another brother was a fellow paratrooper. Johnny initially worked in an ammunition warehouse at Fort Knox as a private but it wasn't long until he saw action overseas. Johnny gave this recount on his jump into a battle zone: "We hit Germany at Witzel about the time the boys broke across the bridge. I landed fine, right out in an open field with plenty of Jerries about. They didn't get me then but five days later I was wounded by shrapnel."

Due to his injuries sustained in battle, Johnny was flown to England and then sent back to the States in October of 1945 on crutches. Doctors insisted he wear a foot-long steel brace because a nerve had been injured in the leg. Despite the injury and the bulky brace, Johnny attended spring training with the Cardinals in 1946. As one could imagine, the war hero was the story of the spring when he attempted a comeback with a large brace fixed to his leg. Although he didn't set the league afire, Johnny pitched for the Cardinals in 1946 and 1947. Never did he allow his injuries to deter him from achieving his dream.

W	L	PCT	G	GS	CG	IP	H	BB	SO	SHO	ERA
2	2	.500	24	1	0	40	31	34	20	0	4.50

Howard Hoffman "Howdy" Groskloss, *Second Base/Shortstop*

Howdy played with his hometown Pirates for three years at the time when the Waner brothers were all the rage in Pittsburgh. Groskloss, a reserve infielder, was more interested in medicine than baseball. His father died when he was a young boy and Howdy wanted to enter the medical field to help people live healthy lives. But it was his father's wish that his son become a baseball player, and Groskloss played ball when he wasn't studying. He was able to both honor his father and do what he wanted.

Groskloss received his doctorate from Yale University and he even taught at the prestigious institute for a time. During the Second World War, Uncle Sam needed men from the medical field and gave Dr. Groskloss a call. Inducted into the navy, Howdy served as a flight surgeon on a navy vessel during the war. After the war, Groskloss returned to the civilian medical field. He was named head of medicine at the University of Minnesota.

G	R	H	2B	3B	HR	RBI	BB	SO	SB	AVG	Slug
72	14	48	7	2	0	21	11	19	1	.261	.321

Benjamin John Guintini, *Outfield*

A noted cut-up who enjoyed pleasing the crowd with antics, Guintini had two cups of coffee at the major league level. He played with the Pirates briefly in 1946 and was a member of the last team that Connie Mack ever managed. Ben served briefly in the military and was discharged in 1944 in time to play in the Pacific Coast League.

G	R	H	2B	3B	HR	RBI	BB	SO	SB	AVG	Slug
5	0	0	0	0	0	0	0	1	0	.000	.000

Harry Edwards Gumbert, *Pitcher*

Harry "Gunboat" Gumbert was a solid major league pitcher before and after the war. His initial trial in the majors came with the 1935 Giants as a 25-year-old. After a year and a half of shifting between the rotation and the bullpen, Gunboat became a regular starter in 1937. He led the Giants in wins during the 1938 and 1939 seasons. He was dealt to the Cardinals early in 1941 and played with the Redbirds through 1944, when he was sent to the Reds. Gunboat was temporarily deferred by his draft board because he was over the age of thirty but received his call in February of 1945. Harry missed one year of baseball as he was stationed at Fort Leonardwood, Missouri.

W	L	PCT	G	GS	CG	IP	H	BB	SO	SHO	ERA
143	113	.559	508	235	96	2,158	2,186	721	709	12	3.68

Randall Pennington Gumpert, *Pitcher*

Connie Mack languished in the American League for a number of years, always trying to rebuild the Athletics after selling off his stars. He wasn't opposed to giving a kid a shot in the majors, and he did just that with an 18-year-old Gumpert in 1936. Randy pitched 62 innings for Mack that year and another 12 in 1937. He was then given the minor league seasoning time he sorely needed and didn't make his return to the majors until after World War II had concluded.

Gumpert served in the U.S. Coast Guard. He applied for an assignment at Allentown, Pennsylvania, and played baseball for a service team named the Meriden Contelcoss. After four years in the minors and three in the service, Randy returned to the highest level with the 1946 Yankees. He finished third on the team in wins and posted a stellar 2.30 ERA. He later saw major league action with the White Sox, Red Sox and Senators.

W	L	PCT	G	GS	CG	IP	H	BB	SO	SHO	ERA
51	59	.464	261	113	47	1,052	1,099	346	352	6	4.17

Berthold John Haas, *Third Base*

A good little ballplayer, Haas had a brief trial with the Dodgers in the late 1930s but couldn't stick. He returned to the majors in 1942 with the daunting task of replacing the great Bill Werber at third base. Bert lost his third-base job the following year to Steve Mesner and was then inducted into the armed forces in late August of 1943. Haas was shipped overseas and saw action in Rome.

G	R	H	2B	3B	HR	RBI	BB	SO	SB	AVG	Slug
721	263	644	93	32	22	263	204	188	51	.264	.355

Robert Julius Habenicht, *Pitcher*

Habenicht had two cups of coffee in the 1950s with his hometown clubs: the Cardinals and the Browns. Called upon to toss only seven innings in his major league career, the St. Louis native had severe command issues. In those seven frames, Bob issued ten walks. Before he made it to the majors, Bob served in the armed forces during World War II. The right-handed pitcher was playing for a minor league team in Lima when he left the club and enlisted in the Army Air Corps. After his playing days, Habenicht attained a law degree from St. Louis University.

W	L	PCT	G	GS	CG	IP	H	BB	SO	SHO	ERA
0	0	—	4	0	0	7	6	10	2	0	6.43

Richard Frederick Hahn, *Catcher*

Hahn spelled regular catchers Rick Ferrell and Jake Early once during the 1940 season, his only game at the highest level. When Uncle Sam needed men, Hahn answered the call and spent time in the United States Navy.

G	R	H	2B	3B	HR	RBI	BB	SO	SB	AVG	Slug
1	0	0	0	0	0	0	0	0	0	.000	.000

Chester Hajduk, *Pinch Hitter*

Chet Hajduk strolled to the plate one time in his major league career, recording an out in the process. He lost several years to service in the United States Army, and the hometown boy was never able to take the field for his native White Sox again.

G	R	H	2B	3B	HR	RBI	BB	SO	SB	AVG	Slug
1	0	0	0	0	0	0	0	0	0	.000	.000

Robert Lewis Hall, *Pitcher*

Hall lost twice as many games as he won at the major league level. During his time in the majors, Bob fashioned one shutout. Before his major league debut, Hall served with the United States Coast Guard during World War II.

W	L	PCT	G	GS	CG	IP	H	BB	SO	SHO	ERA
9	18	.333	89	27	8	276	307	146	133	1	5.41

John Sylvester Hall, *Pitcher*

Hall had a cup of coffee with the 1948 Dodgers. The Oklahoma native appeared in a handful of games without a decision. Before his major league debut, John served in the U.S. Coast Guard during World War II.

W	L	PCT	G	GS	CG	IP	H	BB	SO	SHO	ERA
0	0	—	3	0	0	4	4	2	2	0	6.75

William Anthony "Wild Bill" Hallahan, *Pitcher*

The staff ace of the Cardinals before some kid named Dizzy Dean arrived on the scene, Wild Bill pitched the Cardinals to back-to-back World Series appearances in 1930 and 1931. Although the Redbirds lost to the A's of Connie Mack in 1930, they got their revenge in 1931. A holy terror in the latter Series, Hallahan outperformed Hall of Famer Lefty Grove with two wins and an ERA of 0.49. Hallahan was so highly regarded in the early 1930s that he was named the starting pitcher in the first-ever All-Star Game.

Wild Bill and Dizzy made for a terrific lefty-righty tandem in the Redbirds rotation. But after a rough start in 1936, Hallahan was shipped off to the Reds. He would last pitch in the majors for the last-place Phillies of 1938. When Pearl Harbor was bombed, Wild Bill was pushing 40 years of age but that didn't stop the former All-Star from enlisting. Sent to Fort Niagara to train for army duty, Wild Bill was eager to do his part, saying, "I just want a chance to show the Axis the stuff I've got on a hand grenade." After six months of duty at the Fort Niagara Reception Center, Wild Bill was honorably discharged on the over-38 years of age mandate.

W	L	PCT	G	GS	CG	IP	H	BB	SO	SHO	ERA
102	94	.520	324	224	90	1,740	1,838	777	856	13	4.03

Jack Price Hallett, *Pitcher*

An imposing figure on the mound, Hallett was a large right-hander who pitched with the White Sox, Pirates and Giants. Jack came up with the White Sox in 1940 and struggled in his first three seasons. Right when he had put it all together — a 1.69 ERA in 48 innings — he was inducted into the navy during the 1943 baseball season. Jack served overseas in the South Pacific and also played service ball in Hawaii with a couple stars from Brooklyn: Hugh Casey and Pee Wee Reese.

W	L	PCT	G	GS	CG	IP	H	BB	SO	SHO	ERA
12	16	.429	73	24	11	278	280	106	128	2	4.05

James Sanford Hamby, *Catcher*

A fourth-string catcher for John McGraw in the late 1920s, Hamby was in his forties during World War II. When age requirements were relaxed, Hamby joined up and served in the armed forces.

G	R	H	2B	3B	HR	RBI	BB	SO	SB	AVG	Slug
22	6	10	0	1	0	5	7	7	1	.182	.218

Granville Wilbur Hamner, *Shortstop*

Baseball teams grabbed at straws during the war to find players to fill their rosters. Many teams looked at over-the-hill veterans or career minor leaguers to play while their best and brightest served in the military. Other teams, like the Phillies, scouted the schoolyards and signed kids before they gathered their diplomas. Granny Hamner was one such player. The Phillies brought in a 17-year-old Hamner in 1944 to play during the war. However, when Hamner came of age late in the war years, he too was inducted.

After Granville played fourteen games for the Phillies in 1945, he was inducted into the army as an 18-year-old. The schoolboy shortstop received his pre-induction physical notice by his draft board while he trained with the Phillies before the season. Sent to Fort Lee, Virginia, Granny played some service ball on the installation with pitcher Bob Chakales. After a year in the army, Hamner was discharged when the war ended. He would return to the Phillies and eventually became one of the better offensive middle infielders of his generation. In an odd twist at the end of his career, Granny converted himself into a knuckleball pitcher and saw some action on the mound when he was done as a position player.

G	R	H	2B	3B	HR	RBI	BB	SO	SB	AVG	Slug
1,531	711	1,529	272	62	104	708	351	432	35	.262	.383

Raymond Bernard Hamrick, *Shortstop*

A light-hitting shortstop, Ray served as the Phillies' regular shortstop in 1944 before his induction into the service during the season. Hamrick served as the lead-off man for the 1944 Phillies but was accepted for service in April of that year. Ray served with the navy while his brother, Branlow, was a radio operator on a bomber.

G	R	H	2B	3B	HR	RBI	BB	SO	SB	AVG	Slug
118	34	92	13	2	1	32	31	62	1	.204	.248

Morris Medlock "Buddy" Hancken, *Reserve*

Hancken played one game for Connie Mack's Athletics in 1940. Unable to tally an at-bat in the majors, Buddy instead had a lengthy career as a player, coach and manager in the minor leagues. His baseball duties were interrupted during the war when he left the diamond to serve with the U.S. Marine Corps. After his discharge from the Marines, Buddy began work as a player/manager in the bushes.

G	R	H	2B	3B	HR	RBI	BB	SO	SB	AVG	Slug
1	0	0	0	0	0	0	0	0	0	—	—

Harry Aloysius Hanebrink, *Utilityman*

A versatile ballplayer, Hanebrink made his major league debut after the Braves had relocated to Milwaukee. A teenager during the war, Harry served with the U.S. Navy at the end of the conflict.

G	R	H	2B	3B	HR	RBI	BB	SO	SB	AVG	Slug
177	32	71	7	2	6	25	22	31	1	.224	.315

Loy Vernon Hanning, *Pitcher*

In between Loy's two stints with the Browns he tossed a no-hitter at San Antonio. The slim right-hander from Bunker, Missouri, was given trials with the Browns in 1939 and 1942 but failed to stick. Inducted into the U.S. Army after the 1942 season, Hanning missed minor league action to military service.

W	L	PCT	G	GS	CG	IP	H	BB	SO	SHO	ERA
1	2	.333	15	1	0	27	32	16	17	0	6.33

Donald Thomas Hanski, *Pitcher/First Base*

Hanski was quite a versatile little ballplayer, able to pitch and play first base. However, his major league career was brief, spanning 22 at-bats and four innings pitched. In 1943, he saw action at first base while tossing one inning, and in 1944 he was used exclusively from the mound. He missed the entire 1945 baseball campaign to service in the army after his induction at Camp Sheridan.

G	R	H	2B	3B	HR	RBI	BB	SO	SB	AVG	Slug
11	1	5	1	0	0	2	0	5	0	.227	.273

Paul James Hardy, *Catcher*

A journeyman catcher, Hardy was regarded as a decent defender who offered little with the stick. He was the regular catcher for the Birmingham Black Barons in 1943 when they captured the pennant but he missed out on the World Series when he was inducted into the armed forces. After his military discharge, Hardy returned to the Negro Leagues and played for a couple of years before retiring.

(1932–1947): Chicago American Giants, Birmingham Black Barons, Montgomery Grey Sox, Washington Elite Giants, Kansas City Monarchs and Memphis Red Sox

William Bell Harman, *Pitcher*

Bill Harman pitched five games for the 1941 Phillies and was then inducted into the armed forces. The right-hander never returned to the major leagues after his tour with Uncle Sam had concluded.

W	L	PCT	G	GS	CG	IP	H	BB	SO	SHO	ERA
0	0	—	5	0	0	13	15	8	3	0	4.85

Robert Arthur Harris, *Pitcher*

Harris began his career with the 1938 Detroit Tigers and was dealt to the lowly Browns during the 1939 season. His best year came in 1941, at which time he won 12 games for the American League's St. Louis entry. He was then shuttled to Connie Mack's Athletics and paced that club with a 2.88 ERA. The 1942 season was Bob's last action at the major league level, as he was drafted into the navy after the campaign. Bob served at the Great Lakes and played ball under Mickey Cochrane.

W	L	PCT	G	GS	CG	IP	H	BB	SO	SHO	ERA
30	52	.366	127	89	26	647	770	294	205	4	4.95

Herbert Benjamin Harris, *Pitcher*

A slender southpaw from Chicago, Herb had a cup of coffee with the National League doormat Phillies in 1936. Seven years after his trial in the majors, Harris was inducted into the U.S. Navy and served during World War II.

W	L	PCT	G	GS	CG	IP	H	BB	SO	SHO	ERA
0	0	—	4	0	0	7	14	5	0	0	10.29

Chalmer Luman Harris, *Pitcher*

Lum Harris missed only one year to military duty during World War II, but it proved to be a costly interruption. He had just come into his own in 1944, when he posted 10 wins with a 3.31 ERA. He left near the end of the season for the navy. He spent his navy duty at the Bainbridge Naval Training Station, where he played baseball in his spare time. Lum returned to the Athletics in 1946, as his once-impeccable accuracy had vanished and he played one final year with the Senators before calling it quits. Harris is best known now as a former major league manager. He was at the dugout helm of the Braves, Astros and a brief stint with the Orioles.

W	L	PCT	G	GS	CG	IP	H	BB	SO	SHO	ERA
35	63	.357	151	91	46	819	874	265	232	4	4.16

Maurice Charles Harris, *Pitcher*

Mickey Harris was a solid pitcher throughout his major league career. The southpaw pitched for the Red Sox from 1940 to 1949, with four years missed to service during World War II. Mickey had yet to establish himself before the war, but was clearly making strides when Uncle Sam required his services. He posted a 3.25 ERA in 1941—second on the club to Broadway Charlie Wagner—which was leaps and bounds above his 5.03 mark in his rookie campaign. Just when Harris was putting it all together, he was taken from the Red Sox for a four-year stint in the military.

Harris was inducted at Fort Dix and completed his army training at Fort Eustis. During the holiday season, Harris was slated to be shipped out to Panama. Eager to do his bit in the war effort, Harris said, "If any Jap planes come down this way, I only hope I can bat 1.000 per cent with that anti-aircraft gun."

Preparing for the deployment, Harris was assigned the duty of loading the unit's duffle bags on the ship. Within these duffle bags were each individual soldier's supplies, such as change of clothes and other personal effects. Mickey loaded the duffle bags upon the ship but noticed a discrepancy when his task was completed. Mickey later recalled, "On our trip down I got stuck with handling about 2,000 duffle bags. Sorting them and stowing in the hold. When I got finished I found I was nine short, including one of my own." Mickey spent the majority of his army service time in Central America, where he was stationed in the Canal Zone as a member of the Panama Coast Artillery Command. His artillery unit fielded a baseball team and Mickey was quite fond of its nickname: the Jungle Mudders. Mickey pitched for the Jungle Mudders often—clearly the star of the club—and once struck out 20 batters in a Canal Zone League game. Facing Mickey in that contest was Cardinal star Terry Moore, who Harris sat down on strikes three separate occasions.

When the war was over and the players returned to the game, it was obvious to many baseball observers that the Red Sox were struck hardest by the call to arms. They had finally built a contending team, and the key pieces to their club spent several years in the service. Mickey returned with the likes of Williams, DiMaggio, Doerr, Pesky and Hughson to guide the Red Sox to the World Series in 1946, as he posted a 17–9 record with 131 strikeouts. However, his major league stardom was short-lived. All the innings he toiled for Uncle Sam caught up with him, and he suffered through the 1947 season with a shoulder injury. Mickey played in the majors through 1952 but was never again the force that he was in the mid 1940s.

W	L	PCT	G	GS	CG	IP	H	BB	SO	SHO	ERA
59	71	.454	271	109	42	1,051	1,097	455	534	2	4.18

Robert Ned Harris, *Outfield*

Ned Harris wasn't given much of a trial at the major league level despite some solid stats in his short tenure. He made his debut with the 1941 Tigers and was handed the regular right-field job in 1942. Harris finished second on the team in triples and stolen bases and was later drafted into the United States Navy. Ned missed the 1944 and 1945 seasons to military service and returned to play one final year of major league baseball.

G	R	H	2B	3B	HR	RBI	BB	SO	SB	AVG	Slug
262	107	211	33	14	16	81	102	77	12	.259	.393

Samuel Harshany, *Catcher*

Harshany served as a back-up catcher for the Browns during four seasons. The backstop was back in the minors by the time World War II broke out. During the war, Sam served with the U.S. Navy. In 1944, while stationed at North Carolina, he was commissioned an ensign close to the first of the year. Shortly thereafter, he was married. Harshany played a little service ball while in the navy when he was stationed at the Great Lakes.

G	R	H	2B	3B	HR	RBI	BB	SO	SB	AVG	Slug
61	17	43	3	0	0	15	16	10	0	.238	.254

Christian Henry Hartje, *Catcher*

Hartje had a cup of coffee with the 1939 Dodgers. He spent the next few seasons back in the minors, trying to work his way to the majors. But when World War II needed men, Hartje joined the U.S. Coast Guard. The receiver was discharged from the military after the Japanese surrender and returned to life as normal. Chris went back to baseball, and in June of 1946, he and his wife were expecting a child. He was playing ball in the minors for the Spokane Indians when tragedy struck.

Hartje and a handful of his teammates on the Spokane Indians roster were war veterans who left the military in good health. Some fought on battlefields and lived and returned home to a place of peace. But that peace was disrupted when the Indians were driving through the Cascade Mountains after a ballgame. Their bus driver swerved to avoid a car driving on the wrong side of the street and crashed through the guard-railing. The team bus plummeted 350 feet down the mountainside where many Spokane Indians were tossed from the bus and killed on its deadly descent. Hartje was seriously wounded in the crash and was transported to a Seattle hospital. After two days and nights of plasma transfusions, he died in his hospital bed, leaving behind a pregnant wife and a post-war world that seemed filled with unlimited possibilities.

G	R	H	2B	3B	HR	RBI	BB	SO	SB	AVG	Slug
9	2	5	1	0	0	5	1	0	0	.313	.375

Roy Thomas Hartsfield, *Second Base*

The first manager in Toronto Blue Jays history, Hartsfield played three years for the Boston Braves in the early 1950s. Before Roy made his major league debut, he served with the U.S. Navy during World War II. Stationed at the Great Lakes Naval Training Station, Hartsfield played service ball under Mickey Cochrane for a time. The team had Hall of Famer Billy Herman on its roster, playing Roy's position, but when Herman was injured, Cochrane had Hartsfield fill in for him. Roy looked sharp, and Cochrane predicted a fine future for the kid from Chattahoochee, Georgia.

G	R	H	2B	3B	HR	RBI	BB	SO	SB	AVG	Slug
265	138	266	30	7	13	59	73	146	14	.273	.358

Clinton Clarence Hartung, *Pitcher/Outfield*

Nicknamed "The Hondo Hurricane," Clint was considered a prospect as either a terrific pitcher or a star outfielder. About all anyone could agree on was that Hartung was going to make an amazing major leaguer. One of the young chaps that wasn't known to ballclubs before the war, Hondo reached prospect status while he played service ball. Every baseball man that watched the youngster play knew he was destined for stardom.

Arguably the most highly touted recruit in the service ranks, Hartung played service ball in Texas while with the Army Air Corps. While pitching in the Lone Star state, Cardinals skipper Eddie Dyer saw the kid pitch on several occasions and was wowed by the Texan's ability. Dyer gushed, "Man, oh man, could the Cardinals have used that guy. The first game I saw him in, he struck out 20 men. The next game 18 and the third game 16." The Hondo Hurricane had set the service ranks abuzz with his expert pitching, and when it came time for his discharge, there was bound to be a bidding war for his services.

The New York Giants shelled out the most coin to Clint and he signed with the New Yorkers. The 1946 Giants were a last-place team while Hartung was working in the bushes. They summoned him in 1947 and skipper Mel Ott used him predominantly as a pitcher, even though he hit .309 — better than all the Giants regulars. Writer Harry Grayson was in awe of the rookie, writing, "Hartung [is] reputed to be a combination of a right-handed Ruth and Feller." As a rookie pitcher, Clint went 9–7 with a 4.57 ERA. He was used exclusively as a pitcher in 1948 and 1949 with limited success. When his accuracy abandoned him in 1950, the Giants converted him to the outfield. His hitting ability also went south and Hartung never did reach the immense potential so many saw in the young soldier.

W	L	PCT	G	GS	CG	IP	H	BB	SO	SHO	ERA
29	29	.500	112	72	23	511	529	271	167	3	5.02

Michael Joseph "Mickey" Haslin, *Utility Infielder*

Not a bad hitter, Haslin was used as a backup most of his major league career. He was a member of the Giants when they copped the National League pennant in 1937 but wasn't used in the World Series. The following year, his last in the majors, Mickey hit .324 as a backup for stars Mel Ott and Dick Bartell. During the war, Haslin played minor league ball and drove a brewery truck in the offseason. But he gave up the beer truck job for the khaki of Uncle Sam late in 1943 and spent the next two years in the colors.

G	R	H	2B	3B	HR	RBI	BB	SO	SB	AVG	Slug
318	125	265	33	8	9	109	59	64	8	.272	.350

John Aloysius "Buddy" Hassett, *First Base*

Hassett was a contact-hitting first baseman who possessed little power but rarely struck out. The Brooklyn Dodgers gave Buddy his first major league trial in 1936; he led the team in base hits and triples his rookie year. He was moved to left field in 1938 when Dolph Camilli and his power bat were brought to Brooklyn. Buddy was dealt to the Braves for the 1939 season and made his way to the Yankees in 1942. However, 1942 would be Buddy's last year at the major league level, as he was lassoed by Uncle Sam in 1943.

After breaking his thumb in his last major league game — in the 1942 World Series — Hassett joined the navy. He served as a lieutenant attached to the Navy Pre-Flight School at Chapel Hill. While stationed at Chapel Hill, Buddy was a battalion commander where superiors detected in him an uncanny skill in directing and handling soldiers under his charge. Later during his four-year navy hitch, Hassett served as a recreation officer on an aircraft carrier in foreign waters.

G	R	H	2B	3B	HR	RBI	BB	SO	SB	AVG	Slug
929	469	1,026	130	40	12	343	209	116	53	.292	.362

Charles Eugene "Gene" Hasson, *First Base*

A great minor league hitter, Hasson wasn't given much of a chance at the major league level. He played two years with Connie Mack's Athletics in the late 1930s before he was sent back to the bushes. Gene took his power hitting back to the minors and there he stayed until World War II. Inducted into the army, Hasson was in charge of athletics at Camp Grant. He was later relocated to Camp Lee where he managed the installation's sporting events and played some service ball with pitcher Bob Carpenter.

Gene's stint in the military helped him land a job after his discharge. In 1945, while on furlough, Gene was riding on a train to visit family back home. When he went to the men's room, he bumped into Frank Lawrence, owner of the minor league Portsmouth Cubs. Lawrence told him that he was looking for a manager to guide his club for the upcoming 1946 season. Hasson knew his discharge was coming up so he told Lawrence that he'd be open for the assignment. The two men reached a handshake agreement on the train.

G	R	H	2B	3B	HR	RBI	BB	SO	SB	AVG	Slug
47	22	49	12	5	4	26	25	21	0	.293	.497

Frederick James Hatfield, *Third Base/Second Base*

Before Hatfield made his major league debut, he served in the military during World War II. The portside swinger played with the Red Sox after his discharge but spent the bulk of his playing career in Detroit. After his days as a player Fred spent many years managing at the minor league level.

G	R	H	2B	3B	HR	RBI	BB	SO	SB	AVG	Slug
722	260	493	67	10	25	165	248	247	15	.242	.321

Grady Edgebert Hatton, *Third Base*

A natural talent, Hatton went directly from Uncle Sam's diamonds to the major leagues without a stop in the minors. During the early war years, Grady was working towards a degree at the University of Texas. He left the campus and joined the Army Air Corps. In 1944, Hatton took part in a service baseball tournament that showcased his abilities. During the course of play, Grady was the event's leading hitter. After Hatton was discharged, the Reds paid top dollar for his services and named him their regular third baseman in 1946. He would enjoy a solid playing career and even managed at the major league level for a time with the Houston Astros.

G	R	H	2B	3B	HR	RBI	BB	SO	SB	AVG	Slug
1,312	562	1,068	166	33	91	533	646	430	42	.254	.374

John Arthur Hauger, *Reserve*

Hauger was 18 years old when he made his major league debut in 1912. That cup of coffee with Cleveland was the extent of his major league career. Thirty years later, Art was managing in the White Sox chain but he quit his post to assist in the war effort. He took a job at the shipyard in Brisbane, California, and later joined the service. Although Hauger died during the war, his death wasn't a result of battlefield injuries. He suffered a heart attack that claimed his life.

G	R	H	2B	3B	HR	RBI	BB	SO	SB	AVG	Slug
15	0	1	0	0	0	1	n/a	0	.056	.056	

Christopher Francis Haughey, *Pitcher*

Haughey made only one appearance at the major league level as a seventeen-year-old pitcher for the 1943 Dodgers. The following year, Chris was inducted into the armed forces on January 25. Despite making his debut at such a tender age, Haughey was never asked back to the majors.

W	L	PCT	G	GS	CG	IP	H	BB	SO	SHO	ERA
0	1	.000	1	0	0	7	5	10	0	0	3.86

Philip Donald Haugstad, *Pitcher*

A Wisconsin native, Haugstad split his decisions at the major league level. The wild right-hander pitched with the Dodgers and Reds after the war. He didn't sign his first pro contract until after his military discharge. In the military, Haugstad served as an airplane mechanic in the United States Army Air Corps.

W	L	PCT	G	GS	CG	IP	H	BB	SO	SHO	ERA
1	1	.500	37	2	0	57	51	41	28	0	5.53

Edward Marvin Head, *Pitcher*

As a youngster, Ed was a natural left-hander but due to an injury, he was forced to become a righty. A solid swing pitcher, able to fill in the rotation or the bullpen with equal ability, Head was inducted into the armed forces early in the 1944 baseball season. Ed was inducted into the army at Shreveport and wrote a letter to Branch Rickey informing the general manager that he had been lost to Uncle Sam for the duration.

W	L	PCT	G	GS	CG	IP	H	BB	SO	SHO	ERA
27	23	.540	118	53	22	465	434	174	208	5	3.48

Jehosie "Jay" Heard, *Pitcher*

Built along the lines of Bobby Shantz, Heard was introduced to baseball later than most young men. Due to his late arrival to the diamond sport, Heard had to alter his birthdate in order to become the first black player for the Baltimore Orioles. Jehosie, who learned how to pitch while in the army during World War II, trimmed five years off his actual date of birth in order to sign with the major leagues. It paid off as the mite southpaw won 20 games in the minors before Baltimore gave him a trial. Heard made two appearances with Baltimore before he was returned to the minors. While trying to work his way back to the majors, Heard suffered an arm injury and was forced to retire.

W	L	PCT	G	GS	CG	IP	H	BB	SO	SHO	ERA
0	0	—	2	0	0	3	6	3	2	0	15.00

James Tolbert Hearn, *Pitcher*

A fine major league pitcher, Hearn won 109 career games spent mostly with the New York Giants. The big right-hander from Georgia was a valuable arm for the teams he played for. At the time of Hearn's service hitch, he had yet to reach the major leagues. Jim was in the army and served at Camp Davis. While stationed there, Jim made a name for himself in the service ranks when he no-hit an aggregation from Fort Bragg.

W	L	PCT	G	GS	CG	IP	H	BB	SO	SHO	ERA
109	89	.551	396	229	63	1,704	1,661	655	689	10	3.81

James Edward Hegan, *Catcher*

One of the greatest catchers in the history of the game, he would undoubtedly be a Hall of Famer if only he could have hit for a respectable average. Since he wasn't a luminary with the lumber, Hegan's name is not mentioned with the likes of Cochrane, Bench and Fisk, even though his defensive exploits exceed those of the superior batsmen. Hegan made his debut in 1941 and split time behind the plate in 1942 with Gene Desautels and Otto Denning. He missed three years to service in the U.S. Coast Guard and returned to the Indians in 1946 as their regular catcher. His phenomenal catching skills assisted the Tribe's hurlers; their team ERA of 3.23 in 1948 was the best in baseball, and they copped the World Series title that year. Jim led all Indians with five RBIs during the Fall Classic.

G	R	H	2B	3B	HR	RBI	BB	SO	SB	AVG	Slug
1,666	550	1,087	187	46	92	525	456	742	15	.228	.344

Val Raymond Heim, *Outfield*

Heim got his break in the professional ranks after attending a baseball showcase camp at Jackson, Mississippi. He impressed a scout with the White Sox and signed on the dotted line. Heim started out at Jonesboro, Arkansas, before a promotion to Waterloo, Iowa, where he had to face such pitchers as Warren Spahn and Allie Reynolds. In 1942, Val received a late-season callup to Chicago and had his only stint in the major leagues. World War II prevented him from making the squad in 1943.

The last game of the 1942 season for Heim was a doubleheader against the Browns in St. Louis. He had some friends in St. Louis who inquired about his draft status, and since he was a single man, Val knew his time was short. His chums persuaded him to enlist in the navy where he could get a job in the athletic department and play baseball. His drill master, who eventually became his brother-in-law, organized a team that Val played for at an airfield that boasted the likes of Hal Schumacher, Buddy Blattner and Emil Kush. Heim was able to play ball with those gents until he received orders to be shipped overseas.

After a brief stay in California awaiting his reassignment, Heim was shipped off to the Pacific Theatre of Operations. Sent to Saipan, Val served in the athletic department. He said, "Part of my job was to organize recreational events and stuff like that. I was stationed there for about a year and a half and was able to play some ball." But it wasn't all fun and games for Heim at Saipan. Val said, "What I remember most about my military career was standing guard duty in Saipan, which was a scary deal. All we had for cover were sugarcane fields."

After his discharge, Val caught on with a minor league team in California where he ran into the sister of an old friend—his drill master. They were eventually married and started a family while Heim got back on track in baseball. Although he never did return to the major leagues, Heim harbored no resentment. He said, "Serving in the military was one of those things I knew I had to do. It wasn't something I regretted, but I felt awful bad because when you start playing ball as a kid, your ambition is to play in the big leagues. I reached that point, but I was happy with my position in the service. I didn't regret it at all. It was one of those things that you should do and I did do."

G	R	H	2B	3B	HR	RBI	BB	SO	SB	AVG	Slug
13	6	9	1	1	0	7	5	3	1	.200	.267

Kenneth Alphonse Heintzelman, *Pitcher*

Handcuffed by pitching with some inferior teams in his day, Heintzelman was a decent left-handed pitcher who spent his entire major league career with teams based out of Pennsylvania. Ken joined the Pirates in 1937 and tossed a complete-game victory in his debut. His initial success didn't prove to be a precursor for things to come, as he struggled the next two years. He went 8–8 in 1940 under new skipper Frankie Frisch, and The Fordham Flash used Ken out of the bullpen and as a spot starter. He led the Pirates in strikeouts and shutouts in 1941, but a bum elbow derailed his 1942 season. Ken, however, would have the next three years to rest his elbow under the watchful eye of Uncle Sam.

Ken was inducted into the armed forces at Jefferson Barracks in March of 1943. He was assigned to Fort Riley where he served at the Cavalry Replacement Center with Pistol Pete Reiser. From Fort Riley, Ken was shipped out overseas and served in the European Theatre, attached to the Third Army. While stationed in Europe, he took part in the ETO Baseball Championship held at Nuremburg. Ken also won a service all-star game in Europe against a team managed by Phillies pitcher Subway Sam Nahem. He returned to a seventh-place Pirates club in 1946 but was dealt to the Phillies early in the 1947 season. His finest season came in 1949 when the Phillies, after many years of playing in the second division, began to climb in the standings. A large part of the Phillies' success went to Ken, who was 17–10 with an NL-best five shutouts that year. As a 34-year-old, Ken was one of the oldest players on the Phillies' "Whiz Kids" squad of 1950.

W	L	PCT	G	GS	CG	IP	H	BB	SO	SHO	ERA
77	98	.440	319	183	66	1,502	1,540	630	564	18	3.93

Henry Hartz Helf, *Catcher*

Helf was a power-hitting catcher who hit for a microscopic average. However, when he got hold of a ball, it could soar. Hank spent pieces of two years with the Cleveland Indians before the war and one year with the Browns after the conflict. During his time with Uncle Sam, Hank served in the navy and managed the Gulfport Naval Training Center ballclub.

G	R	H	2B	3B	HR	RBI	BB	SO	SB	AVG	Slug
78	18	36	11	0	6	22	10	41	0	.184	.332

Ralston Burdett Hemsley, *Catcher*

Regarded as an unreliable ballplayer in his early years, Rollie played with four teams prior to catching on with the Indians in 1938. He was obtained by the Tribe at the behest of Bob Feller, a close friend, who believed that Rollie could help the club. Rollie's unreliability stemmed from alcoholism, but when he learned that Feller had requested him as his personal battery mate, he joined Alcoholics Anonymous because he didn't want to let Feller down. Hemsley thus cleaned himself up and caught with the Indians for four years before a transaction sent him to New York. Hemsley assisted Feller in overcoming his wildness and the two men became lifelong friends, as Rollie helped Rapid Robert run his baseball clinic in Tampa.

Nicknamed "Rockin' Chair Rollie" because he caught with ease, Hemsley missed only one year to service in the military. He was inducted into the navy shortly after the close of the 1944 baseball season and attended the physical instructors school at Bainbridge. After graduating from Bainbridge, Rollie was stationed at Memphis for the duration. He returned to the major leagues in 1946 and played two final years with the Phillies. After his retirement from baseball, he purchased a 240-acre farm in Vienna, Missouri.

G	R	H	2B	3B	HR	RBI	BB	SO	SB	AVG	Slug
1,593	562	1,321	257	72	31	555	357	395	29	.262	.360

Thomas David Henrich, *Outfield*

When Yankees of yore are discussed, a name that is rarely mentioned — but should be mentioned often — is that of "Old Reliable" Tommy Henrich. A brilliant hitter, Henrich possessed a supreme batting eye by walking nearly twice as much as he struck out for his career. He made his major league debut a year after Joe DiMaggio and formed, with Charlie Keller in 1941 what is regarded by many as the greatest outfield trio of all-time.

Henrich left for the U.S. Coast Guard late in the 1942 baseball season, and his loss greatly hindered the Yankees' chances of winning the World Series. They ended up losing the 1942 Fall Classic to the Redbirds in five games, unable to fill the void left when Old Reliable joined the armed forces. During his final game in 1942, Henrich came to the plate in the seventh inning. The Yankees public address announcer figured this would be Henrich's last at-bat, so he made this announcement to the crowd: "Ladies and gentlemen, this will be Tommy Henrich's last game with the Yankees until the war is over!" In the clubhouse after the game, Tommy said, "When that crowd started to yell, I just didn't know what to do. I guess I took off my cap to answer them, but my eyes started to get wet because it was awful touching — awful touching. I'll swear I don't know how I hit what [Dizzy] Trout was throwing, because I was still wiping my eyes at first base."

Old Reliable was inducted the following day as a boatswain's mate first class in the United States Coast Guard. He missed three full baseball seasons to service in the armed forces before he received an honorable discharge in October of 1945. He returned to the Yankees the following year as a 36-year-old and finished second on the team with 92 runs scored. He paced the American League in triples during the 1947 and 1948 campaigns, proving that he was still plenty reliable at his advanced age after the war.

G	R	H	2B	3B	HR	RBI	BB	SO	SB	AVG	Slug
1,284	901	1,297	269	73	183	795	712	383	37	.282	.491

Leo "Preacher" Henry, *Pitcher*

One of the smallest pitchers in black baseball history, Henry played for some of the league's lesser teams. As a member of the Jacksonville Red Caps, he worked in the 1941 All-Star Game but struggled against the top-notch competition. During World War II, Preacher served two years in the army and returned to pitch in the Negro Leagues into the 1950s when the level of play had been weakened significantly by the breaking of the color line.

(1938–1947): Jacksonville Red Caps, Cleveland Bears and Indianapolis Clowns

William Jennings Bryan Herman, *Second Base*

A legendary second baseman who played throughout the 1930s with the Chicago Cubs, Herman was dealt to the Dodgers during the 1941 baseball season. His acquisition was instrumental in the Dodgers' championship run as they edged out the Cardinals by two and a half games that season. His numbers declined in 1942, when the 32-year-old Herman hit just .256. However, with the war taking many of the game's stars away, he rebounded in 1943 to hit .330 and paced the Dodgers in RBIs and doubles. He joined the navy after the 1943 Baseball season and played service ball at the Great Lakes Naval Training Station.

G	R	H	2B	3B	HR	RBI	BB	SO	SB	AVG	Slug
1,922	1,163	2,345	486	82	47	839	737	428	67	.304	.407

Eugene Victor Hermanski, *Outfield*

Gene played briefly with the Dodgers prior to his military callup, appearing in eighteen games with Brooklyn in 1943. During the season he was inducted into the U.S. Coast Guard and played service ball with a semi-pro team called the Brooklyn Bushwicks as well as with a club based out of East Orange, New Jersey. Gene completed fifteen months of Coast Guard service before he passed exams for Navy Flight School. He was dropped from flight school and returned to the Coast Guard where he served as an aviation motor mechanic second class.

G	R	H	2B	3B	HR	RBI	BB	SO	SB	AVG	Slug
739	276	533	85	18	46	259	289	212	43	.272	.404

John Edward Hetki, *Pitcher*

A relief pitcher from Kansas, Hetki had an adequate career putting out fires for the Reds of the late 1940s. Hetki was discharged early from the army and was able to play professionally with the Reds when most of the boys were still in the military.

W	L	PCT	G	GS	CG	IP	H	BB	SO	SHO	ERA
18	26	.409	214	23	8	525	557	185	175	0	4.39

James Robert Hickey, *Pitcher*

A war-era pitcher, Hickey pitched briefly for the Braves in 1942 and 1944. He was inducted into the United States Navy in 1945 and missed the baseball season to service.

W	L	PCT	G	GS	CG	IP	H	BB	SO	SHO	ERA
0	1	.000	9	1	0	10	9	7	3	0	7.20

Clarence Walter "Buddy" Hicks, *Utility Infielder*

A teenager throughout the war, Hicks joined the colors near the end of the fighting after high school. The switch-hitting infielder didn't reach the majors until ten years after his military discharge.

G	R	H	2B	3B	HR	RBI	BB	SO	SB	AVG	Slug
26	5	10	2	0	0	5	3	2	0	.213	.255

Walter Kirby Higbe, *Pitcher*

An unheralded star pitcher, Higbe was regarded as the National League's answer to Bob Feller in his prime. The Cubs owned the rights to Higbe from the beginning and used him sparingly for two and a half years. When he was dealt to the Phillies in 1939, he was allowed to cut loose. He paced the Phillies with 14 wins — the 1939 Phillies finished in the cellar — but also led the National League in free passes. In his second year with the Phillies, Kirby led the NL in walks and strikeouts, proving that he possessed a power arm that needed to be harnessed. The Phillies felt they weren't the team capable of harnessing his potential and sent him to Brooklyn in 1941. In his first year in Brooklyn, Higbe led the NL in wins and guided the Dodgers to the World Series, but he also paced the NL in walks.

Higbe lost two years to World War II, taking his blazing fastball to Fort Jackson. He was later reassigned to Camp Livingston where he served in the Infantry. Higbe was shipped overseas to the Pacific Theatre and served in the Philippines. He was able to pitch for a service team named the Manila Dodgers. Eager to return home, Kirby once said while serving overseas, "All I'd be willing to do would be to pitch doubleheaders everyday if they'd let me go back to Ebbets Field tomorrow."

W	L	PCT	G	GS	CG	IP	H	BB	SO	SHO	ERA
118	101	.539	418	238	98	1,954	1,763	979	971	11	3.68

William Travis "Wild Bill" Higdon, *Outfield*

With a devil-may-care flair on the basepaths, Higdon was a hustler of the Pepper Martin mold. During spring training in 1946, Ben Chapman called Higdon "the fastest man on the squad." Before he impressed Chapman, Wild Bill served in the Army Air Corps as a lieutenant. A former star athlete at Auburn before the war, Higdon's major league career consisted of a cup of coffee with Jack Onslow's 1949 White Sox.

G	R	H	2B	3B	HR	RBI	BB	SO	SB	AVG	Slug
11	3	7	3	0	0	1	6	3	1	.304	.435

Michael Franklin "Pinky" Higgins, *Third Base*

Higgins served briefly in the United States Navy during World War II, as the veteran ballplayer was already in his mid-thirties. Despite his advanced age, Pinky was still a productive major leaguer; he hit .297 with a team-best 32 doubles in 1944. He lost the entire 1945 season to the war and returned to the Tigers in 1946. After a rough start, he was replaced by George Kell and then shipped off to the Red Sox. Pinky hit .275 down the stretch for the Sox and guided them to a World Series showdown with the Cardinals. The 1946 World Series was Pinky's last major league action. He later managed the Red Sox for a number of years, including two-third place finishes during his tenure as a skipper.

G	R	H	2B	3B	HR	RBI	BB	SO	SB	AVG	Slug
1,802	930	1,941	375	50	140	1,075	800	590	61	.292	.427

Walter Frank "Whitey" Hilcher, *Pitcher*

A mop-up pitcher for the Reds in the 1930s, Hilcher's last major league assignment came with Cincinnati in 1936. When the United States entered the Second World War, Whitey's days in the majors had been over for some time. The aging right-hander enlisted in the armed forces and worked in the signal corps. Shipped overseas, Whitey saw action in the European Theatre.

W	L	PCT	G	GS	CG	IP	H	BB	SO	SHO	ERA
3	6	.333	31	6	1	85	103	33	28	1	5.29

Jesse Terrill Hill, *Outfield*

A swift outfielder, Hill was one of the top athletes produced by USC. At the college, Jesse excelled at baseball, football and track. He left the campus to join the Yankees and spent three years at the major league level with three different teams before ending his playing days with the 1937 Athletics. Shortly after Pearl Harbor was bombed, Hill enlisted in the armed forces. He joined the navy and was commissioned a lieutenant. While wearing navy blues, Hill was stationed at St. Mary's Pre-Flight Training School and served as an athletic director. After his military discharge, Hill returned to his alma mater and worked many years at USC.

G	R	H	2B	3B	HR	RBI	BB	SO	SB	AVG	Slug
295	175	277	53	12	6	108	115	91	43	.289	.388

William Clyde Hitchcock, *Shortstop*

A notorious scrapper, Hitchcock made a baseball career based largely on grit rather than ability. This tough-as-nails shortstop made his debut with the Tigers in 1942 and then missed the next three seasons to service in the United States Army Air Corps. At the time of his military discharge, Billy had reached the rank of major. Major Hitchcock returned to the Tigers in 1946, but with Eagle-Eye Eddie Lake in town, the Tigers swapped him to Washington. His finest year came in 1948 with the Boston Red Sox, where he hit close to .300 serving as Bobby Doerr and Johnny Pesky's backup.

G	R	H	2B	3B	HR	RBI	BB	SO	SB	AVG	Slug
703	231	547	67	22	5	257	206	230	15	.243	.299

Lloyd Eldon Hittle, *Pitcher*

The southpaw from Lodi, California, pitched two years at the major league level with the Senators after the war. Before he threw his first pitch at the highest level, Hittle served in the United States Army Air Corps with the 11th Replacement Battalion. A light truck driver by trade in the AAC, Hittle was inducted into service in March 1943. The Lodi left-hander was a private first class when he was shipped overseas.

Sent to the Pacific Theatre, Hittle was active in the campaigns at New Guinea, the northern Solomon Islands and Luzon. He spent two years and two months in foreign lands and waters. At the time of his discharge, Hittle was awarded the army's Good Conduct Medal and the Philippine Liberation Ribbon. Separated from the Army Air Corps at Camp Beale, Hittle gravitated toward baseball after his military stint. He signed his first professional contract after his discharge. Summoned to the majors in 1949, Lloyd fired a pair of shutouts in his rookie season, which tied for the team lead in that department with Sid Hudson and Dick Weik.

W	L	PCT	G	GS	CG	IP	H	BB	SO	SHO	ERA
7	11	.389	47	13	4	152	183	74	41	2	4.44

Myril Oliver Hoag, *Outfield*

Known across the baseball circuit as the man with the smallest feet in the game, Hoag had a respectable career on the diamond. His career began in 1931 with the Yankees, and by 1934 he had taken Earle Combs' outfield job. Myril stayed with the Bronx Bombers through 1938 while platooning often and caught on with the

Browns in 1939. He was 35 years old when he was drafted into the army, but he missed only one season to military service. After his discharge, Hoag played sparingly for two more years.

G	R	H	2B	3B	HR	RBI	BB	SO	SB	AVG	Slug
1,020	384	854	141	33	28	401	252	298	59	.271	.364

Donald Albert Hoak, *Third Base*

Associated with the world champion 1960 Pirates, Don "The Tiger" Hoak was a fiery, hustle-by-nature third baseman. A youngster during the heavy fighting during World War II, Hoak leant a hand at the end of the war after he graduated high school. He was a teenage Marine at the end of the war. Mustered out of the U.S. Marine Corps, Hoak broke in at the major league level with the 1954 Dodgers and took playing time away from veteran Billy Cox. Don would play in the excess of 1,200 major league games and even squared off with Cuban dictator Fidel Castro during winter ball.

G	R	H	2B	3B	HR	RBI	BB	SO	SB	AVG	Slug
1,263	598	1,144	214	44	89	498	523	530	64	.265	.396

Melvin Anthony Hoderlein, *Second Base/Shortstop*

Hoderlein spent a short time with the Red Sox in 1951 before he played three years with the Senators. A switch-hitting middle infielder, Mel served in the United States Army Air Force before he made his major league debut.

G	R	H	2B	3B	HR	RBI	BB	SO	SB	AVG	Slug
118	22	74	10	3	0	24	31	37	2	.252	.306

Gilbert Ray Hodges, *Catcher/First Base*

A borderline Hall of Fame performer, Hodges had yet to establish himself at the major league level when World War II got underway. In fact, the Dodgers were still grooming Gil to be a catcher when he left for the armed forces in 1944. He hit just .156 in 1947, his first year back from the war, but showed enough promise to be named the starting first baseman in 1948. His breakout year came in 1949 when he hit 23 home runs and drove in 115 runs. Hodges went on to manage at the major league level, piloting the Washington Senators and the New York Mets. He won a World Series at the helm of the Mets in 1969.

G	R	H	2B	3B	HR	RBI	BB	SO	SB	AVG	Slug
2,071	1,105	1,921	295	48	370	1,274	943	1,137	63	.273	.487

Elmer Ralph Hodgin, *Third Base/Outfield*

Hodgin was a solid hitter who lacked a position. He posted a career batting average of .280. He first reached the majors in 1939 with Casey Stengel's braves, hitting .208 in limited action. Ralph served in the bushes the next few years before Jimmy Dykes gave him a trial with the Pale Hose in 1943. He finished second on the team behind Luke Appling in batting, but his defensive shortcomings forced Dykes to rotate Ralph between third base and the outfield. With Appling gone in 1944, Ralph paced the White Sox in batting average, but he too was lost to the war effort the following year. He served one year with the army and received his discharge in November of 1945. A beaning he sustained in 1947 shortened his season, and he played sparingly after the incident.

G	R	H	2B	3B	HR	RBI	BB	SO	SB	AVG	Slug
530	198	481	79	24	4	188	97	63	7	.285	.367

Francis Joseph Hoerst, *Pitcher*

Hoerst pitched for the Phillies for three years prior to joining the military and came back to the Phillies to toss two more years with the club. Frank was inducted into the military after the close of the 1942 baseball campaign and saw action overseas. He served as a gunnery officer on a merchant ship that completed a round trip to Murmansk.

W	L	PCT	G	GS	CG	IP	H	BB	SO	SHO	ERA
10	33	.233	98	41	8	348	381	175	105	0	5.17

Robert George Hofman, *Utilityman*

Capable of filling in just about anywhere, Hofman was a favorite of Giants skipper Leo Durocher. The versatile St. Louis native could play the infield corners, up the middle and even catcher. Hofman's career in baseball touched all the bases. He was a player, coach, manager, scout and executive. During the Second World War, Bobby served briefly with the army.

G	R	H	2B	3B	HR	RBI	BB	SO	SB	AVG	Slug
341	81	166	22	6	32	101	70	94	1	.248	.442

Robert Clinton Hogue, *Pitcher*

A decent relief pitcher, the stout right-hander had his minor league service time interrupted due to the war. Hogue was drafted into the navy and spent some time playing service ball for Uncle Sam. After his discharge, Bobby was called up and showed flashes of becoming a terrific fireman.

W	L	PCT	G	GS	CG	IP	H	BB	SO	SHO	ERA
18	16	.529	172	3	0	327	336	142	108	0	3.96

James Marbury "Sammy" Holbrook, *Catcher*

Holbrook impressed skipper Bucky Harris during spring training in 1935 and made the Senators club after his strong showing. His 1935 season was his only campaign at the major league level. Holbrook joined the armed forces several years later during World War II.

G	R	H	2B	3B	HR	RBI	BB	SO	SB	AVG	Slug
52	20	35	2	2	2	25	30	16	0	.259	.348

Howard Arthur "Mul" Holland, *Pitcher*

Holland had three brief stints at the major league level with three different teams. His sojourns came in the late 1920s, and his baseball career was in the books by the time World War II broke out. The aging Mul Holland joined the navy and was commissioned in the officer's ranks. He served aboard a ship in the South Pacific during the war.

W	L	PCT	G	GS	CG	IP	H	BB	SO	SHO	ERA
1	1	.500	13	0	0	23	16	15	5	0	6.26

Alva Lee "Bobo" Holloman, *Pitcher*

A most unusual man, Holloman got the itch to pitch in the pro ranks while serving in the navy during World War II. Able to play service ball, Bobo saw how he handled some of the pro players in Uncle Sam's ranks and decided he'd give baseball a shot after his discharge. After a year of action in the South Pacific, Holloman received his discharge and took to baseball. It took him to 1953 before he made the majors, but when he did, he announced his presence with authority. In his first major league start, the confident Bobo tossed a no-hitter. It would be one of only three wins for Bobo at the highest level. He struggled with his command the rest of his career and never achieved the success he had that one magical night.

W	L	PCT	G	GS	CG	IP	H	BB	SO	SHO	ERA
3	7	.300	22	10	1	65	69	50	25	1	5.26

Alexander Marcus Hooks, *First Base*

A big, strapping lad from Texas, Hooks had a long career as a minor league first baseman. Smooth around the bag with the leather, Hooks was a prize first baseman whose batting couldn't quite rival the big bats in the majors. His only trial at the highest level came with the A's when they had the great Jimmie Foxx at first. Alex backed up The Beast for a few weeks in his only major league action. Hooks joined the army during World War II and served in his home state at Fort Sam Houston. After his discharge, Hooks signed on as manager of the Abilene club.

G	R	H	2B	3B	HR	RBI	BB	SO	SB	AVG	Slug
15	4	10	3	0	0	4	3	10	0	.227	.295

Robert Nelson Hooper, *Pitcher*

Although Hooper was born in Canada, he served with the U.S. Army Air Corps during World War II. Hooper, a mop-up pitcher during the 1950s, made his debut with the last team Connie Mack ever managed, the 1950 A's.

W	L	PCT	G	GS	CG	IP	H	BB	SO	SHO	ERA
40	41	.494	194	57	16	620	640	280	196	0	4.80

Richard Lloyd "Dick" Hoover, *Pitcher*

Hoover's major league career consisted of a cup of coffee with the 1952 Braves. The southpaw served in the U.S. Navy during World War II.

W	L	PCT	G	GS	CG	IP	H	BB	SO	SHO	ERA
0	0	—	2	0	0	5	8	3	0	0	7.20

William Horne, *Utility Infielder*

Able to play second base or shortstop with equal skill, Horne played with the Negro League's Columbus Buckeyes around the war years. The scrappy infielder lost just one baseball season to the war effort. After the color line was broken, Horne tried his luck in the minors but barely hit above .200 in his only year in the Mandak League.

(1938–1946): Chicago American Giants, Cleveland Buckeyes and St. Louis Stars

Ralph George Houk, *Catcher*

A seldom-used catcher for the Yankees in the late 1940s and early 1950s, Houk never made his mark as a player. It was at the helm of a ballclub where Houk etched his niche in the game. Nicknamed "Major" because of his war-time heroics, Houk led his first two teams to World Series championships. A borderline Hall of Famer as a manager, Houk had terrific success in New York and managed with the Tigers and Red Sox afterwards. Given the many men that have managed at the major league level, Major Houk is one of the few to have eclipsed 1,000 career wins.

Before Houk started out in the major leagues he was a soldier in Uncle Sam's fighting forces. He enlisted as a buck private but his leadership skills were evident before he ever managed the Yankees to World Series titles. It wouldn't take long for Ralph to join the commissioned officer ranks and become a leader of men. Promoted to the rank of major while in the European Theatre, Houk fought at Omaha Beach and at the defense of Remagen Bridge. Major Houk made it through those campaigns unscathed, but when he was sent to combat in the Battle of Bulge, Houk was wounded in action. His war-time gallantry would allow him to wear the Purple Heart and the Bronze and Silver Stars. The leader of a recon group of Rangers, Houk was discharged at the end of the war and said upon his return to the game, "After the Bulge and Bastogne, baseball has got to be fun."

Major Houk didn't play much in the majors despite spending eight seasons on the Yankees roster. With Yogi Berra around, a horde of catchers was the last thing the Bronx Bombers needed. He was given his first managerial stint with the Yankees in the legendary 1961 season when Roger Maris broke Babe Ruth's single-season home run record. When Major Houk was unveiled as the replacement for the colorful Casey Stengel, Oscar Fraley wrote, "Houk knows the game and he has a reputation for acting with lightning rapidity. He is, after all, a man who made quick decisions under fire and there is no reason to believe that baseball could strip him of that ability."

G	R	H	2B	3B	HR	RBI	BB	SO	SB	AVG	Slug
91	12	43	6	1	0	20	12	10	0	.272	.323

Calvin Earl Howe, *Pitcher*

A mountain of a man, Howe appeared in only one game at the major league level. Given his only shot with the 1952 Cubs, Howe allowed just one base runner in two innings of work. During World War II, the big man from Rock Falls, Illinois, served in the U.S. Army.

W	L	PCT	G	GS	CG	IP	H	BB	SO	SHO	ERA
0	0	—	1	0	0	2	0	1	2	0	0.00

Homer Elliott "Dixie" Howell, *Catcher*

Not to be confused with the pitcher Millard "Dixie" Howell, who was a POW during the war, Homer "Dixie" Howell was a catcher who wasn't captured by the Germans. The two Dixie Howells ended up playing together for a year with the 1949 Reds.

G	R	H	2B	3B	HR	RBI	BB	SO	SB	AVG	Slug
340	98	224	39	4	12	93	87	140	1	.246	.337

Millard "Dixie" Howell, *Pitcher*

During the war years there were a few Dixie Howells of prominence and this gave sportswriters a fit trying to keep them distinguished. Millard "Dixie" Howell was one of two pro baseball players by the name, and there was also a former college football star named Dixie Howell. To make matters more complicated, all three joined the service during World War II. Millard, who made his debut with the 1940 Indians, was inducted into the army as a minor leaguer in 1943. He would eventually be shipped overseas where he saw combat action in France.

Newspapers across the country began to run stories concerning Dixie Howell, the former football star, captured in combat and sent to a German prisoner-of-war camp. But these scoops were only half right. Dixie Howell was indeed captured by the Germans, but it wasn't the former Alabama football great, but Millard "Dixie" Howell, formerly of the Cleveland Indians. Howell spent several months behind the fences as a captured combatant before his POW camp was liberated. Sent home, Dixie tried to return to life as normal. He toiled in the minors until the Reds gave him another trial in 1949. He would last play in the majors with the 1958 White Sox.

W	L	PCT	G	GS	CG	IP	H	BB	SO	SHO	ERA
19	15	.559	115	2	0	226	236	103	99	0	3.78

Roland Edison "Tex" Hoyle, *Pitcher*

Tall and lanky, Hoyle thoroughly impressed skipper Jimmy Dykes in 1952 spring training. However, after coughing up nine base hits in two innings, he was farmed out and never again played in the majors. Tex missed some minor league seasoning time to military service during World War II.

W	L	PCT	G	GS	CG	IP	H	BB	SO	SHO	ERA
0	0	—	3	0	0	2	9	1	1	0	31.50

Otto Huber, *Reserve*

Huber had a cup of coffee with the 1939 Braves. Otto played in eleven games for Casey Stengel's squad that year. Before his military induction, Huber was back in the minors, and after he was discharged he took a job as player/manager in the bushes.

G	R	H	2B	3B	HR	RBI	BB	SO	SB	AVG	Slug
11	2	6	1	0	0	3	0	1	0	.273	.318

Sidney Charles Hudson, *Pitcher*

A baseball lifer, Hudson was an ace pitcher for the Washington Senators who later became a respected pitching coach under his close friend Ted Williams. Hudson's career in baseball was saved by a change in mechanics. After the war, Hudson was suffering from a dead arm and it looked as if his career might be over. Doctors informed him that his shoulder had developed a spur that was restricting his pitching motion. In order to combat the spur, Hudson altered his delivery and became a successful sidearm pitcher.

Hudson was one of the top pitchers on the Senators staff before the war, and Washington was in trouble when they lost Sid to military service. He was one of the few pitchers on the team whose fastball could actually break a pane of glass. Most of the Senators' other hurlers relied heavily on the knuckleball. Hudson took his right arm to the Waco Airfield where he played service ball under Detroit catcher Birdie Tebbetts. Hudson said, "It ended up that we had a good ballclub at Waco with Birdie, myself, and two good outfielders named Hoot Evers and Bruce Campbell, who both played in the major leagues."

But Hudson's stint in the military wasn't all stateside baseball. Shipped overseas to the Pacific Theatre of Operations, Sid was initially sent to Honolulu before he was assigned to Saipan. Attached to the Special Service, Hudson played plenty of baseball in the South Pacific where a unique league was setup. All the islands were in close proximity and they would challenge one another to contests. Hudson said, "They would fly us back and forth for games because the islands were just a few miles from each other." Although Sid served in the Pacific where things were hot, his military duties were in athletics. He said, "I didn't come close to any fighting or anything like that. The pilots used to tell us stories about the missions they flew. On the way back from dropping the bomb at Hiroshima, they tipped their wings to us."

During his stint in the South Pacific, Hudson refrained from pitching because his arm had hurt from his tenure at Waco. He was hoping that a layoff at Saipan would breathe life back into his dead arm, but it didn't seem to work. He said, "I was in charge of conducting calisthenics for the cadets at Waco. Five times a day they had me conduct calisthenics programs for five days a week. So I came up with a sore arm by pitching over 200 innings for the airfield team and conducting calisthenics." When doctors took a look at his arm, they noticed the spur and recommended that he throw sidearm, and Hudson redefined his career.

W	L	PCT	G	GS	CG	IP	H	BB	SO	SHO	ERA
104	152	.406	380	279	123	2,181	2,384	835	734	11	4.28

James Robert Hughes, *Pitcher*

A fireman for the Dodgers of the mid–1950s, Hughes served with the U.S. Marine Corps during World War II before he signed his first pro contract. After his discharge he joined the Dodgers chain and worked his way up the ladder. Summoned by Brooklyn in 1952, he helped them make the World Series in 1952, 1953 and 1955.

W	L	PCT	G	GS	CG	IP	H	BB	SO	SHO	ERA
15	13	.536	172	1	0	297	278	152	165	0	3.82

Samuel Thomas Hughes, *Second Base*

One of the premier second basemen of black baseball, Hughes was a fixture in the Negro League All-Star Games. Unusually tall for a second baseman, Sammy was known for his graceful fielding and gap power at the plate. A star for the Baltimore Elite Giants before the war, he had a tryout with the Pittsburgh Pirates in 1942, before Jackie Robinson broke the color barrier with the Dodgers. Hughes missed some time during World War II when he served with 196th Support Battalion that assisted in the invasion at New Guinea.

(1932–1946): Baltimore Elite Giants, Washington Pilots and Louisville White Sox

Thomas Owen Hughes, *Pitcher*

Hughes pitched at the major league level with the Phillies before and after the war and also tossed a few games with the Reds in the late 1940s. Hughes had his breakout year at an inopportune time — the year before his military induction. While pitching for a lackluster Phillies club in 1942, Tommy led the team in nearly every pitching category. He spent the next three years in the service and returned to the Phillies in 1946. He left baseball for the war at the top of his game but didn't return there. His ERA swelled to 4.38 in 1946 but he rebounded to lower his mark to 3.47 in 1947. He finished out his career with an 0–4 record for the 1948 Cincinnati Reds.

W	L	PCT	G	GS	CG	IP	H	BB	SO	SHO	ERA
31	56	.356	144	87	31	688	698	308	221	5	3.92

Cecil Carlton "Tex" Hughson, *Pitcher*

Just like teammate Bobby Doerr, Hughson missed only one full season during World War II. He appeared in 28 games (23 starts) in 1944 before he was summoned for military duty. With many of the best young players gone, Tex flourished that season, leading the league with a .783 winning percentage while posting a microscopic 2.26 ERA. He was inducted into the navy on August 28, 1944, and returned to the Red Sox in 1946 to post 20 wins. Along with Boo Ferriss and Mickey Harris, the three stud pitchers coupled with their amazing offense brought the World Series to Fenway Park that season. And just like his chums in the rotation, that was Hughson's last effective year at the major league level, as a series of arm injuries hindered his effectiveness.

W	L	PCT	G	GS	CG	IP	H	BB	SO	SHO	ERA
96	54	.640	225	156	99	1,376	1,270	372	693	15	2.94

Frederick Charles Hutchinson, *Pitcher*

Nicknamed "Big Bear," Fred enjoyed a solid career in baseball. He began as a starting pitcher with the 1939 Detroit Tigers and struggled at the major league level until his military callup. Big Bear missed four years to World War II, serving in the United States Navy at Norfolk and playing some ball for Mickey Cochrane at the Great Lakes before he returned, to the Tigers as a reinvented hurler. Unable to get batters out before the war, Fred returned to the majors and stood many batters on their heads. He paced the Tigers with 18 wins in 1947 and only walked 48 batters in 221 innings during the 1948 campaign. After his playing days, Fred managed the Tigers, Cardinals and Reds. Stan Musial once said, "If you couldn't play for Fred, you couldn't play for anyone."

W	L	PCT	G	GS	CG	IP	H	BB	SO	SHO	ERA
95	71	.572	242	169	81	1,465	1,487	388	591	13	3.72

Clarence Eugene "Hooks" Iott, *Pitcher*

A gifted athlete who was able to switch-hit and fling fire from the portside of his anatomy, Hooks' downfall was his lack of accuracy. His first look at the major leagues came in 1941 with the Browns when the left-hander appeared in two games. After a year in the bushes, Hooks joined the armed forces and missed three full years to the military. He returned to the Browns in 1947 but earned his release after walking fourteen batters in eight innings. However, he was left-handed and possessed a brilliant wing, so Giants skipper Mel Ott took a chance on Hooks. He responded by tossing a complete-game shutout in his first start with New York. After the game, Ott was beaming, and said, "All we knew about Hooks was that he had wild spells on the mound." The wild spells returned, and Hooks was out of the major leagues after the season.

W	L	PCT	G	GS	CG	IP	H	BB	SO	SHO	ERA
3	9	.250	26	9	2	82	84	67	53	1	7.02

Monford Merrill "Monte" Irvin, *Outfield*

Many baseball historians feel that Irvin, not Jackie Robinson, was the best prospect the Negro Leagues had to offer the majors after World War II. A gifted natural ballplayer, Irvin was the heart of the powerhouse Newark Eagles' lineup. A two-time batting champ in his brief stay in the Negro Leagues, Monte won his first crown before the war and his second the year after his discharge. When he first tried out with the Eagles, they employed him on the left side of the infield, but he was found wanting and was shifted to the outfield where he excelled. After integration, Monte caught on with the New York Giants and enjoyed a fine career that carried him to the Baseball Hall of Fame.

Irvin missed three seasons to World War II and many believe that his hitch in the army led the Dodgers to sign Robinson instead. But the Eagles were owned by Abe and Effa Manley, and Effa demanded that the Dodgers give her club money as compensation for the signing of Irvin. The Dodgers scoffed at paying Manley as well as the player and refused to sign Monte. The Giants got him instead, and Irvin became a favorite of Giants skipper Leo Durocher. Irvin had injury woes throughout his career in the major leagues and perhaps integrated baseball never saw him at full strength.

G	R	H	2B	3B	HR	RBI	BB	SO	SB	AVG	Slug
764	366	731	97	31	99	443	351	220	28	.293	.475

Anthony Robert Jacobs, *Pitcher*

A fine pitcher at the minor league level, Jacobs didn't have any success in the bigs. Built more like Phil Rizzuto than Don Newcombe, Jacobs was a mite pitcher that major league batters punished. Before he made his big league debut with the 1948 Cubs, Tony served with the U.S. Marines during World War II.

W	L	PCT	G	GS	CG	IP	H	BB	SO	SHO	ERA
0	0	—	2	0	0	4	9	1	3	0	11.25

Sigmund Jakucki, *Pitcher*

Jakucki was a resounding failure when the Browns gave him a trial in 1936. Dejected, the big right-hander gave up the game and enlisted in the United States Army. A peacetime soldier, Jakucki was originally spotted by the Browns while playing ball in the army, but when he failed to make the grade in fast company, he donned the military suit again. The army was Jakucki's home for several years, and the aimless wanderer continued to toil on the crude diamonds of the semipro ranks as a soldier.

Taught how to pitch by an army lieutenant, Jakucki was able to perfect his game while under the employ of Uncle Sam. When the aging right-hander was mustered out of the army he went to work at a Houston shipyard and played ball for a semipro league there. The Browns spotted Sig again, and they signed him to another contract. Jakucki, who writer Jack Hand referred to as a "footloose ex-soldier," became an immediate hit with the war-ravaged Browns and pitched them to their only World Series in 1944. He teamed with Nelson Potter, Jack Kramer and Bob Muncrief to give St. Louis a solid war-time pitching staff. He won a dozen games in 1945, but when the regulars came back, the Browns bid farewell to the 36-year-old war-era hero.

W	L	PCT	G	GS	CG	IP	H	BB	SO	SHO	ERA
25	22	.532	72	50	27	411	431	131	131	5	3.79

LeRoy Gilbert Jarvis, Catcher

Jarvis played briefly at the major league level during three separate seasons. He caught with the Dodgers in 1944 and with the Pirates in 1946 and 1947. Roy missed the entire 1945 baseball season to service in the armed forces.

G	R	H	2B	3B	HR	RBI	BB	SO	SB	AVG	Slug
21	4	8	1	0	1	4	7	7	0	.160	.240

Willie Jefferson, Pitcher

A journeyed right-handed pitcher, Jefferson played in the Negro Leagues, the Mexican League and in the minors after integration. The lean pitcher from Oklahoma won an ERA crown while in the Negro Leagues before the war but was an enigma in the Mexican League. His first year in Mexico, 1940, he went 22–4 but followed that with a poor 9–16 record. He returned to the Negro Leagues but wasn't there long since he was inducted into the army. Jefferson's stint under Uncle Sam was brief and he was discharged before 1943 spring training. His last action came after the color line was broken in the Mandak League.

(1937–1946): Cleveland Buckeyes, Cincinnati Tigers and Memphis Red Sox

William Lee Jennings, Shortstop

Jennings' only major league action came with his hometown Browns in 1951. Part of a shortstop carousel with Johnny Bero and Tom Upton, the Browns received little production from the position that year. During the Second World War, Bill joined the United States Navy as a teenager.

G	R	H	2B	3B	HR	RBI	BB	SO	SB	AVG	Slug
64	20	35	10	2	0	13	26	42	1	.179	.251

Jack Eugene Jensen, Outfield

On the fast track to the Baseball Hall of Fame, Jensen's career was derailed by western expansion. A gifted athlete who could do it all on the ball diamond, Jackie had a phobia about planes and would not step foot on an aircraft. The former University of California standout was forced to quit the game because teams had to fly west to play games against the new California-based teams.

A teenager during the war, Jackie was a highly sought after athlete upon high school graduation. He put his collegiate pursuits on hold when he joined the navy, where he spent one year and had the unusual task of teaching prisoners of war how to swim at Farragut Barracks, Idaho. After his navy discharge, Jensen began his college career at California and was a football and baseball sensation. He led the college to the 1949 Rose Bowl and looked to be a lock for stardom on the gridiron, but he was equally talented on the ball diamond. Jackie opted for the baseball path and was one of the game's greatest stars of the 1950s.

G	R	H	2B	3B	HR	RBI	BB	SO	SB	AVG	Slug
1,438	810	1,463	259	45	199	929	750	546	143	.279	.460

Daniel Edward Jessee, Pinch Runner

Jessee appeared in only one game at the major league level with Roger Peckinpaugh's 1929 Indians. The Kentucky native was already forty years old when World War II broke out but that didn't stop him from joining the colors. He joined the army's athletic department and was shipped overseas to the European Theatre where he conducted clinics for athletic officers.

G	R	H	2B	3B	HR	RBI	BB	SO	SB	AVG	Slug
1	0	0	0	0	0	0	0	0	0	—	—

Arthur Henry Johnson, Pitcher

While many major league baseball players served their country on ball diamonds at various military installations, Johnson served the majority of the war on an aircraft carrier. He went through the battles at Saipan, Tinian, Midway and Iwo Jima and saw many of his close friends killed in action. A humble individual, Johnson does not view himself as a hero, citing instead his departed comrades as the true heroes of the war.

W	L	PCT	G	GS	CG	IP	H	BB	SO	SHO	ERA
7	16	.304	49	19	6	195	203	79	71	0	3.69

William Russell Johnson, Third Base

Johnson participated in four World Series as a member of the Yankees. A small hot corner patrolman, Billy played with the Yankees from 1943 to 1951 and with the Cardinals until 1953. As a rookie in 1943, Johnson played in more games than any other Yankees player and then missed the 1944 and 1945 seasons to service in the army. In the 1947 World Series, Johnson smacked three triples in the seven-game affair, something achieved by only a select few.

G	R	H	2B	3B	HR	RBI	BB	SO	SB	AVG	Slug
964	419	882	141	33	61	487	347	290	13	.271	.391

Byron Johnson, Shortstop

Johnson played briefly with the Kansas City Monarchs in the late 1930s. The Little Rock, Arkansas, native gave up on his baseball career to teach, and was employed as a teacher when Uncle Sam beckoned his services during World War II. Byron served in the Quartermasters Corps and saw action in the European Theatre of Operations. He saw combat action after D-Day, with his unit entering the battle about a week after the initial assault.

(1937–1938): Kansas City Monarchs

Clifford "Connie" Johnson, Pitcher

A star pitcher for the Kansas City Monarchs of the 1940s, Connie made a seamless transition from the Negro Leagues to the majors. Signed out of the Negro Leagues by the White Sox, Johnson was a good power pitcher with Chicago but had control issues. After he was traded to the Orioles in 1956, Connie put it all together and had a couple of good years in Baltimore. He led Baltimore in strikeouts in 1956 and 1957, when he racked up 177 — good for third in the American League. But Connie was already in his mid-thirties and slowed down in 1958. During World War II, Johnson missed a few seasons to military service.

W	L	PCT	G	GS	CG	IP	H	BB	SO	SHO	ERA
40	39	.506	123	100	34	716	654	257	497	8	3.44

Donald Roy Johnson, *Pitcher*

A journeyman pitcher, Big Don Johnson was a teenager during the war. After school, he left the grounds of matriculation for life in the armed forces. He spent some time in Uncle Sam's threads at the end of the war before he signed to play baseball. Don began his nomadic career with the Yankees in 1947 and ended it with the Giants of 1958.

W	L	PCT	G	GS	CG	IP	H	BB	SO	SHO	ERA
27	38	.415	198	70	17	631	712	285	262	5	4.78

Earl Douglas Johnson, *Pitcher*

A lesser-known man on the ball field, Earl Johnson was a legend on the battlefield. Lefty missed four full baseball seasons to service in the United States Army during World War II. He was a non-commissioned officer who served in the 120th Infantry Regiment of the 30th Infantry Division. During his stint in military fatigues, Johnson saw action during the Battle of the Bulge and was awarded the Silver and Bronze Stars. The following paragraph is the citation for the Bronze Star that Johnson earned.

On September 30, 1944, in Germany, during heavy concentration of hostile fire, a friendly truck was struck by an enemy shell and had to be abandoned. The fact that the vehicle contained vital radio equipment made it imperative that it be recovered before falling into enemy hands. Sergeant Earl Johnson and several other members of his unit were assigned to this hazardous mission. They courageously braved severe hostile fire and were completely successful in dragging the vehicle over an area in view of the enemy.

He returned to baseball in 1946, the year the Red Sox went to the World Series, and appeared in three Fall Classic games. He posted a 12–11 record in 1947, serving as a spot starter while Hughson and Harris were on the mend. The bullpen was Johnson's familiar territory and he returned there in 1948, where he posted a 10–4 record while spelling the starting pitchers. Lefty remained in the majors until 1951, at which time he retired as a member of the Detroit Tigers.

W	L	PCT	G	GS	CG	IP	H	BB	SO	SHO	ERA
40	32	.556	179	50	13	546	556	272	250	3	4.31

Ernest Thornwald Johnson, *Pitcher*

Johnson, a longtime relief pitcher for the Boston and Milwaukee Braves, served in the military during World War II prior to his major league debut. Ernie was a member of the Braves' world champion team of 1957 that knocked off the Yankees in the Fall Classic. After his playing days, Johnson had a successful career as a broadcaster.

W	L	PCT	G	GS	CG	IP	H	BB	SO	SHO	ERA
40	23	.635	273	19	3	574	587	231	319	1	3.78

Josh Johnson, *Catcher*

Johnson spent a good deal of his career backing up the best Josh baseball had to offer in Josh Gibson. Stuck behind the Hall of Famer on the Homestead Grays roster, Johnson received more playing time in New York and Cincinnati, where he didn't have to contend with Gibson. At the end of his playing days, Johnson joined the army during World War II and served as a commissioned officer in an antiaircraft outfit. He would later join the Army Reserves and reach the rank of major.

(1934–1942): Homestead Grays, Cincinnati Tigers, New York Black Yankees and Brooklyn Royal Giants

Kenneth Wandersee Johnson, *Pitcher*

During the war, Johnson served in the South Pacific with the United States Army. After leaving the PTO, Ken returned to the minor leagues and worked his way up the Cardinals' cluttered ladder until he reached St. Louis in 1947. Used primarily as a spot-starter/mop-up pitcher, Johnson ended his major league career with the 1952 Tigers.

W	L	PCT	G	GS	CG	IP	H	BB	SO	SHO	ERA
12	14	.462	74	34	8	269	251	195	147	4	4.58

Adam Rankin Johnson Jr., *Pitcher*

Rankin Johnson's father was a star pitcher in the now-defunct Federal League, having played under Hall of Famer Joe Tinker in Chicago. Junior, on the other hand, appeared in seven major league games and was the victorious hurler of his only deciding contest. Rankin Jr. spent the 1942 through 1945 seasons in the military and did not return to the majors after his discharge. He is one of a handful of pitchers to have posted a perfect 1.000 winning percentage in his career.

W	L	PCT	G	GS	CG	IP	H	BB	SO	SHO	ERA
1	0	1.000	7	0	0	10	14	3	0	0	3.60

Silas Kenneth Johnson, *Pitcher*

Ol' Si Johnson was a baseball greybeard at the time World War II started removing players from the major leagues. Silas had been pitching in the majors since 1928, and the veteran was 36 years old when he was inducted into the navy. Johnson had toiled with the Reds in the early 1930s when they were an NL doormat. He used pinpoint control over the course of his career, as the right-hander rarely issued many free passes. His best year came in 1943, the same year he was inducted into the navy, which interrupted a season in which he had his ERA down to 3.27 and posted a .727 winning percentage.

The navy took Silas away from the ball diamond right when he had resurrected his career. He was initially assigned to the Great Lakes and played service ball under the great Mickey Cochrane. Johnson was later transferred to Camp McIntire where he was hospitalized while recovering from a mastoid operation. He received his discharge in 1945 and returned to the Phillies at the tender age of 39. During the season, Si was dealt to the Braves and posted a sparkling ERA of 2.76 for Billy Southworth's boys. Silas owned a 6–8 record in 1947 with the Braves, his last year at the major league level.

W	L	PCT	G	GS	CG	IP	H	BB	SO	SHO	ERA
101	165	.380	492	272	108	2,280	2,510	687	840	13	4.09

Roy Merrill Joiner, *Pitcher*

Joiner's entire major league service came before the war with the Cubs and Giants. A southpaw with easy-to-hit offerings, Roy posted a rather unflattering amount of hits compared to innings pitched. A star in the minors, however, Joiner joined up with Uncle Sam during World War II when his playing days were near their end.

W	L	PCT	G	GS	CG	IP	H	BB	SO	SHO	ERA
3	3	.500	52	4	0	90	133	27	34	0	5.30

Stanley Edward Jok, *Pinch-Hitter*

Jok had only three at-bats with the 1954 Phillies before they traded him to the White Sox, who didn't use him much more than Philadelphia did. Stan played briefly for the Pale Hose in 1955, his last stint in the majors. During the war, the teenage Jok served in the United States Navy.

G	R	H	2B	3B	HR	RBI	BB	SO	SB	AVG	Slug
12	4	3	0	0	1	4	2	5	0	.158	.316

David Jolly, *Pitcher*

A fine relief pitcher who made his debut with the Braves after they relocated to Milwaukee, Jolly was on the staff when they copped the 1957 World Series. Just a few years later, Dave died when he was unable to recover from a brain tumor operation. During World War II, Jolly served in the European Theatre and threw fastballs to the Germans.

W	L	PCT	G	GS	CG	IP	H	BB	SO	SHO	ERA
16	14	.533	159	1	0	291	255	198	155	0	3.77

Arthur Lennox Jones, *Pitcher*

A right-hander from South Carolina, Jones appeared in one major league game with the 1932 Dodgers. In his lone inning, Art surrendered two earned runs. Ten years after his lone appearance, Jones entered the military but was discharged early in 1943.

W	L	PCT	G	GS	CG	IP	H	BB	SO	SHO	ERA
0	0	—	1	0	0	1	2	1	0	0	18.00

Dale Eldon Jones, *Pitcher*

Jones made two appearances in the major leagues with the 1941 Phillies. He then missed the next four years to service in the armed forces. Dale served with the United States Navy. He became a scout after his playing days had ended and signed Rick Rhoden, among others.

W	L	PCT	G	GS	CG	IP	H	BB	SO	SHO	ERA
0	1	.000	2	1	0	8	13	6	2	0	7.88

James Murrell "Jake" Jones, *First Base*

Jake Jones was nothing more than an average major league ballplayer, but his military service time was beyond the ordinary. Jones, who served as a backup for such notable first basemen as Rudy York and Joe Kuhel, entered the military during the 1942 baseball season and didn't receive his discharge until after the 1946 campaign. He spent more time in the armed forces than most other professional athletes, missing the better part of five years to military duty.

Jones enlisted in the Navy Aviation Corps shortly after the bombing of Pearl Harbor and received his summons by the navy during the 1942 baseball season. He spent the majority of his service time in foreign waters, stationed on a carrier that was dubbed "The Fighting Lady." Jones witnessed a lot of fighting in hostile waters but was able to return to the White Sox for the 1947 baseball season. He played one final year at the highest level with the Red Sox before ending his major league career.

G	R	H	2B	3B	HR	RBI	BB	SO	SB	AVG	Slug
224	80	181	31	5	23	117	69	130	8	.229	.368

Vernal Leroy "Nippy" Jones, *First Base*

Some players are remembered for one occurrence on the ball diamond. Fred Merkle is remembered for his famous "bonehead play" as a rookie, and Vic Wertz is recalled today as the guy who hit the ball that Willie Mays made his famous catch against in the 1954 World Series. Nippy Jones falls into that "one-play remembrance" bracket as well. During the 1957 World Series, when Nippy was at the end of his rope, he pinch-hit for the Braves and was hit on the foot by a pitched ball. The umpire wasn't going to allow Nippy first base because he didn't feel that Jones was struck by the pitch. Nippy proved he had been hit when he showed the ump his shoe polish that was smeared on the ball. From that moment on, Nippy was known as "The Shoeshine Kid."

A longtime first baseman with the Cardinals, Nippy would often platoon at first with Stan Musial. Whenever a lefty was on the hill, Jones would start at first, but Musial wouldn't ride the pine—he'd rotate to the outfield and spell a weaker left-handed hitter. Before Nippy made his major league debut, he served with the United States Marine Corps during World War II.

G	R	H	2B	3B	HR	RBI	BB	SO	SB	AVG	Slug
412	146	369	60	12	25	209	71	102	4	.267	.382

Sheldon Leslie Jones, *Pitcher*

Rubber-armed Sheldon Jones was nicknamed "Available" because he was always ready and willing to take the ball. The right-hander from Nebraska served in the military during World War II before he made his major league debut. Jones pitched with the Giants and Braves and ended his career with the 1953 Cubs.

W	L	PCT	G	GS	CG	IP	H	BB	SO	SHO	ERA
54	57	.486	260	101	33	919	909	413	413	5	3.97

Milton Mignot Jordan, *Pitcher*

Big Milt Jordan had a cup of coffee with the 1953 Tigers of Fred Hutchinson. A teenager throughout the war, Jordan enlisted in the Army Air Corps in the latter stages of the conflict.

W	L	PCT	G	GS	CG	IP	H	BB	SO	SHO	ERA
0	1	.000	8	1	0	17	26	5	4	0	5.82

Niles Chapman Jordan, *Pitcher*

Jordan pitched briefly at the major league level in the early 1950s with the Phillies and Reds. The southpaw didn't sign his first professional contract until 1948. After his high school graduation, Niles enlisted in the navy.

W	L	PCT	G	GS	CG	IP	H	BB	SO	SHO	ERA
2	4	.333	8	6	2	43	49	11	13	1	4.19

Walter Franklin Judnich, *Outfield*

There are many exceptional players who lost years to World War II whose names have been forgotten over the years. The legend of some players has been strengthened by their military hiatus, as the mystique shrouding their possible accomplishments adds to their legacy. However, there are several ballplayers, great in their day, whose names have faded through time because they weren't allowed to add to their baseball legacies due to serving their country during time of war. Walter Franklin Judnich is such a player.

For a short time, Walt Judnich was an offensive juggernaut. He broke in with the St. Louis Browns in 1940 and played 137 games as a rookie. He was skipper Fred Haney's regular center fielder during his initial campaign, and Walt finished second to Joe DiMaggio in home runs and RBIs among American League center fielders. He finished third in doubles during the 1941 season, a year in which he posted nearly twice as many walks as strikeouts. Walt out-hit Joe DiMaggio in 1942, as Judnich posted a .313 batting average with a .499 Slugging mark, while the Yankee Clipper hit .305 with a .498 Slugging percentage. At the end of the 1942 campaign, Walt was widely regarded as the Browns' top Slugger and an up-and-coming force in the major leagues when he entered the army.

Judnich was inducted into the army on the exact same day as professional tennis star Donald Budge; they were sworn in together at Monterey, California. He was stationed in upstate California, where Walt played service ball with fellow major leaguer Dario Lodigiani in the Northern California Service League. He and Lodigiani worked at repairing army aircraft at the Sacramento Air Service Command. From California, he was shipped overseas to Hawaii where he smacked five home runs in one service ball game. He reached the rank of staff sergeant but was sent home from Hawaii because he suffered from a severe case of asthma on the islands.

Walt returned to the Browns in 1946 as a 30-year-old veteran. Although he posted strong numbers upon his return — a .262 batting average with 72 RBIs— he wasn't on the same level as he had been prior to the war. Manager Muddy Ruel moved him to first base in 1947. Walt finished second on the team in home runs but his batting average fell to .258. He spent the last two years of his career as a reserve player.

G	R	H	2B	3B	HR	RBI	BB	SO	SB	AVG	Slug
790	424	782	150	29	90	420	385	298	20	.281	.452

Howard Kolls Judson, *Pitcher*

A long relief pitcher/spot starter, Judson pitched a handful of seasons with the Pale Hose in the late 1940s and early 1950s. The Illinois native joined the navy after his high school graduation and spent some time in the military before he signed his first pro contract. A good man with a sense of familial duty, Howie helped pay his brother's way through college with the money he earned in baseball.

W	L	PCT	G	GS	CG	IP	H	BB	SO	SHO	ERA
17	37	.315	207	48	8	615	619	319	204	0	4.29

John Samuel "Red" Juelich, *Second Base/Third Base*

Juelich had a cup of coffee with Pie Traynor's Pirates of 1939. Unable to stick at the major league level, Red was shipped back to the bushes. At the time of Red's military induction, he was playing ball for Syracuse but had to leave the squad when his draft notice came through. Juelich enrolled in the United States Army and was assigned to Camp Phillips, Kansas, where he served as a military police officer.

After Red's discharge from the army, the Syracuse team cut ties with him. Upset by the team's move, Red took action against the Syracuse Chiefs front office. He claimed he was entitled to the same occupation he held before his induction because other men, who held different jobs, had their places waiting for them on account of government mandate. An article in the *Syracuse Post-Standard* read, "Juelich is suing under the selective service act, claiming violation of the rehiring clause when he was told his services would not be needed on his return from the Army." Red won his case, which served as precedence for other men in athletics.

G	R	H	2B	3B	HR	RBI	BB	SO	SB	AVG	Slug
17	5	11	0	2	0	4	2	4	0	.239	.326

George Benedict Jumonville, *Shortstop*

Jumonville played briefly with the Phillies in the early 1940s. He made his debut with the club in 1940 and played his last major league game in 1941. Both seasons the Phillies finished dead last in the senior circuit. George left the game when Uncle Sam needed his presence and he served in the navy. Upon his discharge, he never made it back to the highest level.

G	R	H	2B	3B	HR	RBI	BB	SO	SB	AVG	Slug
17	1	6	0	0	1	2	1	6	0	.146	.220

Kenneth Peter Jungels, *Pitcher*

A mop-up pitcher before the war, Jungels was used intermittently by the Indians and Pirates. Although "Curly" was used in five different seasons, his mop-up duty allowed him to factor in only one decision. During the war, Ken left the Pirates' bullpen and joined the U.S. Army.

W	L	PCT	G	GS	CG	IP	H	BB	SO	SHO	ERA
1	0	1.000	25	0	0	49	56	32	21	0	6.80

Robert Wayne Kahle, *Reserve*

A star in the Pacific Coast League, Kahle never did make the grade in the majors. He had a cup of coffee with the Braves in 1938 — the extent of his major league career. Kahle left the minor league stadiums and joined the navy during World War II. While he served, Bob was able to play plenty of baseball.

G	R	H	2B	3B	HR	RBI	BB	SO	SB	AVG	Slug
8	2	1	0	0	0	0	0	0	0	.333	.333

Owen Earle Kahn, *Pinch-Runner*

Kahn played in one game for Bill McKechnie's 1930 Braves. Employed as a pinch-runner, Owen scored a run at the major league level without ever tallying an official time at-bat. During the Second World War, Owen served in the navy.

G	R	H	2B	3B	HR	RBI	BB	SO	SB	AVG	Slug
1	1	0	0	0	0	0	0	0	0	—	—

Frank Bruno Kalin, *Outfield*

When players of untapped potential are discussed, Kalin should be introduced to the discussion. As an amateur, Frank attended Charlie Dressen's baseball school where he was taught the fine aspects of the game. From Dressen's school, Kalin signed with the Pirates and saw action with them in 1940. He spent the next two years building his stock with strong showings in the Pacific Coast League, and was purchased by the White Sox near the close of the 1943 season. During that short stint with the Pale Hose, he impressed manager Jimmy Dykes. Dykes was fond of Kalin's ability but was unable to use him on a regular basis. Frank was drafted into the army just prior to the 1944 baseball season. After two years in the army, Kalin was never given the look that seemed to be promised him.

G	R	H	2B	3B	HR	RBI	BB	SO	SB	AVG	Slug
7	0	0	0	0	0	1	2	0	0	.000	.000

Alexis William Kampouris, *Third Base*

Kampouris spent the majority of his major league career in the National League. He played with the Reds for five seasons, the Giants for two, and the Dodgers for two and a half. His American League tenure consisted of half a season with the 1943 Washington Senators. After the 1943 season, the Senators sold Alex to the Milwaukee ballclub but the veteran infielder refused to report to the minor league city. He received a call later in the 1944 season that he couldn't refuse — one from Uncle Sam.

Alex joined the army, foregoing a season in the minors, and was stationed at Buckley Field, Colorado. He was later reassigned to a post in Canada where he was able to play some baseball. While stationed north of the border, Alex was asked by a writer which major league pitcher gave him the most trouble. He replied, "All you have to do is take a peak at my batting average and you'll see that I had trouble with them all."

G	R	H	2B	3B	HR	RBI	BB	SO	SB	AVG	Slug
708	272	531	94	20	45	284	244	360	22	.243	.367

Martin Gregory Karow, *Shortstop/Third Base*

Karow had a cup of coffee with the 1927 Red Sox of Bill Carrigan. A legend in the college football ranks, Karow starred for Ohio State but opted to play baseball after he left campus. His days in baseball were short. After he quit the diamond, Karow returned to the football field and built upon his legend as a head coach at the college level.

In 1942, Marty was summoned by the navy and was commissioned a lieutenant. His initial assignment was Annapolis where he was assigned to the naval aviation physical training program. His duties in the navy were to keep sailors in tip-top shape. Transferred to Ward Island, Karow served as the head physical training officer at the Naval Air Technical Training Center based on the island. After his discharge, Marty built a legend as a college coach with Ohio State and Texas A&M.

G	R	H	2B	3B	HR	RBI	BB	SO	SB	AVG	Slug
6	0	2	1	0	0	0	0	2	0	.200	.300

Herbert Karpel, *Pitcher*

On the threshold of the major leagues during World War II, Karpel was added to the Yankees' spring training roster in 1943. A top prospect in the chain, he was a likely candidate to break camp with the pinstripers, but just days after he was added to the roster he received his draft notice. The former Pacific Coast League star served in the army for two and half years and made the majors with New York in 1946 for two games — his only action at the highest level.

W	L	PCT	G	GS	CG	IP	H	BB	SO	SHO	ERA
0	0	—	2	0	0	2	4	0	0	0	9.00

Edward Terrance Kazak, *Third Base*

Few ballplayers witnessed more intense battlefield action than Eddie Kazak. However, the baseball world failed to recognize his sacrifices and heroics when he came home from the European battlefields. At the time of his discharge, he was an unknown in the baseball world, but when he became an unlikely All-Star in 1949, writers began to clamor around Kazak's locker. His journey from the battlefields to baseball's big stage was a writer's dream, but it was a real-life journey that nearly ended the life of the third baseman from Steubenville, Ohio.

Kazak's journey began in Pennsylvania coal country where the boy was raised. He worked in the same coal mines as Andy Seminick, who would reach the major leagues as a power-hitting catcher. Eddie's chance to leave the mines came courtesy baseball. The game was his meal ticket, his chance to make good in life without toiling in the dark, claustrophobic and constrictive mines. But the meal ticket was nearly taken from him during World War II.

His soldiering began at Brooks Field, but the eager young grunt wanted action and applied for service as a paratrooper. Kazak became an airborne infantryman and was shipped overseas where he would see heavy combat action. As a private first class in the European Theatre, Kazak jumped into hostile terrain at Brest. Hand-to-hand combat was the order, and Kazak fought off Germans with his bayonet but suffered bayonet wounds from the Nazis. His left forearm was cut by a bayonet and would need 19 stitches. At Brest, he sought shelter in a building that the Germans would shell and he was buried under rubble after the attack. The debris crushed Kazak's right arm and his elbow was lacerated by shrapnel.

Word came home from France that Eddie had lost his arm in battle, but the reports were false. Although his wounds were severe, they didn't require amputation but did require surgery. Although Kazak was reluctant to talk about his war-time experiences, he detailed his three years in the army when he told a writer, "I started out in the Air Corps, then I was a paratrooper and wound up in the infantry. I spent three years in the army, half of the time in hospitals in England and California." While in the hospitals, doctors did all they could to save Eddie's right arm. His arm was crushed so severely that bone chips and splinters were removed and in their place plastic pieces were inserted. He was given little chance to play baseball again.

But the doctors, who analyzed only the damage done to his arm, failed to take into account the young man's iron resolve. Determined to make it in baseball, Kazak worked himself into condition after his discharge. A second baseman at times, Eddie discovered the snap throws second basemen make during the double play greatly pained his arm and he wound up spending his time learning the subtleties of third base. The Cardinals called up Kazak at the end of the 1948 season but he wasn't satisfied with just reaching the majors: he wanted to excel. He did just that the following year when he made the National League All-Star team.

G	R	H	2B	3B	HR	RBI	BB	SO	SB	AVG	Slug
218	69	165	22	6	11	71	52	45	0	.273	.383

Edward Paul Kearse, *Catcher*

A tough-as-nails catcher, Kearse had the misfortune of breaking into the majors when the Yankees had the great Bill Dickey on their roster. The backstop from the West Coast wasn't about to unseat the great Dickey, so Kearse was used infrequently by the Bronx Bombers in 1942, his only year in the majors. Although given a brief trial at the highest level, Eddie was a star back home on the West Coast. But he put his baseball career on hold when Uncle Sam needed his presence during the Second World War.

Kearse joined the army and served in the Chemical Warfare Division at Fort Campbell, Kentucky. But the "warfare" in his unit's title wasn't an idle boast as his company was shipped overseas to the European Theatre. He saw combat action in the French battlefields and was wounded by shrapnel. The wounds were quite severe and Eddie was removed from the frontlines and sent to army hospitals. The shrapnel did serious damage to Kearse's back and shoulders, and the old catcher would travel to and from fourteen different military hospitals to be treated for his battlefield wounds. He went under the knife many times, leaving nasty scars on his back.

The Purple Heart recipient returned home with little chance to play baseball again. But Kearse wasn't your average man. Not content to sulk, the San Francisco catcher worked his way back to the ball diamonds. In awe of Eddie's courage and determination, scout Joe Devine gushed, "You know how Eddie got back into baseball? Sheer courage, that's what. He wanted to play and he made himself well in spite of any predictions made by a smart doctor. What a guy!"

Although Kearse never did reach the majors again, he was something of a legend in the minors. His grit and determination were the stuff of folktales. Once, during a game on the West Coast, Kearse suffered a nasty spike wound during a collision at home plate. His coaching staff and even the umpires wanted the bleeding Eddie removed from the game so he could be treated. Kearse scoffed at their requests and said, "Spill a little iodine on it if you want but let's get along with the game. I was wounded a few times in the war and this little scratch doesn't mean anything."

G	R	H	2B	3B	HR	RBI	BB	SO	SB	AVG	Slug
11	2	5	0	0	0	2	3	1	1	.192	.192

Robert Charles Keegan, *Pitcher*

Keegan had yet to make his major league debut when the war broke out. The right-hander from Rochester enlisted in the Army Air Corps and served aboard a B-24 during the war. Nicknamed "Smiley," Keegan seemed to be a minor league journeyman after his discharge. He had yet to reach the majors by his thirtieth birthday, but Smiley kept plugging right along. The White Sox finally summoned him in 1953 at the age of 32. The following year, Keegan, as a 33-year-old sophomore, was named to the American League All-Star team.

W	L	PCT	G	GS	CG	IP	H	BB	SO	SHO	ERA
40	36	.526	135	87	29	646	668	233	198	6	3.65

Chester Lawrence Kehn, *Pitcher*

In 1942, Kehn made a boisterous arrival to the big show. A colorful clown, Kehn was said to be a Dizzy Dean clone, not lacking confidence in his abilities. The odd bird was inducted into the military in March of 1943 after making just three appearances with Brooklyn the year before. He served and played ball at Williams Field under skipper Stan Goletz and with Chicago Cubs infielder Lou Stringer. Chet never did make good in the major leagues, at least not on the level of the great Ol' Diz. He didn't return to majors after his discharge.

W	L	PCT	G	GS	CG	IP	H	BB	SO	SHO	ERA
0	0	—	3	1	0	8	8	4	3	0	6.75

Francis Eugene Kelleher, *Outfield*

Kelleher was a light-hitting outfielder during his two-year stint in the major leagues. He entered the army after the 1943 baseball season and missed two years to the war effort. After he returned from the war, Frankie made headlines in a Pacific Coast League game during the 1950 season when he started a brawl that has been regarded as the most violent baseball melee of all-time.

G	R	H	2B	3B	HR	RBI	BB	SO	SB	AVG	Slug
47	14	20	3	1	3	12	18	20	0	.167	.283

Frank William Kellert, *First Base*

A member of the last Browns team and the first Baltimore Orioles squad, Kellert was a power-hitting first baseman who never played regularly at the highest level. Frank was a youngster trying to work his way to the majors when the war broke out. He put his baseball dreams on hold to help in the battle for liberty. Unlike many athletes that were able to play ball in the service, Kellert saw combat action on foreign land and water. His introduction to foreign water nearly ended his life.

Kellert grew up in the Midwest, far removed from any ocean. Given that land surrounded every corner of Oklahoma, Kellert never felt it necessary to learn how to swim. He enlisted in the Army Air Corps, rather than the U.S. Navy or U.S. Marines, but he would nevertheless be introduced to deep bodies of water on his way to the battlefields. Frank was aboard the British troop transport ship, the *HMS Rhona*, which was ferrying servicemen off the North African coast. The *HMS Rhona* was attacked by a German glider and was sunk in the sea. Kellert told the tale to a writer after his discharge, saying, "The bomber got us all right and the ship went down. We were nine and a half hours in the water. There were about 90 of us in the group and 20 were drowned. I couldn't swim ... but I can now. I learned out there."

G	R	H	2B	3B	HR	RBI	BB	SO	SB	AVG	Slug
122	25	57	9	3	8	37	26	36	0	.231	.389

Alexander Raymond Kellner, *Pitcher*

Although Kellner pitched on poor teams throughout his career, he was able to reach 100 victories. The southpaw spent eleven seasons with the Athletics and was with the squad when the franchise relocated to Kansas City in the mid 1950s. Alex made his debut in 1948 when Connie Mack was still at the helm and left the club in 1958. Before his major league career began, Kellner served in the navy during World War II. The Tucson native served aboard a destroyer that was engaged in missions in the Pacific Theater.

W	L	PCT	G	GS	CG	IP	H	BB	SO	SHO	ERA
101	112	.474	321	250	99	1,851	1,925	747	816	9	4.41

William Henry "Big Bill" Kelly, *First Base*

Big Bill had two cups of coffee in the 1920s with both Philadelphia entries. The first baseman failed to hit well enough to stick in the majors in an era when batting was on the rise. Kelly was in his forties during World War II but he served in the military. Discharged in time for the 1945 baseball season, Big Bill signed on as skipper of the Elizabethton nine.

G	R	H	2B	3B	HR	RBI	BB	SO	SB	AVG	Slug
32	6	15	2	1	0	5	7	22	0	.179	.226

Kenneth Frederick Keltner, *Third Base*

The name of Ken Keltner will always be discussed as long as Joe DiMaggio's 56-game hitting streak remains the record. It was Keltner, and his exceptional leatherwork, that stopped Joltin' Joe from making it 57 games straight. Kenny had issues with his draft board, which he greatly benefited from, as he was reclassified 1-A. However, his draft board somehow failed to call him for service and he was returned to his initial 2-A classification. This oversight on the draft board's part was remedied and Keltner was inducted into the navy after the close of 1944 baseball season.

He missed all of the 1945 campaign to service at the Great Lakes but returned to the Tribe in 1946. He enjoyed his breakout year in 1948—the year Cleveland won the World Series—by swatting 31 home runs and driving in 119 runs. Over the years, there have been grumblings to get Keltner into the Hall of Fame, but with more deserving hot corner candidates, such as Lave Cross, Ken Boyer, Ron Santo and Stanley Hack, his name may never be called. Then again, the aforementioned men (with the exception of Boyer), were able to play their careers without a military interruption, while Keltner missed a year to service.

G	R	H	2B	3B	HR	RBI	BB	SO	SB	AVG	Slug
1,526	737	1,570	308	69	163	852	514	480	39	.276	.441

William Gorman Kennedy, *Pitcher*

Kennedy pitched three years in the major leagues and missed three years to military service. A slender southpaw, Kennedy nailed down five saves in his major league career. His first action came with the 1942 Senators, but he was inducted into the army after only eight games at the highest level. While he earned his paycheck under Uncle Sam, Bill served as a paratrooper with the 13th Airborne Division. Kennedy saw action at the battlefields in the European Theatre.

W	L	PCT	G	GS	CG	IP	H	BB	SO	SHO	ERA
1	3	.250	31	4	1	64	71	44	23	0	6.75

Robert Daniel Kennedy, *Third Base*

Bob Kennedy spent the majority of his career with the White Sox (1939–1948) and the Indians (1948–1954) before becoming a nomadic player. His last four years in the major leagues were spent with four different teams, including two separate stops in Chicago. As a 20-year-old, Kennedy was platooning with Dario Lodigiani at third base in 1941 before he took over the starting role in 1942. However, he was drafted into the U.S. Marine Corps at the end of the season and missed the next three years to service under Uncle Sam. He returned to the Pale Hose in 1946 and rotated between left field and third base.

G	R	H	2B	3B	HR	RBI	BB	SO	SB	AVG	Slug
1,483	514	1,176	196	41	63	514	364	443	45	.254	.355

Arthur Joseph Kenney, *Pitcher*

This southpaw from Massachusetts appeared in only two games for the 1938 Braves. Unable to throw a strike, Kenney worked two innings and averaged four walks per frame. With such poor accuracy, Kenney was sent back to the minors. Kenney missed some baseball action to service in the armed forces. Upon his discharge, he wasn't summoned back to the major leagues.

W	L	PCT	G	GS	CG	IP	H	BB	SO	SHO	ERA
0	0	—	2	0	0	2	3	8	2	0	18.00

Wayman William Kerksieck, *Pitcher*

A right-hander from Arkansas, Kerksieck spent one year at the major league level with the last-place 1939 Phillies. Wayman lost two decisions and was unable to pick up a win at the highest level. He left baseball to enlist in the army and by 1942 he had reached the rank of corporeal while he was stationed at Camp Berkeley.

W	L	PCT	G	GS	CG	IP	H	BB	SO	SHO	ERA
0	2	.000	23	2	1	63	81	32	13	0	7.14

Russell Eldon Kerns, *Pinch Hitter*

Kerns' only major league action came with the world champion 1945 Tigers. A war-era ballplayer, Kerns had one pinch hit appearance during his major league stay. Russ served with the United States Army during the war.

G	R	H	2B	3B	HR	RBI	BB	SO	SB	AVG	Slug
1	0	0	0	0	0	0	0	0	0	.000	.000

Horace Kent Kibbie, *Second Base/Shortstop*

Kibbie was the captain of his University of Texas club. The Lone Star recruit played one season at the highest level, with the

1925 Braves. Horace was pushing 40 when the war broke out but that didn't deter him from joining the army.

G	R	H	2B	3B	HR	RBI	BB	SO	SB	AVG	Slug
11	5	11	2	0	0	2	5	6	0	.268	.317

Larry Nathaniel Kimbrough, *Pitcher*

A unique if not star-caliber pitcher, Kimbrough was noted as being ambidextrous. He employed this trait in a few games by pitching with both hands. Essentially a right-hander, Larry signed with his hometown Philadelphia Stars in the early 1940s. His career was interrupted by a two-year stint in the military during World War II. After his discharge he pitched with the Homestead Grays before he took a job with the U.S. Post Office.

(1941–1950): Philadelphia Stars and Homestead Grays

Ellis Raymond Kinder, *Pitcher*

One of the best firemen in the majors in the years directly after the war, "Old Folks" Kinder was a 31-year-old rookie when the Browns gave him his first look in 1946. The year before, Ellis served in the army after his induction at Fort Oglethorpe. Kinder, who would become one of the first pitchers in history to record more than 100 saves, pitched until 1957 when he was in his forties.

W	L	PCT	G	GS	CG	IP	H	BB	SO	SHO	ERA
102	71	.590	484	122	56	1,480	1,421	539	749	10	3.43

Ralph McPherran Kiner, *Outfield*

The greatest power hitter in the National League in the years directly after the war, Kiner led the senior circuit in long balls seven straight years. The brawny blaster from New Mexico had his career cut short by military service and injury. Before he made his major league debut, Kiner was inducted into service and his career came to a halt courtesy of back pains. Despite the interruption and the injury, Kiner still amassed 369 career home runs. His RBI rate was even more impressive given that he played the bulk of his career with the lowly Pirates. Ralph drove home 1,015 mates in just 1,472 career games.

Kiner signed a minor league contract after high school and was playing in the bushes in 1943 when he left the team to join the colors. Ralph joined the navy and served as a Naval Air cadet. Late in 1944, Kiner was promoted to ensign. After his navy discharge, Ralph went directly to the majors. He led the National League in home runs the first year of normalcy after the fighting and did the same the next six years. The Pirates weren't contenders, but with Big Kiner blasting home runs at a Ruthian pace, Pittsburghers had reason to clamor to Forbes Field.

G	R	H	2B	3B	HR	RBI	BB	SO	SB	AVG	Slug
1,472	971	1,451	216	39	369	1,015	1,011	749	22	.279	.548

Lynn Paul King, *Outfield*

Noted as a star flychaser but a poor hitter, King lived up to that billing in the majors with the Redbirds. King joined the squad in the mid–1930s and his last major league action came in 1939. A three-sport star at Drake University, King joined the military in early 1944 even though he had a wife and two children to support.

G	R	H	2B	3B	HR	RBI	BB	SO	SB	AVG	Slug
175	28	43	4	1	0	21	28	18	6	.208	.237

Ernest Alexander Kish, *Outfield*

A war-era ballplayer, Kish was a hot commodity in 1945 after he received his discharge from the U.S. Coast Guard. He had made a name for himself in the service ranks, and teams starved for talent in 1945 fought to acquire his services. Connie Mack won and brought Ernie to Philadelphia in 1945 but he failed to impress. When the regulars returned from their military hitch, Kish wasn't asked back to the majors.

G	R	H	2B	3B	HR	RBI	BB	SO	SB	AVG	Slug
43	10	27	5	1	0	10	9	9	0	.245	.309

Louis Frank Klein, *Second Base*

A second baseman from New Orleans, Klein is remembered best as one of the handful of players barred from the game briefly for playing in the Mexican League. Klein led the Cardinals in stolen bases during the 1943 season and then joined the U.S. Coast Guard after the close of the season. After spending a year and a half in the Coast Guard, stationed at St. Augustine, Lou rejoined the Redbirds midway through the 1945 campaign. He jumped the Cards in 1947 to play south of the border but was reinstated in 1949.

G	R	H	2B	3B	HR	RBI	BB	SO	SB	AVG	Slug
305	162	269	48	15	16	101	105	119	10	.259	.381

Theodore Otto Kleinhans, *Pitcher*

Kleinhans was an old man when he broke into the major leagues. Born in 1899, Ted was 35 years old when the Phillies gave him his first trial in 1934. His rookie season was split between the Phillies and Reds and he would later play with the Yankees. He served in the armed forces during both World Wars. Ted, who coached college ball at Syracuse University, was a captain stationed in England during World War II as a mess officer.

W	L	PCT	G	GS	CG	IP	H	BB	SO	SHO	ERA
4	9	.308	56	12	1	143	185	76	48	0	5.29

Robert Harold Klinger, *Pitcher*

A mainstay with the Pirates from 1938 to 1943, Klinger posted a .706 winning percentage as a 30-year-old rookie. He led the Bucs in wins during the 1939 campaign and was moved to the bullpen in 1941. He enjoyed a comeback year in 1942, when he finished second on the team in wins with a solid 3.24 ERA. His finest year came in 1943, the season before his military induction. Bob had reclaimed a spot in the rotation and led the club with three shutouts. Granted, Klinger had been in the majors for only a few seasons, but he had already reached his thirty-fifth birthday when Uncle Sam called his number.

Bob took his pre-induction physical at Jefferson Barracks, Missouri, and was assigned to the Great Lakes around the same time as teammate Bill Brandt. He spent the 1944 season at the Great Lakes before he received his orders to be shipped overseas. He toured the South Pacific playing for the navy's Fifth Fleet All-Stars with the likes of Hall of Famer Johnny Mize, pitcher Schoolboy Rowe and Athletics infielder Al Brancato. Klinger enjoyed his time spent in the Pacific. He gave a report that pitching on such islands as Saipan had done wonders for his breaking balls.

W	L	PCT	G	GS	CG	IP	H	BB	SO	SHO	ERA
66	61	.520	265	130	48	1,090	1,153	358	357	7	3.68

John Calvin Klippstein, *Pitcher*

A solid relief pitcher throughout his career, Klippstein made his debut with the 1950 Cubs and pitched until 1967. During the war, Johnny was a youngster and he served in the military for one year at the end of the campaign.

W	L	PCT	G	GS	CG	IP	H	BB	SO	SHO	ERA
101	118	.461	711	161	37	1,970	1,915	978	1,158	6	4.24

Austin Jay Knickerbocker, *Outfield*

Before Knickerbocker made his major league debut, he was a combat veteran. Austin enlisted in the army and was stationed at Camp Edwards. A staff sergeant, Knick was in charge of a radio platoon at Camp Edwards until his unit was shipped overseas. He served in the European Theater of Operations and saw combat duty at Normandy, Sicily and North Africa. The decorated war veteran returned home in 1945 and two years later had a cup of coffee with Connie Mack's Athletics.

G	R	H	2B	3B	HR	RBI	BB	SO	SB	AVG	Slug
21	8	12	3	2	0	2	3	4	0	.250	.398

William Hart Knickerbocker, *Shortstop/Second Base*

Bill broke in at the major league level with the 1933 Cleveland Indians. The middle infielder made his rounds in the American League: he also played for the Browns, Yankees, White Sox and A's. His last big league action came with Connie Mack's 1942 Athletics. During the war, the thirty-year-old Knickerbocker served with the enlisted men in the army.

G	R	H	2B	3B	HR	RBI	BB	SO	SB	AVG	Slug
907	423	943	198	27	28	368	244	328	25	.276	.374

John Henry "Jack" Knott, *Pitcher*

Knott had been playing in the major leagues since 1933 when World War II broke out. A longtime member of the St. Louis Browns, Jack was already in his mid-thirties when he joined the army. The right-hander spent three years in the army, initially stationed at Camp Adair, and returned to Connie Mack to pitch in three final major league games for the 1946 Athletics. During his military stint, Knott fought in the Battle of the Bulge and was awarded a Purple Heart for injuries sustained in Belgium.

Few ballplayers experienced as much deep combat action as Knott. The old workhorse pitcher was a high-ranking infantryman in the army. While still stateside, Jack had reached the rank of first sergeant and was in charge of a large number of Uncle Sam's fighting forces. Assigned to the 104th Infantry Division, Knott was shipped overseas where his unit was engaged in numerous battles — most notably the epic Battle of the Bulge. First Sergeant Knott was awarded a battlefield commission and became Lieutenant Knott on hostile land. Wounded in action, Jack nevertheless led his troops through Germany and helped liberate a Nazi concentration camp before the war ended.

W	L	PCT	G	GS	CG	IP	H	BB	SO	SHO	ERA
82	103	.443	325	192	62	1,557	1,787	642	484	4	4.97

Donald Martin Kolloway, *Second Base*

Kolloway was a large, free-swinging second baseman who took over the starting assignment at that position in 1942. After a solid year in 1942, he struggled mightily through the 1943 campaign, which ended with his induction into the military. Don served at Camp Grant, Illinois, and visited his White Sox teammates on one occasion, regaling them with stories of his army training. He said, "Know what we did the other day? Well, after a four-mile hike with full pack we went through an hour of calisthenics. And then did we get to go to our barracks to rest? We did not. We went to the mess hall to scrub for two hours.... Wonder why I ever thought playing a doubleheader at second base was hard work?"

During his stint in the military, Kolloway was shipped overseas and served in Germany. On the enemy's soil, he was introduced to the Cincinnati Reds' young hurler Ewell "The Whip" Blackwell, who was serving with an infantry regiment. He was able to play some baseball against Blackwell and quickly touted Ewell as one of the best pitchers he had ever faced.

G	R	H	2B	3B	HR	RBI	BB	SO	SB	AVG	Slug
1,079	466	1,081	180	30	29	393	189	251	76	.271	.353

Bruno Bruce Konopka, *First Base*

With a major league career that spanned three seasons, Konopka had about as many at-bats as a regular player tallies in a month. At the time Konopka made his debut, Connie Mack needed a young first baseman, but Bruce was lost to the war effort in 1943, missing his chance at the highest level. He was ordered for duty with the naval reserve on April 29, 1943. When the war ended, he returned to Philadelphia hoping to grasp the first-base job, but Mack had found a new youngster in Ferris Fain, and Bruce was left without a job.

G	R	H	2B	3B	HR	RBI	BB	SO	SB	AVG	Slug
45	9	25	4	1	0	10	5	9	0	.238	.295

Casimir James Konstanty, *Pitcher*

Best known for winning the National League's MVP award during the 1950 season, Konstanty was a reliable relief pitcher throughout his career. He remains the only NL relief pitcher to ever win the MVP award, as Rollie Fingers, Guillermo Hernandez and Dennis Eckersley each won the award in the American League. Konstanty missed one year to military service when he was stationed at Sampson Naval Training Center during the 1945 season.

W	L	PCT	G	GS	CG	IP	H	BB	SO	SHO	ERA
66	48	.579	433	36	14	947	957	269	268	2	3.46

Clement John Koshorek, *Utility Infielder*

Descriptive phrases like "pint-sized" were often used regarding the diminutive infielder. Koshorek's height was listed as anywhere from 5'2" to 5'6" but never any higher. The short ballplayer from Royal Oak, Michigan, joined the army before he signed his first pro contract. After his discharge, Clem embarked on his baseball career. He spent two years with the Pirates in the early 1950s when they were the doormat of the National League.

G	R	H	2B	3B	HR	RBI	BB	SO	SB	AVG	Slug
99	27	84	17	0	0	15	26	40	4	.260	.313

George Bernard "Dave" Koslo, *Pitcher*

Koslo was a solid major league pitcher who spent the majority of his career with the Giants. After the Giants let him go in 1953, he pitched half a season with the Orioles and a year and a half with the Braves. As a pup, Koslo posted a 1–2 record with the 1941 Giants, despite a remarkable 1.88 ERA. He regressed mightily in 1942 and was unable to redeem himself as he entered the armed forces after the season.

Dave took his basic training at Fort Sheridan and was then assigned to the 326th Alliance Glider Infantry. His unit was shipped out to the European Theatre, and Koslo was one of many major leaguers who introduced the game to Europeans. He played service ball overseas and once pitched in a game at London in the Harrington Dog Track. While serving in the European Theatre, Koslo was attached to the 13th Airborne Division and met up with fellow major league ballplayer Bill Kennedy of the Senators.

W	L	PCT	G	GS	CG	IP	H	BB	SO	SHO	ERA
92	107	.462	348	189	74	1,592	1,597	538	606	15	3.68

Michael Thomas Kosman, *Reserve*

A war-era ballplayer, Kosman played one game with the 1944 Reds. Mike served briefly with the U.S. Marines during the war and wasn't summoned to Cincinnati after the war ended.

G	R	H	2B	3B	HR	RBI	BB	SO	SB	AVG	Slug
1	0	0	0	0	0	0	0	0	0	—	—

Ernest Anyz Koy, *Outfield*

A stout outfielder from Texas, Koy made his debut with the 1938 Brooklyn Dodgers as their everyday center fielder. He posted an impressive freshman line with a .299 batting average, 29 doubles, 13 triples, 11 homers, and 76 RBIs. Ernie notched 37 doubles in 1939 as an encore but was traded to the Cardinals early in 1940. With St. Louis, Koy hit .310 and finished second on the club in stolen bases. He suffered the same fate, traded midseason, in 1941 when the Cardinals shipped him to the Reds. His last major league action came in 1942 with the Phillies.

Ernie enlisted in the United States Navy in April of 1943 and was sworn in at Fort Sam Houston. He served as an apprentice seaman at the Corpus Christi Naval Air Station. As far as former major league baseball players were concerned, Ernie wasn't alone in Corpus Christi as Athletics star Sam Chapman also served there. After his discharge, Koy did not make a return to the majors. His son, also named Ernie, became a professional football player who quarterbacked for the Giants.

G	R	H	2B	3B	HR	RBI	BB	SO	SB	AVG	Slug
558	238	515	108	29	36	260	137	284	40	.279	.427

Albert Kenneth Kozar, *Second Base*

The Senators regular second baseman at the end of the 1940s, Kozar served in the armed forces before his major league debut. The second baseman served with the 8th Army overseas at the rank of T/5. In his unit were such notable ballplayers as Hugh Mulcahy (the first major leaguer drafted into service), Red Sox first baseman T/4 Al Flair and staff sergeant Erv Dusak of the Cardinals.

G	R	H	2B	3B	HR	RBI	BB	SO	SB	AVG	Slug
285	118	252	41	10	6	94	96	86	6	.254	.334

Joseph Peter Kracher, *Pinch Hitter*

A noted good-time guy and on-field clown, Kracher had a cup of coffee with his hometown Phillies before the war. Joe joined the United States Army during the war, which impeded his minor league career. After his discharge, Kracher returned to the bushes and pleased crowds—but not his managers—with his antics. Writer Ken Johnson detailed one such Kracher clown case in a post-game write-up. Johnson wrote, "Kracher got a home run to score the first Laker run. Apparently manager Sid Gautreaux didn't get quite as much enjoyment out of the clowning as the fans did. Kracher was removed from the game after going through a series of gyrations between first and second base."

G	R	H	2B	3B	HR	RBI	BB	SO	SB	AVG	Slug
5	1	1	0	0	0	0	2	1	0	.200	.200

Joseph Victor Lawrence Krakauskas, *Pitcher*

A southpaw from north of the border, Krakauskas spent four years with the Washington Senators before he made his way to Cleveland in 1941. Wildness was always an issue for Joe during his major league career, but he parlayed his inaccuracy into a seven-year career. Joe served with the Canadian Air Force and was part of the largest group of Royal Canadian Air Force personnel ever to be dispatched overseas. He was stationed in Britain and would have possibly had an opportunity to take part in a few pickup baseball games—had he brought his gear. He said, "This radio mechanic job I've got is a fulltime business."

W	L	PCT	G	GS	CG	IP	H	BB	SO	SHO	ERA
26	36	.419	149	63	22	583	605	355	347	1	4.54

John Henry "Jack" Kramer, *Pitcher*

One of the aces of the 1944 American League pennant-winning Browns staff, Kramer almost missed out on the team's only flag. When the United States became active participants in the war, Kramer left baseball to do his bit in the plants. The right-hander spent the 1942 baseball season working in a defense job but the following year he was accepted into the navy. Kramer didn't last long in the service and was given his discharge, which enabled him to join the Browns of 1944. Jack posted a perfect 0.00 ERA in eleven World Series innings against the Redbirds and accounted for one of the Browns' two victories.

W	L	PCT	G	GS	CG	IP	H	BB	SO	SHO	ERA
95	103	.480	322	215	88	1,638	1,761	682	613	14	4.24

John William "Tex" Kraus, *Pitcher*

Prior to his military induction, Tex had a defense job at Kelly Field during the offseason. He was summoned for military duty on April 8, 1944, and served one year in the army. A solid left-hander, Texas Jack enjoyed his finest season in 1943, when he posted a 3.15 ERA to offset his misleading record of 9–15.

W	L	PCT	G	GS	CG	IP	H	BB	SO	SHO	ERA
15	25	.375	70	39	10	307	318	133	83	1	3.99

Lewis Bernard Krausse Sr., *Pitcher*

Krausse, whose son Lew Junior followed him to the major leagues, spent two years with Connie Mack's Athletics in the early 1930s. The right-hander from Media, Pennsylvania, joined the army ten years after his last major league game. Lewis Krausse Jr. was born early in 1943, but the elder Krausse missed seeing many of the infant's firsts. Off fighting the Germans in the European Theatre, Krausse suffered from trench foot during the battles.

Lew was shipped back home and recuperated at Camp Butler, North Carolina's general hospital. When healthy, he returned home to his wife and young son, trying to regain his form from the injuries he suffered fighting the enemy with the Tenth Armored Division. Signed to manage the ballclub at Federalsburg after the war, Krausse had fourteen war veterans on his roster that year.

W	L	PCT	G	GS	CG	IP	H	BB	SO	SHO	ERA
5	1	.833	23	4	3	68	70	30	17	1	4.50

Albert Joseph "Mickey" Kreitner, *Catcher*

A war-era ballplayer, Kreitner served a few months in the military before he was given a medical discharge. Mickey was the third-string catcher for the Cubs in 1944 after he played a few games with them the year before. When the regulars came back from the war, Kreitner's days in the majors had come to a close.

G	R	H	2B	3B	HR	RBI	BB	SO	SB	AVG	Slug
43	3	16	2	0	0	3	9	18	0	.172	.194

Charles Steven "Chuck" Kress, *First Base*

A minor league star, Kress was given a few trials at the major league level but never did make good. Used mainly as a reserve and a bat off the bench, Kress was stuck behind such notables as Gil Hodges, Ted Kluszewski and Walt Dropo. Chuck missed some minor league action to service in the United States Army during World War II.

G	R	H	2B	3B	HR	RBI	BB	SO	SB	AVG	Slug
175	57	116	20	7	1	52	49	59	6	.249	.328

Louis Henry Kretlow, *Pitcher*

A live-arm pitcher with a blazing fastball but minimal control, Kretlow was an unknown commodity until Uncle Sam's baseball stage made major league clubs take notice. Kretlow, who served in the Army Air Corps during the war, was named MVP of the 1945 National Semipro Baseball Congress tournament while in the service. Given his fine pitching for Uncle Sam's outfit, the Tigers gave Lou a large bonus to sign with Detroit after his discharge. He made his debut with Detorit in 1946 and pitched a complete-game victory in his first outing. But control was always an issue with Kretlow and the Tigers shipped him off to the Browns in 1950.

W	L	PCT	G	GS	CG	IP	H	BB	SO	SHO	ERA
27	47	.365	199	104	22	786	781	522	450	3	4.87

Kurt Ferdinand Krieger, *Pitcher*

Krieger, whose parents came to America when he was a child, was a teenager throughout the war. After school, the Austrian-born right-hander entered the colors and served in the latter stages of the war. He made his debut with Eddie Dyer's 1949 Cardinals.

W	L	PCT	G	GS	CG	IP	H	BB	SO	SHO	ERA
0	0	—	3	0	0	5	6	6	3	0	12.60

Howard Wilbur Krist, *Pitcher*

A relief pitcher with an enviable career winning percentage, Krist didn't stick with the Redbirds at first. He pitched briefly with them in 1937 and 1938, but stuck after a 10–0 season in 1941. He followed up that perfect campaign with a solid 13–3 record in 1942. Howie posted a 2.91 ERA in 1943, his last season before his military callup.

Krist passed his pre-induction physical on February 14, 1944, at the Rochester Induction Center. He went to Camp Croft where he learned how to toss grenades before he was shipped out. Krist went to the European Theatre and saw combat action in the Normandy area as an infantryman. He took part in a battle located at France in which the right-hander was wounded in action. Howie notified his wife of an injury to his leg sustained in battle, and she notified Cardinals president Sam Breadon of the incident. Breadon made this public statement: "Mrs. Krist said it was a leg injury and not a wound and she gave the impression she did not think the injury is serious."

The day after his leg injury made the papers, it was found out that Howie had been awarded the Purple Heart and was convalescing in an English hospital. Krist returned to the Cardinals in 1946 as a war hero but was unable to regain his pre-war form. A proven winner before the war, Howie tossed only fifteen games after the war with a 0–2 record.

W	L	PCT	G	GS	CG	IP	H	BB	SO	SHO	ERA
37	11	.771	128	37	15	444	408	158	150	2	3.32

Richard David "Dick" Kryhoski, *First Base*

A solid yet much-traveled first baseman, Kryhoski was the definition of a stop-gap ballplayer: good enough to play as a regular for a spell but not good enough to ward off a solid prospect. Dick signed his first pro contract after his military discharge and made his debut with the 1949 Yankees. Skipper Casey Stengel loved platoons and employed one at first with Dick and veteran Tommy Henrich. Dick was traded to the Tigers and had his best year in 1951.

G	R	H	2B	3B	HR	RBI	BB	SO	SB	AVG	Slug
569	203	475	85	14	45	231	119	163	5	.265	.403

John Albert Kucab, *Pitcher*

Remembered as the pitcher who recorded the win in Connie Mack's last major league victory, Kucab made his debut in Mack's final season. During the war, Kucab served overseas before he signed on to play ball for the Athletics.

W	L	PCT	G	GS	CG	IP	H	BB	SO	SHO	ERA
5	5	.500	59	3	2	152	169	51	48	0	4.44

Stanislaw Leo Kuczek, *Pinch Hitter*

Kuczek's major league career consisted of one plate appearance. In his only trip to the plate at the highest level, Steve banged out a double. His lone plate appearance came with the 1949 Braves—after the war. During the war, Kuczek, a Colgate graduate, served with the Third Army in the European Theatre of Operations.

G	R	H	2B	3B	HR	RBI	BB	SO	SB	AVG	Slug
1	0	1	1	0	0	0	0	0	0	1.000	2.000

Bernard Carl "Bert" Kuczynski, *Pitcher*

A stellar collegiate football player at the University of Pennsylvania, Bert was persuaded by Connie Mack to sign with the Athletics after college. Mack had an eye for talent and enjoyed experimenting with gifted natural athletes. His gamble with Kuczynski, however, didn't quite pay off like his identical gamble with the great Sam Chapman. Bert only played one year with the Athletics; he only made six appearances with the 1943 squad.

The former captain of the Pennsylvania football club, Bert wrote his former gridiron coach while training to become a U.S. Marine officer at Parris Island, stating that the scrimmages held in football built him up physically to stand the strain of Marine training. After a short time in the Marine Corps, he received a medical discharge and signed to play football with the Detroit Lions. However, Bert had to change his plans as he was called back by his draft board for a re-examination. He was fit enough for duty in the navy, and was inducted early in 1944. While in the Navy, Bert played football in Hawaii.

W	L	PCT	G	GS	CG	IP	H	BB	SO	SHO	ERA
0	1	.000	6	1	0	25	36	9	8	0	3.96

Emil Benedict Kush, *Pitcher*

A reliable relief pitcher, Kush spent his entire major league career with the Chicago Cubs. Before signing his contract with the baby bears, Emil was already familiar with Wrigley Field, having worked there as a peanut vendor as a child. He rarely pitched in the majors prior to World War II, as he appeared in three games over the course of two seasons with the Cubs. He was inducted into the navy and missed the 1943 through 1945 baseball seasons. He built confidence while playing service ball with Val Heim at the Lambert Naval Air Station, and returned to Chicago to post a solid 3.08 ERA in his first full major league season.

W	L	PCT	G	GS	CG	IP	H	BB	SO	SHO	ERA
21	12	.636	150	8	2	347	324	158	150	1	3.48

Robert Leroy Kuzava, *Pitcher*

Throughout his major league career, the big, stern-looking southpaw was nicknamed "Sarge," and it was a moniker well earned. Before Kuzava received his first trial at the major league level, he donned Uncle Sam's khaki. Bob enlisted in the army and his military duties were law enforcement and installation security. Stationed at Camp Maxey with the 792nd Military Police Battalion, Bob was able to play some service ball but he didn't limit his military athletics to the ball diamond. The big Michigan native also took part in a boxing tournament on the installation.

After his discharge from the army, Kuzava hooked up with the Tribe for the 1946 season. Although Bob was joined on Cleveland's staff with some rather quality arms, including Bob Feller, Allie Reynolds and Bob Lemon, the team had the worst aggregate batting average of all American League clubs and finished in the second division. Kuzava is best known today as a member of some strong Yankees teams. Sarge was a hero in the 1952 World Series and was on the mound to record the final out in that Fall Classic. His skipper, Casey Stengel, applauded Bob's fireman work, stating after the game, "That fella Kuzava came in there and really took me out of a jam."

W	L	PCT	G	GS	CG	IP	H	BB	SO	SHO	ERA
49	44	.527	213	99	34	862	849	415	446	7	4.05

Alexander Kvasnak, *Outfield*

Kvasnak appeared in five games for the 1942 Senators—the extent of his major league career. The right-handed outfielder missed three years to service during World War II.

G	R	H	2B	3B	HR	RBI	BB	SO	SB	AVG	Slug
5	3	2	0	0	0	0	2	1	0	.182	.182

Clement Walter Labine, *Pitcher*

Perhaps the greatest relief pitcher of the 1950s, Labine spent every year of that decade putting out fires for the Dodgers. A great fireman, Labine was a fixture in the Dodgers' bullpen, first in Brooklyn and later in Los Angeles. Before his major league debut, Clem, who was a teenager throughout the war, served in the military in the conflict's latter stages.

W	L	PCT	G	GS	CG	IP	H	BB	SO	SHO	ERA
77	56	.579	513	38	7	1,080	1,043	396	551	2	3.63

Doyle Marion Lade, *Pitcher*

Short and stocky, Lade was nicknamed "Porky" by his peers. He spent five years at the major league level, all with the Cubs. Used as a long relief man and spot starter, Porky left the game for military duty during World War II. During the war, Lade served with the U.S. Coast Guard.

W	L	PCT	G	GS	CG	IP	H	BB	SO	SHO	ERA
25	29	.463	126	64	20	537	583	221	178	2	4.39

Joseph Lafata, *Outfield/First Base*

Lafata was notorious for his short temper. The Detroit native was often fined and thrown out of games for his disputes with umpires. One of his favorite pastimes was the throwing of baseball bats. Hot temper aside, Lafata served his country for a little over a year but was discharged early in 1944. His early heave-ho, unlike the ejections given by the umpires, was medical in nature, and he was able to play the 1944 season with the minor league Minneapolis Millers.

G	R	H	2B	3B	HR	RBI	BB	SO	SB	AVG	Slug
127	31	54	3	2	5	34	24	42	2	.229	.322

Richard Edward "Dick" Lajeskie, *Reserve*

A bonus-baby bust, Lajeskie was a talented, trim young ballplayer before the war but became the poster child for military training versus baseball training. During the war, Dick served in the U.S. Marine Corps and bulked up in the service, putting on muscle mass that he didn't have prior to his joining the Marines. Uncle Sam's fighting men needed to be strong and Dick adhered to the rigorous physical regimen of the Marine Corps. But the Giants weren't happy. After his discharge, Lajeskie had a new muscular body that the Giants felt was proper for war but poor for baseball. They only played their bonus baby in six games after the war and Lajeskie never reached his ball diamond potential.

G	R	H	2B	3B	HR	RBI	BB	SO	SB	AVG	Slug
6	3	2	0	0	0	0	3	2	0	.200	.200

Alfred Anthony LaMacchia, *Pitcher*

After LaMacchia's playing days he became a super scout with a long list of star players that he discovered. As a senior citizen baseball scout, Al was criticized when he backed a young ballplayer few thought would make it in fast company. But LaMacchia stuck behind the kid and Andre Ethier has become one of the top young stars in the National League. Al was a mop-up pitcher for the Browns during the war years and had a brief trial in the armed forces before an early discharge.

W	L	PCT	G	GS	CG	IP	H	BB	SO	SHO	ERA
2	2	.500	16	1	0	31	38	14	7	0	6.39

Frank Lamanna, *Pitcher*

A wild relief hurler, Lamanna spent three years at the major league level with the Braves before the war and didn't return to the club after his discharge. Frank was inducted into the army at Pittsburgh on February 19, 1943. He was assigned to the Overseas Replacement Depot in Kearns, Utah, after basic training. In Utah, Lamanna was able to continue playing baseball but was shipped overseas where he served in the South Pacific. He was part of a service team overseas named the Manila Dodgers.

W	L	PCT	G	GS	CG	IP	H	BB	SO	SHO	ERA
6	5	.545	45	5	1	93	95	67	28	0	5.23

Raymond Simond Lamanno, *Catcher*

Lamanno supplanted the great Ernie Lombardi as the Reds' starting catcher in 1942. He led all National League backstops in long balls in his rookie season while hitting the apple at a .264 clip. Ray was unable to build off his solid rookie campaign and was inducted into the navy after the season. He was stationed at Livermore Naval Air Station where he was asked to manage a service ball club. Lamanno played in a benefit game on the West Coast under his skipper, Hall of Fame second baseman Charlie Gehringer.

At Livermore, Ray took a training course in the refrigeration department. After his training had concluded, he was shipped overseas. Ray played service ball in Hawaii and participated in a navy all-star game held on Pearl Harbor. In the contest, Ray played with Stan Musial, and he and the Cardinal great swatted a long ball apiece. He returned to the Reds in 1946, four years after his solid rookie showing. Having led all NL catchers in home runs the year before the war, all Ray could muster upon his return was a single long ball during the entire 1946 campaign.

G	R	H	2B	3B	HR	RBI	BB	SO	SB	AVG	Slug
442	122	355	57	5	18	150	118	151	2	.252	.338

William Harmong Lamar, *Outfield*

"Good Time" Bill Lamar served his country in both World Wars. He missed a large portion of the 1918 season as a 21-year-old rookie major leaguer. Good Time Bill was a prototypical contact hitter — not drawing many walks and not striking out often. The bulk of his major league playing time came in the mid 1920s with Connie Mack's Philadelphia Athletics. Lamar's high-water season came in 1925 when he hit .356 as. Mack's regular left fielder.

G	R	H	2B	3B	HR	RBI	BB	SO	SB	AVG	Slug
550	303	633	114	23	19	245	86	78	25	.310	.417

Clayton Patrick Lambert, *Pitcher*

Lambert was one of the many young ballplayers who had his major league debut pushed back because of the war. When he finally received his call to the highest level, Clay was pushing thirty years of age. He only pitched two years at the major league level. Before his stint in the majors, Clay served with the Army Air Corps during World War II.

W	L	PCT	G	GS	CG	IP	H	BB	SO	SHO	ERA
2	2	.500	26	4	2	59	60	26	21	0	5.34

Eugene Marion Lambert, *Pitcher*

Lambert was another of the many ballplayers who saw the briefest of action at the major league level but served his country for three years during the war. Lambert made three appearances with the Phillies prior to the war and then was inducted into the army after the 1942 season. He never again reached the majors after his military discharge.

W	L	PCT	G	GS	CG	IP	H	BB	SO	SHO	ERA
0	1	.000	3	1	0	10	14	2	4	0	2.70

Jerald Hal Lane, *Pitcher*

Lane didn't make the major leagues until 1953, eight years after his discharge. Lane served with the navy during the war, in the conflict's latter stages as a teenager, and used the GI Bill to go to college. After matriculating at the university level, Jerry signed to play professional baseball. He spent one year with the Senators and two with the Reds.

W	L	PCT	G	GS	CG	IP	H	BB	SO	SHO	ERA
2	6	.250	31	2	0	79	84	25	33	0	4.44

Walter Oswald Lanfranconi, *Pitcher*

A mighty-mite, Little Lanfranconi stood at 5'7" and weighed just 155 pounds. With those dimensions, he was one of the slightest pitchers of his time. Walt pitched only two years at the major league level but lost four years to World War II. He made four appearances prior to the war and spent his military years with a combat outfit. He was initially able to play service ball at Fort Campbell, assigned to the 12th Armored Division, but was later shipped overseas and saw action in the European Theatre. Walt earned a pair of Battle Stars for his wartime heroics while serving on the frontlines with the 12th Armored Division.

W	L	PCT	G	GS	CG	IP	H	BB	SO	SHO	ERA
4	5	.444	38	5	1	70	72	29	19	0	2.96

Donald Charles Lang, *Third Base*

Don Lang played two years at the major league level. His first trial came with the 1938 Reds before the war and his second look was with the 1948 Cardinals after the conflict. Lang enlisted in the Army Air Corps during the Second World War. After training, he was shipped out to the Pacific Theatre. Able to play some service ball, Don participated in a service all-star game on the Hawaiian Islands with such notables as Hugh Casey, Enos Slaughter, Stan Musial and Billy Herman.

G	R	H	2B	3B	HR	RBI	BB	SO	SB	AVG	Slug
138	35	100	17	2	5	42	49	45	2	.268	.365

Hubert Max Lanier, *Pitcher*

Like his battery mate Walker Cooper, Lanier was able to play in the majors through most of the fighting. He and Cooper were both called to the colors early in the 1945 season and missed time on the ball diamond during the war's final year. A star southpaw, Lanier served in the army at Fort Bragg. After his discharge Max was one of a handful of players blacklisted by the majors for signing to play ball in Mexico. He was banished from the majors for two seasons until the ban was lifted in 1949.

W	L	PCT	G	GS	CG	IP	H	BB	SO	SHO	ERA
108	82	.568	327	204	91	1,619	1,490	611	821	21	3.01

John Young Lanning, *Pitcher*

A strike-thrower, Lanning, who was nicknamed "Tobacco Chewin' Johnny," pitched at the major league level with the Pirates and Braves. After posting a 2.33 ERA early in the 1943 baseball season, Lanning was inducted into the army before the All-Star break. He was stationed at Fort Riley with teammate Ken Heintzelman and returned to the Pirates at the end of the 1945 season.

W	L	PCT	G	GS	CG	IP	H	BB	SO	SHO	ERA
58	60	.492	278	104	30	1,072	1,078	358	295	4	3.58

Paul Edmore LaPalme, *Pitcher*

A southpaw knuckleball pitcher, LaPalme pitched at the major league level in the 1950s. Before he journeyed to the big league diamonds, LaPalme served with the United States Army at Camp McCoy, Wisconsin. The little southpaw made his debut with Billy Meyer's 1951 Pirates and his major league tenure came to a close with the 1957 White Sox of Hall of Famer Al Lopez.

W	L	PCT	G	GS	CG	IP	H	BB	SO	SHO	ERA
24	45	.348	253	51	10	616	645	272	277	2	4.42

Andrew Lapihuska, *Pitcher*

"Apples" pitched for the Phillies briefly in the 1942 and 1943 campaigns. He was ordered to report for military induction on July 7, 1943. Apples lost two and a half years to service in the army.

W	L	PCT	G	GS	CG	IP	H	BB	SO	SHO	ERA
0	2	.000	4	2	0	23	22	16	8	0	7.04

Ralph Robert LaPointe, *Shortstop/Second Base*

One of the few University of Vermont graduates to have played at the major league level, LaPointe would return to the campus after his playing days to coach the baseball club. But the war would come first and Ralph joined the Army Air Corps. Due to Ralph's French-Canadian heritage, the army groomed him to be a linguist. He was serving at Camp Ritchie at the time of his discharge. After the war, Ralph was promptly signed by the Phillies, who farmed him out and then called him up in 1947. He spent one year with the Phillies and the next season with the Cardinals. At the University of Vermont after his playing days, Ralph was a respected baseball coach whose life was cut short in his forties due to cancer.

G	R	H	2B	3B	HR	RBI	BB	SO	SB	AVG	Slug
143	60	115	10	0	1	30	35	34	9	.266	.296

Stephen Patrick Larkin, *Pitcher*

A power pitcher with a live arm and minimal accuracy, Larkin had a cup of coffee with the 1934 Tigers. The Tigers copped the American League pennant that year with a terrific pitching staff of Schoolboy Rowe, Tommy Bridges, Firpo Marberry and Eldon Auker. Given that sort of talent on the mound, Larkin's role was minimized. Steve joined the army during World War II and served in the European Theatre as one of the few ballplayers stationed at Greenland.

W	L	PCT	G	GS	CG	IP	H	BB	SO	SHO	ERA
0	0	—	2	1	0	6	8	5	8	0	1.50

Thomas Charles Lasorda, *Pitcher*

Hall of Fame skipper Tommy Lasorda had a wild career in the majors as a pitcher. The squat southpaw pitched 58 innings in the majors and walked an alarmingly high total of batters—nearly one walk per inning. A teenager when the war began Lasorda served briefly during the latter stages of the great conflict.

W	L	PCT	G	GS	CG	IP	H	BB	SO	SHO	ERA
0	4	.000	26	6	0	58	53	56	37	0	6.52

Harry Arthur "Cookie" Lavagetto, *Third Base*

Cookie was a major league veteran when World War II broke out, having spent three years with the Pirates and five years with the Dodgers before the United States got involved. Showing praiseworthy patriotism, Lavagetto enlisted in the Naval Reserve despite his 3-A classification before the start of the 1942 baseball season. A good third baseman who led the Dodgers in hitting during the 1939 campaign, Lavagetto was a multi-faceted ballplayer who possessed modest pop and often stole more than ten bases a season.

Upon his enlistment, Lavagetto sought an occupation with the Naval Air Corps, as the hot corner man owned an amateur pilot's license. He was inducted as a machinist's mate in the Naval Reserve and was sent to a base in Oakland. While serving at the Oakland Naval Base, Cookie was named the manager of a service ballclub on the installation. He was later shipped overseas and managed a service team in the Hawaiian League that boasted the amazing talents of Stan Musial. Cookie received his discharge from the navy in October of 1945 and played two more years with the Dodgers—his talents almost completely eroded from his long stint in the service.

G	R	H	2B	3B	HR	RBI	BB	SO	SB	AVG	Slug
1,043	487	945	183	37	40	486	485	244	63	.269	.377

John Leonard "Doc" Lavan, *Shortstop*

With the advent of the Lively Ball Era in 1920, batting averages across America began to spike. Lavan, never much of a hitter before, saw his batting mark rise to .289 in 1920, but he was the only member of the Redbirds infield that failed to hit .300. His average fell below .260 in 1921 while his infield mates, Rogers Hornsby, Jack Fournier and Milt Stock, all easily eclipsed the .300 mark again. He lost his job to Specs Toporcer in 1922 and was done as a major leaguer by 1924. Doc joined the navy during World War II. During the Second World War Lavan served as the senior medical officer at the Toledo Training Station.

G	R	H	2B	3B	HR	RBI	BB	SO	SB	AVG	Slug
1,162	338	954	134	45	7	377	209	376	71	.245	.308

Garland Fred Lawing, *Outfield*

Considered a top outfield prospect when inducted into the service, Lawing was hampered greatly by the interruption in his career. The top flight recruit never could get his timing back and failed to hit during his trial in 1946, spent with the Giants and Reds.

G	R	H	2B	3B	HR	RBI	BB	SO	SB	AVG	Slug
10	2	2	0	0	0	0	5	0	.133	.133

Brooks Ulysses Lawrence, *Pitcher*

During World War II it looked as if Brooks Lawrence was going to become a career soldier. He joined the army during the war, but when the war ended and many young men returned to their pre-war occupations, Lawrence stayed in the service. He remained with Uncle Sam until 1948 when he signed a contract to pitch in the Negro Leagues. The right-hander quickly attracted the attention of major league scouts and joined the Cardinals chain. Brooks was nicknamed "Bull" because he projected a no-nonsense demeanor and had an unrivalled work ethic. He pitched for St. Louis and the Reds during the 1950s and amassed 69 career wins.

W	L	PCT	G	GS	CG	IP	H	BB	SO	SHO	ERA
69	62	.527	275	127	42	1,041	1,034	385	481	5	4.25

Alfred Voyle "Roxie" Lawson, *Pitcher*

A wild mop-up pitcher during the 1930s, Lawson was the type of pitcher a team would bring in to chew up innings in a lost affair. Roxie's right arm packed little accuracy but it could be stretched out. His last big league trial came with the Browns in 1940. With the war underway, Lawson enlisted in the navy the same day as outfielder Hub Walker. Roxie, who claimed that Bill Dickey was the toughest batter he ever faced, served as a recruiter during the war.

W	L	PCT	G	GS	CG	IP	H	BB	SO	SHO	ERA
47	39	.547	208	83	34	852	963	512	258	2	5.37

Peter John Layden, *Outfield*

A gifted natural athlete, Layden played one year in the major leagues with the 1948 Browns. His career in professional football lasted quite a bit longer. The Texan was able to play some sports in the service during World War II.

G	R	H	2B	3B	HR	RBI	BB	SO	SB	AVG	Slug
41	11	26	2	1	0	4	6	10	4	.250	.288

Ivoria Hillis Layne, *Third Base*

Layne played professional baseball at peak capacity for a short amount of time. While an All-Star in the minor leagues and one of Washington's top prospects, Hillis was diagnosed with Typhus Fever. The illness settled in his left leg and he had to be operated on, which reduced his mobility and limited his baseball skill. Layne said, "I have had, and still have it now, an aluminum plate in my leg. I'm not trying to cry over it, but I think about how easy it would have been to be able to play in top-notch shape—without any pain." Although the affliction hindered his baseball playing, Layne was still a perennial .300 hitter in the minors.

With World War II underway in 1942, Layne was summoned by his draft board for a physical. The year before, Layne was an All-Star third baseman at his hometown of Chattanooga, but he'd have to put his baseball career on hold. Layne said, "I was called to military service in 1942 but the army turned me down because of my leg. But a month or two later they recalled me to take more tests and accepted me for service." Inducted into the Army Air Corps, Layne was stationed at Keesler Field, Mississippi. He found that his surgically repaired leg couldn't withstand the intense army training of constant ruck-marches and war preparation. When the pain became too much to tolerate, Layne was hospitalized for a time before receiving his medical discharge.

Hillis Layne missed two years of baseball to the army but returned to the Senators in 1944 to help their war ravaged roster. Gone were star hitters Cecil Travis and Buddy Lewis, and Layne helped fill their void when he hit a point under .300 in the Senators' second-place finish in 1945. Meanwhile, his former AAF unit was sent overseas and was engaged in combat action. Reminiscing, Layne said, "I went into service with many boys at Keesler Field, and most all my buddies didn't come home. They gave their lives while I was playing a game. I'll always think about the loss of the kids I went into service with. Most all my buddies were killed at Normandy, so what I'm trying to say is that I was fortunate to have something happen to me or I would have been right there with them."

At the end of the war, Lewis and Travis returned to Washington and Layne was pushed to a reserve capacity. He could have easily made the Senators team in 1946 but their top farm club was his hometown of Chattanooga and the Lookouts owner, Joe Engel, requested that the Senators send him the hometown boy for a drawing card. So back to the minors Layne went, but not before he fulfilled a promise he made to his mother as a boy. His hero was Babe Ruth, and he once told his mother that someday he'd hit a home run at Yankee Stadium just like Ruth. The record books show that Layne hit all of one home run in the majors, but it was the shot that he promised his mother. Hillis said, "I told myself that I'd better fulfill my promise, so I hit a home run and when I got to second base I started crying. I said, 'Momma, I made it.' It seemed like the end of the world. I got teared up a little bit, then said to myself, 'These are men, they're not sissies.' So I couldn't do that, but got by with it anyway."

G	R	H	2B	3B	HR	RBI	BB	SO	SB	AVG	Slug
107	37	75	9	4	1	28	20	22	3	.264	.335

Lester Lee Layton, *Outfield*

An underused outfielder with a solid Slugging percentage, Layton spent one season at the major league level with the 1948 Giants. Layton legged out four triples in under 100 at-bats. During the war, Les served with the United States Navy.

G	R	H	2B	3B	HR	RBI	BB	SO	SB	AVG	Slug
63	14	21	4	4	2	12	6	21	1	.231	.429

Wilfrid Henry "Bill" Lefebvre, *Pitcher*

Lefebvre pitched briefly for the Boston Red Sox in the late 1930s and didn't resurface at the major league level until World War II had opened roster space. A tremendous hitting pitcher, Bill belted a home run in his first major league at-bat. With the war raging overseas, Bill took an off-season job at a New England defense plant. He received his draft notice after the 1944 baseball season and missed the 1945 campaign to service in the army. The former Holy Cross star was inducted at Fort Banks and served his time at Fort Devens.

W	L	PCT	G	GS	CG	IP	H	BB	SO	SHO	ERA
5	5	.500	36	10	3	132	162	51	36	0	5.05

Paul Eugene Lehner, *Outfield/First Base*

The Alabama native served in the Army Air Corps before he made his major league debut. Stationed at the San Antonio Aviation Cadet Center, Paul played plenty of service ball and was on a squad with Hall of Famer Enos Slaughter for a time. Lehner was then transferred to the Pre-Flight School, which forced him to quit the San Antonio ballclub. After a stint at Kelly Field, Paul was shipped overseas where he was stationed at Guam. He returned stateside in 1945 and was mustered out in Alabama.

Lehner would break into the majors the following year with the Browns. He played briefly but impressed the team in 1947 spring training. New skipper Muddy Ruel, a World War I veteran, named Paul his everyday center fielder in 1947 and he was the toughest strikeout victim among Brownie regulars. Lehner would play with the Browns through 1949. His career became nomadic as he played with the A's, White Sox, Indians, Red Sox and a return to the Browns from 1950 to 1952.

G	R	H	2B	3B	HR	RBI	BB	SO	SB	AVG	Slug
540	175	455	80	21	22	197	127	118	6	.257	.364

Edgar Ellsworth Leip, *Second Base*

Leip was a reserve infielder for four seasons at the major league level, first with the Washington Senators in 1939 and with the Pirates from 1940 to 1942. Never able to play regularly, Ed had a reputation on the ball diamond for his gritty play and fighting spirit. He took that fighting spirit to Uncle Sam late in 1942, which officially ended his major league career.

Inducted as a private in 1942, Leip was the first Pirates player to be sent overseas. He took part in the African Campaign and saw combat action in several battlefields at Italy. Although he joined the army as a private, Ed had aspirations of joining the commissioned officer ranks. While serving overseas, Ed received his commission in 1945. After the promotion, Ed wrote Pirates president William Benswanger, stating that he hoped he would be "able to fill [the position] satisfactorily."

G	R	H	2B	3B	HR	RBI	BB	SO	SB	AVG	Slug
30	7	17	1	2	0	5	3	6	1	.274	.355

Robert Granville Lemon, *Pitcher/Third Base*

Hall of Fame pitcher Bob Lemon was a poor-hitting third baseman at the time of his military induction. He spent three years in the navy and returned to the Tribe as a far-from-finished product. The Indians still viewed Lemon as a position player, and skipper Lou Boudreau named him the 1946 Opening Day starter in center field. However, when he couldn't raise his average over .200, Boudreau sent Bob to the bullpen — and the rest is history.

W	L	PCT	G	GS	CG	IP	H	BB	SO	SHO	ERA
207	128	.618	460	350	188	2,849	2,559	1,251	1,277	31	3.23

Donald Eugene Lenhardt, *Outfield*

A power-hitting outfielder with good plate discipline, Lenhardt was nicknamed "Footsie" on account of his lack of speed. Minus the feet of Mercury, Don was still a solid offensive force in the Browns lineup in the early 1950s. The tall outfielder from Illinois served in the military prior to reaching the major leagues. In 1942, Lenhardt joined the Merchant Marines at St. Louis and was sent to Sheepshead Bay, New York. The following year, he transferred to the navy and served at the Great Lakes Naval Training Station.

G	R	H	2B	3B	HR	RBI	BB	SO	SB	AVG	Slug
481	192	401	64	9	61	239	214	235	6	.271	.450

John Joseph Leovich, *Reserve*

Leovich played in one game at the major league level and legged out a double for his only big league hit. John played with Connie Mack's 1941 Athletics before the war. During the war, Leovich, a baseball and football star at Oregon State, joined the U.S. Coast Guard and played some service ball with major leaguers Sibby Sisti and Marv Rickert.

G	R	H	2B	3B	HR	RBI	BB	SO	SB	AVG	Slug
1	0	1	1	0	0	0	0	0	0	.500	1.000

George Edward Lerchen, *Outfield*

Before Lerchen made his major league debut, he served in the navy during World War II. George reported to the Great Lakes Naval Training Station in 1943 and served for the duration. It took him seven years after his discharge to make the majors with his hometown Tigers.

G	R	H	2B	3B	HR	RBI	BB	SO	SB	AVG	Slug
36	3	10	2	0	1	5	12	16	1	.204	.306

Charlie Letchas, *Utility Infielder*

Letchas played sporadically at the major league level; his first action came with the 1939 Phillies. He spent the 1940 season in the bushes and returned to the majors in 1941 with the Senators. It was back to the bushes for the 1942 and 1943 seasons but the Phillies reacquired him in 1944, when he played in 116 games. Charlie was lost to the military in 1945 when he was inducted into the army on March 23, 1945. He was stationed at Fort McPherson and returned to the Phillies in 1946 to play briefly under skipper Ben Chapman. After his playing career ended, Letchas managed at the minor league level with Anniston and Richmond.

G	R	H	2B	3B	HR	RBI	BB	SO	SB	AVG	Slug
136	32	108	10	0	1	37	35	31	0	.234	.262

Jesse Roy Levan, *Reserve*

One of baseball's noted scabs, Levan was blacklisted from the game in 1959 when he was accused of serving as a go-between for gamblers who fixed games. A member of the Chattanooga Lookouts when he took part in underhanded action, Jesse was expelled from the game due in large part to testimony given by Lookouts coach Sammy Meeks. During the war, the young Levan served in the military in the conflict's latter stages.

G	R	H	2B	3B	HR	RBI	BB	SO	SB	AVG	Slug
25	5	10	0	0	1	5	0	2	0	.286	.371

Edward Clarence Levy, *First Base/Outfield*

Levy saw the bulk of his playing time with the Yankees during the war years. A natural first baseman, Levy had to patrol the outfield because New York had one of the best Sluggers during the war-era manning first in Nick Etten. Levy had joined the U.S. Coast Guard but was deemed unfit for duty and was medically discharged.

G	R	H	2B	3B	HR	RBI	BB	SO	SB	AVG	Slug
54	17	42	11	2	4	32	10	24	2	.215	.354

John Kelly "Buddy" Lewis, *Outfield/Third Base*

A tremendous offensive talent, Buddy Lewis made his major league debut as an 18-year-old with the 1935 Senators. In his first full major league season, Lewis smacked 175 base hits—topped only by Red Rolfe and Odell Hale as far as AL third basemen were concerned. He led the American League in at-bats during the 1937 season and stole seventeen bases in 1938. He paced the league in triples during the 1939 campaign while he hit at a hefty .319 clip. Buddy continued to hit for a robust average in 1940, when he batted .317 and rotated between right field and third base. In his last year before the war, Lewis drew a team-high 82 walks and legged out eleven triples. Given all these impressive ball diamond credentials, one would figure Lewis to be in the class of baseball's elite. However, he lost the better part of four years to service in the military, where John Kelly Lewis became a true hero.

Buddy Lewis applied for deferment to earn his 1941 baseball salary to support his parents. Of the deferment request, Lewis said, "They just smiled and I knew what that meant." He was, however, granted two deferments to support his folks but was inducted into the Army Air Corps after the end of the 1941 baseball season. He took his basic training at Fort Knox, Kentucky. Concerning basic training, Buddy said, "Spring training never was like this, and neither were the hours."

Although he had to get boot camp out of the way, Lewis was eager to get inside a cockpit and start flying. After he finished basic training, he was reassigned to Lubbock Army Flying School in Texas. While in Texas the hours of ground school made Lewis forlorn as he said, "So far, we haven't even been close to a plane." He would go on to earn his wings at Lubbock and looked forward to doing his part overseas. Buddy said, "Maybe I can bat 1.000 against that Japanese pitching. It should be a cinch after swinging at Marius Russo's sinker."

Buddy Lewis was shipped overseas and served as a transport pilot in the CBI Theatre. He flew material to Burma over some of the toughest military terrain and even dropped down to a base at the exact moment the Japanese were trying to recapture it. Unlike many ballplayers, Lewis saw heavy action in the war zone, as he participated in the Allied Airborne Flanking Attack in Northern Burma during March of 1944. He flew one of the first troop carrier towing transports that made the hazardous attack on the Japanese rear positions in Burma. In total, Lewis flew 368 missions during World War II.

A friend of Buddy Lewis' named Johnny Derr, a sportswriter, was stationed overseas near him for a time. Derr wrote, "Buddy's only 1,200 miles away from where I'm stationed. I send him a special baseball roundup each day. He's a captain now and one helluva flyer. He's probably in this war deeper than any ballplayer in uniform."

Buddy was awarded three Distinguished Flying Crosses and three Air Medals for his heroics during the war. His citation for one of his Distinguished Flying Crosses read,

For extraordinary achievement in aerial flight during which exposure to enemy fire was probable and expected. Flying transport aircraft carrying a normal load, in addition to towing two heavy-loaded gliders, he took off at night for a point 200 miles behind enemy positions in Burma.... Due to the proximity of the enemy and the necessity of surprise, the entire flight was made without radio aid, requiring the highest degree of piloting skill to avoid mid-air crashes either with aircraft in the towing unit or other nearby units on the mission.

A favorite Buddy Lewis story concerns one written by Sergeant Ed Cunningham for *Stars and Stripes*. Cunningham wrote an article about Lewis' visit to Griffith Stadium, home of his beloved Washington Senators, while on furlough from the Army Air Corps. Lewis participated in fielding drills and took batting practice that day but was unable to stay for the game because he was due to report back to his unit. Before he left the stadium, he told teammate George Case, the fleet-footed outfielder, that he would swing back by for a final curtain call.

Lewis told Case, "I'll be back precisely at 4:30, and then it will be 'so long' until the war is over."

"Can you find the field?" Case asked.

"Sure," Buddy replied. "I'll zoom down across center field on the dot of 4:30, split the diamond and cross over home plate."

As fate would have it, Case was at bat at 4:29 during the second game of a doubleheader. While standing in the batter's box, he could see a plane approaching the diamond in the distance. Knowing exactly who it was, Case stepped out of the box and casually tapped his cleats, knocking loose the built-up dirt on his footwear. He didn't want to take a chance of having a play in progress as Lewis said his final goodbye to Griffith Stadium. Cunningham writes, "Just as the scoreboard clock struck 4:30, the huge transport plane roared over the centerfield fence, dipped low over the diamond, then zoomed upward as it passed home plate. Case threw a resin bag high in the air as his own farewell."

G	R	H	2B	3B	HR	RBI	BB	SO	SB	AVG	Slug
1,349	830	1,563	249	93	71	607	573	303	83	.297	.420

Rufus Lewis, *Pitcher*

A former Negro League All-Star Game starting pitcher, Lewis was noted for his knuckleball and fine control of the pitch. Although Rufus had a brief trial in the Negro Leagues before the war, he failed to establish himself. That all changed in the army. While serving in the Army Air Corps, Lewis mastered his repertoire of pitches and signed with Newark after his discharge. He had to play third fiddle to Leon Day and Max Manning, but the three pitching stars led the Eagles to a World Series win in 1946. When the Negro Leagues began losing players to the majors, Rufus was a sought-after pitcher but he couldn't agree to terms with the Dodgers and went to Mexico to play. Nearly killed in a game in the Mexican League, Lewis was beaten with a bat when a player he low-bridged charged the mound and clubbed him.

(1936–1952): Newark Eagles, Pittsburgh Crawfords and Houston Eagles

Donald Eugene Liddle, *Pitcher*

The wiry southpaw enlisted in the navy after high school graduation. It would take Liddle another ten years to make the major league level. Don eventually got his first look with the Braves in 1953 — their first year in Milwaukee. Liddle is best known today as the pitcher Vic Wertz tagged in the World Series when Willie Mays made his famous over-the-shoulder catch. Right after Mays hauled the ball in, the Giants skipper came out to the mound to relieve Liddle. Liddle casually surrendered the ball and told the manager, "Well, I got my man."

W	L	PCT	G	GS	CG	IP	H	BB	SO	SHO	ERA
28	18	.609	117	54	13	428	397	203	198	3	3.74

Charles Edwin "Dutch" Lieber, *Pitcher*

Lieber was called up to Philadelphia in 1935 after Connie Mack had traded away most of his talent from his dynasty of earlier years. The following year, Lieber's last in the majors, Mack traded Jimmie Foxx to Boston, and the talent pool in the Athletics chain was shallow. Dutch took what he learned from Mack and applied it at the minor league level as a skipper in the bushes.

When the war broke out, Lieber was managing the Medford entry in the Oregon-California Baseball League. His Oakland draft board gave him his notice in the fall of 1942 and he left the Medford dugout for the duration. Dutch would spend the next three years in the army; when he was mustered out, he had reached the rank of sergeant.

W	L	PCT	G	GS	CG	IP	H	BB	SO	SHO	ERA
1	2	.333	21	1	0	59	62	25	15	0	3.97

William Beverly Lillard, *Shortstop*

After Ted Williams signed with the Red Sox, Lillard was regarded as the best prospect the Pacific Coast League had to offer. While the Splendid Splinter was tearing up the American League, the Athletics decided to sign the consolation prize in Bill Lillard late in the season. He didn't reach his potential and the A's were done with him after the 1940 season. Bill went back to the bushes but had an interruption in his career courtesy the war. He joined the colors but wasn't able to make his way back to the majors after his discharge.

G	R	H	2B	3B	HR	RBI	BB	SO	SB	AVG	Slug
80	30	55	9	2	1	22	31	29	0	.244	.316

Robert Eugene "Gene" Lillard, *Pitcher*

The elder brother of former PCL star Bill Lillard, Gene played briefly at the major league level with the Cubs and Cardinals before the war. When the war broke out, Gene was back in the bushes. In 1943, he wired Sacramento Solons president Phil Bartelme and informed him that he was quitting baseball to remain on his defense job. However, shortly after that wire was sent, Uncle Sam sent Gene a wire that informed him of his draft notice.

W	L	PCT	G	GS	CG	IP	H	BB	SO	SHO	ERA
3	6	.333	22	8	2	60	76	40	33	0	7.05

Louis Limmer, *First Base*

A big power-hitting first baseman, Limmer was a top-notch athlete in many sports in high school. Lou was the captain of his basketball, swimming, boxing and track teams. Limmer left the schoolyard and joined the Army Air Corps before he signed his first pro contract. After his discharge, he signed with the Athletics and played for the first A's team not managed by Connie Mack.

G	R	H	2B	3B	HR	RBI	BB	SO	SB	AVG	Slug
209	66	107	19	4	19	62	63	77	3	.202	.360

Lyman Gilbert Linde, *Pitcher*

Linde had yet to make his major league debut before the war. Removed from the minor leagues to help out during World War II, Lyman served in the United States Army Signal Corps. The right-hander pitched a few games with the 1948 world champion Indians.

W	L	PCT	G	GS	CG	IP	H	BB	SO	SHO	ERA
0	0	—	4	0	0	11	12	5	0	0	6.55

John Harlan Lindell, *Outfield*

Considered by many critics to be a war-era ballplayer, Lindell did play before the mass exodus and stuck around after the war.

His best years clearly came during the war, but Lindell was a fine ballplayer regardless the era he played in. Johnny led the American League in triples in both the 1943 and 1944 seasons but was unable to make it a hat trick in 1945 when he was inducted into the service. In June of 1945, Johnny was accepted for service. On the same day that Lindell was okayed by Uncle Sam, he rejected Lindell's New York teammate Snuffy Stirnweiss once again on account of ulcers.

G	R	H	2B	3B	HR	RBI	BB	SO	SB	AVG	Slug
854	401	762	124	48	72	404	289	366	17	.273	.429

Walter Charles Linden, *Catcher*

Linden's major league career consisted of three games with the 1950 Braves. The stout catcher Slugged at a Ruthian clip in his short trial. Before he made his major league debut, Walt served in the military during World War II.

G	R	H	2B	3B	HR	RBI	BB	SO	SB	AVG	Slug
3	0	2	1	0	0	0	1	0	0	.400	.600

Royce James Lint, *Pitcher*

A southern left-hander who married a northern lady, Lint's bride wasn't steeped on baseball lingo when she met Royce. She had often heard her beau referred to as a "southpaw" and just assumed the term was a comment on his heritage. Wilma Lint said, "I once thought a southpaw meant someone from the South, and when I learned this was wrong, I was ashamed to show my ignorance."

A fine pitching prospect before the war, Lint was leading the Interstate League in wins at the time he received his draft notice from Uncle Sam. Inducted into the military, Royce played some service ball at New Cumberland before he was assigned to Maxwell Field. While playing service ball there, Lint tossed a no-hitter against a team of soldiers from Craig Field. The southpaw was then transferred to Smyrna Army Airfield in Tennessee.

W	L	PCT	G	GS	CG	IP	H	BB	SO	SHO	ERA
2	3	.400	30	4	1	70	75	30	36	1	4.89

John Joseph Lipon, *Shortstop*

Nicknamed "Skids," Johnny Lipon was a sure-handed, underrated shortstop who possessed a keen batting eye. Skids walked twice as much as he struck out during his career, something rarely witnessed in the modern swing-and-miss era that the game has devolved into. Birdie Tebbetts said, "He would have been the greatest shortstop who ever lived if his career hadn't been interrupted by the war when he was flying planes for three years in the navy. He had the greatest baseball hands I ever seen and he could hit a baseball."

Lipon was just a kid of nineteen years when he made his major league debut in 1942. Skids played in 34 games that year for the Tigers before he was drafted into the United States Navy Air Corps. Johnny graduated from the air gunner school and received the coveted Naval Air Crewman's Wings. He was then assigned to the naval airbase at Jacksonville but before long was shipped overseas to a location described as "somewhere in action." Before getting shipped out, Johnny said, "I'll bet laying my 50-caliber machine gun on those Jap-a-Nastys won't hurt my eye any when I get back at home plate with my favorite bat in hand."

A prolific gunner, Skids set a record for striking moving targets with a 50-caliber machine gun at Yellow River Gunnery School. He packed up his keen eye and took it with him overseas, as Johnny flew casualties out of the Okinawa region during the war. Skids returned to the game in 1946 but played sparingly until a place was cleared for him in 1948. In his first year as a regular at the major league level, Skids hit .290 and posted an amazing 68-to-22 walks to-strikeouts ratio. His finest year came in 1950 as a 27-year-old; he hit .293 with 104 runs scored and posted an eye-popping walks to-strikeouts ratio of 81-to-26.

He was traded to the Red Sox in 1952 and finished his playing days with the Reds in 1954. With his playing career concluded, Skids embarked on a stellar minor league coaching career. Having learned a lot about the game from his minor league coach, catching star Steve O'Neill, Skids took his lessons learned and applied them to his charges. He is widely regarded as assisting Sudden Sam McDowell through his early bouts of wildness and making the southpaw one of the game's most dominant hurlers.

G	R	H	2B	3B	HR	RBI	BB	SO	SB	AVG	Slug
758	351	690	95	24	10	266	347	152	28	.259	.324

Daniel Webster Litwhiler, *Outfield*

In the same fashion as Phillies outfielder Ron Northey, Litwhiler was rejected by the military due to medical issues. There was a media fiasco regarding athletes who had been placed on limited duty, as both Northey and Litwhiler were inducted into the armed forces in 1945 despite failing numerous military medical exams. Danny was initially classified 4-F due to a knee injury, but after five re-examinations he was accepted for duty. Litwhiler was sent to the New Cumberland Reception Center under limited service guidelines and missed one year of baseball to military service.

Danny became a case study for an Illinois politician named Price who felt there were "draft discriminations against professional athletes." Price protested that some athletes were inducted even though they failed to meet physical requirements. To make his case, Price cited Litwhiler's service record, which read, "This registrant cannot be considered a soldier against your quota whether he is called by the army or navy because he does not meet the minimum requirements for military training." Although politicians spoke on the behalf of players like Danny and Ron Northey, the players were eager to do their part. Litwhiler said, "[I'm glad] it's over with. Now I know where I stand after a year of uncertainty."

G	R	H	2B	3B	HR	RBI	BB	SO	SB	AVG	Slug
1,057	428	982	162	32	107	451	299	377	11	.281	.438

Everett Adrian "Buddy" Lively, *Pitcher*

A spot starter-long relief pitcher for three years with the Reds in the late 1940s, Lively was a strong-armed Birmingham native with good speed. Buddy threw a one-hitter against the vaunted Brooklyn Dodgers squad when he was a rookie. Before his major league days began, Lively served in the United States Army during the war.

W	L	PCT	G	GS	CG	IP	H	BB	SO	SHO	ERA
8	13	.381	79	27	6	249	230	127	94	2	4.15

Wesley Amos Livengood, *Pitcher*

Livengood had a cup of coffee with the National League pennant-winning Reds of 1939. The tall right-hander from North Carolina pitched five games at the major league level. During the war, Wes served at the Bainbridge Naval Training Station where he shut out Connie Mack's Athletics in a pick-up game in 1944. Later, he was shipped out and served in the Pacific Theatre.

W	L	PCT	G	GS	CG	IP	H	BB	SO	SHO	ERA
0	0	—	5	0	0	6	9	3	4	0	9.00

Thompson Orville "Mickey" Livingston, *Catcher*

A journeyman catcher, Mickey played with the Senators, Phillies, Cubs, Giants, Braves and Dodgers. He served as Bennie Warren's backup in Philadelphia but was the Cubs regular catcher in 1945, the year they went to the World Series. Mickey hit the apple at a .364 clip in the 1945 Fall Classic. He was inducted into the army in 1944, but after spending a year there, he received a medical discharge and returned to catch for the Cubs.

G	R	H	2B	3B	HR	RBI	BB	SO	SB	AVG	Slug
561	128	354	56	9	19	153	144	141	7	.238	.326

Robert Kenneth Loane, *Outfield*

Loane's major league career consisted of two cups of coffee with the 1939 Senators and the 1940 Boston Braves. A swift outfielder with a decent eye at the plate, Bob didn't hit for the robust averages that players of the day were registering. A minor league veteran, Loane left the bushes during World War II to cast his lot with Uncle Sam. Bob joined the army and like many former players kept in touch with old ball-playing chums stateside. While in the service, Loane kept former teammate George Barnicle abreast of his endeavors.

When Loane was to be married, he was toiling in the minor leagues for a team owned by quick-thinking Joe Cambria. Cambria, like most executives, was always looking for ways to make a buck and when he heard Bob's plans to wed, he convinced the outfielder to perform the ceremony at the ball diamond. One of the first players to get married on the dirt field of a baseball diamond, Loane was able to persuade his bride to take the vows within the white lines because Mr. Cambria promised the couple a portion of the gate receipts.

G	R	H	2B	3B	HR	RBI	BB	SO	SB	AVG	Slug
16	6	5	3	0	0	2	6	9	2	.161	.258

Carroll Walter "Whitey" Lockman, *Outfield*

A solid left-hand bat for the Giants, Lockman was with the club from 1945 to 1956 and returned to the team after a brief look with the Cardinals. Lockman was a teenager when the war began and saw action in the military in the conflict's latter stages. He served in the Merchant Marines from September 15, 1944, to May of 1945 and saw his first major league action in the 1945 season. At the tender age of 18, Whitey paced the Giants with a .341 batting average but left for the army in August of that season. He missed the entire 1946 campaign to the army and was discharged in January of 1947. A broken ankle limited his baseball duties in 1947, but by 1948 Lockman became a valuable ingredient of the Giants, leading the club in hits, runs scored and triples in his first full season.

G	R	H	2B	3B	HR	RBI	BB	SO	SB	AVG	Slug
1,666	836	1,658	222	49	114	563	552	383	43	.279	.391

Dario Joseph Lodigiani, *Third Base*

Originally signed by Connie Mack for the Athletics, Lodigiani had a couple of good years in Philadelphia before the war. Traded to the White Sox, Dario had to fight for playing time on the infield with Don Kolloway and Bob Kennedy. He bested his teammates with a .280 batting average in 1942 but would be lost to the war effort the next three seasons.

Inducted into the Army Air Corps, Lodigiani was able to play some service ball stateside with Browns center fielder Walt Judnich. He would later get shipped overseas, where he was stationed at Hawaii for a time. He said, "I served in the B-29 outfit, the 73rd Palm Service Group. We watched the big B-29s take off and come back. We took care of the planes and all so it was kind of interesting." Dario would later see service at various Pacific locales, such as Saipan and Guam. After his days in the military, Lodigiani returned to baseball where he remained until his passing, still an active scout with the White Sox into his nineties.

G	R	H	2B	3B	HR	RBI	BB	SO	SB	AVG	Slug
405	142	355	71	7	16	156	141	86	12	.260	.358

John Logan, *Shortstop*

One of the best shortstops of the 1950s, Logan was a member of the final Boston Braves team as well as the inaugural Milwaukee Braves club. Logan was a teenager throughout the war as he joined the colors near the end when he came of age. Johnny was a terrific shortstop on into the early 1960s and was famous for his Yogi Berra-like malapropisms.

G	R	H	2B	3B	HR	RBI	BB	SO	SB	AVG	Slug
1,503	651	1,407	216	41	93	547	451	472	19	.268	.378

Jack Wayne Lohrke, *Utility Infielder*

Many of Jack Lohrke's baseball cards list his nickname of "Lucky." He wasn't the type of man who came about his alias via comical reasons. The nickname stuck with Lohrke throughout his career, although it was a moniker he didn't approve of. He knew he was lucky and didn't feel it was necessary to explain to those not in the know why he was referred to by such a handle. But his good fortune began while he was serving his country during World War II.

A combat soldier during the Great War, Lohrke was engaged in the Battle of the Bulge. The third-base prospect witnessed heavy fighting in the ETO but was able to return home unscathed. While he was being mustered out at Camp Kilmer, Jack was bumped from a military flight when they unexpectedly reached full capacity on the vessel. The plane, which was en route to the West Coast, crashed after refueling; there were no survivors. But that was only the beginning of how Lohrke came across the nickname.

After his military discharge, Jack caught on with the Spokane Indians. One of the top players on the club, Lohrke received notice of his callup to the majors at the nick of time. He was aboard the

Indians' bus but stepped off after he received word that the Giants needed him right away. In the most tragic event in baseball history, the Spokane Indians bus was traveling in the mountains, shortly after Lohrke departed the vehicle, when the driver swerved to avoid a car that was driving in the wrong lane. The bus crashed through the guard railing and plummeted hundreds of feet down the mountain. Most of the players on the bus died in the crash while Lohrke escaped his brush with death for the second time.

G	R	H	2B	3B	HR	RBI	BB	SO	SB	AVG	Slug
354	125	221	38	9	22	96	111	86	9	.242	.375

Victor Alvin Lombardi, *Pitcher*

A diminutive southpaw, Lombardi served briefly with the United States Navy during the war. He made his debut during the war-interrupted season of 1945 after he was mustered out of the navy. Lombardi pitched three seasons with Brooklyn, followed by three more with the Pirates. He ended his career one victory below a .500 win percentage.

W	L	PCT	G	GS	CG	IP	H	BB	SO	SHO	ERA
50	51	.495	223	100	42	945	919	418	340	5	3.68

Stanley Edward Lopata, *Catcher*

One of the top power-hitting catchers of his era, Lopata was a young man when he joined the colors during World War II. The Slugging backstop from Delray, Michigan, enlisted in the army and after basic training was assigned to the 14th Armored Division. Lopata and his battle buddies were shipped overseas to the European Theatre of Operations where they were actively engaged in combat maneuvers. He witnessed first hand the fighting that so many athletes were able to avoid.

After Lopata returned home, he was given an honorable discharge and took up baseball. Behind the dish, where batted balls and foul tips run amok, Lopata was one of the few receivers to perform bespectacled. A glasses-wearing catcher was an unusual sight on the ball diamond, as was one with the raw power of Lopata. Stan had to bide his time behind another Slugging backstop, Andy Seminick, before his chance at starting, duty came about. After Seminick was shipped away, he platooned with Smoky Burgess for a couple of years before Seminick returned and Lopata platooned with him. Stan blasted 22 homers in 1955 and then followed that up with a team-high 32 dingers in 1956 when he was the everyday catcher.

G	R	H	2B	3B	HR	RBI	BB	SO	SB	AVG	Slug
853	375	661	116	25	116	397	393	497	18	.254	.452

Arthur Joseph Lopatka, *Pitcher*

A graduate of the University of Chicago, Art gathered his college diploma before he joined the military. The southpaw from Chicago spent some time in the armed forces but was discharged early and was able to participate in the war-interrupted campaign of 1945. Art's first taste of the major leagues came that year, but when 1946 rolled around and the war had ended, he knew the battle for a major league job would be arduous. Lopatka was asked by an editor to write a column for a newspaper concerning the spring training battles that players fought during 1946. Art wrote, "Almost a new team has returned from the wars and I knew them only by their pictures in the newspapers or by reading of their exploits on the diamond a few years back. They were stars in their own right, coming back for their jobs."

W	L	PCT	G	GS	CG	IP	H	BB	SO	SHO	ERA
1	1	.500	8	2	1	17	20	7	9	0	6.35

Omar Joseph "Turk" Lown, *Pitcher*

One of the top relief pitchers of the 1950s, Lown spent all but half of a season in Chicago. Originally a Cubs fireman, Turk was traded to the Reds where he pitched briefly before joining the White Sox. An unknown commodity before the war, Turk missed out on some valuable seasoning time in the minors to service in the armed forces during World War II.

W	L	PCT	G	GS	CG	IP	H	BB	SO	SHO	ERA
55	61	.474	504	49	10	1,031	978	590	574	1	4.12

Harry Lee "Peanuts" Lowrey, *Outfield*

A small and gritty ballplayer, Peanuts spent the majority of his career with the Cubs and Cardinals. A versatile ballplayer, Lowrey was the starting center fielder for the 1943 Cubs while also playing in the infield on occasion. Despite the loss of his four-year-old son to an illness during spring training of 1943, Peanuts led the team with thirteen steals and twelve triples. He lost the entire 1944 season to military service but received a medical discharge late in the year due to weak knees.

G	R	H	2B	3B	HR	RBI	BB	SO	SB	AVG	Slug
1,401	564	1,177	186	45	37	479	403	226	48	.273	.362

Samuel Joseph Lowry, *Pitcher*

Sam Lowry played sparingly in two years with the Mackmen, as he saw limited action in 1942 and 1943. He was then inducted into the armed forces and missed the next three seasons to military service.

W	L	PCT	G	GS	CG	IP	H	BB	SO	SHO	ERA
0	0	—	6	0	0	21	21	10	3	0	5.14

Hugh Max Luby, *Utility Infielder*

Luby was little more than a war-era ballplayer, and the majority of his major league playing time came with the 1944 Giants. His only other action in the majors came with the 1936 Athletics, as Connie Mack used Hugh sparingly. Regarded as a soft-spoken ballplayer, Hugh set a minor league record for playing in 866 consecutive games. He passed his pre-induction physical in January of 1945 and spent a year in the navy.

G	R	H	2B	3B	HR	RBI	BB	SO	SB	AVG	Slug
120	33	89	11	2	2	38	52	22	4	.247	.305

John Lucadello, *Utility Infielder*

Initially a third baseman, Johnny had to add other posts to his resume in an effort to get in the lineup. In the late 1930s, the Browns had Harlond Clift manning the hot corner, and he was one of the best in baseball. With Clift's presence, Lucadello experimented up the middle while splitting time at second base and shortstop with Johnny Berardino and Don Heffner. His major league career was interrupted by World War II, and he lost a total of four years to service in the United States Navy. He wired skipper Luke Sewell during 1942 spring training and informed his manager that he had enlisted.

The first stop on Johnny's service map was the Great Lakes Naval Training Station. While serving his country in the upper regions of the nation, he played ball for the great Mickey Cochrane. He met up with two high school chums, Aldo Forte and Rudy Mucha, and the trio aided in the physical training department at the Great Lakes. He was later reassigned to Bainbridge and from there was sent overseas. Johnny was shipped out to Hawaii on January 3, 1944. A solid baseball player, Lucadello was once described as a "hustling, chatter-box type."

G	R	H	2B	3B	HR	RBI	BB	SO	SB	AVG	Slug
239	95	181	36	7	5	60	93	56	6	.264	.359

Joseph Earl Lucey, *Pitcher*

A two-way player, Lucey made his debut with the 1920 Yankees as a middle infielder but played only in a couple games. Five years later the Red Sox called Joe up and employed him as a pitcher. He had little success in either capacity. During the Second World War, the forty-year-old Lucey served with the army.

W	L	PCT	G	GS	CG	IP	H	BB	SO	SHO	ERA
0	1	.000	7	2	0	11	18	14	2	0	9.00

Edward Paul Lukon, *Outfield*

"The Mongoose," as Lukon was referred to by his peers, wasn't an imposing physical specimen but possessed modest pop in his lumber. He was summoned by the Reds in 1941 and played for Bill McKechnie in a handful of games. He spent the 1942 season in the bushes and was in the service from 1943 to late 1944. Eddie's brother, John, saw combat action in the Italian Campaign; the two Lukon boys worked in the Pennsylvanian mines as youths.

G	R	H	2B	3B	HR	RBI	BB	SO	SB	AVG	Slug
213	64	143	19	9	23	70	60	72	4	.236	.408

Ulysses John "Tony" Lupien, *First Base*

Lupien was essentially a war-era ballplayer. He had a brief trial with the 1940 Red Sox, but the young Ulysses Lupien wasn't about to unseat Jimmie Foxx. When the war began taking players from major league rosters, the Red Sox brought Lupien back to Boston in 1942 and he played with the Sox until he joined the Phillies in 1944. Tony hit a respectable .283 in 1944 but early in the 1945 season he was inducted into the military. After a few months of military service, Lupien was discharged when the war ended and returned to baseball. But he created waves upon his return.

Frank McCormick, a much better player than Lupien, beat out Tony for the Phillies' first base job in 1946 spring training and the Phillies opted to farm Tony out. Lupien wasn't about to let this happen without a fight. Lupien, a Harvard graduate, challenged the Phillies assignment and used the GI Bill of Rights as his defense. He felt that since men in other occupations were given their jobs back after their discharge, ballplayers should have their jobs back as well. When he tried to contact commissioner Happy Chandler for assistance in the suit, Tony was told by Chandler's associates that he couldn't be found.

With the commissioner sitting this one out for the time being, Lupien was on his own. His defense was simple. Lupien stated, "A baseball player's span of usefulness is comparatively short, so why take a cut in pay at this stage, when under the GI Bill I am entitled to the full amount I was receiving when I entered the service?" After hearing Lupien out, Happy came out from the rock he was hiding under and tossed his two cents into the debate. The commissioner sided with Lupien, to an extent, stating, "A player shall receive the same salary as previously paid him and his contract shall not be assigned to a club of lower classification until the player has been retained for fifteen days."

Happy Chandler tried to walk the line on the issue. He wanted to appease Lupien and the boys coming back from war but knew that forcing a team to hold onto a lesser player, at the expense of their pennant hopes, was a suicidal gesture. The Phillies had their first baseman in McCormick and had no room for Lupien, but the Harvard man created a stir that writer John Kenney feared would afflict every team. Kenney assumed that every major league club would have a "Lupien case" on their hands.

Hoping that his reply on the issue would lead to a resolve, Chandler waited for a reply from Lupien, and when it came, it wasn't pleasant. Tony was dismayed at Chandler's fifteen-day trial to make good statement. He said, "Veterans returning to other lines of work get one year to make good and I can't see how a baseball player can be judged in fifteen days." But the Lupien headache ended quietly as Tony dropped the case because he didn't have enough funds to pursue it further. In the end, Lupien was farmed out and didn't play with the Phillies all year. He didn't make it back to the majors until 1948, with the Chicago White Sox.

G	R	H	2B	3B	HR	RBI	BB	SO	SB	AVG	Slug
614	285	632	92	30	18	230	241	111	57	.268	.355

Rollin Joseph Lutz, *First Base*

The first American to manage in the Nippon Pro Baseball League of Japan, Lutz lasted only fifteen games because the Japanese media criticized the way he wore his trousers and scratched his head. Joe had a cup of coffee with the 1951 Browns. He served as Hank Arft's backup during his brief trial at the highest level. During the war, Lutz served with the U.S. Marine Corps.

G	R	H	2B	3B	HR	RBI	BB	SO	SB	AVG	Slug
14	7	6	0	1	0	2	6	9	0	.167	.222

Louis William "Red" Lutz, *Pinch-Hitter*

Lutz had one plate appearance at the major league level and legged out a double in that lone at-bat. Red's sojourn to the majors came in 1922. Twenty years later, Lutz entered the navy for service during World War II.

G	R	H	2B	3B	HR	RBI	BB	SO	SB	AVG	Slug
1	0	1	1	0	0	0	0	0	0	1.000	2.000

Japhet Monroe "Red" Lynn, *Pitcher*

An adequate relief pitcher, Red spent three years with three separate teams at the major league level. He initially came up with the 1939 Tigers but was dealt to the Giants during the season. After some time in the bushes, Lynn returned to the majors in 1944 with the Cubs. He was inducted into the military and missed the 1945 season to service with Uncle Sam.

W	L	PCT	G	GS	CG	IP	H	BB	SO	SHO	ERA
10	8	.556	85	7	4	184	175	85	85	1	3.96

Albert Harold Lyons, *Pitcher*

Lyons made eleven appearances with the 1944 Yankees as a rookie before he received his draft notice during the baseball season. He left the Bronx Bombers and caught on with the navy, where he was able to play baseball as a player-manager on the Hawaiian Islands. He returned to pitch another year and a half with the Yankees before he ended his career in 1948 with the Braves.

W	L	PCT	G	GS	CG	IP	H	BB	SO	SHO	ERA
3	3	.500	39	1	0	100	125	59	46	0	6.30

Edward Hoyte Lyons, *Second Base*

"Mouse" had a cup of coffee with the 1947 Senators—the extent of his major league career. The diminutive middle infielder served with the navy before he made his major league debut. After his playing days, Lyons became a rather successful skipper. In his first three years as a minor league manager, Mouse captured three pennants.

G	R	H	2B	3B	HR	RBI	BB	SO	SB	AVG	Slug
7	2	4	0	0	0	0	2	2	0	.154	.154

Herschel Englebert Lyons, *Pitcher*

Lyons pitched one game at the major league level and walked the bases loaded in his only frame. The right-hander pitched with the Redbirds before the war. A graduate of Occidental College where he lettered in four sports, Herschel joined the navy during World War II. He played some service ball at Bainbridge Naval Training Station with Dick Sisler. Commissioned a 2nd Lieutenant, Lyons was sent to Daniel Field. When asked about baseball's prospects for the 1944 season, concerning whether it would survive or not, Herschel said, "They'll be playing ball as long as they have the go-ahead signal from the White House. After all, theaters and other amusements can't take care of all that trade."

W	L	PCT	G	GS	CG	IP	H	BB	SO	SHO	ERA
0	0	—	1	0	0	1	3	1	0	0	0.00

Theodore Amar Lyons, *Pitcher*

Baseball Hall of Fame right-hander Ted Lyons was born and raised in the bayou, and is remembered by his peers as being quite a troublemaker. Ted Williams spoke of the shenanigans that Lyons would pull on the ball diamond in his biography, *My Turn at Bat*. He was always quick with the insults and enjoyed razzing the opposition, much like his longtime skipper, Jimmy Dykes.

When World War II broke out, Lyons was already 40 years old. Despite his age, which could be seen as a handicap, Lyons paced all American League pitchers with a 2.10 ERA in 1942. With the war raging overseas, Lyons was eager to do his part, saying, "I want to do the most possible good when called." At the age of 41, the control artist entered the U.S. Marine Corps for service during World War II. Ted's logic behind joining the Marines was as simple as the desire to see action. Lyons picked the Marines "because they do things—they don't fool around."

Quantico was the first stop on Ted's training map and after his days there he was assigned to a pier off Lake Michigan. This assignment kept him close to his old teammates in Chicago, who kept his uniform hanging in the clubhouse while he served under Uncle Sam. The 41-year-old Lyons dropped 20 pounds during his Marine training and had this to say about his White Sox teammates while he was at the pier: "I understand Luke Appling and some of those other gents I used to bounce around are getting a little flabby. So I will devote my Sundays off, when the Sox are in town, to tossing Luke and his tough pals around the clubhouse—Marine style. I'll get 'em in shape!"

The bayou boy showed remorse when questioned about his time in the military and how it differed from his days as a civilian. Lyons said that his military duty was the "first time in my life I haven't had a bird dog to go hunting with me or tramping through the woods." On August 13, 1943, Ted was ordered detached from the pier for duty described as "in the Pacific Coast area." He was later shipped out to Hawaii where he was able to play some baseball for the Marine Flyers ballclub that he managed.

Ted Lyons returned to baseball at the age of 45 with every intention of picking up where he left off. After the White Sox got off to a dismal 10–20 start to the 1946 season, Ted was tabbed as the successor to Jimmy Dykes when he was fired. As a manager, Ted went 64–60 after Dykes had the team buried with their poor start. On the mound, Ted won just one game—his 260th career victory—with a miniscule 2.30 ERA, a mark bested only by Earl Caldwell and Gordon Maltzberger.

W	L	PCT	G	GS	CG	IP	H	BB	SO	SHO	ERA
260	230	.531	594	484	356	4,161	4,489	1,121	1,073	27	3.67

Raymond James Mack, *Second Base*

Mack, whose real last name was Mickovsky before he anglicized it, played with the Indians from 1938 through 1946 with a brief military interruption in 1945. Never much to brag about with lumber in his hands, Mack made his debut as Bad News Odell Hale's backup in 1938. He won the second-base job in 1940 and proceeded to post his fluke season by smacking 12 home runs and hitting .283. His batting average dipped to .228 in 1941, to .225 in 1942, and fell another five points in 1943. He began to split time with Rusty Peters in 1944 and was inducted into the army in 1945. Before his induction, Mack quit baseball to remain on his war job as an engineer. Uncle Sam beckoned his presence, and he donned khaki for a year.

G	R	H	2B	3B	HR	RBI	BB	SO	SB	AVG	Slug
791	273	629	113	24	34	278	261	365	35	.232	.330

John Joseph Mackinson, *Pitcher*

Mackinson had two brief trials at the major league level. Initially summoned by the A's in 1953, John failed to make the grade and was sent back to the bushes. He returned to the highest level in 1955 with the Cardinals—his last major league service. He missed some minor league seasoning to service during the war.

W	L	PCT	G	GS	CG	IP	H	BB	SO	SHO	ERA
0	1	.000	9	1	0	22	25	12	8	0	7.36

Max Cullen Macon, *First Base*

Macon was that rare baseball player, much like the modern Rick Ankiel or Ron Mahay, who played regularly as a position player and made regular appearances on the mound. A multi-talented southpaw, Macon posted a career ERA of 4.24 in 297 innings of work. Macon entered the army after the close of the 1944 baseball season and served as a private with the Fourth Service Command Medics.

G	R	H	2B	3B	HR	RBI	BB	SO	SB	AVG	Slug
226	54	133	17	4	3	46	16	32	9	.265	.333

Clarence James Maddern, *Outfield*

Before Maddern made his major league debut, he was engaged in combat action in the European Theatre during World War II. Attached to the same outfit as Washington Senators great Cecil Travis, Maddern was able to play some service ball with Travis before their unit took to less leisurely pursuits. With the 76th Infantry Division, Maddern was sent to Camp McCoy as a private first class to undergo cold weather training with his company. They were preparing for the harsh winters of the European Theatre.

After their training at Camp McCoy was complete, the 76th was shipped overseas where they would be engaged in combat maneuvers. The unit took part in the Battle of the Bulge as they marched through the frozen terrain of Europe. Maddern's battle buddy, Cecil Travis, suffered frostbite on his feet and would never again be the star player he was before the war. When the war ended, Maddern returned home and to the game of baseball. In his first year back from the war, Clarence set a minor league record for most consecutive games played in left field without an error. His flawless defense earned him a callup to Chicago. Maddern would play his last major league game with the 1951 Cleveland Indians.

G	R	H	2B	3B	HR	RBI	BB	SO	SB	AVG	Slug
104	17	59	12	1	5	29	12	26	0	.248	.370

David Pledger Madison, *Pitcher*

Like Ted Williams and Jerry Coleman, Madison also served in two separate wars— he missed minor league action to World War II and major league service time to the Korean War. Dave missed the entire 1951 season to service in the Army Reserves, where he served as a lieutenant, and returned to the Browns in 1952. His last major league action came in 1953 with the Detroit Tigers.

W	L	PCT	G	GS	CG	IP	H	BB	SO	SHO	ERA
8	7	.533	74	6	0	158	173	103	70	0	5.70

Jack Maguire, *Outfield/First Base*

Maguire played with three different teams during his two-year major league career. Called up by the Giants in 1950, Jack had been discharged from the military five years prior.

G	R	H	2B	3B	HR	RBI	BB	SO	SB	AVG	Slug
94	25	46	5	2	2	21	18	36	1	.240	.318

Forrest Harry "Woody" Main, *Pitcher*

A mop-up pitcher for the Pirates in the early 1950s, Main was a serviceable long arm out of the bullpen. He made his debut with the Bucs in 1948. During the war, Main served with the United States Marine Corps.

W	L	PCT	G	GS	CG	IP	H	BB	SO	SHO	ERA
4	13	.235	79	11	2	204	210	84	107	0	5.16

Henry Majeski, *Third Base*

A decent-hitting third baseman, Majeski earned his stripes as a superior defender — he established the single-season fielding percentage record at the hot corner with a .989 mark in 1947. Hank played with the Braves from 1939 to 1941 and then missed the 1943 through 1945 seasons to service in the armed forces. He returned to the diamond in 1946 with the Yankees but was dealt to the Athletics after only eight games with Joe McCarthy's men. It was under Connie Mack when Hank set the fielding record and helped the A's finish above .500, a feat they rarely accomplished after 1933.

G	R	H	2B	3B	HR	RBI	BB	SO	SB	AVG	Slug
1,069	404	956	181	27	57	501	299	260	10	.279	.398

Anthony Francis Malinosky, *Third Base/Shortstop*

Malinosky played one year with the Dodgers in the late 1930s. A trim utility infielder, Tony had a decent batting eye. With his major league service all but over, Malinosky was drafted into the army for duty during World War II. The former Brooklyn Dodger trained with a combat outfit and was shipped overseas where he saw action at the Battle of the Bulge.

G	R	H	2B	3B	HR	RBI	BB	SO	SB	AVG	Slug
35	7	18	2	0	0	3	9	11	0	.228	.253

Cyrus Sol Malis, *Pitcher*

Cy Malis wore many hats during his life: baseball player, navy sailor, film actor and recovered addict. Malis lived a tortured life but was able to clean himself up and help others battling the same addictions. Malis pitched one game of mop-up duty with the 1934 Phillies. With his baseball career in the books, Malis went west and dabbled in the film industry for a time. However, when Pearl Harbor was bombed, Malis was quick to enlist in the navy.

While stationed on a battleship in the navy, Malis suffered a serious freak injury that would alter his life. Cy was working on a ship, assisting in the anti-aircraft outfit, when a gun mount was dislodged and struck him in the back. Severe damage was done to Cy's spine, and his neck was broken in the accident. Sent to military hospitals, Malis, who was suffering from severe pain, was prescribed morphine by the doctors. After he was medically discharged, Malis left the navy but couldn't discharge his morphine addiction. It took Malis some time but he was able to kick his habit. Spurred by his trials and tribulations, Cy founded Narcotics Anonymous, which he modeled after Alcoholics Anonymous. He dedicated the last years of his life to helping others fight their addictions.

W	L	PCT	G	GS	CG	IP	H	BB	SO	SHO	ERA
0	0	—	1	0	0	4	4	2	1	0	4.50

James Baugh Mallory, *Outfield*

Mallory played two years at the major league level with three separate teams. He made his debut with the Senators in 1940 and then split the 1945 season with the Cardinals and Giants. Sunny Jim spent the 1942 through the 1944 baseball campaigns on Uncle Sam's roster.

G	R	H	2B	3B	HR	RBI	BB	SO	SB	AVG	Slug
54	15	40	3	0	0	14	7	10	1	.268	.289

Robert Paul Malloy, *Pitcher*

A serviceable relief pitcher, Malloy spent a year and a half with the Reds before his tour in the military. He was inducted into the navy on April 13, 1944, and missed the next year and a half to military service. He returned to the Reds in 1946 and posted a solid 2.75 ERA over 72 innings of work.

W	L	PCT	G	GS	CG	IP	H	BB	SO	SHO	ERA
4	7	.364	48	3	1	116	116	52	35	0	3.26

Harry William Malmberg, *Second Base*

Harry played one year at the major league level, ten years after his military discharge, with the 1955 Tigers. Used in a platoon capacity, Malmberg played second when left-handed-hitting Fred Hatfield was withheld from the lineup.

G	R	H	2B	3B	HR	RBI	BB	SO	SB	AVG	Slug
67	25	45	5	2	0	19	29	19	0	.216	.260

Edward Russell Malone, *Catcher*

A back-up catcher with the Pale Hose for two seasons, Malone possessed a terrific batting eye. Eddie, who served in the navy during World War II, drew 39 walks in 241 plate appearances.

G	R	H	2B	3B	HR	RBI	BB	SO	SB	AVG	Slug
86	19	62	9	2	1	26	39	27	2	.257	.324

Gordon Ralph Maltzberger, *Pitcher*

Widely regarded as the American League's top relief pitcher during the World War II era, Maltzberger served as a coach in the Pacific Coast League once his playing days were over. Gordon's major league career wasn't extensive, he played two years before his military induction and two years after. He paced the AL in saves with 14 in 1943 — his rookie season — as the only pitcher to post a double-digit total. In 1944, he tied with George Caster and Jittery Joe Berry for the AL lead in saves. In two years in the majors, Maltzberger was atop the leader board in saves, but Uncle Sam beckoned him for 1945. He was inducted into the army at Rialto, California, and received his discharge during the 1946 baseball season.

W	L	PCT	G	GS	CG	IP	H	BB	SO	SHO	ERA
20	13	.606	135	0	0	294	258	75	136	0	2.69

Frank Octavius Mancuso, *Catcher*

Mancuso, brother of star backstop Gus Mancuso of the Giants, had a military injury to thank for his arrival on the baseball scene. Before the younger Mancuso made his major league debut, he served in the army during World War II. But Frank found out the hard way that servicemen train like they fight, and that wartime simulations can be as arduous as the real thing.

Mancuso enlisted in the Army Air Corps in 1942 and was sent to Randolph Field, where his military duties were to be in vehicular maintenance. Not content to be an enlisted mechanic, Mancuso sought his commission and then looked for more exciting opportunities. He sought airborne wings and went to jump training to acquire them. While learning how to jump out of an aircraft at Fort Benning, Mancuso suffered a freak injury that led to a medical discharge from the army. Mancuso described his airborne accident: "You're supposed to stick your head out of the plane and spot your field. Then you're supposed to look at the sky and jump — feet first. Well, when I looked down my body just sort of followed my head out of the plane. When my chute opened, it wrapped around my foot, so instead of my shoulders taking the shock, the yank came in my leg, pulled my knee out of joint and hurt my spine. I was in the hospital three months."

Due to the injury, Mancuso was mustered out of the army on medical grounds and returned home. He tried out with the Browns in 1944 and made good. During that war-torn season, Mancuso played fine defense and helped the Browns reach their only World Series. In the Fall Classic, Frank hit a robust .667. Although Mancuso was back home playing the game he loved, he often thought about his airborne chums and his time in the military fondly. He said, "Although I am glad to get back in baseball, I am also glad for my experience in the paratroops. It's kind of hard to leave at first, because we all had that urge to get overseas. I'd do it again if I could."

G	R	H	2B	3B	HR	RBI	BB	SO	SB	AVG	Slug
337	85	241	37	7	5	98	101	118	2	.241	.306

Maxwell Manning, *Pitcher*

A supply man in the U.S. Army during World War II, Manning served in the Quartermaster's Corps. After training at Fort Dix, Max was assigned to Richland Airfield with the 316th Air Squadron. Shipped overseas from there, the big right-hander from Georgia served in France as a truck driver, hauling supplies to the frontlines for the Third Army. After Manning's discharge, he helped the Newark Eagles win the Negro National League World Series in 1946. A tall, rangy right-hander with a side-arm motion, Manning stood out on the ball diamond because he wore the thickest glasses in any league.

(1938–1949): Newark Eagles and Houston Eagles

Richard Wesley "Dick" Manville, *Pitcher*

A Christmas baby, Manville had two cups of coffee in the majors. His first came with the Braves in 1950 and his last with the 1952 Cubs. Before Dick made his debut, he served in the navy during World War II. After his discharge, the young Iowa native enrolled at Yale University where he played ball and became friends with future president George Bush.

W	L	PCT	G	GS	CG	IP	H	BB	SO	SHO	ERA
0	0	—	12	0	0	19	25	15	8	0	7.11

Cliff Franklin Mapes, *Outfield*

With a thundering bat capable of swatting home runs at any ballpark, Mapes had the power to stick at the major league level. Never a regular player in the majors, Cliff had to be content with offering his heavy bat off the bench. Mapes took his pre-induction physical early in 1944 and was accepted for duty in the United States Navy. He served on the West Coast and was able to play plenty of service ball.

G	R	H	2B	3B	HR	RBI	BB	SO	SB	AVG	Slug
459	199	289	55	13	38	172	168	213	8	.242	.408

Howard Albert Maple, *Catcher*

A short yet solidly built athlete, Maple had cups of coffee in both professional baseball and football. Unable to stick in either sport, Maple was nonetheless a two-sport professional. Ten years after he made his debut with the Senators, Howard joined the army for duty during World War II. He served with the Army Engineers and was stationed in Alaska.

G	R	H	2B	3B	HR	RBI	BB	SO	SB	AVG	Slug
44	6	10	0	1	0	7	7	7	0	.244	.293

Philip Edward Marchildon, *Pitcher*

War presents many hardships, but fewer are greater than serving as a prisoner of war. Marchildon, who served in the Royal Canadian Air Force, was a prisoner in a Nazi concentration camp for ten months. He finished seventh (other sources list him as finishing ninth) in MVP voting after the 1942 season, when he posted 17 wins for a team that lost one shy of 100. The 28-year-old rising star was then inducted into the Canadian military, and he missed three years to World War II.

Marchildon was commissioned as an officer in the Royal Canadian Air Force on July 27, 1943. His initial taste of military life wasn't unlike other major leaguers, as Phil played service ball for the Trenton Air Base nine in Ontario. His military occupation was that of a tail-gunner on a Halifax bomber. The right-hander was shipped overseas and began flying missions for the Canadian Air Force. He played baseball in the European Theatre and was the hero of a contest by swatting a walk-off home run. Then, just three days after his heroic deeds on the ball diamond, his crew flew their 27th and final mission.

Marchildon was reported missing in action on August 17, 1944, after his plane was shot down over Kiel. His plane was brought down near the Danish coast, and Phil had to tread water for three hours before he was picked up. However, his rescuers were detained by enemies, and Phil became a POW under the Nazi regime. He stated that all he was fed at the concentration camp were three slices of black bread a day. The image that Phil could never shake about his ordeal in the war was watching as SS Troops shot and murdered approximately 50 of his buddies without trial.

When Marchildon returned to the Athletics late in 1945, he visited his teammates and many saw a "new nervousness in his speech and gesture." Although he had been released from the concentration camp, a hopeless feeling weighed upon Phil. He said, "Only a few weeks ago I was on my way to the ballpark and suddenly something seemed to grab at my nerves. I wanted to pick up a brick and toss it through a window. But I'm not setting myself up as a lone individual. We've all been through a lot and we've come home with that sense of futility — a sort of vacant feeling."

Connie Mack used Phil in three games at the end of the 1945 season, easing the former prisoner of war back into the game. Baseball proved to be a soothing elixir for Marchildon, a way to get his mind off his troubles. Phil said, "The medicine of competitive sports is doing its work and I'm relaxed again. The tension of baseball is similar enough to grasp and hold my interest, and yet it is a pleasant tension. I realize that if Greenberg hits me for a homer, I'll still be able to go back to the hotel, eat a good meal, see a movie and laugh about the whole thing the next morning."

In 1946, Marchildon reasserted himself as Connie Mack's ace, leading the club in wins, innings pitched, complete games and strikeouts. More importantly, he was able to live on his own terms, to discuss the war and keep the horrors he witnessed in the back of his mind. To Athletics coach Earle Brucker, Phil said, "What a shellacking those Germans took. Why those Lancasters hit a town 20 miles away and the ground rocked under us like a canoe!"

W	L	PCT	G	GS	CG	IP	H	BB	SO	SHO	ERA
68	75	.476	185	162	82	1,214	1,084	684	481	6	3.93

Cleneth Eugene "Gene" Markland, *Second Base*

Markland had a cup of coffee with the 1950 A's, the last team Connie Mack would manage. Gene scratched out only one hit at the highest level. Before he joined the Mackmen, Markland was a soldier in the United States Army. Stationed at Camp McCoy with the 1620 Headquarters and Service Company, Gene was the captain of the installation's baseball club. In 1944, he was named the best athlete on the installation.

G	R	H	2B	3B	HR	RBI	BB	SO	SB	AVG	Slug
5	2	1	0	0	0	0	3	0	0	.125	.125

Harry Sylvester Marnie, *Utility Infielder*

Marnie played with the Phillies in three separate seasons, but after a three-year stint in the service, he failed to return to the majors. Hal was inducted into the army in 1943 and played service ball at the New Cumberland Reception Center with fellow Phillies player Bill Peterman.

G	R	H	2B	3B	HR	RBI	BB	SO	SB	AVG	Slug
96	19	49	3	3	0	15	18	29	1	.221	.261

Robert Rudolph Marquis, *Outfield*

Marquis offered a solid power bat off the bench for the 1953 Reds, the only major league squad he'd play for. In limited duty, he Slugged a nifty .477. Before Bob made it to the majors, he served in the armed forces during World War II.

G	R	H	2B	3B	HR	RBI	BB	SO	SB	AVG	Slug
40	9	12	1	1	2	3	4	11	0	.273	.477

Fred Francis Marsh, *Third Base*

Marsh served with the United States Navy during World War II before his major league career began. The infielder from Valley Falls, Kansas, was a journeyed ballplayer who made his rounds in the American League. Marsh debuted with the 1949 Indians and played his last game with the 1956 Orioles.

G	R	H	2B	3B	HR	RBI	BB	SO	SB	AVG	Slug
465	148	296	43	8	10	96	125	171	13	.239	.311

Charles Anthony "Chip" Marshall, Reserve

Marshall played in one game with the 1941 Cardinals without recording an official at-bat. Chip would leave the game and serve in the armed forces during World War II.

G	R	H	2B	3B	HR	RBI	BB	SO	SB	AVG	Slug
1	0	0	0	0	0	0	0	0	0	—	—

Milo May "Max" Marshall, Outfield

Marshall saw all of his major league action during the war years as he didn't return to the majors after his one-year stint in the colors. Max took his pre-induction physical at Sidney, Iowa, and was inducted into the navy shortly thereafter.

G	R	H	2B	3B	HR	RBI	BB	SO	SB	AVG	Slug
329	140	311	41	16	15	105	89	100	15	.245	.339

Willard Warren Marshall, Outfield

Marshall enjoyed a decent major league career, beginning when he was inserted as the Giants' regular center fielder in 1942, his rookie season. He posted as many home runs as doubles and triples combined in his first year. His good start at the major league level was impeded when Uncle Sam plucked him for military duty. Marshall served three years with the U.S. Marine Corps and returned to the Giants in 1946, where he stroked the onion for a .282 average. His greatest season came in 1947, as Willard hit 36 home runs with 107 RBIs. He played in the majors through 1955 but never again came close to posting as many long balls as he did in 1947.

G	R	H	2B	3B	HR	RBI	BB	SO	SB	AVG	Slug
1,246	583	1,160	163	39	130	604	458	219	14	.274	.423

Barney Robertson Martin, Pitcher

Martin pitched in one game with the 1953 Reds, the extent of his major league career. Before he signed his first professional contract, Barney served overseas with the United States Navy during World War II.

W	L	PCT	G	GS	CG	IP	H	BB	SO	SHO	ERA
0	0	—	1	0	0	2	3	1	1	0	9.00

Morris Webster Martin, Pitcher

The fact that Martin even reached the major leagues is a testament to his courage and work ethic. A Missouri farm boy, Martin was quick to enlist in the army and do his bit for his country. Morrie served with the 49th Engineer Battalion that was shipped overseas to the European Theatre. Not an idle unit, the 49th saw heavy combat action at Omaha Beach and other locales. When the unit was engaged in the Battle of the Bulge, Martin was wounded in battle and suffered a severe leg injury. Awarded the Purple Heart for his bravery, Martin was honorably discharged from the army.

Martin went back home and tried to strengthen his leg in order to pitch again. He knew that a pitcher's legs were just as important as his arm, and he worked tirelessly to get back into condition. The Dodgers were impressed with Morrie and gave him his first big league trial in 1949. Although he failed to make good with the first-place Dodgers, Morrie eventually achieved success at the highest level with Jimmy Dykes' Athletics. Employed primarily as a long arm out of the bullpen, Martin would pitch in the majors until 1959.

W	L	PCT	G	GS	CG	IP	H	BB	SO	SHO	ERA
38	34	.528	250	42	8	604	607	251	245	1	4.29

Raymond Joseph Martin, Pitcher

Martin appeared in five major league games over the course of three years. He was only 18 years old when he made his debut with the 1943 Braves, but he was whisked away by Uncle Sam during the baseball season that year. He stayed in the military through 1946 and rejoined the Braves for a spell in 1947.

W	L	PCT	G	GS	CG	IP	H	BB	SO	SHO	ERA
1	0	1.000	5	1	1	14	10	6	3	0	2.57

Joseph Anton Marty, Outfield

A lean outfielder from Sacramento, Marty played in the majors with the Cubs and Phillies. He hit .290 as a rookie with Charlie Grimm's 1937 Cubs and enjoyed his finest hour in the 1938 World Series. Joe led all participants with a .500 batting average (6-for-12), but his heroics couldn't bring the Cubs a single victory over the powerful Yankees. After a shaky start in 1939, Marty was traded to the Phillies and tied with Emmett Mueller for the team lead in long balls. He spent the next two years as the Phillies' starting center fielder but finished his major league career when he enlisted in the army after the 1941 season. Joe played in one of the first service baseball games that utilized major league players. His coaches for the game were Hall of Fame catcher Mickey Cochrane and World War I hero Hank Gowdy.

G	R	H	2B	3B	HR	RBI	BB	SO	SB	AVG	Slug
538	223	478	78	22	44	222	142	187	14	.261	.361

Walter Edward Masterson, Pitcher

Masterson pitched the majority of his solid career with the Senators, and his career winning percentage proves how inefficient the club was at providing him with run support. He made his debut with the 1939 Senators as a 19-year-old kid. The following year he posted a 3–13 record and combated control issues. In 1942, Walt pieced it all together and harnessed his ability, trimming his walk total substantially. However, with World War II well underway, Masterson was called to the colors after the close of the season.

Walt served with the United States Navy and was stationed at the Norfolk Naval Training Station. He didn't stay stateside long as he was shipped out to Hawaii. His claim to fame, regarding his military playing days, was tossing the first no-hitter in Hawaiian League history. For his feats on the Hawaiian ball diamonds, Masterson was named Athlete of the Year of the Hawaiian Islands for the 1944 season. He returned to the Senators late in the 1945 season and outpitched Bob Feller, who had also made a late return, in a contest during the campaign. Like most pitchers of his time, Walt was squeamish in regards to pitching to Ted Williams. When asked how he pitched to Williams, Masterson replied, "I wound up, threw and then ducked behind the mound."

W	L	PCT	G	GS	CG	IP	H	BB	SO	SHO	ERA
78	100	.438	399	184	70	1,648	1,613	886	815	15	4.15

Francis Oliver Mathews, *First Base*

A first baseman with a brief tenure in the Negro Leagues, Mathews manned the initial sack for the Newark Eagles for a spell in the 1940s. Inducted into the military in 1942, Mathews didn't serve for the duration but was discharged in time to play the 1945 season, his last in black baseball.

(1938–1945): Newark Eagles and Baltimore Elite Giants

Gene William Mauch, *Second Base*

Best known for his managerial work, Mauch piloted such franchises as the Philadelphia Phillies, Montreal Expos, Minnesota Twins and California Angels. Mauch was still receiving his high school education when World War II broke out, and the kid reached the majors as an 18-year-old in 1944. He was handed the starting assignment at shortstop in 1944 but he was enrolled in the Army Air Corps and was sworn in early in the season.

G	R	H	2B	3B	HR	RBI	BB	SO	SB	AVG	Slug
304	93	176	25	7	5	62	104	82	6	.239	.312

Merrill Glend "Pinky" May, *Third Base*

Pinky ascended from the bushes in 1939 to be named the everyday third baseman by skipper Doc Prothro. He showed a remarkable batting eye — his most notable trait throughout his career — by fanning only twenty times in 464 at-bats. He cemented himself as one of the National League's top hot corner men in 1940, and his .293 batting mark was bested only by Stan Hack, the Cubs third baseman who should be a cinch for the Hall of Fame. By 1941, in his third year in the major leagues, Pinky was already 30 years old. He hit .282 in 1943, his last year in the majors, while striking out twenty-one times.

After the 1943 baseball season, Pinky was inducted into the armed forces, which signaled the end of his professional baseball career. The wiry third baseman played service ball for Mickey Cochrane at the Great Lakes. May's military duties entailed supervising the general issue of gear at the Great Lakes Naval Station.

G	R	H	2B	3B	HR	RBI	BB	SO	SB	AVG	Slug
665	210	610	102	11	4	215	261	121	13	.275	.337

James Walter "Buster" Maynard, *Outfield*

Buster spent pieces of four years at the major league level, all with the New York Giants. Just prior to spring training in 1944, Maynard received his draft notice and was inducted into the army. He was stationed at Fort Bragg and played service ball with a remarkable former major leaguer named Van Lingle Mungo as well as a gabby catcher named Jake Early.

G	R	H	2B	3B	HR	RBI	BB	SO	SB	AVG	Slug
224	68	136	14	5	14	66	46	53	6	.221	.328

William Glenn McCahan, *Pitcher*

A gifted natural athlete, McCahan pitched for Connie Mack's Athletics after the war and also played some professional basketball in 1946 and 1947. Before Bill played sports at the highest level, he served in the Army Air Corps. As a young lieutenant, McCahan may have had the most interesting military occupation among professional athletes. While stationed at Maxwell Field, McCahan, who had advanced through pre-flight school, was engaged as a test pilot for Uncle Sam.

W	L	PCT	G	GS	CG	IP	H	BB	SO	SHO	ERA
16	14	.533	57	40	17	291	297	145	76	2	3.84

Robert Leonard "Dutch" McCall, *Pitcher*

A two-way star as an amateur, McCall didn't know which path he wanted to walk: that of a pitcher or position player. He decided to let the Cubs make the decision for him. The Cubs chose the mound for Dutch and he pitched one year at the major league level. McCall had his military induction pushed back on account of a hernia operation.

W	L	PCT	G	GS	CG	IP	H	BB	SO	SHO	ERA
4	13	.235	30	20	5	151	158	85	89	0	4.83

Jerome Francis McCarthy, *First Base*

McCarthy had a cup of coffee with the 1948 Browns that netted him three trips to the plate. The former University of Pennsylvania football star served with the Army Air Corps during World War II.

G	R	H	2B	3B	HR	RBI	BB	SO	SB	AVG	Slug
2	0	1	0	0	0	0	0	0	0	.333	.333

John Joseph McCarthy, *First Base*

A contact hitter who rarely drew a walk or struck out, McCarthy had been in the league ten years before he was summoned for military duty. McCarthy served as the regular first baseman for the National League champion New York Giants in 1937, hitting .279 for Bill Terry's boys. He lost his job to Zeke Bonura in 1939 and left the Giants to join the Braves in 1943. He began the year as the regular first baseman but was drafted into the navy before the season came to a close. In the navy, Johnny played service ball for Mickey Cochrane's Great Lakes naval powerhouse.

G	R	H	2B	3B	HR	RBI	BB	SO	SB	AVG	Slug
542	182	432	72	16	25	209	90	114	8	.277	.392

Clinton Hill "Butch" McCord, *First Base*

McCord was a young man during World War II when he lost two years to military service. At the right age during baseball's integration period, Butch left the Chicago American Giants and entered the minor leagues. A fine ballplayer in the minors throughout the 1950s, Butch didn't have the build of the brawny blasters in the majors who manned first base, players like Joe Adcock, Luke Easter and Dick Stuart. Because of his wiry physique, he was never asked up to the majors.

(1948–1950): Baltimore Elite Giants and Chicago American Giants

Myron Winthrop "Mike" McCormick, *Outfield*

McCormick was an adequate major league hitter who batted an even .300 in his rookie season of 1940. During that season's

World Series, Mike hit .310 in a winning effort for Cincy. From there, Mike's numbers began to dip as it appeared that he would never regain his freshman stroke. He was inducted into the navy early in the 1943 baseball season and spent two and a half years with Uncle Sam. During his navy stay, McCormick served at McClellan Field.

G	R	H	2B	3B	HR	RBI	BB	SO	SB	AVG	Slug
748	302	640	100	29	14	215	188	174	16	.275	.361

William Barney McCosky, *Outfield*

One of the better outfielders of his day, it was said of McCosky that he "covered center field like a tent." Barney joined the Tigers in 1939 and was immediately inserted as the everyday center fielder. He hit .311 as a rookie while leading the team with 120 runs, 190 hits and 14 triples. Unfamiliar with the sophomore jinx, McCosky led the American League with 200 hits and 19 triples in 1940, only his second major league season. McCosky then started to struggle. His batting average fell to .324 in 1941 and then fell further in 1942. He was unable to redeem himself in 1943, when he was drafted into the navy.

In the fall before he was drafted, Barney made headlines when he was wounded on a hunting trip. While hunting pheasant in Bad Axe, Barney was shot in the face by his hunting companion. Two pellets that struck just beneath his left eye had to be removed by a doctor. Other pellets lodged in his forehead, ear and the side of his nose. It turned out that Barney joined the navy with scars on his face, having endured a scrape with fate before his military induction.

His navy career mirrored that of Bob Seeds' baseball career—rather nomadic. He served at the Bainbridge Naval Training Station as a physical instructor and also saw action with Mickey Cochrane's powerhouse Great Lakes baseball club. He attended a Navy Pre-Flight School but didn't bring his baseball gear along since he thought he wasn't eligible to play for the team. He was later shipped overseas where he was stationed at Hawaii and took part in the Hawaiian Baseball League.

McCosky returned to the Tigers in 1946, but after an abysmal start to the season, he was dealt to the Athletics. The trade rejuvenated him, as Barney hit at a .354 clip for Connie Mack. He was the best hitter in Mack's last years, and he teamed with two other solid hitters in Ferris Fain and Elmer Valo. A serious back injury, which sidelined him the entire 1949 season, all but ended his career. Although Barney enjoyed a very good career, the war may have interrupted a Hall of Fame–caliber tenure.

G	R	H	2B	3B	HR	RBI	BB	SO	SB	AVG	Slug
1,170	664	1,301	214	71	24	397	497	261	58	.312	.414

Benjamin Jenison McCoy, *Second Base*

McCoy was a solid little second baseman who made his debut with the 1938 Tigers. A decent grasp on baseball history reveals Detorit had Hall of Famer Charlie Gehringer manning that post in 1938. Benny played briefly for the Tigers and even saw action at shortstop in 1939 before he was dealt to the Athletics. In his last major league season, 1941, Benny tied Indian Bob Johnson for the team lead in walks with 95. After the 1941 season, McCoy enlisted in the navy and never returned to the major league level.

He never made an announcement concerning his desire to enlist, and he shocked the Athletics by voluntarily signing up. On February 4, 1942, McCoy became a coxswain in the United States Navy. His initial assignment was at the Norfolk Naval Training Station, where the small second baseman was able to play some baseball. He also served at the Great Lakes, where he played ball for Mickey Cochrane, before he was reassigned to the West Coast. Out west, Benny met with Red Sox legend Dom DiMaggio and together the two major leaguers built a recreation center on Luzon. McCoy served in the South Pacific and played ball when he was able before the war ended. Although he was a decent second baseman with a remarkable batting eye, Benny never laced up his spikes in a major league dugout after the war.

G	R	H	2B	3B	HR	RBI	BB	SO	SB	AVG	Slug
337	182	327	52	18	16	156	190	122	8	.269	.381

Clyde Edward McCullough, *Catcher*

Clyde spent two years in the service and was in the process of receiving his discharge while the Cubs wrapped up a National League pennant. The Cubs went to the World Series, and McCullough, who spent the entire regular season in the military, returned to the team during the Fall Classic. Skipper Charlie Grimm used Clyde as a pinch-hitter against the Tigers, showing immense faith in a backstop that had been away from the game for a couple of years.

McCullough joined the Cubs in 1940, when Chicago had three catchers who were over the age of 30 on their roster. He took over the regular catching chore from the greybeards in 1941, finishing third on the team in home runs that year. Clyde remained the Cubs' regular catcher until he was summoned by Uncle Sam. McCullough served in the navy and was stationed at the Great Lakes. He was part of a program that indoctrinated new recruits to navy life.

G	R	H	2B	3B	HR	RBI	BB	SO	SB	AVG	Slug
1,098	308	785	121	28	52	339	265	398	27	.252	.358

Pinson Lamar "Phil" McCullough, *Pitcher*

McCullough made one appearance at the major league level and tossed three innings for the 1942 Senators. The big right-hander was drafted into the navy at the close of the season and served his country for three years.

W	L	PCT	G	GS	CG	IP	H	BB	SO	SHO	ERA
0	0	—	1	0	0	3	5	2	2	0	6.00

Frank McElyea, *Outfield*

Much like fellow Brave Sam Gentile, Frank made four major league plate appearances in his career. However, McElyea didn't record a base hit in his four sojourns to the batter's box. He made his plate appearances in 1942 and then missed the next three seasons to service in the armed forces. A mountain of a man—Frank stood 6'6" and weighed 220 pounds—he transferred from Camp Sheridan to Camp Grant for a change in military training late in 1943.

G	R	H	2B	3B	HR	RBI	BB	SO	SB	AVG	Slug
7	0	0	0	0	0	0	0	0	0	.000	.000

Ezra Mac "Pat" McGlothin, *Pitcher*

The tall right-hander from Tennessee pitched briefly with the Dodgers at the major league level. He made his debut with them in their NL pennant-winning 1949 season and last pitched in 1950. McGlothin served in the navy before his major league debut. While employed by Uncle Sam, Pat worked in the navy's athletic department. His tasks were to referee navy basketball games, prepare the ball diamond by laying out the chalk lines, and keep tabs on the athletic gear. During his stint in the navy, McGlothin was stationed at Corpus Christi, Texas, Jacksonville, and the Bainbridge Naval Training Center. While in the colors, he was able to play some service ball with Ted Williams, Sam Chapman and Joe Coleman.

W	L	PCT	G	GS	CG	IP	H	BB	SO	SHO	ERA
1	1	.500	8	0	0	18	18	6	13	0	5.50

Rogers Hornsby McKee, *Pitcher*

With a handle like Rogers Hornsby McKee, it's obvious that McKee's father was a baseball fan. A portside chucker, Rogers made his major league debut as a 16-year-old with the 1943 Phillies. The kid won his only decision that year, which would turn out to be his only career decision at the highest level. McKee was inducted into the navy after the 1944 baseball season and spent a year in the colors. McKee never reached the majors again after his navy discharge.

W	L	PCT	G	GS	CG	IP	H	BB	SO	SHO	ERA
1	0	1.000	5	1	1	15	14	6	1	0	6.00

Albert Elrod McLean, *Pitcher*

Sometimes listed as Mac McLean, Al had a cup of coffee with the 1935 Senators. After his sojourn in the major leagues, McLean would join the Army Air Corps during World War II.

W	L	PCT	G	GS	CG	IP	H	BB	SO	SHO	ERA
0	0	—	4	0	0	9	12	5	3	0	7.00

Wayne Gaffney McLeland, *Pitcher*

McLeland pitched pieces of two seasons in the majors with the Tigers in the early 1950s. Wayne served in the United States Army during the Second World War.

W	L	PCT	G	GS	CG	IP	H	BB	SO	SHO	ERA
0	1	.000	10	1	0	14	24	10	0	0	8.38

Ralph Alton McLeod, *Outfield*

McLeod had a cup of coffee with the 1938 Braves. In six games, he had just seven at-bats. During the war, Ralph served with the U.S. Army.

G	R	H	2B	3B	HR	RBI	BB	SO	SB	AVG	Slug
6	1	2	1	0	0	0	0	2	0	.286	.429

Calvin Coolidge Julius Caesar Tuskahoma McLish, *Pitcher*

One of four teenage pitchers the Dodgers used in 1944, McLish logged more innings than any other teen on the staff. An ambidextrous Choctaw Indian, McLish was listed by his draft board as available for service in July of 1944. His Brooklyn teammates collected a $160 purse for him before he left for the navy. Of the kind gesture, McLish said, "Gosh, fellows, I'd like to take you all down to the corner store and have sodas on me." The man of many names enjoyed a long major league career — he pitched through 1964 — and ended his career with the Philadelphia Phillies.

W	L	PCT	G	GS	CG	IP	H	BB	SO	SHO	ERA
92	92	.500	352	209	57	1,609	1,685	552	713	5	4.01

Carl Mac McNabb, *Pinch-Hitter*

A war-era ballplayer, McNabb had one at-bat with the world champion Tigers of 1945. The Alabama native struck out in his only plate appearance. Carl was injured overseas while serving in the armed forces and was shipped stateside in 1943. Sent to Sulphur Springs, West Virginia, to recuperate, McNabb received a medical discharge and joined the minor league Hagerstown Owls. Considered a nifty fielder but weak hitter, Carl made the majors in 1945.

G	R	H	2B	3B	HR	RBI	BB	SO	SB	AVG	Slug
1	0	0	0	0	0	0	0	1	0	.000	.000

Glenn Richard McQuillen, *Outfield*

McQuillen was just beginning to establish himself at the major league level when World War II broke out. A free-swinging batter, Glenn led the Browns in triples in 1942 and struck out the fewest times among Browns regulars, with seventeen whiffs in 100 games played. However, the following year, he was sworn into the navy after he passed his physical examination at Jefferson Barracks, Missouri.

Glenn's two brothers, Jack and James, each served in the war. Glenn and James served in the Pacific Theatre while their brother, Jack, served in Holland with the army. A headline for the *Frederick Post* read, "Three McQuillen Brothers Scattered over the World." Glenn met up with James in Hawaii and the brothers were able to spend two days together after they had just missed meeting each other by a day at Guam. While serving in the South Pacific, Glenn toured with a navy all-star team, making stops in the Marianas.

G	R	H	2B	3B	HR	RBI	BB	SO	SB	AVG	Slug
210	82	176	24	16	4	75	34	49	1	.274	.379

Samuel Mack Meeks, *Utility Infielder*

Meeks joined the armed forces after school in 1941 and didn't sign his first pro contract until he was discharged from the service. The South Carolina native played briefly at the major league level with Washington and the Reds but made headlines when he played in Chattanooga. His testimony against Jesse Levan got Levan barred for life for cavorting with gamblers.

G	R	H	2B	3B	HR	RBI	BB	SO	SB	AVG	Slug
102	25	50	8	0	3	18	9	36	3	.251	.337

Russell Harlan Meers, *Pitcher*

A short southpaw, Meers pitched for parts of three years with the Chicago Cubs; he never saw major league action in any other uniform. Russ missed four full Baseball seasons to service during World War II and was the first Cubs player to enlist in the colors. Meers served his time under Uncle Sam in the navy where he was stationed at Norfolk. While playing an exhibition game with Norfolk against the Philadelphia Athletics, Meers tossed a two-hitter.

W	L	PCT	G	GS	CG	IP	H	BB	SO	SHO	ERA
3	3	.500	43	4	0	83	76	48	35	0	4.01

Henry William "Heinie" Meine, *Pitcher*

Nicknamed "The Count of Luxembourg," Meine pitched briefly with the Browns in the early 1920s. When his pet pitch, the spitball, was outlawed, Meine became so despondent that he quit the game. Meine opened a tavern but many of his patrons pressured him to give baseball another chance, leading the Count to brush aside the joy juice and take up pitching again. It was a wise choice on Meine's part since he tied for the National League lead in wins during the 1931 season. His last year in the majors came in 1934, and as a man in his forties he joined the army to help out during World War II.

W	L	PCT	G	GS	CG	IP	H	BB	SO	SHO	ERA
68	50	.569	165	132	60	998	1,125	287	199	7	3.96

Reuben Franklin Melton, *Pitcher*

A big pitcher who missed his share of bats, Melton played six years at the major league level. He originally came up with the 1941 Phillies and made his way to Brooklyn for the 1943 season. Melton struggled with his accuracy in his first year at Brooklyn but made strides in finding the strike zone in 1944. He finished second on the team in games started and strikeouts. He lost the 1945 season to service in the armed forces, as Rube served as a private with the Third Regiment at Fort McClellan. Melton was a large man, and writer Harry Grayson once referred to him as "an oversized Ichabod Crane."

W	L	PCT	G	GS	CG	IP	H	BB	SO	SHO	ERA
30	50	.375	162	87	25	704	624	395	363	6	3.62

Lloyd Archer Merriman, *Outfield*

A gifted natural athlete, Merriman was a highly touted prospect for the Reds who missed action on the ball diamond to two separate military campaigns. The Clovis, California, native missed time as a minor leaguer to service during World War II. Since he was a pilot, and thus in demand, he was called back to the military for the Korean War. For more on Merriman, see his listing in the section on the Korean War.

G	R	H	2B	3B	HR	RBI	BB	SO	SB	AVG	Slug
455	140	291	64	12	12	117	126	124	20	.242	.345

John Warren "Jack" Merson, *Second Base/Third Base*

Jack served in the military before he joined the professional baseball ranks. After his discharge he caught on with Pinky May's Albany Senators. He made his major league debut with the 1951 Pirates and played his last game with the 1953 Red Sox.

G	R	H	2B	3B	HR	RBI	BB	SO	SB	AVG	Slug
125	47	116	22	4	6	52	23	45	1	.257	.363

James Verlin Mertz, *Pitcher*

In Jim's only season at the major league level, he appeared in 33 games for the 1943 Senators. Skipper Ossie Bluege used Mertz out of the bullpen and also in the rotation; Jim made ten starts in his only major league campaign. Mertz, who grew up playing ball on the sandlots of Lima, Ohio, was reclassified 1-A before the start of the 1944 baseball season. He was inducted into the armed forces shortly thereafter and served at Camp Blanding, Florida.

W	L	PCT	G	GS	CG	IP	H	BB	SO	SHO	ERA
5	7	.417	33	10	2	117	109	58	53	0	4.62

William Andrew Metzig, *Second Base*

Bill Metzig appeared in only five major league games—all in 1944—and he missed the entire 1945 baseball season to service in the United States Navy. He played all five of his major league games at second base.

G	R	H	2B	3B	HR	RBI	BB	SO	SB	AVG	Slug
5	1	2	0	0	0	1	1	4	0	.125	.125

Lambert Daniel "Dutch" Meyer, *Second Base*

Meyer appeared in one game for the 1937 Chicago Cubs and didn't resurface at the major league level again until the Tigers called him up in 1940. Dutch's task with the Tigers was serving as the great Charlie Gehringer's backup. He was drafted into the army after the 1942 baseball season and missed the entire 1943 and 1944 seasons to the war. In 1945 Dutch returned to baseball, but not to the Tigers. He enjoyed his finest year as the Indians' everyday second baseman that season.

G	R	H	2B	3B	HR	RBI	BB	SO	SB	AVG	Slug
286	113	262	49	12	10	93	82	75	5	.264	.367

Russell Charles Meyer, *Pitcher*

The "Mad Monk," Meyer was one of baseball's most noted eccentrics. Quick-tempered and quick-witted, Meyer was remembered by Oscar Fraley for "his proclivity toward impromptu donnybrooks." During the war, before Russ had made his major league debut, he served briefly during the 1943 season before he was discharged. Meyer returned to Illinois where he operated a Christmas tree farm. When the minor league club in Milwaukee planted evergreens beyond the center-field fence as a backdrop for hitters, Meyer spotted the trees and cooed, "Man, look at those big babies! I'd get about 35 bucks apiece for them back home around Christmas time."

W	L	PCT	G	GS	CG	IP	H	BB	SO	SHO	ERA
94	73	.563	319	219	65	1,531	1,606	541	672	13	3.99

Edward Thomas Miksis, *Utilityman*

Much like Gene Mauch, Miksis was a fresh-faced teenager with the 1944 Dodgers, having just walked off the high school grounds prior to trying on his Dodgers uniform for the first time. He hit .220 as a 17-year-old in 1944 but was inducted into the armed forces shortly after the close of the season.

G	R	H	2B	3B	HR	RBI	BB	SO	SB	AVG	Slug
1,042	383	722	95	17	44	228	215	313	52	.236	.322

Robert John Miller, *Pitcher*

A tall, stoutly built Michigan boy, Miller left the schoolyard to enlist in the armed forces during World War II. A teenager throughout his service, the young Miller saw combat action overseas. Miller patrolled the South Pacific and took part in campaigns at New Guinea and Japan. After his discharge, the Detroit native took to baseball and became a fixture in the Phillies mound corps throughout the 1950s. He was a member of the Phillies' staff for ten years.

W	L	PCT	G	GS	CG	IP	H	BB	SO	SHO	ERA
42	42	.500	261	69	23	821	889	247	263	6	3.97

Roland Arthur "Ronnie" Miller, *Pitcher*

Like teammate Phil McCullough, Miller appeared in only one major league game. His lone major league action came with the 1941 Senators. The thin right-hander missed four years to service in the armed forces during World War II.

W	L	PCT	G	GS	CG	IP	H	BB	SO	SHO	ERA
0	0	—	1	0	0	2	2	1	0	0	4.50

Colonel Buster Mills, *Outfield*

Many players throughout baseball history have been described as nomadic, but Buster gives the term a whole new meaning. In his first six major league seasons, Mills played with six different teams. After his sixth year in the bigs, Buster was given the come-hither by Uncle Sam. While serving in the military, Buster played ball under Birdie Tebbetts at the Waco Army Airfield. He left Birdie after a spell and sought out his commission by attending the Officer Candidate School held at Miami. He graduated and was given his bar and a reassignment to the San Antonio Aviation Cadet Center.

His second assignment kept him close to Tebbetts, who was eager to field a solid team for a service tournament. The entire time that Buster played under Birdie, he tried in vain to obtain a golden cigarette case from the catcher, who didn't smoke. When Birdie was assembling his roster for the tournament, he desired Buster's services and gave his chum a call at San Antonio. He made Mills an offer to join his team for the tournament by saying, "Name your price." Mills replied, "I won't take any money. But if I play, it will cost you that gold cigarette case." In the end, Buster played.

G	R	H	2B	3B	HR	RBI	BB	SO	SB	AVG	Slug
415	200	396	62	19	14	163	131	137	23	.287	.390

Albert Joseph Milnar, *Pitcher*

Al Milnar made an outrageous prediction in May of 1944 that the famed soothsayer Nostradamus would have found insane. Al predicted, while in basic training at Fort McClellan, Alabama, that his former St. Louis Browns teammates would win the pennant. The Browns had been nothing short of a laughingstock in the game for decades, but Milnar's prediction bore fruit, and the Browns took the pennant and went to the 1944 World Series.

Milnar was merely a serviceable major league southpaw. He made his debut with the 1936 Indians. He and teammate Bob Feller paced the league in shutouts during the 1940 season, but after struggling for a couple of years, the Tribe sent Al to the Browns in 1943. He appeared in just three games for the Browns near the close of the season, and was then summoned by Uncle Sam in 1944.

Milnar took his basic training at Fort McClellan with Yankees outfielder Stormy Roy Weatherly. They served in the Infantry Replacement Center at the army installation. Milnar said, "If I can pitch grenades the way I do baseballs, the Nazis are going to streak for home fast." He later entered a specialist company that trained men for intelligence work. Of his army duty, Al said, "You get regular hours, plenty of physical training and exercise and good chow. I feel that undoubtedly there'll be a physically tougher group of men playing ball after the war because they've been in the services."

W	L	PCT	G	GS	CG	IP	H	BB	SO	SHO	ERA
57	58	.496	188	127	49	996	1,043	495	350	10	4.22

Paul Edison Minner, *Pitcher*

An unknown commodity before the war, Minner took the stage in the service ranks. All the rage in Uncle Sam's baseball circuit, Minner pitched for the New Cumberland Army Reception Center squad. Minner was the star attraction there as he beat the great Negro League team, the Homestead Grays, as well as a service squad made up of major leaguers, such as Dom DiMaggio, Phil Rizzuto and Benny McCoy. The public relations officer at New Cumberland raved about their young, stout southpaw. He wrote, "Minner is doing a pretty fair job these days stealing the spotlight from eight former major league stars on the New Cumberland team."

After his discharge, the Brooklyn Dodgers brought Paul up to the major leagues in 1946. His time was cut short due to an arm injury, which may have originated with all the innings Uncle Sam asked him to log at New Cumberland. He made good with the Dodgers in 1948 as a relief pitcher and he tossed a scoreless inning in the 1949 World Series. Dealt to the Cubs, Minner established himself as a fine pitcher at Wrigley. Minner led the Cubs in wins in 1953 and logged a lot of innings each year as the Cubs' top left-handed starter.

W	L	PCT	G	GS	CG	IP	H	BB	SO	SHO	ERA
69	84	.451	253	169	64	1,311	1,428	393	481	9	3.94

John Robert Mize, *First Base*

A tremendous Slugger who was unlike modern-day mashers, Mize fanned only 538 times over the course of 1,884 games. Current home run threats can reach 538 whiffs in three seasons of play. "The Big Cat" broke in with the 1936 Cardinals, stealing the first-base job away from Ripper Collins — no slouch himself, as Ripper hit .313 with 23 home runs and 122 RBIs the year before losing his job to Mize. Johnny hit .329 as a rookie and had already developed the keen batting eye that would be his trademark throughout his career; he fanned just 32 times in 414 at-bats. He finished ten points behind the NL leader in batting average in 1937, as the Big Cat posted a remarkable average of .364. Mize led the league in Slugging during the 1938 campaign and won the batting title in 1939. He led the league in home runs, RBIs and Slugging in 1940 and was dealt to the Giants after an off-year — which would have been a tremendous year for anyone else — in 1941.

The Big Cat played one year with the Giants, in which he led the NL in RBIs and Slugging, before he was inducted into the service. He was almost rejected for military service because of an enlarged heart and high blood pressure. Despite his ailments, Mize was sworn into the navy as a seaman at St. Louis in early 1943. Mize missed the next three years to military service and was initially stationed at the Great Lakes, where he was able to play service ball under the eye of Mickey Cochrane. From the Great Lakes Mize attended a physical instructor's course at Bainbridge and was transferred to an undisclosed point in 1944. That "undisclosed point" turned out to be the South Pacific, where Mize toured the area playing exhibition games at various islands.

G	R	H	2B	3B	HR	RBI	BB	SO	SB	AVG	Slug
1,884	1,118	2,011	367	83	359	1,337	856	524	28	.312	.562

Michael Modak, *Pitcher*

Modak joined the colors at the end of World War II, and he missed the 1946 baseball season to service in the army. Mike spent a year at Fort Meade and played service ball for the Second Army.

W	L	PCT	G	GS	CG	IP	H	BB	SO	SHO	ERA
1	2	.333	20	3	1	42	52	23	7	1	5.79

John Henry Mohardt, *Outfield*

One of professional sports' most educated players, Mohardt was an honor graduate from Notre Dame. John spent just one year with the Tigers and was unable to crack their legendary outfield of Ty Cobb, Harry Heilmann and Bobby Veach. Since there weren't any Cobbs in the football ranks, John left baseball and played a handful of years in professional football. Mohardt used his wages in baseball and football to pay his way through medical school. It was as a doctor that John Mohardt received his greatest fame.

Dr. Mohardt studied under the famous Mayo Brothers at their prestigious clinic. After his studies were complete, John opened his own clinic in the Chicago area. Specializing in brain surgery, Mohardt had a thriving practice, but he gave up his practice after the Japanese bombed Pearl Harbor. Mohardt closed the doors to his clinic and enlisted in the Army Medical Corps. With the rank of major, Mohardt was assigned overseas where he performed surgeries on wounded soldiers in a hospital based in North Africa.

G	R	H	2B	3B	HR	RBI	BB	SO	SB	AVG	Slug
5	2	1	0	0	0	0	1	0	0	1.000	1.000

William Joseph Moisan, *Pitcher*

Described as a "bespectacled junk pitcher," Moisan had a cup of coffee with the 1953 Cubs. During the war, Bill served in the European Theatre of Operations. After his discharge he signed his first pro contract.

W	L	PCT	G	GS	CG	IP	H	BB	SO	SHO	ERA
0	0	—	3	0	0	5	5	2	1	0	5.40

Alex Monchak, *Shortstop*

A fiery competitor who had a short playing career but a lengthy coaching and managing career, Monchak had a cup of coffee with the last-place 1940 Phillies. The type of player that got by on grit and hustle, Monchak expected the same level of enthusiasm from his players. Gus Schrader described Monchak's managerial approach as that of a "strict disciplinarian." Alex missed some minor league service time to duty in the armed forces during World War II.

G	R	H	2B	3B	HR	RBI	BB	SO	SB	AVG	Slug
19	1	2	0	0	0	0	0	6	1	.143	.143

Anselm Winn Moore, *Outfield*

Moore spent one year at the highest level with the defending world champion Tigers of 1946. Detroit wasn't able to make it back to the Fall Classic the year Anse was with them, as Boston captured the AL pennant that season. Moore missed minor league seasoning time to service during World War II.

G	R	H	2B	3B	HR	RBI	BB	SO	SB	AVG	Slug
51	16	28	4	0	1	8	12	9	1	.209	.261

Dee Moore, *Catcher*

Dee saw most of his major league action in 1943, a season he split with the Dodgers and Phillies. He had played briefly in the mid–1930s with the Reds but was able to play more during the war years. Moore was inducted into the military after the 1943 season and spent two years in the U.S. Marine Corps where he managed a service ball team.

G	R	H	2B	3B	HR	RBI	BB	SO	SB	AVG	Slug
98	29	53	9	2	1	22	34	24	1	.232	.303

Euel Walton Moore, *Pitcher*

Moore, a full-blooded Chickasaw Indian, pitched in the majors before World War II. He pitched for the Phillies in 1934 and 1935 but was traded to the Giants during the latter season. The Phillies reacquired him, and his last major league action came with the Phillies of 1936. In January of 1943, Euel was inducted into service at Oklahoma City. In the army, Moore was stationed at Camp Grant in the physical education rehabilitation program. He was able to play some service ball with major leaguer Heinie Mueller.

W	L	PCT	G	GS	CG	IP	H	BB	SO	SHO	ERA
9	16	.360	61	29	5	224	293	77	75	0	5.50

Ferdinand De Paige Moore, *First Base*

Not much is known about Ferdie Moore, including which hand he threw with and how he batted. What is known is that he made his debut as an 18-year-old with Connie Mack's 1914 A's and played in only two games. Thirty years later, when he was in his forties, he joined the navy during World War II.

G	R	H	2B	3B	HR	RBI	BB	SO	SB	AVG	Slug
2	1	2	0	0	0	1	0	2	0	.500	.500

James "Red" Moore, *First Base*

Moore was the type of first baseman that made the rest of his infield look better than they actually were. He was a brilliant defender who was adept at picking errant throws out of the dirt. Because of his talent, he was often accused of showboating, making plays look harder than they were to appease the crowd. At the plate, however, Moore couldn't hit with other first basemen like Buck

Leonard, and was employed simply for his glove. Red served in the military for the duration of World War II. Attached to the Third Army in Europe, Moore served with the combat engineers and saw action in France and Belgium.

(1935–1940): Newark Eagles, Atlanta Black Crackers, Indianapolis ABCs and Baltimore Elite Giants

Terry Bluford Moore, *Outfield*

Arguably the best National League center fielder of his time, Terry Moore may have missed out on a Hall of Fame career due to his three-year hitch in the military. Moore was inserted as the Redbirds' center fielder from day one. Skipper Frankie Frisch gave rookie Terry Moore the job over incumbent Ernie Orsatti, who hit .300 the year before. He enjoyed his breakout year in 1939, when he hit .295 with 17 home runs and 77 RBIs. He followed up that season with a .304 batting average and finished third in the league in stolen bases in 1940. He led the Cardinals to a World Series victory over the Yankees in 1942, when Terry hit .294 in the contest. Once he had reached his peak, Uncle Sam gave him the heave-ho.

Moore spent the majority of his military stint stationed in Panama. Terry served with the Sixth Air Force in Panama, constantly on alert for fear of an enemy air raid. Terry was the batting champion in the Panama Canal Zone League, which also boasted the talents of Red Sox southpaw Mickey Harris. Moore returned to the Redbirds at the age of 34 and suffered a knee injury that hindered him throughout the season. His batting average fell to .263 in 1946 but he raised it to .283 in 1947. He struggled mightily in 1948 and began to lose playing time to Erv Dusak, which forced Moore to call it quits after the season.

G	R	H	2B	3B	HR	RBI	BB	SO	SB	AVG	Slug
1,298	719	1,318	263	28	80	513	406	368	82	.280	.399

Lloyd Albert "Whitey" Moore, *Pitcher*

Moore enjoyed a relatively lengthy career. He pitched at the major league level for seven years. A mainstay with the Cincinnati Reds from 1936 to 1941, Whitey was traded to the Cardinals during the 1942 season. Whitey appeared in nine games for St. Louis and then missed the next three years to military service. After Moore was discharged, he didn't make a return trip to the majors.

W	L	PCT	G	GS	CG	IP	H	BB	SO	SHO	ERA
30	29	.508	133	60	18	514	450	292	228	4	3.75

Robert Morris Morgan, *Utility Infielder*

A teenager during the war, Morgan joined the army in the latter stages of the great conflict. Bobby had a long shelf life in the game of baseball. He played throughout the 1950s and then became a scout after his playing career. He spent time scouting for the Kansas City Royals.

G	R	H	2B	3B	HR	RBI	BB	SO	SB	AVG	Slug
671	286	487	96	11	53	217	327	381	18	.233	.366

Willard Blackmer Morrell, *Pitcher*

Morrell made his major league debut with the Senators in 1926 and then pitched two years with the Giants in the early 1930s. When the United States entered World War II, Morrell was ten years removed from his last major league action. The right-hander enlisted in the Army Air Corps and served as a commissioned officer. Shipped overseas, Bill saw action in Northern Africa during the war. After the fighting ceased, Morrell opted to remain in the Army Air Corps and made the military a career.

W	L	PCT	G	GS	CG	IP	H	BB	SO	SHO	ERA
8	6	.571	48	9	3	144	172	57	35	0	4.63

Newell Obadiah Morse, *Second Base*

Morse had a cup of coffee with the world champion Athletics of 1929. Since the A's had Camera Eye Max Bishop as their regular second sacker, Morse received little work. Newell was approaching 40 when he joined the colors. Afterwards, Morse became a lifelong worker for the Department of Veterans Affairs. While he was working at the Reno Veteran's Hospital later in life, Newell was awarded an exceptional service medal for heroism when he subdued a deranged former hospital security guard that went on a shooting spree at the VA hospital.

G	R	H	2B	3B	HR	RBI	BB	SO	SB	AVG	Slug
8	1	2	0	0	0	0	0	2	0	.074	.074

Arnold Robert Moser, *Pinch Hitter*

Moser had a cup of coffee with the 1937 Reds. The trim Texan would join the U.S. Coast Guard several years later during World War II.

G	R	H	2B	3B	HR	RBI	BB	SO	SB	AVG	Slug
5	0	0	0	0	0	0	0	2	0	.000	.000

Howard Glenn Moss, *Outfield*

A feared Slugger in the minor leagues, Moss never did make good in the majors. Howie was given a trial by the Giants in 1942 but failed to impress. He was then shipped back to the bushes where he had his greatest season in the International League during the 1944 campaign. That year he led the league in hits, doubles, triples, home runs and RBIs. After the close of the season, he was inducted into the navy and was greeted by Stan Musial at the Bainbridge Naval Training Center. He spent one year in the navy and received his last look in the majors during the 1946 season, split between the Reds and Cleveland.

G	R	H	2B	3B	HR	RBI	BB	SO	SB	AVG	Slug
22	3	7	0	0	1	3	17	0	.097	.097	

Charles Malcolm Moss, *Pitcher*

Moss had a cup of coffee with the 1930 Cubs in the year teammate Hack Wilson set the still-standing record for RBIs in a season. The southpaw from Indiana would join the navy during World War II. A sailor of high rank, Moss attained the level of lieutenant commander.

W	L	PCT	G	GS	CG	IP	H	BB	SO	SHO	ERA
0	0	—	12	1	0	19	18	14	4	0	6.16

William Lawrence Mueller, *Outfield*

Bill Mueller was little more than a war-era ballplayer. He played with the White Sox in pieces of the 1942 and 1945 seasons—

unable to reach a career batting average of .150. He served two years in the United States Navy during the war.

G	R	H	2B	3B	HR	RBI	BB	SO	SB	AVG	Slug
39	8	14	1	0	0	5	14	10	3	.149	.160

Emmett Jerome Mueller, *Utilityman*

Mueller lost as many years to World War II as he had playing ball in the majors. As a rookie in 1938, Emmett became the regular second baseman when he supplanted the weak-hitting Delmer Young. Mueller was pushed aside in 1939 when the Phillies acquired Jeep Hughes, which forced Emmett to become a "Jack of all trades." Mueller became a reliable and valuable reserve, filling in wherever he was needed on the ball diamond.

Emmett was inducted into the army shortly after his contract was sold to Montreal, which voided the deal. His initial station was Jefferson Barracks, Missouri, where he served with former Washington Senator George Archie and Hall of Famer Johnny Mize. During his first year in the military, Mueller joined Dizzy Dean's All-Stars, a group that consisted of the finest service ballplayers. While stationed at Jefferson Barracks, Emmett married Joan Lorraine Black. The newlywed was shipped overseas and saw combat action in the European Theatre. He had reached the rank of sergeant at the time he was wounded in a German battlefield and was returned stateside shortly after convalescing in Europe. Although he was through as a player, Emmett was hired as the manager of the Lynchburg Cardinals in the Piedmont League after his discharge.

G	R	H	2B	3B	HR	RBI	BB	SO	SB	AVG	Slug
441	144	324	55	11	17	127	156	124	10	.253	.353

Joseph Gordon Mueller, *Pitcher*

Built along the lines of Don Newcombe, Mueller was an intimidating presence on the mound. Couple his size with his complete absence of accuracy, and he was a certifiable nightmare on the hill. Gordy had a cup of coffee with the 1950 Red Sox. He missed valuable minor league seasoning time to the war.

W	L	PCT	G	GS	CG	IP	H	BB	SO	SHO	ERA
0	0	—	8	0	0	7	11	13	1	0	10.29

Leslie Clyde Mueller, *Pitcher*

Mueller pitched briefly with the Tigers in 1941 and 1945, missing time in between to service in the United States Navy. Les showed promise in 1945, when he posted fewer hits allowed than innings pitched. With the return of the game's stars, he wasn't given another look at the highest level.

W	L	PCT	G	GS	CG	IP	H	BB	SO	SHO	ERA
6	8	.429	30	18	6	148	126	68	50	2	3.77

Ray Coleman Mueller, *Catcher*

Mueller set a record in 1944 for consecutive games caught, as the loss to Ray Lamanno and Dick West cost the Reds their two best options for a platoon partner for Mueller. His record earned him the nickname "Iron Man." After the 1944 season, in which Ray caught 155 games, he was inducted into the army. Iron Man Mueller was sworn in at New Cumberland Reception Center. He spent one year in the service after having been rejected in the past for stomach ulcers.

G	R	H	2B	3B	HR	RBI	BB	SO	SB	AVG	Slug
985	281	733	123	23	56	373	250	322	14	.252	.368

Joseph Allen Muir, *Pitcher*

A Marine during the Second World War, Muir made it to the majors in 1951 with the Pirates. When the ex-Marine was playing ball in the minors late in his career, he decided to quit because there was an age limit placed on new police recruits in the state of Maryland. Believing he was never going to return to the show, he left the game and enrolled in the Maryland State Police Academy while he still met the age requirements.

W	L	PCT	G	GS	CG	IP	H	BB	SO	SHO	ERA
2	5	.286	21	6	1	52	53	25	22	0	5.19

Hugh Noyes Mulcahy, *Pitcher*

Hugh was handed the absolute worst nickname in baseball history due to pitching for a lackluster Phillies team in the late 1930s. The moniker was "Losing Pitcher." Hugh tossed his first fastball at the major league level with the 1935 Phillies. He led all NL pitchers with 59 appearances in 1937, although he posted a poor 8–18 record. Hugh followed up that season by leading the league with 20 losses in 1938. His ERA fell to 3.60 in 1940, but his loss total climbed to 22 since the Phillies hit .238 as a team. Mulcahy was saved from further losses before the 1941 season began when he became the first major leaguer drafted for military service.

Mulcahy became a case study for baseball when he was pressured to seek deferment on grounds of being a major league ballplayer. When his request was denied, every player in the game became subject to a call from Uncle Sam. His request was denied on grounds that baseball, or any sport for that matter, wasn't a necessary wartime occupation. Hugh wasn't bitter about being the first player drafted, saying, "It would not only help me to stay in shape, but I also could instruct some of the younger fellows who might be baseball-minded. There must be plenty of kids from eighteen up who were thinking about starting in baseball when they were called up by Uncle Sam."

His lone regret wasn't baseball-oriented at all. He had yet to complete payments on a new home that he had bought for his parents. Had he played ball at the major league level in 1941, like nearly every other professional, he would have finished the payments, but he was unable to pay off the house on a soldier's salary. When he was inducted, Hugh was under the misconception that he wouldn't remain in the service for long. He said, "I won't be 28 until September and they say that a pitcher's prime comes between the ages of 28 and 31. So, by the time I come out of the army I should be just about reaching my peak."

Mulcahy took his basic training at Camp Edwards on Cape Cod and was assigned to the 101st Field Artillery. He was later reassigned to Fort Jackson in 1943 and was placed in charge of the 28th Division's recreation program. While serving in the army, Hugh wrote a sports column. He had this to say in his column in 1944: "The old wing is as good as new—yes sir, I think she'd be ready to go right now. It's been more than three years now but as for my arm, it's as good as it ever was. I pitched a little with the Second Army this spring, you know. I found I still had all my stuff—hadn't lost any of my speed and control."

Hugh was later shipped overseas and managed a service ballclub in New Guinea. After four and a half years of service in the army, he received his discharge with the rank of master sergeant. When Hugh received his discharge, he said, "I don't think I have anything extra on the ball but I'm halfway hoping all those needles that got punched into my arm put an extra curve in there." When he was asked about rejoining the Phillies, Hugh said, "I plan to report to the Phillies on August 18th but in the meantime I'd like to regain some of the weight I have lost since I left baseball. I don't suppose I'll meet up with enough steaks but maybe I can fatten myself up on a diet of milk and cheese and plenty of rest."

On August 12, 1945, Hugh made his long-awaited return to baseball; the first player selected by Uncle Sam returned home to a hero's reception. Hugh said, "Gee, how I wish I could walk out on the field the first day and start one and win it. I wouldn't ask for anything more than just to go out there and bear down and let those people in the stands know I appreciated them. They were sure swell."

An extremely humble man, Mulcahy made four starts down the stretch with the last-place Phillies, and true to his nickname, picked up three losses courtesy of lousy run support. Early in his stint in the military, Hugh said that a pitcher's prime years were from 28 to 31, ages that the unlucky right-hander spent in the army. However, he wasn't bitter and knew the fans adored him despite his career-long handicap with poor run support. Hugh said shortly after his army discharge, "The fans were always good to me. They were great. I used to think about it when I'd get kind of low. They were pretty fine, I thought, to a fellow who didn't win many ball games."

W	L	PCT	G	GS	CG	IP	H	BB	SO	SHO	ERA
45	89	.336	220	145	63	1,163	1,271	487	314	5	4.48

Ford Parker "Moon" Mullen, *Second Base*

Moon Mullen played one year at the major league level, serving as the Phillies' regular second baseman in 1944. Knowing he was soon to be inducted into the armed forces, Moon sent a letter to general manager Herb Pennock before spring training of 1945 announcing his retirement.

G	R	H	2B	3B	HR	RBI	BB	SO	SB	AVG	Slug
118	51	124	9	4	0	31	28	32	4	.267	.304

Richard Charles Mulligan, *Pitcher*

Dick played with three separate clubs in as many years at the major league level, beginning with the 1941 Senators before playing with the Phillies and the Braves after his four-year stint in the military. Mulligan was stationed at the San Antonio Aviation Cadet Center where he worked and played service ball.

W	L	PCT	G	GS	CG	IP	H	BB	SO	SHO	ERA
3	3	.500	25	6	2	81	82	39	23	0	4.44

Patrick Joseph Mullin, *Outfield*

One of a handful of major league players to lose four full seasons of baseball to the war, Mullin spent his entire career with the Tigers. He was initially summoned to Detroit in 1940 and made only four plate appearances. He showed immense promise the next year, hitting .345 in limited playing time. However, with the war raging overseas, Mullin felt it was his duty to fight. On March 13, 1942, Pat enlisted in the United States Army at Pittsburgh.

Pat served in the United States Army and played ball for the New Cumberland Reception Center team. At New Cumberland, he played in an exhibition game against an all-girls team named the Roxborough Bobbies. He later became the player-manager of the 1,301st Service Unit and received his promotion to corporeal in October of 1942. Dubbed a "celery addict" by sportswriter friend Phil Short, Pat appeared in several army relief shows during his military tenure.

G	R	H	2B	3B	HR	RBI	BB	SO	SB	AVG	Slug
864	381	676	106	43	87	385	330	312	20	.271	.453

George David Munger, *Pitcher*

A Texan with a thick build, Munger missed one year to service during World War II. As a rookie, he pitched with the National League champion Cardinals of 1943. He didn't appear in that World Series, and even though the Cards returned to the Fall Classic in 1944, George missed out on that contest as well due to his late-season military callup. Had he not been called up by Uncle Sam, he would have been an asset in the World Series with his 1.34 ERA over 121 innings.

W	L	PCT	G	GS	CG	IP	H	BB	SO	SHO	ERA
77	56	.579	273	161	54	1,229	1,243	500	564	13	3.83

Edward Joseph Murphy, *First Base*

Murphy hit .250 in limited action with the 1942 Phillies. He was inducted into the armed forces and missed the next three years to service in the military during World War II.

G	R	H	2B	3B	HR	RBI	BB	SO	SB	AVG	Slug
13	2	7	2	0	0	4	2	4	0	.250	.321

Joseph Ambrose Murray, *Pitcher*

Murray had a cup of coffee with the 1950 Athletics, the last team Hall of Fame skipper Connie Mack managed. During World War II, Murray served in the navy.

W	L	PCT	G	GS	CG	IP	H	BB	SO	SHO	ERA
0	3	.000	8	2	0	30	34	21	8	0	5.70

Raymond Lee Murray, *Catcher*

"The Deacon" served in the military during World War II before he made his major league debut. The war's intrusion into Ray's career certainly gave him the impression that he'd never make the majors. When he reached thirty years of age, Ray was still beating around the minors. Cleveland called Murray up in 1948 and he played in the majors until 1954.

G	R	H	2B	3B	HR	RBI	BB	SO	SB	AVG	Slug
250	69	184	37	6	8	80	55	67	1	.252	.352

Daniel Edward Murtaugh, *Second Base*

A scrappy ballplayer in his heyday, Murtaugh is now best known for managing the Pittsburgh Pirates during their finer years in the 1960s and 1970s. His work as a skipper has placed him on the doormat to Cooperstown, as his induction would be a deserving one. A baseball lifer, Murtaugh had a fondness for the dugout and leading the boys. His no-nonsense demeanor led to health issues, as doctors warned Danny about his elevated stress level due to managing. In spite of his doctors' advice, he once said, "I'd rather die of a coronary in the dugout than of boredom in the front office." Murtaugh lost two years of baseball while serving in the Army Air Corps.

G	R	H	2B	3B	HR	RBI	BB	SO	SB	AVG	Slug
767	263	661	97	21	8	219	287	215	49	.254	.317

Stanley Frank Musial, *Outfield*

The greatest player in St. Louis Cardinals' history, Stan "The Man" Musial missed one year to military service. Before the war, Stan had set the National League on fire — he hit for a .347 batting average and led the league with 197 base hits, 51 doubles and a .548 Slugging percentage. Despite those lofty numbers, he was unable to garner his second straight MVP award, which was given to his teammate, Marty Marion, a slick-fielding shortstop.

Musial was inducted into the armed forces after he led the Cardinals to a World Series title over their city rival, the Browns, in 1944. Stan reported to the Bainbridge Naval Training Center where he showed soldiers his batting technique. Musial's batting stance can easily be described as unorthodox, and when a young soldier who didn't know who Musial was spotted his stance, he said, "You'll never get a hit if you hold a bat that way!" Stan the Man was shipped out to Pearl Harbor in the summer of 1945 where he served as a Seaman Second Class. He returned to the Redbirds in 1946 and the rest is history — history found in Cooperstown, that is.

G	R	H	2B	3B	HR	RBI	BB	SO	SB	AVG	Slug
3,026	1,949	3,630	725	177	475	1,951	1,599	696	78	.331	.559

Stephen Nagy, *Pitcher*

The pride of Sussex County, Nagy saw action at the major league level with the 1947 Pirates and the 1950 Senators. The slim southpaw served in the navy during World War II before his major league debut. In the athletic department, Nagy was responsible for providing sporting events and exercise for the sailors. But his stint in the armed forces wasn't all stateside baseball and jumping jacks—Steve was shipped out to the ETO.

His trip to the European Theatre took him to such locales as Newfoundland and St. Davids, Wales. As a chief petty officer in the navy, Nagy later stopped off in Honiton, England, and assisted in the construction of a baseball field. Although Nagy was missing valuable time in baseball, he had no regrets because he met his bride-to-be in England, Ruth Wakeman, and they were wed in December 1944. The following year, he and his bride were shipped to the States where Steve was mustered out of the navy at Mayport, Florida. Nagy said, "I might have missed some of my best years for pitching, but I gained all great years for the rest of my life."

W	L	PCT	G	GS	CG	IP	H	BB	SO	SHO	ERA
3	8	.273	15	10	2	67	87	38	21	0	6.45

Samuel Ralph "Subway Sam" Nahem, *Pitcher*

Nahem earned his nickname not by throwing in the fashion of Tekulve and Quisenberry, but by commuting to Brooklyn during his playing days to obtain his law degree at St. John's University. Subway Sam pitched for the 1938 Dodgers, 1941 Cardinals, and with the Phillies in 1942 and 1946. He lost three years to service in the military and was stationed at Fort Totten, New York. As a corporeal late in 1943, Sam became a sportswriter for *The Alertman*, a publication of the Eastern Anti-Aircraft Forces. He posted a 0.85 service ERA in 1943 and was shipped overseas where he served in the European Theatre. Sam was able to play some service ball in Europe, and he once played on an integrated team with Negro League great Leon Day.

W	L	PCT	G	GS	CG	IP	H	BB	SO	SHO	ERA
10	8	.556	90	12	3	225	222	127	101	0	4.68

Earl Eugene Naylor, *Outfield*

Naylor played briefly at the major league level with the Phillies and Dodgers. Although he was on the Cardinals' service roster, Naylor never played a game in a Redbird uniform. Earl missed the 1944 and 1945 seasons to service in the armed forces.

G	R	H	2B	3B	HR	RBI	BB	SO	SB	AVG	Slug
112	22	54	6	1	3	28	23	35	2	.186	.245

Robert Otis Neighbors, *Reserve*

Neighbors had a cup of coffee with the last-place Browns of 1939. In his only year at the highest level, Bob made just eleven plate appearances but managed to make one of them a home run. Shortly after the bombing at Pearl Harbor, Neighbors enlisted in the armed forces. Eager to get overseas and do some fighting, he enlisted in the Army Air Corps and was commissioned a lieutenant. Lieutenant Neighbors was a co-pilot on a C-54 transport craft. While stateside, Bob served at Sheppard Airfield and played some service ball with Dave Short in 1942.

Shipped out in 1943, Neighbors and his flight crew battle buddies served in hostile territory. An article in the *San Antonio Light* read, "Bob Neighbors is an army lieutenant in air transport in a lonesome part of the world." But Neighbors made it through the war unscathed. However, when Uncle Sam needed pilots again during the Korean War, Bob answered the call once more. During the Korean War, Neighbors was engaged in flight missions over hostile terrain but wouldn't be as lucky as he was in the Second World War. His plane was shot down in August of 1952, and his body was never recovered. Designated as "missing in action," Neighbors' body still remains unclaimed to this day.

G	R	H	2B	3B	HR	RBI	BB	SO	SB	AVG	Slug
7	3	2	0	0	1	1	0	1	0	.182	.455

Glenn Richard "Rocky" Nelson, *First Base*

A three-time MVP in the minor leagues, Rocky had a decent major league career but never did quite reach his potential. A solid batsman with good power despite his smaller-than-Mize stature, Nelson made his debut with the Redbirds after the war.

G	R	H	2B	3B	HR	RBI	BB	SO	SB	AVG	Slug
620	186	347	61	14	31	173	130	94	7	.249	.379

Ernest Alonzo Nevers, *Pitcher*

An American golden boy, Ernie Nevers remains one of the greatest athletes in the nation's history. Built like a Greek god, Nevers seemed to lack any deficiencies. He was a top-flight football player at Stanford whom the legendary Pop Warner called "the greatest football player of all-time." Ernie also acted in movies, playing himself in *The Spirit of Stanford* and starring opposite Richard Arlen and Gloria Stuart in *The All-American*. He pitched in the majors for three years with the Browns, but it was the battlefield that Nevers was born for.

When the war broke out, Nevers was quick to enlist in the U.S. Marine Corps despite his advanced age. Although he was pushing forty, Ernie was the definition of physical fitness and in far greater condition than boys half his age. Commissioned a captain in the Marine Corps, Nevers was eager to get overseas and do some fighting. He wanted little of the stateside athletics programs many athletes were engaged in. He got his wish early on in the war, as writer Nelson Cullenward saw him off when he was shipped out. Cullenward wrote, "You can safely say that Captain Ernie Nevers has left for the South Pacific. We said goodbye and the big guy looked like a graphite commando with pistol in shoulder holster, a long knife on his belt and a tin helmet."

Nevers left behind a wife, Mae, who died while Ernie was fighting overseas. Many a writer said she died courtesy of a broken heart, but she had suffered from pneumonia, which claimed her life. Meanwhile, in the South Pacific, Captain Nevers was engaged in combat duty with the Marines. He served ten months in battle areas in the Pacific Theater and was once cutoff entirely from radio communications, which forced Marine brass to label his squadron "missing in action." But Nevers fought his way out of the Pacific and was able to recount his ordeals to writers. He discussed the flora and fauna of the region with Russ Newland. A bit of a snake enthusiast, Newland asked Ernie about the snakes the region had to offer, to which Nevers said, "I never saw any big snakes. The only ones I saw were pink coral snakes. They are little but they pack an awful wallop. I heard there were big snakes in the jungle but I never went looking for any."

When Nevers returned stateside in 1945, he was approached by the owners of the Chicago football club to sign on as a coach for the upcoming season. He signed a contract with them while he was still in the Marine Corps, serving as an athletic officer at the San Diego Marine base while waiting for his discharge. A war hero, Nevers returned home to a cold house, having lost his bride while he was fighting the enemy. In his early forties, Nevers returned to the gridiron to take his mind off the love he lost while serving in that hostile theatre.

W	*L*	*PCT*	*G*	*GS*	*CG*	*IP*	*H*	*BB*	*SO*	*SHO*	*ERA*
6	12	.333	44	12	6	179	196	61	39	0	4.63

Floyd Elmo Newkirk, *Pitcher*

The Yankees billed Newkirk as the next Mordecai "Three Finger" Brown when they called him up in 1934. Used in just one game, Floyd kept all runners from crossing the plate in his only frame. Newkirk lost two fingers on his pitching hand during a steel mill accident as a young man in Gary, Indiana. Despite the injury, it didn't stop Floyd from pitching ... or from enlisting. When men were rejected for service on many grounds, such as ulcers and punctured eardrums, it seemed unlikely that Floyd, who was missing two fingers, would be accepted. But he was welcomed into the army and served with Battery A, 78th Division of the 308th Field Artillery at Camp Butler, North Carolina.

W	*L*	*PCT*	*G*	*GS*	*CG*	*IP*	*H*	*BB*	*SO*	*SHO*	*ERA*
0	0	—	1	0	0	1	1	1	0	0	0.00

Maurice Milton Newlin, *Pitcher*

Newlin pitched only fifteen games at the major league level over the course of two seasons. The right-hander notched one win and one save in his career. He entered the navy after the 1941 baseball season and spent four years in the armed forces. Newlin served with the Seabees and was able to pitch occasionally for Price's Neck Gunners while in the service. Before his transfer to Quonset, Maury gave demonstrations of control, curves and grips at the recreation department's baseball school at Cardines Field. While he served in the navy, Newlin wed the former Edith Outlaw.

W	*L*	*PCT*	*G*	*GS*	*CG*	*IP*	*H*	*BB*	*SO*	*SHO*	*ERA*
1	2	.333	15	1	0	34	47	14	13	0	6.35

Constantine Gregory "Gus" Niarhos, *Catcher*

On Kansas City's war list during World War II, Niarhos played for the Yankees' top farm system. A top catching prospect, Gus owned an exceptional batting eye but was in the wrong chain. After his discharge, he had to contend with another war veteran, Yogi Berra, for catching duties, and Berra won out. Niarhos would later be shipped to the White Sox, and he spent his major league career as a reserve backstop.

G	*R*	*H*	*2B*	*3B*	*HR*	*RBI*	*BB*	*SO*	*SB*	*AVG*	*Slug*
315	114	174	26	5	1	59	153	56	6	.252	.308

Milton Robert Nielsen, *Reserve*

Used as a pinch-runner and pinch-hitter, Nielsen had two cups of coffee with Cleveland in 1949 and 1951. Milt missed some seasoning time to service in the armed forces during World War II.

G	*R*	*H*	*2B*	*3B*	*HR*	*RBI*	*BB*	*SO*	*SB*	*AVG*	*Slug*
19	2	1	0	0	0	0	3	5	0	.067	.067

Jacob Leland Niemes, *Pitcher*

A man of mystery, what little information there is to be found on Jack Niemes is interesting. Niemes pitched three games at the major league level with the 1943 Reds and then joined the armed forces. The southpaw served as a motor machinist's mate third class in the navy and saw action overseas. As for the mysterious information about Niemes, the only date that could be gathered on the ex-ballplayer was that he was labeled missing in action in the South Pacific in 1945. Nothing else is written about Jack Niemes other than his obituary that boasts his date of death as March 4, 1966, twenty years after the war.

W	*L*	*PCT*	*G*	*GS*	*CG*	*IP*	*H*	*BB*	*SO*	*SHO*	*ERA*
0	0	—	3	0	0	3	5	2	1	0	6.00

Alfred Joseph Niemiec, *Second Base/Shortstop*

Niemiec picked up where Phillies first baseman Tony Lupien left off in his suit against baseball. Lupien had sued the Phillies under the GI Bill of Rights, which stated that returning servicemen were entitled to their positions and same salaries after their discharge from active military duty. Lupien's case was highly publicized since he was suing a major league club, while Niemiec received less press because he was suing the minor league club in Seattle. Although Lupien eventually dropped his case, Niemiec saw his through and won.

Niemiec played briefly in the 1930s with the Red Sox and Athletics and mustered a career .200 batting average at the highest level. At the time of his military induction, he was simply a minor league journeyman. Al served in the navy as a commissioned officer at St. Mary's Pre-Flight School but when he was discharged, Seattle's owner Emil Sick released Al from his baseball contract. Niemiec sued Sick under the Selective Service Act of the GI Bill of Rights and his case was heard by Judge Lloyd L. Black. Judge Black awarded Al his $750 monthly salary with Seattle and said of his decision, "The ball club need not play, but must pay, the petitioner."

G	R	H	2B	3B	HR	RBI	BB	SO	SB	AVG	Slug
78	24	47	3	2	1	23	29	20	2	.200	.243

Ronald James Northey, *Outfield*

Short and husky, Ron was known around the league as "The Round Man." A solid hitter, Northey led the Phillies in nearly every offensive category during the 1943 baseball season. His finest year came in 1944 when Ron posted a remarkable offensive line of a .288 batting average, 35 doubles, 22 home runs, and 104 RBIs. Ron was able to put his off-field problems aside while on the diamond, as he was under constant pressure from his draft board. The Round Man was initially refused by the military due to high blood pressure, to which writer Harry Grayson quipped, "They get that way playing with the Phillies." He was later classified 1-AL, meaning he was suitable for limited service.

There was a big to-do regarding men who had been placed in limited service or who were classified 4-A in late 1944 and early 1945. The War Department was pressured to reevaluate the men listed as suitable for limited service. Ron took his re-examination physical in January of 1945 and was sent to a naval hospital for further checkups to determine whether he should retain his 1-AL classification. After the checkups and exams, Ron became the first major league ballplayer drafted into the armed forces after the War Department's crackdown.

To go along with his high blood pressure, Ron's re-examination physical also discovered that he had a punctured ear drum as well as a heart condition. Despite his ailments, the Round Man was inducted into the army and was glad to get the draft fiasco over and done with. Northey said, "It was not my fault that I was not in the army long ago and now that I am here I want to do my part the same as any other American, to get this war over in a hurry." After a few short months of service at Fort Lewis, Ron received a medical discharge from the army on account of his punctured ear drum.

G	R	H	2B	3B	HR	RBI	BB	SO	SB	AVG	Slug
1,084	385	874	172	28	108	513	361	297	7	.276	.450

Ralph Joseph "Rube" Novotney, *Catcher*

Rube played one year at the major league level with the 1949 Cubs. A reserve catcher, Novotney served with the U.S. Marine Corps during World War II.

G	R	H	2B	3B	HR	RBI	BB	SO	SB	AVG	Slug
22	4	18	2	1	0	6	3	11	0	.269	.328

Walter Andrew Ockey, *Pitcher*

A war-era pitcher, Ockey appeared in two games with the war-ravaged Giants of 1944. Walter had served in the army the year before but was given a medical discharge in time to participate in spring training of 1944.

W	L	PCT	G	GS	CG	IP	H	BB	SO	SHO	ERA
0	0	—	2	0	0	3	2	2	1	0	3.00

David Everett Odom, *Pitcher*

A war-era pitcher, "Porky" quit baseball in 1940 due to a dead arm and enlisted in the army. Odom served with the Army Engineers for a little over two years but was medically discharged before 1943. After a couple years in the army, with his arm rested up, Odom found he could pitch again and tried out with the Braves in 1943. He made the squad and pitched that season — his only year in the majors — out of the Boston bullpen.

W	L	PCT	G	GS	CG	IP	H	BB	SO	SHO	ERA
0	3	.000	22	3	1	55	54	30	17	0	5.24

Leonard Joseph Okrie, *Catcher*

A back-up catcher in the majors, Okrie spent a few seasons with the Senators but rarely received much playing time. After his playing days Okrie had a lengthy career as a respected minor league manager. Before he made his major league debut, Len served in the military during World War II.

G	R	H	2B	3B	HR	RBI	BB	SO	SB	AVG	Slug
42	3	17	1	1	0	3	9	16	0	.218	.256

Thomas Noble Oliver, *Outfield*

Many southern ballplayers were given the nickname "Dixie" during the post–Civil War decades but Oliver was handed the moniker of "Rebel" by his peers. An Alabama native, Oliver was the Red Sox's everyday center fielder during the early 1930s. As a rookie in 1930, Tom led the American League in at-bats. Rebel was the type of batter that never saw a pitch he didn't like — he rarely walked and hardly ever struck out. When the U.S. entered battle during World War II, Tom's major league career had been over for some time. He entered the navy and served aboard a destroyer that was engaged in maneuvers around the Solomon Islands.

G	R	H	2B	3B	HR	RBI	BB	SO	SB	AVG	Slug
514	202	534	101	11	0	176	105	61	12	.277	.340

Bernard Charles "Barney" Olsen, *Outfield*

Olsen had a cup of coffee with the Cubs just before the war. After Pearl Harbor was bombed, Barney left the game and joined the United States Navy. He enlisted in 1942 as a storekeeper third class and took his training at the Great Lakes Naval Training Station. Olsen was eventually relocated to the West Coast where he served in supply.

G	R	H	2B	3B	HR	RBI	BB	SO	SB	AVG	Slug
24	13	21	6	1	1	4	4	11	0	.288	.438

Vern Jarl Olsen, *Pitcher*

A lean southpaw from Oregon, Olsen pitched with the Cubs prior to World War II for four years and played just one year after the war. His finest season came in 1940 when he went 13–9 with a 2.97 ERA. He joined the United States Navy after the completion of the 1942 Baseball season and played service ball while he was stationed in Hawaii.

W	L	PCT	G	GS	CG	IP	H	BB	SO	SHO	ERA
30	26	.536	112	60	23	517	547	192	201	7	3.39

John Jordan "Buck" O'Neil, *First Base*

A trailblazer in his own right, Buck may have been too long in the tooth to play in the major leagues after Jackie Robinson broke the color barrier, but O'Neil broke another barrier afterwards. He became the first black coach in the majors when the Chicago Cubs brought him into the dugout. A warm, genial man throughout his life, O'Neil was the perfect goodwill ambassador for the game of baseball. He bridged the gap between the Negro Leagues and the majors, and while he served on the Baseball Hall of Fame's Veterans Committee, he kept alive the spirit of the long disbanded Negro Leagues.

A kid from Florida, O'Neil escaped the life of a farmhand through baseball. While boxing celery as a teen, Buck, who worked with his father in the celery fields, muttered, "Damn, there's got to be something better than this." His father urged him to find it and he eventually did, on the ball diamond. After a couple of years playing for teams of lesser quality, such as the Zulu Cannibals, Buck caught on with the Kansas City Monarchs and found a new home in Missouri. A fine all-around ballplayer, O'Neil was a decent hitter and fielded first base well, but his leadership qualities were his greatest asset. They would serve him well as a manager in black baseball, a coach in the majors and a scout for the Kansas City Royals, as well as a non-commissioned officer in the navy.

Buck manned first base for the Monarchs until he was inducted into the navy in 1943. A supply man, O'Neil entered the navy at Norfolk and was later assigned to a ship. Although Buck missed out on the better part of three years to World War II, he made up for lost time upon his return to the diamond. Buck led the Monarchs to the World Series by capturing the batting title during his finest season in 1946. He hit the Newark Eagles vaunted staff of Leon Day and Max Manning quite handily in the World Series with a pair of home runs and a .333 batting average, but his Monarchs lost the series in seven games.

Afterwards, Buck's main task was leading the Monarchs in the years after integration. As player-manager for the Monarchs, Buck was a fixture in the All-Star Games when the talent level in the Negro Leagues began to dry up because of the majors. He participated in eight All-Star Games as either a player or a manager. In the 1950s, Buck would sign and send such stars as Ernie Banks, George Altman and Elston Howard to the major leagues. Upon his death a few years ago, Buck was widely regarded as the face of black baseball, the man who kept history alive through his work in museums and his role as an ambassador.

(1937–1955): Kansas City Monarchs and Memphis Red Sox

Harry Mink O'Neill, *Reserve*

When a reader scans the *Baseball Encyclopedia*, he is likely to run across the name Harry O'Neill without stopping. O'Neill played in one game with his hometown Athletics in 1939 without an official at-bat. Although O'Neill's baseball career was less than stellar, a person would shortchange Lieutenant O'Neill if they glossed over his life. One of only two former major league ballplayers to have been killed in action, Harry O'Neill paid the ultimate price for freedom and liberty. A big, physical individual, O'Neill attended Gettysburg College before Connie Mack brought him home to Philadelphia. The war and major league baseball were far from O'Neill's mind when he quit the game to work as a high school coach at Upper Darby Junior High School in Pennsylvania. When Pearl Harbor was bombed, Harry bid his wife, Ethel, and his new occupation farewell to do his bit for his country. He enlisted in the U.S. Marine Corps and was commissioned a lieutenant before his squad was shipped overseas.

Shipped out to the Pacific Theatre, O'Neill was engaged in heavy combat action with his Marines. Lieutenant O'Neill led his troops on land while they fought at Iwo Jima. Under intense enemy fire, O'Neill was struck and killed on the sands of that faraway land. The Marine Corps notified his widow that he had died while serving his country on March 6, 1945, at Iwo Jima. Baseball writers, who barely knew the man, mourned his passing as the game's fraternity lost one of its own.

G	R	H	2B	3B	HR	RBI	BB	SO	SB	AVG	Slug
1	0	0	0	0	0	0	0	0	0	—	—

Manuel Dominguez Onis, *Catcher*

A longtime minor league catcher, Onis had one at-bat at the major league level. The backstop from Florida slapped a single in that trip, which gave him a perfect 1.000 batting average. Known by a multitude of names, Manuel is also referred to as Ralph, Manny and Curly Onis. During the war, Manuel served in the U.S. Coast Guard.

G	R	H	2B	3B	HR	RBI	BB	SO	SB	AVG	Slug
1	0	1	0	0	0	0	0	0	0	1.000	1.000

Frederick Raymond "Fritz" Ostermueller, *Pitcher*

A solid major league pitcher for the Red Sox during the late 1930s, Fritz was a good southpaw with a sharp wit. After he struggled in 1940, the Bosox traded him to the Browns where he was a seldom-used pitcher by skipper Luke Sewell. When Uncle Sam began to claim players for the war effort, Fritz returned to prominence. With the Pirates in 1944, Fritz posted a 2.72 ERA. Ostermueller wanted to join the military but was rejected for service on medical grounds early in the war. In 1945 he was summoned by his draft board again and accepted for duty. Fritz spent about half a year in the military at the end of the fighting.

W	L	PCT	G	GS	CG	IP	H	BB	SO	SHO	ERA
114	115	.498	390	246	113	2,068	2,170	835	774	11	3.99

Joseph Paul Ostrowski, *Pitcher*

Nicknamed "Professor" because the University of Scranton grad taught school before he became a pro baseball player, Ostrowski possessed a serious, bespectacled appearance that did the moniker justice. The professor gave up teaching and baseball pursuits during World War II when he joined the Army Air Corps. Joe served in the European Theatre of Operations and spent plenty of his service time in the Mediterranean waters. After his discharge, Ostrowski gave baseball a chance and made good with the 1948 Browns. He ended his major league career in 1952 as a member of the world champion Yankees.

W	L	PCT	G	GS	CG	IP	H	BB	SO	SHO	ERA
23	25	.479	150	37	12	455	559	98	131	0	4.55

Don Wilson Padgett, *Catcher*

A versatile player capable of filling in behind the plate, in the outfield or at first base, Padgett missed four years to service in the United States Navy. When Padgett was inducted into the navy, the Dodgers had recently purchased his contract from the Cardinals. However, in the contract that was signed, a clause stated that if he was inducted into the military before the 1942 season began, the Cardinals would refund the Dodgers their purchase price of $25,000. He was inducted before the season, and the Cardinals seemed obligated to refund the Dodgers' money. But this was baseball under the Landis regime. The commissioner stepped in and ruled the Cardinals should keep the money spent on Padgett while the Dodgers retained his rights as he served in the navy.

During his stint in the navy, Padgett was one of many major league ballplayers to be cycled through the Norfolk Naval Training Station. He was able to play some baseball at Norfolk before his reassignment to the West Coast. Don Padgett is best remembered for being one of baseball's greatest "fluke players." A decent hitter throughout his early years, Padgett hit .399 in 92 games for the 1939 Cardinals. He watched his average fall 157 points the following year and remain in the .240 range the rest of his career.

G	R	H	2B	3B	HR	RBI	BB	SO	SB	AVG	Slug
699	247	573	111	16	37	338	141	130	6	.288	.415

Richard Paul "Mike" Palm, *Pitcher*

Palm had a cup of coffee with his hometown Red Sox in 1948 — the extent of his major league career. Before he reached the bigs, Mike served in the military during World War II.

W	L	PCT	G	GS	CG	IP	H	BB	SO	SHO	ERA
0	0	—	3	0	0	3	6	5	1	0	6.00

Alfred Thomas Papai, *Pitcher*

With a different team every year, the tall, slender right-hander was used almost exclusively in mop-up situations. Papai pitched in the majors during the late 1940s and intermittently throughout the 1950s. Al, who became a mail carrier after his playing days, spent time in the army during World War II.

W	L	PCT	G	GS	CG	IP	H	BB	SO	SHO	ERA
9	14	.391	88	18	8	240	281	138	70	0	5.36

Francis James "Salty" Parker, *Shortstop/First Base*

A baseball lifer, Parker may have played only a few games in the majors but he spent a lifetime in the game. Salty's only major league playing time came with the 1934 Tigers, who finished second in the American League. With his career as a player about to end, Parker shifted gears and became a coach. Salty was managing the St. Paul Saints at the time he left for the military during World War II.

Parker walked away from the Saints dugout and entered the clubhouse of Uncle Sam. He served at Fort Bliss, Texas, for a time before he was moved out west to Camp Callan, California. A commissioned officer, Salty served in an anti-aircraft outfit in the army. After his military discharge, Salty returned to the minor leagues. He left the frozen regions of St. Paul and took a job close to his old army stomping grounds when he assumed the manager's post at Shreveport. Parker would have a lengthy coaching and managing career, which included interim gigs in the majors with the Mets and Astros.

G	R	H	2B	3B	HR	RBI	BB	SO	SB	AVG	Slug
11	6	7	2	0	0	4	2	3	0	.280	.360

Thomas Parker, *Pitcher*

A heavyset pitcher from Alexandria, Louisiana, Parker pitched for the powerhouse Homestead Grays of the late 1930s but was essentially a journeyman hurler. With the St. Louis Stars in 1943, Parker was inducted into the military but didn't last long. After less than a year in the armed forces, the husky pitcher was discharged. At the end of his career, he pitched a couple of seasons in the minors after the game was integrated.

(1929–1949): Homestead Grays, Memphis Red Sox, Indianapolis ABCs, Toledo Crawfords, St. Louis Stars, New York Black Yankees, New York Cubans and Birmingham Black Barons

Charles Edison Parks, *Catcher*

An average catcher, Parks played a few years with the Newark Eagles sandwiched around his stint in the armed forces during World War II. With a rather weak bat, Parks was a backup when he first joined the Negro Leagues but had worked his way into a regular role just before the war. Inducted into the army, Charlie saw combat action in the European Theatre and was awarded three Bronze Stars for his war-time heroics. Discharged with the rank of sergeant, Parks returned to the Eagles and caught Leon Day's Opening Day no-hitter.

(1939–1947): Newark Eagles and New York Black Yankees

Melvin Lloyd Parnell, *Pitcher*

Like many young ballplayers that entered the service, Parnell took full advantage of the stage that was military baseball. An unknown commodity before the war, Mel stood batters on their ears throughout his tenure with Uncle Sam's fighting forces. Parnell was the talk of athletics at the Blytheville Army Air Base where he was stationed. After the southpaw was mustered out of the army, he joined the Red Sox in 1947 and was one of their best pitchers during his heyday. He led the American League in wins during the 1949 season.

W	L	PCT	G	GS	CG	IP	H	BB	SO	SHO	ERA
123	75	.621	289	232	113	1,752	1,715	758	732	20	3.50

Roy Robert Partee, *Catcher*

Roy made his major league debut in 1943 as a war-era receiver. The Red Sox gave open auditions at the catcher post when Frankie Pytlak entered the navy, but Boston never could find a suitable replacement. Partee played regularly for Joe Cronin his rookie year, splitting time with veteran Johnny Peacock, and caught the majority of the Red Sox's games in 1944 as well. On his initial draft physical, he was found unfit for duty due to a bad ankle, but he was drafted into the army after the 1944 baseball season. Roy reported to Fort MacArthur and lost one baseball campaign to the war.

G	R	H	2B	3B	HR	RBI	BB	SO	SB	AVG	Slug
367	89	273	41	5	2	114	132	120	2	.250	.303

Robert Lee Patrick, *Outfield*

Bob Patrick played briefly for the Tigers in 1941 and 1942. The Arkansas native spent three years in the military and never returned to the major league level after his discharge.

G	R	H	2B	3B	HR	RBI	BB	SO	SB	AVG	Slug
9	3	4	1	0	1	3	1	1	0	.267	.533

Andrew L. "Pat" Patterson, *Third Base*

A graduate of Wiley College, Patterson became a high school superintendent in the Houston area after baseball. A switch-hitting third baseman with a nomadic career, Pat spent the majority of his time in the Negro Leagues with the Philadelphia Stars. Noted more as a contact hitter than a hitter for power, Patterson left the Stars in 1942 when he was inducted for military duty. After three and a half years in the military, Pat returned to the Negro Leagues and signed with the Newark Eagles, who would win the World Series in 1946.

(1934–1949): Philadelphia Stars, Kansas City Monarchs, Cleveland Red Sox, Homestead Grays, Pittsburgh Crawfords and Newark Eagles

Gene Tunney Patton, *Utility Infielder*

Patton's major league career mirrors that of the fabled Archie "Moonlight" Graham, in that he appeared in one game and wasn't able to record an official at-bat. Patton's day in the majors came in 1944 as a seventeen-year-old kid. He then entered the military in 1945 and never resurfaced at the major league level.

G	R	H	2B	3B	HR	RBI	BB	SO	SB	AVG	Slug
1	0	0	0	0	0	0	0	0	0	—	—

Theodore John Pawelek, *Pinch Hitter*

Nicknamed "Porky" on account of his short and chunky build, Pawelek had a cup of coffee with the 1946 Cubs directly after the war. Ted, a longtime manager in the minor leagues, spent three years in the U.S. Marine Corps during the Second World War.

G	R	H	2B	3B	HR	RBI	BB	SO	SB	AVG	Slug
4	0	1	1	0	0	0	0	0	0	.250	.500

Isaac Overton Pearson, *Pitcher*

A hard-luck pitcher like most Phillies hurlers, Pearson lost thirteen games his rookie year, fourteen as a sophomore and junior, and posted a .143 winning percentage in his fourth year. He joined the military in 1943, four years after he joined the Phillies directly from Ole Miss. Ike served in the U.S. Marine Corps and was stationed at Quantico with former White Sox Hall of Famer Ted Lyons. Pearson pitched in only four service games at Quantico because his Marine training kept him far too busy for recreational sporting events.

W	L	PCT	G	GS	CG	IP	H	BB	SO	SHO	ERA
13	50	.206	165	54	10	558	611	268	149	2	4.84

Stephen George Peek, *Pitcher*

Peek pitched one year in the major leagues, but his greatest ball diamond success came for Uncle Sam. During World War II, Steve served in the army at Fort Niagara. While pitching for the Niagara ballclub, Steve faced the Negro League champion Kansas City Monarchs in an exhibition game. He proceeded to stand black baseball's finest squad on its ears, beating the Monarchs with a total of ten strikeouts. He was later shipped overseas and pitched in a contest against Philadelphia Athletics palmball expert Bob Savage at Salzburg, Austria.

W	L	PCT	G	GS	CG	IP	H	BB	SO	SHO	ERA
4	2	.667	17	8	2	80	85	39	18	0	5.06

Edward Charles Pellagrini, *Utility Infielder*

A terrific fielder with a weak stick, Pellagrini was the second-best fielding shortstop in the Pacific Coast League the year before his navy induction. Eddie left the game and went to the Great Lakes Naval Training Station where he served in the athletic department and played service ball under Mickey Cochrane. Later, Pellagrini and National League Slugger Johnny Mize were shipped to the Pacific Theatre. After his naval discharge, Pellagrini broke in with the 1946 Red Sox that captured the AL pennant. A Boston College graduate, Eddie would return to the campus after his playing days and coach the university's baseball club for four decades.

G	R	H	2B	3B	HR	RBI	BB	SO	SB	AVG	Slug
563	167	321	42	13	20	133	128	201	13	.226	.316

Ralph Foster "Cy" Perkins, *Catcher*

A favorite of manager Connie Mack, Perkins caught with the Mackmen for three decades. He broke in with the A's in 1915 and was cut loose in 1930. His last major league action came with the 1934 Tigers. A valuable, intelligent reserve catcher, Cy mentored Mickey Cochrane when the Hall of Fame backstop was a youngster in Philadelphia. Already past forty when the war broke out, Perkins enlisted nonetheless and served as a yeoman in the navy. After his discharge he was signed to manage the minor league Burlington Bees.

G	R	H	2B	3B	HR	RBI	BB	SO	SB	AVG	Slug
1,171	329	933	175	35	30	409	301	221	18	.259	.352

Harry Walter Perkowski, *Pitcher*

Originally signed by the Giants in 1941, Harry was cut loose by the club when the war depleted its farm system. Inducted into the armed forces, Perkowski served with the navy and was assigned to the amphibious forces. The southpaw was in the transportation services and his duties centered on sending troops and supplies to the frontlines. In total, Harry spent thirty months overseas in such faraway locales as Normandy and the North African region. After his discharge, Perkowski was picked up by the Reds and he pitched seven seasons for Cincinnati.

W	L	PCT	G	GS	CG	IP	H	BB	SO	SHO	ERA
33	40	.452	184	76	24	698	719	324	296	4	4.37

Leonard John Perme, *Pitcher*

A difficult-to-hit southpaw, Perme initially signed in 1937 and enjoyed getting paid for something he loved doing. He served three of his baseball seasons in the navy and played ball for the navy during the war, which took him to many installations. After his baseball career was over, Perme worked for the city of Los Angeles.

W	L	PCT	G	GS	CG	IP	H	BB	SO	SHO	ERA
0	1	.000	8	1	1	17	11	11	6	0	3.18

William Andrew Pertica, *Pitcher*

Pertica broke in with the Red Sox during the Deadball Era but spent most of his time with the Cardinals in the early stages of the Lively Ball Era. Bill, who fashioned a pair of shutouts in his career, was well past the age of service during World War II, but the former major leaguer enlisted in the army nonetheless. The old right-hander was a 40-plus-year old buck private.

W	L	PCT	G	GS	CG	IP	H	BB	SO	SHO	ERA
22	18	.550	74	47	17	330	370	138	98	2	4.28

John Michael Pesky, *Shortstop*

The year before Pesky entered the military, he as a rookie led the American League in base hits. He then lost the 1943 through 1945 seasons to service in the navy and returned to lead the American League in hits in 1946. In 1942 Pesky totaled 205 hits and amassed 208 in 1946. It seems reasonable to assume that Pesky would have reached the two hundred hits plateau each year he missed to the war, therefore giving him a possible 600 he missed out on in his career. Factoring in those extra 600 base hits to his career total, Pesky would have 2,055 for his career. Not a poor sum by anyone's estimate.

Johnny Pesky entered the navy and was initially sent to Amherst College for training. From there, he was assigned with teammate Ted Williams to the Naval Pre-Flight School at Chapel Hill, North Carolina, where the two Boston ballplayers completed six weeks of training. He was transferred from the Pre-Flight School to Bainbridge Naval Training Station late in 1943. His career in the navy proved to be rather nomadic but also beneficial, for Pesky met and married his wife, Ruth Hickey, at Gordon Field in Atlanta. In addition to meeting his future bride at Gordon Field, he was also able to manage the installation's baseball club.

He attended and graduated from the Assistant Operations Officers School held at the Atlanta Naval Air Station and was commissioned an ensign in the Naval Reserves. From the southern United States, Pesky was shipped out to the South Pacific. While stationed on foreign soil, Pesky let it be known that he had no intention of returning to baseball upon his discharge from the navy. An offer to enter the lumber business in his native Oregon seemed too perfect to pass, but when Johnny received his discharge, he returned to Boston and proceeded to pace the AL in base hits.

As a youth, Pesky was quite adept at another sport: hockey. He was so good on the rink that the Bruins (I have also read that the hockey team in question was the New York Rangers.) allowed the swift little shortstop to train with them after his baseball duties had been met. He trained with the Bruins under his given name, Paveskovich, but when Red Sox skipper Joe Cronin received news of this, he was less than happy. Cronin told Pesky, "Pesky, Paveskovich, or whatever your name is, get off the ice and stay off!"

G	R	H	2B	3B	HR	RBI	BB	SO	SB	AVG	Slug
1,270	867	1,455	226	50	17	404	662	218	53	.307	.386

William David Peterman, *Pinch-Hitter*

Not many former players can say they were perfect hitters at the major league level, but Bill Peterman can. Bill strode to the plate one time in his career, with the 1942 Phillies, and slapped a single. Bill was inducted into the army in 1943 and played service ball in 1943 with Philadelphia teammate Hal Marnie for the New Cumberland Reception Center club.

G	R	H	2B	3B	HR	RBI	BB	SO	SB	AVG	Slug
1	0	1	0	0	0	0	0	0	0	1.000	1.000

Russell Dixon Peters, *Utility Infielder*

Peters made his major league debut in 1936 with Connie Mack's Athletics. It was around this time that Mack had unloaded his pricy stars, leaving him in the star department only Indian Bob Johnson. Rusty showed his versatility by playing at four different positions in his rookie season. In 1937, he was able to play regularly, but by 1938, Dario Lodigiani had taken his job. Rusty then caught on with the Indians and played in Cleveland through the early 1940s. He was inducted into the armed forces on April 20, 1945, and received his discharge late in the 1946 baseball season. Shortly after his discharge, Rusty was traded to the Browns where he played one final season.

G	R	H	2B	3B	HR	RBI	BB	SO	SB	AVG	Slug
417	123	289	53	16	8	117	98	199	9	.236	.326

Kent Franklin Peterson, *Pitcher*

The Reds brought Peterson directly to Cincinnati after his high school graduation in 1944. He wasn't the youngest player used by the Reds that year, as 15-year-old Joe Nuxhall tossed one wild inning for them as well. The next year, Kent was inducted into the army and missed the 1945 and 1946 seasons to service under Uncle Sam.

W	L	PCT	G	GS	CG	IP	H	BB	SO	SHO	ERA
13	38	.255	147	43	7	420	434	215	208	1	4.95

David Earl Philley, *Outfield*

The Texas-born Philley enjoyed a decent major league career, finding his niche as a pinch-hitter. The switch-hitter was the type of player who kept his suitcases packed, as Dave was constantly dealt from team to team. He played with eight teams over the course of his long career, spending the majority of his time with the White Sox. Philley was in his early twenties when he was drafted into the United States Army, and he spent three years serving under Uncle Sam.

G	R	H	2B	3B	HR	RBI	BB	SO	SB	AVG	Slug
1,904	789	1,700	276	72	84	729	594	551	102	.270	.377

Jack Dorn Phillips, *First Base*

Tall with long, lanky arms, Phillips was nicknamed "Stretch" by his peers. The Clarkson University graduate spent time in the armed forces before the Yankees called him up in 1947. Stretch would play on into the 1950s with the Pirates and Tigers before retiring from the game. He would later return to Clarkson University and serve as head baseball coach for a number of years.

G	R	H	2B	3B	HR	RBI	BB	SO	SB	AVG	Slug
343	111	252	42	16	9	101	85	86	5	.283	.396

Urbane Henry Pickering, *Third Base*

Pickering was a slap-hitting third baseman for the Red Sox during their greatest period of struggle. The Kansas native quit baseball to enroll in the Modesto police force in 1934. He made law enforcement his career, starting out as a traffic officer before becoming a patrolman then a sergeant. By the start of World War II, he had been named captain of the Modesto Police Department. But with the war raging overseas, Pickering left Modesto and joined the army. After his army discharge, Urbane returned to Modesto and was given the title of police chief.

G	R	H	2B	3B	HR	RBI	BB	SO	SB	AVG	Slug
235	95	205	41	9	11	92	72	124	6	.257	.372

Aloysius Edward Piechota, *Pitcher*

Piechota broke in at the major league level in 1940 with the Braves. A second-division club the two years Al played in Boston, skipper Casey Stengel was denied the cellar in 1940 and 1941 by the woeful Phillies. During the war, Piechota joined the navy and played service ball at Bunker Hill Naval Training Station.

W	L	PCT	G	GS	CG	IP	H	BB	SO	SHO	ERA
2	5	.286	22	8	2	62	68	42	18	0	5.66

William Leonard "Wild Bill" Pierro, *Pitcher*

During many battles there are often young boys that wish they were of age so they could take part in the fighting. Their only obstacle to duty is their failure to meet a certain age requirement. But this failure can be overcome if the young man passes himself off as older than his actual age. In earlier days, before things like Social Security numbers were the norm, it was much easier for a person to lie about who they were and when they were born. Young William Pierro did such a thing in 1942.

With the war in its early stages, Wild Bill, just sixteen, was eager to fight the enemy after the bombing on Pearl Harbor. The Brooklyn schoolboy left home and enlisted in the U.S. Marine Corps, claiming to be eighteen rather than his actual sixteen years of age. His real age wasn't determined at his induction physical, and the Marines welcomed the eager young soldier into their flock. The kid Marine's real age was later uncovered but not before he spent some time working for Uncle Sam.

After the war Wild Bill signed on to play professional baseball. He did the moniker "Wild Bill" justice as the right-hander had a live arm but lacked control. Pierro spent one year with the Pirates, 1950, and he walked nearly a batter an inning. The following year, during spring training, Wild Bill nearly died when he fell ill at Pirates training camp. The doctors didn't know what ailed Pierro at the moment but tests revealed that he suffered from inflammation of the brain lining.

W	L	PCT	G	GS	CG	IP	H	BB	SO	SHO	ERA
0	2	.000	12	3	0	29	33	28	13	0	10.55

Leonard Pigg, *Catcher*

A soldier during peacetime, Pigg served in the military before his debut in the Negro Leagues and a year before Pearl Harbor was bombed. Stationed at Fort Sill with the Quartermasters Corps, Pigg played plenty of service baseball, which would prepare him for the Negro Leagues. During the war, Leonard was shipped out to the Philippine Islands but wasn't engaged in combat maneuvers. After his discharge, the short and stocky Pigg caught on with the Indianapolis Clowns and spent a few years there after Jackie Robinson had broken the color line. After his military discharge, Pigg's weight became more of an issue each season until he finally ate his way out of a job.

(1947–1951): Indianapolis Clowns and Cleveland Buckeyes

Antone James "Andy" Pilney, *Reserve*

Pilney had a cup of coffee with the 1936 Braves and never got to play the field. He had all of two at-bats and struck out in one of them. Pilney, a star football player at Notre Dame, was an ensign in the navy who coached service football at Georgia's Navy Pre-Flight School.

G	R	H	2B	3B	HR	RBI	BB	SO	SB	AVG	Slug
3	0	0	0	0	0	0	0	1	0	.000	.000

Henry Harold "Cotton" Pippen, *Pitcher*

A good minor league pitcher who was hit quite handily in the majors, Pippen was deferred by his draft board because of his age and family status—he was married with two children. But in 1944, more soldiers were needed and Cotton answered the call. He joined the navy that July. Eager to do his part, Pippen was happy when the navy accepted him, saying, "That's what I was shooting for."

W	L	PCT	G	GS	CG	IP	H	BB	SO	SHO	ERA
5	16	.238	38	25	5	175	253	64	55	0	6.38

Mizell George "Whitey" Platt, *Outfield*

Whitey played sparingly at Wrigley Field prior to the war. The outfielder missed two full baseball campaigns to military service. Platt served with the navy and was stationed briefly at the Great Lakes with baseball great Schoolboy Rowe and fellow Cub Al Glossop. He was later shipped overseas and served in the South Pacific. Whitey ended his major league career as a member of the St. Louis Browns.

G	R	H	2B	3B	HR	RBI	BB	SO	SB	AVG	Slug
333	117	256	41	17	13	147	81	122	2	.255	.369

Clarence Anthony "Bud" Podbielan, *Pitcher*

Podbielan served in the armed forces during World War II before he signed his first pro contract. The Dodgers gave Bud his first look when they called him up in 1949. He pitched throughout the 1950s, mostly with the Reds.

W	L	PCT	G	GS	CG	IP	H	BB	SO	SHO	ERA
25	42	.373	172	76	20	641	693	245	242	2	4.49

Cletus Elwood "Boots" Poffenberger, *Pitcher*

With a name like Boots Poffenberger, it's only fitting that the man was as odd as his name. Boots was a noted entertainer with a healthy image of his own worth to a ballclub. Only a middling pitcher, Boots used to get upset when Detroit skipper Mickey Cochrane would "waste him" against lesser teams like the Browns and Athletics. He felt that he was a giant slayer, capable of humbling such big guns as the Yankees and Indians.

Writer Dick Killy referred to Boots as "The Lou Costello of the ball diamond." A crowd pleaser, Poff was a fan favorite who could often be found after games reminiscing with fans at the local tavern about his ball diamond heroics. Heavy drinking and personal boasting were Poffenberger's vices, and these character deficiencies earned Boots the tag of an unreliable, undisciplined ballplayer. Despite his lifestyle, Boots was simply a fun-loving fellow who enjoyed the wind-down as much as the wind-up. Once, when Boots missed a game in which he was slated to start, Cochrane asked Boots what happened to him. Ever the honest chap, Boots looked Mick square in the eye and said, "Oh, Skip, I just got cockeyed."

Poffenberger's last major league action came with the 1939 Dodgers, which was cut short due to a suspension for his undisciplined lifestyle. During the war, Boots pitched a little here and there before his draft notice came. He shocked everyone that knew him when he opted to join up with the U.S. Marine Corps. The general public views the Marines as the most disciplined of Uncle Sam's fighting forces, which seemed backwards to Poff's way of life. His unreliability and propensity to imbibe a few seemed adverse to the Marine Corps creed. But Boots joined with the Marines and took his basic training at Paris Island.

Shipped overseas in 1945, Boots was stationed on the Hawaiian Islands. The former major league hurler was active in Marine duties and played some service ball there. More importantly, Boots had finally gained the discipline he needed. Flabbergasted, sportswriter Oscar Fraley wrote, "Boots, the baron of sauerkraut and the disciple of the flowing cup, has got discipline. Don't take my word for it. It comes right out of the Marine Corps Dispatch from that usual somewhere in the South Pacific."

Although the Marine Corps gave Boots his needed dose of discipline, Poffenberger was still the character he had always been. Boasting and jaw-wagging were still his favorite pastimes and many a Marine thoroughly enjoyed the antics of Boots Poffenberger. Marine Corps Lieutenant Bob Crosby wrote a letter home to a newspaperman chum in which he described life on the Hawaiian Islands. Never much of a baseball fan, the Marine lieutenant claimed that he enjoyed going to ballgames on the islands simply to hear Boots pop-off and ride the opposition. After his discharge, Baron Boots never made it back to the majors.

W	L	PCT	G	GS	CG	IP	H	BB	SO	SHO	ERA
16	12	.571	57	32	13	267	301	149	65	0	4.75

Hugh Reid Poland, *Catcher*

Poland played for three teams in his major league career, usually slotted as a third-string catcher. He backed up Gus Mancuso in New York, Phil Masi in Boston, and Ray Lamanno in Cincinnati. Hugh missed one year, 1945, to service in the United States Army during World War II.

G	R	H	2B	3B	HR	RBI	BB	SO	SB	AVG	Slug
83	8	39	10	1	0	19	6	16	0	.185	.242

Kenneth Lyle Polivka, *Pitcher*

Ken had a cup of coffee with the 1947 Reds — the extent of his major league career. The southpaw from Chicago spent time in the U.S. Navy before he made the majors.

W	L	PCT	G	GS	CG	IP	H	BB	SO	SHO	ERA
0	0	—	2	0	0	3	3	3	1	0	3.00

Nathaniel Hawthorne Pollard, *Pitcher*

A short and chunky pitcher for the Birmingham Black Barons after World War II, Pollard pitched in the Negro Leagues when the quality of play was rapidly declining thanks to integration. Nat spent two years in the navy during the war.

(1943–1950): Birmingham Black Barons

Howard Joseph Pollet, *Pitcher*

Pollet was discovered and developed by Cardinals skipper Eddie Dyer. The lanky lefty made a strong first impression in St. Louis by posting a 1.92 ERA in eight starts, two of which were shutouts. He led the National League with a 1.75 ERA in 1943 but was kept from building off that year due to his military callup. Pollet was assigned to the Santa Ana Army Air Field, the same stomping grounds as Joe DiMaggio, after his induction. From Santa Ana, Howie went to Las Vegas where he tutored in aerial gunnery. Kept on the move, Howie was reassigned to the Amarillo Army Air Field where he tossed a no-hitter. He received his discharge in November of 1945.

W	L	PCT	G	GS	CG	IP	H	BB	SO	SHO	ERA
131	116	.530	403	278	116	2,106	2,096	745	934	25	3.51

Harlin Welty Pool, *Outfield*

The Reds' regular left fielder as a rookie in 1934, Pool hit a nifty .327 as a freshman. The following year he failed to hit .200 and his major league career was over. A batter with a swing-happy approach, Harlin rarely struck out or took a free pass. He held a bat for one purpose: to swing it. When World War II broke out, Pool joined the Army Air Corps. Harlin was a non-commissioned officer in the USAAF.

G	R	H	2B	3B	HR	RBI	BB	SO	SB	AVG	Slug
127	46	129	28	7	2	61	19	20	3	.303	.415

Raymond Herman Poole, *Outfield*

Poole had a brief major league career. He appeared in just fifteen games for the Philadelphia Athletics in 1941 and 1947. A native of Salisbury, North Carolina, Poole enjoyed reminiscing about his days playing for Connie Mack before his death. During the war, Poole served south of the border in Panama, missing four full baseball seasons to military service.

G	R	H	2B	3B	HR	RBI	BB	SO	SB	AVG	Slug
15	1	3	0	0	0	1	1	5	0	.200	.200

David Pope, *Outfield*

Pope spent the bulk of World War II in school. The Talladega native was studying medicine when he left for the military in 1945. Dave spent one year in the military, and after his discharge he opted to make baseball a career. Pope signed with the Homestead Grays of the Negro League but quickly attracted the attention of major league scouts and joined affiliated ball. Dave spent a few years in the majors with Cleveland and Baltimore. Although he was rarely a starter, he offered a solid bat off the bench.

G	R	H	2B	3B	HR	RBI	BB	SO	SB	AVG	Slug
230	75	146	19	7	12	73	40	113	7	.265	.390

William John Posedel, *Pitcher*

Barnacle Bill Posedel was in his mid thirties when he entered the armed forces during World War II, and was in the tail end of his baseball career. He missed out on his twilight years in the major leagues, as Posedel spent four years in the United States Navy during the war. Barnacle Bill was stationed at Treasure Island and later became the chief of a gun crew on a merchant vessel in the Pacific. He returned to the major leagues in 1946 as a 39-year-old and posted a perfect 2–0 record.

W	L	PCT	G	GS	CG	IP	H	BB	SO	SHO	ERA
41	43	.488	138	87	45	679	757	248	227	6	4.56

Louis Thomas Possehl, *Pitcher*

A teenager throughout the war, Possehl joined the navy in the campaign's latter stages. The young right-hander from Chicago was stationed close to home at the Great Lakes Naval Training Station. While at the Great Lakes, Lou was able to play some service ball. Playing the game in the service kept him in shape for the 1946 baseball season; he made his debut that year with Ben Chapman's Phillies.

W	L	PCT	G	GS	CG	IP	H	BB	SO	SHO	ERA
2	5	.286	15	8	1	52	62	24	22	0	5.19

William H. Powell, *Pitcher*

A teenager throughout the war, Powell served in the military near the end of the fighting. After his discharge, he signed with his hometown Birmingham Black Barons and pitched in the Negro Leagues before he entered integrated baseball. A fine minor league pitcher, Powell didn't show enough to earn a callup to the majors.

(1946–1950): Birmingham Black Barons

John Steven Pramesa, *Catcher*

Pramesa platooned behind the dish for the Reds with Walker Cooper and Dixie Howell several years after the war. During World War II, Johnny served two years with the U.S. Marine Corps. A big catcher, Pramesa had modest pop with the bat.

G	R	H	2B	3B	HR	RBI	BB	SO	SB	AVG	Slug
185	29	141	17	3	13	59	31	41	0	.268	.386

James Bartholomew Prendergast, *Pitcher*

The southpaw from Brooklyn had a cup of coffee with the 1948 Braves after the war and fashioned a 1–1 record with an ERA above 10.00. Before he made his major league debut, Prendergast served with the 36th Infantry at Fort Benning, Georgia. His unit was shipped overseas and served in the ETO.

W	L	PCT	G	GS	CG	IP	H	BB	SO	SHO	ERA
1	1	.500	10	2	0	17	30	5	3	0	10.06

John T. Reid "Jackie" Price, *Shortstop*

Always one to seek out attractions, Bill Veeck, owner of the Indians after the war, signed minor league shortstop Jackie Price to a contract for the 1946 season. It was understood by Cleveland skipper Lou Boudreau that Price wasn't brought in to play but to clown. A good crowd-pleaser, one of Jackie's routines was to take batting practice by dangling from the top of the batting cage. Remarkably, he hit nearly all thrown balls that way.

A minor league sensation for his clown antics before the war, Price gave up the comedy for a trip with Uncle Sam's fighting forces. Price joined the Army Air Corps and was a T/5 during World War II. Veeck, who was an admirer of the odd, signed Price after the army discharged him. Veeck described Jackie's routine, saying, "He'll stand in the pitcher's box and throw two balls with one hand, one a curve and the other a fastball. That's just his way of warming up. He'll stand on second base and throw the ball between his legs—all the way to home plate, and a perfect strike. He's a riot!"

G	R	H	2B	3B	HR	RBI	BB	SO	SB	AVG	Slug
7	1	3	0	0	0	0	0	0	0	.231	.231

Gerald Edward Priddy, *Second Base*

Priddy had the reputation of being a seedy character, both on the diamond and off. He was nabbed by the FBI for extortion in 1973, which proved he was just as dirty off the ball field as he was on it. He trolled through the Yankees organization with Phil Rizzuto, but while Scooter was able to win a job with the Bronx Bombers, the Yankees sent Jerry to Washington. He played with the Senators for three years and missed two to World War II. During the war, Priddy served in the Army Air Corps and was stationed in Hawaii.

G	R	H	2B	3B	HR	RBI	BB	SO	SB	AVG	Slug
1,296	612	1,252	232	46	61	541	624	639	44	.265	.373

Frank Anthony Pytlak, *Catcher*

Pytlak spent the bulk of his career with the Cleveland Indians; he played for the Tribe from 1932 to 1940. While there, he and stellar third baseman Willie Kamm developed a foolproof plan on pop flies. During a game, they put their plan to action when a pop-up was lofted in foul territory between the two players. Kamm raced for the high pop fly, shouting, "I got it!" He felt safe when he heard no response from Frankie. However, when the ball reached his awaiting mitt, he collided with Pytlak — dropping the ball. Annoyed, Kamm asked Frankie if he hadn't heard him call him off, to which Pytlak replied, "Sure I did, and didn't you hear me wave you off?"

One of the top catchers of the 1940s, Pytlak was an exceptionally difficult strikeout victim — he fanned only 97 times in nearly 800 games. Modern baseball fans have grown accustomed to players striking out 100 times in a single 162-game season. He wielded a solid stick for a catcher, hitting higher than .300 in four separate campaigns. Also possessing great speed for a backstop, Frankie paced the Indians in stolen bases on one occasion. He was already 32 years old when he was lost to the military, he served three and a half years in the navy and returned to the Red Sox late in 1945 after he received his discharge. His baseball career was all but over with, as he hit .118 in limited action for Boston in 1945 and appeared in only a handful of games for their 1946 AL champion squad.

G	R	H	2B	3B	HR	RBI	BB	SO	SB	AVG	Slug
795	316	677	100	36	7	272	247	97	56	.282	.363

Melvin Joseph Queen, *Pitcher*

Mel Queen spent the majority of his major league career with the Pittsburgh Pirates, where he worked out of their bullpen and also served as a spot starter. He made his debut with the Yankees in 1942, winning his only decision, and spent all of 1943 in the minors. He made ten starts with the 1944 Yankees and then missed all of the 1945 season to service in the armed forces. He took his physical exam at Huntington and was inducted shortly thereafter. Queen returned to the diamond in 1946 and was dealt to the Pirates during the 1947 season. He played with the Bucs until 1952. When he retired from the game, Mel took a job in an aircraft plant.

W	L	PCT	G	GS	CG	IP	H	BB	SO	SHO	ERA
27	40	.403	146	77	15	556	567	329	328	3	5.10

James Harold "Hal" Quick, *Shortstop*

Quick had his cup of coffee with the 1939 Senators. Washington's best player at the time was shortstop Cecil Travis, which meant Quick's road to everyday duty was blocked by the fellow Georgian. Quick was returned to the minors in 1940 and remained there until he enlisted in the army during World War II. Commissioned a lieutenant in the Army Air Corps, Quick was shipped to the European Theatre in 1944. He was listed as "seeing action somewhere in the ETO" early that year. After some lengthy combat action in Europe, Hal returned stateside in 1945 where he was sent to Douglas Army Air Base. He played some service ball there with Clay Lambert but made a decision to quit baseball and make the military a career.

In the military, Quick didn't have to contend for a position with guys like Cecil Travis, which made the job security, although hostile at times, seem better than baseball. Hal served in peacetime until war broke out in Korea. Quick lent his hand in that war as well and was still active in the Air Force during Vietnam. At the time of the Vietnam War, Quick had reached the rank of lieutenant colonel. He would retire from the Air Force but died shortly after his retirement.

G	R	H	2B	3B	HR	RBI	BB	SO	SB	AVG	Slug
12	3	10	1	0	0	2	1	1	1	.244	.268

Wellington Hunt "Wimpy" Quinn, *Pitcher*

A two-way player in the minors, Quinn was brought up by the Cubs strictly to pitch in 1941. Wimpy appeared in only three games and failed to impress. He thoroughly impressed Hall of Fame second baseman Billy Herman, however, when the two played service ball on the Hawaiian Islands during the war. Quinn served with the U.S. Marines.

W	L	PCT	G	GS	CG	IP	H	BB	SO	SHO	ERA
0	0	—	3	0	0	5	3	3	2	0	7.20

Raymond Allen "Rip" Radcliff, *Outfield*

A ballplayer who rarely struck out, Radcliff was already in his upper thirties when he entered the military. Before he was drafted, Rip spent the offseasons working at an airplane manufacturing plant in Enid, Oklahoma. He was drafted into the navy and took his basic training at San Diego. He didn't make a return to the majors after his navy discharge, retiring with more than twice as many walks as strikeouts.

G	R	H	2B	3B	HR	RBI	BB	SO	SB	AVG	Slug
1,081	598	1,267	205	50	42	533	310	141	40	.311	.417

Theodore Roosevelt "Double Duty" Radcliffe, *Catcher/Pitcher*

Radcliffe earned the nickname "Double Duty" because he could pitch the first game of a doubleheader and then work behind the dish the second game. Although Double Duty was regarded more for defense than his hitting, he occasionally hit .300 and once notched 19 victories in a season. A native of Mobile, Alabama, Radcliffe had plenty of mobility in his blood. The catcher-pitcher would often play with a different team each season and sometimes played for numerous squads in a given campaign. A colorful character with a quick wit and healthy self-image, Radcliffe might be regarded as the most famous self-promoter of the Negro Leagues if it weren't for Satchel Paige.

Double Duty made his debut in the Negro Leagues during the late 1920s and was quite advanced in years when World War II broke out. In his early forties, Radcliffe spent most of the war playing ball for Birmingham before he joined the army as a cook. He served less than a year in the army because he was given a medical discharge due to asthma. After his discharge he returned to the Negro Leagues and slowly switched from player to manager. When the Negro Leagues was depleted of talent after integration, Radcliffe made headlines when he signed a few white ballplayers to play for his Chicago American Giants. Double Duty lived to be 103 years old.

(1928–1950): Chicago American Giants, Detroit Stars, Homestead Grays, Pittsburgh Crawfords, St. Louis Stars, Columbus Blue Birds, New York Black Yankees, Cincinnati Tigers, Memphis Red Sox, Birmingham Black Barons, Kansas City Monarchs and Louisville Buckeyes

Kenneth David Raffensberger, *Pitcher*

A southpaw with impeccable accuracy, Raffensberger was able to play throughout most of the war. Ken led the Phillies in wins, innings pitched and strikeout during the war-interrupted 1944 campaign. In 1945, Ken was inducted into the military early in the baseball season. He was able to play service ball in the navy for half a year before he was discharged at the end of the war. A good pitcher throughout his career, Ken has a losing record because he was saddled to some rather lousy teams.

W	L	PCT	G	GS	CG	IP	H	BB	SO	SHO	ERA
119	154	.436	396	262	133	2,152	2,257	449	806	31	3.60

Robert Louis Ramazzotti, *Utility Infielder*

A modest man who never liked to discuss the things he accomplished in life, Ramazzotti was a decorated war veteran who saw action in the European Theatre. In his mid-twenties when the war broke out, Bob had yet to make his debut in the major leagues. Inducted into the army during the war, Ramazzotti was stationed at Fort Myer, near Arlington National Cemetery, for a time. He served with Company K of the 176th Infantry. While Bob was a grunt in the army, his brother, Paul, was at Camp Wheeler.

Ramazzotti's 176th Infantry Regiment would be sent overseas to the European Theatre. Attached with Uncle Sam's fighting forces, Bob witnessed combat action on the shores of Europe. A staff sergeant in the infantry while he served overseas, Bob marched through hostile terrain but came out of the war unscathed. When he reported back home after his discharge, a writer asked Bob how much baseball he had played in the service. He answered, "I haven't played a great deal and when I did play, it was against what you would term Sunday school picnic pitching." The Dodgers called Ramazzotti up in 1946 for a brief trial but he would get more playing time later as a member of the Cubs.

G	R	H	2B	3B	HR	RBI	BB	SO	SB	AVG	Slug
348	86	198	22	9	4	53	45	107	15	.230	.291

Frank Robert Donald "Ribs" Raney, *Pitcher*

Ribs Raney pitched in four major league games and was credited with the decision in each contest. A tall, lanky right-hander from Detroit, Raney pitched in pieces of two seasons for the Browns. During the war, Raney served in the U.S. Navy.

W	L	PCT	G	GS	CG	IP	H	BB	SO	SHO	ERA
1	3	.250	4	3	1	18	25	14	7	0	7.50

Earl Wellington Rapp, *Outfield*

A nomadic reserve outfielder, Earl Rapp played with five teams in three major league seasons. He broke in with the Tigers in 1949 but was traded to the White Sox during the season. In his second year, 1951, he split the campaign between the Giants and Browns, and in 1952 he played for the Browns before he was dealt to the Senators to end the season. Rapp left baseball during World War II to enlist in the army. In 1943, he was a private stationed in Alabama.

G	R	H	2B	3B	HR	RBI	BB	SO	SB	AVG	Slug
135	27	73	16	4	2	39	25	41	2	.262	.369

Victor John Angelo Raschi, *Pitcher*

One of the Yankees' top guns in the years right after the war, Rifle Vic Raschi helped the team reach the World Series and win it every year from 1949 to 1953. Over that span, Rifle won 92 games for the Bronx Bombers. Raschi remains one of the best pitchers in Yankees history. During the war, Vic lost two years in the minors to service in the military.

W	L	PCT	G	GS	CG	IP	H	BB	SO	SHO	ERA
132	66	.667	269	255	106	1,820	1,666	727	944	26	3.72

John Anthony Reder, *First Base*

A terrific natural athlete, Johnny Reder had a cup of coffee with the 1932 Red Sox. A two-way player in the minors, Reder could hit and pitch, but the Bosox used him exclusively at the infield corners. The foreign-born Reder was also regarded as a stellar soccer goalkeeper. During the war, Johnny served in the armed forces.

G	R	H	2B	3B	HR	RBI	BB	SO	SB	AVG	Slug
17	4	5	1	0	0	3	6	6	0	.135	.162

William Joseph Reed, *Second Base*

A gifted athlete, Reed was a star basketball player at Notre Dame who played pro basketball instead of baseball after his military discharge. During the war, Reed served in the U.S. Army and opted to play on the hardcourt after his discharge. He played one year of baseball in the majors with the 1952 Braves.

G	R	H	2B	3B	HR	RBI	BB	SO	SB	AVG	Slug
15	4	13	0	0	0	0	0	5	0	.250	.250

William Edgar Reeder, *Pitcher*

Reeder was a big, strong lad from Texas who did some quality pitching in his day. A minor league pitching ace, Bill was used by the Cardinals in a relief capacity during the 1949 season, his only year in the major leagues. A lack of accuracy was his downfall in the majors averaging close to one walk issued per inning. However, as wild as Reeder was, he made sure he got the job done. A strong-armed man known for his strength, Reeder could toss a baseball for great distance, which served him well in combat at Okinawa.

After Reeder enlisted in the U.S. Army he attended basic training and from there went to AIT where he wowed in the art of grenade pitching. The young Texan pitcher was assigned to Company E of the 381st Regiment that was deployed to the Pacific Theatre of Operations. A fighting unit, Reeder was as deep in combat as any former athlete during the war. On a mission, when Reeder and his platoon couldn't get close enough to a Japanese fighting position to acquire a good line of fire with their rifles, Bill's battle buddies looked to him. With his gifted right arm, Reeder lobbed grenades an amazing distance to subdue the enemy. Gordon Cobbledick wrote, "The Jap target was a good 300 feet away. Small arms fire couldn't reach them, and nobody could pitch a grenade that far. Nobody but PFC Reeder."

Private First Class Bill Reeder lobbed grenades toward the enemy until the fire coming from that position ceased. They advanced on the Jap nest and found a pair of dead soldiers, blasted to death by Reeder's grenades. After his discharge, Bill returned to baseball, and when a writer learned of Reeder's heroics at Okinawa, he asked Bill if he had any reservations about lobbing those heavy grenades without any form of warmup. The arm of a pitcher is his meal ticket, the writer thought. Reeder just shook his head at the naïve scribe and answered, "Way I look at it, it's better to have a dead arm on a live body than vice versa."

W	L	PCT	G	GS	CG	IP	H	BB	SO	SHO	ERA
1	1	.500	21	1	0	34	33	30	21	0	5.03

James Herman Reese, *Second Base*

Baseball's darling senior citizen in the early 1990s, the elderly Reese was still suiting up in his baseball uniform at the age of ninety. At the time he was one of the final links to Babe Ruth because the two played together with the Yankees in the early 1930s. Reese, a left-handed-hitting second baseman, spelled Hall of Famer Tony Lazzeri while he was a member of the Bronx Bombers. During the Second World War, Reese served briefly but was given a medical discharge in 1943.

G	R	H	2B	3B	HR	RBI	BB	SO	SB	AVG	Slug
232	123	209	39	4	8	70	48	37	7	.278	.373

Harold Henry "Pee Wee" Reese, *Shortstop*

Reese earned his nickname because he was a superior marbles player as a kid. He cast the marbles aside later in life and took up a larger round object, one he mastered in Brooklyn. Reese was inserted as the regular shortstop in 1940 but a broken foot sidelined the rookie for a large portion of the season. He came back in 1941 and suffered through the famous "sophomore jinx" as his batting average dipped to .229. His numbers rebounded in 1942, but the 23-year-old was inducted into the armed forces prior to spring training the following year.

In January of 1943, Pee Wee said it would be "very improbable" that he would play in the upcoming baseball season. During his induction physical, Reese said, "I'll try to join either the Marines or the navy." He was inducted into the navy in late January as an apprentice seaman with aspirations of becoming a chief petty officer in the physical training division. Reese was assigned to the Norfolk Naval Air Station where he played baseball under former major leaguer Homer Peel. Peel, a former New York Giants player, was eager to manage a hated Brooklyn Dodger, but the two men left the rivalry in the majors and got along swimmingly in the navy.

In 1944, Pee Wee, a gifted natural athlete and leader, was asked to manage the Norfolk basketball team. Reese took his ball diamond leadership skills to the hardcourt and guided the navy's cage luminaries. While stationed at Norfolk, Reese and his wife gave birth to daughter Barbara Lee. Shortly after his daughter's birth, Pee Wee was shipped overseas to Hawaii. At the sunny islands, Reese was borrowed by the U.S. Marine Corps to coach the 3rd Marine Division baseball club but wasn't allowed to play because he wasn't a Marine.

G	R	H	2B	3B	HR	RBI	BB	SO	SB	AVG	Slug
2,166	1,338	2,170	330	80	126	885	1,210	890	232	.269	.377

Herman Charles Reich, *First Base/Outfield*

Reich spent one year at the major league level but played with three teams that season. In 1949, the Senators called Herm up initially but dealt him to the Indians. After a game in Cleveland, he was sent to the Cubs where he played regularly at first base while splitting time with veteran Phil Cavaretta. An early inductee into the army during World War II, Herm was stationed at Fort Lewis where he was able to play some service ball with Giants outfielder Morrie Arnovich.

G	R	H	2B	3B	HR	RBI	BB	SO	SB	AVG	Slug
111	43	109	18	2	3	34	14	33	4	.279	.359

Thomas Edward Reis, *Pitcher*

Reis was given a trial in the majors before the war in 1938 with the Phillies and Braves but failed to make good with either club. He allowed far too many base runners, via the walk and the base hit. It was back to the bushes for Tommy in 1939 and there he remained until the war. Reis enlisted in the army and was assigned to Uncle Sam's fighting forces. In the army, Tommy served with the 76th Infantry Regiment based out of Camp McCoy.

While stationed at Camp McCoy, Reis was able to play some service ball with Senators All-Star Cecil Travis and fellow former major leaguer Bama Rowell. But the three former ballplayers weren't attached to the special services—bullets, not baseball, was made to order for them. With the 76th, Reis was shipped overseas to the European Theatre of Operations, attached to the Third Army. His unit marched through the harsh winter landscape of Europe and took part in the Battle of the Bulge. When the war was over, Reis and his chums participated in a ball game at Zwickau where Tommy beat the Ninth Armored Division in a pick-up match.

W	L	PCT	G	GS	CG	IP	H	BB	SO	SHO	ERA
0	1	.000	8	0	0	11	16	9	6	0	12.27

Harold Patrick "Pistol Pete" Reiser, *Outfield*

The original "Wallbanger," Pistol Pete always gave it his all on the ball diamond. A person could make a valid argument that the ball diamond was as hazardous for Reiser as a battlefield. Many times did Brooklyn gasp in horror and concern as their fearless center fielder, Pistol Pete, was carried off the field on a stretcher.

It's because of players like Reiser and Elmer Valo that every ballpark across America possesses a warning track — a beacon for fly-chasers informing them that danger awaits. Of Pistol Pete, Los Angeles *Times* columnist Jim Murray wrote, "They haven't invented the bones he hasn't broken."

Pistol Pete hit .293 as a rookie in 1940, but the outfield picture in Brooklyn that year was quite stable with the Hall of Famer Joe Medwick, the great Dixie Walker and hit-machine Joe Vosmik as the regular men in the pasture. The next year, Reiser moved Walker to right field and Pistol Pete set the National League afire, leading the league with 39 doubles, 17 triples, 117 runs scored, a .343 batting average and a Slugging percentage of .558. A star was born in Brooklyn. He followed up that season by leading the league in stolen bases despite missing time to an injury. Although he had eclipsed Terry Moore as the best center fielder in the National League, he missed the next three years to service in the military.

Much like Ted Williams, who suffered from overexposure, Reiser was reclassified by his draft board to 1-A status early in 1942, but he appealed the reclassification because he supported his parents and five siblings. His appeal was accepted and he returned to 3-A, but he was returned to 1-A late in 1942 and inducted into the service shortly thereafter. He was sworn into the army at Jefferson Barracks, Missouri, as photographers and writers were there to capture his likeness and gather quotes. Pistol Pete was tight-lipped that day, as he said, "Well, this is it." His only other comment was, "Gee, it's a nice day — could play baseball today."

He was sent to Fort Riley and played for a service ballclub at the Kansas installation. Reiser was assigned as a physical training instructor in the Second Regiment at Fort Riley. While playing service ball, Reiser, whose only way of playing the game was the all-out manner, broke his throwing shoulder while diving for a fly ball. Someone asked Pete what he would do if he couldn't throw the ball when he returned to the diamond. He answered, "I'll just throw left-handed." Because of the injury, Pistol Pete had his shoulder wired together, and his reconstructed wing hindered his play the rest of his career. He visited the 1944 World Series and returned to the army where he was reassigned to Camp Livingston. As a corporeal, he was named the manager of a service ballclub at his new stomping grounds. After his promotion to sergeant, he left Camp Livingston in the summer of 1945 for a new assignment with the Army Special Services in their expanding athletic program. He was stationed in California late in 1945 and was slated to be sent to Japan when the war ended. At the time of his discharge, Reiser was in serious need of a shoulder operation before rejoining the Dodgers for the 1946 season.

Pistol Pete returned to the Dodgers in 1946 and led the league in stolen bases, finishing twelve higher than his runnerup, Cincinnati's Bert Haas. He suffered a severe concussion in 1947 but helped guide the Dodgers to the World Series. During the 1947 Fall Classic, Reiser showed immense fortitude by playing sparingly on two broken ankles. Reiser was injured throughout 1948, only appearing in a handful of games, and lost his job to Duke Snider in 1949. He stuck around the majors for another three years, playing briefly when his numerous ailments allowed.

G	R	H	2B	3B	HR	RBI	BB	SO	SB	AVG	Slug
861	473	786	155	41	58	368	343	369	87	.295	.450

Robert Willis Repass, *Utility Infielder*

Repass had a cup of coffee with the Cardinals in 1939 and was sent back to the bushes afterwards. He didn't resurface at the major league level again until 1942 with the Senators. Washington had just lost the cornerstones of their club, shortstop Cecil Travis and third baseman-outfielder Buddy Lewis, to the war and Repass was brought in to help out. But in the summer of 1943, it was Bob's turn to join the colors. Repass was able to play some service ball with George Yankowski at the Fort Devens Reception Center before he was shipped overseas in 1944. Bob spent the rest of the war in foreign lands.

G	R	H	2B	3B	HR	RBI	BB	SO	SB	AVG	Slug
84	30	64	12	1	2	24	33	32	6	.242	.317

Dino Paul Restelli, *Outfield*

Before Restelli made his major league debut, he served in the military at the end of the war. Shipped overseas in 1945, Dino was stationed in Italy for a time. Sent back to the States in 1946, Restelli returned to the game of baseball. Dino made an immediate splash in the majors with the 1949 Pirates when he clubbed six home runs in his first ten games. Pittsburgh sportswriters got carried away and likened him, as a center fielder of Italian descent, to the great Joe DiMaggio.

G	R	H	2B	3B	HR	RBI	BB	SO	SB	AVG	Slug
93	42	65	12	0	13	43	37	30	3	.241	.430

Harold Housten Rice, *Outfield*

A fourth outfielder his entire major league career, Rice always played second fiddle to someone else. The Cardinals had a bevy of outfielders when Rice came up with the club after the war, and he was employed as a reserve gardener. Before Rice made his major league debut, he served with distinction in the United States Navy during the Great War. Hal's unit was shipped overseas where they were engaged in combat action in the South Pacific. When members of his outfit died in combat, Hal was given a battlefield commission to see his troops through the fighting.

G	R	H	2B	3B	HR	RBI	BB	SO	SB	AVG	Slug
424	129	307	52	12	19	162	94	133	1	.260	.372

Woodrow Earl Rich, *Pitcher*

Rich played at the major league level for both Boston affiliates and missed one full season to the war effort. The right-hander was inducted into the armed forces after the close of the 1944 baseball season and missed the entire 1945 campaign. Woody Rich didn't return to the majors after the war.

W	L	PCT	G	GS	CG	IP	H	BB	SO	SHO	ERA
6	4	.600	33	16	5	118	127	50	42	0	5.03

Donald Lester Richmond, *Third Base*

Don Richmond was dubbed "Scholarly" by his teammates. He played briefly at the major league level with the Athletics and Cardinals, and missed four years to World War II.

G	R	H	2B	3B	HR	RBI	BB	SO	SB	AVG	Slug
56	11	32	6	2	2	22	6	17	1	.211	.316

Allen Gordon Richter, Reserve

Used sparingly in his two trips to Boston in the early 1950s, Richter was just a teenager during World War II. Al served in the military at the end of the war.

G	R	H	2B	3B	HR	RBI	BB	SO	SB	AVG	Slug
6	1	1	0	0	0	0	3	0	0	.091	.091

Marvin August Rickert, Outfield

Nicknamed "Twitch," Rickert tallied 26 pre-war at-bats for the Cubs. He was inducted into the military after the 1942 baseball season and spent three years in the U.S. Coast Guard. Marv served with a Coast Guard unit based out of Seattle. He returned to the game in 1946 and played two years with the Cubs. Marv finished his career in nomadic fashion, playing with four different clubs in his last three years.

G	R	H	2B	3B	HR	RBI	BB	SO	SB	AVG	Slug
402	139	284	45	9	19	145	88	161	4	.247	.352

Harvey Donald "Hank" Riebe, Catcher

Riebe spent a handful of seasons at the major league level with the Tigers during the 1940s while serving as a backup to Birdie Tebbetts and Bob Swift. Hank missed three full baseball seasons to World War II by serving with the United States Army.

G	R	H	2B	3B	HR	RBI	BB	SO	SB	AVG	Slug
61	2	29	4	0	0	11	3	18	1	.212	.241

Lewis Sidney Riggs, Third Base

Riggs spent the majority of his major league career with the Cincinnati Reds, where he served as their regular third baseman throughout the mid to late 1930s. He lost his job to star Bill Werber in 1939 and was dealt to the Dodgers for the 1941 season. Lew played with the Dodgers until 1943, when he was inducted into the military, and returned for one final stint with Brooklyn in 1946.

Growing up with his older brother, Hurley, in rural North Carolina, Lew's country mindset never vanished. Riggs said, "I was always just a country boy, even when I was in the big cities." The two country boys entered the armed forces during World War II, as Lew enlisted in the Army Air Corps while Hurley joined the U.S. Marines. Lew was inducted at Fort Jackson and from there went to Fort Myers, Florida, for basic aviation crew training. Late in 1942, he was assigned to the orderly room of the base headquarters squadron but put in a request for an airplane mechanic assignment.

About his service stint, Lew said, "It's a more important series that has to be won here—of course, we don't get any series cut, but this looks like it will be a better fight and besides, it's for keeps." He became a mechanic at the Army Air Force Flexible Gunnery School at Fort Myers. Although he had a new occupation, Lew still remained optimistic regarding a return to the majors. When asked if he planned on returning to the game, Lew said, "Unless something crops up and in times like these, one is never sure of what tomorrow will bring."

Riggs was later shipped out to the Pacific Theatre. He led a group of service all-stars with 19 RBIs on a tour of Iwo Jima, Saipan, Tinian and Guam. He received his discharge in October of 1945 and played one final season with Brooklyn in 1946 at the age of 36.

G	R	H	2B	3B	HR	RBI	BB	SO	SB	AVG	Slug
760	298	650	110	43	28	271	181	140	22	.262	.375

William Joseph Rigney, Utility Infielder

Better known today as a major league manager, Rigney won more than 1,200 career games at the highest level. A scrappy little infielder during his playing days, "Cricket" was the type of player that extracted as much as possible out of his modest skill set. Bill was on the cusp of making the majors when the war broke out and Cricket joined the navy to do his bit. In 1943, Rigney was stationed at the St. Mary's Navy Pre-Flight School where he was able to play service ball. The Giants liked Rigney and cut a deal for him while he was still in the service. The trade, due to its unusual circumstances (Rigney wasn't going to the club but had to remain in the navy.), had to be signed off by Commissioner Landis.

G	R	H	2B	3B	HR	RBI	BB	SO	SB	AVG	Slug
654	281	510	78	14	41	212	208	208	25	.259	.376

John Dungan Rigney, Pitcher

Johnny Rigney was an underrated pitcher throughout his career. After a rough debut in 1937, Rigney settled down and posted a 9–9 record in 1938 and then led the Pale Hose in victories the following year. His misfortune of pitching for a losing aggregation like the White Sox showcased itself in 1940, when his brilliant efforts netted him a losing record of 14–18. He led the White Sox that season in ERA, innings pitched and strikeouts but still couldn't muster a winning record.

Near the beginning of the 1942 baseball season, Rigney entered the United States Navy and remained there until the war concluded. Sailors enjoyed having the White Sox star around, as he was commonly referred to as a "swell guy." Rigney was able to play baseball for Mickey Cochrane at the Great Lakes for a time and later met up with Hall of Fame teammate Ted Lyons at Pearl Harbor.

To prove that the military wasn't in the conserving of pitchers' arms business, Rigney once tossed a complete 21-inning game in the navy as a chief specialist, striking out 22 batters. Johnny served 42 months in the navy—including South Pacific assignments—and returned to the White Sox and future wife Dorothy Comiskey in 1946 with an injured shoulder.

W	L	PCT	G	GS	CG	IP	H	BB	SO	SHO	ERA
64	64	.500	197	132	66	1,188	1,101	450	605	9	3.58

Culley Rikard, Outfield

Rikard played with the Pirates in pieces of two seasons prior to his military stint and played one year after his discharge. The bulk of his playing time came with the 1947 Pirates when he hit .287 in an outfield platoon with Wally Westlake. Culley was a fleet-footed minor league sensation at Memphis in 1941, and he saw brief action with the Pirates in that season and again in 1942. In March of 1943, he was inducted into the armed forces. Culley was the tenth Pirates player to join the colors as he served with the Fourth Ferrying Command in the same city where he enjoyed his greatest baseball success—Memphis.

G	R	H	2B	3B	HR	RBI	BB	SO	SB	AVG	Slug
153	64	107	19	5	4	37	58	48	1	.270	.374

John T. Ritchey, *Catcher*

A good hitting catcher, Ritchey lacked the defensive skills behind the dish to make the major leagues. During World War II, John joined the army and saw combat action at Normandy. He fought in the European Theatre and was then reassigned to lend a hand in the Pacific Theatre near the end of the war. After his military discharge, Ritchey spent one year in the Negro Leagues before entering the minor leagues. Although scouts felt he could hit major league pitching, he was deemed an inferior catching prospect and was never called up.

(1947): Chicago American Giants

Arthur Bernard "Tink" Riviere, *Pitcher*

Riviere was given two trials at the major league level, first with the 1921 Cardinals and later with the 1925 White Sox, and failed to make the grade in either instance. With his ball playing days in the books by the 1940s, Tink had turned his attentions to executive work in baseball. He tried, successfully at first, to bring a semi-pro team to Big Spring, Texas, in 1941 but the team relocated the next year. He served as a business manager in the minor West Texas-New Mexican League before he served in the United States Army during World War II.

W	L	PCT	G	GS	CG	IP	H	BB	SO	SHO	ERA
1	0	1.000	20	2	0	40	51	27	16	0	7.65

John Costa Rizzo, *Outfield*

Despite his great raw power, Rizzo made his rounds in the major leagues. As a rookie with the 1938 Pirates, he paced the club in home runs and RBIs. In fact, Rizzo tripled the second-highest long ball output on the club while hitting .301 for the season. His power mysteriously vanished in 1939 and he was quickly dealt to the Phillies early in the 1940 season, where he found his power stroke and swatted 20 long balls for the last-place club. He joined the Dodgers in 1942 and then spent the next four years in the armed forces.

Johnny enlisted in the navy in December of 1942 as a Seaman First Class. He was stationed at the Norman Naval Air Station in Oklahoma and played service ball with pitcher Al Benton. An avid golfer, Rizzo participated in the Oklahoma City Invitational Golf Tournament while stationed at the Norman Naval Air Station. During the head-to-head tournament, Johnny was defeated by R.M. Selby. After his discharge from the navy, Rizzo didn't return to the major leagues.

G	R	H	2B	3B	HR	RBI	BB	SO	SB	AVG	Slug
557	268	497	90	16	61	288	200	197	7	.270	.435

Philip Francis Rizzuto, *Shortstop*

During his first tryout with a major league team, Rizzuto, who was affectionately referred to as "Scooter," was told by Brooklyn Dodgers manager Casey Stengel that he was too small and informed the diminutive kid to take up the art of shoe shining. Obviously not heeding Stengel's advice, Rizzuto later tried out with the Yankees and became an MVP Award winner, proving that Stengel's eye for talent was wanting.

Scooter was once referred to by a writer as one of the first "bonus babies." In response to this false comment, Rizzuto said, "If you call 15 cents a bonus, I guess you'd say I was a bonus player. Hamburgers cost a dime apiece in those days and the Yankees bought me a hamburger and a cup of coffee the day I signed." Rizzuto had a tremendous rookie season; he hit .307 with a team-high fourteen stolen bases. His batting average regressed the following year, but he finished third in the American League with 22 thefts, behind two Senators, George Case and Mickey Vernon.

After two solid years at the major league level, Scooter was drafted into the United States Navy. He met his bride-to-be in the service and they were married while Phil was at the rank of Seaman First Class. Rizzuto spent an ample amount of time in foreign lands during the war. He played for Bill Dickey's Navy All-Star team in Hawaii and spent a combined 19 months service in Australia and the Philippines. In the land down under, Scooter played for and managed the top club in the Australian Service League. For one contest in Australia, Phil was forced to pencil himself in the lineup as the starting catcher. A spectator quipped, "The catching equipment nearly swallowed him."

G	R	H	2B	3B	HR	RBI	BB	SO	SB	AVG	Slug
1,661	877	1,588	239	62	38	563	651	398	149	.273	.355

Thomas Vardasco "Tony" Robello, *Second Base/Third Base*

A hitter for power at the minor league level, Robello was given only a brief look by the Reds in 1933 and 1934. By the time of the war, Tony was preparing himself for life after playing; he served as playing manager of the Twins Falls Cowboys before his military induction. Tony served in the navy and was the recreation director at the Norfolk Naval Training Station. His military duties couldn't take his mind off the game, as Tony said, "I'm getting that itchy baseball feeling again" as spring training approached. After his navy discharge, Robello, finished as a player, began a lengthy tenure as a scout with the Reds.

G	R	H	2B	3B	HR	RBI	BB	SO	SB	AVG	Slug
16	1	7	3	0	0	3	1	6	0	.219	.313

Joseph Albert Armand "Skippy" Roberge, *Utility Infielder*

Roberge spent three years at the major league level with the Braves and was able to step in at any post on the infield. The majority of his playing time came in 1942, when Skippy played 29 games at second base, 27 games at third base and six at shortstop. When he returned from the war, Roberge spent his last year in the major leagues as a third base platoon partner with Nanny Fernandez.

Roberge enlisted in the army in January of 1943. Of Skippy, Casey Stengel said, "He was one of the nicest young men I've ever met." The player was also fond of the manager, as Skippy enjoyed playing under the aloof Stengel. Roberge said, "Stengel was a clown and always will be. I remember the time in 1941 when he filled my glove with pebbles and when I went out to my position at third, I didn't know what was going on."

Skippy was stationed at Fort Devens and worked in the mess hall. While he wasn't busy peeling potatoes, Roberge played ball for the Fort Devens Recruit Reception Center squad. He was also an advocate for baseball during the war when many thought the game should be closed so that able-bodied ballplayers could serve their country. Skippy said, "Just because I have been taken away from the game doesn't mean that I have soured on it or that I believe it should be dropped for the duration. People have become accustomed to big league ball and they look at it as part of their day, just like three meals and a little rest. To take it away from them now would only serve to deprive them of something they've come to look on as essential."

From Fort Devens, Roberge was transferred to Camp Reynolds in 1944. He wasn't stationed at Camp Reynolds long, as his unit was sent overseas. Skippy served and saw action in the European Theatre while also playing a little service ball in England. The private first class was wounded in action in Germany and was sent to Belgium to recover. He returned stateside after his convalescence in Belgium and made his way back to a Stengel-less Braves team in 1946, his last year in the majors.

G	R	H	2B	3B	HR	RBI	BB	SO	SB	AVG	Slug
177	35	112	19	2	3	47	25	49	2	.220	.283

Robin Evan Roberts, *Pitcher*

Hall of Famer Robin Roberts was a teenager during World War II. The youngster joined the army at the end of the fighting. After his discharge, Roberts took to baseball and showed enough early promise that the Phillies called him up in 1948. One of the game's greatest workhorses, Roberts was an innings-eater deluxe.

W	L	PCT	G	GS	CG	IP	H	BB	SO	SHO	ERA
286	245	.539	676	609	305	4,689	4,582	902	2,357	45	3.41

Sherrard Alexander Robertson, *Utilityman*

Robertson had yet to establish himself at the major league level when he was summoned by Uncle Sam. His military stint cost him the 1944 and 1945 baseball seasons when Sherry served with the United States Navy. He was stationed at the Bainbridge Naval Training Center with fellow major leaguer Elbie Fletcher. The light-hitting versatile player returned to the Senators in 1946 and made 38 starts at third base, fourteen at second base and twelve at shortstop.

G	R	H	2B	3B	HR	RBI	BB	SO	SB	AVG	Slug
597	200	346	55	18	26	151	202	238	32	.230	.342

Aaron Andrew Robinson, *Catcher*

Nothing more than a stop-gap catcher, Robinson served as the bridge between two Hall of Famers in the Bronx: Bill Dickey and Yogi Berra. Aaron made his debut with the Yankees in 1943 and then missed the 1944 and a small portion of the 1945 seasons to service in the U.S. Coast Guard. Just like Dickey and Berra, Robinson was a left-handed-hitting receiver, but his time in pinstripes was brief because he was dealt to the White Sox in 1948. He ended his major league career with the Red Sox in 1951.

G	R	H	2B	3B	HR	RBI	BB	SO	SB	AVG	Slug
610	208	478	74	11	61	272	337	194	0	.260	.412

William Edward Robinson, *First Base*

While serving in the navy, Robinson had surgery to remove a bone tumor but the military doctors severed a nerve that affected Eddie's play throughout the rest of his baseball career. He had played briefly with the Tribe in 1942 but was inducted into the navy shortly after the close of that season and missed the next three years to military duty. He was able to participate in a little service baseball action by playing for a team based at the Norfolk Naval Training Station. Eddie returned to the majors in 1946 and began a rather nomadic but solid career. He wore the uniforms of the Indians, Senators, White Sox, Philadelphia Athletics, Yankees, Kansas City Athletics, Tigers and Orioles.

G	R	H	2B	3B	HR	RBI	BB	SO	SB	AVG	Slug
1,315	546	1,146	172	24	172	723	521	359	10	.268	.440

Henry Frazier Robinson, *Catcher*

A reserve catcher throughout his career in black baseball, Robinson caught with the Monarchs and Black Yankees before the war and the Baltimore Elite Giants after the fighting. Inducted into the U.S. Navy in 1943, Frazier missed two years of baseball to the war effort.

(1942–1950): Baltimore Elite Giants, Kansas City Monarchs and New York Black Yankees

Jack Roosevelt Robinson, *Shortstop*

Although Jackie Robinson only played in the Negro Leagues one season with the Kansas City Monarchs, he is one of the most recognizable names of black baseball. A standout college athlete, Jackie was an exceptional running back in football and a pretty fair collegiate baseball player, too. A pro football player in 1941, the college-educated Robinson attended officer's candidate school in Kansas after Pearl Harbor was bombed. Commissioned an officer, Jackie was a 2nd Lieutenant at the time of his discharge.

Discharged before the war was over, Jackie was able to play the 1945 season with Kansas City. Some of the better players in the Negro Leagues were still in the service, but Dodgers general manager Branch Rickey found his man in Robinson. He signed Jackie to a contract with his Dodgers and farmed him out to Montreal in 1946. The following year, Jackie became the first black player in the major leagues when he broke the color line and carried Brooklyn to an NL pennant. Robinson enjoyed a terrific career with the Dodgers, and on his first year listed on the Baseball Hall of Fame ballot, he was inducted into Cooperstown.

G	R	H	2B	3B	HR	RBI	BB	SO	SB	AVG	Slug
1,382	947	1,518	273	54	137	734	740	291	197	.311	.474

Louis Joseph Rochelli, *Utility Infielder*

Rochelli appeared in just five major league ballgames, as the thin infielder missed two full seasons to service in the military. Lou joined the navy during the 1944 baseball season but was able to leave the Navy Pre-Flight School late in 1944 under an alternative provided by the Naval Aviation Program. However, Lou returned to the colors in 1945 and was stationed at the Great Lakes Naval Training Center as an apprentice seaman.

G	R	H	2B	3B	HR	RBI	BB	SO	SB	AVG	Slug
5	0	3	0	1	0	2	2	6	0	.176	.294

Lester Henry Rock (Schwarzrock), *First Base*

Box scores spurred many a ballplayer with a lengthy last name to anglicize their surname, and Les set the table for later players like Johnny Pesky and Charlie Metro to shorten their names. Rock had a cup of coffee with the 1936 White Sox, who employed heavy-hitting Zeke Bonura at his station. Cast back to the bushes, Rock joined the military early during World War II and served with Cardinals star center fielder Terry Moore with the 825th Flyers in Panama. The duo led the Flyers to the Panama Canal Department baseball championship in 1944.

G	R	H	2B	3B	HR	RBI	BB	SO	SB	AVG	Slug
2	0	0	0	0	0	1	0	0	0	.000	.000

Joseph Anthony Rogalski, *Pitcher*

Rogalski had a cup of coffee with the 1938 Tigers. Back in the minors at the time of the war, Rogalski left the diamond in 1942 and enlisted in the army. Sent to Camp Grant, Joe was able to play some service ball during his military hitch. After his discharge, Rogalski's health began to decline and he was diagnosed with Lou Gehrig's disease, which claimed his life in 1951.

W	L	PCT	G	GS	CG	IP	H	BB	SO	SHO	ERA
0	0	—	2	0	0	7	12	0	2	0	2.57

Lee Otis Rogers, *Pitcher*

Rogers spent one year at the major league level split between the Dodgers and Red Sox. His only action came in 1938. During the war, Lefty left the minors and joined the army.

W	L	PCT	G	GS	CG	IP	H	BB	SO	SHO	ERA
1	3	.250	26	4	0	51	55	28	18	0	6.16

Stanley Frank "Packy" Rogers, *Utility Infielder*

Packy served as a reserve infielder with the Dodgers in 1938, his only major league season. During the war, Packy was in the navy and played some service ball with Clyde Shoun and Chet Hajduk. The trio was eventually transferred from the Great Lakes and sent to the Pacific Theatre.

G	R	H	2B	3B	HR	RBI	BB	SO	SB	AVG	Slug
23	3	7	1	1	0	5	6	6	0	.189	.270

Stanley Andrew Rojek, *Utility Infielder*

A confident individual, Rojek was vying for the shortstop post in 1946 after he had spent three years in the service. He had some solid competition for the job with the likes of Hall of Famer Pee Wee Reese on the roster, but the ever-assured Rojek knew he belonged. He took Branch Rickey aside and said, "Why, Mr. Rickey, I don't think those fellows will be able to carry my glove at the end of spring training."

Rojek's pre-war career consisted of one game played for the 1942 Dodgers. He was summoned by his draft board late in 1942 and reported to Buffalo for his induction. He had enlisted in the Army Air Corps prior to the 1942 baseball season but was placed on the inactive list and didn't get summoned until after the season closed. Rojek's military occupation was as a ground mechanic, but Stan was able to take up a glove when he wasn't repairing aircraft. He was shipped out and toured the South Pacific with a group of service all-stars. This aggregation went on a 27-game exhibition series that took Stan to such locales as Iwo Jima, Tinian, Saipan and Guam. Of all the players participating in the series, Rojek led them all in batting.

G	R	H	2B	3B	HR	RBI	BB	SO	SB	AVG	Slug
522	225	470	67	13	4	122	152	100	32	.266	.326

Robert L. Romby, *Pitcher*

A southpaw pitcher from Shreveport, Romby served in the military during World War II before he made his debut in black baseball. Romby signed with the Baltimore Elite Giants after his discharge and played in the Negro Leagues when the talent pool was drying up due to integration.

(1946–1950): Baltimore Elite Giants

Albert Leonard Rosen, *Third Base*

One of the greatest third basemen of all-time, had Rosen's career lasted a little longer, he would be a strong Hall of Fame candidate. He played only ten years at the major league level but was quite a star in that short span. His career was pushed back due to service in the military during World War II. Cleveland called him up for the first time in 1947 when Kenny Keltner was still producing. When Keltner had his greatest year in Cleveland's championship 1948 season, it looked like "Flip" would never get a chance. But Keltner mysteriously lost his hitting ability in 1949, which opened the door for Al in 1950. He led the league in home runs that year, topped the AL in RBIs in 1952, and was named the MVP in 1953 when he paced the circuit in runs, home runs, RBIs and Slugging percentage.

G	R	H	2B	3B	HR	RBI	BB	SO	SB	AVG	Slug
1,044	603	1,063	165	20	192	717	587	385	39	.285	.495

Simon Rosenthal, *Outfield*

When Si Rosenthal played for his hometown Red Sox in the mid–1920s, they were the laughingstock of major league baseball. The two years Si played in Boston, the Red Sox lost more than 100 games each season. They were the only team in the majors in 1925 and 1926 to eclipse 100 losses. Rosenthal was in his early twenties then, and when World War II was underway, his fortieth birthday was right around the corner. But his age didn't deter him from enlisting. With his teenage son, he joined the military to do their bit for their country: Si with the navy and his son with the U.S. Marine Corps.

The war was a great hardship for many, but for Si Rosenthal it was a tragic ordeal that completely altered his life. Attached to a mine-sweeping unit in the U.S. Navy, Si was shipped overseas to the ETO. All the while Si was in the service, he kept in touch with his son as the two would shoot off letters to one another. When Si stopped receiving letters from his boy he feared the worst. While stationed in Europe, Si received a bulk of his letters that were addressed to his son but returned when he learned that his teenage son was killed in action with the Marines.

With his son gone, Rosenthal had one other person on this earth to correspond with: his ex-wife. After his son's death, he wrote his ex-wife and they rekindled their love for one another. But Rosenthal would suffer a brush with fate on the battlefields that would alter his life. While engaged in his mine-sweeping duties, the enemy struck and Si was the victim of a shell that left him paralyzed from the waist down. Lifted from battle, Si spent the remainder of the war in French hospitals. Sent home, he was bound to a wheelchair for the rest of his life. He and his ex-wife remarried, and Si kept his attitude upbeat despite his crippling injury and his son's death. Later in life he would be actively engaged in several charity events for handicapped individuals.

G	R	H	2B	3B	HR	RBI	BB	SO	SB	AVG	Slug
126	40	95	17	5	4	42	26	21	5	.266	.375

Chester James Ross, *Outfield*

Ross played with the Braves from 1939 to 1944 and missed one lone season — the 1945 campaign — to service in the armed forces. In 1945, Chet served in the United States Navy and played service ball for the Sampson Naval Training Center. One of the first "all-or-nothing" hitters in the game, Ross' best season came in 1940 when he paced the Braves in runs, hits, triples, home runs and RBIs — yet also led the National league with 127 strikeouts.

G	R	H	2B	3B	HR	RBI	BB	SO	SB	AVG	Slug
413	156	316	53	21	34	170	124	281	6	.241	.392

Francis James Rosso, *Pitcher*

A war-era pitcher, Rosso had a cup of coffee with the 1944 Giants. Ravaged by the war with the loss of ace pitchers Hal Schumacher and Bob Carpenter, the Giants gave Frank a brief trial in that war-interrupted 1944 campaign. He failed to make good. Rosso served briefly with the U.S. Marines during the war but was discharged and spent most of 1944 pitching at Jersey City.

W	L	PCT	G	GS	CG	IP	H	BB	SO	SHO	ERA
0	0	—	2	0	0	4	11	3	1	0	9.00

Lynwood Thomas "Schoolboy" Rowe, *Pitcher*

One of the greatest all-around talents in baseball history, Rowe posted a career winning percentage over .600 while hitting .263 for his career. A marvelous pitcher for the Tigers in the 1930s, Schoolboy became a sensation in 1934 when he won 24 games for a .750 winning percentage. That season he equaled a record with 16 consecutive wins. He didn't walk a batter in 21 World Series innings on his 2.95 ERA. It was in the 1934 World Series when Rowe became a household name, along with his sweetheart, Edna Skinner. While mowing down the Redbirds, Schoolboy called out to his love, asking, "How'm I doin,' Edna?" His lovelorn inquiry became the origin of the Cardinals' catcalls and rhubarbs, as whenever Rowe took the hill, the Redbirds would yell, "Yoohoo, Edna! How'm I doin,' Edna?"

Schoolboy married Edna after the World Series, and he pitched with the Tigers into the 1940s. He caught on with the Phillies in 1943 and led the team with 14 wins; 1937 was the last time any Phillies pitcher had notched more. He was sworn into the navy on February 19, 1944. Upon his induction, Rowe said, "There's just a helluva lot more to work for in this here uniform, and it brings out every ounce of drive a feller has."

The Great Lakes Naval Training Station was Schoolboy's first stop and he met up with a familiar face in Mickey Cochrane, Rowe's former teammate and manager. He played service ball at the Great Lakes but also proved to be a brilliant soldier. Schoolboy was an honor student in naval training, which allowed him to be assigned to the Great Lakes Security Watch.

Like many ballplayers, Rowe received his orders to be shipped overseas. He went to Hawaii where he served as a player-manager of a navy ballclub. During one contest, Schoolboy's team took on a club managed by Yankees pitcher Al Lyons. The two former ballplayers got together before the game and enjoyed a major league conversation.

"How many points you got?" Schoolboy asked Lyons.

"Oh, I'm short a few," Lyons replied, "but I hear you're planning to stay out this way."

Flabbergasted, Rowe exclaimed, "Stay here! Why man, if there weren't some spots in that ocean that are over my head, I'd start walking right now!"

After 21 months of service in the navy, Rowe was discharged in November of 1945. He said, "I believe my arm is as good as it ever was. I won fourteen games with the Philadelphia Phillies in 1943. I believe I can top that next year." Although he was unable to reach fourteen wins in 1946, Schoolboy returned to the majors with a 2.16 ERA in 136 innings of work. A gifted baseball sensation, Schoolboy was one of the best players of his time, and taking into account the two years he lost to the war, he remains a borderline Baseball Hall of Fame inductee.

W	L	PCT	G	GS	CG	IP	H	BB	SO	SHO	ERA
158	101	.610	382	278	137	2,219	2,332	558	913	22	3.87

Carvel William "Bama" Rowell, *Second Base*

A colorful southern gentleman, Rowell enlisted in the army three days before the attack on Pearl Harbor. Bama was beginning to establish himself in the major league ranks, and he led all National League second basemen in RBIs during the 1941 season, but that didn't deter him from serving his country. He missed a combined four years to service in the army, a stint that was anything but idle.

Rowell was assigned to the 76th Infantry Division and didn't mind the strenuous army training. He said, "This is an interesting game down here and I like it. But I sort of miss those big steaks." He was stationed at Camp Sibert and served in the same outfit as Washington Senator great Cecil Travis. The two portside-swinging infielders were shipped out to the European Theatre where they saw combat action attached to the Third Army.

G	R	H	2B	3B	HR	RBI	BB	SO	SB	AVG	Slug
574	200	523	95	26	19	217	113	105	37	.275	.382

Richard Louis "Dick" Rozek, *Pitcher*

Rozek joined the navy fresh out of high school at the end of the war. His induction into the navy was a boon for the young man as he met fellow Iowan pitcher Bob Feller when he was stationed at the Great Lakes. Feller took the young Rozek under his wing and they trained together at the Great Lakes when the war was near its end. The chance meeting led to a job for Dick because his pitching impressed Rapid Robert. Feller made certain the Indians got the jump on the talented young southpaw and recommended they sign him. He made his debut with the Indians in 1950.

W	L	PCT	G	GS	CG	IP	H	BB	SO	SHO	ERA
1	0	1.000	33	4	0	65	65	55	26	0	4.57

Charles Leon Ruffin, *Catcher*

An elite defensive catcher, Ruffin's glaring weakness was his inability to hit. He enjoyed a sporadic career in the Negro Leagues, spent predominately with the Newark Eagles. A smart catcher with a terrific throwing arm, Ruffin made up for some of his offensive deficiencies by playing superior defense. During World War II, Leon joined the U.S. Navy and missed 2½ seasons of baseball.

(1935–1950): Newark Eagles, Pittsburgh Crawfords, Philadelphia Stars and Houston Eagles

Charles Herbert "Red" Ruffing, *Pitcher*

Ruffing had been in the major leagues since 1924 and the Hall of Fame right-hander was 39 years old when he was inducted into the army. Although he was a grizzled veteran by World War II, Red was still getting the job done at the major league level, indicated by his 14–7 record in 1942. In the military, Ruffing played service baseball with the Sixth Ferrying Command, which won the Southern California Service Championship. He was labeled by the army as a non-combatant because he had lost four toes in a coal mining accident as a teenager. After Red received his discharge, he reminisced on his first day of boot camp. Ruffing said, "A sergeant said me to me, 'Ruffing, I understand you can pitch.' That's right I answered and the sergeant said 'Okay, buddy, see how fast you can pitch this tent.'" Red returned to the Yankees in the middle of the 1945 baseball season as a 41-year-old man. Despite his advanced age — or perhaps because of it — he came back as good as ever, posting a 7–3 record with a 2.90 ERA.

A favorite Red Ruffing story concerns his days as a rookie in the Boston Red Sox chain. He was a rather light kid, minus four toes and all, so the Red Sox demanded that he add weight. Red decided to combine his favorite leisure activity, beer drinking, with his baseball training. Ruffing said, "When I won a game I'd consume a quart of rye celebrating and when I'd lose I'd drink a quart consoling myself."

W	L	PCT	G	GS	CG	IP	H	BB	SO	SHO	ERA
273	225	.548	624	538	335	4,344	4,284	1,541	1,987	45	3.80

James Edward "Pete" Runnels, *Utility Infielder*

A terrific average hitter whose glove left a bit to be desired, Pete played all over the infield in an effort to keep his bat in the lineup. A kid throughout the war, Runnels enlisted in the U.S. Marine Corps at the end of the great conflict when he came of age.

G	R	H	2B	3B	HR	RBI	BB	SO	SB	AVG	Slug
1,799	876	1,854	282	64	49	630	844	627	37	.291	.378

Lloyd Opal Russell, *Pinch Runner*

Russell's major league career consisted of two games with the 1938 Indians. A gifted college athlete, Lloyd quit baseball shortly after his sojourn to Cleveland to accept a football and track coaching job at the University of North Texas. When the war broke out, Russell left the campus and enlisted in the U.S. Navy Reserves. Commissioned an ensign, Lloyd was assigned to the naval base at Hollywood, Florida. After his discharge he accepted a job at Baylor University as the head of the physical and health education department.

G	R	H	2B	3B	HR	RBI	BB	SO	SB	AVG	Slug
2	0	0	0	0	0	0	0	0	0	—	—

Marius Ugo Russo, *Pitcher*

An unheralded hurler, Russo was a solid major league pitcher for a handful of years with the Yankees. Marius made his debut with the 1939 Yankees. That year he won eight games and missed more bats on average than any other pinstripe pitcher. He posted back-to-back 14-win seasons in 1940 and 1941 before a sore arm interrupted his 1942 campaign. Russo struggled through the 1943 season and retired from the game in January of 1944 to focus on his defense job at Republic Aircraft. Shortly thereafter, Marius was inducted into the army and served at Camp Crowder, Missouri.

W	L	PCT	G	GS	CG	IP	H	BB	SO	SHO	ERA
45	34	.570	120	84	48	681	618	253	311	6	3.13

Henry Alexander Ruszkowski, *Catcher*

Hank took his pre-induction physical in April of 1945. He was inducted into the armed forces shortly thereafter, cutting short the young catcher's rookie season. He spent the entire 1946 baseball season in the military and returned for a brief trial with the Tribe in 1947.

G	R	H	2B	3B	HR	RBI	BB	SO	SB	AVG	Slug
40	8	20	2	0	3	10	6	16	0	.238	.369

John Collins "Blondy" Ryan, *Utility Infielder*

The starting shortstop for the world champion 1933 Giants, Ryan filled in quite admirably for Hall of Famer Travis Jackson. Blondy, who was a star athlete at Holy Cross University, was done as a ballplayer by the time World War II broke out. In fact, he was done with baseball altogether, as he began work with the IRS shortly after the bombing at Pearl Harbor. But Ryan desired to do his bit during the war despite his advanced age and joined the navy. Commissioned a lieutenant, Ryan was assigned to the Boston Navy Yard during the latter stages of the war.

G	R	H	2B	3B	HR	RBI	BB	SO	SB	AVG	Slug
386	127	318	36	13	8	133	57	184	6	.239	.304

Cornelius Joseph Ryan, *Second Base*

Ryan played in the majors from 1942 to 1954 and had brief stints as a major league manager with the 1975 Braves and the 1977 Texas Rangers. Connie was the hero of the 1944 All-Star Game, a year in which he hit .295 with 13 steals. However, a few days after his mid-season heroics against the American League, Connie was inducted into the navy. Ryan served at the Sampson Naval Training Station.

G	R	H	2B	3B	HR	RBI	BB	SO	SB	AVG	Slug
1,184	535	988	181	42	56	381	518	514	69	.248	.357

Frank Sacka, *Catcher*

Sacka played briefly with the Senators in the early 1950s. The sturdy catcher from Romulus, Michigan, served in the military during World War II before he signed his first pro contract.

G	R	H	2B	3B	HR	RBI	BB	SO	SB	AVG	Slug
14	3	9	0	0	0	6	3	6	0	.265	.265

Thomas Judson Saffell, *Outfield*

Although the Pirates weren't much of a team when Saffell played for them, they had quite a solid outfield. Saffell had to serve as a fourth outfielder behind Ralph Kiner, Gus Bell and Wally Westlake for a time. Tom, who would have a long career in the minors as a manager and executive, served in the armed forces during World War II. A pilot in the navy, Saffell served his stint in a cockpit.

G	R	H	2B	3B	HR	RBI	BB	SO	SB	AVG	Slug
271	91	143	15	1	6	40	59	108	9	.238	.296

John Franklin Sain, *Pitcher*

Together with Hall of Fame left-hander Warren Spahn from 1946 to 1951, the formidable righty-lefty duo was referred to as "Spahn and Sain and pray for rain." As far as praying for rain was concerned, the two military veterans were the only reliable hurlers on the Boston staff. Sain, a big man from Arkansas, joined the colors after the 1942 baseball season. He attended the Navy Pre-Flight School at Chapel Hill with Ted Williams, Johnny Pesky and teammate Buddy Gremp. From there, Johnny attended flight courses at Amherst.

Sain returned to the Braves in 1946 a completely different pitcher. Before he left for the navy, Johnny struggled mightily with his control; he walked 63 batters in 97 innings during the 1942 campaign. He returned to the Braves to toss 265 innings—one short of league-leader Howie Pollet—while he issued just 87 free passes. Johnny led the National League in complete games that year while posting a microscopic 2.21 ERA. Also a terrific hitting pitcher, Sain batted .346 for the 1947 Braves, a mark that eclipsed every position player not named Frank McCormick.

W	L	PCT	G	GS	CG	IP	H	BB	SO	SHO	ERA
139	116	.545	412	245	140	2,125	2,145	619	910	16	3.49

Edward Joseph "Ebba" St. Claire, *Catcher*

A brawny catcher in the early 1950s with the Braves, Ebba was a member of the team when it relocated to Milwaukee. The switch-hitting receiver from Whitehall, New York, left Colgate University to join the military during World War II. St. Claire's son, Randy, became a pitcher with the Montreal Expos, but Ebba died shortly before his son made his major league debut.

G	R	H	2B	3B	HR	RBI	BB	SO	SB	AVG	Slug
164	39	112	23	2	7	40	35	52	0	.249	.356

Manuel Salvo, *Pitcher*

A decent pitcher for the Braves before the war, Salvo led the staff in shutouts in 1940. Able to play a good chunk of the war years before his military induction, Salvo pitched with the Braves in 1943 but spent 1944 back home in California with the PCL. Philadelphia A's manager Connie Mack was making preparations for Salvo to pitch for him in 1945 when Salvo was inducted into the armed forces. Manny served briefly overseas at the end of the war with the army in occupied Japan after the bombing at Hiroshima.

W	L	PCT	G	GS	CG	IP	H	BB	SO	SHO	ERA
33	50	.398	135	93	40	722	723	284	247	9	3.69

Michael Joseph Sandlock, *Utilityman*

A valuable man to have on a team, Sandlock could fill in anywhere. The switch-hitter from Connecticut came up as a third baseman but during the war years he played all over in diamond and was the Dodgers' primary catcher in 1945. The versatile player had a brief service hitch during the war and spent most of the war years in the majors.

G	R	H	2B	3B	HR	RBI	BB	SO	SB	AVG	Slug
195	34	107	19	2	2	31	38	45	2	.240	.305

John Frederick Sanford, *Pitcher*

Sanford was a serviceable right-hander for a number of years at the major league level. He was equally capable coming out of the bullpen as he was starting games. He missed the entire 1944 and 1945 seasons in the armed forces and returned to baseball to pitch for the Browns, Yankees and Senators.

W	L	PCT	G	GS	CG	IP	H	BB	SO	SHO	ERA
37	55	.402	164	98	26	744	768	391	285	3	4.45

John Doward Sanford, *First Base*

A tall first baseman, Jack Sanford played briefly with the Washington Senators in 1940 and 1941. He missed four years to service during World War II and then appeared in a handful of games with the Senators in 1946.

G	R	H	2B	3B	HR	RBI	BB	SO	SB	AVG	Slug
47	13	32	4	4	0	11	9	24	0	.209	.288

Edward Robert Sanicki, *Outfield*

Sanicki is the answer to a fun trivia question, one very few people would ever get right. Of all the players in baseball history with at least twenty plate appearances to their credit, Sanicki leads all with a .882 Slugging percentage. Ed was a terror in his brief trial at the major league level, but the Phillies of the early 1950s were well stocked in the outfield with Hall of Famer Richie Ashburn, Del Ennis (who could be in the Hall of Fame), and Dick Sisler—not a bad hitter, either.

At the time of the war, Sanicki was attending Seton Hall University but took time out from his studies to enlist in the navy. During his stint in the war, Ed served on a ship as a signalman. After his discharge, Sanicki returned to campus to finish up his studies before he chose to play baseball. The outfielder received his first trial with the Phillies in 1949 but failed to make the club in

1950. The Phillies made the World Series that year with a fellow named Richie Ashburn manning Ed's natural position.

G	R	H	2B	3B	HR	RBI	BB	SO	SB	AVG	Slug
20	5	5	1	0	3	8	2	5	1	.294	.882

William Florine Sarni, *Catcher*

Sarni made headlines on the West Coast during the war when he signed his first professional contract with the war-ravaged Los Angeles Angels of the PCL. He was only fifteen years old at the time. Back then, during the war, there weren't restrictions on a player's age like there are now. If a team needed a catcher — like the Angeles did in 1943 — they could look to high school cafeterias and gymnasiums if the mood struck them. But once Sarni came of age, he was inducted into the army at the end of the war.

G	R	H	2B	3B	HR	RBI	BB	SO	SB	AVG	Slug
390	107	311	50	11	22	151	89	135	6	.263	.380

Frank Field Saucier, *Outfield/Catcher*

Every man leaves behind a legacy, no matter how small, and Saucier is best remembered for being the injured player that midget Eddie Gaedel pinch-hit for in 1951. Upon completion of high school, at the age of 16, he quickly enlisted in the navy. Saucier was commissioned an officer in the navy as an 18-year-old as part of the V-12 Program during World War II, which made him one of the youngest deck officers ever commissioned by the United States Navy. During the Second World War, Saucier was initially assigned as the skipper of Beach Party Team No. 76 of the Amphibious Forces. This assignment took him to the Philippines and Japan. He later served in China as a deck watch officer and second division officer on the flagship *USS Mt. Olympus*. For more on Saucier, see his listing in the section on the Korean War.

G	R	H	2B	3B	HR	RBI	BB	SO	SB	AVG	Slug
18	4	1	1	0	0	1	3	4	0	.071	.143

Henry John Sauer, *Outfield*

A big-time long ball threat, Hank wasn't given much of a chance to prove himself in Cincinnati. He played briefly for the Reds in 1941 and 1942 and despite their noticeable lack of thunder in the lineup, skipper Bill McKechnie never gave Sauer regular playing time. He was inducted into the Coast Guard in 1944 and served at Curtis Bay. He returned to the Reds as a 28-year-old midway through the 1945 season and hit a team-best .293 down the stretch. Despite his prolific hitting, Hank spent the next two years in the bushes. He resurfaced in 1948 as a 31-year-old and swatted 35 home runs, just behind three Hall of Famers in Ralph Kiner, Johnny Mize and Stan Musial. Sauer was dealt to the Cubs in 1949 and posted 30 or more homers from 1950 to 1953, the last one cut short to injury. Sauer led the NL with 37 home runs and 121 RBIs in 1952 at the tender age of 35.

G	R	H	2B	3B	HR	RBI	BB	SO	SB	AVG	Slug
1,399	709	1,278	200	19	288	876	561	714	11	.266	.496

Russell Collier Saunders, *Outfield*

Although Saunders had only a cup of coffee with the 1927 Athletics, he had a lengthy playing career in pro sports. Rusty was a cage luminary and spent many years playing professional basketball. At the time Connie Mack summoned Rusty to the A's, he was a star in the pro basketball ranks. Still active in basketball when World War II broke out, Rusty left the hardcourt and joined the navy.

G	R	H	2B	3B	HR	RBI	BB	SO	SB	AVG	Slug
5	2	2	1	0	0	2	3	2	0	.133	.200

John Robert Savage, *Pitcher*

Sometimes the pitcher's life is one of plight. Bob Savage had a pretty fair season in 1946 after the war, but his record was a dismal 3–15. This was before fellows like Fain, Valo and Joost gave a little character to the A's offense, and the punchless attack had a negative effect on Savage and his mound mates. Noted for his palmball, Savage was a solid long relief pitcher in the majors who filled in quite capably in the rotation when needed. But his career was interrupted by World War II, and Savage witnessed action on the European battlefields.

A top-flight pitching recruit at Staunton Military Academy before the war, Savage had scouts fawning over him in 1941. He agreed to sign with the Tigers, but when Detroit's delegate failed to get in touch with him, Savage opted to sign with Connie Mack's Athletics the following year. In 1942, baseball had a different feel and Savage was rushed to the majors. He said, "I went straight to the big leagues because the war was taking players away. There was a manpower need — both for the service and for baseball." Savage got into only a handful of games with the A's in 1942 before it was his turn to join the armed forces.

Having attended Staunton Military Academy as a teen, Savage was better prepared for army life than most young men. After the baseball season, Bob returned to the academy to complete his military training. He aspired to be an officer in the army and put in a request for Officer's Candidacy School, but things didn't go as planned for the New Hampshire native. Savage said, "I volunteered with some friends thinking we'd go to Officer's Training School. One of my friends was the son of President Roosevelt's chief of staff. He went to Officer's Training, but the rest of us were shipped off to Texas for boot camp."

After stateside training, Savage was sent overseas to the European Theatre of Operations. Engaged in combat missions, the war was more intense for him than other young athletes. While fighting in Europe, Savage was hit in the back by shrapnel his first day in combat maneuvers. He said, "The war was tough. I got hit the very first day of action and spent six months in and out of hospitals — in and out of the war really."

With shrapnel embedded in his back, Savage returned to his military duties. However, between fighting, he was asked to pitch a service game near Anzio and tossed a no-hitter. Savage said about the game, "We played in a makeshift ballpark with foxholes all around the foul lines. My catcher was the company commander. They had all kinds of money bet on the game — I'd say upwards to four grand. I threw a no-hitter and the captain asked if there was anything he could do for me since I won him a lot of money. So I told him about my back, with the shrapnel embedded in it, and how I'd like to get in his motor department. So he said, 'Here's a Jeep.' And I had a ball in that thing."

Able to drive a Jeep during the war to help ease the pain in his back, Savage ran missions in his motor vehicle. On one such mission, he came across a fork in the road and opted to turn into an area that was off limits: Rome. Instead of going around Rome, like all soldiers were supposed to, Savage accidentally chose the route that cut through the heart of Rome. When he spotted the Coliseum, he knew he was somewhere he wasn't supposed to be. Savage said, "I turned around to head back before I was caught, but then here comes the general to take the town. The city had been vacated at the time, so I didn't see any action there, but I was the first soldier in and out of Rome. The general even saluted me as I rode out of Rome with a girl in my Jeep ... and there were rules against that as well."

With the shrapnel in his back causing more and more discomfort, Savage was scheduled for a medical reassignment to the States. But much like his plans to enroll in Officer's Training School, his plans of finally getting the shrapnel removed had to be put on hold. He said, "I was scheduled to be transferred to Walter Reed to get the shrapnel out of my back when the breakthrough for Anzio hit. I was in line at the hospital when the breakthrough was announced and then I knew that I wasn't going anywhere. So I went back to Anzio."

The war was a hardship for all. It either put dreams on hold or dashed them entirely. A young pitching recruit in professional baseball, Savage's future was bright, but his present was an obstacle toward his goals. Like many young men engaged in the war, his thoughts drifted back home and to the life that was frozen, waiting for him. Savage said, "When I went into the service I was gung-ho to get over there and do it, even though I had a chance to stay in Virginia and play baseball. I was a major league ballplayer so I was in demand. I thought about that many times when I was in Europe during the war. In Anzio and Rome I thought about still living in Virginia and playing baseball. I thought about that so often."

A decorated war hero, Savage was awarded several medals and citations for his war-time gallantry. Among his medals was the Purple Heart, which he was awarded on three separate occasions. Although the war was a hardship for Savage, he had the good fortune of playing for a great man in Connie Mack, who took care of his boys in the service. Savage said, "When I was overseas I received a letter from Connie Mack. It meant a lot to me because I knew how long it took him just to sign his name. He was a wonderful person—just great to play for. Instead of playing for Mr. Mack, I went overseas and they gave me three Purple Hearts because I couldn't get out of the way."

W	L	PCT	G	GS	CG	IP	H	BB	SO	SHO	ERA
16	27	.372	129	31	10	423	433	215	171	2	4.32

William Nisbeth Sayles, *Pitcher*

Sayles pitched for three teams in two seasons at the major league level, as the right-hander saw action with the Red Sox, Giants and Dodgers. Bill split the 1943 season with the two National League clubs based in New York and was summoned into the armed forces after the season. Sayles missed the 1944 and 1945 seasons to the war.

W	L	PCT	G	GS	CG	IP	H	BB	SO	SHO	ERA
1	3	.250	28	3	1	79	87	46	52	0	5.58

Ray Wilson Scarborough, *Pitcher*

Throughout his career, Scarborough bounced between the rotation and bullpen. He made nearly as many relief appearances, five of which were starts, as starts. Ray made seventeen appearances as a rookie under Hall of Fame skipper Bucky Harris in 1942. He was enjoying a solid season in 1943 when he was inducted into the navy late in the season. He served and played ball at St. Mary's Pre-Flight School.

W	L	PCT	G	GS	CG	IP	H	BB	SO	SHO	ERA
80	85	.485	318	168	59	1,429	1,487	611	564	9	4.13

Sidney Schacht, *Pitcher*

No relation to Al Schacht, the Clown Prince of Baseball, Sid pitched briefly with the Browns and Braves in the early 1950s. Beaten like a drum in the majors, Schacht had little success at the highest level. During the war, he served with the United States Army Air Corps.

W	L	PCT	G	GS	CG	IP	H	BB	SO	SHO	ERA
0	2	.000	19	1	0	22	44	21	12	0	13.91

Harold Schacker, *Pitcher*

A war-era pitcher, Schacker played with the Braves in 1945 after his military discharge. A side-armer with a good curveball, Hal wasn't asked back to the majors after the war.

W	L	PCT	G	GS	CG	IP	H	BB	SO	SHO	ERA
0	1	.000	6	0	0	15	14	9	6	0	5.40

Harry Edward Schaeffer, *Pitcher*

Schaeffer served in the U.S. Navy during World War II prior to his major league debut. The Yankees called up the wild southpaw in 1952 and used him in seventeen innings—the extent of his major league career.

W	L	PCT	G	GS	CG	IP	H	BB	SO	SHO	ERA
0	1	.000	5	2	0	17	18	18	15	0	5.29

LeRoy John Schalk, *Second Base*

Schalk made his major league debut in 1932 with the Yankees—he appeared in three games—and then was cast back into the vast sea of the minor leagues. He didn't resurface at the highest level until 1944, a year after his hitch in the army, and the 35-year-old ballplayer spent his first full year at the majors. Even though his numbers weren't robust, Schalk is one of many able to return to the major leagues due to the military taking the younger stars.

G	R	H	2B	3B	HR	RBI	BB	SO	SB	AVG	Slug
282	100	259	38	5	2	109	79	95	8	.233	.281

Arthur Lawrence Schallock, *Pitcher*

A diminutive southpaw, Schallock was a mop-up pitcher for the Yankees in the early-to-mid–1950s. Before he tried on the pinstripes, Art served in the United States Navy. He pitched in the newly formed Peninsula League in the winter of 1942–1943 for a team called the San Mateo Blues. After that off-season league had concluded, Art signed up with the navy. His military duties were in the radar department of an aircraft carrier he served on that circled the Pacific Ocean.

W	L	PCT	G	GS	CG	IP	H	BB	SO	SHO	ERA
6	7	.462	58	14	3	169	199	91	77	0	4.05

Robert Boden Scheffing, *Catcher*

Scheffing spent the majority of his career as Clyde McCullough's backup but also saw action in Cincinnati and with the Cardinals. After his playing days, Bob managed the Cubs and Tigers and served as the Mets' general manager for a time. Scheffing spent his military time in the navy. He was stationed at Bainbridge and at Lambert Field with fellow Cubs player Emil Kush.

G	R	H	2B	3B	HR	RBI	BB	SO	SB	AVG	Slug
517	105	357	53	9	20	187	103	127	6	.263	.360

Carl Alvin Scheib, *Pitcher*

Scheib made his major league debut with the 1943 Athletics as a sixteen-year-old kid. Up to the task, Carl posted a respectable 4.26 ERA in nineteen innings. His numbers were nearly identical in 1944, as he lowered his ERA one point, to 4.25. After pitching nine innings in 1945, Scheib was inducted into the armed forces at Harrisburg and received his orders to the New Cumberland Reception Center in May of 1945. Carl played service ball for a semi-pro club based out of Indiantown Gap, Pennsylvania.

W	L	PCT	G	GS	CG	IP	H	BB	SO	SHO	ERA
45	65	.409	267	107	47	1,072	1,130	493	290	6	4.88

Gerard Anthony "Jim" Schelle, *Pitcher*

Schelle appeared in one game with the 1939 A's and failed to record an out. The wild right-hander served in the U.S. Army during the war.

W	L	PCT	G	GS	CG	IP	H	BB	SO	SHO	ERA
0	0	—	1	0	0	0	1	3	0	0	n/a

Henry Leonard Schenz, *Utility Infielder*

A pepper-pot sparkplug, Hank Schenz could fill in anywhere on the infield. The gritty ballplayer wasn't regarded as much of a prospect before the war, but when he showed his stuff while playing for the navy, the Cubs were impressed and brought him into the Wrigley Field fold in 1946. Hank received a late-season callup by the Cubs that year after he won the MVP Award in the Texas League as the captain of the Tulsa squad.

G	R	H	2B	3B	HR	RBI	BB	SO	SB	AVG	Slug
207	70	133	22	3	2	24	27	25	6	.247	.310

Robert Elmer Scherbarth, *Catcher*

A teenager throughout the war, Scherbarth left the schoolyard after graduation and joined the navy. After his discharge, Bob signed his first professional contract. The catcher was used in one game with the 1950 Red Sox.

G	R	H	2B	3B	HR	RBI	BB	SO	SB	AVG	Slug
1	0	0	0	0	0	0	0	0	0	—	—

Frederick Albert Schmidt, *Pitcher*

Schmidt missed the 1945 baseball season to service in the army. The right-hander ran afoul of a sergeant on his first day in the army when he spoke about the Cardinals' chances when he was supposed to be quiet. He and his conversation buddy were ordered KP duty for their infraction. Freddy was discharged from Fort Chaffee and returned to baseball after his year-long hiatus.

W	L	PCT	G	GS	CG	IP	H	BB	SO	SHO	ERA
13	11	.542	85	15	3	225	206	122	98	2	3.76

John Albert Schmitz, *Pitcher*

Johnny "Bear Tracks" Schmitz pitched for the Cubs from 1941 to 1951 and missed the 1943 through 1945 seasons to military service. Johnny enjoyed a solid debut season, posting a 1.29 ERA in 21 innings of work with the 1941 Cubs. Skipper Jimmie Wilson used the young left-hander out of the bullpen and in the rotation during the 1942 season, but Bear Tracks was unable to build off his solid showing and was inducted into the navy after the season. Johnny joined the navy in 1943 and played service ball under Mickey Cochrane at the Great Lakes Naval Training Station.

W	L	PCT	G	GS	CG	IP	H	BB	SO	SHO	ERA
93	114	.449	366	235	86	1,813	1,766	757	746	16	3.54

Henry Alrives Schmulbach, *Pinch Runner*

Hank Schmulbach appeared in one major league game, scoring a run without tallying an official at-bat. He was inducted into the army in November of 1943.

G	R	H	2B	3B	HR	RBI	BB	SO	SB	AVG	Slug
1	1	0	0	0	0	0	0	0	0	—	—

Albert Frederick "Red" Schoendienst, *Second Base*

Hall of Famer Red Schoendienst began his major league career as a war-era ballplayer. The skinny switch-hitter had served nine months in the military but received an early discharge due to an eye injury. Red led the National League in steals as a rookie in 1945 while skipper Billy Southworth used him mostly in left field. However, when Musial, Moore and Slaughter returned from the military, Southworth switched the young Schoendienst to second, where he became a Hall of Famer.

G	R	H	2B	3B	HR	RBI	BB	SO	SB	AVG	Slug
2,216	1,223	2,449	427	78	84	773	606	346	89	.289	.387

Edward Wesley Schulmerich, *Outfield*

Schulmerich broke in with Hall of Fame skipper Bill McKechnie's 1931 Braves. He was a 29-year-old rookie who split time with veteran Lance Richbourg that year. The following year, Wes finished second on the team in home runs, behind thumper Wally Berger, as the Braves reached the .500 mark after years of futility. After struggling early in 1933, he was traded to the Phillies and rebounded to hit .334 the rest of the season. He finished his major league career as a member of Chuck Dressen's last-place 1934 Reds.

With his playing career in the books, the stocky outfielder turned his attention toward coaching. But when the war interrupted things in the 1940s, Wes became a coach in the U.S. Navy. The former outfielder was commissioned a lieutenant and sent to the Iowa Navy Pre-Flight School where he coached athletics. Schulmerich was then transferred to Chapel Hill in 1945 and his duties were essentially the same. At Chapel Hill, Wes managed a service ballclub called the Cloudbusters.

G	R	H	2B	3B	HR	RBI	BB	SO	SB	AVG	Slug
429	169	417	73	20	27	192	118	197	7	.289	.424

Robert Duffy Schultz, *Pitcher*

A wild southpaw, Schultz spent two and a half years with the Cubs and a little time with the Pirates and Tigers. Schultz, whose ball diamond deficiency was a lack of accuracy, served with the U.S. Marines during World War II.

W	L	PCT	G	GS	CG	IP	H	BB	SO	SHO	ERA
9	13	.409	65	19	3	182	179	125	67	0	5.19

Harold Henry Schumacher, *Pitcher*

A great innings-eating pitcher during his heyday, Schumacher pitched from 1931 to 1946 with the New York Giants. His only baseball duty outside of a Giants uniform came in the khaki of Uncle Sam. After a disastrous rookie season in 1931, Prince Hal settled down in 1932 to post a 3.56 ERA. He enjoyed a breakout year in 1933 when he teamed with the legendary Carl Hubbell and Fat Freddie Fitzsimmons to give the Giants three pitchers with 16 or more wins. The three hurlers were instrumental in guiding the Giants to a World Series championship over the Senators. Hal allowed only 199 hits in 259 innings over the regular season with a sparkling 2.15 ERA. He notched 23 wins in 1934 and 19 in 1935. He helped pitch the Giants back to the World Series in 1936, where he struck out eleven batters in twelve Fall Classic innings. He pitched serviceable baseball for the Giants until his military callup.

Hal applied for a commission in the navy shortly after the close of the 1942 baseball campaign. He was later sworn into the Naval Reserve as a lieutenant in December of 1942. Hal was named the athletic officer at a base near Memphis and received his transfer to Lambert Field in the summer of 1943 to serve as a player-manager for a service club there. While serving in the navy, Prince Hal experimented with a knuckleball. With Hall of Famer Charlie Gehringer, Schumacher attended a one-month course for naval indoctrination at Chapel Hill.

The war presented a great hardship for Hal and his family when word came back from overseas that his brother, Herman J. Schumacher, had been killed in battle. Herman was killed in action at France on the first day of July, 26 years after his uncle for whom he was named died in action on the western front in World War I. Hal was released to inactive duty at Camp Shelton Separation Center in November of 1945. During the offseason, he visited Rhoads Hospital in Utica to discuss baseball as seen through the eyes of servicemen. He pitched one final year with the Giants in 1946 — he went 4–4 with a 3.90 ERA — before hanging up his spikes for good.

W	L	PCT	G	GS	CG	IP	H	BB	SO	SHO	ERA
158	121	.566	391	329	138	2,482	2,424	902	906	28	3.36

Ralph Richard "Blackie" Schwamb, *Pitcher*

One of the most despicable people to ever play professional sports, Blackie Schwamb was sent to prison in San Quentin after he was convicted of murder. Before his conviction, Blackie was always in trouble with the law. As a youth, he was in constant scrapes and was a common face to police officers. Under probation at the time of World War II, one of his conditions was that he enlist in the service for discipline. Forced to follow Uncle Sam, Blackie joined the navy near the end of the war.

The navy may have instilled discipline in young Blackie Schwamb, but if it did, he quickly forgot it. He pitched a dozen games with the Browns in 1948 before he was convicted of murder and sent to San Quentin. In Eric Stone's book *The Wrong Side of the Law*, he details the prison life of Blackie Schwamb. Blackie became a legend at San Quentin, courtesy of his baseball feats. Even though many people thought he had ties to the mob, Blackie was released on good behavior in the mid–1970s. The disgraced ballplayer was free to walk the streets and lived out the rest of his days in relative obscurity.

W	L	PCT	G	GS	CG	IP	H	BB	SO	SHO	ERA
1	1	.500	12	5	0	32	44	21	7	0	8.44

Joseph Scott, *First Base*

A soldier before he became a pro baseball player, Scott was deep in combat action in the European Theatre of Operations. Attached to the 46th Brigade with the 350th Field Artillery Company, Scott entered battle about a week after the Normandy Invasion. His unit pushed through France, drove the Germans back, and were stationed in Belgium for a time until the war ended. After his discharge, Scott spent a couple of years with the Birmingham Black Barons but never established himself as a regular.

(1947–1950): Birmingham Black Barons and Chicago American Giants

Kenneth Eugene Sears, *Catcher*

Ken was the son of National League umpire Ziggy Sears. The younger Sears spent two years at the major league level, with the 1943 Yankees and the 1946 Browns. While still on the Yankees roster, Ken missed the 1944 and 1945 seasons to service in the navy.

G	R	H	2B	3B	HR	RBI	BB	SO	SB	AVG	Slug
67	23	57	7	0	2	23	14	18	1	.282	.347

Richard William Seay, *Second Base*

Considered a defensive wiz, Seay had to work hard to remain in black baseball despite his exceptional fielding. Unable to hit his weight his first few years in the Negro Leagues, Dick's career in baseball was almost over before it really began. A workaholic, Seay was a baseball rat who played to better himself and worked diligently to correct his offensive weaknesses. He became an expert bunter and a good hit-and-run man to offset his weak batting averages.

Because of his weak stick, Seay made his rounds in black baseball. Able to find a job each year because of his terrific defense, Dick finally caught on with the Newark Eagles in the late-1930s. But even hitting as low as .200 was oftentimes a chore for Dick, and he was let go to join the Black Yankees. He left New York in 1943 to serve in the military during World War II, and after his discharge he was at the end of his rope. He played two more years with the Black Yankees before calling it a career.

(1925–1947): New York Black Yankees, Newark Eagles, Brooklyn Royal Giants, Baltimore Black Sox, Philadelphia Stars and Pittsburgh Crawfords

George Alexander Selkirk, *Outfield*

"Twinkletoes," as Selkirk was nicknamed, was a 34-year-old man in the twilight of his baseball career when he was drafted. A solid if not spectacular hitter throughout his career, George spent the 1941 and 1942 seasons as the Yankees' fourth outfielder. He had been a starter in the past, but Henrich and Charlie Keller had passed him by on the depth chart. He joined the Naval Reserves in 1943 and served as a boatswain. After his discharge, Selkirk didn't return to the major leagues but later became the general manager of the Washington Senators.

G	R	H	2B	3B	HR	RBI	BB	SO	SB	AVG	Slug
846	503	810	141	41	108	576	486	319	49	.290	.483

Theodore Walter Sepkowski, *Second Base*

Ted made his major league debut as a fresh-faced 18-year-old with the 1942 Indians. The kid then joined the U.S. Coast Guard and served in the military until 1945. His major league career spanned three years—1942, 1946 and 1947—but Ted only played in 19 games.

G	R	H	2B	3B	HR	RBI	BB	SO	SB	AVG	Slug
19	3	6	2	0	0	1	1	4	0	.231	.308

William Robert Serena, *Third Base/Second Base*

A power-hitting third baseman with the Cubs in the early-1950s, Bill had the hot corner job in Wrigley until he broke his wrist. When he came back, Randy Jackson had taken over and Bill was used as a reserve bat off the bench with good power. Before Serena signed his first pro contract, he served in the armed forces during World War II.

G	R	H	2B	3B	HR	RBI	BB	SO	SB	AVG	Slug
408	154	311	57	16	48	198	177	235	2	.251	.439

Walter Anthony Sessi, *Outfield*

A giant man, Sessi stood at 6'3" and weighed 225 pounds. Although that isn't a very large frame nowadays, he was much bigger than the average player of the 1940s. Sessi played with the Cardinals in 1941 and 1946 and missed the in-between years to military service. He was inducted into the armed forces shortly after the close of the 1941 season and returned to the 1946 Redbirds to sock his only major league home run.

G	R	H	2B	3B	HR	RBI	BB	SO	SB	AVG	Slug
20	4	2	0	0	1	2	2	6	0	.074	.185

Walter Dedaker Shaner, *Outfield*

Noted for his speed, Shaner played with the Red Sox during their weakest period in the 1920s and finished up as a member for the 1929 Reds. Wally was a 40-year-old man when he joined the armed forces during World War II.

G	R	H	2B	3B	HR	RBI	BB	SO	SB	AVG	Slug
207	80	175	45	8	4	74	43	54	13	.278	.394

Wilmer Ebert "Billy" Shantz, *Catcher*

The kid brother of Athletics star southpaw Bobby Shantz, Billy was a backstop for two years with the A's. A teenager throughout the war, Billy joined the navy in the conflict's latter stages. After his naval discharge, Billy signed his first pro contract.

G	R	H	2B	3B	HR	RBI	BB	SO	SB	AVG	Slug
131	31	98	13	4	2	29	28	37	0	.257	.328

Robert Clayton Shantz, *Pitcher*

Perhaps the greatest defensive pitcher of all-time, Shantz had the market cornered on Gold Gloves for the position. A gifted natural athlete, Shantz was also a fine hitter, belying his vest-pocket stature. The slim southpaw won an MVP Award at the major league level. But before he was a baseball star, he was just another grunt in Uncle Sam's army.

Shantz left high school and joined the army's fighting forces. An infantryman, Bobby served with the 86th Infantry's Chemical Division. Shipped out to the Pacific Theatre, Shantz saw combat action on foreign lands. His unit was stationed for a time on the Philippine Islands. When Shantz came back from the service, his size turned off many scouts, but the A's took a chance on the mite pitcher. Bobby became a star until arm injuries limited his effectiveness.

W	L	PCT	G	GS	CG	IP	H	BB	SO	SHO	ERA
119	99	.546	537	171	78	1,936	1,795	643	1,072	15	3.38

Robert Sharpe, *Pitcher*

Sharpe had a brief career in the Negro Leagues, spent predominately with the Memphis Red Sox. The right-hander served in the army at the end of the war.

(1941–1948): Memphis Red Sox and Chicago American Giants

Hollis Kimball "Bud" Sheely, *Catcher*

Sheely, the son of former major leaguer Earl Sheely, spent three years in the early-1950s as a back-up catcher with the White Sox. Chicago at the time had all-star Sherm Lollar handling the catching duties, and a platoon situation wasn't an option. During the war, Bud served in the navy. He was a yeoman second class stationed at Treasure Island, where he played service ball under the great Dick Bartell.

G	R	H	2B	3B	HR	RBI	BB	SO	SB	AVG	Slug
101	7	44	5	0	0	12	27	22	0	.210	.233

Bert Robert Shepard, *Pitcher*

The story of Bert Shepard is perhaps the greatest baseball story ever told. One thing is for certain: it surely was the best during World War II. Shepard was nothing more than a minor league drifter before the war. The southpaw had yet to make the majors when Uncle Sam needed boys to help fight the Japanese and Germans. Shepard was one of the first pro ballplayers to answer the call. Bert joined the armed forces and became a fighter pilot with the 55th Fighter Group. His unit was sent overseas where they were engaged in missions over hostile territory.

His fighter group was stationed in England, and while there, Shepard was able to play a little baseball. He was widely regarded as the best player on his service team, but the 55th would lose its pitching ace in May 1944. On May 21, Bert flew his 34th mission — it would be his last. Shot down over enemy territory, Bert was taken captive by the Germans and sent to a prisoner-of-war camp. Unconscious the entire trip to the camp, Shepard later came to and found that he was missing a leg, which he lost during his crash landing. Bert would recall later, "I was flying on a mission and was shot down. The next thing I knew, I was in a hospital north of Berlin and my leg was gone. While I was in prison camp, I had a crude artificial leg made for me by a Canadian prisoner. I practiced on it and maintained my muscle tone."

Liberated from the prison camp, Bert was sent home and was placed in an army hospital. A better artificial leg was made for him, and he also met Senators owner Clark Griffith while convalescing in Washington. Determined to play baseball again, Bert said, "I had been an athlete all my life and I promised myself the day I found my leg was off that I would continue to be one." Impressed by Shepard's determination, Griffith signed Bert to a contract, wishing the amputee the best but not expecting much production.

He joined the Senators in 1945 and was an instant sensation. During drills, Shepard peppered the ball across the plate like a major leaguer and even fielded his position well. The Senators were afraid that teams would exploit Shepard's handicap by laying down bunts, assuming Bert couldn't field. But when a teammate placed a bunt down in drills, Bert fielded it flawlessly and retired the batter at first. The army saw what a great example Bert would be for fellow war amputees and filmed Bert during practice and showed the home movies to casualties of war.

Preparing for the 1945 baseball season, Bert said he had two objectives: to gain a place in baseball and to be an example to all who were handicapped. Shepard's big test came during the season when the Senators called on him to pitch mop-up duty during a contest. The war hero took the hill to an ovation and pitched soundly for five innings. Although he was never called on to pitch for the Senators again, Bert achieved the unthinkable and became the darling of the nation.

W	L	PCT	G	GS	CG	IP	H	BB	SO	SHO	ERA
0	0	—	1	0	0	5	3	1	2	0	1.80

Edward Christopher Shokes, *First Base*

Shokes played briefly at the major league level, hitting 50 points under his weight. He made his debut with the 1941 Reds and then missed the 1943 through 1945 seasons to military service. Shokes, who was regarded as a defensive whiz, served at the Norfolk Naval Air Station during the war. During his navy stint, Eddie married his sweetheart from Duke University. He reached the rank of chief specialist early in 1944. Shokes operated an apple orchard after his retirement from baseball. A great minor league ballplayer, Eddie was inducted into the Syracuse Chiefs' Wall of Fame in 2000.

G	R	H	2B	3B	HR	RBI	BB	SO	SB	AVG	Slug
32	3	10	1	0	0	5	18	22	1	.119	.131

David Orvis Short, *Outfield*

Short went 1-for-11 in his major league career, which spanned two years with the Chicago White Sox. He missed four years to the war effort; Dave enlisted in the United States Army Air Corps before play began in 1942. After his stint in the military, he never again reached the major leagues.

G	R	H	2B	3B	HR	RBI	BB	SO	SB	AVG	Slug
7	1	1	0	0	0	0	3	3	0	.091	.091

Clyde Mitchell Shoun, *Pitcher*

A reliable left-handed relief pitcher throughout his career, Hardrock Clyde Shoun missed one year to service in the navy. Shoun was sworn into the colors at Fort Oglethorpe and pitched in a navy all-star game against Ted Williams. His claim to fame is tossing a no-hitter against the Braves on April 15, 1944. Hardrock, who began his career with the Cubs, was one of the players the Cardinals stole in the Dizzy Dean trade.

W	L	PCT	G	GS	CG	IP	H	BB	SO	SHO	ERA
73	59	.553	454	85	34	1,286	1,325	404	483	3	3.91

Roy Edward Sievers, *Outfield/First Base*

One of the most underrated Sluggers of the 1950s, Sievers was named Rookie of the Year in 1949. The perfect example of hometown boy makes good, Roy was a rookie sensation for the Browns. Before he exploded on the major league scene, Sievers served in the armed forces near the end of the war. A teen during the fighting, Roy did his bit in the great conflict's latter stages. Sievers would enjoy a borderline Hall of Fame career. A terrific Slugger during the height of his career, he played in relative obscurity with the Browns and Senators.

G	R	H	2B	3B	HR	RBI	BB	SO	SB	AVG	Slug
1,887	945	1,703	292	42	318	1,147	841	920	14	.267	.475

Charles Anthony Ryan Silvera, *Catcher*

Although Silvera played ten years in the majors, his offensive line looks more like a player who only had one full season of play. Charlie spent the bulk of his career as Yogi Berra's backup. With the Hall of Fame backstop on the roster, Silvera managed a lot of miles on the bench. During the war, Silvera played on a service all-Star team at McClellan Field with Walt Judnich, Ferris Fain and Bob Dillinger.

G	R	H	2B	3B	HR	RBI	BB	SO	SB	AVG	Slug
227	34	136	15	2	1	52	53	32	2	.282	.328

Kenneth Joseph Silvestri, *Catcher*

Silvestri was one of five major league catchers the Yankees lost to World War II. On the catching totem pole, he was the last man. "Hawk" spent parts of eight years in the majors but only strode to the plate 203 times. Never a regular, Silvestri lost four years to service in the army. He served with the Second Army in Memphis and even played with Dizzy Dean's All-Stars while in the service.

G	R	H	2B	3B	HR	RBI	BB	SO	SB	AVG	Slug
102	26	44	11	1	5	25	31	41	0	.217	.355

Albert Sima, *Pitcher*

A southpaw from New Jersey, Sima was a decent mop-up pitcher in the early-1950s. Sima made his debut with the 1950 Senators and would later pitch for the A's and White Sox. During the war, Al served in the U.S. navy.

W	L	PCT	G	GS	CG	IP	H	BB	SO	SHO	ERA
11	21	.344	100	30	4	308	343	132	11	0	4.62

Harry Leon Simpson, *Outfield*

Simpson earned the nickname "Suitcase" because he was a journeyed ballplayer. Often found in the transaction section of the newspaper, Harry was a sought-after left-handed bat during the 1950s. The Atlanta native could hit for a decent average and offered some power. Before Simpson joined the majors, he served in the U.S. Army during World War II and had a brief trial in the Negro Leagues.

G	R	H	2B	3B	HR	RBI	BB	SO	SB	AVG	Slug
888	343	752	101	41	73	381	271	429	17	.266	.408

Richard Allan "Dick" Sisler, *Outfield*

Dick's father, George, was a sensation in St. Louis around the time of the First World War. Father Sisler was a Hall of Fame first baseman who could hit .400 with the slightest of effort. Dick was built a little sturdier than his old man and therefore had a little more power. Before the younger Sisler made the major leagues, he served in the U.S. Navy during World War II. An ensign in the navy, Sisler was a company commander at Bainbridge. Later, he was transferred to the Great Lakes where he was mustered out. To get in shape for the upcoming baseball season, Dick ventured to Cuba and played winter ball on the island.

G	R	H	2B	3B	HR	RBI	BB	SO	SB	AVG	Slug
799	302	720	118	28	55	360	226	253	6	.276	.406

Sebastian Daniel "Sibby" Sisti, *Shortstop*

Sisti played in two cities during his major league career but wore only one uniform. He made his debut with the 1939 Boston Braves and was still a member of the club when they relocated to Milwaukee in 1953. With injuries to Tony Cuccinello and Eddie Miller, Sibby was given a prolonged trial by Casey Stengel in 1939 as an 18-year-old. He hit for a relatively weak batting average but did finish third on the club in the stolen base department. He became the regular third baseman in 1940 and slapped 24 doubles in 1941. He moved to second base in 1942 and entered the military after the close of the season. Sisti served in the U.S. Coast Guard and was stationed in Buffalo with Yankees star Tommy Henrich.

G	R	H	2B	3B	HR	RBI	BB	SO	SB	AVG	Slug
1,016	401	732	121	19	27	260	283	440	30	.244	.324

Enos Bradsher Slaughter, *Outfield*

Although Slaughter was a terrific player with a career's worth of highlights, he is best remembered now as the man who scored on "The Mad Dash" during the 1946 World Series. Country Slaughter was already an established major leaguer when the war broke out, having hit .320 in his second major league season. After he led the NL in hits in 1942 and guided the Redbirds to a Fall Classic victory over the Yankees, Enos joined the colors.

While the Cardinals were racing toward the NL pennant, Country was making his own "mad dash" toward the military. In August of 1942, Slaughter enlisted as an aviation cadet but wasn't called to duty until after the World Series was completed. He served as a sergeant with the 509th Base Headquarters Squadron at the San Antonio Army Air Field. Country was transferred from San Antonio to Kearns, Utah, in early 1945 and then rejoined the Redbirds after his military discharge. The next year, Enos, while playing against the Red Sox in the World Series, made his famous mad dash home to win the Series for St. Louis.

G	R	H	2B	3B	HR	RBI	BB	SO	SB	AVG	Slug
2,380	1,247	2,383	413	148	169	1,304	1,018	538	71	.300	.453

Dwain Clifford Sloat, *Pitcher*

A slim southpaw, Sloat pitched briefly in the majors in the late-1940s. Dwain served in the Army Air Corps before his major league debut. Stationed at the Waco Army Airfield, Sloat was able to play baseball under great catcher Birdie Tebbetts.

W	L	PCT	G	GS	CG	IP	H	BB	SO	SHO	ERA
0	1	.000	9	2	0	16	21	11	4	0	6.75

Roy Frederick Smalley Jr., *Infielder*

Smalley, whose son, Roy III, had a fine career with the Twins, played throughout the 1950s with the Cubs and Phillies. A decent infielder with modest power, Smalley was a teenager during World War II. He served in the armed forces at the end of the war. Roy's brother-in-law was former manager and fellow war veteran Gene Mauch.

G	R	H	2B	3B	HR	RBI	BB	SO	SB	AVG	Slug
872	277	601	103	33	61	305	257	541	4	.227	.360

Joseph Paul Smaza, *Reserve*

Smaza played only two games at the major league level with the 1946 White Sox. He had yet to make the majors when he left the game for the military. While playing ball at the Norman Navy Airfield, Smaza made quite a name for himself in the service ranks.

G	R	H	2B	3B	HR	RBI	BB	SO	SB	AVG	Slug
2	2	1	0	0	0	0	0	0	0	.200	.200

Edgar Smith, *Pitcher*

In the same fashion as Ted Lyons, Ted Williams remembered Edgar Smith in his biography *My Turn at Bat* as a player who enjoyed razzing the opposition. The Splendid Splinter even recalled that Smith was a notorious "elbow hunter," always trying to strike a batter's wing with a fastball. Smith made his debut with Connie Mack's Athletics in 1936 and was dealt to the White Sox during the 1939 baseball season. He pitched for the Pale Hose until he was inducted into the army after the 1943 campaign. He spent two years in the army and returned to the major leagues to pitch two more years before calling it quits.

W	L	PCT	G	GS	CG	IP	H	BB	SO	SHO	ERA
73	113	.392	282	197	91	1,595	1,554	739	694	7	3.82

Eugene Smith, *Pitcher*

A journeyman pitcher, Smith was with a different team every other year. He played for a number of teams in black baseball and even left the States to pitch in the Mexican League. During World War II, Smith spent three years in the army, and after his discharge he joined the once-powerful Homestead Grays. Gene's brother, Quincy, also played in the Negro Leagues.

(1938–1951): Cleveland Buckeyes, Atlanta Black Crackers, Ethiopian Clowns, St. Louis Stars, Kansas City Monarchs, New York Black Yankees, Pittsburgh Crawfords, Homestead Grays and Chicago American Giants

John Ford Smith, *Pitcher*

A fastball pitcher from Phoenix, Smith had yet to establish himself in black baseball before World War II. He left the Kansas City Monarchs in 1942 to join the war effort and was commissioned a lieutenant in the Army Air Corps. After his discharge he returned to the Monarchs but showed enough promise for the New York Giants to buy his contract. Ford played some minor league ball in the Giants chain with fellow former Negro Leaguer Monte Irvin. Too inconsistent in the minor league ranks, the Giants never called Smith up to New York.

(1939–1948): Kansas City Monarchs, Chicago American Giants and Indianapolis Crawfords

Vincent Ambrose Smith, *Catcher*

Smith missed four years to the war effort. He played in nine games before the war and seven after the fighting had stopped. Smith enlisted in the navy after the 1941 baseball season and served at the Norfolk Naval Training Station. He remained stateside for a spell before he received his orders, which shipped him overseas. Vinnie served in the South Pacific and played service ball with the Third Fleet All-Stars managed by Yankees great Bill Dickey.

G	R	H	2B	3B	HR	RBI	BB	SO	SB	AVG	Slug
16	5	14	1	0	0	5	2	10	0	.259	.278

Edwin Donald "Duke" Snider, *Outfield*

Hall of Fame center fielder Duke Snider was a teenager during World War II. The young Silver Fox served in the armed forces in the great conflict's final stages. Quick to make the major leagues, Snider was called up in 1947 to begin his Hall of Fame career with Brooklyn.

G	R	H	2B	3B	HR	RBI	BB	SO	SB	AVG	Slug
2,143	1,259	2,116	358	85	407	1,333	971	1,237	99	.295	.540

William Sodd, *Pinch Hitter*

Sodd had one at-bat with the 1937 Indians—the extent of his major league career. While playing ball in the minors during the war, Sodd quit the game in order to remain on his war plant job. However, he was inducted shortly thereafter in the U.S. Army.

G	R	H	2B	3B	HR	RBI	BB	SO	SB	AVG	Slug
1	0	0	0	0	0	0	0	1	0	.000	.000

William Dunn Sommers, *Third Base/Second Base*

Sommers played only one year in the majors, 1950, with the Browns. Sommers was used in a third-base carousel by skipper Zack Taylor with the likes of Roy Sievers, Leo Thomas and Snuffy Stirnweiss, as the Browns didn't have a regular hot corner custodian that season. Bill missed minor league tenure to service in the military during World War II.

G	R	H	2B	3B	HR	RBI	BB	SO	SB	AVG	Slug
65	24	35	5	1	0	14	25	14	0	.255	.307

Stephen Souchock, *Outfield*

When Souchock's career was about to take flight, he was inducted into the United States Army. The big basher was named the MVP of the Eastern League in 1942 but that offseason, before he could hang the award in his den, he was off to boot camp. A big, strong man from Pennsylvania, Steve entered the army and missed the next three baseball seasons to the war. When he returned from the military, the Yankees gave him a few trials in the late-1940s but he didn't stick in the majors until the Tigers got their mitts on him. The home run threat was described by writer Jim Hubbert as "a strapping truck foreman who likes tall women and Beethoven."

G	R	H	2B	3B	HR	RBI	BB	SO	SB	AVG	Slug
473	163	313	58	20	50	186	88	164	15	.255	.457

Warren Edward Spahn, *Pitcher*

This Hall of Fame left-hander was one of the few major league players to see action in the Battle of the Bulge. A famous Spahn story concerns another Hall of Famer, his skipper, Casey Stengel. In 1942 with Spahn's Braves facing the Dodgers, Stengel ordered Spahn to knock down Pee Wee Reese with a pitch. Spahn refused to throw at Reese, which forced Stengel to call the rookie southpaw "gutless." The next three years, Spahn was off to war, where he earned a Purple Heart and a Bronze Star for his war-time heroics. Stengel's "gutless" scouting report proved to be the greatest inaccuracy the game has ever known.

The lanky left-hander pitched briefly for the Braves prior to the war. He tossed sixteen innings in his cup of coffee with the 1942 Braves. Spahn then entered the colors and tossed a no-hitter at Fort Chaffee. In the service, Warren became a star pitcher, striking out 73 batters in four straight service games. Spahn served with the 115th Engineers in Heidelberg, Germany, during the war. He saw action at the Battle of the Bulge with the 115th years before he became the winningest southpaw in major league history.

W	L	PCT	G	GS	CG	IP	H	BB	SO	SHO	ERA
363	245	.597	750	665	382	5,244	4,830	1,434	2,583	63	3.08

Stanley Orvil Spence, *Outfield*

A left-handed fly-chaser who possessed an eagle's eye in the batter's box, Spence totaled twice as many bases on balls than strikeouts for his career. Unable to crack the Red Sox's amazing 1940 outfield of Williams, Dom DiMaggio and Doc Cramer, Spence was shipped to the Senators in 1942. He paced the league in triples his first year in Washington while he hit for a lofty .323 batting average—better than every Red Sox player other than Williams and

Pesky. When a lot of the players received their draft notices, Spence continued to play in the major leagues. He was one of four American League players to tally at least 100 RBIs in the war-stricken season of 1944. Stan joined the colors in 1945, just prior to spring training, and was inducted into the navy where he was stationed at the Bainbridge Naval Training Station.

G	R	H	2B	3B	HR	RBI	BB	SO	SB	AVG	Slug
1,112	541	1,090	196	60	95	575	520	248	21	.282	.437

Robert Oberton Spicer, *Pitcher*

An all-star his first year in professional baseball, Spicer missed time in the bushes to service with the army during World War II. The right-hander served in the infantry at Camp Wheeler and Camp Robinson, and at the time of his discharge, had reached the rank of staff sergeant. Spicer was called up by the Athletics after they had relocated to Kansas City.

W	L	PCT	G	GS	CG	IP	H	BB	SO	SHO	ERA
0	0	—	4	0	0	5	15	5	2	0	27.00

Homer Franklin Spragins, *Pitcher*

In spring training during the 1943 season, Homer's skipper, Doc Prothro, was optimistic regarding the upcoming season even though Uncle Sam had taken away many boys. When he looked at Spragins, Prothro felt confident that he'd have something in 1943. Prothro said, "He may be my meal ticket. I'm going to have good pitching." Shortly after Prothro uttered those words, Homer was inducted into the army. Spragins, a Mississippi State graduate, served in the Army Air Corps and was stationed at Florida.

W	L	PCT	G	GS	CG	IP	H	BB	SO	SHO	ERA
0	0	—	4	0	0	5	3	3	3	0	7.20

Gerald Lee Staley, *Pitcher*

At the time of the war, Staley was just another quality arm in the Cardinals' vast minor league stable. He pitched in the Pioneer League before the war to some acclaim but was inducted into service before St. Louis called him up. After boot camp, Staley was shipped overseas, where he was stationed at an evacuation hospital of an advanced base Service Command in the Bougainville Theatre. After his discharge, Gerry joined the Cardinals in 1947 and had a solid major league career that ended with the 1961 Tigers.

W	L	PCT	G	GS	CG	IP	H	BB	SO	SHO	ERA
134	11	.547	640	186	58	1,981	2,070	529	727	9	3.70

Thomas Virgil Stallcup, *Shortstop*

At the time of the war, Stallcup was in the Red Sox chain and was considered by many scouts to be a better shortstop than Johnny Pesky. Regarded as a defensive whiz, Stallcup was fine in the field but didn't have the solid bat that Pesky wielded. Stallcup, a free-swinger at the plate, lacked the great discipline that Pesky owned in spades. Carter Latimer wrote of the young prospect, "He has tremendous speed and is also one of the league's best base stealers. Defensively, he leaves little to be desired."

But the Red Sox lost their shortstop prospect to the war. Virgil joined the United States Navy and served in foreign waters on a destroyer for the duration. After his discharge, the Reds obtained his services from Boston and gave him his first look in the majors in 1947. The Reds had all-star Eddie Miller, who led the National League in doubles in 1947, entrenched at short, but they were confident enough in Stallcup's abilities to move Miller after the season. Inserted as the everyday shortstop in 1948, Stallcup impressed with his glove, but his bat couldn't match Miller's. He played into the early-1950s as a solid glove man with minimal offensive production.

G	R	H	2B	3B	HR	RBI	BB	SO	SB	AVG	Slug
587	171	497	99	13	22	214	51	181	9	.241	.334

George Walborn Staller, *Outfield*

Staller showed immense promise with the Athletics in 1943, swatting three home runs with as many triples in just 85 at-bats. Oddly enough, those 85 turns at the dish would be his only at-bats at the major league level. George entered the U.S. Marine Corps and missed the 1944 and 1945 seasons to service in the military. During his stint with the Marines, Staller spent time in the South Pacific.

G	R	H	2B	3B	HR	RBI	BB	SO	SB	AVG	Slug
21	14	23	1	3	3	12	5	6	1	.271	.459

Charles Stanceau, *Pitcher*

Charley's major league career spanned two seasons with two different teams: the Yankees and Athletics. Stanceau missed four full Baseball seasons to service in the United States Army. Shortly after the bombing at Pearl Harbor, Charley enlisted and was inducted at Canton, Ohio.

W	L	PCT	G	GS	CG	IP	H	BB	SO	SHO	ERA
5	7	.417	39	13	1	122	135	79	47	0	4.94

Richard Eugene "Dick" Starr, *Pitcher*

A mop-up pitcher for the Yankees in the late-1940s and the Browns afterwards, Starr served in the military before his major league debut. The right-hander joined the U.S. Army and missed valuable minor league seasoning to service in the armed forces.

W	L	PCT	G	GS	CG	IP	H	BB	SO	SHO	ERA
12	24	.333	93	45	7	344	390	198	120	2	5.26

Henry John Steinbacher, *Outfield*

Perhaps no manager had a greater impact on his team than Jimmy Dykes. The White Sox immediately turned things around when they acquired Dykes, and he rarely had much talent at his disposal. Steinbacher played for Jimmy in the late-1930s and gave Dykes a terrific 1938 season, in which he hit over .330. But when he failed in 1939, Hank was done as a major leaguer. During the war, Steinbacher served at Fort Lee in the battle's final stage.

G	R	H	2B	3B	HR	RBI	BB	SO	SB	AVG	Slug
203	88	170	29	10	6	85	66	34	3	.292	.407

Joseph Chester Stephenson, *Catcher*

One of six catchers the Cubs lost to the war, Stephenson played with three clubs in as many seasons. He spent the 1943 season with the Giants, 1944 with the Cubs, and 1947 with the White Sox. Joe missed one full year to military service.

G	R	H	2B	3B	HR	RBI	BB	SO	SB	AVG	Slug
29	8	12	1	0	0	4	2	15	1	.179	.194

Charles Augustus Stevens, *First Base*

A switch-hitting first baseman, Stevens made his debut before the war but got into only four games. He would have to wait until after the fighting to add to his numbers. Chuck, who had to play against such legends as Bobby Doerr, Bob Lemon, Jackie Robinson and Ted Williams while in high school, seemed ready for the task in affiliated ball with that kind of background. He signed with the Browns in 1937 and worked his way up the ladder until he made the parent club in 1941. He then spent 1942 in the minors and the next three years in the armed forces.

Stevens left the ball diamond and joined the fighting forces of Uncle Sam in 1943. Like so many young men, he put his dreams on hold. He reached the major leagues before the war and was determined to stay there, but the war interrupted things. Rather than feeling resentment, Stevens felt a sense of duty that permeated the nation, as personal dreams were miniscule when it came to the well being of a nation. He said, "You're in a short-term career in baseball, so you know that military service has taken away some of your time. But that wasn't the issue. We were in the service because the country was in trouble and your career becomes secondary then."

Shipped overseas to the Pacific Theatre, Stevens served with the Army Air Corps and stepped foot on such far-flung locales as Tinian, Saipan and Guam. He had some detached service on Iwo Jima after the land was taken by the Allies. Looking back on his tenure in the military during World War II, Stevens said, "The experience didn't hurt me a bit. It made you appreciate the things that you take for granted, and it had a very quick way of making you grow up with their values."

G	R	H	2B	3B	HR	RBI	BB	SO	SB	AVG	Slug
211	89	184	29	8	4	55	88	89	6	.251	.329

Edward Perry "Bud" Stewart, *Outfield*

Stewart came into his own after his retirement from baseball — his first retirement that is. With the war raging overseas, Bud announced his retirement in 1943 as a 26-year-old. He quit baseball so he could remain on his defense job but received his orders to report for induction in 1944. After the war, Stewart returned to baseball in 1948 with the Yankees and enjoyed some decent years with the White Sox in the early-1950s.

G	R	H	2B	3B	HR	RBI	BB	SO	SB	AVG	Slug
773	288	547	96	32	32	260	252	157	29	.268	.393

Lee Elbert Stine, *Pitcher*

Stine made his major league debut well before the war with the 1934 White Sox. The Pale Hose was a last-place team until they gave Jimmy Dykes control of the ship, and he guided them out of the doldrums. Stine's major league career was rather brief, as he tossed his last pitch with the 1938 Yankees. During the war, the Oklahoma native quit baseball to work for a shipyard where he built ships for the armed forces. However, in 1944, Stine joined the navy and used the knowledge he gained in the shipyards to help as a ship repairman.

W	L	PCT	G	GS	CG	IP	H	BB	SO	SHO	ERA
3	8	.273	49	12	5	144	179	55	39	0	5.06

William Arthur "Tige" Stone, *Outfield*

A standout at Mercer University, Stone had a cup of coffee with the 1923 Cardinals. A defensive replacement in the outfield, Tige had just one major league at-bat and slapped a single. The Georgian was also used on the mound in one contest. During the war, the 40-year-old Stone served in the armed forces.

G	R	H	2B	3B	HR	RBI	BB	SO	SB	AVG	Slug
5	0	1	0	0	0	0	2	0	0	1.000	1.000

George Bevan Strickland, *Shortstop*

Although Strickland knew how to draw walks, he was labeled an all-field, no-hit shortstop. George had a lengthy career in the 1950s, spent predominantly with Cleveland. He later managed the Indians for a spell after his playing days concluded. During the war, the teenage Strickland served in the Pacific Theatre.

G	R	H	2B	3B	HR	RBI	BB	SO	SB	AVG	Slug
971	305	633	84	27	36	284	362	453	12	.224	.311

Louis Bernard Stringer, *Second Base*

Stringer became the Cubs' everyday second baseman in 1941, his rookie season, when he took over for the veteran Billy Herman. He led all National League second basemen in home runs during the 1942 campaign and then missed the next three years to military service. Lou was inducted into the Army Air Corps shortly after the close of the 1942 baseball season when he served in the ground crew. He played service ball in the Arizona Valley Service League during 1943 for the William Field Fliers. In that league, Lou's club played against a service team that Joe DiMaggio was part of. He earned his discharge in 1945 at the rank of staff sergeant.

G	R	H	2B	3B	HR	RBI	BB	SO	SB	AVG	Slug
409	148	290	49	10	19	122	121	192	7	.242	.348

Ted R. Strong, *Outfield*

A gifted natural athlete, the tall outfielder may have been a better basketball player. At 6'6", he was the ideal height for the hardcourt and starred with the original Harlem Globetrotters basketball team. Although he was a good bit taller than the average outfielder, Strong was a star performer on the ball diamond. A switch-hitter with good power and solid defense, Ted's only weakness seemed to be a lack of speed. But he had a greater weakness than that — an absence of team loyalty. While he was with the Monarchs after the war, Kansas City won their division and went to the World Series. Strong and teammate Satchel Paige, the most flighty man in the history of professional sports, didn't bother showing up for the final two World Series games.

Due to the absence of Paige and Strong, the Monarchs lost the World Series to the Newark Eagles despite the best efforts of

Buck O'Neil and Hilton Smith to fill the two wayward stars' shoes. Before his disappearing act with Paige, Ted served three years in the armed forces during the Second World War. In 1950, when he was past his prime, he tried his luck in the low minor leagues but batted only .236.

(1937–1951): Kansas City Monarchs, Indianapolis ABCs and Chicago American Giants

Marlin Henry Stuart, *Pitcher*

A long arm out of the bullpen who was capable of offering a spot start, Stuart missed minor league seasoning to the war effort. At the time Detroit called Marlin up, he had reached his thirtieth birthday. Stuart later pitched with the Browns/Orioles, and when the Yankees brought him in during the 1954 season, he recommended that they acquire a kid fireballer named Ryne Duren.

W	L	PCT	G	GS	CG	IP	H	BB	SO	SHO	ERA
23	17	.575	196	31	7	486	544	256	185	0	4.65

Paul Herrington Stuffel, *Pitcher*

Like teammate Robin Roberts, Stuffel served at the end of the war when he came of age. A teenager throughout the fighting, Paul had a handful of trials with the Phillies in the 1950s but couldn't stick.

W	L	PCT	G	GS	CG	IP	H	BB	SO	SHO	ERA
1	0	1.000	7	1	0	11	9	12	6	0	5.73

Robert Harwood Sturgeon, *Shortstop*

Bobby became the Cubs' starting shortstop in 1941 after they bid adieu to their previous keystone combination of Billy Herman and Bob Mattick. He lost his starting job to Lennie Merullo in 1942 and was inducted into the navy prior to the 1943 baseball season. Sturgeon played on a service ballclub with St. Louis Browns first baseman Chuck Stevens. During his stint in the military, Sturgeon also played on a service all-star team with Joe DiMaggio.

G	R	H	2B	3B	HR	RBI	BB	SO	SB	AVG	Slug
420	106	313	48	12	1	80	34	79	7	.257	.318

John Peter Joseph Sturm, *First Base*

Johnny Sturm served as the Yankees' regular first baseman in 1941, the only year he played in the major leagues. After Babe Dahlgren was dealt to the Braves, Sturm was handed the first-base job. He appeared in 124 games that year and finished it by hitting .286 in the World Series. Soon thereafter, Johnny enlisted in the army and missed the next four years to military duty. He was the first married major league player to join the colors.

During his induction, Johnny said, "In my six years of baseball I was fortunate enough to reach the top. I haven't given up any more than countless fellows now working for Uncle Sam. All these men have given up their jobs, postponed careers." Before he left for basic training, Johnny was given a scrapbook by a fan detailing his career in baseball from the minors to the Big Apple. Sturm said, "It's one of the nicest presents I've ever received."

His initial military assignment was an engagement in public relations and recreation work at Jefferson Barracks, Missouri. While he served at Jefferson Barracks, Johnny suffered a mishap that was originally reported as a training accident. He underwent amputation of two joints of his right index finger at the infirmary because of the accident. Sturm was driving a tractor when a loose wire became entangled in a tractor wheel. He leaned over to dislodge it and his finger was mangled between the wheel and the wire.

Sturm later became a physical training instructor for the 33rd Training Group at Jefferson Barracks, able to continue his army duties despite the injury he sustained. Johnny also served as a drill instructor at the installation before his reassignment to Kearns, Utah. In 1945, Johnny served in the Pacific Theatre. Of his military stint, Johnny said, "I felt that as long as I was going to be a soldier, I wanted to be a good one. Baseball taught me to do my best; it's no different in the army." His return to baseball was short-lived, as he suffered a fractured wrist his first season after the war while playing for Kansas City.

G	R	H	2B	3B	HR	RBI	BB	SO	SB	AVG	Slug
124	58	125	17	3	3	36	37	50	3	.239	.300

Charles Morris Suche, *Pitcher*

Charley's major league career consisted of one ugly inning with the 1938 Indians. He allowed four hits and walked three batters in his lone frame. During the war, Suche served at Camp Crowder and played some service ball with Tigers great Tommy Bridges.

W	L	PCT	G	GS	CG	IP	H	BB	SO	SHO	ERA
0	0	—	1	0	0	1	4	3	1	0	36.00

Peter Suder, *Second Base*

A lifelong Athletic, Suder made his debut with the club in 1941 and played with them until they relocated to Kansas City in 1955. Never a goliath in the offensive departments, Suder was a slick-fielding second baseman whose fielding averages were usually in the upper .980s. He had a fondness for Yankee southpaw Joe Page, saying, "Ever since I can remember I've gotten just one bloop hit off Page. That hit was a real fluky, but every time Page gives out an interview he says, 'Suder gives me more trouble than anyone in the league.' Guys like that I like."

Suder went for his pre-induction physical in February of 1944 and told Connie Mack, "I don't think I'll be playing any ball this year." He was inducted into the armed forces on March 27 of the same year and missed two full seasons to the war effort. He returned to the Athletics in 1946 and enjoyed a fine year at the plate, hitting .281 while playing at every infield position. Suder settled in as the regular second baseman in 1947 and was a fixture in their infield on into the 1950s with Eddie Joost and Ferris Fain.

G	R	H	2B	3B	HR	RBI	BB	SO	SB	AVG	Slug
1,421	469	1,268	210	44	49	541	288	456	19	.249	.337

William Joseph Sullivan Jr., *Catcher*

The son of the great White Sox catcher of the same name, Sullivan Jr. was a journeyman backstop who wielded solid lumber in his heyday. Billy Jr. was the recipient of a poor hand dealt by fate, as he made his major league debut with the same club that his father became famous playing for. He played for the Pale Hose in three separate seasons before he made his way to Cleveland. After one season with the Tribe, he caught on with the Browns. Keeping his suitcases packed, Billy was shipped off to the Tigers and then to the

Dodgers before he was inducted into the service. He served three years in the military and played out one final season with the Pirates after his discharge.

G	R	H	2B	3B	HR	RBI	BB	SO	SB	AVG	Slug
962	347	820	152	32	29	388	240	119	30	.289	.395

John Paul Sullivan, *Shortstop*

A light-hitting shortstop, Sullivan was brought up to Washington in 1942 to replace Cecil Travis, who had entered the armed forces before the season. The slap-hitter drove in 55 runs as the regular shortstop in 1943 and hit the apple at a .251 clip in 1944. He missed the 1945 and 1946 baseball campaigns to service in the army and returned to Washington in 1947 to serve as Mark Christman's backup.

G	R	H	2B	3B	HR	RBI	BB	SO	SB	AVG	Slug
605	203	422	52	9	1	162	216	206	18	.230	.270

Lonnie Summers, *Catcher*

Summers didn't have much of a career in the Negro Leagues. He spent more time playing in Mexico and the minor leagues than he did in black baseball. Before the war he was unable to crack the roster of a Negro League team and played on the West Coast in the amateur ranks before joining the U.S. Army during World War II. Lonnie served with the 614th Tank Battalion that saw action in the ETO. After his discharge he played south of the border for a few years before trying his luck in the minor leagues. Overmatched in the Pacific Coast League, he had a little better luck in the lower Pioneer League in the Northwest.

(1938–1951): Chicago American Giants and Baltimore Elite Giants

Stephen Richard Sundra, *Pitcher*

Smokey Steve Sundra made his debut with the 1936 New York Yankees. His finest year came in 1939 when he posted an 11–1 record with a 2.75 ERA. However, with Lefty Gomez, Red Ruffing and Atley Donald around, Smokey was used out of the bullpen more often than he was as a starter. He struggled through a horrendous season in 1940, which forced the Yankees to send him to Washington. After his stint with the Senators, Steve was dealt to the Browns where he remained until he received his draft notice early in the 1944 season. Smokey was stationed at Camp Patrick Henry, Virginia, where he was able to play baseball.

W	L	PCT	G	GS	CG	IP	H	BB	SO	SHO	ERA
56	41	.577	168	99	47	858	944	321	214	4	4.17

Matthew Constantine "Max" Surkont, *Pitcher*

A big-bodied pitcher from Rhode Island, Surkont had his troubles before he made the major leagues. After his service discharge, Max was traded to the Braves, but the deal was voided when they learned that Max's arm was dead due to overwork in the armed forces. It took him some time before he was able to get back into condition. When he did, he was a part of the White Sox chain, and they gave him his first trial in 1949. A starting pitcher who was also used as a long arm out of the bullpen, Surkont spent the bulk of his career with the Braves.

During the war, Max played a lot of softball early in the service. Baseball took over for softball and then battle replaced recreation. Surkont was shipped overseas as he served as a gunner's mate in charge of artillery equipment on a landing craft. Transporting gear and bodies was Surkont's main duties in the military. Many of those bodies were captive soldiers of the enemy. Max wrote a letter to Ford Frick, detailing his military experiences with prisoners of war. Surkont wrote, "We've hauled many Jap prisoners back to our advanced bases. I started a conversation with one who talked fairly good English. I mentioned baseball and he was all smiles. He said he attended many games in Tokyo before the war and misses the game very much."

W	L	PCT	G	GS	CG	IP	H	BB	SO	SHO	ERA
61	76	.445	236	149	52	1,194	1,209	481	571	7	4.38

Charles Inigo "Butch" Sutcliffe, *Catcher*

Sutcliffe had a cup of coffee with the 1938 Braves. The reserve catcher slapped out one base hit in four at-bats. During the war, Butch served in the armed forces.

G	R	H	2B	3B	HR	RBI	BB	SO	SB	AVG	Slug
4	1	1	0	0	0	2	2	1	0	.250	.250

Howard Alvin "Dizzy" Sutherland, *Pitcher*

Before the war, Sutherland harbored ambitions of a career in baseball, but those dreams almost failed to come to life. The southpaw from DC had yet to sign professionally when he enlisted in the U.S. Army for service during World War II. Eager to do his bit, Dizzy joined the fighting forces of the army and earned his airborne wings. Attached to a fighting outfit, Sutherland was shipped out and served in the European Theatre of Operations.

Dizzy jumped into battle on the Italian fields. The paratrooper took part in heavy combat action and was overrun by the Germans and had to surrender. Taken prisoner, Dizzy and his captive battle buddies were marched to a POW camp. The Nazis kept Sutherland behind the barbed fences and fed him just enough to survive. Sutherland, who had always had a thick, strong body, lost a lot of weight in the camp and was sapped of much of his strength. When his camp was finally liberated, Sutherland was sent home to recover. The recovery process took Dizzy some time, and he didn't achieve his dream of signing a baseball contract until 1949. He appeared in one game for the Senators that season, overcoming the odds to achieve his dream.

W	L	PCT	G	GS	CG	IP	H	BB	SO	SHO	ERA
0	1	.000	1	1	0	1	2	6	0	0	45.00

Oadis Vaughn Swigart, *Pitcher*

Swigart lost more baseball time than most other major league players, as the right-hander enlisted after the 1940 season and missed the 1941 through 1945 seasons to the war effort. Upon his discharge, the Missouri native did not return to the major league ranks.

W	L	PCT	G	GS	CG	IP	H	BB	SO	SHO	ERA
1	3	.250	10	5	1	46	54	16	17	1	4.50

Joseph Szekely, Reserve

Szekely had a cup of coffee with the 1953 Reds. The Cleveland native missed valuable seasoning time in the minors to service in the armed forces during World War II.

G	R	H	2B	3B	HR	RBI	BB	SO	SB	AVG	Slug
5	1	1	0	0	0	0	0	3	0	.077	.077

James Reubin "Rawhide Jim" Tabor, Third Base

A tough and gritty ballplayer from the South, Tabor manned the hot corner in Boston from 1939 to 1944. He led the Bosox in stolen bases in 1939, 1940 and 1941. During the 1944 baseball season, Tabor received his orders to report to the United States Army. Rawhide was able to play in 116 games for the Red Sox that year before he had to report for his induction at Fort Devens. He served his tour of duty at Camp Croft, North Carolina. When he was discharged, Rawhide began his stint with the National League doormat Phillies and played with Ben Chapman's boys for two full seasons.

G	R	H	2B	3B	HR	RBI	BB	SO	SB	AVG	Slug
1,005	473	1,021	191	29	104	598	286	377	69	.270	.418

Vitautis Casimirus "Vito" Tamulis, Pitcher

A fine pitcher who played in an age when pitching was at one of its weaker points, Vito was a strong southpaw during the late-1930s. Tamulis began with the Yankees in 1934 before he caught on with Brooklyn in 1938. Vito led the team in winning percentage his first year there when the Dodgers were still a poor team. With Vito on the staff and help coming from others, the Dodgers began to turn things around and finished second in 1940. They captured the National League pennant in 1941, Vito's final year in the majors.

With his baseball career at its end, Tamulis entered the armed forces. He chose to join the Army Air Corps and was sent to Drew Field early in 1943. While stationed at Drew Field, the prospects for the 1943 baseball season looked bleak, but Vito felt the game would survive the war years. Tamulis said, "Sure, they'll play baseball this year, and it'll be an interesting race." Transferred to Sherman Field, Kansas, Vito reached the rank of staff sergeant before he was mustered out.

W	L	PCT	G	GS	CG	IP	H	BB	SO	SHO	ERA
40	28	.588	170	70	31	692	758	202	294	6	3.97

V. T. "Tommy" Tatum, Outfield

Tatum made his debut with the National League champion Dodgers in 1941. The Texas native would then spend the next four years in the army. Tommy served with the Army's Signal Corps and was stationed at Hawaii.

G	R	H	2B	3B	HR	RBI	BB	SO	SB	AVG	Slug
81	20	50	6	2	1	17	17	20	7	.258	.325

Fred Joseph Tauby (Taubensee), Outfield

A heady ballplayer, Tauby had modest skills but baseball brains. A well-respected man in the game, Fred had two cups of coffee at the major league level. Given his first look by the White Sox in 1935, Tauby failed to stick, and his last trial in the majors came with the 1937 Phillies. Unable to hit major league pitching, Tauby had to settle for a good career in the minor leagues. With Fred's baseball career near its end at the start of the war, Uncle Sam took the final playing Tauby had left in his frame.

On the Oakland Oaks' military reserve list throughout the war, Tauby knew he wasn't going to return to play in the fast Pacific Coast League after his discharge. He made the shift to managing while in the service, stationed at the Oakland Naval Training Station. Tauby managed a service ballclub that had major leaguers Ray Lamanno and Joe Hatten on its roster. After his discharge, Fred was still on Oakland's military list and stenciled to return to play. But his days as a player were done. Still, he was envied across the baseball circuit for his savvy and knowledge of the game. Writer Lee Dunbar said, "He's as smart as a tree full of owls and could be of great value to the Oaks in either of three jobs—coach, scout or manager of a farm team."

G	R	H	2B	3B	HR	RBI	BB	SO	SB	AVG	Slug
24	7	4	1	0	0	5	2	8	1	.077	.096

Harry Warren Taylor, First Base

"Handsome Harry" Taylor had a cup of coffee with the 1932 National League champion Cubs. Chicago had the great Charlie Grimm at first base, which meant the sharp-looking Taylor wasn't needed. During the war, Handsome Harry served with the U.S. Navy.

G	R	H	2B	3B	HR	RBI	BB	SO	SB	AVG	Slug
10	1	1	0	0	0	0	1	1	0	.125	.125

John Taylor, Pitcher

A wiry right-handed pitcher with vast potential that essentially went unfulfilled, Taylor was a flighty hurler who made the rounds during his career. He showed promise with the New York Cubans in the late 1930s before running off to Mexico. A sensation in Mexico his first year there, he won eleven games on a 1.19 ERA. However, it wasn't a hairbinger of things to come. He was a train wreck his next season in Mexico, when he issued 150 walks in less than 200 innings of work. Taylor then quit baseball and was inducted into the service for a two-and-a-half-year stint. After his discharge he tried to work his way back in Mexico but had limited success.

(1935–1945): New York Cubans and Pittsburgh Crawfords

Olan "Jelly" Taylor, First Base

Originally nicknamed "Satan" because he "played like the devil," Taylor had his nicknamed changed to "Jelly" because his mother didn't quite approve of his first ball diamond moniker. A gifted defender at first base, Jelly was a bit of a liability offensively. He had little power and hit for low batting averages. A showman with the Memphis Red Sox before World War II, Taylor was noted for his fancy glovework and was regarded as the best defender at first base in black baseball. Jelly missed three-plus years of baseball while he served in the armed forces during the war.

(1934–1946): Memphis Red Sox, Birmingham Black Barons, Cincinnati Tigers and Pittsburgh Crawfords

George Robert "Birdie" Tebbetts, *Catcher*

A genuinely likable character, Birdie had a very good career as a catcher and became a successful manager after his playing days had concluded. Tebbetts was capable of employing psychology as a catcher and manager. Ted Williams said that Birdie came as close as anyone ever had to get the temperamental Splendid Splinter to tip his cap to the Boston fans.

Tebbetts made his major league debut in 1936 with Mickey Cochrane's Tigers. Cochrane was one of baseball's top catchers when he played. After serving a couple years as Rudy York's backup, the Tigers had to move York to accommodate Birdie, who was clearly superior to the Slugging York in regards to defense. This move allowed the Tigers to win the 1940 American League pennant, as the team ERA dropped 28 points and York's heavy lumber was still in the lineup at a different position. His major league career was interrupted in 1943 when Birdie enlisted in the army.

After Birdie enlisted, he stated, "It would do untold good to some great and slightly temperamental players I've known if they could have six months of life in the army." These words weren't spoken at anyone in particular, but they seem to conjure up images for a certain ballplayer or two. Birdie, who held a degree in psychology (other sources list his degree as being in philosophy), was sent to the Waco Army Airfield where he managed a ballclub dubbed "The Birdie Boys." His official military duty was in recruiting, and Birdie was adept at offering the army sales pitch. One story concerning Birdie's uncanny knack for persuasive jaw-wagging centers on a visit he made to a young lady he knew. Birdie paid his female friend a social call one evening, and before the night was over, he had convinced four of her brothers into enlisting in the army. His recruiting excellence became general knowledge in the major league baseball circles, and Birdie was once asked to leave a major league city by club officials who felt that Birdie had come to recruit their entire roster.

During his first year in the army, in 1943, Birdie guided his airfield ballclub to a 52–10 record. He left Waco briefly to attend the Army Air Force Officer Candidate School at Miami Beach. When he returned to Waco, Birdie was an officer in the Special Service, heading the physical training department. In 1944, Birdie played baseball sporadically, as the backstop dealt with a number of health issues. He suffered a broken toe, sprained ankle and twisted knee, all injuries sustained on the baseball diamond and not on a battlefield or during military training. He was called to New York with his ace pitcher Sid Hudson, a Washington Senator great, and the two major league stars assisted in a ten-day war bond campaign.

Birdie returned to the Tigers in 1946 as a 33-year-old man. He platooned that year with Paul Richards and was dealt to the Red Sox early in the 1947 campaign. After the trade, Birdie raised his batting average 109 points and filled a glaring deficiency on Boston's roster. He hit .280 in 1948 and .270 in 1949 as a 36-year-old backstop. He retired in 1952 and accepted a managing job two years later with the Cincinnati Reds.

Fond of psychology, Birdie enjoyed distracting batters while they awaited the pitcher's offering in the batter's box. He later revealed there was one player he gave up on distracting altogether: Jimmie Foxx. Birdie said, "We'd get to talking and Jimmie would start to say something as the pitcher threw the ball. That big lug would just wham the ball out of the park and turn his head casually to me as he started toward first and say, 'I'll tell you about it when I get back.'"

G	R	H	2B	3B	HR	RBI	BB	SO	SB	AVG	Slug
1,162	357	1,000	169	22	38	469	389	261	29	.270	.358

John Ellis Temple, *Second Base*

The Reds' star second baseman during the 1950s, Temple was a youngster throughout the war. After high school graduation, Temple joined the service at the very end of the war. A gifted little ballplayer, Temple was one of the top second basemen of his time. Johnny was quick, hit for a good average, and had a terrific batting eye.

G	R	H	2B	3B	HR	RBI	BB	SO	SB	AVG	Slug
1,420	720	1,484	208	36	22	395	648	338	140	.284	.351

Joseph John Tepsic, *Pinch Runner*

A gridiron great at Penn State, Tepsic chose baseball over football after the war. The gifted natural athlete was employed as a pinch-runner by the Dodgers in 1948, his only season in the majors. To persuade Joe off the football field, Brooklyn offered him a hefty $17,000 signing bonus. Although he failed to make it in the baseball ranks, Tepsic earned acclaim on the battlefields while fighting the enemy with the U.S. Marine Corps.

Tepsic left the Penn State campus and enlisted in the Marine Corps for service during World War II. Short but strong and ideally built, Joe became a fighting man in Uncle Sam's outfit. After his boot camp, Tepsic was shipped overseas where he was engaged in combat action at Guadalcanal. Many American soldiers died in that region, and Tepsic was nearly one of that total. Engaged in hand-to-hand combat, Joe sustained a bayonet wound to the right arm and shoulder. Lifted from the battlefield, Tepsic was sent to a military hospital where doctors informed him that his shoulder was permanently damaged. He was advised against playing sports, but after his discharge Tepsic went right back to the life he knew best.

G	R	H	2B	3B	HR	RBI	BB	SO	SB	AVG	Slug
15	2	0	0	0	0	0	1	1	0	.000	.000

Willard Wayne Terwilliger, *Second Base*

The definition of a baseball rat, "Twig" has been in the game since the 1940s with little interruption since the turn of the century. A solid fielding, modest hitting second baseman for the Cubs and Senators, Wayne had a respectable playing career that ended in the early 1960s. He then ventured to the dugout where he coached for his chum Ted Williams on the Senators, helped the Twins build a dynasty in the 1980s, and managed in the minor and independent leagues. His career in baseball has been a lengthy and successful one. But before it began, he was a young Marine engaged in battle at foreign lands.

Two months after Twig turned eighteen, he was off to San Diego for boot camp. After his basic training, Wayne was sent to radio school to learn Morse code. This matriculation led to an assignment as a radioman in a tank where he also served as a machine gunner. His tank duties fell under the Second Armored Amphibian Battalion, which was attached to the second Marine Battalion. Mustered out after training, Terwilliger went to Saipan where he was actively engaged in the deadly Saipan Invasion.

His tank was unloaded onto the island and they pushed inland via armored vehicle. But when their tank bottomed out in a deep shell hole, they were sitting ducks and had to abandon their vehicle. The fight was on foot for Terwilliger and his battle buddies, who provided support for the infantrymen. Later, Terwilliger would participate in missions on Tinian before the big push on Iwo Jima. His squad was in charge of removing wounded soldiers and taking them to transport ships to be sent to hospitals. After a few days of this mission, Terwilliger witnessed the flag rise on Iwo Jima. From there, he was sent to Hawaii where he prepared for an even larger assault on the Japanese, but it never happened as Hiroshima was bombed and the Japanese surrendered. Sent back home, Twig's battalion was deactivated in November of 1945. The young man witnessed some severe war-time battles but managed to come out ablebodied and eager to face the challenges of a post-war world. He used the GI Bill to enroll in college, married his high school sweetheart, and played ball for the Western Michigan baseball team. Life was back to normal for Terwilliger, as the sounds of battle became a memory. But they were a dear memory that shaped a high school boy from Michigan into a man of character.

G	R	H	2B	3B	HR	RBI	BB	SO	SB	AVG	Slug
666	271	501	93	10	22	162	247	296	31	.240	.325

Keith Marshall "Kite" Thomas, *Outfield*

A strong outfielder from Kansas City, Kite had good power and a decent batting eye. He served with the U.S. Navy during World War II and used the GI Bill to attend college after his discharge. Kite was called up to the Athletics and played some outfield for them in the early 1950s when they had solid players like Elmer Valo, Gus Zernial and Dave Philley in the pasture.

G	R	H	2B	3B	HR	RBI	BB	SO	SB	AVG	Slug
137	35	52	9	3	7	32	34	40	0	.233	.395

Leo Raymond Thomas, *Third Base*

Third base was a gaping hole for the Browns in the early 1950s, and they tried everyone at the position. Leo received his look there in 1950 and 1952 but failed to impress. Before his major league debut, he served in the armed forces during World War II.

G	R	H	2B	3B	HR	RBI	BB	SO	SB	AVG	Slug
95	32	57	11	1	1	27	43	25	2	.212	.271

Raymond Joseph Thomas, *Reserve*

Thomas played one game at the major league level and scratched out a single for his only hit. He left baseball to enlist in the navy before the United States was actively engaged in the war. By the time of his discharge, Thomas had reached the rank of lieutenant commander.

G	R	H	2B	3B	HR	RBI	BB	SO	SB	AVG	Slug
1	1	1	0	0	0	0	0	0	0	.333	.333

Henry Curtis Thompson, *Utilityman*

Like fellow Negro Leaguer Lemuel Hawkins, Thompson wasn't about to win any "Man of the Year" awards. A violent individual with a history of criminal behavior, Hank carried a pistol almost everywhere he went and wasn't afraid to use it. Thompson murdered a man he didn't want dating his sister, and many teammates felt he was an evil hoodlum with no business in polite society. However, Hank played professional baseball in the Negro Leagues and was a very poor selection to play for the Browns shortly after Jackie Robinson broke the color line. Thompson didn't possess Jackie's demeanor and he was quickly let go by St. Louis. Hank missed just a year and half of baseball to service in the military.

G	R	H	2B	3B	HR	RBI	BB	SO	SB	AVG	Slug
933	492	801	104	34	129	482	493	337	33	.267	.453

John Samuel "Jocko" Thompson, *Pitcher*

When Curt Simmons was removed from the Phillies roster during their push to the World Series in 1950 courtesy of the Korean War, the team selected Jocko to take his place on the roster. Thompson could relate to what Simmons was going through, having been a soldier himself. Before Jocko reached the majors, he served in the army during World War II and saw plenty of combat action as a paratrooper. Always modest, whenever Jocko was asked by writers how many jumps he made during the war, he'd answer with "umpteen."

During World War II the young Thompson served with the 82nd Airborne Division. Jocko and his battle buddies would jump into hostile regions and engage the enemy in combat. The 82nd entered the fray during the Battle of the Bulge and Jocko was wounded during the famous battle. When he returned home, Thompson was able to wear the Purple Heart and both the Silver and Bronze Stars on his uniform.

W	L	PCT	G	GS	CG	IP	H	BB	SO	SHO	ERA
6	11	.353	41	21	5	167	151	83	81	2	4.26

Eugene Earl "Junior" Thompson, *Pitcher*

Junior was a pretty good pitcher for a couple years in Cincinnati. He was the fresh blood in the 1939 NL champion pitching staff that boasted solid veterans in Bucky Walters, Paul Derringer and Lee Grissom. Thompson, who was a rookie that year, posted a swell 13–5 record with a 2.55 ERA. He became a full-fledged starting pitcher in 1940, fashioning a 16–9 record as the Reds won the World Series that year. He struggled mightily in 1941, suffering the "junior jinx," but rebounded to have a respectable 1942 season. However, with the war raging overseas, Junior voluntarily retired from baseball after the 1942 season.

Thompson was inducted into the military in 1944 and missed two years to the navy. He was stationed at the Great Lakes and set a record for number of assignments handled in one day at the receiving regiment. Thompson returned to major league baseball in 1946 and enjoyed his finest year out of Mel Ott's bullpen. Junior posted a microscopic ERA of 1.29 in 63 innings during the 1946 season — while surrendering a total of 36 base hits.

W	L	PCT	G	GS	CG	IP	H	BB	SO	SHO	ERA
47	35	.573	185	68	27	687	602	328	315	6	3.26

Charles Lemoine "Tim" Thompson, Catcher

A longtime scout after his playing days, Thompson made his debut with the Dodgers in 1954. The bulk of his playing time came with the Kansas City A's two years later. Thompson missed valuable minor league seasoning time to service in the armed forces during World War II.

G	R	H	2B	3B	HR	RBI	BB	SO	SB	AVG	Slug
187	49	123	24	2	8	47	39	52	2	.238	.338

Robert Brown Thomson, Outfield/Third Base

Forever remembered as the Slugger who hit the famous "Shot Heard Round the World" in 1951, Thomson was a lot more than a one-game ballplayer. One of the top Sluggers of the 1950s, "The Staten Island Scot"—as Bobby was warmly referred to—was a perennial All-Star threat. As a child, Bobby's parents left Scotland and came to Staten Island where they raised young Robert. When he came of age during World War II, he joined the Army Air Corps and served his new homeland.

G	R	H	2B	3B	HR	RBI	BB	SO	SB	AVG	Slug
1,779	903	1,705	267	74	264	1,026	559	804	38	.270	.462

Benjamin Robert Thorpe, Outfield

A member of the last Boston Braves team and the first Milwaukee Braves club, Thorpe was a regular for just one major league season. A free-swinger in the batter's box, Thorpe served in the U.S. Navy during World War II.

G	R	H	2B	3B	HR	RBI	BB	SO	SB	AVG	Slug
110	22	83	9	3	3	32	6	48	3	.251	.323

James Francis Thorpe, Outfield

Widely regarded as the greatest athlete of his generation—or any generation for that matter—Thorpe, the Native American legend, was a pro baseball and football player as well as a gold medal winner in the Olympics. Thorpe last played major league baseball in 1919 with the Braves of George Stallings. When his son, Philip, enlisted in the navy during World War II, Jim was so overcome with a sense of national pride that he wanted to join up with his boy. Given that Thorpe was 57 years old, the only branch that would accept him was the Merchant Marines. During the last year of the war, Thorpe worked on an ammunition ship.

G	R	H	2B	3B	HR	RBI	BB	SO	SB	AVG	Slug
289	91	176	20	18	7	82	27	122	29	.252	.362

Louis Charles Frank Thuman, Pitcher

Lou Thuman's baseball career ended tragically in the European Theatre while engaged in combat. The right-handed pitcher served in the infantry during the war and participated in the Normandy Invasion. During combat, Thuman was shot in his right shoulder. For his military heroics, he was awarded the Purple Heart, but his career in baseball was officially over. Unable to throw, he was forced to retire upon his stateside return. He pitched overseas in England, participated in service ball, and taught nonprofessionals the art of the game. Thuman was forced to give up Baseball having pitched only nine innings at the major league level. He never was able to collect his first big league win because his dreams were dashed due to the wounds he suffered while serving his country.

W	L	PCT	G	GS	CG	IP	H	BB	SO	SHO	ERA
0	1	.000	5	0	0	9	12	9	1	0	12.00

Robert Burns Thurman, Outfield

Thurman had a rather brief career in baseball since he was discovered in his mid-twenties while playing service ball during World War II. The big left-hander enlisted in the army during World War II and served in the Pacific Theatre. He was sent to such locales as New Guinea and Luzon, but it was on the Philippine Islands where Bob was discovered by baseball folks. He was a solid pitcher in the army, and after his discharge he joined the Homestead Grays as a hurler. Only a modest pitcher, Thurman moved to the Kansas City Monarchs in 1949 where skipper Buck O'Neil began to use him in the outfield.

O'Neil's tutelage paid off, and after just one season in Kansas City, Thurman was sold to the New York Yankees. But in order to attract scouts from the majors, Bob lied about his age. He was already in his early thirties when he signed, and he knew no team would take a chance on an aging player who had just found his niche. The Yankees officially scrapped the mound work and Thurman became a full-time outfielder. Sold to the PCL by the Yankees, Thurman was a member of the Reds when he finally made the majors in 1955 at the age of 38. With an outfield of young Slugging sensations Gus Bell, Wally Post and Frank Robinson, Thurman was employed simply as a power bat off the bench.

G	R	H	2B	3B	HR	RBI	BB	SO	SB	AVG	Slug
334	106	163	18	11	35	106	62	112	1	.246	.465

Joe Hicks Tipton, Catcher

A decent catcher with a good eye and some power, Tipton made his major league debut with the world champion 1948 Indians. He hit .289 as a rookie and even had a pinch-hit at-bat in the World Series. Dealt to the White Sox the following year, Tipton would also play for the A's and Senators. During the war, Joe served with the United States Navy.

G	R	H	2B	3B	HR	RBI	BB	SO	SB	AVG	Slug
417	116	264	36	5	29	125	186	142	3	.236	.355

William Harrel "Hal" Toenes, Pitcher

Hal Toenes had a cup of coffee with the 1947 Senators of Ossie Bluege. The Mobile, Alabama, native lost his only major league decision. A right-handed pitcher, Hal served under Uncle Sam before he made his debut with Washington. Toenes served with a transport outfit in the Army Air Corps during the war. A high-ranking official, Hal was a non-commissioned officer with the 4th Ferrying Command.

W	L	PCT	G	GS	CG	IP	H	BB	SO	SHO	ERA
0	1	.000	3	1	0	7	11	2	5	0	6.43

Andrew John Tomasic, *Pitcher*

Better known for his work on the football field than the baseball diamond, Tomasic was a pro football player during the war. A member of the Pittsburgh Steelers in 1942, Tomasic left the gridiron for the U.S. Army. Stationed at Miami Beach, Florida, with the 46th Wing, Andy served with the Army Air Corps. Shipped out in 1944, Tomasic was sent to the Philippines, where the 46th was placed at Clark Field. While stationed at Clark Field, Philippine Islands, Tomasic coached a football team that participated in what was termed the Bamboo Bowl. After his discharge, Andy returned to the Steelers. His baseball career consisted of a cup of coffee with the 1949 Giants.

W	L	PCT	G	GS	CG	IP	H	BB	SO	SHO	ERA
0	1	.000	2	0	0	5	9	5	2	0	18.00

Clifford Earl Torgeson, *First Base*

"The Earl of Snohomish," Torgeson was a gifted natural athlete who played basketball during the offseason to stay in shape. A terrific all-around talent, Torgeson was a solid defensive first baseman with good power and a supreme batting eye. His impeccable pitch recognition skills allowed him to post some rather enviable on-base percentages over the course of his career. But that career, as good as it was, didn't begin until Torgeson ended another career: a fighting soldier in Uncle Sam's army.

An unknown commodity in the pro baseball ranks before the war, Earl made a name for himself in the service ranks. When he was spotted blasting the sphere at army installations, baseball birddogs took notice. But army life wasn't all baseball and recreation for the Earl of Snohomish. Torgeson was a fighting man who was shipped overseas for combat duty. When he first arrived overseas, Earl was able to continue with baseball for a time. Torchy Torrance, business manager of the PCL's Seattle club, was a major in the Marine U.S. Corps who saw Earl play in Europe. Torrance said, "We are sending Torgeson into the major leagues soon. He's liable to make them forget the other good ones. He can do just about everything. He's been in the service since 1942, but you'll hear about him."

First things first, Torgeson had to make it through the war unscathed. Earl was attached to a company that saw combat action in the ETO. Engaged in the Battle of the Bulge, Earl was wounded during that great battle and thus awarded the Purple Heart. Pulled from the frontlines to recover, his wounds kept him out of action until the armistice was signed. At that time, while still in the army, Earl was inked to a contract by the Braves.

G	R	H	2B	3B	HR	RBI	BB	SO	SB	AVG	Slug
1,668	848	1,318	215	46	149	740	980	653	133	.265	.417

Louis Eugene Tost, *Pitcher*

Tost pitched briefly at the major league level, two years with the Braves and a season with Pittsburgh. The southpaw was ordered for induction on April 13, 1943, and sought to be assigned to the ground crew of the Naval Air Force. Lou missed the better part of three years to service in the navy where he was able to play ball on a navy All-Star aggregation.

W	L	PCT	G	GS	CG	IP	H	BB	SO	SHO	ERA
10	11	.476	39	23	5	156	159	56	46	1	3.63

Stephen Joseph "Red" Tramback, *Outfield*

Red had a cup of coffee with the 1940 Giants. A second-division club that year, Tramback was used in only two games. Shipped back to the minors, Red won MVP honors in the Western Association and appeared poised for a return trip to the majors before the war interceded and Tramback joined the colors. Red enlisted in the navy. Shipped overseas, he was sent to Hawaii where he played some service ball with Mickey Vernon and Buddy Blattner. After his discharge, Tramback was not called back up to the majors.

G	R	H	2B	3B	HR	RBI	BB	SO	SB	AVG	Slug
2	0	1	0	0	0	0	1	1	1	.250	.250

Cecil Howell Travis, *Shortstop*

Quiet and unassuming, Travis played his entire baseball career in the obscurity of Griffith Stadium as a member of American League doormat Washington Senators. A stellar shortstop in his time, Travis' career batting average of .314 ranks behind only Honus Wagner and Arky Vaughan on the all-time list of shortstops. However, had the portside-swinging Travis not have attempted a return to baseball after his tour in the military, he would be tied with the great Flying Dutchman as the best hitting shortstops in history with identical marks of .328.

Travis was a respected player by peers and former players alike. Hall of Famer Joe Cronin once stated about Travis: "He's another fellow who can hit in his sleep. There's one way to pitch to him — pitch — and duck." Rogers Hornsby, a cantankerous Hall of Fame second baseman not known for issuing statements of praise, had this to say about Travis: "Now there's a guy you can tell is a fine hitter by everything he does. He's relaxed and still tough."

During the 1941 baseball season, Senators owner Clark Griffith was afraid he was going to lose his star shortstop to the military draft. However, Travis was able to play the entire season, the season in which Ted Williams, with his chase for .400, and Joe DiMaggio, with his hitting streak, made all the headlines. Travis kept on pace with the two legends, playing with that ominous "W" on his cap, and proceeded to best the two in the base hit department with 218 — a league-leading total. One might also be interested to learn that Travis' .359 batting average also eclipsed the Yankee Clipper's own batting mark. Not even a famed fortune teller could predict that 1941 season would be Travis' last in the sun. His career was taking off like a ball connecting with his lumber of choice, but he was called by Uncle Sam and reported to Fort McPherson for his induction physical on January 7, 1942.

Travis would be assigned to Camp Wheeler, Georgia, with the 15th Battalion where he was able to play baseball for the installation. He played with Dizzy Dean, the great hurler of the famous St. Louis Gashouse Gang, and batted against legendary Negro League twirler Satchel Paige. His days of playing baseball for Uncle Sam came to an end when he was reassigned to Camp McCoy, Wisconsin, in 1944 where he served with the 76th Infantry Division. While stationed in Wisconsin, Travis underwent cold weather training with his unit, as he was undoubtedly going to witness harsher conditions across the ocean. Across the ocean he went in late 1944 as his unit moved through Le Havre, France and set up their headquarters at Limesy.

The 76th was an infantry group and thus saw action in

conflicts. Travis and his mates arrived during the latter stages of the Battle of the Bulge and kept marching toward the enemy. Travis recalls the harsh winter nights as thus: "It was the cold that got to us.... You slept where you could, in a barn, anyplace, but there was no heat. We just shivered all night long. I'll never forget that cold as long as I live."

Travis' unit relieved a weary 87th Division late in January. Later, he developed trenchfoot and frostbite on his left foot and was ordered to a hospital in Metz, France, to allow his feet to heal. After three weeks of healing, Travis rejoined his unit and helped them take the Siegfried Line in one week's time. During their march to Trier, Travis' 76th Infantry Division captured 28 towns and took more than 1,600 enemy prisoners. The 76th also achieved the deepest penetration into German soil of any allied force on April 16. In all, the 76th saw 110 days of combat action before Major General Schmidt ordered the unit dissolved on June 15.

Cecil Travis was discharged from the army as a sergeant and was awarded four Battle Stars, one of which being the Bronze Star. He returned home to a new son and to a pennant-chasing Senator club late in the 1945 season. Travis contributed ten RBIs in 15 games down the stretch but the Senators still finished a game and a half behind Steve O'Neill's Tigers. Although Travis played for another two seasons, he never again resembled the player he was before the war. Never one to make excuses, Travis stated that his decline in production was the result of a lack of timing instead of blaming his frostbitten appendage. Manager Ossie Bluege, however, noted how Travis didn't have his usual spring in his step after his tour in the military.

Travis played through the 1946 and 1947 seasons. The ailment greatly affected the player and he underwent treatment in 1946 to restore proper circulation to his feet. This ailment proved critical in his slide from all-star performer to average player and was apparent one contest when Travis failed to score from third on a deep flyball to right field. Fans, the collection of the forever fickle, jeered Travis for not scoring on the drive. However, legendary sports scribe Shirley Povich reprimanded the fans in the sports page the following day when he said they should be ashamed for booing a man who fought the Germans on their own soil.

Cecil Travis officially announced his retirement on September 27, 1947, and returned to his family farm in Riverdale, Georgia. It was later revealed that the humble Southern star informed owner Clark Griffith while still an active player in 1946 that he should decrease his pay for playing so poorly. He felt that he did not deserve to be paid such a lofty price for not producing like he had in the past. This great game could exist for another hundred years, but it will never again produce another quite like Cecil Howell Travis, a man who *should* be in the Baseball Hall of Fame.

G	R	H	2B	3B	HR	RBI	BB	SO	SB	AVG	Slug
1,328	665	1,544	265	78	27	657	402	291	23	.314	.416

Nicholas Joseph Tremark, *Outfield*

A pocket-sized outfielder who played with the Dodgers in the mid–1930s, Tremark stood all of 5'5" and was generously listed at 150 pounds. The diminutive outfielder was a slap hitter who played pieces of three seasons for Brooklyn. During his stint with the Dodgers, he had to back up such outfielders as Len Koenecke, Frenchy Bordagaray and Johnny Frederick. Nick's last action at the major league level came in 1936.

During the war, the Manhattan College graduate served in the U.S. Navy. During his stint in the navy, Nick was stationed at such bases as Norfolk, Sampson and Pensacola. When it was learned that the little outfielder had been accepted for duty by the navy, writer Roy Shudt quipped, "I didn't think Nick was big enough to meet the navy's requirements." At Bronson Field in Pensacola, Nick was a chief athletic specialist who worked in ground training at the Naval Air Training Station. On the service club there, Tremark was able to play with none other than Ted Williams.

G	R	H	2B	3B	HR	RBI	BB	SO	SB	AVG	Slug
35	10	18	4	0	0	10	6	5	0	.247	.301

Robert Lee Trice, *Pitcher*

A tall right-hander from Newton, Georgia, Trice was with the Athletics when they moved from Philadelphia to Kansas City. Bob pitched three years at the major league level with the A's after a one-year stint in the navy during World War II. After his naval discharge, Bob joined the Homestead Grays of the Negro Leagues before the Athletics bought his contract. A 20-game winner in the minors, Trice struggled in the majors and ended his playing days in Mexico.

W	L	PCT	G	GS	CG	IP	H	BB	SO	SHO	ERA
9	9	.500	26	21	9	152	185	60	28	1	5.80

Kenneth Wayne Trinkle, *Pitcher*

An adequate relief pitcher over the course of his career, Ken Trinkle missed two full seasons to service in the armed forces. After spending the 1944 and 1945 seasons in the military, Ken returned to the Giants in 1946 and led the National league in games pitched.

W	L	PCT	G	GS	CG	IP	H	BB	SO	SHO	ERA
21	29	.420	216	19	3	436	442	208	130	0	3.74

Virgil Oliver Trucks, *Pitcher*

Much like teammate Tommy Bridges, Trucks is a vastly underrated pitcher whose name is lost to the modern fan. This southern flamethrower possessed a hard one that legendary catcher Mickey Cochrane compared it with Bob Feller's fastball. His heat, as well as his last name, earned him the nickname "Fire." Virgil made his debut with the 1941 Tigers, fanning three men in two innings, and then led the Tigers in wins the following season.

Trucks became a 16-game winner in 1943 — his last season before his military callup — as he teamed with Dizzy Trout, Tommy Bridges and Hal Newhouser to give the Tigers a dynamic front four. With the war raging overseas, the Tigers' stellar rotation was disbanded, as both Virgil and Bridges entered the service in 1944. Virgil served in the navy's shipping department and was able to play some baseball in the service. While stationed at Pearl Harbor, Virgil shut out an army all-star team. He returned to the majors late in 1945, so late in fact that he made only one start during the regular season. But the Tigers made the World Series and Virgil doubled his season's workload with two appearances, collecting a complete-game victory in Game 2.

With teammate Hal Newhouser, he gave the Tigers a solid righty-lefty combination in the rotation on into the 1950s. Virgil paced the American League in both strikeouts and shutouts in 1949 but suffered an arm injury in 1950. He rebounded the next year to pace the Tigers in wins, but his left-handed partner Newhouser had suffered an arm ailment that season. After his days in Detroit, Trucks became a nomadic player. He saw action with the Browns, White Sox, Athletics and Yankees before he announced his retirement.

W	L	PCT	G	GS	CG	IP	H	BB	SO	SHO	ERA
177	135	.567	517	328	124	2,684	2,416	1,088	1,534	33	3.38

Thurman Lowell Tucker, *Outfield*

Sharing the same physical appearance as a noted comedian of the day, Thurman Tucker was affectionately referred to as Joe E., after funnyman Joe E. Brown. Tucker was an adequate hitter who knew how to draw a walk, and he split his career with the White Sox and Indians. After the 1944 baseball season, he was drafted into the navy and missed the 1945 campaign to service in the armed forces. Tucker was handed the starting center-field job upon his return from the navy and finished behind Luke Appling as the club's top hitter for average.

G	R	H	2B	3B	HR	RBI	BB	SO	SB	AVG	Slug
701	325	570	79	24	9	179	291	237	77	.255	.325

George Elkins Turbeville, *Pitcher*

Turbeville pitched for the A's during their lean years of the mid–1930s. They had already surrendered most of their talent to other clubs to survive the Great Depression by the time George debuted with them. A lack of accuracy was Turbeville's downfall in the majors. In three years with Philadelphia, George struggled to find the plate each season. Inducted into the military for service during World War II, George gained a level of accuracy while he pitched for a service team at the Shaw Field Aviation Cadet Training Station.

W	L	PCT	G	GS	CG	IP	H	BB	SO	SHO	ERA
2	12	.143	62	15	4	185	196	157	47	0	6.13

Earl Edwin Turner, *Catcher*

A back-up catcher during his two-year sojourn at the major league level, Turner missed valuable minor league time to service in the army.

G	R	H	2B	3B	HR	RBI	BB	SO	SB	AVG	Slug
42	10	18	0	0	3	5	4	13	1	.240	.360

Thomas Richard Turner, *Catcher*

Turner spent three and a half years with the Chicago White Sox, where he served as Mike Tresh's backup. He was dealt to the Browns late in the 1944 season and platooned with Ray Hayworth and Frank Mancuso while the Browns won the pennant. He missed the entire 1945 season to service in the army.

G	R	H	2B	3B	HR	RBI	BB	SO	SB	AVG	Slug
233	63	165	29	4	7	63	51	84	4	.237	.320

Elmer Strange Tutwiler, *Pitcher*

Tutwiler had a cup of coffee with the Pirates in 1928. The right-hander appeared in only two major league games. During World War II, Elmer joined the U.S. Marine Corps.

W	L	PCT	G	GS	CG	IP	H	BB	SO	SHO	ERA
0	0	—	2	0	0	4	4	0	1	0	4.50

John Anthony Tyler, *Outfield*

Tyler's baseball career came several decades too soon. A gifted natural hitter who was capable of hitting the ball out of sight, Johnnie was a train wreck on the field. The batter's box was his home, but he was as lost in the outfield as a golf ball in a farmer's cotton field. He would have made an ideal designated hitter, but the DH wasn't adopted until well after Johnnie's career was over. He served in the armed forces during World War II.

G	R	H	2B	3B	HR	RBI	BB	SO	SB	AVG	Slug
16	7	17	2	1	2	12	4	6	0	.321	.509

Robert Royce Usher, *Outfield*

When Usher signed with the Reds, it was anyone's guess where he would play. A gifted pitcher who was also an adept batsman, Bob could have gone either way: pitcher or hitter. At the time of the war, it looked as if Usher would be a pitcher. Bill McKechnie predicted a fine pitching career for him in spring training in 1943, and when he joined the navy, Cardinals Hall of Famer Stan Musial was impressed by his pitching ability. Stan the Man said, "I think he's about ready. He's fast, has pretty good control, and is a good hitter to boot." After his discharge, the Reds pressed Bob towards the outfield and he was essentially done as a pitcher.

G	R	H	2B	3B	HR	RBI	BB	SO	SB	AVG	Slug
428	133	259	41	4	18	102	90	136	9	.234	.329

Elmer William Valo, *Outfield*

Elmer Valo was a ballplayer of a dying breed, one that seems all but extinct in the age of big contracts and never taking risks on the ball diamond. He was the textbook definition of a wallbanger. He went all-out every inning of the game, making catches on flyballs that soared into dangerous territory. Fearless, Valo would crash into walls, oftentimes catching the drives while smacking into obstacles. It is because of players like Valo and Pistol Pete Reiser that every ballpark across the nation now has a warning track.

Valo made his debut with the 1940 Philadelphia Athletics as a 19-year-old. He hit .348 in his short trial in 1940 and .420 the following year after he spent most of the season in the minor leagues. He was up to stay in 1942, when he paced the club with ten triples and thirteen stolen bases. After he played in 77 games for Mack in 1943, Valo was drafted into the army.

Born in Czechoslovakia, Valo's parents came to the States when he was a boy. He said, "I came over here when I was still a youngster but I remember Czechoslovakia well — still have cousins there and I identify with the people." Valo, who was the only Czechoslovakian-born player in the major leagues at the time, played service ball for the New Cumberland Reception Center nine. He was commissioned as a second lieutenant in the medical corps and earned his discharge in time to participate in the 1946 spring training.

He returned to the diamond in solid fashion. Always a contact hitter who often posted three times as many walks as strikeouts, he hit .307 upon his return. Valo was also an enigma for fireball hurlers, as evidenced in a game against the Indians when he stroked two hits off Bob Feller. Despite Athletics hurler Bob Savage pitching a great game of his own, the other Philadelphia players couldn't muster but a single hit off Rapid Robert, and Savage was handed a 1–0 loss.

G	R	H	2B	3B	HR	RBI	BB	SO	SB	AVG	Slug
1,806	768	1,420	228	73	58	601	942	284	110	.282	.391

John Henry Van Cuyk, *Pitcher*

Van Cuyk was with the Dodgers for three years in the late-1940s but rarely pitched. The southpaw from Wisconsin served in the U.S. Army during World War II and played service ball at Camp Grant, Illinois.

W	L	PCT	G	GS	CG	IP	H	BB	SO	SHO	ERA
0	0	—	7	0	0	10	12	3	3	0	5.40

Maurice Rene Van Robays, *Outfield*

Bomber Van Robays played his entire major league career with the Pirates, which began in 1939 and ended in 1946. His finest year came in 1940 when Maurice drove in 116 runs, good for third in the National League behind Johnny Mize and Frank McCormick. Bomber left the Pirates in 1944 to join Uncle Sam's roster, as he served with Company A of the 38th Signal Training Battalion at Camp Crowder, Missouri. At Camp Crowder, Bomber was in charge of running sporting events.

G	R	H	2B	3B	HR	RBI	BB	SO	SB	AVG	Slug
529	232	493	94	27	20	303	139	155	2	.267	.380

John Samuel Vander Meer, *Pitcher*

One of the most dominating pitchers in baseball annals, Johnny "The Dutch Master" Vander Meer is the only pitcher in the game's history to toss consecutive no-hit ballgames. Johnny blanked the Boston Braves on June 11, 1938, and then no-hit the Dodgers his next start, on June 15. Vander Meer's only drawback on the ball diamond was his lack of accuracy, as he oftentimes walked a large amount of batters.

The Dutch Master, who was also referred to as "Double No-Hit," walked 69 batters in his first 84 innings of major league work. He became the talk of baseball in 1938 when he tossed his back-to-back no-hit games, but he finished third in the NL in the walks department, behind a couple fellas who tossed in the access of 260 innings. After he struggled in 1939, Cincinnati gave up on him and farmed him out for the majority of the 1940 season. The banishment to the bushes was effective, as Johnny came back hotter than a skillet on the range top. He struck out an NL-best 202 batters in 1941 and allowed only 172 hits in 226 innings of work. Again, in 1942, the Dutch Master led all National League hurlers in strikeouts, but more importantly, he began to trim his alarmingly high base on balls total.

For the three years prior to his military induction, Vander Meer led the NL in strikeouts each season. Although his accuracy would waver, Johnny's ERA was usually low, always hovering near 3.25. Vander Meer was eager to do his part in the war but had been rejected by the military on medical grounds. During a telephone interview conducted with writer Jack Cuddy, Johnny said, "If you're looking for superlatives in my life, I'll tell you the lowest I ever felt was last summer when I was rejected for service because Colitis— a stomach condition—brought on by the muscular tenseness of pitching in major league games. I wanted to get in. Everyone else is getting in. And I don't see why I should be an exception."

After his previous rejection, Johnny was taken into service with the United States Navy in 1944. At the time of his induction, Vander Meer had become the 200th National League player summoned by Uncle Sam. Johnny took his boot camp at Sampson Naval Training Station. He was shipped out overseas and spent twelve months of service in the South Pacific before he received his discharge in December 1945 as a coxswain at the Lido Beach Separation Center. Johnny returned to the Reds in 1946, minus the trademark zip on his fastball. For the first time, Johnny failed to strike out 100 batters in a full season's worth of work.

W	L	PCT	G	GS	CG	IP	H	BB	SO	SHO	ERA
119	121	.496	346	286	131	2,104	1,799	1,132	1,294	30	3.44

Cecil Porter Vaughan, *Pitcher*

A trim southpaw, Porter Vaughan spent pieces of three seasons at the major league level with the Athletics. His son, Leroy B. Vaughan, who followed his father into the real estate business, mentioned that one of his father's most memorable experiences was facing Ted Williams on the final day of 1941—the day the Splendid Splinter finished the season with a batting average over .400. Vaughan surrendered two of Ted's hits that day, which allowed Williams to end the season with a batting mark of .406.

During the war, Vaughan served in the United States Army at Camp Lee. He was inducted as a private on January 14, 1942. He was one of the first Athletics to join the colors. During an Army-Navy game, Porter squared off against the great Bob Feller. Vaughan, who attended the University of Richmond, became a successful realtor after his playing days had concluded.

W	L	PCT	G	GS	CG	IP	H	BB	SO	SHO	ERA
2	11	.154	24	18	6	122	137	74	52	0	5.83

Albert Alfred Verdel, *Pitcher*

A war-era pitcher, Verdel was in the army and served at Fort Dix, New York. While stationed there, Al went 36–6 in service league play but was discharged early in the fall of 1943. He joined the Phillies and pitched one perfect inning for them in the war-interrupted 1944 campaign.

W	L	PCT	G	GS	CG	IP	H	BB	SO	SHO	ERA
0	0	—	1	0	0	1	0	0	0	0	0.00

James Barton "Mickey" Vernon, *First Base*

One of the best first basemen left out of the Baseball Hall of Fame, Vernon won two batting titles in his major league career. A slick fielder who never exploited his power, he was just as capable of slapping the ball to the opposite field as he was at ripping the offering to right field. He made his debut with the 1939 Washington Senators and platooned with Jimmy Wasdell as a rookie. His initial lack of offense forced the Senators to acquire all-hit, no-field Zeke Bonura in 1940. Manager Bucky Harris then gave Vernon the everyday chore in 1941 and he responded with 93 RBIs. He led all first basemen in stolen bases in 1942 and 1943.

Vernon was summoned by Uncle Sam after the close of the 1943 baseball season; his loss forced the Senators to use an aging Joe Kuhel at the initial sack. Mickey spent the next two years in the United States Navy. He initially reported to the physical instructor's school at Bainbridge. After his discharge, Vernon set the American League ablaze with his hitting. Most fans would have bet that Williams or DiMaggio would pace the AL in batting the year after the war, but it was Mickey who outdistanced them all with his tremendous .353 batting mark in 1946.

G	R	H	2B	3B	HR	RBI	BB	SO	SB	AVG	Slug
2,409	1,196	2,495	490	120	172	1,311	935	869	137	.286	.428

George Steve Vico, *First Base*

A slick-fielding first baseman for the Tigers in the late-1940s, Vico became property of Detroit after tearing up the PCL following his military discharge. Portland sold his contract to Detroit for a hefty sum and George played regularly with the club in 1948 and 1949.

G	R	H	2B	3B	HR	RBI	BB	SO	SB	AVG	Slug
211	65	166	28	11	12	76	60	56	2	.250	.380

Antonio Joseph "Joe" Vitelli, *Pitcher*

A war-era pitcher, Vitelli served briefly at Camp Livingston with a recon company before he was medically discharged. The Pirates took a look at Vitelli in 1944 and signed him to be a batting practice pitcher. Despite his batting practice duties, the Bucs got Joe into a few games in 1944 and 1945.

W	L	PCT	G	GS	CG	IP	H	BB	SO	SHO	ERA
0	0	—	4	0	0	7	5	7	2	0	2.57

Clyde Frederick Vollmer, *Outfield*

Vollmer usually served as a fourth outfielder, but when he was a regular, he showcased above-average power. Clyde played briefly before the war with the Reds in 1942, and then missed the next three years to service in the army. However, despite his brief stay in Cincinnati, he left a lasting impression by swatting a home run in his first major league at-bat. Vollmer was shipped overseas and served in Iran. He wrote a letter to Reds general manager Warren Giles that stated, "It's plenty hot. The other night it dropped to 110 and we had to use blankets."

G	R	H	2B	3B	HR	RBI	BB	SO	SB	AVG	Slug
685	283	508	77	10	69	339	243	328	7	.251	.402

Philip Vance Voyles, *Outfield*

Voyles spent one year in the majors with the last-place 1929 Boston Braves. Phil only had two extra-base hits in his career but they were both triples. Before he made his major league debut he served in the navy during World War I. When America was involved in the Second World War, Voyles rejoined the navy and worked as an electrician.

G	R	H	2B	3B	HR	RBI	BB	SO	SB	AVG	Slug
20	9	16	0	2	0	4	6	8	0	.235	.294

Jacob Fields Wade, *Pitcher*

Whistlin' Jake Wade was a wild southpaw who pitched in the late 1930s and on through the mid–1940s. With a dynamite left wing, the Tigers gave him his initial trial at the major league level in 1936 and inserted him into the rotation the following year. His trademark inaccuracy was obvious from the onset, as Whistlin' Jake walked 107 batters in just 165 innings in 1937. Detroit gave up on him in 1938 and he was subsequently shipped off to the Red Sox—then the Browns and later the White Sox. Wade was inducted into the navy after the completion of the 1944 baseball season and spent one year at Bainbridge. He returned to the game to play one final season split between the Yankees and Senators.

W	L	PCT	G	GS	CG	IP	H	BB	SO	SHO	ERA
27	40	.403	171	71	20	669	690	440	291	3	4.99

Charles Thomas Wagner, *Pitcher*

Nicknamed "Broadway" because he enjoyed dressing in style, Wagner was the road roommate of a young Ted Williams. Broadway began his major league career in 1938 and ended it in 1946, playing with only one team. After a terrible debut season in 1938, Charlie was used sparingly by skipper Joe Cronin until 1941. That year, Wagner led the club with three shutouts while his roommate chased the .400 batting milestone. His finest year came in 1942, as Wagner posted a 14–11 record with a respectable 3.29 ERA. He missed the following three years to service in the navy where he was stationed at Norfolk before he played one final season in the majors in 1946.

W	L	PCT	G	GS	CG	IP	H	BB	SO	SHO	ERA
32	23	.582	100	67	30	527	532	245	157	5	3.91

Harold Edward Wagner, *Catcher*

Only the Yankees lost as many catchers to the war effort as the Red Sox in the American League, and Wagner was one of the last to be called to arms. He played with Connie Mack's Athletics from 1937 to 1944—he spent most of that time as Frankie Hayes' backup—and was swapped to Boston early in the 1944 campaign. Never much of a hitter under Mack, Wagner's move to Fenway paid great dividends as he smacked the apple at a .332 clip. Despite his newfound hitting skill, Wagner was drafted into the navy shortly before the close of that season. He lost the entire 1945 baseball season and returned to Boston—and his usual low batting average—in 1946.

G	R	H	2B	3B	HR	RBI	BB	SO	SB	AVG	Slug
672	179	458	90	12	15	227	253	152	10	.248	.334

Kermit Emerson Wahl, *Utility Infielder*

Wahl was inducted into the armed forces despite a bad knee that hindered him throughout his baseball career. The knee also kept him from becoming an effective soldier, and he was medically discharged after just a few months of service. Classified 4-F by his draft board, Kermit joined the Reds in 1944 and played with them through the duration of the war. After the war, Kermit was farmed out but he returned in 1947 and played some in the 1950s with the A's and Browns.

G	R	H	2B	3B	HR	RBI	BB	SO	SB	AVG	Slug
231	58	145	23	6	3	50	68	72	3	.226	.294

Eddie Stephen Waitkus, *First Base*

Waitkus gained notoriety when a deranged female fan named Mary Ann Sternhagen shot him in a hotel room during the year of 1949. Doctors felt that Eddie would never play baseball again, but the determined first sacker ventured south to Clearwater, Florida, in an attempt to rehab. He made a valiant return to baseball after spending four months in Clearwater, recovering from his gunshot wounds. Of his recovery, Waitkus said, "Looking back now, they were the four most horrible months of my life. Worse than anything in the army— worse than New Guinea or anything in the Philippines. The pain was so severe that more than once I found myself wishing that the girl had finished the job."

Eddie played briefly with the Cubs prior to the war. He registered for the draft at Cambridge, Massachusetts, and was inducted into the army shortly thereafter. Waitkus was a corporeal with the Engineer Amphibian Command at Camp Edwards when he broke his right arm in the first inning of the first service game he played in. After his recovery, he was shipped overseas and served in New Guinea where he received Cubs box scores. Eddie said, "Every time we get a box score out here, I have to sneak around corners."

His military time wasn't spent idle, as the young first baseman wrote baseball bigwig Ford Frick on several occasions detailing the missions he had been on. One of Eddie's letters to Frick concerned a treacherous and unorthodox assignment that he was a part of in the Netherlands East Indies. Waitkus wrote, "I can't help but respect the man who planned this one for the amphibious force, and the strategy gave us a surprise and saved a lot of lives. It was like stealing home in a ball game. If it worked, swell! If it failed, it looked idiotic!"

Concerning the same operation, Eddie wrote

As the boats circle and head for shore, you get a feeling like Opening Day. You check your rifle a hundred times. I was in one of the first waves. We hit in deep water, had to go in over our heads. It's a seemingly endless stretch through the water to the shore, but finally we made it. A machine gun got a Jap sniper pinned up in a tree just as we hit. On shore there wasn't much opposition, and right now things are coming under control. I don't know where or when we hit again. All our bats, balls and gloves are packed away. The fellows would like to break them out in the Philippines, but that's up to the fates and General MacArthur. All I can say about the place we hit is that it's in the Netherlands East Indies. Nothing like Wrigley Field, either!

Eddie took a war-time breather to participate in a pick-up ball game in Manila at the shell-damaged Rizal Stadium. He was discharged in time to rejoin the Cubs for the 1946 season. He paced all Cubs players with a .304 batting average and struck out only fourteen times in 441 at-bats. An expert batsman, Waitkus' lone ball diamond drawback was his lack of power at a run-producing position.

G	R	H	2B	3B	HR	RBI	BB	SO	SB	AVG	Slug
1,140	528	1,214	215	44	24	373	372	204	28	.285	.374

Richard Cummings Wakefield, *Outfield*

One of baseball's first "bonus babies," Wakefield was signed by the Tigers at the price of a $52,000 bonus. To sweeten the deal, Dick also received a brand-new automobile. At about this time, Hank Greenberg was the highest-paid player in baseball, making just $3,000 more than was paid the amateur. Although he was a good ballplayer, Dick never did quite live up to his vast potential. Referred to as a "carbon copy of Ted Williams," Dick missed one year to the war while serving in the navy.

G	R	H	2B	3B	HR	RBI	BB	SO	SB	AVG	Slug
638	334	625	102	29	56	315	360	270	10	.293	.447

Edwin Joseph Walczak, *Second Base/Shortstop*

Ed only played at the major league level during the war-interrupted 1945 season, but "Husky" wasn't your typical war-era ballplayer. Most players that wear the "war-era" tag were guys that didn't serve in the military and were thus able to make the majors because of the manpower shortage. Walczak was a soldier who served with distinction in the European Theatre. A waist gunner on a flying fortress, Husky was engaged in bombing operations over Germany. A sergeant during the fighting, Ed received the Air Medal for Excellence while serving his country.

G	R	H	2B	3B	HR	RBI	BB	SO	SB	AVG	Slug
20	6	12	3	0	0	2	6	9	0	.211	.263

Harry William Walker, *Outfield*

There are varying accounts depicting how Harry "The Hat" Walker came by his nickname. Some say that he was called "The Hat" because he owned a substantial array of headgear, while the most common answer presents the fact that he tugged at his cap while in the batter's box. Either way, Walker was a tremendous ballplayer who was a sensational slap hitter under any moniker. Walker missed the 1944 and 1945 seasons to military service when the left-handed hitter served at Fort Riley and also served overseas in the European Theatre. His most famous hour coincides with that of Enos Slaughter, as Walker was the man who got the base hit that Slaughter scored on his "mad dash" in the 1946 World Series.

G	R	H	2B	3B	HR	RBI	BB	SO	SB	AVG	Slug
807	385	786	126	37	10	214	245	175	42	.296	.383

Harvey Willos "Hub" Walker, *Outfield*

Hub enjoyed a scattershot career at the major league level; he never could quite stick. His first action came with the 1931 Tigers, and after three years in the bushes, Hub returned for nine games in 1935. He spent the next two years with the Reds, where he served as a backup to Hall of Famers Kiki Cuyler and Chick Hafey, before another prolonged stint in the minors. He joined the navy in 1942 and spent three years in the service before he saw his last action with the world champion Tigers of 1945. His last major league hit was a pinch-hit double in the Fall Classic. During the war, one of Hub's brothers was killed in action.

G	R	H	2B	3B	HR	RBI	BB	SO	SB	AVG	Slug
297	117	205	43	6	5	60	104	89	26	.263	.353

James Harold "Lefty" Wallace, *Pitcher*

A slight southpaw, Wallace made his major league debut with the 1942 Braves. Manager Casey Stengel, a World War I veteran, used Lefty in nineteen games as a rookie. He lost the next two years to the war effort but received an early discharge from the army with a CDD.

W	L	PCT	G	GS	CG	IP	H	BB	SO	SHO	ERA
5	6	.455	51	14	4	144	133	64	51	0	4.13

John "Jack" Wallaesa, *Shortstop*

Wallaesa was a tall shortstop before they became fashionable. He had trouble sticking in the major leagues given his propensity for the strikeout while he saw action with the Athletics and White Sox during his career. Jack played briefly before the war and missed three full seasons to service in the armed forces. He served in the ground crew of the Army Air Corps during the war.

G	R	H	2B	3B	HR	RBI	BB	SO	SB	AVG	Slug
219	56	120	17	4	15	61	39	138	3	.205	.325

James Gerald "Junior" Walsh, *Pitcher*

A mop-up pitcher for the Pirates after the war, Walsh missed some time in the minors to service in the armed forces during World War II. The year after his discharge, Junior was brought up for a look by the Bucs but failed to impress. He was able to stick after the 1948 season and pitched through 1951.

W	L	PCT	G	GS	CG	IP	H	BB	SO	SHO	ERA
4	10	.286	89	12	1	192	201	111	91	1	5.91

Lonnie Warneke, *Pitcher*

A great pitcher, Warneke was dubbed "The Arkansas Hummingbird." Warneke was a grizzled veteran by the time World War II broke out. He made his major league debut with the 1930 Chicago Cubs. After his terrible debut—five walks in one inning—the Cubs were reticent in using the wild kid from Arkansas. He overcame his wildness in 1932 by pitching the Cubs to the World Series. Lon posted a 22–6 record, and led the National League in wins, winning percentage, shutouts and earned run average. The Cubs' pitching imploded in the Fall Classic, as Warneke was the only pitcher used by Chicago for more than three innings whose ERA was below 10.00.

Writer George Kirksey called Warneke an "Arkansas hillbilly and cracker box philosopher." The colorful right-hander led the NL with 26 complete games in 1933 on a miniscule 2.01 ERA. He netted 22 wins in 1934 and an even 20 in 1935, pitching the Cubs to the World Series again. Despite Lon's October brilliance, including a pair of wins with a 0.54 ERA, the Cubs lost to the Tigers in six games. He tied for the league lead in shutouts during the 1936 season and was dealt to the Cardinals, where he won 18 games in his first season with the Redbirds. His numbers began to dip in St. Louis even though he was still a credible major league hurler. He rebounded in 1940 to post a 16–10 record and won 17 the following year. Warneke was sent back to the Cubs in 1942 and was inducted into the armed forces as a 35-year-old in 1944.

Warneke took his screening exam before his draft board in early January of 1944. He informed the Cubs not to expect his services for the 1944 baseball season. At his induction physical, the Arkansas Hummingbird said, "They gave me a thorough examination, but they didn't tell me the result. I don't know whether I'm in or out. I don't know whether I'll be throwing grenades at the Germans or Japs or baseballs at opposing National League batsmen." During the war, Warneke worked for a naval ordinance plant.

W	L	PCT	G	GS	CG	IP	H	BB	SO	SHO	ERA
192	121	.613	445	343	192	2,781	2,726	739	1,140	31	3.18

Harold Charles Warnock, *Outfielder*

A highly educated ballplayer, Warnock didn't start playing ball professionally until after he had earned his law degree. Hal had a cup of coffee with the 1935 Browns of Rogers Hornsby. Unable to stick in baseball, Warnock had a safety net and became an attorney in Tucson. He closed up shop during World War II to enlist in the navy as a commissioned officer. At the time of his discharge, Hal had attained the rank of lieutenant commander.

G	R	H	2B	3B	HR	RBI	BB	SO	SB	AVG	Slug
6	1	2	2	0	0	0	0	3	0	.286	.571

Bennie Louis Warren, *Catcher*

A power-hitting catcher, Warren served as the Phillies' regular backstop from 1940 to 1942. His weakness was his inability to hit for a high average, but he once posted twice as many home runs compared to doubles in one season. Bennie was inducted into the military after the 1942 baseball season and played service ball at the Norman Naval Center in Oklahoma.

G	R	H	2B	3B	HR	RBI	BB	SO	SB	AVG	Slug
377	97	217	26	7	33	104	129	177	1	.219	.360

Thomas Gentry Warren, *Pitcher*

One of the first diamond performers to return home a war hero, Warren was essentially a war-era ballplayer. He pitched for the war-ravaged Dodgers of 1944—his only major league action. A good drawing card that season nonetheless, Warren was a war casualty wounded in action overseas. A navy commando, Tommy trained for heavy fighting and saw such action in Northern Africa. While engaged in missions at Casablanca, Warren was wounded in combat. Awarded a Purple Heart among other distinguished service medals, Tommy was sent home. He signed with Brooklyn in 1944 and played that season only in the majors.

W	L	PCT	G	GS	CG	IP	H	BB	SO	SHO	ERA
1	4	.200	22	4	2	69	74	40	18	0	4.96

John G. Washington, *First Base*

A terrific hitting first baseman, Johnny was mentored by Hall of Famer Oscar Charleston to take his first-base job. Although merely serviceable on the field, Washington was a stellar hitter for average. The first baseman typically batted in the heart of the order. At the height of his career, however, Johnny was inducted into the service during World War II and missed four years of baseball. After the long layoff, Johnny had plenty of rust to knock off. He struggled his first year back before rounding into form in 1947. When Jackie Robinson broke the color barrier, Johnny was an aging veteran and major league clubs steered clear of him.

(1933–1951): Baltimore Elite Giants, Houston Eagles, Montgomery Grey Sox, Birmingham Black Barons, Pittsburgh Crawfords and New York Black Yankees

John Thomas Watson, *Reserve*

Watson had a cup of coffee with the 1930 Tigers of Bucky Harris. The Tazewell, Virginia, native appeared in only four games. When the war broke out, Watson's baseball career was already over, and he was employed as a coach at Marshall University. He left the campus to join the navy.

G	R	H	2B	3B	HR	RBI	BB	SO	SB	AVG	Slug
4	1	3	2	0	0	3	1	2	0	.250	.417

Andrew Watts, *Third Base*

Andy's military induction during World War II benefited him as a ballplayer. He had yet to make the Negro Leagues when the war broke out but he played service ball for a championship squad at the Great Lakes Naval Training Station his first year in service. He was later shipped out to Guam with the U.S. Navy and played ball in the Pacific Theatre. After his naval discharge, Watts signed with the Cleveland Buckeyes but never firmly established himself in black baseball.

(1946–1952): Cleveland Buckeyes, Birmingham Black Barons and Indianapolis Clowns

Cyril Roy Weatherly, *Outfield*

A diminutive outfielder who cared little for drawing walks or striking out, Stormy was a slap hitter who posted more career triples than home runs. He spent the majority of his major league career with the Cleveland Indians. As a rookie, Stormy hit .335 before suffering a severe case of the sophomore jinx, when he watched his batting average fall 134 points in 1937. He enjoyed a comeback year in 1940, hitting .303 with 12 home runs, but was dealt to the Yankees after struggling again in 1942. He spent the 1943 season with the Yankees and missed the next two years to service in the United States Army.

Stormy took his basic training with former Cleveland teammate Al Milnar after the major league duo traded their baseball uniforms for the khaki of infantrymen. He was part of a heavy weapons outfit where he learned how to fire mortars at Fort McClellan. While serving at the Alabama installation, Stormy said, "We've got to out-hit the enemy first if I'm ever going back to baseball and my wife and two children." We did out-hit the enemy, and Stormy did return to baseball. He played briefly for pieces of two years before ending his baseball career.

G	R	H	2B	3B	HR	RBI	BB	SO	SB	AVG	Slug
811	415	794	152	44	43	290	180	170	42	.286	.418

Monte Morton Weaver, *Pitcher*

A successful pitcher during the 1930s with the Washington Senators, Monte won 22 games in 1932. He helped the Senators reach the World Series in 1933 and locked horns with Hall of Famer Carl Hubbell in an extra-inning pitchers' duel in Game 4. He ended his career as a mop-up pitcher with Joe Cronin's 1939 Red Sox. During the war, the aging Weaver was a ground officer at a fighter wing headquarters.

W	L	PCT	G	GS	CG	IP	H	BB	SO	SHO	ERA
71	50	.587	201	135	57	1,052	1,137	435	297	2	4.36

Ralph Richard Weigel, *Catcher*

A native of Coldwater, Ohio, Weigel played with a different team every year he was in the majors. Ralph made his debut directly after the war with the 1946 Indians. Before he tried on his first major league uniform, Ralph served in the U.S. Coast Guard during the war. Initially stationed in Alabama, Ralph was shipped overseas and spent time in the PTO. He was actively engaged in combat maneuvers in hostile Pacific waters.

G	R	H	2B	3B	HR	RBI	BB	SO	SB	AVG	Slug
106	12	54	9	3	0	30	21	26	2	.230	.294

Edwin Nicholas Weiland, *Pitcher*

Weiland's military chore was to lead exercises at the Great Lakes Naval Training Station. He appeared briefly in the major leagues in two seasons— the 1940 and 1942 baseball campaigns— with the Chicago White Sox. Ed missed three years to the war, stationed at a post in Iowa as well as the Great Lakes, and didn't return to the majors after his discharge.

W	L	PCT	G	GS	CG	IP	H	BB	SO	SHO	ERA
0	0	—	10	0	0	24	33	10	7	0	8.25

John Ludwig Welaj, *Outfield*

A speedy outfielder, Welaj played three years with the Senators and one with the Athletics. He made his debut with the 1939 Senators. That year he finished second to speed merchant George Case with thirteen thefts. In 1941, Johnny struggled and spent the entire 1942 season in the bushes. He resurfaced at the major league level in 1943 with the Athletics. Despite receiving his draft notice midway in the 1943 season, Welaj was able to pace the club in stolen bases. Johnny played service baseball as a corporeal stationed at Camp Roberts.

G	R	H	2B	3B	HR	RBI	BB	SO	SB	AVG	Slug
293	115	198	40	3	4	74	53	73	36	.250	.323

Robert Joseph Wellman, *First Base/Outfield*

Big Bob Wellman signed with Connie Mack after his discharge from the navy. Given Bob's size, it's no doubt Mack thought he might have another Jimmie Foxx on his hands. Wellman had two trials, in 1948 and 1950, but failed to stick.

G	R	H	2B	3B	HR	RBI	BB	SO	SB	AVG	Slug
15	2	7	0	1	1	3	5	0	.280	.480

Leo Donald Wells, *Third Base*

Leo Wells received a brief look in the big leagues prior to his military induction. He split time between third base and shortstop for the 1942 White Sox. He lost the next three years to service in the U.S. Coast Guard. When Wells came back to baseball, he platooned at third base with Dario Lodigiani and Cass Michaels.

G	R	H	2B	3B	HR	RBI	BB	SO	SB	AVG	Slug
80	19	36	6	1	2	15	16	39	4	.190	.265

Roy Horace Welmaker, *Pitcher*

A maddeningly talented pitcher, Welmaker had the Hall of Fame arm but questionable accuracy. In the late 1930s, Welmaker pitched for the powerhouse Homestead Grays and appeared in seven World Series games for the team during their championship run through World War II. Roy missed only a small portion of baseball to the war effort while he was stationed at Fort Benning. Roy had some success in black baseball, and he ventured down to Mexico to play there in the early 1940s. South of the border, Welmaker's accuracy abandoned him, but he settled down when he rejoined the Grays. After integration, Roy had some success in the low minors, but when he was moved to the fast company of the PCL, he was simply a modest pitcher.

Players like Welmaker were regarded as case studies as to how the major leagues should compensate the Negro Leagues when they signed their players. After the signings of Robinson and Doby, Negro League owners watched as their best players left for the greener pastures of the major leagues. Neil Lanctot, in his book *Negro League Baseball: The Rise and Ruin of a Black Institution*, wrote, "For an industry in desperate need for positive publicity, the uncompensated signings of Welmaker [and others] contributed to a perception that black baseball was a poorly run business ill-prepared for integration." Some owners, like the Manleys, would demand compensation from the major league teams, but the major league clubs would often balk because they felt they were being swindled by paying the player to sign while also throwing money to the team for the player's services. Major league owners for decades had bought players from minor league teams, paying the club the price for its player, while the player would report without receiving any of the purchase price. The major league owners obviously wanted to write one check and be done with the transaction, but the Negro League owners, justifiably, didn't want to see their talent taken away without reimbursement.

(1936–1945): Homestead Grays, Atlanta Black Crackers, Toledo Crawfords and Philadelphia Stars

Charles William "Butch" Wensloff, *Pitcher*

Wensloff's career numbers look very pleasing, even though he pitched for just three years in the major leagues. The war unquestioningly hindered what could have been a solid major league career. Butch retired in 1944 to work in a defense job, and then was drafted into the armed forces where he spent two years under Uncle Sam. Butch's wife was a die-hard baseball fan who followed her husband during his days in the minors. She willingly sacrificed her wants to allow Butch the opportunity to pursue his dream. She once said, "Charlie has new spikes and a new glove ... there goes my new dress."

W	L	PCT	G	GS	CG	IP	H	BB	SO	SHO	ERA
16	13	.552	41	32	19	277	222	95	125	1	2.60

William George Werle, *Pitcher*

Classified 4-F by his Stockton draft board, Werle was listed as a non-combatant because of damaged vertebrae. He was an intelligent ballplayer who studied insects at college, and a writer for the *Oakland Tribune* referred to Werle as a "bugologist from the University of California." His studies in insects led to his nicknamed "Bugs." The southpaw, despite being 4-F in the draft, was inducted in 1945 after working in a war plant in 1944. Bugs served a year in the army before he was discharged. He made his debut with the 1949 Pirates.

W	L	PCT	G	GS	CG	IP	H	BB	SO	SHO	ERA
29	39	.426	185	60	18	666	770	194	283	2	4.69

Victor Woodrow Wertz, *Outfield/First Base*

A terrific power threat throughout his career, Wertz thoroughly impressed the Tigers brass in spring training during 1943. Fresh from school, Vic wasn't able to build off his strong showing in the spring as he was inducted into the navy. A big, strong lad, Wertz was shipped overseas after boot camp. The young man ascended in rank quickly and was a sergeant by his twentieth birthday, which he spent in the South Pacific.

G	R	H	2B	3B	HR	RBI	BB	SO	SB	AVG	Slug
1,862	867	1,692	289	42	266	1,178	828	842	9	.277	.469

Richard Thomas West, *Catcher*

West spent pieces of six years at the major league level with the Reds, often serving as a third-string catcher and emergency outfielder. After he was inducted into the navy, Dick never returned to the majors. He was stationed at the Great Lakes and played service ball under the legendary Mickey Cochrane.

G	R	H	2B	3B	HR	RBI	BB	SO	SB	AVG	Slug
119	30	66	10	2	3	35	12	42	6	.221	.296

Max Edward West, *Outfield*

West provided the Braves with some modest power in the late 1930s and early 1940s. He socked ten home runs as a rookie in 1938 and led the club in the long ball department in 1939. Chet Ross took over West's left-field post in 1940, moving Max to right field, and his power production dropped off, although he did lead the team with 65 walks. When Ross hit .120 to start the 1941 season, Max moved back to left field and regained his power swing, indicated by his team-leading stats in doubles, home runs and walks. Max swatted sixteen home runs in 1942, again pacing the team, but was summoned by his draft board after the close of the season.

West missed three full baseball seasons to the war effort. The left-handed-hitting and right-handed-throwing outfielder lent his talents to Uncle Sam and served with the Sixth Ferrying Command in California, the same outfit as Yankees Hall of Fame pitcher Red Ruffing. Max returned to the Braves in 1946 but was quickly dealt to the Reds, as the 29-year-old could not regain his pre-war stroke. His batting average dipped to .213 in 1946 and a career low of .178 in 1948, his last year in the majors.

G	R	H	2B	3B	HR	RBI	BB	SO	SB	AVG	Slug
824	338	681	136	20	77	380	353	340	19	.254	.407

Samuel Filmore West, *Outfield*

Sammy West was a remarkable batsman, and just like Hall of Famer Charlie Gehringer, was summoned by Uncle Sam at the twilight of his baseball career. He retired one point shy of .300 for his career, as the lean outfielder was a triples machine. He began his career in 1927 with the Washington Senators, where he served as a backup to a trio of Hall of Fame flychasers in Tris Speaker, Sam Rice and Goose Goslin. He took over the center-field job in 1929 — slapping eight triples — and suffered an elbow injury during his breakout campaign in 1930. Sammy paced the Senators with a .333 batting average in 1931 but was dealt to the Browns for the 1933 season. He was the Browns' top hitter in 1934 and he drew 94 walks in 1936.

Sammy returned to the Senators in 1938 and finished his career with the White Sox in 1942 after a couple of years serving as a part-time player in the nation's capital. After the 1942 season, the 37-year-old West joined the United States Army and spent three years serving in khaki. He didn't attempt a comeback as a 41-year-old when he was given his discharge in 1945.

G	R	H	2B	3B	HR	RBI	BB	SO	SB	AVG	Slug
1,753	934	1,838	347	101	75	838	696	540	53	.299	.425

Waldon Thomas "Wally" Westlake, *Outfield*

Before Westlake made his major league debut, he served in the U.S. Coast Guard for three years. After his discharge, Westlake joined the Pirates and had a solid showing with them in 1947. He added a solid bat to a lineup that featured Hall of Fame Sluggers Ralph Kiner and Hank Greenberg. When Hammerin' Hank retired after the season, Pittsburgh's offense revolved around Kiner and Wally for the next few years.

G	R	H	2B	3B	HR	RBI	BB	SO	SB	AVG	Slug
958	474	848	107	33	127	539	317	453	19	.272	.450

Wesley N. Westrum, *Catcher*

An interesting ballplayer, Westrum was an elite defensive catcher who hit for very poor batting averages. Despite his lifetime .217 batting average, Wes caught at the major league level for eleven seasons. His work behind the dish, coupled with his above-average power and great batting eye, allowed him to survive in the game despite his weak batting marks. When Westrum retired, he boasted a rather good career .356 on-base percentage. He missed some minor league duty to service in the armed forces during World War II.

G	R	H	2B	3B	HR	RBI	BB	SO	SB	AVG	Slug
919	302	503	59	8	96	315	489	514	10	.217	.373

Ernest Daniel White, *Pitcher*

An effective pitcher during his major league days, White pitched with the Cardinals for three years before the war and finished his career with three post-war seasons on the Braves' roster. Ernie's career year came in 1941 when he led the Cardinals with 17 wins and finished one strikeout behind team leader Mort Cooper. His arm gave out during the 1942 season, but the southpaw soldiered on through two years of pain. After the 1943 season, Ernie was slated to receive shoulder surgery, but his military induction came before he could undergo the procedure. Ernie said, "They sent those greetings a month too soon. Now I'll have to wait [for the operation]."

White was inducted into the army on February 11, 1944, and sent to Fort Bragg. He served as an assistant athletic director with the rank of T/5. Despite his arm woes, Ernie took part in service ball, saying of his Fort Bragg team, "We had more pitchers than we knew what to do with, so I played first base and the outfield." He was shipped overseas and while in transient on European waters, he was eager to hear how his Cardinals were doing back home. He wanted to know the outcome of the 1944 World Series and he asked a radio technician if he had heard who won. The tech replied, "Don't know. But Creighton played Essex in cricket — rousing game."

W	L	PCT	G	GS	CG	IP	H	BB	SO	SHO	ERA
30	21	.588	108	57	24	490	425	188	244	5	2.77

Albert Eugene "Fuzz" White, *Outfield*

A fleet-footed outfielder who had a cup of coffee before the war with the Browns and another cup after the war with the Giants, White served with the U.S. Army during the war. A throwback player who liked to run, White wasn't of the brawny blaster mold that characterized baseball of the time. While in the minors, Fuzz had more than 70 stolen bases in a season and was accused of "padding his stolen base total like a sofa."

G	R	H	2B	3B	HR	RBI	BB	SO	SB	AVG	Slug
9	3	3	0	0	0	0	0	0	0	.200	.200

Harold George White, *Pitcher*

White was a valuable relief pitcher for the Tigers in the 1940s and into the early 1950s. He served as the fifth arm in Detroit's rotation prior to his military callup, and he missed the 1944 and 1945 seasons to the navy. It took Hal a full year to get adjusted to the major leagues again while he suffered through the 1946 campaign, but he became a respectable arm out of Steve O'Neill's bullpen in 1947. White pitched for the Tigers through 1952 and then ended his career in St. Louis.

W	L	PCT	G	GS	CG	IP	H	BB	SO	SHO	ERA
46	54	.460	336	67	23	921	875	450	349	7	3.78

Burgess Urquhart Whitehead, *Second Base*

In the *Baseball Encyclopedia*, Burgess is listed as missing the entire 1938 season to an illness. The in-depth story regarding Whitehead's ailment concerns a dispute between Burgess' dog and another canine. Burgess, who two days prior to the canine quarrel had his appendix removed, was at home convalescing in Lewiston, North Carolina, when his dog picked a fight with another dog. Eager to keep the dogs from harming one another, Burgess tried to separate the dogs with his hands to no avail, so he tried to kick them apart. The kicking motion caused an adhesion in his new operation, and he suffered for many weeks. He even had a nervous breakdown because of the ordeal, which forced him to miss the entire 1938 season.

After he had fully recovered, Burgess had little desire to return to the Giants. He felt guilty for having missed an entire season. When he did make his return to New York, Burgess said, "I wasn't going to play. I had made up my mind to quit baseball entirely. I felt that my illness in 1938 had let down the Giants and the New York fans. I was ashamed to show up again at the Polo Grounds."

Whitehead returned to the Giants in 1939 and played with them through 1941. He was traded to the Pirates after the 1941 season but was inducted into the army before he was able to play a game for the Bucs. Burgess was inducted at Fort Bragg and served as a physical instructor in the Army Air Corps. He was transferred to Daniel Field, Georgia, in 1944 and attended non-commissioned officer's school at Miami Beach. He was reassigned to Colorado Springs in 1945 and served with the Second Air Force. While stationed in Colorado, he also served as the trainer for the Second Air Force football team. Late in 1945, Whitehead received his discharge at Lowry Field.

G	R	H	2B	3B	HR	RBI	BB	SO	SB	AVG	Slug
924	415	883	100	31	17	245	150	138	51	.268	.331

Charles Evis Whitehouse, *Pitcher*

Whitehouse pitched in the Federal League during its two years of operation and made six appearances with the 1919 Senators after the Feds closed up shop. The slender Illinoisan did his bit in both World Wars.

W	L	PCT	G	GS	CG	IP	H	BB	SO	SHO	ERA
4	3	.571	25	6	3	78	93	28	33	0	4.50

Dick Corwin Whitman, *Outfield*

A top prospect in the Dodgers chain before the war, Whitman was almost denied his trial in the major leagues. Quick to join the military during the war, Whitman wanted action and enlisted in the U.S. Army infantry. A University of Oregon graduate, Dick took his boot camp that prepared him for the hostile fields he would see overseas. The Brooklyn recruit had to contend with such men as Pete Reiser, Dixie Walker and Carl Furillo for playing time in the Dodgers' outfield, but the competition he would see in the ETO was far more severe. Whitman saw heavy combat action in the European Theatre. His unit took part in the Battle of Bulge where Dick was wounded in action. Shrapnel struck Dick and tore through his back and neck during that famous battle. Removed from the frontlines to treat his wounds, Whitman recovered in army hospitals. Given the Purple Heart, Dick made his way back to the States where sportswriters fabricated tales of Dick learning how to play baseball on crude German fields. He was under control of the Dodgers before the war, and he knew his way around a ball diamond before he set foot on German soil. In 1946 spring training, Dick thoroughly impressed skipper Leo Durocher and made the Opening Day roster. He played with Brooklyn through 1949 before a two-year stint with the Phillies.

G	R	H	2B	3B	HR	RBI	BB	SO	SB	AVG	Slug
285	93	165	37	3	2	67	51	46	10	.259	.335

Charles John Wiedemeyer, *Pitcher*

Tall and lanky, Wiedemeyer had a cup of coffee with the 1934 Cubs. The southpaw got into four games with his hometown team. During the war, Charlie served in the armed forces.

W	L	PCT	G	GS	CG	IP	H	BB	SO	SHO	ERA
0	0	—	4	1	0	8	16	4	2	0	10.13

William Robert Wight, *Pitcher*

Wight was a highly touted prospect after his military discharge in 1946. A good prospect for the Yankees before the war, Bill became a sensation in the service ranks. He was stationed at the St. Mary's Pre-Flight School where he played service ball with Giants infielder Bill Rigney. In a game against the Stockton Air Base squad, Bill fanned 25 batters. But it wasn't all baseballs and fastballs for Bill—he had to perform some soldierly duties as well. A photograph in the *Oakland Tribune* showed Bill and Rigney busy at work mopping the barracks between games.

When Wight was discharged, the Yankees had a good southpaw on their hands. They were hoping he'd be the heir apparent to Lefty Gomez, but Bill struggled mightily with his control in 1946. He spent most of 1947 in the bushes, and by 1948 the Yankees gave up on him and shipped him to Chicago, where he put things together in 1949. After his playing career, Wight became a successful scout in the Braves chain who signed such players as Dusty Baker and Dale Murphy for the club.

W	L	PCT	G	GS	CG	IP	H	BB	SO	SHO	ERA
77	99	.438	347	198	66	1,532	1,656	714	574	15	3.95

Delbert Quentin Wilber, *Catcher*

A decent power-hitting catcher, Wilber wasn't able to show off his strength on a regular basis in the majors. Employed chiefly as a backup, Del played with the Cardinals, Phillies and Red Sox over the course of his career but rarely as a starter. During the war, Wilber served in Texas as a lieutenant stationed at the San Antonio Aviation Cadet Center. He managed the installation's baseball team and had such notables as Enos Slaughter, Paul Lehner and Howie Pollet on his roster.

G	R	H	2B	3B	HR	RBI	BB	SO	SB	AVG	Slug
299	67	174	35	7	19	115	44	96	1	.242	.389

James Hoyt Wilhelm, *Pitcher*

At the time of Wilhelm's retirement from the game, he was the last World War II veteran still active in the majors. With the 1972 Dodgers, Hoyt was 49 years old. Able to hang on for a number of years, Hoyt's pet pitch was the easy-on-the-arm knuckleball. The greatest sportswriter of his time, Jim Murray, once joked about Wilhelm's knuckler when he wrote, "The ball comes to the plate like a kid on his way to the bath. It takes more detours than a dog with a block full of hydrants." But the fact that Hoyt was able to make the majors, let alone pitch for so long, seemed unlikely when World War II broke out.

Wilhelm joined the army during World War II and enlisted as an infantryman. A terrific soldier with great leadership skills, Hoyt ascended in rank quickly, and by the time his unit was shipped overseas, he had already attained his sergeant's stripes. Engaged in fighting at the Battle of the Bulge, Staff Sergeant Wilhelm was wounded in action when he was struck by shrapnel. Pulled from the frontlines and treated, Hoyt would eventually return to his unit and serve for the duration. Awarded the Purple Heart for his heroics, Wilhelm was discharged but to little fanfare. He wasn't a top prospect in the baseball ranks, and given that he fought instead of played in the army, the military wasn't a stage for him to show off his baseball skills. He didn't reach the major leagues until 1952 but he held on for twenty years by baffling many batters with his knuckleball.

W	L	PCT	G	GS	CG	IP	H	BB	SO	SHO	ERA
143	122	.540	1,070	52	20	2,253	1,757	778	1,610	5	2.52

Aldon Jay "Lefty" Wilkie, *Pitcher*

Wilkie rarely notched a strikeout during his brief stay in the majors. During the 1942 season, Lefty pitched 107 innings and fanned only eighteen batters. After the 1942 season, Lefty went to work in a Portland war plant, and his wife gave birth to twins in October. However, shortly after the arrival of his two children, Wilkie was summoned by Uncle Sam. Lefty was stationed at Camp Roberts where he excelled at tossing grenades. From Camp Roberts he was shipped overseas to the European Theatre, where he was transferred to Special Services at Geislinger, Germany.

W	L	PCT	G	GS	CG	IP	H	BB	SO	SHO	ERA
8	11	.421	68	12	5	194	215	80	37	1	4.59

Robert Fulton "Ace" Williams, *Pitcher*

Ace Williams had a forgettable career at the major league level; he worked nine innings and coughed up twenty-two base hits. The southpaw's career came to a close with an ERA well above 9.00. During World War II, Williams served in the army.

W	L	PCT	G	GS	CG	IP	H	BB	SO	SHO	ERA
0	0	—	6	0	0	9	22	13	5	0	16.00

Almon Edward Williams, *Pitcher*

Williams pitched two years with the A's after Connie Mack had shipped off all his stars from the dynasty just a few years prior. Gone were Foxx, Grove, Cochrane and Simmons when Almon came to Philadelphia. He pitched for the A's in 1937 and 1938. During the war, Williams served in the armed forces.

W	L	PCT	G	GS	CG	IP	H	BB	SO	SHO	ERA
4	8	.333	46	16	3	169	216	103	52	0	6.23

Earl Baxter Williams, *Catcher*

Williams had a cup of coffee with the 1928 Braves, the extent of his major league career. A reserve catcher, Earl was used in three games. During World War II, he served in the armed forces.

G	R	H	2B	3B	HR	RBI	BB	SO	SB	AVG	Slug
3	0	0	0	0	0	0	1	0		.000	.000

Theodore Samuel Williams, *Outfield*

Nicknamed "The Splendid Splinter," Williams was oftentimes brash and arrogant but he remained the darling of the Red Sox fans. Never on the best of terms with the sportswriters of his time, Williams was labeled a draft dodger by the Knaves of the Newspaper. He was the sole supporter of his mother, which garnered him the III-A classification. When his classification was switched to I-A, the young and impressionable star, who lacked a person whose guidance he trusted, was urged to fight the classification. After a lengthy ordeal, Williams was returned to his initial III-A classification. Although many other stars of the day were classified III-A along with Williams, the seething Boston media made him out to be a draft-dodging villain when his lone concern was looking after his mother's well-being.

Later, Williams entered the military and attended Amherst College for ground school in the navy's aviation wing. Williams put in a hundred hours of flight time at Kokomo, Indiana, before he saw advanced training in Pensacola. From there, he attended combat training at Jacksonville and set the student gunnery record. He missed the 1943–1945 seasons to military service, where he served as a pilot. He returned to Boston in 1946 and won his first AL MVP Award after having been denied the accolade by the writers who detested him in previous years despite Ted enjoying far better production than the men who actually won the award.

The Splendid Splinter's time in military fatigues was not over. The Hall of Famer was recalled for the Korean War at the age of 34. He flew 39 missions during that war while missing out on the better part of two more seasons. In Williams' autobiography *My Turn at Bat*, he informs his readers on what he thought about being a "retread" pilot and how he felt about politicians—all in his usual brash, unflinching commentary. Had Williams not missed five seasons to military service, he would have amassed stats that few other players could fathom reaching. For more on Williams, see his listing in the section on the Korean War.

G	R	H	2B	3B	HR	RBI	BB	SO	SB	AVG	Slug
2,292	1,798	2,654	525	71	521	1,839	2,021	709	24	.344	.634

Alfred Gardner Wilmore, *Pitcher*

A right-handed pitcher for the Philadelphia Stars after World War II, Wilmore caught his break in black baseball when the talent level was waning. Al would join the exodus as well when he signed with the Philadelphia Athletics, but an arm injury in the minors prevented him from making the major leagues. During the war, Al played service ball with Charlie Biot for an infantry team.

(1946–1950): Philadelphia Stars and Baltimore Elite Giants

Archie Clifton Wilson, *Outfield*

Wilson played two years at the major league level with three different American League teams. He spent 1951 with the Yankees, and during the 1952 season, Archie played with New York, Washington and the Red Sox. Wilson, a USC graduate, served with the U.S. Navy during the war.

G	R	H	2B	3B	HR	RBI	BB	SO	SB	AVG	Slug
51	9	31	5	3	0	17	7	14	0	.221	.300

Edward Francis Wilson, *Outfield*

A top outfield recruit in the mid 1930s, Wilson never reached his potential. In 1936, Eddie was hitting a robust .347 before he fractured his skull during the season and wasn't the same player afterwards. The Holy Cross graduate served with the Merchant Marines during World War II.

G	R	H	2B	3B	HR	RBI	BB	SO	SB	AVG	Slug
88	39	72	12	2	4	33	31	39	4	.317	.441

Emmett Dabney Wilson, *Outfield*

Noted for his speed and little else, Wilson was essentially a fourth outfielder who platooned occasionally. A weak hitter,

Emmett spent two years in the armed forces during World War II.

(1937–1946): Pittsburgh Crawfords, Cincinnati Clowns and Boston Blues

George Washington Wilson, *Outfield/First Base*

A teenager when he joined the army during World War II, Wilson served with Uncle Sam's forces in the European Theatre of Operations. A star at the minor league level, Wilson never settled in at the major league ranks.

G	R	H	2B	3B	HR	RBI	BB	SO	SB	AVG	Slug
145	15	40	8	0	3	19	14	32	0	.191	.273

John Samuel Wilson, *Pitcher*

Wilson pitched briefly with the Red Sox in the late 1920s. The right-hander from Coal City, Alabama, served as an enlisted man in the United States Army during World War II.

W	L	PCT	G	GS	CG	IP	H	BB	SO	SHO	ERA
0	2	.000	3	0	0	4	4	3	1	0	4.50

Max Wilson, *Pitcher*

Standing at 5'7" and weighing 160 pounds, Wilson made for a less-than-intimidating presence on the pitcher's mound. The southpaw made his debut with the 1940 Phillies and missed four years to World War II. He served in the United States Navy and was stationed at the Norfolk Naval Training Station, among other locales. He returned to baseball in 1946 and pitched sparingly for the Senators.

W	L	PCT	G	GS	CG	IP	H	BB	SO	SHO	ERA
0	1	.000	12	0	0	20	32	11	11	0	9.00

James Head "Cowboy" Winford, *Pitcher*

The right-handed knuckleballer from Tennessee pitched for the Cardinals in the mid 1930s with a fair amount of success. The Cardinals of the time received the bulk of their mound chores from the Dean brothers and Wild Bill Hallahan, but Cowboy was always ready to fill in. When Daffy Dean's arm went south in 1936, Cowboy stepped into the number-two starter's shoes and did quite well—he finished second to Dizzy in staff wins. Winford's last major league action came with the 1938 Dodgers. During the war, Cowboy served at Norman Airfield with the Army Air Corps.

W	L	PCT	G	GS	CG	IP	H	BB	SO	SHO	ERA
14	18	.438	68	31	10	276	307	115	107	1	4.57

John Thomas Winsett, *Outfield*

A native of McKenzie, Tennessee, Winsett was a reserve outfielder/pinch-hitter throughout the 1930s. Tom played with the Red Sox, Cardinals and Dodgers during the decade. When the United States entered World War II, Winsett's major league career had ended but he was able to play some service ball in the colors. With the Army Air Corps, Winsett was shipped overseas and played baseball on the Hawaiian Islands with Joe DiMaggio.

G	R	H	2B	3B	HR	RBI	BB	SO	SB	AVG	Slug
230	60	134	25	5	8	76	69	113	3	.237	.341

Archibald Edwin Wise, *Pitcher*

Wise had a cup of coffee with the 1932 White Sox. The right-hander from Texas joined the U.S. Navy during World War II.

W	L	PCT	G	GS	CG	IP	H	BB	SO	SHO	ERA
0	0	—	2	0	0	7	8	5	2	0	5.14

Francis Michael "Whitey" Wistert, *Pitcher*

A mountain of a man, Wistert was a collegiate gridiron star before his trial with the Reds. He appeared in only two games for Cincinnati in 1934, losing his lone decision. During World War II, Whitey enlisted in the U.S. Navy and was commissioned a lieutenant. He served two years as a naval officer.

W	L	PCT	G	GS	CG	IP	H	BB	SO	SHO	ERA
0	1	.000	2	1	0	8	5	5	1	0	1.13

Nicholas Joseph "Mickey" Witek, *Second Base*

Mickey played regularly in his rookie year, rotating between shortstop and second base in 1940. A singles hitter, only ten of his 111 hits were of the extra-base variety. He settled in as the everyday second baseman in 1942. His break-out year came a season later as Witek finished second in the league in hits, behind Hall of Famer Stan Musial, while he led the Giants with a .314 average. However, like many ballplayers, Mickey was unable to build off that season because he lost the next two years to military service.

Prior to his induction in the U.S. Coast Guard, Mickey had a defense job working in a Newark plant. He was sworn into the Coast Guard in early 1944 and played service ball with actor-athlete Chuck Connors for a team named the Poughkeepsie Roe Movers. Witek returned to the Giants in 1946 eager to build off his .314 average prior to his military induction, but a broken arm suffered during the season all but ended his career.

G	R	H	2B	3B	HR	RBI	BB	SO	SB	AVG	Slug
581	239	595	65	9	22	196	148	84	7	.277	.347

Jerome Charles Witte, *First Base*

Witte was the type of player that had nothing left to prove in the minors but never could quite figure out major league pitching. Jerry, who played service ball in the military at Kelly Airfield, was the MVP of the American Association in 1946, the year after his discharge. He swatted 43 home runs and was even considered the heir apparent to Hall of Famer Hank Greenberg. With the Browns after the war, Witte showed some power but failed to make consistent contact.

G	R	H	2B	3B	HR	RBI	BB	SO	SB	AVG	Slug
52	11	28	4	1	4	16	11	40	0	.163	.267

John Carl Wittig, *Pitcher*

Wittig's major league career was sporadic, as the right-hander made his debut with the Giants in 1938 and appeared in only five games in 1939. Johnnie spent the entire 1940 season in the bushes and then logged 85 innings for Bill Terry's club in 1941. To the minors Wittig went for more seasoning in 1942, and he returned to the offensively challenged Giants to post fifteen losses in 1943. He took his pre-induction physical exam on March 28, 1944, and entered the military shortly thereafter. After two years in the service and another three years in the minors, Johnnie was called up by the Red Sox in 1949 for his last taste of the big show.

W	L	PCT	G	GS	CG	IP	H	BB	SO	SHO	ERA
10	25	.286	84	39	7	307	342	163	121	1	4.90

Joseph Perry Wood, *Utility Infielder*

Nicknamed "The Little General," Joe Wood was quite a little hitter at the major league level. He played only one year in the majors but hit for a .323 average. Wood rotated between second base and third base with the 1943 Detorit Tigers and then lost the next two years to service in the United States Navy.

G	R	H	2B	3B	HR	RBI	BB	SO	SB	AVG	Slug
60	22	53	4	4	1	17	6	13	2	.323	.415

Kenneth Lanier Wood, *Outfield*

Wood gave the Browns a decent corner outfield power combo with Dick Kokos before Kokos was inducted into the army for service in the Korean War. During World War II, Wood served with the U.S. Coast Guard. Ken, who had decent power, later played with the Red Sox and Senators.

G	R	H	2B	3B	HR	RBI	BB	SO	SB	AVG	Slug
342	110	223	52	7	34	143	102	141	1	.224	.393

Eugene Richard Woodling, *Outfield*

Woodling was an unknown commodity before World War II—he appeared in just eight games before his military callup in 1943. Gene served in the navy and trained at the Great Lakes Naval Training Station. While there, he was able to play ball for legendary catcher Mickey Cochrane, who gave the youngster his seal of approval, predicting a bright future for him. Gene lived up to Mickey's assumptions of his skills and became a great player after his naval discharge. A left-handed batter who possessed an eagle's eye at the plate, Gene was a valuable ingredient to the Yankees' five straight AL championships from 1949 to 1953.

During his time playing for the Bronx Bombers, Gene got to know the great Joe DiMaggio on a personal level. They became good friends, and Gene said of Joe, "[He was a] great ballplayer and also a great person." After his playing days had concluded, Gene became a farmer.

G	R	H	2B	3B	HR	RBI	BB	SO	SB	AVG	Slug
1,796	830	1,585	257	63	147	830	921	477	29	.284	.431

Robert Lee "Red" Worthington, *Outfield*

A decent outfielder in the early 1930s before he suffered a broken leg, Worthington starred in the pasture for the Braves. After the injury, he tried to make a comeback with the Braves in 1934 and was dealt to the Cardinals at the end of the year, but he wasn't the same player. Red served in the armed forces during World War II.

G	R	H	2B	3B	HR	RBI	BB	SO	SB	AVG	Slug
292	118	298	69	18	12	111	48	71	2	.287	.423

Forrest Glenn Wright, *Shortstop*

One of the top shortstops of his day, "Buckshot" played just before the All-Star Game became a yearly occurrence. Had there been a mid-summer classic, Wright assuredly would have participated in a few. He broke in with the Pirates in 1924 and was the best shortstop they had since the days of Honus Wagner. As a rookie in 1924, Buckshot was the only middle infielder in the National League to have a 100-RBI season. The following year, Glenn led the Pirates to a World Series title with a team-best 121 RBIs—the fourth-best total in the senior circuit. After an injury-shortened season in 1928, he was sent to the Dodgers and had a 22-homer, 126-RBI season at short with Brooklyn in 1930. His last major league action came with the White Sox in 1935.

With his career in the books by the time World War II broke out, Buckshot was quick to join the military despite his advanced age. Born in Archie, Missouri, Glenn, who operated free baseball clinics for boys before the war, enlisted in the U.S. Navy. One of the greatest run-producing shortstops in baseball history, Wright became an apprentice seaman in 1942. He served at the naval base in Farragut, Idaho, where his military duties were instructing at the quartermaster's school on the installation.

G	R	H	2B	3B	HR	RBI	BB	SO	SB	AVG	Slug
1,119	584	1,219	203	76	94	723	209	407	38	.294	.447

John Richard Wright, *Pitcher*

The second black player signed by the major leagues, Wright joined Jackie Robinson in Dodgers camp in 1946 but wasn't as willing as Robinson to subject himself to verbal abuse. Wright lasted only one year in the minor leagues before he returned to black baseball. Nicknamed "Needle Nose," Wright was a terrific pitcher with a solid assortment of pitches. A star with the Homestead Grays before the war, Johnny was inducted into service and spent two years in the navy. He played service ball at the Great Lakes Naval Training Station and Bennett Airfield.

(1937–1948): Homestead Grays, Newark Eagles, Atlanta Black Crackers and Pittsburgh Crawfords

Taft Shedron "Taffy" Wright, *Outfield*

Of all the players in baseball, only Ted Williams and Joe DiMaggio bested Taffy's combined .328 batting average for the five years before World War II. The portside-swinger named Chubby Dean as the pitcher who gave him the greatest fit in the batter's box. Wright said of Dean, "He throws a nothing ball and fools you with his motion."

Taffy initially came up to the major leagues with the Senators in 1938, leading the team with a .350 batting average as a reserve. The Senators were long on offense, with the likes of Al Simmons, Cecil Travis, Buddy Lewis, George Case and Buddy Myer, but were noticeably weak at pitching. After the 1939 season, Wright was dangled as trade bait and the White Sox bought. Taffy proceeded to stroke .337 in his first year with the White Sox and paced the club with 97 RBIs in his second year. In 1942, Taffy hit the apple at a .333 clip and fanned just nine times all year. The sweet-swinging outfielder then entered the military and missed the next three years to service in the United States Army.

Army training was a grueling endeavor, and Taffy said, "I'm down to 185 pounds. That's my playing weight — and my fighting weight too." Wright served as a physical training instructor at the Army Air Force's Eastern Technical Training Command. He later attended non-commissioned officer's school at Miami Beach to earn his stripes. Unlike some other players, Taffy refused to visit his old baseball teammates while he was on furlough. He knew that his old chums would give him a hero's reception, and Taffy didn't view himself as a hero; he was just doing his part like so many other boys.

G	R	H	2B	3B	HR	RBI	BB	SO	SB	AVG	Slug
1,029	465	1,115	175	55	38	553	347	155	32	.311	.423

Thomas Everette Wright, *Outfield*

A reserve outfielder/pinch-hitter throughout his major league career, Wright served with the Army Air Corps in the Pacific Theatre during the war. After his discharge, he made the Red Sox squad late in 1948 and kept the bench warm for Ted Williams, Dom DiMaggio and Stan Spence. Only after he joined the White Sox did Tom see any real playing time.

G	R	H	2B	3B	HR	RBI	BB	SO	SB	AVG	Slug
341	75	175	28	11	6	99	76	123	2	.255	.355

Early Wynn, *Pitcher*

Hall of Fame pitcher Early Wynn spent the majority of the war in the major leagues. He enjoyed his break-out year in 1943, when he paced the Senators in nearly every pitching category, but he suffered from a lack of run support in 1944. At the end of the 1944 baseball season, Wynn was inducted into the armed forces. Despite missing some time to the war, he still paced the American League in losses. Early served in the South Pacific and played ball in the Philippines.

W	L	PCT	G	GS	CG	IP	H	BB	SO	SHO	ERA
300	244	.551	691	612	290	4,564	4,291	1,775	2,334	49	3.54

John Barney Wyrostek, *Outfield*

Just like Earl Naylor, Johnny was on the Cardinals' service roster but never played a game with the team. Prior to his military induction, he played with the Pittsburgh Pirates and became property of the Redbirds after the 1943 season. Johnny was then inducted into the army before the 1944 season began and served with the Third Army in Europe. He returned to the ball diamond in 1946 after the Cardinals had shipped him off to the Phillies.

G	R	H	2B	3B	HR	RBI	BB	SO	SB	AVG	Slug
1,221	525	1,149	209	45	58	481	482	437	33	.271	.383

George Edward Yankowski, *Catcher*

A reserve catcher who had two cups of coffee that sandwiched his military tenure, Yankowski was a Boston kid who grew up at Fenway Park and Braves Field. In one of Yankowski's first games in the major leagues, Connie Mack started George in a contest at Fenway Park, knowing that the hometown kid really wanted to play before his Boston friends. His biggest thrill in baseball was doubling off the Green Monster in his first trip to the plate.

Yankowski made the A's in 1942 and one of his two hits at the end of the season was that Fenway two-bagger. The next four years he'd be off to war. George didn't worry about losing time in baseball to the war. He said, "Serving your country dwarfs playing baseball." So off Yankowski went to boot camp after the 1942 baseball season. From there, he would be assigned to the Third Army in December of 1942 and spent the duration of the war in the European Theatre.

The ETO was a hot area where many of the war's most famous battles occurred. Yankowski was in the area and leant his support. He was fortunate enough to keep free of the enemy and made it through Europe without serious injury. He said, "Luckily I never was wounded or anything like that. The winters were tough, but I consider myself lucky to have come out of the war unscathed." But a four-year layoff upset Yankowski's timing and he couldn't get started in baseball after his discharge. He didn't return to the majors until 1949 with the White Sox.

G	R	H	2B	3B	HR	RBI	BB	SO	SB	AVG	Slug
18	0	5	2	0	0	4	0	4	0	.161	.226

Waldo Ward "Rusty" Yarnall, *Pitcher*

The University of Vermont grad was a star football player on campus who only appeared in one major league game. Rusty pitched one inning for the 1926 Phillies. With his baseball career over the moment it began, Yarnall returned to school and eventually became a football coach. Before the war he was the head football coach at the Lowell Textile Institute. But after Pearl Harbor was bombed, the aging Yarnall joined the U.S. Navy. While training, the former ballplayer wrote a letter home to the *Lowell Sun*, which marveled at the drive and determination of the average soldier. Rusty wrote, "The sustained physical and mental courage of the American boy is something wondrous to behold."

Shipped overseas, Yarnall was a naval officer who served in an air rescue unit based in the South Pacific. His camp was deep in the heart of jungle country, and Yarnall felt that the local flora and fauna were just as much a threat as the human enemy. In a letter home, he wrote, "Only 100 feet away from the field on which our blimps take off, frequently on rescue missions, one can walk right into the loving embrace of a boa constrictor. Yes sir, in this country, there is more than one kind of enemy."

Service in the Pacific Theatre was unlike stateside or even European assignments. The weather was a constant nuisance, with severe storms cropping up so often the soldiers had little time for leisure between the storms. Yarnall wrote, "There isn't much opportunity for diversion. We have wrinkled the playing cards to crumble paper. Torrential rains prevent any kind of set athletic program." Rusty's military duties centered on finding and rescuing downed aircraft. Pilots had to make certain that Yarnall's unit could find them when they crashed. In order to be found, they had to fully expose their position. Yarnall said, "Pilots of planes adopt a measure of emergency while hoping never to use it. It is this: when it is inevitable that they will crash, they attempt to hit the jungle in a low, lengthy sweep, the purpose of which is to give rescuing blimps a chance to see a scar in the growth from the air later."

W	L	PCT	G	GS	CG	IP	H	BB	SO	SHO	ERA
0	1	.000	1	0	0	1	3	1	0	0	18.00

Raymond Austin Aloysius Yochim, *Pitcher*

Yochim received two brief trials at the major league level with the Cardinals after the war. The southern right-hander struggled with his command and walked more than two batters an inning. Before his wild sojourn to the majors, Ray played service ball with the U.S. Marine Corps. Yochim was stationed in Hawaii and played on the same service team as noted cut-up Boots Poffenberger. A case of false reporting circulated after the battle at Iwo Jima in which Ray was listed as killed in action. Yochim, who didn't see combat action, was playing ball in Hawaii at the time.

W	L	PCT	G	GS	CG	IP	H	BB	SO	SHO	ERA
0	0	—	4	0	0	3	3	7	4	0	12.00

Tony Batton York, *Utility Infielder*

York played one year in the major leagues, 1944, and then missed the entire 1945 season to service in the armed forces. After his discharge, York didn't return to the Majors.

G	R	H	2B	3B	HR	RBI	BB	SO	SB	AVG	Slug
28	4	20	1	0	0	7	4	11	0	.235	.247

Edward Frederick Joseph Yost, *Third Base*

The Senators called up Eddie Yost in 1944 as a 17-year-old kid. He played briefly with Washington that year but was summoned by Uncle Sam in 1945. Yost spent a year and a half in the navy and was credited as the sparkplug of the Sampson Naval Training Center ballclub. The kid, who would eventually become known as "The Walking Man," rejoined the Senators late in 1946 and became their regular third baseman in 1947. In 1948, Yost began to display his supreme batting eye, as he paced the club with 82 walks.

He eclipsed the 100-walk plateau for the first time in 1950, as Eddie paced the American League with 141 free passes. His 114 runs scored was the best total of any second-division team, which proved that his ability to get on base through the walk enabled his teammates to drive him in. Often criticized for accepting too many bases on balls, Eddie retaliated, "I just can't relish the idea of swinging at bad pitches."

G	R	H	2B	3B	HR	RBI	BB	SO	SB	AVG	Slug
2,109	1,215	1,863	337	56	139	683	1,614	920	72	.254	.371

Norman Robert "Babe" Young, *Outfield/First Base*

Babe spent a good deal of his major league career as man without a position. He first came up with the Giants in 1936 but was unable to crack the lineup. His next stint at the Polo Grounds came in 1939 when the Giants had Zeke Bonura blocking his path. In 1940 Babe was handed the starting first-base post and did an admirable job: he hit .286 and led the team with 101 RBIs. He socked 25 home runs in 1941, but despite his heavy hitting, the Giants acquired legendary masher Johnny Mize to take his job in 1942. Young was relegated to a reserve role, and he saw occasional time in the outfield. Babe was inducted into the U.S. Coast Guard in 1943 and served 21 months as an executive officer of the Corvette Brisk on convoy and patrol duty.

G	R	H	2B	3B	HR	RBI	BB	SO	SB	AVG	Slug
728	320	656	121	17	79	415	274	161	9	.273	.436

Richard Ennis Young, *Second Base*

As a rookie, Dick was part of a second-base carousel with Putsy Caballero and Eddie Pellagrini for the 1951 Phillies. They brought in Connie Ryan the following year and Dick hardly played thereafter. During the war Young served at the end of the fighting as a teenager.

G	R	H	2B	3B	HR	RBI	BB	SO	SB	AVG	Slug
20	10	18	6	0	0	2	4	9	1	.234	.312

Albert Clyde "Chief" Youngblood, *Pitcher*

A Native American from Texas, Albert Youngblood made two mound appearances for the 1922 Senators. A large man, Youngblood struggled with command in his major league sojourn and never again played at the highest level after his initial trial. Albert served in the army as a teenager during the First World War and returned to Uncle Sam's outfit for more action during the Second World War.

W	L	PCT	G	GS	CG	IP	H	BB	SO	SHO	ERA
0	0	—	2	0	0	4	9	7	0	0	15.75

Floyd Edwin "Eddie" Yount, *Outfield*

Yount had two cups of coffee in the late 1930s, his first with the Athletics in 1937 and his last with the 1939 Pirates. Eddie failed to reach ten at-bats in his brief major league tenure. A minor league ballplayer at the time of the war, Yount joined the army and served with the 12th Armored Division. He served in the ETO for a time.

G	R	H	2B	3B	HR	RBI	BB	SO	SB	AVG	Slug
6	1	2	0	0	0	1	0	3	0	.222	.222

John Edward "Eddie" Yuhas, *Pitcher*

Before Yuhas made his major league debut, he served in the United States Army during World War II. Stationed at Camp Battle, Eddie was a private first class in 1943 before he was shipped overseas to the European Theatre. Able to make it home unscathed, Yuhas later signed with the Cardinals and made his debut in 1952. A strong relief pitcher in '52, Eddie blew out his arm in 1953 and never pitched in the majors again.

W	L	PCT	G	GS	CG	IP	H	BB	SO	SHO	ERA
12	2	.857	56	2	0	100	93	35	39	0	2.88

Salvador Anthony Yvars, *Catcher*

Longtime back-up to Wes Westrum, Yvars enlisted in the Army Air Corps directly after high school graduation. He missed some valuable minor league seasoning to service in the Air Corps. After his discharge, he was called up by the Giants in 1947 and remained with them through 1953. His last major league action came with the Cardinals the following year.

G	R	H	2B	3B	HR	RBI	BB	SO	SB	AVG	Slug
210	44	102	12	0	10	42	37	41	1	.244	.344

James Zapp, *Outfield*

A big, power-hitting outfielder in the latter years of black baseball, Zapp learned to play baseball while in the navy. Inducted into service during World War II, Zapp joined the U.S. Navy and was shipped overseas to Hawaii where he played service ball. After his discharge, Jim caught on with the Baltimore Elite Giants and played in the Negro Leagues through the early 1950s, when black baseball was nearing its demise. He joined the minor leagues and had some success in the low levels but never got a call to the majors.

(1945–1954): Baltimore Elite Giants, Birmingham Black Barons and Atlanta Black Crackers

Allen Lee Zarilla, *Outfield*

Zarilla usually platooned in the outfield during his stay in the majors, which allowed him to wear the uniforms of the Browns and the Sox — both the crimson and chalky variety. He played with the Browns through 1944 and even saw action in that season's Fall Classic, but the outfielder missed the entire 1945 campaign to service in the army. Al was stationed briefly at Cheyenne, Wyoming.

G	R	H	2B	3B	HR	RBI	BB	SO	SB	AVG	Slug
1,120	507	975	186	43	61	456	415	382	33	.276	.405

Gus Edward Zernial, *Outfield*

Nicknamed "Ozark Ike," Zernial was one of the top power hitters of the 1950s. He led the American League in both home runs and RBIs in 1951 and missed another home run crown by one dinger to Al Rosen in 1953. He was the first player to club 30 home runs for the Kansas City Athletics and has one of the greatest home run-per-at-bat ratios in the game's history. When all that is taken into account, Zernial is a little known former star.

Before his major league debut, Gus served in the armed forces during World War II. A supporter of the VFW throughout his life, he joined the Greater Pullman Post No. 2240 Veterans of Foreign Wars while an active player. A tall, strapping power hitter, Zernial was a hit in the box score but may have been a bigger hit with the ladies. At the height of his career, he had a photo shoot with Marilyn Monroe. A ravishing beauty named Dagmar, who was referred to as "the blonde torpedo of television," placed Gus on her top ten list of handsomest men in sports. When she introduced her roster, she gave a description of each man. While unveiling Ozark Ike, Dagmar simply purred, "Wow!"

G	R	H	2B	3B	HR	RBI	BB	SO	SB	AVG	Slug
1,234	572	1,093	159	22	237	776	383	755	15	.265	.486

Benedict Joseph Zientara, *Second Base*

Benny appeared in nine pre-war games for the Reds. He enlisted in the armed forces after the 1941 baseball season, which made him the first Reds major leaguer to enter the colors. He served in the United States Army as an infantryman, stationed at Fort Benning. After his baseball playing career had concluded, he became a scout for the Cleveland Indians.

G	R	H	2B	3B	HR	RBI	BB	SO	SB	AVG	Slug
278	106	230	29	5	2	49	50	48	5	.254	.304

William Francis Zinser, *Pitcher*

A war-era pitcher, Zinser was with the Senators in spring training in 1942 but left the club to enlist in the U.S. Coast Guard. Discharged early in 1944, Zinser returned to the Senators and had a cup of coffee with them in the war-ravaged 1944 season.

W	L	PCT	G	GS	CG	IP	H	BB	SO	SHO	ERA
0	0	—	2	0	0	1	1	5	1	0	18.00

George Zuverink, *Pitcher*

One of the top firemen of the 1950s, Zuverink was an unusual relief pitcher during the decade in that he possessed good accuracy. The tall right-hander from Michigan served in the South Pacific with the Army Air Corps before he made his major league debut. George broke in with the Indians in 1951 but didn't establish himself until the Tigers claimed him in 1954. He would later pitch effectively out of the Orioles' pen as well.

W	L	PCT	G	GS	CG	IP	H	BB	SO	SHO	ERA
32	36	.471	265	31	9	642	660	203	223	2	3.54

Korean — Vietnam Wars

Albert Julius Aber, *Pitcher*

A stout southpaw, Aber was one of the first major league players drafted into duty for the Korean War. Given his resemblance in stature to fellow Cleveland hurler Mike Garcia, Aber claimed Big Bear Garcia as his mentor when he trained with him. A Cleveland boy, Aber was ecstatic when he signed his contract with the Indians. His older brother served as a bullpen catcher briefly for the Tribe.

Al was inducted into the army on October 11, 1950, and served at Fort Knox, where he was the installation's player-manager. After he signed with the Indians during the mid 1940s, Al sent a clipping of his signing to his brother who was serving in the military during World War II. Several weeks after he sent the clipping, Al was notified that his brother was killed in action by a kamikaze. He never knew if his brother received the letter he had sent. Al spent his career playing for his deceased sibling's memory.

W	L	PCT	G	GS	CG	IP	H	BB	SO	SHO	ERA
24	25	.490	168	30	7	390	398	160	169	0	4.18

Theodore Wade Abernathy, *Pitcher*

Before Abernathy made his major league debut, he was lifted from the minor leagues to serve during the Korean War. Ted reported to Fort Jackson on May 19, 1953, and served two years in the army. After his discharge, Abernathy, property of the Senators, went to training with Washington where skipper Chuck Dressen compared him to former Reds star Ewell Blackwell. In an odd stipulation, the Senators were allowed to carry Ted on their 1955 roster without sacrificing roster space because he was a returnee from the army draft. He was essentially an extra man in 1955.

W	L	PCT	G	GS	CG	IP	H	BB	SO	SHO	ERA
63	69	.477	681	34	7	1,148	1,010	592	765	2	3.46

Thomas James Acker, *Pitcher*

A mountain of a man, Tom was nicknamed "Shoulders" because he didn't have any. Built like an army tank, Acker was a highly regarded prospect by skipper Birdie Tebbetts when he reported for 1954 spring training after his army discharge.

W	L	PCT	G	GS	CG	IP	H	BB	SO	SHO	ERA
19	13	.594	153	23	5	381	365	150	256	1	4.13

Herbert Loren Adams, *Outfield*

Adams was an oft-injured player whose playing time was limited due to assorted ailments. He was the regular left fielder his rookie season with Jack Onslow's White Sox when he missed action due to a broken finger. He was never again a regular player at the major league level. Adams lost his job in 1950 to power hitter Gus Zernial. He missed the 1951 and 1952 seasons while serving during Korea.

G	R	H	2B	3B	HR	RBI	BB	SO	SB	AVG	Slug
95	39	88	8	6	0	18	22	24	4	.261	.320

Harry Agganis, *First Base*

One of the game's most famous tragic figures, Agganis played baseball while he knew he was dying. The "Golden Greek" was suffering from a massive pulmonary embolism, but he played through the pain until he passed away in June of 1955. A former star quarterback at Boston University, Agganis served with the U.S. Marine Corps during the Korean War.

G	R	H	2B	3B	HR	RBI	BB	SO	SB	AVG	Slug
157	65	135	23	9	11	67	57	67	8	.261	.404

Victor Albury, *Pitcher*

At the time Albury was drafted for the Vietnam War, he was a first baseman in the minors. Vic missed the 1966 through 1968 seasons to military service. Shortly after his discharge, Albury was converted into a pitcher and made his major league debut with the 1973 Twins.

W	L	PCT	G	GS	CG	IP	H	BB	SO	SHO	ERA
18	17	.514	101	37	6	372	338	220	193	1	4.11

Matthew Alexander, *Outfield*

The swift Shreveport native holds the records for most runs scored and bases stolen by a pinch-runner. Although he was rarely used as a regular player, Matt saw much more game action than Oakland's star pinch-runner Herb Washington in the 1970s. During the Vietnam War, Alexander served with the U.S. Navy and was stationed in Alaska. Able to play some service ball in Alaska, Matt played for a team called the SubPac Goldpanners.

G	R	H	2B	3B	HR	RBI	BB	SO	SB	AVG	Slug
374	111	36	4	2	0	4	18	26	103	.214	.262

John August Antonelli, *Pitcher*

A "bonus baby," Antonelli served in the army during his stint in the Korean War. He saw his first action with the NL champion Boston Braves in 1948, but the youngster was used sparingly on a staff that boasted Warren Spahn, Johnny Sain, Vern Bickford and Bill Vioselle. He missed the 1951 and 1952 seasons to service in the army, as the southpaw was stationed at Fort Myer. While Hall of Famer Willie Mays was also in the service, he played ball against Antonelli and claimed that Johnny was the best pitcher the service ranks had to offer.

W	L	PCT	G	GS	CG	IP	H	BB	SO	SHO	ERA
126	110	.534	377	268	102	1,992	1,870	687	1,162	25	3.34

Kenneth Joseph Aspromonte, *Second Base*

Before Aspromonte made his major league debut, he served in the armed forces during the Korean War. The infielder from Brooklyn served with the army and was stationed at Fort Monmouth. He was eventually shipped overseas to France where he served in Paris with the SHAPE Headquarters. He made his major league debut with the Ted Williams led Red Sox of 1957. After his playing days, Ken managed briefly with the Indians.

G	R	H	2B	3B	HR	RBI	BB	SO	SB	AVG	Slug
475	171	369	69	3	19	124	179	149	7	.249	.338

Lomas Edgar Bailey, *Catcher*

One of the best power-hitting catchers of the 1950s, Bailey platooned with Smoky Burgess for a time, giving the Reds a terrific one-two punch behind the dish. Shortly after Ed was discharged from the military, he made his debut with Cincinnati.

G	R	H	2B	3B	HR	RBI	BB	SO	SB	AVG	Slug
1,212	432	915	128	15	155	540	545	577	17	.256	.429

Frank Baker, *Outfield*

A stocky outfielder, Baker played with the Indians in 1969 and 1971. He missed the 1967 and 1968 seasons to service in the military during the Vietnam War.

G	R	H	2B	3B	HR	RBI	BB	SO	SB	AVG	Slug
125	39	82	17	4	4	38	26	68	3	.232	.337

Ernest Banks, *Shortstop/First Base*

Always delighted to hear the call to "play ball," Banks was a member of the Negro League Kansas City Monarchs at the time he was drafted for military duty. Before he was drafted, Dodgers bird dog Andy High had his eye on Banks and was ready to recommend him to the Dodgers, but Ernie received his draft notice and High watched him leave for the army. When Banks returned, the Monarchs showcased him and he signed with the Cubs. The power-hitting shortstop would make his way to Cooperstown and was rewarded by Wrigley Field fans with the moniker of "Mr. Cub."

G	R	H	2B	3B	HR	RBI	BB	SO	SB	AVG	Slug
2,528	1,305	2,583	407	90	512	1,636	763	1,236	50	.274	.500

Curtis Cordell Barclay, *Pitcher*

A big right-handed pitcher, Barclay was equally adept on the basketball court. Before he made his debut with the Giants in 1957, Curt was drafted for service during the Korean War. A University of Oregon basketball sensation, Barclay was sent to Fort Jackson where he played athletics. Curt was a regular on Fort Jackson's basketball team, which was nicknamed the Red Raiders.

W	L	PCT	G	GS	CG	IP	H	BB	SO	SHO	ERA
10	9	.526	44	29	5	199	214	55	73	2	3.48

Anthony Joseph Bartirome, *First Base*

The Pittsburgh-born Bartirome was able to fulfill his boyhood dream of playing for his hometown Pirates, but a war intervened and cut his dream short. A first baseman of light build, Tony wasn't of the Ted Kluszewski or Joe Adcock mold. He knew his game didn't revolve around the long ball and worked hard at becoming a fine defensive first baseman. With his smaller body size, he felt that a transition to the outfield might be his best bet to stick in the majors, but an accident in the army kept him from making the move.

After the 1952 season, his dream year with the Pirates, Bartirome was inducted into service for the Korean War. Sent to Fort Knox for basic training, Tony became a truck driver under Uncle Sam. After boot camp, Tony had no idea where he was going to be sent. He said, "The war was very hot in Korea at that time, so in basic training we were all wishing that we didn't have to go over there. A lot of soldiers coming out of Fort Knox were getting assigned to Germany, so we were hoping we'd get sent there instead. As it turned out, they assigned us by alphabetical order. The As, Bs, Cs and Ds went to Germany, so I was fortunate that time."

Orders to Germany were a lot like orders at basic training — a soldier still didn't know where he was going. He could be shipped north and spend time close to Russia or he could get orders further south, away from northern enemies. When Bartirome went to the Reception Center at Germany, he handed the officer making assignments his MOS Card, which showed what his military duties were as well as some background information. Bartirome said, "I handed this lieutenant my card and he looked at it. He said, 'Oh, you played big league baseball? You know what, I'm going to do you a favor. I'm going to send you to a nice place; you're really going to like it.' Well, he sent me to Berlin. That was 125 miles behind the Iron Curtain. He must have hated baseball to send me there."

As a truck driver, Bartirome spent his days in Berlin assisting in escorts and performing maintenance on his vehicles. During his stint in Berlin, he had made up his mind to request the Pirates to switch him to the outfield where his lack of power wouldn't be as exploited as it was at first base. Instead, he suffered a freak injury that prevented that from happening. Bartirome said, "We were cleaning our tanks and I slipped between two tanks and tried to hold myself up. I felt something pop in my left shoulder but I didn't think much anything of it because it didn't really bother me that bad. After a couple days the pain went away. But I didn't realize until I got out that I couldn't throw overhand anymore."

With a damaged arm, Bartirome couldn't make the long throws from the outfield, and as a southpaw, he was relegated to first base. In his first spring training after his army discharge, Tony suffered a hamstring tear to go along with his wounded wing and his career was essentially over. He limped through a painful season in the minors before ending his playing days. He would make it back to the majors to stay as a trainer with the Pirates, a job he held for more than twenty years.

G	R	H	2B	3B	HR	RBI	BB	SO	SB	AVG	Slug
124	32	78	10	3	0	16	26	37	3	.220	.265

Frank Matt Baumann, *Pitcher*

At the time of Baumann's military induction, he was a top pitching prospect in the Red Sox chain. The pitching-starved Red Sox in 1954 had the second-worst staff ERA in the American League and could have used the southpaw from St. Louis. Johnny Keane was thoroughly impressed with Frank as he said, "Possibly the best young pitcher I have seen in many years is Frank Baumann. He entered the service but I believe he would have pitched for the Red Sox very shortly."

Baumann was initially rejected for service by his draft board. After taking the induction physical, it was revealed that Frank had a perforated eardrum. The deficiency was unknown to Baumann. He thought it was a temporary affliction that he received while swimming and that he'd be fine for military duty. After healing for a time, Frank reported back to his draft board for a second physical and was deemed suitable for induction. Frank missed some important minor league seasoning time to service in the armed forces during the Korean War. His left-handed presence could have helped offset the injury to staff ace Mel Parnell.

W	L	PCT	G	GS	CG	IP	H	BB	SO	SHO	ERA
45	38	.542	244	78	19	798	856	300	384	4	4.11

Michael Baxes, *Shortstop/Second Base*

Baxes, whose older brother, Jim, also played in the majors, spent two years with the Kansas City A's. A middle infielder, Mike served in the armed forces during the Korean War before his major league debut. Stationed in the European Theatre, Mike played some service ball overseas at such locales as Bremerhaven.

G	R	H	2B	3B	HR	RBI	BB	SO	SB	AVG	Slug
146	40	73	13	2	1	13	39	39	1	.217	.276

Richard Henry Beck, *Pitcher*

The Yankees dropped in the standings during the mid 1960s; their need for pitching was obvious. Whitey Ford's career was over and two youngsters named Stottlemyre and Downing showed promise, but they needed another arm. It looked as if Rich Beck would be that man when he won two of his three starts late in the 1965 season on a microscopic 2.14 ERA. However, fate had other plans as Beck lost the next two seasons to service in the Army Finance branch at Fort Hood, Texas. Upon his return from the military, Beck, who said that he suffered from a lack of confidence, never again reached the major leagues.

W	L	PCT	G	GS	CG	IP	H	BB	SO	SHO	ERA
2	1	.667	3	3	1	21	22	7	10	1	2.14

Melvin Brian Behney, *Pitcher*

Behney enjoyed a blink-and-you-missed-it major league career, as he appeared in a handful of games for the National League champion Cincinnati Reds. His 1970 season was cut short due to service in the armed forces. When he tried to make his way back to the major leagues, Behney broke his arm in Pawtucket while throwing a pitch.

W	L	PCT	G	GS	CG	IP	H	BB	SO	SHO	ERA
0	2	.000	5	1	0	10	15	8	2	0	4.50

William Samuel Bell, *Pitcher*

A minor league phenom, Bell is credited with tossing three no-hitters in the lower ranks. Despite his minor league accomplishments, the player nicknamed "Ding Dong" only appeared in five major league games. Bell lost the entire 1953 and 1954 seasons to service in the army as the hurler was stationed at Fort Jackson.

W	L	PCT	G	GS	CG	IP	H	BB	SO	SHO	ERA
0	1	.000	5	1	0	17	16	14	4	0	4.24

John "Zeke" Bella, *Outfield*

One of the many players who began his career with the Yankees but was shipped to the Kansas City Athletics, Bella was that unusual left-handed thrower but right-handed batter. Before Zeke made his debut with the 1957 Yankees, he served with the 7th army overseas and played some service ball at such locales as Leipheim.

G	R	H	2B	3B	HR	RBI	BB	SO	SB	AVG	Slug
52	10	18	2	1	1	9	10	16	0	.196	.272

Louis Joseph Berberet, *Catcher*

A catcher who made his debut with the Yankees in the mid 1950s, Lou didn't have a chance with Yogi Berra and Elston Howard on the roster. Only after he was sent to the Senators did he get to play. Before Berberet made his major league debut, he served at Fort Bliss, Texas, with the 4052nd ASU during the Korean War.

G	R	H	2B	3B	HR	RBI	BB	SO	SB	AVG	Slug
448	118	281	34	10	31	153	200	195	2	.230	.350

William "Fireball" Beverly, *Pitcher*

A flamethrower in the latter stages of the Negro Leagues, Beverly made his debut in black baseball in 1950. Two years later, he was drafted for service in the military during the Korean War. After his discharge, "Fireball" played a year in Canada before returning to black baseball where he ended his career.

(1950–1955): Birmingham Black Barons, Houston Eagles and Chicago American Giants

James Blair Bibby, *Pitcher*

A mountain of a man, Bibby was claimed to have been built more like the Incredible Hulk than a pitcher. The big fellow was an All-Star pitcher and two-time winning percentage champ at the major league level. A solid starting pitcher who could also eat innings out of the bullpen, Jim was a member of the world champion 1979 Pirates. That year Bibby led the league in winning percentage and had a solid 2.61 ERA to end the year on a high note. But Bibby's road to the majors was a rocky one with detours and stops he had little control over.

Jim's back had always ailed him and while pitching in the minors he had to have it operated on. A big man already, with a back that was surgically repaired his mobility was limited. But he was able to soldier through the back pain — quite literally — when he was drafted into the army during the Vietnam War. After boot camp, Jim was shipped out to Vietnam where his unit was engaged in transport missions. Bibby said, "In Vietnam I was a truck driver. We handled everything from dead bodies to plastic forks. My unit never got hit, and I didn't see anybody get killed so things weren't bad for me." Discharged from the army, Jim returned home and back to baseball. He was finally called up to the majors in 1972 by the Cardinals and pitched until 1984.

W	L	PCT	G	GS	CG	IP	H	BB	SO	SHO	ERA
111	101	.524	340	239	56	1,723	1,565	723	1,079	19	3.76

Lawrence David Biittner, *Outfield/First Base*

A good average hitter with solid bat control, Biittner was a decent fourth outfielder/pinch-hitter/first baseman over the course of his career. Before he began playing professionally, he was a college student at Buena Vista College, Iowa. He left the school to enlist in the army during the Vietnam War. After his tour in Vietnam, Larry decided to remain in the army on a limited basis and enrolled in the Army Reserves. While he played ball in the minor leagues, he had to leave for a weekend training stint each month.

G	R	H	2B	3B	HR	RBI	BB	SO	SB	AVG	Slug
1,217	310	861	144	20	29	354	236	287	10	.273	.358

William Carroll Black, *Pitcher*

Black appeared in ten major league games, with his first action on the 1952 Tigers roster. He missed the 1953 and 1954 seasons to military service and returned to appear in three games in 1955 and five games in 1956 to close out his career in the Majors.

W	L	PCT	G	GS	CG	IP	H	BB	SO	SHO	ERA
2	3	.400	10	5	1	32	36	18	14	1	4.22

Ronald Hamilton Blackburn, *Pitcher*

Blackburn had a short career. He pitched for parts of two years with the Pittsburgh Pirates. Ron showed promise as a 23-year-old out of Danny Murtaugh's bullpen with a 3.38 ERA in 1958 but missed six months to service in the army. After the 1959 season, Blackburn never again tossed another inning at the major league level.

W	L	PCT	G	GS	CG	IP	H	BB	SO	SHO	ERA
3	2	.600	64	2	0	108	111	42	50	0	3.50

John Edwin Blanchard, *Catcher/Outfield*

A solid role player for the Yankees during their great Mantle and Maris days, Blanchard was often employed as a pinch-hitter. Perhaps the greatest power bat off the bench in baseball history, Blanchard was stuck as a reserve with the Yankees when he could have been blasting 35 home runs a year elsewhere with regular duty. But Blanchard would be the first to admit that he wasn't that great of a baseball player. The story goes that when he learned the Yankees had traded him to Kansas City, Johnny began to sob. Mickey Mantle reassured his old teammate, informing Johnny that he'd get a chance to play regularly with KC, to which Johnny replied, "That's just it, Mick. I can't play."

A big power hitter, Blanchard served in the military during the Korean War before the Yankees called him up in 1955. The Slugger from Minneapolis was with the 47th Regiment stationed in Germany. While stationed in Europe, Blanchard was able to play plenty of baseball. He took part and was the hero in the 1954 USAREUR GI World Series held at Stuttgart, Germany. In the early innings, Johnny blasted a towering home run that gave his squad an early lead that would hold until the last out. After his discharge, Blanchard played briefly with the Yankees in 1955 but didn't stick until 1959.

G	R	H	2B	3B	HR	RBI	BB	SO	SB	AVG	Slug
516	137	285	36	2	67	200	136	163	2	.239	.441

Michael John Blyzka, *Pitcher*

Blyzka was a member of the last St. Louis Browns team and a charter member of the new Baltimore Orioles. A right-handed mop-up pitcher, Mike pitched two seasons at the highest level. During the Korean War, Blyzka served at Fort Sam Houston and tossed a no-hitter there against a squad from the 43rd Division from Fort Pickett. A lifetime supporter of the VFW, Mike was a member of his Cheyenne, Wyoming, branch for many years.

W	L	PCT	G	GS	CG	IP	H	BB	SO	SHO	ERA
3	11	.214	70	9	2	180	193	107	58	0	5.60

Frank Elmore Bolling, *Second Base*

A solid major league second baseman for many years in Detroit and with the Braves, Bolling missed the entire 1955 season to service in the army. He received his discharge at Fort McPherson and returned to the Tigers to hit .281 for Bucky Harris' club. He led all American League second basemen with 15 home runs in 1957 while Boston's Ted Lepcio finished second with nine.

G	R	H	2B	3B	HR	RBI	BB	SO	SB	AVG	Slug
1,540	692	1,415	221	40	106	556	462	558	40	.254	.366

Edward Francis Bouchee, *First Base*

A highly underrated first baseman for the Phillies in the late 1950s, Bouchee brought to his team decent power, good run production and great plate discipline. A good on-base percentage guy, Bouchee drew plenty of walks and often led the Phillies in doubles. Before the Phillies called Ed up in 1956, he served in the armed forces during the Korean War.

G	R	H	2B	3B	HR	RBI	BB	SO	SB	AVG	Slug
670	298	583	114	21	61	290	340	401	5	.265	.429

Kenton Lloyd Boyer, *Third Base*

As a teenager, his older brother, Cloyd, served briefly during World War II, and Ken was called to service later for the Korean War. Cloyd played for the Cardinals a few years before they unveiled Ken while their younger brother, Clete, would make the majors and achieve some fame as a gifted defender with the Yankees. But when Cloyd was pitching ball professionally in the early 1950s, Clete was still in school and Ken was wearing Uncle Sam's khaki uniforms.

Ken served with the 28th Artillery Division in USAREUR during the Korean War. The strong third baseman played some service ball overseas with Lou Skizas at such locales as Schwaebisch-Gmuend. After his hitch with Uncle Sam was complete, Boyer returned stateside and began a prosperous baseball career. A terrific third baseman, Kenny was a fixture at third in the All-Star Games and won a handful of Gold Glove Awards. A strong Hall of Fame candidate, Boyer's only real peer during his playing days was Ron Santo.

G	R	H	2B	3B	HR	RBI	BB	SO	SB	AVG	Slug
2,034	1,104	2,143	318	68	282	1,141	713	1,017	105	.287	.462

Eugene Matthew Brabender, *Pitcher*

A member of the only Seattle Pilots team, Gene was with the club when it relocated close to home in Wisconsin. A large man, Brabender stood at 6'5" and tipped the scales at 225 pounds. Drafted into the army during the Vietnam War, Gene remained stateside and played service ball at Aberdeen. While pitching for Aberdeen, the nearby Orioles took notice of Gene and made an unusual claim when they selected him in the 1966 Rule V Draft. Brabender had been in the army the last two years, but Baltimore saw enough in him at Aberdeen to make a claim and Gene made good. He pitched with Baltimore for three years before he joined the Pilots.

W	L	PCT	G	GS	CG	IP	H	BB	SO	SHO	ERA
35	43	.449	151	80	15	621	570	282	440	4	4.25

John George "Jackie" Brandt, *Outfield*

Brandt was a noted clown who was dubbed by the press "The Marvelous Flake" on account of his antics. An exceptional athlete, Jackie gave management fits due to his behavior. An indication of how odd Brandt was can be seen when the outfielder worked as an electrician during the offseason. He said of his initial wiring job, "The first house I wired somebody pushed the doorbell and all the toilets flushed."

During Brandt's stint in the army he served at Fort Chaffee, Arkansas, as a clerical typist. Constantly running afoul of Oriole manager Hank Bauer, a decorated veteran of World War II, Brandt was benched by Hank and later dealt to the Phillies. While in Philadelphia, a teammate once said of Jackie, "He begged me to drive 20 miles to a certain ice cream stand because it was the only one that carried 29 flavors ... and then he ordered vanilla."

G	R	H	2B	3B	HR	RBI	BB	SO	SB	AVG	Slug
1,221	540	1,020	175	37	112	485	351	574	45	.262	.412

Edward Francis Bressoud, *Shortstop*

Bressoud made his debut with the New York Giants and two years later he was a member of the San Francisco Giants after their relocation. A tall shortstop with some modest power, Eddie helped pave the way for larger shortstops. During the time, most middle infielders were short and swift, like Luis Aparicio and Nellie Fox, but Eddie helped redefine the position. When Bressoud served in the military during the Korean War, he was in his early twenties.

G	R	H	2B	3B	HR	RBI	BB	SO	SB	AVG	Slug
1,186	443	925	184	40	94	365	359	723	9	.252	.401

Thomas Austin Brewer, *Pitcher*

A good pitching prospect for the Red Sox before he was drafted for service, Brewer spent two years in the army during the Korean War. Tom served at Camp Atterbury, Indiana, where he became a service ball legend. Against the Offutt Air Force Base nine, Tom tossed a no-hitter. Later, he would win Camp Atterbury's final game in the Indiana Semi-Pro Baseball tournament. With his army accolades under his belt, Tom reported to Red Sox training camp in 1954 and thoroughly impressed skipper Lou Boudreau, who called Brewer "the find of the year." Tom would have a good major league career and was a reliable innings-eater with the Bosox.

W	L	PCT	G	GS	CG	IP	H	BB	SO	SHO	ERA
91	82	.526	241	217	75	1,509	1,478	669	733	13	4.00

Leon Clarence Brinkopf, *Shortstop*

A shortstop from southern Missouri, Brinkopf had a cup of coffee with the 1952 Cubs. During the Korean War, Leon served with the United States Marine Corps.

G	R	H	2B	3B	HR	RBI	BB	SO	SB	AVG	Slug
9	1	4	0	0	0	2	4	5	0	.182	.182

Richard Stanley Brodowski, *Pitcher*

A humble man who views his career in baseball and the military as "not very exciting," Brodowski served two years during the Korean War at Fort Dix. Although he may consider his career as a yawn-inducing moment in time, he might be surprised to learn that his strikeout rate in 1958 was bested by only one American League hurler: Ryne Duren of the champion Yankees.

W	L	PCT	G	GS	CG	IP	H	BB	SO	SHO	ERA
9	11	.450	72	15	5	216	212	124	85	0	4.75

James Patrick Brosnan, *Pitcher*

Although Jim was a decent major league pitcher, he is best known for the books he published on the game. His works include the best-seller, *The Long Season*, and his second volume, titled *Pennant Race*. Known as "Professor" by his peers, Brosnan served at Fort Meade in the army before he made his major league debut with the Cubs.

W	L	PCT	G	GS	CG	IP	H	BB	SO	SHO	ERA
55	47	.539	385	47	7	832	790	312	507	2	3.54

Robert William Brown, *Third Base*

A graduate of Tulane's School of Medicine, Brown lost the majority of the 1952 season as well as the entire 1953 campaign to service in Korea as an army doctor. He returned late in the 1954 season to finish out his playing career as a member of the second-place Yankees, who posted a remarkable record of 103–51 but still finished eight games behind Cleveland. After Brown's playing career was over, he served as the president of the American League.

G	R	H	2B	3B	HR	RBI	BB	SO	SB	AVG	Slug
548	233	452	62	14	22	237	214	88	9	.279	.376

Donald Thomas Buddin, *Shortstop*

Buddin was the Red Sox's regular shortstop in 1956 but that didn't stop Uncle Sam from claiming him in 1957. The loss of Buddin forced manager Pinky Higgins to tinker with his lineup. He had to rotate third baseman Billy Klaus to short to fill in for Buddin, which opened third base for Frank Malzone. With Billy Goodman gone, the new second baseman was Ted Lepcio. The Red Sox's new-look infield in 1957 was an area of concern for Higgins. Before the season he said, "Our chief problem is in the infield, of course. The loss of Buddin to the service has hurt us a lot. He was a good shortstop for us and he would have been much better for us this year."

Inducted into the army, Don took his basic training and AIT at Fort Jackson. From there he was assigned to Fort McPherson, where he worked as a supply clerk for the Hospital Detachment. Buddin knew he'd get a chance to play plenty of baseball after duty hours and wasn't disappointed by his military induction. He said, "I hope to be better when my army service ends than I was when I came in. I have a wonderful opportunity here and I intend to work on my batting and ball-handling as much as I can."

While playing service ball with fellow professionals Steve Korcheck and Al Spangler, Buddin was able to stay in game shape. Discharged after a year of army service, Buddin returned to Boston a better player than he was before his induction. A modest hitter in 1956 when he hit .239 with five home runs, he showed additional power by swatting a dozen home runs his first year back from the service.

G	R	H	2B	3B	HR	RBI	BB	SO	SB	AVG	Slug
711	342	441	123	12	41	225	410	404	15	.241	.359

Robert Ray Buhl, *Pitcher*

A star pitcher for the Milwaukee Braves, Buhl teamed with Warren Spahn, Lew Burdette and Ray Crone to give the team a fine pitching staff. In 1956, Spahn won 20 games, Burdette 19, and Buhl netted 18. World champions in 1957, Buhl led the National League in winning percentage with an 18–7 record to his credit. Bob tied for the league lead in shutouts in 1959, and then the great trio was in fine form again in 1960 when Spahn won 21 games, Burdette 19, and Buhl chipped in 16. Bob Buhl had a terrific career but was always overshadowed by Spahn and Burdette. However, before his baseball career began, he spent time in the U.S. army.

Inducted into the army at Fort Campbell, Kentucky, in 1951, Buhl missed two baseball seasons to the Korean War. During his stint in the military, Bob earned his airborne wings and was assigned to the 11th Airborne Regiment. Jumping out of planes helped Bob develop nerves of steel that would come in handy in the game of baseball. When he returned from his stint in the army, he impressed in 1953 spring training. Ben Phlegar wrote, "Parachute jumping isn't included in the normal course of instruction on how to become a winning major league pitcher, but young hurlers may consider it when they study the amazing development of Blazing Bob Buhl."

W	L	PCT	G	GS	CG	IP	H	BB	SO	SHO	ERA
166	132	.557	457	369	111	2,587	2,446	1,105	1,268	20	3.55

Alonza Benjamin Bumbry, *Outfield*

The American League's Rookie of the Year in 1973, Al "The Bumble Bee" Bumbry was a solid lead-off man throughout his career with the Orioles. A longtime favorite of skipper Earl Weaver, Bumbry was the dependable center fielder for the Orioles during the 1970s and the early 1980s. In 1985, his only season at the major league level while not in Baltimore, Al played for the defending National League champion San Diego Padres. But the Bumble Bee almost never made it to the majors. After his stint in the ROTC in college, Bumbry was shipped overseas and saw combat action as a platoon leader in Vietnam.

Bumbry arrived in Vietnam in June 1970 and was assigned as a platoon leader for a reconnaissance group in Region Three. A young commissioned officer, Al was in charge of an entire platoon, ranging from young buck privates to seasoned sergeants. When he first arrived in Vietnam, his commanding officer introduced him to life in the foreign area and his duties as a lieutenant team leader. Bumbry said, "When I got to Vietnam, my commander said, 'You probably won't win this war while you're here so just take care of and be responsible for your men. See that they get back home.' I always kept that in the back of my mind."

His platoon patrolled the area of Region Three and met hostile fire on many occasions. The battle presented many hardships for Bumbry and his troops, most notably the inability to read the people. He said, "There were physical and mental strains that were different from other wars because it was a war where it was difficult to distinguish friend from foe. Someone who was a farmer by day could be mining the roads at night." But Lieutenant Bumbry persevered and led his troops through the thick of battle with minimal casualties. Decorated for his work in battle, Al was awarded the Bronze Star when his platoon stopped a shipment of rations that was headed for a hidden group of Vietcong.

After his discharge, Bumbry returned stateside and was able to do his best bumble bee routine in the minor leagues while awaiting his trial in the majors. A speedy, pesky hitter, Bumbry could lay down a bunt with the best of them and was also capable of sending drives to the wall. Baseball helped Bumbry transition back to civilian life and forget the horrors of war. He said, "When I got back the strain was no longer there. I was doing something that I wanted to do. I had my arms, legs and could run around and enjoy myself. In a sense it was like the world had been lifted off my shoulders."

G	R	H	2B	3B	HR	RBI	BB	SO	SB	AVG	Slug
1,496	778	1,422	220	52	54	402	471	709	254	.281	.378

Mack Edwin Burk, *Catcher*

Burk was a $40,000 bonus baby bust as the catcher only had two major league at-bats. He played in fifteen games for Mayo Smith's Phillies of 1956 with only one at-bat and missed the entire 1958 and the majority of the 1959 season to service in the armed forces.

G	R	H	2B	3B	HR	RBI	BB	SO	SB	AVG	Slug
16	3	1	0	0	0	0	0	1	0	.500	.500

Peter Willits Burnside, *Pitcher*

A journeyed left-handed mop-up pitcher, Burnside spent the bulk of his major league action with the Giants and Senators. A member of the last New York Giants squad and the inaugural San Francisco Giants, Burnside typically worked in long relief but made quite a few starts as well. Before he tossed his first major league pitch, the Dartmouth grad played service ball at Fort Leonard Wood while in the army.

W	L	PCT	G	GS	CG	IP	H	BB	SO	SHO	ERA
19	36	.345	196	64	14	589	607	230	203	3	4.79

Samuel Francis Calderone, *Catcher*

Calderone was stationed at Fort Dix, where he played on the installation baseball team. While he was serving in Tokyo, Sammy was a member of the winning club in the Service World Series. A member of the New York Giants, Calderone couldn't supplant power-hitting receiver Wes Westrum and was dealt to the Braves, where he served briefly behind an even better catcher in Del Crandall.

G	R	H	2B	3B	HR	RBI	BB	SO	SB	AVG	Slug
91	16	41	5	0	1	25	7	13	0	.291	.348

Thomas Edward Carroll, *Third Base*

Carroll played briefly with the Yankees in 1955 and 1956 and despite posting batting averages above .300 in both years, he couldn't supplant modest-hitting Andy Carey at third base. He served in the army in 1958, and upon his return to the game, he was dealt to the lowly Kansas City Athletics, where he finished out his major league career.

G	R	H	2B	3B	HR	RBI	BB	SO	SB	AVG	Slug
64	15	9	0	0	0	1	1	6	1	.300	.300

Jerry Joseph Casale, *Pitcher*

Casale broke in with the Red Sox of the late 1950s, which is why he has gotten away with displaying Red Sox memorabilia in his New York City restaurant called Pino's. The Brooklyn right-hander missed some minor league seasoning time when he was drafted for duty during the Korean War. Casale was shipped overseas, where he served in Germany attached to the Combat Command team of the Third Army. Shipped back home after his overseas stint, Jerry was mustered out at Fort Dix.

W	L	PCT	G	GS	CG	IP	H	BB	SO	SHO	ERA
17	24	.415	96	49	10	371	376	204	207	3	5.07

Foster Ephraim Castleman, *Third Base*

Castleman played third base for the New York Giants just before they drifted out west. A corner infielder with some pop, Foster served in the military during the Korean War and was discharged in time to participate in spring training in 1953.

G	R	H	2B	3B	HR	RBI	BB	SO	SB	AVG	Slug
268	58	136	24	3	20	65	35	99	4	.205	.341

Arthur Edward Ceccarelli, *Pitcher*

Art broke in with the 1955 Kansas City Athletics after a stint in the armed forces during the Korean War. A spot starter/long relief pitcher, "Chic" last pitched at the major league level with the 1960 Cubs.

W	L	PCT	G	GS	CG	IP	H	BB	SO	SHO	ERA
9	18	.333	79	42	8	307	309	147	166	3	5.04

Darrel Lee Chaney, *Shortstop*

Sometimes being a major league baseball player is like looking into a brick wall. Chaney spent the bulk of his major league career with Cincinnati's Big Red Machine dynasty and therefore, as a middle infielder, served as a backup to Joe Morgan and Dave Concepcion. Noted for his fine fielding, he was stuck on the depth chart behind a Hall of Famer and a shortstop with some Hall of Fame credentials. Only after he was traded to Atlanta did Chaney get to climb that brick wall and play a little.

Chaney enlisted in the Army Reserves during the Vietnam War era and took his basic training at Fort Campbell, Kentucky. From there it was off to Fort Sill for AIT. The switch-hitting shortstop's military duties were as a cannoneer, working with the 105 Howitzer. Reflecting on his enlistment, Chaney said, "One of the reasons I enlisted is because I wanted the discipline of the army. At the time I was young and immature, just thinking about myself and baseball. I didn't think about my country and protecting it until I enlisted and got the discipline from basic training. It sure made a man out of me."

Working with cannons at Fort Sill, Oklahoma, Chaney's military occupation seemed a likely fit for service in the war regions. While training in Oklahoma, he was fully prepared for a deployment to Vietnam, but the orders never came. He said, "The Vietnam War was pretty hot then, so I was thinking, since the 105 Howitzer was a popular weapon in Vietnam, I thought I'd go over there and shoot that thing. But we never did get called to active duty."

Army life put more meat on Chaney's bones and worked him in the best condition of his life. The training was strenuous, but Chaney was always a fit individual; the thing that bothered him the most was getting sand in his contacts. At the time of his discharge, Chaney was twenty pounds heavier, carrying the added muscle that Uncle Sam put on his frame. He quickly found out in the Reds organization that middle infielders should carry as little weight as possible. Chaney said, "It was difficult returning to baseball because I bulked up in the service. I had put on twenty pounds, and as a middle infielder, I was carrying too much weight. The scout that signed me pulled me aside and told me if I wanted to make the big leagues I had to lose the weight I put on in the army."

A lifelong admirer of Cubs legend Ernie Banks, one of Chaney's fondest memories is playing against Mr. Cub as a rookie and Banks giving him a hug, welcoming him to the majors. When he visited the Baseball Hall of Fame and saw a plaque commemorating the Hall of Famers who served in the war, including his hero's name, Chaney said, "It put chills up and down my spine."

G	R	H	2B	3B	HR	RBI	BB	SO	SB	AVG	Slug
915	237	458	75	17	14	190	238	471	19	.217	.288

Edwin Douglas Charles, *Third Base*

The longtime third baseman for the Kansas City A's, Charles enjoyed a solid career at the major league level. He possessed tools, although not of the high grade; he got by with above-average speed and power. A good defender at the hot corner as well, Charles served in the army during the Korean War for several years before he made his major league debut.

G	R	H	2B	3B	HR	RBI	BB	SO	SB	AVG	Slug
1,005	438	917	147	30	86	421	332	525	86	.263	.397

Thomas Edgar Cheney, *Pitcher*

Cheney's claim to fame was striking out 21 Orioles in a 16-inning contest. The right-hander was a classic swing-and-miss-type hurler who possessed minimal control. He missed the entire

1958 season to service in the army where he was stationed at Fort McPherson. While serving his time in the military, Cheney was stabbed in Atlanta, but the injury wasn't serious enough for him to lose any baseball time. The wild right-hander spent his offseasons as a peanut farmer.

W	L	PCT	G	GS	CG	IP	H	BB	SO	SHO	ERA
19	29	.396	115	71	13	466	382	245	345	8	3.77

Harry Chiti, *Catcher*

Chiti holds the distinction of being traded for himself. He was acquired in a trade for a player to be named later, but when he failed to impress, he was shipped back to the club that initially dealt him away. The journeyman catcher was inducted into the army on December 11, 1952, and missed the following two baseball seasons to the war effort. While serving in the army at Fort Lee, Chiti played for the Service Champions of that installation with Wes Covington.

G	R	H	2B	3B	HR	RBI	BB	SO	SB	AVG	Slug
502	135	356	49	9	41	179	115	242	4	.238	.365

Bruce Ray Christensen, *Shortstop*

Before Bruce made his major league debut he served in the armed forces during the Vietnam War. Stationed in Alaska, he was able to play some service ball with outfielder Matt Alexander for a SubPac club. After his discharge he made the majors with the 1971 Angels, who had former All-Star Jim Fregosi entrenched at his position.

G	R	H	2B	3B	HR	RBI	BB	SO	SB	AVG	Slug
29	4	17	1	0	0	3	6	5	0	.270	.286

Clarence Nottingham Churn, *Pitcher*

Sometimes listed as "Chuck" Churn to give his name more of a melodic ring, Clarence played three years at the major league level with three different teams. The big right-hander from Virginia played some service ball with Rudy Minarcin at Fort Eustis during the Korean War. Thereafter, he was shipped out and listed as serving in the Korean Theatre. After his discharge, Churn made his first major league appearance with the 1957 Pirates.

W	L	PCT	G	GS	CG	IP	H	BB	SO	SHO	ERA
3	2	.600	25	0	0	48	49	19	32	0	5.06

Philip James Clark, *Pitcher*

Before Clark made his major league debut, he missed the 1952 and 1953 seasons to military service during the Korean War. He would pitch two years in the late 1950s with the Cardinals.

W	L	PCT	G	GS	CG	IP	H	BB	SO	SHO	ERA
0	2	.000	14	0	0	15	19	11	6	0	7.80

Hyman Cohen, *Pitcher*

Cohen had a cup of coffee with the 1955 Cubs after his tour of duty in the military during the Korean War. While working under Uncle Sam, Hy played service ball at the Brooke Army Medical Center with Joe Margoneri and Owen Friend.

W	L	PCT	G	GS	CG	IP	H	BB	SO	SHO	ERA
0	0	—	7	1	0	17	28	10	4	0	7.94

Gordon Calvin Coleman, *First Base*

A power-hitting first baseman for the Reds of the 1960s, Coleman missed some minor league action during the 1950s when he served at Fort McPherson. Coleman was able to play service ball with the likes of Don Buddin and Steve Korcheck, and the Fort McPherson squad was an army powerhouse. After his discharge, Gordy played briefly with the Cleveland Indians, but most of his major league at-bats came in Cincinnati.

G	R	H	2B	3B	HR	RBI	BB	SO	SB	AVG	Slug
773	282	650	102	11	98	387	177	333	9	.273	.448

Gerald Francis Coleman, *Second Base*

Coleman saw action in World War II, which took away valuable seasoning time as a minor leaguer. During the Second World War, Coleman flew 57 dive-bombing missions. He was awarded two distinguished Flying Crosses and seven Air Medals while flying Douglas attack bombers during the great conflict. With Ted Williams, Coleman became a "retread" pilot, as both baseball players were asked to serve their country in two separate conflicts.

During the Korean War Coleman flew 67 missions and won six Air Medals. The newspapers across the country kept tabs on Coleman's heroics during the war as his first flight in Korea made its way to the presses. In his initial flight in the Korean War, Coleman took out an enemy bridge and earned two Gold Stars for his work in the war to go along with his Air Medals. A captain in the First Marine Air Wing, Coleman was sent to El Toro for a refresher flying course prior to his deployment. A highly decorated war hero, Coleman won the Ford C. Frick Award for his work as a baseball broadcaster.

G	R	H	2B	3B	HR	RBI	BB	SO	SB	AVG	Slug
723	267	558	77	18	16	217	235	218	22	.263	.339

Charles Edward Coles, *Outfield*

Coles had a cup of coffee with the 1958 Reds. Before his major league debut he missed some minor league action to service in the armed forces during the Korean War.

G	R	H	2B	3B	HR	RBI	BB	SO	SB	AVG	Slug
5	0	2	1	0	0	2	2	6	0	.182	.273

Daniel Bernard Coombs, *Pitcher*

Coombs was a decent left-handed relief pitcher throughout the mid-to-late 1960s with the Houston Astros. He missed a portion of the 1964 season to service in the Army Reserves. His best year came in 1968 when he posted a 3.26 ERA and a pair of saves for the cellar-finishing Astros.

W	L	PCT	G	GS	CG	IP	H	BB	SO	SHO	ERA
19	27	.413	144	5	2	393	433	162	249	1	4.08

John Wesley "Wes" Covington, *Outfield*

A fine power hitter for the Braves of the late 1950s and the Phillies of the early 1960s, Covington was a nice complement to

Aaron, Mathews and Adcock in Milwaukee and to Johnny Callison and Roy Sievers in Philadelphia. The strong man from South Carolina missed some minor league action to military service during the Korean War. Wes played service ball at Fort Lee with Harry Chiti and put up monster numbers at the installation. In just 53 games, Covington hit .411 with 94 RBIs.

G	R	H	2B	3B	HR	RBI	BB	SO	SB	AVG	Slug
1,075	355	832	128	17	131	499	247	414	7	.279	.466

Roger Lee Craig, *Pitcher*

The best pitcher on the worst team in baseball history, Craig was Casey Stengel's go-to guy on the terrible 1962 Mets squad. Taken away from the contending Dodgers, Craig toiled for the Mets for two seasons before he was shipped off to St. Louis. After his playing days, Roger would enjoy some success as a manager with the San Francisco Giants. Before he made his major league debut, however, Craig served in the army during the Korean War. Stationed at Fort Jackson, he was able to play some service ball after his duties were completed at the Reception Center.

W	L	PCT	G	GS	CG	IP	H	BB	SO	SHO	ERA
74	98	.430	368	186	58	1,537	1,528	522	803	7	3.82

Delmar Wesley Crandall, *Catcher*

Crandall was widely regarded as the best catcher in the National League during the late 1950s when he was a member of the Braves. An astute game-caller, Crandall also managed at the major league level for six years, first with the Milwaukee Brewers and later with the Seattle Mariners. During Crandall's stint in the military, which took away the 1951 and 1952 Baseball seasons, he spent eleven months at Fort Ord, California, and also served in Japan.

G	R	H	2B	3B	HR	RBI	BB	SO	SB	AVG	Slug
1,573	585	1,276	179	18	179	657	424	477	26	.254	.404

Jerome Alex Dahlke, *Pitcher*

Dahlke had a cup of coffee with the Go-Go White Sox of Aparicio and Fox in 1956. Before his stint in the Windy City, Jerry served in the military during the Korean War. Stationed at the Brooke Army Medical Center, he was able to play service ball for the military powerhouse.

W	L	PCT	G	GS	CG	IP	H	BB	SO	SHO	ERA
0	0	—	5	0	0	2	5	6	1	0	22.50

Peter Harvey Daley, *Catcher*

Ted Williams was Daley's teammate in the late 1950s when the Splendid Splinter was at the end of his terrific career. Pete would then spend a year with the Kansas City A's before he played with the expansion Washington Senators in 1961. Before Daley made his major league debut, he served in the armed forces during the Korean War. Stationed overseas in the Pacific Theatre, Daley served at Eta Jima and participated in the Japan Logistical Command Baseball Tournament. His squad was defeated in the tournament by the Camp Drake team that boasted the likes of Bob Speake and Herb Plews.

G	R	H	2B	3B	HR	RBI	BB	SO	SB	AVG	Slug
391	93	259	49	8	18	120	87	187	2	.239	.349

Bennie Daniels, *Pitcher*

A decent pitcher for the Pirates and Senators of the late 1950s and early 1960s, Daniels was an adequate back-of-the-rotation starter. Before Bennie threw his first pitch with the Pirates, he was drafted for military service during the Korean War. He served with the 1st Division Artillery and was shipped overseas. While on foreign ground, Daniels was able to play some service ball when it didn't conflict with his military duties.

W	L	PCT	G	GS	CG	IP	H	BB	SO	SHO	ERA
45	76	.372	230	139	26	997	1,004	383	471	5	4.44

Gerald Lee Davie, *Pitcher*

Davie pitched briefly with his hometown Tigers in 1959, which was the extent of his major league career. He missed the 1953 and 1954 seasons to military service during the Korean War.

W	L	PCT	G	GS	CG	IP	H	BB	SO	SHO	ERA
2	2	.500	11	5	1	37	40	17	20	0	4.14

Michael Lynn Davison, *Pitcher*

Mike was the pitching sensation in Giants training camp during the 1966 season. With Mike poised to make the Giants' Opening Day roster, San Francisco had to alter its plans when Davison was inducted into the military before the season began. During instructional league play, Mike paced all Giants pitchers in strikeouts and looked to be a lock to make the team before Uncle Sam had other ideas. He was inducted into the army. The Giants, however, had hopes that his tour wouldn't last long and that he'd receive an early discharge because of an arthritic condition Mike had. But the condition didn't prevent him from serving, and he was lost through the 1968 season.

W	L	PCT	G	GS	CG	IP	H	BB	SO	SHO	ERA
3	5	.375	32	0	0	38	48	22	23	0	6.39

David Albert DeBusschere, *Pitcher*

Better known for his time in the NBA, the tall DeBusschere played and coached basketball from 1962 to 1974. His baseball career was short-lived, as he pitched in two seasons for the White Sox. He missed the 1964 season to military service but was later rejected by the armed forces because he was too tall.

W	L	PCT	G	GS	CG	IP	H	BB	SO	SHO	ERA
3	4	.429	36	10	1	102	85	57	61	1	2.91

Lawrence Edward Dierker, *Pitcher*

The former ace of the Houston Astros and later their manager and broadcaster, Dierker pitched for the Astros for thirteen years. He tossed a no-hitter against the Montreal Expos on July 9, 1976, a feat many Hall of Fame pitchers never accomplished. An extremely intelligent man, Dierker missed time in 1967 to service with Company B, 2nd Battalion of the 143rd Infantry, 36th Division of the Texas Army National Guard. He spent his basic training time in Fort Ord, California. Just two years after his stint in the armed forces, Dierker became a 20-game winner.

W	L	PCT	G	GS	CG	IP	H	BB	SO	SHO	ERA
139	123	.531	356	329	106	2,334	2,130	711	1,493	25	3.30

Arthur John Ditmar, *Pitcher*

One of the many players to have purchased a ticket on the Kansas City to New York express, Ditmar was traded to the Yankees when he became too good for the Athletics. Later in his career, when he was no longer good enough for the Yankees, he made a return trip to Kansas City. Ditmar was a solid pitcher who could log innings out of the rotation or chew them up as a middle relief pitcher. During his five-year stint with the Yankees, he played for four AL pennant-winnings teams.

Before he made his major league debut with the Athletics, Art served in the military during the Korean War. In 1951, Ditmar was a private first class at Fort Jackson, with military duties as a clerk in the personnel division. While stationed at Fort Jackson, military life was kind to the right-hander. He tacked on fifteen pounds of muscle while training with Uncle Sam's fighting forces. Later, Ditmar was reassigned to Camp Atterbury, where he served with the 31st Infantry Division. While stationed at Camp Atterbury, Art was able to play his share of service baseball.

W	L	PCT	G	GS	CG	IP	H	BB	SO	SHO	ERA
72	77	.482	287	156	41	1,267	1,237	461	552	5	3.99

Henry John "Dutch" Dotterer, *Catcher*

A back-up catcher for four seasons with the Reds and one with the expansion Senators of 1961, Dotterer came from a baseball family. When Dutch was serving with the army in the Korean War, he was property of the Reds, who also employed his father, also named Dutch. The Reds then signed Dutch Junior's kid brother Tom, which gave the Reds three Dotterer gentlemen in their ranks.

G	R	H	2B	3B	HR	RBI	BB	SO	SB	AVG	Slug
107	27	74	15	0	5	33	35	44	0	.247	.348

Joseph Vann Durham, *Outfield*

Durham got his start with the old Chicago American Giants of the Negro Leagues after Jackie Robinson had broken the color line. The Negro Leagues at the time were of a low minor league caliber, and any player with talent, like Durham, was quickly snatched up by a major league team. He made his major league debut with the Baltimore Orioles in 1954 but would spend the next two years in the United States Army as an MP.

As soon as Durham had reached the majors, his career was put on hold to help out Uncle Sam. Drafted into the armed forces, Durham ventured off to the army and took his basic training and AIT to learn the duties of a military police officer. Shipped overseas to Germany, Joe was able to play some service ball while stationed at Stuttgart. A star on the basketball court as well as the ball diamond, Durham was a top athlete for the Seventh Army. He was able to take advantage of the old European scenery while over there. Durham said, "When I went to Germany, I had a chance to tour a lot of places and various countries that I had heard of behind the Iron Curtain. So I saw some war-damaged buildings and it was like a history lesson for me."

But Durham's time in the MP Corps wasn't all baseball, basketball and history lessons. As a military police officer, his duties entailed law enforcement, security and crowd and traffic control. Stationed at Stuttgart, where the winters can be unbearable, the duties of an MP didn't cease when Mother Nature became unfriendly. Recalling his work at Stuttgart, Durham said, "I didn't pull too much duty, but I did work that winter, directing traffic at Robinson Barracks. It was just outside of Stuttgart and the temperatures were anywhere from thirty-five to forty below zero at times. And I was out there directing traffic, which got a little tough in those conditions."

The tough conditions of military life have a tendency to bring soldiers closer together. They build a camaraderie the likes of which folks in the civilian sector could never understand. Soldiers are exposed to men and women of various walks of life and learn from one another. Where else can a young high school graduate from Yakima befriend a coal miner's son from Nanty-Glo, Pennsylvania? The ball diamond perhaps, but such acquaintances are built more often in the armed forces. Durham said, "In the military you meet guys from all over the country and you work with them, you eat with them and you sleep in the same barracks. The camaraderie in the military is something you never forget."

G	R	H	2B	3B	HR	RBI	BB	SO	SB	AVG	Slug
93	25	38	2	0	5	20	20	50	1	.188	.272

Carl Robert Duser, *Pitcher*

Duser appeared in only three games at the major league level with the Kansas City A's. The southpaw served in the military during the Korean War before he made his major league debut.

W	L	PCT	G	GS	CG	IP	H	BB	SO	SHO	ERA
1	1	.500	3	2	0	8	19	3	5	0	7.88

Arnold Carl Earley, *Pitcher*

A serviceable left-handed relief pitcher for the Red Sox during the 1960s, Earley missed some minor league action to military service during the Korean War.

W	L	PCT	G	GS	CG	IP	H	BB	SO	SHO	ERA
12	20	.375	223	10	1	381	400	184	310	0	4.49

Don Lee Erickson, *Pitcher*

Erickson's major league career consisted of a cup of coffee with the 1958 Phillies. Before he made the majors, Don served in the military during the Korean War. In the U.S. Army, Erickson pitched for a service ballclub named the Lackland Warhawks.

W	L	PCT	G	GS	CG	IP	H	BB	SO	SHO	ERA
0	1	.000	9	0	0	12	11	9	9	0	4.50

Samuel Esposito, *Utility Infielder*

A longtime reserve infielder with the Chicago White Sox, Sammy spelled some rather noteworthy stars during his major league career. He served as a backup for Luis Aparicio, Nellie Fox, Billy Goodman and Jerry Lumpe. Sammy was inducted into the army in August of 1953 and was discharged in May of 1955.

G	R	H	2B	3B	HR	RBI	BB	SO	SB	AVG	Slug
560	130	164	27	2	8	73	145	127	7	.207	.227

Darcy Rae Fast, *Pitcher*

With a better name for a pitcher than, say, Bob Walk, Fast was signed by scout George Freese, a former third baseman for the Pittsburgh Pirates. Fast appeared in six games for the 1968 Chicago Cubs and lost the 1969 season to service in the Army Reserves.

W	L	PCT	G	GS	CG	IP	H	BB	SO	SHO	ERA
0	1	.000	6	1	0	10	8	8	10	0	5.40

Frank Fernandez, *Catcher*

A weak-hitting reserve catcher, Fernandez missed a portion of the 1967 season to the Army Reserves. He made 727 plate appearances in his career, first with his hometown Yankees and later with the Oakland Athletics, Washington Senators and Chicago Cubs.

G	R	H	2B	3B	HR	RBI	BB	SO	SB	AVG	Slug
285	92	145	21	2	39	116	164	231	4	.199	.395

Donald Hugh Ferrarese, *Pitcher*

Although he towered over such ballplayers as Rabbit Maranville and Buster Caton, Don was nicknamed "Midget" because he was shorter than the big pitchers that characterized baseball in the 1950s. Baseball 1950s-style was a much different animal than the game today. Back then, players had to supplement their income with an off-season job, and Don did that with the Thompson Electric Store in Walnut Creek. A clerk in the offseason and a pint-sized pitcher during the summer, Don was forced to give up both jobs when his draft notice came through.

Inducted into the army during the Korean War, Ferrarese was shipped overseas and was stationed on the sunny islands of Hawaii. Don worked at the Tripler Army Hospital and was able to stay in baseball shape by pitching for a service team called the Waikiki Surfers. After he was discharged, Don went to camp where he impressed old-timer Mel Harder. The former Cleveland star said, "He's fast. His fastball is fast, his curve's fast, and his slider's fast." The quick little southpaw made his major league debut with the 1955 Orioles and had a solid career as a long relief pitcher and spot starter.

W	L	PCT	G	GS	CG	IP	H	BB	SO	SHO	ERA
19	36	.345	183	50	12	507	449	295	350	2	3.99

Eduardo Figueroa, *Pitcher*

The first Puerto Rican-born pitcher to win 20 games in the major leagues, Figueroa served briefly in the military during the Vietnam War. Eduardo made his debut with the 1974 Angels and enjoyed his best years with the Yankees in the late 1970s.

W	L	PCT	G	GS	CG	IP	H	BB	SO	SHO	ERA
80	67	.544	200	179	63	1,310	1,299	443	571	12	3.51

James Leroy Finigan, *Second Base/Third Base*

Finigan was a rookie sensation for the Philadelphia A's in 1954 but two shifts the following season burst his bubble. First, the A's relocated to Kansas City; secondly, they moved Jim from third base to second. The Rookie of the Year runner-up in 1954, Finigan struggled in 1955 and never regained his form. Before his major league debut, Jim served in the U.S. Army during the Korean War at Fort Leonard Wood, Missouri, and played service ball for a team called the Hilltoppers.

G	R	H	2B	3B	HR	RBI	BB	SO	SB	AVG	Slug
512	195	422	741	17	19	168	190	176	8	.264	.367

Gene Arlan Fodge, *Pitcher*

A terrific natural athlete, Fodge was equally skilled on the football field as he was on the diamond. Gene, who spent one year at the major league level with the 1958 Cubs, served with the U.S. Marines during the Korean War. Stationed at the El Toro Marine Base, Gene played service ball—baseball, basketball and football. A star pitcher on the base's baseball squad, he might have been even better as the team's quarterback. After his career, Fodge enjoyed attending his grandchildren's sporting events. All seven of the kids followed Gene to the pitcher's mound.

W	L	PCT	G	GS	CG	IP	H	BB	SO	SHO	ERA
1	1	.500	16	4	1	40	47	11	15	0	4.73

Richard Nevin Folkers, *Pitcher*

A left-handed relief pitcher during the 1970s, Folkers pitched for the Mets, Cardinals, Padres and Brewers. The southpaw was a reliable set-up man who bridged the gap between the starters and the closer. Before Rich made his major league debut, he served with the Marine Reserves during the Vietnam War. His unit was activated in 1969, and Rich missed an entire season of baseball to military duty. Many ballplayers in the service were able to play baseball throughout their hitch with Uncle Sam in previous wars, but most ballplayers drafted for service during Vietnam kept their ball gloves in the closet.

Folkers reported to the Marine Recruit Depot at San Diego for training. He was assigned to a combat attachment unit and his training was nothing but serious business. Attached to the 7th Howitzer Battery, Folkers spent his time in the Marine Corps preparing for war; he hardly ever picked up a baseball. Near the end of his stint, when he was close to his discharge, Rich pitched a little service ball at San Diego and noticed he had some rough edges he needed to address. He said, "I was a little wild but not bad considering the amount I've pitched."

W	L	PCT	G	GS	CG	IP	H	BB	SO	SHO	ERA
19	23	.452	195	28	5	422	416	170	242	0	4.12

Theodore Henry Ford, *Outfield*

A former first-round pick who never did make good at the major league level, Ford had an interruption in his minor league career that cost him some valuable seasoning time. Unlike many young baseball prodigies that have continuous game action before they reach the majors, Ford was inducted into the service during the Vietnam War. When he could have been honing his skills in preparation for his callup to the Majors, Ted was engaged in warfare in the Vietnam jungles. When the Indians called him up in 1970, he hardly resembled the first-round pick he was a few years before.

G	R	H	2B	3B	HR	RBI	BB	SO	SB	AVG	Slug
240	66	156	26	2	17	68	51	134	7	.219	.333

Edward Charles "Whitey" Ford, *Pitcher*

Arguably the most famous pitcher in New York Yankees history, Ford missed two years to service in the armed forces during the Korean War. Whitey still remains the career leader in innings pitched, wins, strikeouts and shutouts in Yankees history — by a comfortable margin in most categories. During his stint in the military, Ford served at Fort Devens and also managed a service all-star team.

W	L	PCT	G	GS	CG	IP	H	BB	SO	SHO	ERA
236	106	.690	498	438	156	3,171	2,766	1,086	1,956	45	2.74

John Patsy "Tito" Francona, *Outfield*

A fine outfielder during his playing days, Tito is the father of current Red Sox manager Terry Francona. A gifted natural hitter who could reach solid batting averages and hit with modest power, Tito enjoyed a journeyed career. He played with nine major league teams. Before Francona made his major league debut with the 1956 Orioles, he served in the United States Army at Fort Benning, Georgia.

Like many athletes inducted into the service during the Korean War, Tito played a lot of baseball. Stationed at Fort Benning, known for its airborne school, Tito was on an installation baseball club. He led his team to the Third Army Championship before he was discharged in August of 1955. Although he played plenty of baseball at Fort Benning, Tito wanted some action against fast company and ventured to Colombia in order to play winter ball. While with the Colombian team, Tito played under former major leaguer Bootnose Hofmann, who mentored the young Francona and helped him become a dynamo during 1956 spring training. Tito raved about Bootnose, saying, "He helped me with everything. My hitting. My fielding. He's sure a great fellow."

G	R	H	2B	3B	HR	RBI	BB	SO	SB	AVG	Slug
1,719	650	1,395	224	34	125	656	544	694	46	.272	.403

Lawrence Herbert French, *Pitcher*

One of the top southpaws in the years before World War II, French was denied 200 career wins because he lost the last couple years of his career to the war. French, who possessed excellent control, quit baseball after his discharge due to age. He then opted to return to the military and became a career soldier. For more on French, see his listing in the section on World War II.

W	L	PCT	G	GS	CG	IP	H	BB	SO	SHO	ERA
197	171	.535	570	383	198	3,152	3,375	819	1,187	40	3.44

Owen Lacey Friend, *Second Base*

A utility infielder whose best position was second base, Friend missed the 1951 and 1952 seasons to service in the Army Medical Corps. Owen played for five different major league clubs in as many years while getting by with his ability to handle numerous posts.

G	R	H	2B	3B	HR	RBI	BB	SO	SB	AVG	Slug
208	69	136	24	2	13	76	55	109	2	.227	.339

William John Froats, *Pitcher*

A southpaw, Froats appeared in just one major league game and kept the opposition from stomping on home plate during the contest. Bill, who attended the University of Notre Dame, was drafted during the Korean War and was stationed at Camp Breckinridge.

W	L	PCT	G	GS	CG	IP	H	BB	SO	SHO	ERA
0	0	—	1	0	0	2	0	2	0	0	0.00

Robert Mitchell Garber, *Pitcher*

Garber had a cup of coffee with the 1956 Pirates in his lone major league activity. Before he was summoned to Pittsburgh, Bob was a star in the service ranks during the Korean War. Stationed in Alaska with the 196th Regimental Combat Team at Fort Richardson, Bob was the team's ace pitcher. His commanding officer wrote a letter home that praised Garber, which read: "Our ace is none other than Bob Garber. He is averaging 17 strikeouts a game. Bob is a sergeant first class and a really fine soldier."

W	L	PCT	G	GS	CG	IP	H	BB	SO	SHO	ERA
0	0	—	2	0	0	4	3	3	3	0	2.25

Ronald Wayne Garrett, *Third Base*

Garrett, a longtime New York Mets third baseman, posted a solid 28-to-31 walk-to-strikeout ratio in his abbreviated 1971 campaign. The abbreviation was due to serving in the Army National Guard. During his tenure in the guard, Garrett was stationed at Fort Leonardwood, Missouri, as a clerk. Packing his baseball gear along for the ride, Garrett was dismayed to learn that the installation was without baseball facilities. Never much of a hitter for average, Garrett was known for his selective eye at the plate, allowing him to draw more walks than strikeouts.

G	R	H	2B	3B	HR	RBI	BB	SO	SB	AVG	Slug
1,092	438	786	107	22	61	340	561	529	38	.239	.341

Paul Robert Giel, *Pitcher*

Giel missed the 1956 and 1957 seasons to the military after he was inducted into the army. A solid relief man for the New York Giants prior to leaving for the war, Giel served with the 7th Army at Germany with the rank of lieutenant. While Giel was serving overseas, his Giant teammates relocated to San Francisco, and Paul rejoined them in 1958. He was sent to the Pirates in 1959 and pitched for their championship club of 1960. After his baseball career was over, Giel served as the athletic director at the University of Minnesota.

W	L	PCT	G	GS	CG	IP	H	BB	SO	SHO	ERA
11	9	.550	102	11	0	240	249	148	145	0	5.40

Roy William Gleason, *Outfield*

Compared to Frank Howard when he was in the minor leagues, Gleason certainly had the build to place fear in the heart of any pitcher he faced. A devastating power threat, Gleason's blasts were of the Mantle variety. However, Roy had a glaring weakness. There were years in the minors when it looked like he was about to put it all together and become the next Howard, but he'd also have seasons where his batting average would level out around the dismal .150 line. Gleason never did reach his baseball potential, but he had an interruption no prospect would desire when he saw heavy combat action during the Vietnam War.

Gleason had already reached the majors at the time he was drafted into service and was trying to fight his way back. The Dodgers employed him briefly as a pinch-runner and scare tactic, given his immense size. But Roy left the Dodgers and ventured into Uncle Sam's fighting forces. He took his boot camp at Fort Polk, Louisiana, where he trained to be an infantryman. After basic training Roy was assigned to Company A, 3rd Battalion, 39th Infantry of the 9th Division, known as the Fighting Falcons. The Fighting Falcons were shipped overseas and served in the combat regions of Vietnam.

Gleason had been lucky through his first eight months in Vietnam until the worm turned. A sergeant and a squad leader, Gleason took the point on a mission when they were hit by the enemy. An unexploded artillery shell, booby trapped by the Vietcong, was detonated and wounded Roy while killing ten of his soldiers. Shrapnel from the shell penetrated Sergeant Gleason's left leg and wrist. Gleason said, "I didn't even know I was hit until I saw the blood. It was a funny feeling. I thought it would be more painful, but it just began to ache a bit. I wasn't thinking so much of myself as about the rest of the squad. I wasn't badly hurt."

The injuries were severe enough that Roy was removed from the frontlines and sent to an army hospital. While recuperating at Camp Drake, Sergeant Gleason still had baseball on his mind. He said, "I threw a few grenades and tossed around an old ball in my spare time. My baseball training helped, particularly when it came to running, throwing those grenades, and even diving head-first when trouble started." Mustered out of the service, Sergeant Gleason was awarded the Purple Heart, Bronze Star and the Army Commendation Medal for his heroics. But what was foremost on his mind was his unit. The Fighting Falcons sent 80 boys into battle at Vietnam and only two returned home without injuries.

G	R	H	2B	3B	HR	RBI	BB	SO	SB	AVG	Slug
8	3	1	1	0	0	0	0	0	0	1.000	2.000

Charles Francis "Chuck" Goggin, *Utilityman*

A solid hitter at the major league level despite not having a position, Goggin was tried out at second base and the outfield and even caught a game. Although Goggin only racked up 99 at-bats at the highest level, he hit just under the coveted .300 mark. Chuck played pieces of three seasons in the majors with the Pirates, Braves and Red Sox. Before he made his debut with the 1972 Pirates, Goggin was in the middle of heavy combat action in Vietnam.

A member of the U.S. Marine Corps, Goggin patrolled the jungle regions of Vietnam with his unit. His squad came under heavy fire on several occasions, and Chuck was hit while in the line of duty. Wounded, Chuck was removed from the frontlines and treated. Awarded the Purple Heart, Goggin never did speak about his Vietnam injuries to writers. A modest man, Chuck was awarded the Vietnamese Cross of Gallantry, the Bronze Star and the Presidential Unit Citation to accompany his Purple Heart. As a rookie with the 1972 Pirates, the VFW honored Chuck before a game, and he played by the script when he knocked in the winning run with a walk-off hit.

G	R	H	2B	3B	HR	RBI	BB	SO	SB	AVG	Slug
72	19	29	5	0	0	7	10	21	0	.293	.343

David Allan Goltz, *Pitcher*

Most major league teams get upset when their players report late for spring training, but the Twins had to subdue their anger when Dave was a late arrival for camp in 1970. The year prior, he spent the entire season in the military and was held back from early spring action due to his military commitments. A tall right-hander, Dave enjoyed a solid career at the major league level spent predominately with his hometown Twins.

W	L	PCT	G	GS	CG	IP	H	BB	SO	SHO	ERA
113	109	.509	353	264	83	2,039	2,104	646	1,105	13	3.69

Charles Perry Gorin, *Pitcher*

A veteran of World War II, Gorin enlisted in the Navy Reserves after the Second World War and was called back to service for the Korean War. With his reserve unit activated, Gorin was shipped to the Pensacola Pre-Flight School where he conducted physical training. For more on Gorin, see his listing in the section on World War II.

W	L	PCT	G	GS	CG	IP	H	BB	SO	SHO	ERA
0	1	.000	7	0	0	10	8	9	12	0	3.60

Rodney Blaine Graber, *Outfield*

Graber had a cup of coffee with the 1958 Cleveland Indians. Before his major league sojourn, Rod served in the armed forces during the Korean War. Graber was able to play some service ball with a team called the Military District of Washington Colonials. But baseball played second fiddle to army training. A photograph circled the country, courtesy of the Associated Press, which showed Rod and fellow ballplayer Johnny Antonelli engaged in simulated combat maneuvers. They were training in house-to-house combat at A.P. Hill Camp near Bowling Green, Virginia, simulating an invading force attempting to recapture a village.

G	R	H	2B	3B	HR	RBI	BB	SO	SB	AVG	Slug
4	0	1	0	0	0	0	1	2	0	.125	.125

Milton Edward Graff, *Second Base*

Although Graff played in only pieces of two seasons with the Kansas City A's, he had a lengthy career in baseball. After he was done as a player, Milt joined the Pirates organization and became a coach and executive for the club. During the Korean War, Graff served with the U.S. Army.

G	R	H	2B	3B	HR	RBI	BB	SO	SB	AVG	Slug
61	16	28	4	3	0	10	15	10	2	.179	.244

Richard Benjamin Gray, *Utility Infielder*

Capable of filling in anywhere on the infield, Gray offered some solid pop for the Dodgers and Cardinals of the late 1950s. He missed some minor league seasoning time to service in the armed forces during the Korean War.

G	R	H	2B	3B	HR	RBI	BB	SO	SB	AVG	Slug
124	43	73	7	6	12	41	33	52	4	.239	.420

William Henry Greason, *Pitcher*

Greason was a pitcher in the Negro Leagues during the Second World War. He left the diamond during the great conflict and joined the U.S. Marine Corps. After his discharge, Bill returned to the Negro Leagues and wasn't part of the mass exodus to the major leagues after Jackie Robinson and the Dodgers broke the color barrier. Instead, Bill remained in the Negro Leagues until he was summoned by the Marines again for duty during the Korean War.

During Bill's military hitch in the Korean War, most baseball executives failed to take notice of Greason. One sergeant did, who recommended him to the Okalahoma City club. The sergeant watched Bill tame Dodgers star Don Newcombe in a service contest by a 1–0 score, which spurred him to inform his pal with the Okahoma City ball team. When Bill joined the integrated minor leagues, he became a star. The sports editor for a paper in Oklahoma City wrote, "How Greason came out of the Marine Corps unnoticed by the majors I'll never know. He joined the club the last day of July and practically pitched the team into the playoffs."

After his hot stint in Oklahoma City, major league teams took notice, and it was reported that both the Yankees and Red Sox offered Oklahoma City $100,000 for Bill. He would eventually catch on with the St. Louis Cardinals and was given a brief trial in 1954. He struggled with his command and lasted only three games at the highest level. After baseball, Greason became a pastor in Alabama, where he still lives to this day.

W	L	PCT	G	GS	CG	IP	H	BB	SO	SHO	ERA
0	1	.000	3	2	0	4	8	4	2	0	13.50

Leonard Charles Green, *Outfield*

Green was inducted into the army before he set foot on a major league diamond. During the Korean War, Lenny was stationed at Fort Carson with the 5th Army. While at Fort Carson he was able to play some service ball with Zack Monroe. The duo was named to the 5th Army All-Star team in 1954. After his discharge, Lenny made the Majors in 1957 with the Orioles. A swift outfielder with a keen batting eye, Green played through the 1968 season, when he was a member of his hometown Tigers.

G	R	H	2B	3B	HR	RBI	BB	SO	SB	AVG	Slug
1,136	461	788	138	27	47	253	368	260	78	.267	.379

Douglas Lee Griffin, *Second Base*

The Red Sox's regular second baseman on their American League pennant-winning team of 1975, Doug was a sound infielder during the 1970s. Before Griffin made his major league debut, he spent some time in the military during the Vietnam War. Doug was shipped overseas with the U.S. Navy and was stationed at Hawaii. While serving on the islands, he was able to stay in baseball shape by playing service ball for his SUBPAC 5 squad.

G	R	H	2B	3B	HR	RBI	BB	SO	SB	AVG	Slug
632	209	524	70	12	7	165	158	204	33	.245	.299

Robert Anton Grim, *Pitcher*

The most unlikely of Rookie of the Year Award winners, Grim wasn't even in organized ball the year before he won the coveted award. Instead, Grim was a Marine at Camp Lejeune, North Carolina. After his discharge from the U.S. Marine Corps, Grim went to spring training with the Yankees in 1954 and was the talk of the Grapefruit League. He won a job with the New Yorkers out of spring training and led the squad with 20 wins during the regular season.

W	L	PCT	G	GS	CG	IP	H	BB	SO	SHO	ERA
61	41	.598	268	60	18	759	708	330	443	4	3.62

Richard Morrow Groat, *Shortstop*

Upon completion of college, Dick Groat was a highly sought-after commodity. A star basketball player at the collegiate level, Groat played two seasons in the NBA before he made baseball his permanent trade. A star shortstop, arguably the best not in the Baseball Hall of Fame, Groat led the National League in batting the year the Pirates shocked the world when they beat the heavily favored Yankees in the 1960 Fall Classic. During his stint in the military, Groat served at Fort Belvoir and played on the basketball team.

G	R	H	2B	3B	HR	RBI	BB	SO	SB	AVG	Slug
1,929	829	2,138	352	67	39	707	490	512	14	.286	.366

Conrad George Grob, *Pitcher*

A minor league veteran, Grob may have been hurt greatly by the Rule V Draft. While Grob was a young pitcher freshly discharged from the army, the Washington Senators plucked Conrad in the draft and held on to him throughout the 1956 season. Clearly overmatched after two seasons of pitching against servicemen, Grob struggled that year and was never again summoned to the majors. During the Korean War, Conrad served at Camp Roberts, California, where he played service ball and married his sweetheart.

W	L	PCT	G	GS	CG	IP	H	BB	SO	SHO	ERA
4	5	.444	37	1	0	79	121	26	27	0	7.86

Harvey Haddix, *Pitcher*

Famous for pitching the "Greatest Game Ever Lost," Haddix was one of the most dominant pitchers of his era. A left-handed strikeout artist, "Kitten" once pitched a perfect game through nine innings with his Pirates, but his mates couldn't get him a run and he lost the contest in extra innings. Usually saddled to some rather weak teams, it's a testament to his worth as a pitcher that he ended his career with an above even winning percentage.

One of the first players inducted into service during the Korean War, Haddix was on the threshold of the majors when Uncle Sam called his name. When he was drafted, his skipper, Marty Marion, lamented, "We lost a good prospect to the army in Haddix." Inducted into the army, Kitten, so nicknamed because he resembled star left-hander Harry "The Cat" Brecheen, served at Fort Dix, New York. When Haddix was discharged in the summer of 1952, the Cardinals wasted little time in bringing him to St. Louis. He started six games at the end of the season. The following year, he established himself as one of the game's elite pitchers when he paced the team with 20 wins, led the National League with six shutouts, and finished fourth in strikeouts.

W	L	PCT	G	GS	CG	IP	H	BB	SO	SHO	ERA
136	113	.546	453	285	99	2,235	2,154	601	1,575	20	3.63

Douglas William Hansen, *Pinch Runner*

Used as a pinch runner in three games by the 1951 Indians, Hansen missed some valuable seasoning time in the minors to service during the Korean War.

G	R	H	2B	3B	HR	RBI	BB	SO	SB	AVG	Slug
3	2	0	0	0	0	0	0	0	0	—	—

Billy Womble Harrington, *Pitcher*

Harrington's major league career consisted of three seasons, all with the Athletics. He made his debut with the Philadelphia A's in 1953 — he missed the majority of the campaign to military service — and returned to the Athletics, who had relocated to Kansas City in 1955.

W	L	PCT	G	GS	CG	IP	H	BB	SO	SHO	ERA
5	5	.500	58	2	0	117	114	67	40	0	5.00

James Michael Hegan, *First Base/Outfield*

Mike, the son of catching legend Jim Hegan, enjoyed a rather nomadic major league career. A first baseman with minimal power must keep his suitcases packed, and is not unfamiliar with taking it on the heel and toe. The younger Hegan made his debut with the Yankees in 1964 and spent the entire 1965 season in the minors. He returned in 1966, right when the Yankees hit rock bottom, and spent the 1967 season teaching Mickey Mantle the fine art of first base. He had to take leave of educating Mantle during the season when his National Guard unit out of Stoughton was activated for duty. He served six months on active duty, stationed at Fort Dix, and returned to baseball worse for wear. Concerning his early struggles after his military discharge, Hegan said, "I didn't join the club until mid-May because of the army and I haven't seen enough good pitching to catch up."

G	R	H	2B	3B	HR	RBI	BB	SO	SB	AVG	Slug
965	281	504	73	18	53	229	311	489	28	.242	.371

Thomas Kenneth Heintzelman, *Utility Infielder*

The son of former major league pitcher and World War II veteran Ken Heintzelman, Tom played briefly in the majors as a reserve infielder. He made his debut with the 1973 Cardinals, and after playing in the minors a few more years, he was given his last trial with the Giants in the late 1970s. During the Vietnam War, Tom spent some time in the U.S. Army.

G	R	H	2B	3B	HR	RBI	BB	SO	SB	AVG	Slug
90	17	34	5	0	3	12	14	22	0	.243	.343

Phillip Winston Hennigan, *Pitcher*

A decent right-handed relief pitcher throughout his major league career, Hennigan was playing minor league ball at Reno when he was inducted into the armed forces. His trip to Reno in the minors proved beneficial as he met and wed Carolyn Martini before his military induction. The pitcher from Texas was drafted into the U.S. Army and was shipped overseas where he saw combat action in the jungles of Vietnam. With Uncle Sam's fighting forces, Hennigan served a fourteen-month hitch in hostile territory. He saw plenty of the enemy while patrolling the Mekong Delta as a sergeant in the army. When Phil was discharged, he returned to Reno and to a young infant son he had never met. Able to pick up where he left off in life, Phil returned to the Reno ball club for a spell and was nicknamed "Combat" on account of his tour in Vietnam. Combat Hennigan made the majors with the Indians in 1969 and collected 26 saves in a five-year major league career.

W	L	PCT	G	GS	CG	IP	H	BB	SO	SHO	ERA
17	14	.548	176	2	0	280	267	133	188	0	4.27

Raymond Ernest Herbert, *Pitcher*

Herbert made his major league debut with his hometown Tigers in 1950. Although he struggled initially in Detroit, he had success after his military stint with the Kansas City A's and the Chicago White Sox. A 20-game winner in 1962, Herbert could log plenty of innings—four times exceeding 220 innings of work—and posted his highest total with Kansas City in 1960 when he reached 257. But the right-hander missed some action when he served during the Korean War.

When Herbert received his draft notice, he was a member of the Tigers rotation and started the 1951 season 4–0 with a 1.38 ERA. Denied his chance to continue on his brilliant start, Ray was inducted into the armed forces after five starts. The draft notice didn't bother him; he simply viewed it as a bump in the road. Herbert said, "Back then, it never really occurred to us, having our major league careers interrupted to military service. It was just a part of life, you know, people getting drafted into service. At my age, I knew it was only a matter of time until I got drafted, so I didn't really think too much about it. When you go, you'd say that you were going to serve your two years the best you can."

Herbert's father drove him down to the Reception Center at Battle Creek, Michigan, just a short drive from their home. Ray would never leave Battle Creek, as it became his duty station. Although he was able to play service ball, he wasn't fortunate like the fellows down at Fort McPherson or over on the coast at Fort Ord who played on stocked rosters and had plenty of talent around them. At Battle Creek, Herbert was the star attraction of the Reception Center team and the competition was lacking. He suffered greatly after his return to the Tigers because he played against very weak competition for two years. Herbert said, "It was difficult returning to the majors even though I played a lot in the army. You know, I was pitching against high school kids and none of them were very good. So I didn't stay sharp."

W	L	PCT	G	GS	CG	IP	H	BB	SO	SHO	ERA
104	107	.493	407	236	68	1,883	2,000	571	864	13	4.01

William Troy Herriage, *Pitcher*

Herriage spent one season at the major league level with the last-place 1956 Kansas City A's. Managed by Hall of Famer Lou

Boudreau, the A's lost more than 100 games that season, and Art Ditmar was the only pitcher with more than ten wins. Before Herriage made the major leagues he served in the armed forces during the Korean War. As a PFC in the U.S. Army, Troy attended a baseball clinic with major leaguer J.W. Porter at Camp Stoneman that was conducted by Senators skipper Chuck Dressen and his lieutenant, Cookie Lavagetto.

W	L	PCT	G	GS	CG	IP	H	BB	SO	SHO	ERA
1	13	.071	31	16	1	103	135	64	59	0	6.64

Dorrel Norman Elvert "Whitey" Herzog, *Outfield*

Hall of Fame skipper Whitey Herzog was a good fourth outfielder during his playing days who could fill in as a starter in the pasture. His fame wouldn't come until later. He managed the Royals through their successful run in the 1970s and then guided the St. Louis Cardinals to a few World Series appearances. However, before Herzog set foot in a major league dugout, he served in the armed forces during the Korean War. A soldier in the U.S. Army, Herzog played service ball while stationed at Fort Leonard Wood, Missouri.

G	R	H	2B	3B	HR	RBI	BB	SO	SB	AVG	Slug
634	213	414	60	20	25	172	241	261	13	.257	.365

William Joseph Hicks, *Outfield*

Hicks was a reserve outfielder and pinch-hitter for a couple of years in the early 1960s. A member of the expansion Washington Senators of 1961, he would move on the Mets in 1963 — their second year of existence. They weren't much better in 1963 than they were in their hapless season of 1962. Before Joe played in the Majors, he served in the armed forces and missed the 1956 and 1957 seasons to military service.

G	R	H	2B	3B	HR	RBI	BB	SO	SB	AVG	Slug
212	41	92	11	3	12	39	29	73	3	.221	.349

James William Holt, *Outfield/First Base*

Holt enlisted in the U.S. Army during the mid 1960s and was shipped overseas to Germany. He was able to play some service ball while stationed in the European Theatre with hopes of a tryout with Organized Baseball after his discharge. When Jim was sent home, he received a tryout with the Kansas City A's and looked good to the team until they learned he still had some service time left. Holt said, "I went to spring training with the A's in 1965. I still had six months left to go in the service and I couldn't get out early because of Vietnam. So the A's told me to wait until next year."

With half a year of army duty left, Holt was rejected by the A's. He took their advice and "waited," but the wait didn't lead to a stint with the A's. Instead, Jim made his major league debut with the Twins in 1968. The left-handed-hitting, right-handed-throwing Holt spent many years with the Twins as a reserve outfielder/bat-off-the-bench before he gave the A's another shot. Sent to the A's in 1974, Jim played a couple of seasons with the team that casually rejected him years before.

G	R	H	2B	3B	HR	RBI	BB	SO	SB	AVG	Slug
707	174	428	64	10	19	177	93	166	8	.265	.352

Kenneth Dale Holtzman, *Pitcher*

A vastly underrated pitcher, Holtzman is the lesser-known Oakland star on a staff that boasted Catfish Hunter, Vida Blue and Rollie Fingers. During Oakland's three consecutive championship seasons, 1972 through 1974, Holtzman won 59 games for Charlie Finley's brigade — more than Blue and Fingers. Holtzman's military tenure was brief as he served only on the weekends in the Illinois National Guard during the 1967 baseball season.

W	L	PCT	G	GS	CG	IP	H	BB	SO	SHO	ERA
174	150	.537	451	410	127	2,867	2,787	910	1,601	31	3.49

Henry Franklin House, *Catcher*

After House's playing career concluded, the former backstop became a state legislator. Nicknamed "Pig," House was inducted into the army on April 12, 1952, and stationed at Fort Jackson. The left-handed-hitting receiver became Detroit's regular catcher after his return from the armed forces and finished third on the club in home runs his first season back. He caught 21-game-winner Frank Lary in 1956, as the "Yankee Killer" paced the AL in victories that season. He was later sent to the Kansas City Athletics, where he platooned with fellow former soldier Harry Chiti.

G	R	H	2B	3B	HR	RBI	BB	SO	SB	AVG	Slug
653	202	494	64	11	47	235	151	147	6	.248	.362

Arthur Joseph Houtteman, *Pitcher*

Dubbed "Hard Luck" Houtteman by the Detroit press, Art posted a 2–16 record for the Bengals in 1948. He received more run support in 1949, which allowed him to post an impressive 15–10 record. However, at the end of that season, Houtteman was involved in a severe auto accident in which he was read his last rites. Not given much of a chance to survive the ordeal, Houtteman showed immense personal courage and fully recovered to pace the Tigers with 19 wins the following season.

Houtteman left for the military two days after his marriage and served in the 169th Infantry Regiment of the 43rd Division. When he was inducted into the military, Art stated that he wanted to be treated as "just Joe Doakes" and desired no special treatment on account of his status as a major league baseball player. His base pay in the military at the time was just $80 a month, most of which was deferred to his wife. After he served the entire 1951 baseball season, Houtteman was medically discharged due to recurring injuries sustained in his 1949 automobile accident. He returned to the Tigers in 1952 and dropped a league-high 20 contests. The abysmal Tigers couldn't score any runs for any of their pitchers, as fellow Bengal hurler Virgil Trucks posted 19 losses while also pitching well for the poor offensive club.

W	L	PCT	G	GS	CG	IP	H	BB	SO	SHO	ERA
87	91	.489	325	181	78	1,556	1,646	516	639	14	4.14

Elston Gene Howard, *Catcher/Outfield*

When Howard came up with the Yankees in the mid 1950s after his military discharge, the natural catcher would have to shadow Hall of Famer Yogi Berra. But the Yankees soon found out that Elston Howard could play, and they needed to get him into the lineup. This was no problem for skipper Casey Stengel, the master of the platoon, who was obsessed with juggling his lineup. Ellie kept his catcher's mitt in his locker through his early years with the Yankees and wore an outfielder's glove. But once Yogi started to slow down, Howard was there to remove his catcher's mitt from his locker and put it to use.

A borderline Hall of Famer, Howard won an MVP Award during his career and was widely regarded as a top-flight catcher. Not only was he good defensively, his bat was stellar as well. But before Howard played with the Yankees, he created quite a controversy at Camp McCoy during the Korean War. In order to play more baseball, Elston requested to play off the installation for a semipro team in his free time. The post commander didn't see any harm in this and granted Ellie's wishes. However, when Howard's semipro outfit played the Camp McCoy team, Ellie and his non-soldier chums beat the Camp McCoy outfit handily. Supporters of the camp's athletic department wondered why their top player was allowed to play off post for a team on their schedule. The commanding officer saw the error of his ways and ordered Howard to play only for Camp McCoy.

G	R	H	2B	3B	HR	RBI	BB	SO	SB	AVG	Slug
1,605	619	1,471	218	15	167	762	373	786	9	.274	.427

Alan Thomas Hrabosky, *Pitcher*

One of baseball's noted "wild men," Al, known as "The Mad Hungarian," has made a career out of broadcasting. This bizarre southpaw made constant headlines in the St. Louis newspapers for his appearance, as the hurler sported a Fu Manchu and an unkempt mane of brown hair. During the 1971 season, the Mad Hungarian was one of only three major league players to serve in the military. He was in the Army Reserves and stationed at Fort Ord, California.

W	L	PCT	G	GS	CG	IP	H	BB	SO	SHO	ERA
64	35	.646	545	1	0	722	619	315	548	0	3.10

Richard Elde "Dick" Hyde, *Pitcher*

The forerunner for such star fireman as Dan Quisenberry and Kent Tekulve, Hyde was a submarine relief pitcher for the Senators of the late 1950s. The stopper enjoyed a solid career with Washington, but before he made his major league debut he missed the 1951 and 1952 seasons to military service.

W	L	PCT	G	GS	CG	IP	H	BB	SO	SHO	ERA
17	14	.548	169	2	0	298	273	137	144	0	3.56

Mike Warren Jackson, *Pitcher*

A wild left-handed relief pitcher, Mike pitched pieces of four seasons at the major league level with four different teams. Before his stint at the highest level, Jackson missed the 1966 and 1967 seasons to service in the military.

W	L	PCT	G	GS	CG	IP	H	BB	SO	SHO	ERA
2	3	.400	23	3	0	50	57	39	33	0	5.76

Raymond Arnold Jarvis, *Pitcher*

A decent young pitcher for the Red Sox in 1970, Jarvis looked poised to turn the page and achieve his potential. An arm injury derailed his career, however, and he was done by 1971. Before he made his major league debut, Jarvis spent the 1966 season in the U.S. Army.

W	L	PCT	G	GS	CG	IP	H	BB	SO	SHO	ERA
5	7	.417	44	12	2	116	122	57	44	0	4.66

Robert Dale Johnson, *Pitcher*

Although Bob Johnson missed the entire 1968 season to military service during the Vietnam War, it didn't adversely affect his pitching. The Mets called him up the next season and then made an ill-advised move when they traded him to Kansas City. With the second-year Royals, Johnson was a terror. The first good pitcher for the fledgling franchise, Bob was the first Royal pitcher to eclipse 200 strikeouts.

W	L	PCT	G	GS	CG	IP	H	BB	SO	SHO	ERA
28	34	.452	183	76	18	693	644	269	507	2	3.48

Richard Allan "Footer" Johnson, *Pinch-Hitter*

Footer had a cup of coffee with the 1958 Chicago Cubs. Before he made his major league debut, Johnson served in the military during the Korean War.

G	R	H	2B	3B	HR	RBI	BB	SO	SB	AVG	Slug
8	1	0	0	0	0	0	0	1	0	.000	.000

Robert Oliver Jones, *Outfield/First Base*

Jones spent a number of years with the Texas Rangers as a power bat off the bench. A fairly versatile ballplayer despite being left-handed, Jones could play the outfield and first base but was employed mostly as a pinch-hitter and occasional designated hitter. He broke in with the Rangers in 1974 before he was sent to the Angels. When he failed to make the grade, Bob ventured off to Japan to play overseas for a couple of seasons. When he returned stateside with the Rangers, Jones found his niche as a role player. He currently works in the Rangers organization as a minor league manager.

A teenager when he was inducted into the military during the Vietnam War, Jones was shipped overseas and saw heavy combat action. While fighting the Vietcong in the jungle, Jones sustained damage to his hearing courtesy of the battlefield noise, leaving him nearly deaf in one ear. When he returned to baseball after the war, teammates had to employ their loudest voice when coaxing Bob off a fly ball or pop-up.

G	R	H	2B	3B	HR	RBI	BB	SO	SB	AVG	Slug
314	35	133	17	0	20	86	50	117	5	.221	.348

Gordon Bassett Jones, *Pitcher*

A decent relief pitcher in the late 1950s with the Giants, Jones was with the team when it relocated to San Francisco. He would later pitch for the Orioles, A's and Houston Colt .45s. After his playing days, he coached for a time with Houston, which changed its name to the Astros. Before he made his major league debut,

Gordon served in the U.S. Coast Guard during the Korean War. Stationed at Alameda, Jones was able to play some service ball while in the military.

W	L	PCT	G	GS	CG	IP	H	BB	SO	SHO	ERA
15	18	.455	171	21	4	379	405	120	232	2	4.16

Ronald Lee Keller, *Pitcher*

Keller received a brief taste of the major leagues in parts of two seasons for the Minnesota Twins. He missed the majority of the 1968 season to service in the Army Reserves.

W	L	PCT	G	GS	CG	IP	H	BB	SO	SHO	ERA
0	1	.000	9	1	0	21	25	5	12	0	3.43

Harold Patrick Kelly, *Outfield*

Kelly was plucked out of the Twins' system by the Kansas City Royals in the expansion draft of 1969 and paced the Royals with 40 stolen bases. The fleet outfielder would go on to play for the White Sox in the early 1970s and fell into the wrong crowd, becoming a drug abuser. Kelly, who served a six-month stint in the U.S. Army in 1967, cleaned up his act and became a born-again Christian, founding the Life Line Ministries after his career in baseball was over. Prior to his death from a heart attack, one of Kelly's favorite stories was when he urged manager Earl Weaver to walk with the Lord; Weaver replied that he'd rather Kelly walk with the bases loaded.

G	R	H	2B	3B	HR	RBI	BB	SO	SB	AVG	Slug
1,385	620	1,147	189	35	76	418	588	768	250	.264	.377

Gerald Tennyson Kenney, *Utilityman*

Kenney made his debut with the Yankees in 1967 but spent the following year in the U.S. Navy. Summoned by Uncle Sam during the Vietnam War, Jerry left the Yankees shortly after he reached the highest level. Stationed overseas, Kenney played some service ball on the Hawaiian Islands with Red Sox second baseman Doug Griffin. When Kenney returned from his one-year hitch in the navy, skipper Ralph Houk, a decorated World War II veteran, liked the kid and worked Jerry into the lineup as much as possible. The swift St. Louis native played regularly at third base for the Yankees before they upgraded with the addition of Graig Nettles.

G	R	H	2B	3B	HR	RBI	BB	SO	SB	AVG	Slug
465	165	325	38	13	7	103	184	139	59	.237	.299

James Lester Kern, *Pitcher*

A nightmare on the hill for both opposing batters and his manager, Kern had an electric arm but a complete absence of control. The "Texas Tornado" was a power pitcher fireman during the 1970s and 1980s who tallied his fair share of saves. Standing at 6'5", Kern made for an imposing figure on the mound; when added with his wild, live arm, he was a certifiable night terror. Jim, known for hunting pigeons at Cleveland Stadium with his .22 rifle, served briefly in the military during the Vietnam War.

W	L	PCT	G	GS	CG	IP	H	BB	SO	SHO	ERA
53	57	.482	416	14	1	793	670	644	651	0	3.32

Leo Patrick Kiely, *Pitcher*

Kiely was inducted into the U.S. Army and stationed at Camp Kilmer. His Class 3-C status, due to a chronic bad back, couldn't keep him out of the military, as he served eleven months in the Far East. He missed two full seasons, the 1952 and 1953 campaigns, to military service but returned to the Red Sox in 1954. He was used exclusively out of the bullpen by skipper Pinky Higgins and enjoyed his finest season in 1958 when he paced the Sox with 12 saves.

W	L	PCT	G	GS	CG	IP	H	BB	SO	SHO	ERA
26	27	.491	209	39	8	523	562	189	212	1	3.37

Nelson Joseph King, *Pitcher*

Best known as an insightful broadcaster for the Pittsburgh Pirates in the 1960s and 1970s, King was a pretty fair relief pitcher during his playing days. Nellie put out fires for the Buccos in the mid 1950s. Tall and lanky, King missed two years of minor league action while he served in the military during the Korean War.

W	L	PCT	G	GS	CG	IP	H	BB	SO	SHO	ERA
7	5	.583	95	4	0	173	193	50	72	0	3.59

Joseph John Kirrene, *Third Base*

Kirrene's major league career was rather brief, but he did miss three full seasons to service in the U.S. Coast Guard. He made his major league debut with the 1950 White Sox — he went 1-for-4 in his only game that year. The next three seasons were lost to the military, and Joe returned to the Sox in 1954 to hit .304 in limited action.

G	R	H	2B	3B	HR	RBI	BB	SO	SB	AVG	Slug
10	4	8	1	0	0	4	5	3	1	.296	.333

Ronald Lee Kline, *Pitcher*

Kline served his country well. He wore fatigues when the need arose and made USO trips to greet wounded soldiers while he played baseball. Kline used to phone wounded soldiers' parents, keeping their next of kin abreast on how their son was doing. A solid major league pitcher for over seventeen years, Kline netted 108 career saves. During his stint in the U.S. Army, Kline was stationed at Camp Breckenridge, Kentucky, and Aberdeen, where he played baseball with pitcher Danny McDevitt.

W	L	PCT	G	GS	CG	IP	H	BB	SO	SHO	ERA
114	144	.442	736	203	44	2,078	2,113	731	989	8	3.75

Darold Duane Knowles, *Pitcher*

One of the top relief pitchers of the 1970s, Knowles was a member of Oakland's three consecutive World Series-winning teams from 1972–1974. Knowles lists his greatest thrill in baseball as recording the final out in the 1973 World Series.

During the Vietnam War, Knowles was a member of the Air National Guard. His unit was activated while he was a major league pitcher, and he split his military duties with his baseball career. Life as a two-career man drained the young southpaw fireman. Knowles said, "It was tough that first year because I played for the Senators during the night and went to the base during the day — so I was a worn-out puppy. I had to be on base at seven every morning, and we had a ballgame almost every night."

The baseball-military shuffle that Knowles was engaged in came to an end when he received orders to be shipped overseas. The left-handed fireman had to say goodbye to baseball when he was shipped to Japan. He said, "I was stationed at an airbase in Japan. I enjoyed the camaraderie I had with other guardsmen from around the country—we bonded a bit. They called us 'Fangs,' which was true. We were Federalized Air National Guardsmen and that was our nickname: FANGS."

While stationed overseas, the military made certain that Darold stayed in tip-top shape, but as a major league pitcher, he needed more specialized physical training. One of his guardsmen pals was a catcher and would take time to receive Knowles' offerings as part of his extra P.T. Knowles said, "I had a good friend over in Japan with me who I have to give a lot of credit to. He and I played catch every other day. He would catch me just like a bullpen session and that helped keep me in shape." When his two-year service hitch expired, Knowles returned to Washington and to a former war hero manager. Darold said, "You know, I've always read about guys like Ted Williams missing time to the military, and what's kind of funny was when I came back from the military he was my manager."

W	L	PCT	G	GS	CG	IP	H	BB	SO	SHO	ERA
66	74	.4711	765	8	1	1,092	1,006	480	681	1	3.12

Richard Jerome Kokos, *Outfield*

A power hitter with a short, compact build, Kokos swatted his first major league home run off the legendary Bob Feller. Kokos was a member of the St. Louis Browns when they switched locales to play in Baltimore as the Orioles. He was the top left-handed-hitting power slugger for the Browns of the early 1950s when he paced all portside swingers with 18 long balls in 1950. He missed the 1951 and 1952 seasons to service in the army. He served at the Brooke Army Medical Center with his St. Louis Browns teammate Owen Friend.

G	R	H	2B	3B	HR	RBI	BB	SO	SB	AVG	Slug
475	239	410	82	9	59	223	242	252	15	.263	.441

Alexander James Konikowski, *Pitcher*

The New York Giants lost their star center fielder, Willie Mays, to the war effort and a week later lost up-and-coming hurler Konikowski to the draft as well. Alex served his basic training at Indiantown Gap, Pennsylvania, and was assigned to the 5th Infantry upon completion of training. He played baseball at Fort Myer while in the service and returned to the Giants in 1954. His return to the major leagues was short-lived, as Konikowski credits Leo Durocher for his demise as a major leaguer. While riding on a train after a game, Konikowski defeated Leo the Lip in a game of cards, which infuriated the detestable manager, and he sent Alex packing soon thereafter.

W	L	PCT	G	GS	CG	IP	H	BB	SO	SHO	ERA
2	3	.400	35	1	0	49	58	29	20	0	6.98

Jerome Martin Koosman, *Pitcher*

A borderline Hall of Fame pitcher, Koosman was always overshadowed on those strong Mets teams by Tom Seaver. The pair gave New York fans one of the best righty-lefty duos in the game's history. But clubhouse friction led to Seaver's trade to Cincinnati, and afterwards the Mets became a second-division club. Koosman bore the brunt of the Mets' futility in 1978 when he went 3–15 despite solid peripheral stats. Saved the following year, Jerry won 20 games with the Twins despite the same kind of production he gave the lowly Mets. He would go on to win 222 games at the major league level.

It was by accident that Koosman even reached the major leagues. When he was spotted playing baseball, he wasn't tossing for a college campus or on the high school sandlots—he was in the military. Jerry was in the army when a soldier he worked with, whose father was employed by the Mets, was impressed by his pitching ability. The soldier tipped off his father and Jerry signed with New York after his discharge. During his stint in the army, Koosman served in Texas with a Hawk Missile unit that was shipped out to Vietnam after Jerry had fulfilled his military commitment.

W	L	PCT	G	GS	CG	IP	H	BB	SO	SHO	ERA
222	209	.515	612	527	140	3,839	3,635	1,198	2,556	33	3.36

Stephen Joseph Korcheck, *Catcher*

A reserve catcher for a handful of years with the Washington Senators, Korcheck was called to the military after he had made his major league debut. He took his basic training at Fort Jackson before he was assigned to Fort McPherson, Georgia. The southern army installations had an athletic system that Korcheck was wise to. He said, "General Edward Hickey was the Third Army Commander and somewhere along the way he made the decision that Fort McPherson would get all the baseball players, Fort Jackson would get the football players, and Fort Benning got the basketball players."

Stationed at Fort McPherson during the Korean War, Korcheck was part of a strong service team. On the same roster as the Washington catcher were Don Buddin, Norm Siebern, Al Spangler, Billy O'Dell, Vinegar Bend Mizell and a few other gents that made the major leagues. Named the manager of the ballclub, Korcheck had plenty of talent at his disposal, which made his task quite easy. Korcheck said, "I didn't do a lot of managing with all the major league players we had, but I made out the lineup card and said who was going to pitch, and that was about it."

Korcheck had no regrets about his time in the service. He said, "I just felt it was something you do if you're an American." Baseball was his orders and he got to play plenty of the sport while also working on his golf swing in a pseudo-security capacity. After Fort McPherson's golf shop was vandalized, Korcheck was summoned into General Hickey's office for some unusual orders. Korcheck said, "General Hickey called me and told me about the vandalism done at the golf shop and asked me if I would mind if they constructed an apartment there for me. He said that I could work in the shop during the day and conduct baseball drills at night. So I did, and I spent a little over a year living in the golf clubhouse. And I learned how to play golf there."

After his discharge, Korcheck returned to the Senators in a reserve capacity and essentially wasted away on the bench. After losing two years to the military, a young ballplayer would probably have been best served by a stint in the minors to play everyday and get back into baseball shape, but that's not how the Senators managed Korcheck. But his time with the Senators after his discharge helped him keep in touch with baseball crazed General Hickey. He said, "Any time he came to Washington during the summer, he'd call me and would attend a Senators game and then we'd have dinner. He was probably one of the nicest individuals I ever met. He was a three-star general, but you'd never know it, and there I was, a private, and just because of his love for baseball, we became good friends."

G	R	H	2B	3B	HR	RBI	BB	SO	SB	AVG	Slug
58	12	23	6	1	0	7	6	36	0	.159	.214

William John Koski, *Pitcher*

Bill Koski's major league career was rather brief and rather wild. He issued more free passes than innings worked during his lone season at the highest level. He saw his only major league action in 1951 as a nineteen-year-old with a poor Pirates club. He missed the next three years to service in the armed forces and was unable to return to the majors to clean up his poor statistics.

W	L	PCT	G	GS	CG	IP	H	BB	SO	SHO	ERA
0	1	.000	13	1	0	27	26	28	6	0	6.67

Daniel Kravitz *Catcher*

Usually a third-string catcher when he played in the majors, Danny was traded to the Kansas City A's from the Pirates during Pittsburgh's championship season of 1960. Kravitz missed minor league action to military service during the Korean War.

G	R	H	2B	3B	HR	RBI	BB	SO	SB	AVG	Slug
215	52	130	22	7	10	54	35	64	1	.236	.355

Theodore Rodger Kubiak, *Middle Infielder*

A switch-hitting infielder, Kubiak always seemed to be blocked at the major league level. With the A's he was stuck behind Bert Campaneris and John Donaldson, and was later dealt to the Brewers where he rotated between short and second with Roberto Pena and Gus Gil. He played behind Toby Harrah and Dave Nelson in Texas, and returned to Oakland to back up Campy once again. He finished out his career as a San Diego Padre, where he backed up Doug Rader and Tito Fuentes. Kubiak missed a portion of the 1968 season to service with a National Guard unit based in Yakima.

G	R	H	2B	3B	HR	RBI	BB	SO	SB	AVG	Slug
977	238	565	61	21	13	202	271	272	13	.231	.289

John Charles Kucks, *Pitcher*

Kucks was a pretty fair starting pitcher for the powerhouse Yankees of the late 1950s. Like many Yankees that were no longer needed, he was traded to the Kansas City A's in 1959 in a deal that brought Hector Lopez to the Bronx. Kucks, whose last name is pronounced "cooks," last pitched at the major league level with the 1960 Athletics. The right-hander from Hoboken made an immediate splash in the majors by turning heads directly after his military discharge.

While in the service during the Korean War, Johnny was sent overseas to the European Theatre. Attached to the 311th Engineers, Kucks was able to play some service ball in the Rhine Sector. In a game against the 2nd Armored Division at Kaefertal, he fanned a dozen batters. A star in the service ranks, Kucks was discharged and went to spring training with the Yankees in 1955. He impressed everyone at camp and made the Opening Day roster. Dismayed by the Yankees' knack for acquiring talent, Harry Grayson quipped, "The Yankees even use the army as a farm team."

W	L	PCT	G	GS	CG	IP	H	BB	SO	SHO	ERA
54	56	.491	207	123	30	938	970	308	338	7	4.10

William Henry Landis, *Pitcher*

Tall and slender, Landis made his major league debut with the 1963 Kansas City Athletics. It took Bill another four years before he returned to the majors— with the Red Sox — and saw a portion of his baseball career interrupted to service in the armed forces in 1968.

W	L	PCT	G	GS	CG	IP	H	BB	SO	SHO	ERA
9	8	.529	102	7	0	170	154	91	135	0	4.45

James Henry Landis, *Outfield*

A terrific center fielder the slim Landis was quick on the bases, spelled death to flyballs, and also had some modest pop in his stick. Landis' debut was pushed back a couple of years due to service in the army during the Korean War. Jim was stationed at Fort Ord, California, and played service ball under catcher J.W. Porter. Fort Ord was a military powerhouse and Landis was a large reason why. But the club had more than enough strength to contend when Jim was given orders elsewhere.

Landis was transferred to Alaska where he played service ball when the weather permitted with the Pioneers of Camp Richardson. Although he was no longer surrounded by the likes of Bob Lillis and J.W. Porter, Landis turned the Pioneers into contenders in the Alaskan Service League. In 1955, Jim was the leading hitter in the Alaskan armed forces Baseball Tournament. After his discharge, Landis returned to baseball and would eventually win five Gold Glove Awards.

G	R	H	2B	3B	HR	RBI	BB	SO	SB	AVG	Slug
1,346	625	1,061	169	50	93	467	588	767	139	.247	.375

Don James Larsen, *Pitcher*

Larsen may never have company as the only pitcher to throw a perfect game in World Series play. He achieved this legendary feat in 1956, and no pitcher has done it since. Before his World Series heroics, Larsen served in the military during the Korean War. He was an unusual find for the Browns in 1953. After two years of military duty, Don joined the Browns for spring training and pitched like a seasoned veteran. However, the highest classification of ball Don played before the military was Class A ball. But skipper Marty Marion and pitching coach Harry Brecheen liked what they saw and Larsen made his debut that year.

W	L	PCT	G	GS	CG	IP	H	BB	SO	SHO	ERA
81	91	.471	412	171	44	1,549	1,442	725	849	11	3.78

Frank Strong Lary, *Pitcher*

One of the most hated men in Yankees history, Lary was so adept at turning back the Bronx Bombers that he earned the nickname "Yankee Killer." A terrific pitcher for the better part of a decade in Detroit, Frank tallied more than 20 career shutouts and was one of the best pitchers for WHIP of his generation. He missed some minor league action to service in the U.S. Army during the Korean War. While wearing khaki, Lary was stationed at Camp Atterbury and was able to play plenty of service ball. After his discharge, Frank fired a no-hitter in the minors.

W	L	PCT	G	GS	CG	IP	H	BB	SO	SHO	ERA
128	116	.525	350	292	126	2,162	2,123	616	1,099	21	3.49

Charles Richard Lau, *Catcher*

A catcher during his playing days, Lau spent the bulk of his playing career as a backup or in platoon situations. Lau was a decent ballplayer but he was a legend as a hitting instructor. He took a raw kid named George Brett and turned him into a Hall of Fame ballplayer — perhaps the best third baseman of all-time. After his stint with the Royals, Charley caught on with the White Sox and was praised for his work with Harold Baines. But before Lau taught Brett and Baines, he served in the army during the Korean War. Charley was stationed at Fort Lewis where he played service ball with long ball hitter Dick Stuart and pitcher Conrad Grob.

G	R	H	2B	3B	HR	RBI	BB	SO	SB	AVG	Slug
527	105	298	63	9	16	140	109	150	3	.255	.365

Vernon Sanders Law, *Pitcher*

A hero of the Pirates' championship season of 1960, Law — known as "The Deacon" — nailed down 162 career wins. He made his debut with the 1950 Pirates, a last-place team, and stuck with the organization through thick and thin. His last major league game was played in 1967, and between his debut and final bow, Vern only wore Pirate black and gold. Law had yet to establish himself at the major league level when he was drafted into the armed forces prior to the 1952 baseball campaign. He missed the 1952 and 1953 seasons to military service and was shelled to the tune of a 5.50 ERA upon his return. He took his lumps that year, learned from his mistakes, and became a reliable starter in 1955. With Bob Friend and Roy Face, Law was instrumental in turning the Pirates around late in the 1950s. He won 14 games in 1958, 18 in 1959, and became a 20-game winner in the 1960 season — every Pirate fan's favorite year.

W	L	PCT	G	GS	CG	IP	H	BB	SO	SHO	ERA
162	147	.524	483	364	119	2,673	2,833	597	1,092	28	3.76

William Francis "Spaceman" Lee, *Pitcher*

To those readers who are familiar with the Spaceman, it may come as a shock to find out that the zany southpaw was once in the employ of Uncle Sam. A typical odd southpaw, the lefty — who became a modest star during the Red Sox's postseason of 1975 — missed a portion of the 1970 baseball season to service in the armed forces. A noted soft-tosser, Lee prided himself on keeping the batter off-balance — as off-balance as he generally was.

W	L	PCT	G	GS	CG	IP	H	BB	SO	SHO	ERA
119	90	.569	416	225	72	1,944	2,122	531	713	10	3.62

Kenneth Karl Lehman, *Pitcher*

One of the few players to have enlisted in the service during the Korean War rather than wait for a draft notice, Lehman left his PCL club to sign up with Uncle Sam. The southpaw from the Pacific Northwest took his basic training stateside and was then shipped overseas to the Pacific Theatre. Stationed in Japan, Ken served with the 4th Infantry Division. Although he was a grunt, Lehman was able to play some service ball in the Far West. He once tossed a no-hitter in Japan against an aggregation of troops from Camp Sendai. After his discharge, Ken would have a decent career as a fireman for the Brooklyn Dodgers.

W	L	PCT	G	GS	CG	IP	H	BB	SO	SHO	ERA
14	10	.583	134	13	2	264	273	95	134	0	3.82

James Robert Lemon, *Outfield*

A mountain of a man, Lemon was one of the most feared Sluggers of the 1950s. With his unusual, erect stance, Lemon generated immense power with his upper body. Not one to stride into a pitch or employ a high leg kick like Mel Ott, Lemon just let muscle do its job. And his muscles clubbed many home runs for the Washington Senators. He blasted 26 homers in 1958, tattooed 33 the following year, and smacked 38 in 1960. When the Senators moved to Minnesota and became the Twins, Lemon suffered from injuries and had to surrender his crown as the club's top Slugger to a kid named Killebrew.

Jim had a couple of brief trials with the Indians in the early 1950s and had his career interrupted by service in the army during the Korean War. The brawny Slugger was inducted into the army on January 18, 1951, and spent two years flexing for Uncle Sam on military lots. Assigned to Fort Meade, Lemon was named the installation's player-manager and led a decent service team. After his discharge, Cleveland gave him another trial in 1953 but lacked patience with the free-swinging Slugger. He was then brought into the Senators' fold and after a high strikeout total start, he became more selective and thus a top power hitter in the American League.

G	R	H	2B	3B	HR	RBI	BB	SO	SB	AVG	Slug
1,010	446	901	121	35	164	529	363	787	13	.262	.460

Robert Albert Lennon, *Outfield*

A Triple Crown winner in the minor leagues, Lennon was given three trials in the majors but failed to impress. The Giants called Bob up twice and the Cubs gave him his final look in 1957. He missed some minor league service time to the military during the Korean War. He served in the U.S. Army and was discharged as a junior non-commissioned officer.

G	R	H	2B	3B	HR	RBI	BB	SO	SB	AVG	Slug
38	5	13	2	0	1	4	5	26	0	.165	.228

Robert Perry Lillis, *Utility Infielder*

Bob "The Flea" Lillis was a scrappy little infielder who extracted the most out of his modest tools. During the Korean War, Bob served at Fort Ord, California, and played service ball with J.W. Porter. After his discharge, Lillis joined the Dodgers and played sparingly on the West Coast. His playing time became more substantial after the 1962 expansion. He caught on with the newly formed Houston Colt .45s and was a regular on their infield. After his career, he managed the Houston Astros a few seasons.

G	R	H	2B	3B	HR	RBI	BB	SO	SB	AVG	Slug
817	198	549	68	9	3	137	99	116	23	.236	.277

Stuart Carlton Locklin, *Reserve*

Locklin played briefly at the major league level with the Indians in the late 1950s. During the Korean War, Stu served in the Air Corps and played some service ball.

G	R	H	2B	3B	HR	RBI	BB	SO	SB	AVG	Slug
25	4	4	1	0	0	0	3	5	0	.167	.208

William Loes, *Pitcher*

Cut from the same cloth as Dizzy Dean, Loes was offered $6,000 as an amateur by the New York Giants, to which he replied, "I can triple that for you at the gate the first game I pitch." Loes is now best remembered for uttering this famous quote, concerning why he never desired to be a twenty-game winner: "If you win twenty games one year, then they expect you to do it every year."

He missed the entire 1951 season to service in the army, as Billy was attached to the 514th Quartermaster Subsistence Company at Fort Devens. Loes had this to say about serving in the army: "I put on weight in the army and it helped my speed. A good curve makes a good fast one possible." He received a hardship discharge because his father was ill and unable to provide for the family. Billy returned to the Dodgers in 1952 and pitched them to a World Series.

W	L	PCT	G	GS	CG	IP	H	BB	SO	SHO	ERA
80	63	.559	316	139	42	1,190	1,135	421	645	9	3.88

Joseph Paul Lonnett, *Catcher*

Lonnett played four years in the majors and served as a backup to some pretty fair backstops. While with the Phillies he had to spell Stan Lopata and Andy Seminick. At the time Joe was inducted into the army for the Korean War, Phillies owner Bob Carpenter called him "the outstanding young prospect in our organization." But Lonnett would lose two valuable years to the military. Stationed at Fort Eustis, Lonnett played in the All-Army Baseball Tournament with Willie Mays.

G	R	H	2B	3B	HR	RBI	BB	SO	SB	AVG	Slug
143	22	54	8	0	6	27	40	74	0	.166	.246

Arturo Lopez, *Outfield*

The only Puerto Rican-born major league ballplayer to serve during the Korean War, Lopez was a diminutive slap-hitting outfielder for the 1965 Yankees. Well before his major league debut, Arturo served in the navy near the end of the war.

G	R	H	2B	3B	HR	RBI	BB	SO	SB	AVG	Slug
38	5	7	0	0	0	0	1	6	0	.143	.143

John Lee Lowenstein
Outfield/First Base

Lowenstein had a fine career with the Indians and Orioles as an outfielder/pinch-hitter. With a keen batting eye, John was an ideal bat-off-the-bench who could work the count and draw a walk or hit for authority, as indicated by his 116 career home runs. He debuted with the 1970 Indians, but the year prior the UC Riverside alum was with the U.S. Marine Corps. A member of the Marine Corps Reserves, John's unit was activated in 1969 and he spent six months on active duty.

G	R	H	2B	3B	HR	RBI	BB	SO	SB	AVG	Slug
1,368	510	881	137	18	116	441	446	596	128	.253	.403

Duane Frederick "Duke" Maas, *Pitcher*

A swing pitcher who could start or work in long relief, Maas made his major league debut with the 1955 Tigers. Just before he reached Motown, Duke served in the military during the Korean War.

W	L	PCT	G	GS	CG	IP	H	BB	SO	SHO	ERA
45	44	.506	195	91	21	734	745	284	356	7	4.19

William Paul Macdonald, *Pitcher*

Macdonald played only two seasons in the major leagues. He received his initial trial in 1950 with the Pirates. As a rookie, he tied with Cliff Chambers for the team lead in shutouts. He spent the next two seasons in the military and returned to Pittsburgh to toss his final seven major league innings.

W	L	PCT	G	GS	CG	IP	H	BB	SO	SHO	ERA
8	11	.421	36	21	6	160	150	96	64	2	4.67

Garry Lee Maddox, *Outfield*

One of the greatest defensive center fielders of all-time, Maddox won the Gold Glove Award for his position eight times. Hall of Famer Ralph Kiner, when employed as a play-by-play man, once quipped, "Two-thirds of the earth is covered by water, the other third is covered by Garry Maddox." Noted for his glove, Garry was no slouch in the batter's box either. A career .285 hitter, Garry eclipsed 300 doubles, 100 home runs and 240 stolen bases. But his baseball stardom almost failed to take shape. He quit the game and joined the army during the Vietnam War.

Unlike many players that were drafted into service, Maddox felt like his baseball career had stalled and that he'd never climb the minor league chain. He said, "I was leading the league in strikeouts and errors and I hated those thirteen-hour bus trips. It got so I disliked baseball. So I quit and joined the army." Maddox enlisted in the Army Engineers and began to change from a self-professed "150-pound weakling who couldn't hit a curveball" into a soldier. He was later shipped out to the Vietnam region where he would serve guard duty.

In Vietnam, Maddox's main duties centered on guard watch. Of his stint in Vietnam, Garry said, "I had perimeter guard duty. That's about as close to the action as you can get without actually being in it. We got fired on a lot of times." A corporeal in the Army Engineers, Garry was stationed near the Chu Lai district of Vietnam. While he played ball, Garry always kept a beard, and many writers claimed that he kept the facial whiskers because his skin suffered a reaction from chemicals he was exposed to in Vietnam. After his discharge, the stronger Maddox returned to baseball and made his debut with the Giants in 1972. He would later spend a dozen years as a star patrolling center field with the Phillies.

G	R	H	2B	3B	HR	RBI	BB	SO	SB	AVG	Slug
1,749	777	1,802	337	62	117	754	323	781	248	.285	.413

David Pledger Madison, *Pitcher*

Like Ted Williams and Jerry Coleman, Madison also served in two separate wars — he missed minor league action to World

War II and major league service time to the Korean War. Dave missed the entire 1951 season to service in the Army Reserves, where he served as a lieutenant, and returned to the Browns in 1952. His last major league action came in 1953 with the Detroit Tigers.

W	L	PCT	G	GS	CG	IP	H	BB	SO	SHO	ERA
8	7	.533	74	6	0	158	173	103	70	0	5.70

James Robert Magnuson, *Pitcher*

A left-handed pitcher who appeared briefly with the White Sox and Yankees in the early 1970s, Magnuson missed some minor league action to military service during the Vietnam War.

W	L	PCT	G	GS	CG	IP	H	BB	SO	SHO	ERA
2	7	.222	36	10	0	102	113	41	40	0	4.59

Robert Edward Malkmus, *Utility Infielder*

An Independence Day baby, Malkmus was a solid infielder who could fill in at any position. Bobby broke in with the Braves in their 1957 championship season but was shipped off to the Senators after the campaign. Following his discharge from the service during the Korean War, Bobby was sent to Evansville where he made the league's all-star team.

G	R	H	2B	3B	HR	RBI	BB	SO	SB	AVG	Slug
268	69	123	15	5	8	48	38	90	3	.215	.301

Frank James Malzone, *Third Base*

Although Malzone was born in the Bronx, it would be difficult to find a Red Sox fan that despised the man. Frank grew up in Yankee country but became a star with Boston. The fine third baseman made six All-Star teams and won three Gold Glove Awards over the course of his career. But before his career began, Malzone served in the army during the Korean War. Stationed in Hawaii, Corporeal Malzone played some service ball on the islands when it didn't conflict with his military duties.

G	R	H	2B	3B	HR	RBI	BB	SO	SB	AVG	Slug
1,441	647	1,486	239	21	133	728	337	434	14	.274	.399

James Daniel Mangan, *Catcher*

In 1952, Mangan was called up by the Pirates and made his major league debut. Jim served as a third-string catcher behind Joe Garagiola and Clyde McCullough. He missed the entire 1953 season to service in the navy and was discharged midseason in 1954 and farmed out to Hollywood before he returned to the Pirates at the end of the year. Mangan saw his last major league action in 1956 with the Giants.

G	R	H	2B	3B	HR	RBI	BB	SO	SB	AVG	Slug
45	5	9	0	0	0	5	9	18	0	.153	.153

Joseph Emanuel Margoneri, *Pitcher*

The southpaw pitched two years at the major league level with the Giants—the last two seasons they were stationed in New York. Before he was drafted for military duty during the Korean War, Joe was considered a top pitching prospect in the Giants chain. Margoneri served at the Brooke Army Medical Center and played some service ball with Marv Rotblatt.

W	L	PCT	G	GS	CG	IP	H	BB	SO	SHO	ERA
7	7	.500	36	15	3	126	132	70	67	0	4.29

Fred Daniel Marolewski, *First Base*

Fred appeared in one game at the major league level and didn't record a time at bat. During the Korean War, Marolewski served in the Pacific Theatre and was stationed for a time in Yokohama where he played baseball and basketball.

G	R	H	2B	3B	HR	RBI	BB	SO	SB	AVG	Slug
1	0	0	0	0	0	0	0	0	0	—	—

Clarence Westly "Cuddles" Marshall, *Pitcher*

The unusually nicknamed pitcher made his major league debut directly after World War II. He was a rarity for the Korean War in that his major league career was practically over when he joined the service for the latter campaign. During the Korean War, Cuddles served overseas with the 11th AAA Battalion and was able to play some service ball at Salzburg as well as other locales in the ETO.

W	L	PCT	G	GS	CG	IP	H	BB	SO	SHO	ERA
7	7	.500	73	15	1	185	216	158	69	0	5.98

Alfred Manuel "Billy" Martin, *Second Base*

A solid, scrappy second baseman, Martin's claim to fame is interpreted differently by many people. Some people may state that Martin is famous for winning a World Series MVP Award, while the more acerbic might tell you that Billy's career is more notable for managing the Yankees ... on several occasions. Billy was initially placed at the helm in the Bronx in 1975 and managed New York until he was ousted in the middle of the 1978 season. He returned the following year, when he replaced his former replacement, Bob Lemon, only to be issued his walking papers after the year. Dick Howser took over in 1980 and guided the Yankees to an AL East pennant before he was replaced for his troubles. Billy came back in 1983 to guide the Bronx Bombers to a third-place finish and was replaced by Yogi Berra the following year. When Yogi was canned, Martin replaced him as skipper. His last stint as Yankees manager came in 1988, one year before his death.

Billy Martin served in the military briefly prior to his induction for the Korean War. He was released from service in that instance due to a hardship discharge in order to support his mother, siblings and ill stepfather. When Martin was inducted in 1954, he was giddy regarding his prior military stint on record, which allowed him to serve a lesser stint than other soldiers. He said, "I've got five months in already, if they allow for this, maybe I'll be able to get out in about thirteen months." Martin was initially assigned to Fort Ord, California, where he trained before a reassignment to Camp Carson, Colorado, where his main chore was KP duty.

Upset that he received "more severe" treatment than other soldiers, Martin's perceived injustice prompted a letter to be written to politician William E. Russ. Russ served as the head of a subcommittee that looked into the treatment of athletes in the military. In Martin's letter to Russ, Billy wrote, "When stationed at Fort Ord, I would have greatly enjoyed trying out for the camp baseball team. I found, however, that I was not to be permitted to try out for that team although a place on the ball team was supposedly available to any soldier on the post who could successfully fill the position after qualifying through the tryouts." Martin finished his letter to Russ by writing, "I do not wish this letter interpreted as a complaint or belly-aching. I do wish to emphasize that my treatment has never been preferential in any way or form."

Martin remained in the military but returned earlier than previously expected to the Yankees due to accumulated leave time. The wiry second baseman hit .300 upon his return to the majors and finished his career a lifetime .257 hitter.

G	R	H	2B	3B	HR	RBI	BB	SO	SB	AVG	Slug
1,021	425	877	137	28	64	333	188	355	34	.257	.369

Thomas Eugene "Gene" Martin, *Pinch-Hitter*

Martin was given only a nine-game trial with the Senators in 1968. The bulk of his playing time came in Japan, where he starred as a power hitter deluxe. Gene missed two years in the minors to military service during the Vietnam War.

G	R	H	2B	3B	HR	RBI	BB	SO	SB	AVG	Slug
9	1	4	1	0	1	1	0	1	0	.364	.727

John Albert "Buck" Martinez, *Catcher*

A backstop who spent a great deal of time platooning at the major league level, Martinez has found a second calling as a highly respected and informative broadcaster. Buck made his major league debut with the expansion Kansas City Royals in 1969, and missed a portion of that season in order to finish his education. In his second year at the highest level, Buck served four and a half months in the army stationed at Fort Benning during his stint under Uncle Sam. Martinez played with the Royals through 1977 before he left the club for the Milwaukee Brewers. He ended his playing career in 1986 with the Toronto Blue Jays and later managed the Canadian club for two years.

G	R	H	2B	3B	HR	RBI	BB	SO	SB	AVG	Slug
1,049	245	618	128	10	58	321	230	419	5	.225	.343

Robert Gordon Martyn, *Outfield*

An outfielder who spent three years with the Kansas City A's, Martyn served in the armed forces during the Korean War. Shortly after his discharge, the wiry Martyn was optioned to Norfolk, where he swatted three home runs in one game. The headline in the paper the following day read, "Army Training Helps" make Bob a Slugger.

G	R	H	2B	3B	HR	RBI	BB	SO	SB	AVG	Slug
154	35	94	12	11	3	35	37	56	2	.263	.383

Gordon Richard Massa, *Catcher*

When one looks in the record books, jaws drop when coming across the career batting average of Gordon Massa. He appeared in only eight major league games before his military induction but hit a resounding .412 in that brief trial. A big, strong left-handed-hitting catcher, Massa was a prospect in the Cubs chain when he served two stints in the military. A national guardsman his first tour with the military, Massa was in the reserves when he was summoned for the Berlin callup.

Massa's stint in the military was quite brief. Assigned to the Special Services, his duties revolved around athletics and playing baseball. During his first tour, he was stationed at Fort Ord, California, and when he was summoned again, he spent his second callup at Fort Bragg. Massa regarded his time in the military as doing his bit for Uncle Sam, regardless how little was asked of him. He said, "I felt that it was something that was necessary. You know, I was doing what the country needed me to do."

G	R	H	2B	3B	HR	RBI	BB	SO	SB	AVG	Slug
8	2	7	1	0	0	3	4	5	0	.412	.471

Edwin Lee Mathews, *Third Base*

Still regarded by some as the greatest third baseman of all-time, Eddie certainly hit circles around his position peers. One of the few players to hit in the excess of 500 home runs without any artificial help, Eddie was an instant major leaguer after his navy discharge. He served at the San Diego Naval Training Station with Boston teammate Pete Whisenant. The duo rejoined the Braves after their discharge in 1952. Mathews was with the club during its last year in Boston, its entire tenure in Milwaukee, and the Braves' first year in Atlanta.

G	R	H	2B	3B	HR	RBI	BB	SO	SB	AVG	Slug
2,391	1,509	2,315	354	72	512	1,453	1,444	1,487	68	.271	.509

Willie Howard Mays, *Outfield*

Arguably the greatest all-around talent in baseball history, Mays could do it all. He could hit for power as well as average; he could run, catch and throw with the best of them. Despite his current legacy, the story of Willie Mays could have been more legendary had he not missed a year and a half to the military. Given the time that Mays missed, it is feasible that he could have broken Babe Ruth's home run record before Hank Aaron. Then again, fate also robbed Ted Williams of several years, therefore Mays could have been chasing the Splendid Splinter rather than the Bambino.

Mays was still a rather raw product in 1952 when he was summoned by his draft board. At the time he was drafted, Mays was hitting a feeble .236 through 34 games. The year before, at the age of 20, Willie stroked the apple at a .274 clip with 20 long balls. Although he was in the midst of a rut when Uncle Sam beckoned his presence, Mays was quickly becoming a star and exploded into superstardom upon his return from the service, when he won the National League batting title and swatted 41 home runs.

Willie Mays was on the Montgomery, Alabama, draft board, and when his number was called, he applied for deferment on grounds of dependency. However, his draft board denied his appeal, and Mays accepted his call to arms. As a rookie soldier, Mays said, "Maybe I'll learn some baseball in the army."

Despite his draft board denying his deferment request, he put in another hardship discharge request while stationed at Fort Eustis. Mays claimed no fewer than nine dependents at Fort Eustis, but again, Mays was denied discharge on grounds that his "dependency did not exist to a degree that warrants a discharge." He remained in the army and was able to play some service ball. During a ballgame for the army, Willie suffered a fracture in his left foot and his injured appendage was set in a cast for five weeks. Upon his discharge, Mays said, "Playing ball in the army has definitely helped keep me in condition."

G	R	H	2B	3B	HR	RBI	BB	SO	SB	AVG	Slug
2,992	2,062	3,283	523	140	660	1,903	1,463	1,526	338	.302	.557

Roger Morton McCardell, *Catcher*

McCardell had a cup of coffee with the 1959 Giants, which was the extent of his major league career. He missed valuable minor league action to service in the armed forces during the Korean War.

G	R	H	2B	3B	HR	RBI	BB	SO	SB	AVG	Slug
4	0	0	0	0	0	0	0	0	0	.000	.000

Daniel Eugene McDevitt, *Pitcher*

Originally signed by his hometown Yankees, Danny was released by the team on account of his lack of control. He would eventually make good with the Dodgers and was on their first Los Angeles-based squad. Before McDevitt reached the major leagues, he served in the armed forces during the Korean War.

W	L	PCT	G	GS	CG	IP	H	BB	SO	SHO	ERA
21	27	.438	155	60	13	456	461	264	303	4	4.40

Donald John McMahon, *Pitcher*

One of the greatest relief pitchers of all-time, McMahon was arguably better than the recent crew of firemen inducted into the Baseball Hall of Fame. Don was a workhorse who logged 153 career saves when the stat didn't hold the weight it does now. He broke in with the Braves in 1957 and threw his last pitch with the 1974 Giants. Before Don put out his first major league fire, he served during the Korean War.

W	L	PCT	G	GS	CG	IP	H	BB	SO	SHO	ERA
90	68	.570	874	2	0	1,312	1,054	579	1,003	0	2.96

David Olin Melton, *Reserve*

Melton played briefly at the major league level with the Kansas City A's in the late 1950s. Before Dave was given his trial in western Missouri, he was a power-hitting outfielder in the lineup at Fort Ord, California, during the Korean War.

G	R	H	2B	3B	HR	RBI	BB	SO	SB	AVG	Slug
12	0	1	0	0	0	0	5	0	.111	.111

Lloyd Archer Merriman, *Outfield*

The casual baseball fan has heard of Ted Williams and the serious fan has heard of Jerry Coleman, but Lloyd Merriman's name rests on the tongues of but a few, even though he is forever linked with the two stars. Along with Williams and Coleman, Merriman was a pilot in both World War II and the Korean War, as the three ballplayers were "retread pilots." Williams was the only one of the trio who was an active major league ballplayer during World War II; both Merriman and Coleman were still in the bushes at that time. However, all three were legitimate major league ballplayers when the Korean War broke out.

Merriman made his major league debut with the 1949 Cincinnati Reds after a stellar football career at Stanford University. The All-America fullback was courted by professional football teams, but he accepted the Reds' offer upon graduation. Professional athletics was forced to the side when Merriman entered the armed forces as a Marine Corps pilot. When the Second World War concluded, Merriman returned to the diamond and played with the Reds from 1949 to 1951. He put his baseball career on hold once again when the Marine Air Corps summoned him for duty during the Korean War.

He held a reserve commission as a first lieutenant from World War II and was assigned to the Kaneohe Marine Corps Air Station. When he was asked about how he felt regarding his retread status, Merriman showed more concern for Williams and Coleman than he did for himself, stating, "Naturally, I'd like to have kept on with baseball. It's kind of a short life. It would not have made so much difference if I had been younger. (Merriman was 27 at the time.) But it isn't as tough on me as it is on Williams and Coleman. Especially Williams. He's older. He won't be going back to baseball. Jerry can go back, but it's going to be rough. He was just coming into his own."

When Merriman was shipped out to Korea, he found himself in the same squadron as Ted Williams. Together, the two baseball stars flew missions in the same outfit, as Merriman was an established Panther jet pilot. Even though Lloyd and Ted were unable to play baseball overseas, at the request of their commanding officer they entertained soldiers once in Korea with batting exhibitions. Lloyd flew 85 missions in seven months of service in Korea, where he was promoted to the rank of captain. At the time of his return to the States, Merriman had earned four Air Medals, with another four pending. Prior to his discharge, Merriman was awarded the Distinguished Flying Cross for his actions in Korea, as he flew more combat missions than any other athlete in the war.

His impending return to baseball posed problems for Merriman, saying, "My big problem is that I'm not established. If there are two of us trying for a position and the other guy has a better batting average, he gets the job. But I'll give 'em a battle when I get back."

To prepare himself for his return to baseball, Lloyd ventured south into Latin America for some winter league action. While playing ball in the southern reaches, Merriman said, "I want to be in top shape when I report to the Cincinnati Reds next spring. I know 1954 will be a do-or-die year for me in the majors." Despite his concern, Merriman found encouragement in Ted Williams, saying, "We had no chance to play baseball over there. The way Ted picked up the game again is encouraging to me."

As a 29-year-old, Merriman returned to the Reds but was unable to crack their outfield of Gus Bell, Wally Post and Jimmy Greengrass and served as a reserve all season. He hit .268 upon his return to the majors, but even more encouraging was his exceptional 10-to-23 strikeout-to-walk ratio. He played one final season in the major leagues before retiring.

G	R	H	2B	3B	HR	RBI	BB	SO	SB	AVG	Slug
455	140	291	64	12	12	117	126	124	20	.242	.345

Lloyd Wesley Merritt, *Pitcher*

Merritt pitched one season in the majors with his hometown Cardinals in 1957. Effective out of the bullpen, Lloyd saved seven games as a rookie. Before his major league debut, he served in the armed forces during the Korean War.

W	L	PCT	G	GS	CG	IP	H	BB	SO	SHO	ERA
1	2	.333	44	0	0	65	60	28	35	0	3.32

Robert Peter "Mickey" Micelotta, *Reserve*

Given two brief trials in the majors with the Phillies after his discharge from the service, Mickey was regarded as a weak hitter until he donned glasses.

G	R	H	2B	3B	HR	RBI	BB	SO	SB	AVG	Slug
17	2	0	0	0	0	0	1	1	0	.000	.000

Larry Don Miller, *Pitcher*

A left-handed long arm-spot starter, Miller pitched for the Dodgers and Mets in the mid 1960s. He missed two years to military service while still in the minors.

W	L	PCT	G	GS	CG	IP	H	BB	SO	SHO	ERA
5	14	.263	48	20	1	145	162	57	93	0	4.72

Norman Calvin Miller, *Outfield*

A longtime Houston Astro, Miller missed a piece of the 1967 baseball season to service in the armed forces. Norm was only 21 years old at the time of his military call-up and was able to play a full season in 1968. Rarely a regular player, Miller offered the Astros a decent left-handed bat off the bench and was also capable of filling in as an emergency catcher.

G	R	H	2B	3B	HR	RBI	BB	SO	SB	AVG	Slug
540	166	325	68	10	24	159	160	265	16	.238	.356

Rudolph Anthony Minarcin, *Pitcher*

A baseball player and butcher before his army induction for the Korean War, Minarcin was on the verge of making the majors when Uncle Sam called his number. When prospects for the upcoming season in 1952 were discussed, Rudy was initially mentioned until it was learned that he was inducted into the army. An Associated Press article read, "I see where Uncle Sam likes Minarcin, so he is out." Taken from the baseball ranks, Rudy was mustered into the armed forces on February 5, 1952.

Assigned to the army's transportation branch, Rudy served his time at Fort Eustis. While there, he was able to play some service ball with Willie Mays, Joe Lonnett and Chuck Churn, but an injury put an end to baseball and greatly restricted his military duties. While training to be a calisthenics instructor, Minarcin damaged his ACL and was out of commission for sixteen months. Doctors at the time didn't know how to operate on the ACL so rest was prescribed. After his discharge, Rudy made his debut with the 1955 Reds. He would also pitch for the Boston Red Sox of the late 1950s.

W	L	PCT	G	GS	CG	IP	H	BB	SO	SHO	ERA
6	9	.400	70	13	3	171	169	89	70	1	4.63

Donald Athey Minnick, *Pitcher*

A tall right-hander from Virginia, Minnick had a cup of coffee with the 1957 Senators. Before his major league sojourn, Minnick served in Korea with the 101st Airborne Division.

W	L	PCT	G	GS	CG	IP	H	BB	SO	SHO	ERA
0	1	.000	2	1	0	9	14	2	7	0	5.00

George Eugene Mitterwald, *Catcher*

Nicknamed "The Baron," Mitterwald was a good backstop in the 1970s with the Twins and Cubs. The Baron packed a decent amount of power in his bat. A member of the Army Reserves, Mitterwald's unit was activated during the Vietnam War for a brief stint. He was stationed at Fort Carson, Colorado, while he served on active duty.

G	R	H	2B	3B	HR	RBI	BB	SO	SB	AVG	Slug
887	251	623	93	7	76	301	222	607	14	.236	.362

Wilmer David "Vinegar Bend" Mizell, *Pitcher*

Wilmer Mizell came from the small town of Vinegar Bend, Alabama, played professional baseball, and became a congressman later in life. The small Alabama town, with its population of 37, was a utopia for Mizell. The personable southpaw liked to say of his hometown, "This is the only town in Alabama that has its city limits signs back to back."

Wilmer, who played under the handle of "Vinegar Bend"— as homage to his little Alabama community—made his major league debut in 1952 with the Cardinals. Ben Phlegar wrote this about the rookie from the South during his initial campaign: "Mizell is the greatest character, in the true sense of the word, to find his way into the Cardinal organization since Dizzy Dean." Anyone familiar with the great Diz can paint a picture in their mind regarding how eccentric Vinegar Bend might have been.

Mizell started 30 games as a rookie for the Redbirds and then paced the team with 173 strikeouts—good for third in the league—in his sophomore season. Prepared to build off two solid years in the major leagues, Mizell had to forego his baseball dreams when Uncle Sam phoned him in Vinegar Bend. Mizell answered the call to colors and missed the 1954 and 1955 baseball campaigns to service in the United States Army. He was inducted at Jackson, Mississippi, and took his basic training at Fort Jackson. From basic training, Vinegar Bend was assigned to Fort McPherson, where he took a handful of minor league ballplayers under his wing. Always personable and easy-going, Mizell said, "Every day in the army is like Sunday on the farm. Really though, I've been pretty lucky in the army. I've got to play a good bit of baseball and that's helped me stay in shape. Also I think that I've improved my pitching."

Military service, which could be seen as a crutch for a major league ballplayer, was perceived as a blessing for the sunny Mizell. Vinegar Bend said, "I've got to experiment moving the ball around the plate. I could never do that in the majors. Against those guys you just concentrate on staying alive."

After he received his discharge, Mizell ventured to Cuba to play winter ball and sharpen his pitches for the upcoming 1956 baseball season. Despite the amount of innings he logged in the military, Mizell knew that Cuba offered better competition than he faced in the service. The extra work paid off, and he returned to the Cardinals to lead the team in wins, innings pitched and strikeouts. The excessive work caught up with Mizell by 1958, as his once-high strikeout totals began to slide closer to league average.

The man from Vinegar Bend ended his major league career after splitting the 1962 season with the Pirates and Mets. Reminiscing with writer Gene Karst, Mizell told him that Ted Williams was the best hitter he ever saw. Vinegar Bend also had a special fondness for teammate Stan Musial, stating, "I used to tell Stan he was the nicest rich man I know."

W	L	PCT	G	GS	CG	IP	H	BB	SO	SHO	ERA
90	88	.506	268	230	61	1,528	1,434	680	918	15	3.85

Zachary Charles Monroe, *Pitcher*

Monroe pitched two years with the Yankees in the late 1950s. Before he made his major league debut, Monroe served in the U.S. Army during the Korean War. Stationed at Fort Carson, he played service ball with outfielder Lenny Green.

W	L	PCT	G	GS	CG	IP	H	BB	SO	SHO	ERA
4	2	.667	24	6	1	61	60	29	19	0	3.39

William Nelson Moran, *Second Base*

Before Moran made his major league debut he served in the army during the Korean War. Stationed at Fort McPherson, Billy played service ball with Vinegar Bend Mizell and Norm Siebern. The trio led their ballclub to victory in the Third Army's Double Elimination Baseball Tournament. After his discharge, Moran played some with the Indians in the late 1950s but failed to stick. When the American League expanded, Billy joined the newly formed Angels in 1961 and had a few goods years in Los Angeles.

G	R	H	2B	3B	HR	RBI	BB	SO	SB	AVG	Slug
634	242	545	88	10	28	202	133	218	10	.263	.355

Thomas Stephen Morgan, *Pitcher*

"Plowboy" was an adequate major league relief pitcher for a number of years, first with the Yankees and later with the Tigers and Angels. He made his major league debut in 1951 with the Bronx Bombers and even tossed two scoreless innings in that year's World Series. Although the Yankees won the pennant again in 1952, Morgan was unable to participate in that year's Fall Classic because he had been summoned by Uncle Sam.

Plowboy was able to play some ball in the service with Fort Ord and he took part in the 18th Annual National Semipro Baseball Tournament. He returned to the Yankees in 1954 and went 11–5 for the second-place team. In 1957 he became one of the many players to be swapped by the Yankees to the Kansas City Athletics, and he spent one year in KC before he was shuttled off to Detroit. He ended his major league career in 1963 with the Los Angeles Angels.

W	L	PCT	G	GS	CG	IP	H	BB	SO	SHO	ERA
67	47	.588	443	61	18	1,025	1,040	300	364	7	3.60

Vernon Thomas Morgan, *Third Base*

In Morgan's two years in the majors, he was stuck behind power-hitting Randy Jackson on the Cubs roster. The year before Vern made his major league debut, he was the player-manager on the Fort Eustis baseball team.

G	R	H	2B	3B	HR	RBI	BB	SO	SB	AVG	Slug
31	4	16	2	0	0	3	4	14	0	.225	.254

Ross Allen Moschitto, *Outfield*

Ross appeared in more than 100 major league games but is only credited with 36 career at-bats. He earned his paycheck by serving as Mickey Mantle's defensive replacement late in Mick's career. Much like Sammy Byrd was dubbed Babe Ruth's legs, the same could be said for Moschitto, only substituting the Sultan of Swat with the Commerce Comet. A "bonus baby" outfielder, Ross missed the entire 1966 baseball campaign to service in the armed forces.

G	R	H	2B	3B	HR	RBI	BB	SO	SB	AVG	Slug
110	13	6	0	0	1	3	1	14	0	.167	.250

Curtell Howard Motton, *Outfield*

A longtime Baltimore Orioles outfielder who never saw regular action, Motton was used mostly as a power bat off the bench. Short with a compact build, Motton packed solid power in his tank-like frame. The Darnell, Louisiana, native missed a season in the minors to military service.

G	R	H	2B	3B	HR	RBI	BB	SO	SB	AVG	Slug
316	85	121	20	1	25	89	86	116	5	.213	.384

Billy Arnold Muffett, *Pitcher*

Used as a mop-up pitcher in the late 1950s and early 1960s, Muffett played mostly with the Cardinals and Red Sox. Before he made his major league debut, Muffett served in the U.S. Army at Fort Sill during the Korean War. The right-hander participated in the Fourth Army Baseball Tournament held at Fort Hood. In that tournament, he tossed a three-hit shutout against a team from Fort Bliss.

W	L	PCT	G	GS	CG	IP	H	BB	SO	SHO	ERA
16	23	.410	125	32	7	377	407	132	188	1	4.32

Thurman Lee Munson, *Catcher*

A borderline Hall of Famer, "Tugboat" served a brief hitch in the armed forces during the Vietnam War. One of the game's most recognizable tragic figures, Thurman, who owned a pilot's license, died during the 1979 baseball season when he was flying his private plane. One of the top catchers of the 1970s, Thurman gave baseball fans a star-studded foursome to choose from behind the dish with Johnny Bench, Carlton Fisk and Ted Simmons.

G	R	H	2B	3B	HR	RBI	BB	SO	SB	AVG	Slug
1,423	696	1,558	229	32	113	701	438	571	48	.292	.410

Bobby Ray Murcer, *Outfield*

The former outfield star for the New York Yankees, Murcer entered the Bronx baseball scene when Mantle was bowing out. The portside-swinger made his debut in 1965 and played sparingly for the bottom-finishing Yankees of 1966. He was destined to replace Mantle in the outer garden but was summoned by Uncle Sam and missed the entire 1967 and 1968 seasons to service in the armed forces. He made a brilliant return to the majors in 1969 while swatting 26 homers for Ralph Houk's Yankees. He became the everyday center fielder in 1970, as the Oklahoma boy—from the same state as Mantle—became the Yankees star player. Murcer began his career as a Yankee and finished it in the Bronx, with stops in San Francisco and Chicago in between. He served at Fort Huachuca.

G	R	H	2B	3B	HR	RBI	BB	SO	SB	AVG	Slug
1,908	972	1,862	285	45	252	1,043	862	841	127	.277	.445

Richard Lee Murphy, *Pinch Runner*

Murphy appeared in six major league games during his career, all with the Cincinnati Reds, and strolled to the plate just one time. Rarely found with lumber in his mitts, Murphy's only major league action came in 1954. After that, it was duty under Uncle Sam for Dick, who was on the Reds' military service list from 1955 to 1957.

G	R	H	2B	3B	HR	RBI	BB	SO	SB	AVG	Slug
6	1	0	0	0	0	0	0	1	0	.000	.000

Harold Richard Naragon, *Catcher*

A portside-swinging catcher, Naragon played throughout the late 1950s with the Cleveland Indians. Followers of great catchers will note that Cleveland boasted stellar backstop Jim Hegan during that timeframe, and Hal held the dubious honor of serving as Hegan's backup. Naragon missed the 1952 and 1953 baseball campaigns to military service and returned to play nine more years in the majors, mostly as a reserve.

G	R	H	2B	3B	HR	RBI	BB	SO	SB	AVG	Slug
424	83	262	27	11	6	87	76	62	1	.266	.334

Peter Alphonsus Naton, *Pinch Hitter*

Naton's only major league action came with the 1953 Pittsburgh Pirates, a season that was interrupted to military service. Pete missed the majority of the 1953 season as well as the entire 1954 baseball campaign. The Holy Cross graduate, who received offers from fourteen major league clubs upon his college graduation, appeared in only six games at the highest level.

G	R	H	2B	3B	HR	RBI	BB	SO	SB	AVG	Slug
6	2	2	0	0	0	1	2	1	0	.167	.167

Ronald Andrew Necciai, *Pitcher*

Few pitchers have had the promise of Ron Necciai, a flame-thrower in the Bob Feller mold. While he played ball at the Class D level with Bristol, Ron tossed a no-hitter and fanned an unheard-of total of 27. However, fate dealt Ron a poor hand when he was drafted into the armed forces and missed the 1953 season. When the Pirates were training the following year, Branch Rickey, who by then was running the show in Pittsburgh, felt Necciai was the cream of the crop. Rickey said, "The one who should be the best of all is Ron Necciai. He's our greatest young talent. There are factors, of course, in his case—military service ulcers." Despite Branch Rickey's boast, Necciai never fulfilled his potential as a future Bob Feller and played only one season of major league ball.

W	L	PCT	G	GS	CG	IP	H	BB	SO	SHO	ERA
1	6	.143	12	9	0	55	63	32	31	0	7.04

Robert Otis Neighbors, *Reserve*

Neighbors had a cup of coffee with the last-place Browns of 1939. In his only year at the highest level, Bob made eleven plate appearances but managed to hit a home run. Shortly after the bombing at Pearl Harbor, Neighbors enlisted in the armed forces. Eager to get overseas and do some fighting, he enlisted in the Army Air Corps and was commissioned a lieutenant. Lieutenant Neighbors was a co-pilot on a C-54 transport craft. While stateside, Bob served at Sheppard Airfield and played some service ball with Dave Short in 1942.

Shipped out in 1943, Neighbors and his flight crew battle buddies served in hostile territory. An article in the *San Antonio Light* read, "Bob Neighbors is an army lieutenant in air transport in a lonesome part of the world." But Neighbors made it through the war unscathed. However, when Uncle Sam needed pilots again during the Korean War, Bob answered the call once more. During the Korean War, Neighbors was engaged in flight missions over hostile terrain but wouldn't be as lucky as he was in the Second World War. His plane was shot down in August of 1952 and his body was never recovered. Designated as "missing in action," Neighbors' body remains unclaimed to this day.

G	R	H	2B	3B	HR	RBI	BB	SO	SB	AVG	Slug
7	3	2	0	0	1	1	0	1	0	.182	.455

Donald Newcombe, *Pitcher*

One of the game's greatest all-around talents, Newcombe could beat a team on the mound and in the batter's box. The legendary Brooklyn hurler closed out his career with an astounding .623 winning percentage as well as a .271 batting average—a mark that eclipses a handful of Hall of Fame position players. Newcombe's major league career began in 1949 when he tied the National League lead with five shutouts. He played with Brooklyn until the club moved west to Los Angeles. Don only played half a season with the Los Angeles-based Dodgers before a trade sent him to Cincinnati. His major league career ended after he split the 1960 season with the Reds and Indians.

Newcombe was on the Elizabeth, New Jersey, draft board and was inducted into the army three weeks after signing a $25,000 contract for the 1952 baseball season. Upon his induction into the army, Newcombe said, "It's just one of those things. Uncle Sam comes first. I'm no better than anybody else. It's up to him if I do any pitching this spring."

Camp Pickett was Newk's initial assignment from Uncle Sam, as the big right-hander was assigned to a medical replacement training center at the Virginia installation. During his time at Camp Pickett, Newk served as a platoon leader, and said, "I don't think the layoff will affect my pitching. I'll only be 27 years old when I get out." Although he accepted his fate, Newcombe showed remorse for missing what he thought was certain to be a special season, stating, "I thought this would be my top year in the Majors—and a pennant-winning one for the Dodgers."

While serving at Camp Pickett, there were reports that Newk would receive his discharge from the army earlier than previously thought. He was discharged for medical reasons by the navy during World War II, which led to speculation concerning an early dismissal from the army. But the army found him fit for duty and retained his services despite the publicity surrounding a discharge.

Later in his military stint, Newcombe was transferred to Brooke Army Medical Center. After his reassignment to an installation with plenty of major league-caliber ballplayers, Newcombe was approached with an offer to join the Brooke Center nine. Newcombe said, "I always had occasional arm trouble and I don't know how I'm going to be when I get out of this uniform. I hope to do some pitching this year, but I'm not going to really cut loose. Sure, I want to keep in shape, but there's no sense doing any damage to the ol' meal ticket."

Don Newcombe received his discharge from the army in February of 1954 with plenty to prove for the upcoming season. In his last year prior to his military call-up, Newk won 20 games and led the NL with 164 strikeouts. The fear of many struck Newk when he was ineffective upon his return to Brooklyn from the army. He posted a 9–8 record with a 4.56 ERA, the worst mark on the club among pitchers with at least 70 innings of work. However, Newk rebounded the following year when he won 20 games for the Dodgers and paced the National League with an .800 winning percentage.

W	L	PCT	G	GS	CG	IP	H	BB	SO	SHO	ERA
149	90	.623	344	294	136	2,155	2,102	490	1,129	24	3.56

Raymond Francis Newman, *Pitcher*

A hulking southpaw, Newman pitched three years at the major league level in the early 1970s. While still in the minor leagues, the large left-hander missed the 1967 and 1968 seasons to service in the U.S. Navy during the Vietnam War.

W	L	PCT	G	GS	CG	IP	H	BB	SO	SHO	ERA
3	3	.500	45	0	0	63	53	24	46	0	3.00

Chester Raymond Nichols Jr., *Pitcher*

Nichols spent the better part of nine years in the major leagues as a relief pitcher and spot starter. The southpaw made his debut with the 1951 Boston Braves and led the league with a 2.88 ERA as a rookie. However, Nichols was unable to build off his solid rookie showing when he missed the next two seasons to the armed forces and the Korean War. Nichols took his physical exam at the Providence armed forces Center in January 1952 and was sworn into the army on April 7, 1952. He served at Fort Lee, where his baseball battery mate was major leaguer Harry Chiti.

When Nichols was asked how he'd fair on his return to the majors, he said, "Wait 'til I get out and I'll tell you." After he spent two years under the control of Uncle Sam, Chet returned to the Braves—who had relocated to Milwaukee—in 1954 and had a poor 9–11 record with a team-high 4.43 ERA. He rebounded somewhat the following year when he lowered his ERA to an even 4.00, but he made only two appearances in 1956. Nichols was out of the majors for a time until he returned in 1960 with the pitching-starved Red Sox. Nichols' last major league action came in 1964 with the Reds, but he never was able to duplicate his pre-war success.

W	L	PCT	G	GS	CG	IP	H	BB	SO	SHO	ERA
34	36	.486	189	71	23	604	600	280	266	4	3.64

Scott Richard Northey, *Outfield*

From the same family as former World War II-era Slugger "Round Man" Ron Northey, Scott's only major league service came with the expansion Kansas City Royals in 1969. Before his major league sojourn, Scott served in the military during the Vietnam War.

G	R	H	2B	3B	HR	RBI	BB	SO	SB	AVG	Slug
20	11	16	2	2	1	7	7	19	6	.262	.410

Edward Joseph O'Brien, *Utilityman*

Eddie and his twin brother, Johnny, were a pair of cage luminaries at Seattle University. Despite their prolific basketball skills, the O'Brien brothers signed to play baseball with the Pittsburgh Pirates out of college. They were rookies in 1953 with the worst team in baseball, the twins served as Fred Haney's Pirates' starting middle infield. They missed the entire 1954 baseball season and a portion of the 1955 campaign to military service. When they returned, Haney switched Eddie to the outfield.

G	R	H	2B	3B	HR	RBI	BB	SO	SB	AVG	Slug
231	64	131	10	4	0	25	37	45	11	.236	.269

John Thomas O'Brien, *Second Base*

Johnny served with twin brother Eddie as the Pirates' regular double-play duo in 1953, a year before they were summoned by Uncle Sam. Johnny's major league career lasted a year longer than brother Eddie's, as Johnny played a final year with the Milwaukee Braves in 1959 while Eddie was out of the bigs. Johnny's basketball legacy overshadowed his baseball accomplishments. He set the University of Seattle's single-season scoring record with 1,051 points. He also beat Goose Tatum's Harlem Globetrotters in a game when he racked up more than 40 points, which left the eccentric Tatum stunned.

G	R	H	2B	3B	HR	RBI	BB	SO	SB	AVG	Slug
339	90	204	35	5	4	59	59	82	2	.250	.320

Daniel Francis O'Connell, *Third Base*

O'Connell made his major league debut in 1950 with the Pittsburgh Pirates and then lost the next two seasons to service in the army. He was inducted into the army on February 21, 1951, and took his basic training at Fort Myer, Virginia, with pitcher Johnny Antonelli. Danny served his country for two years as an infantryman before he returned to the Pirates' lineup in 1953. Not missing a beat, Danny paced the Bucs in games played, at-bats, runs scored, hits, doubles, triples and batting average. Despite those lofty credentials, he was shipped off to the Braves for the 1954 season. He played in the major leagues until 1962. His last action at the highest level was with the Washington Senators.

G	R	H	2B	3B	HR	RBI	BB	SO	SB	AVG	Slug
1,143	527	1,049	181	35	39	320	431	396	48	.260	.351

William Oliver O'Dell, *Pitcher*

During his major league career, Billy "Digger" O'Dell combated Addison's disease. Before every outing, he had to consume an extra half tablet of cortisone to keep his illness from interfering with his pitching.

O'Dell was a highly touted prospect out of Clemson University, and the Orioles bought his services with a $20,000 signing bonus. Although that total seems skimpy compared with modern bonuses, it was quite a sign of confidence in an amateur during the 1950s. He posted a 1–1 record in his first major league action during the 1954 season and was drafted into the army shortly after the close of the baseball campaign. Billy missed the entire 1955 season and all but four games in 1956 to service in the army. While donning Uncle Sam's threads, Digger played service ball for the 3rd Army based at Fort McPherson. A student of legendary pitching coach and Cardinals hurler Harry "The Cat" Brecheen, O'Dell was discharged from the army early in September of 1956.

W	L	PCT	G	GS	CG	IP	H	BB	SO	SHO	ERA
105	100	.512	479	199	63	1,816	1,697	556	1,133	13	3.30

Charles Francis Oertel, *Outfield*

Oertel, an avid duck hunter, had a cup of coffee with the 1958 Baltimore Orioles of Paul Richards. The small outfielder from Coffeyville, Kansas, joined the U.S. Marine Corps during the Korean War. Oertel was stationed at Camp Pendleton where he was able to play some service ball.

G	R	H	2B	3B	HR	RBI	BB	SO	SB	AVG	Slug
14	4	2	0	0	1	1	1	1	0	.167	.417

Karl Arthur Olson, *Outfield*

Steve O'Neill, a great major league catcher in his day and Olson's first manager at the highest level, said this of Karl: "He can do anything. Olson is a ballhawk in center field…. He's a good prospect." However, prospects in the early 1950s had a tendency to get plucked by Uncle Sam, and Olson entered the colors in 1952. During his time in the military, Olson served at Fort Ord, California, where he played several sports, including starting for the 63rd Infantry Regiment's basketball squad. A charitable man, Olson took leave from the army to take part in a benefit baseball game for the March of Dimes to raise money for a polio cure.

G	R	H	2B	3B	HR	RBI	BB	SO	SB	AVG	Slug
279	74	160	25	6	6	50	43	94	3	.235	.316

Ernest Eugene Oravetz, *Outfield*

A diminutive ballplayer who served as a fourth outfielder with the Senators for two years, Ernie was the target of some writers' puns about his not-quite-Jim Lemon-like frame. Small enough to easily fit in a cigar box, Oravetz was one of the smallest players of any generation. But he was a solid little ballplayer with a good batting eye. He played in the majors in 1955 and 1956 after he paid his way into the pro ranks. Ernie attended a tryout camp in Cocoa, Florida, with the Senators, and the price of admission came out of his pocket. He was a backup to such heavy hitters as the aforementioned Lemon and Roy Sievers.

Ernie missed some minor league seasoning time to service in the armed forces during the Korean War. He served with the 42nd Field Artillery and was stationed overseas for fifteen months in Europe. A service baseball sensation, Oravetz posted the second-best batting average among players in the USAREUR League in 1954. Active in other sports, Ernie was a member of the 42nd Field Artillery's football squad, but his duties didn't entail suiting up for games. Rather, the pint-sized soldier was employed by the team as the equipment manager.

G	R	H	2B	3B	HR	RBI	BB	SO	SB	AVG	Slug
188	44	105	8	3	0	36	53	39	2	.263	.298

Milton Darrell Osteen, *Pitcher*

Osteen pitched briefly — and ineffectively — at the major league level for pieces of four seasons. Darrell was initially called up by the 1965 Cincinnati Reds and pitched sparingly with that club through 1967. He toiled in the bushes until the Athletics summoned his services in 1970, the same year Uncle Sam called his number. The sinkerball specialist was reclassified in the draft due to his divorce, and was called to colors shortly thereafter.

Upon his discharge from the army, Osteen ventured to Puerto Rico to take part in the island's winter league action to prepare for the upcoming baseball season. Despite his preparations, Darrell never again tossed another sinkerball at the major league level. Darrell said, "I thought I had a good enough spring to stay up this year, but they said after two years in the army they couldn't tell enough from spring training to keep me."

W	L	PCT	G	GS	CG	IP	H	BB	SO	SHO	ERA
1	4	.200	29	1	0	38	47	29	34	0	8.05

James Philip Owens, *Pitcher*

A long reliever and spot starter, Owens played with the Phillies, Reds and Astros at the major league level. Originally beckoned to the bigs in 1955 to play under Mayo Smith, Owens didn't savor his first cup of coffee. He was given another chance in 1956 but struggled just the same before he was drafted into the army. Owens lost the 1957 and the majority of the 1958 season to service at Fort McPherson, where he played baseball with Steve Korcheck. However, 1958 would prove to be a season of firsts for Jim, as he appeared in one major league game that year and netted his first career win. Owens pitched with the Phillies through 1962 and ended his career as a reliever out of Grady Hatton's bullpen in Houston.

W	L	PCT	G	GS	CG	IP	H	BB	SO	SHO	ERA
42	68	.382	286	103	21	886	932	340	516	1	4.31

James Vincent Pagliaroni, *Catcher*

This stout catcher from Michigan began his major league career with the 1955 Boston Red Sox. Pags then lost the next two years to the armed forces and later took over the starting catcher role in 1961. He finished second on the team in home runs his first full season at the major league level, besting teammate Carl Yastrzemski by five long balls. He was dealt to the Pirates in 1963 to platoon with an aging Smoky Burgess and ended his career in 1969 as a member of the only Seattle Pilots club to take the field.

G	R	H	2B	3B	HR	RBI	BB	SO	SB	AVG	Slug
849	269	622	98	7	90	326	330	494	4	.252	.407

Phillips Steere Paine, *Pitcher*

Paine was a career relief pitcher at the major league level. Of his 94 games played, all came out of the bullpen. He went 2–0 as a rookie in 1951 and then missed all of the 1952 and 1953 baseball seasons to military service. When he made his return to the ball diamond, his Boston Braves teammates had moved west to Milwaukee, and Phil joined them for fourteen games in 1954. He was rarely used by the Braves. Paine saw brief action with the organization from 1954 through 1957 and then enjoyed his finest, and last, season in 1958 with the Cardinals.

W	L	PCT	G	GS	CG	IP	H	BB	SO	SHO	ERA
10	1	.909	95	0	0	149	144	80	101	0	3.38

Ervin Martin Palica, *Pitcher*

Palica spent the majority of his major league career with the Brooklyn Dodgers. His career began in 1945 as a fresh-faced 17-year-old and ended in 1956 after a short stint with the Orioles. Often used out of the bullpen, Palica missed the entire 1952 baseball season and returned to Brooklyn late in 1953 to appear in just four contests. During his stint in the military, Erv served in the army at Fort Dix.

W	L	PCT	G	GS	CG	IP	H	BB	SO	SHO	ERA
41	55	.427	246	80	20	839	806	399	423	3	4.23

Stanley Francis Palys, *Outfield*

A big power-hitting outfielder, Palys spent four years in the majors but was never a regular. Stan won an MVP Award in the Southern Association, but his trials in the majors were always in a reserve capacity. Before Palys made his major league debut, he served in the military during the Korean War.

G	R	H	2B	3B	HR	RBI	BB	SO	SB	AVG	Slug
138	42	79	17	0	10	43	26	54	2	.237	.378

Harry William Parker, *Pitcher*

The year before Parker made his major league debut with the Cardinals, he lost the season to military service during the Vietnam War. The right-hander from Illinois had some success as a long arm-spot starter with the Redbirds and Mets in the early 1970s.

W	L	PCT	G	GS	CG	IP	H	BB	SO	SHO	ERA
15	21	.417	124	30	1	315	315	128	172	0	3.86

Daryl Alan Patterson, *Pitcher*

A tall relief pitcher of the late 1960s and early 1970s, Patterson once spent one baseball season with three separate major league clubs. The bullpen flinger was a remarkable hurler his rookie year — he posted a 2.12 ERA — and pitched three scoreless innings in a World Series championship for the Detroit Tigers in 1968. His accuracy betrayed him the following year when he walked 19 batters in 22 innings before the reserve unit he served with was activated early in the 1969 baseball season.

W	L	PCT	G	GS	CG	IP	H	BB	SO	SHO	ERA
11	9	.550	142	3	0	231	223	119	142	0	4.09

Donald Stephen Pavletich, *First Base/Catcher*

Short and stocky, Pavletich enjoyed an up-and-down career with the Cincinnati Reds. He made his debut in 1957. Don missed a portion of the season to military service and returned to play briefly for the Reds in 1959. He spent 1960 and 1961 in the bushes and returned to the majors to stay in 1962. He played with the Reds through 1968 and finished his career with brief stints in Chicago and Boston.

G	R	H	2B	3B	HR	RBI	BB	SO	SB	AVG	Slug
536	163	349	73	8	46	193	148	237	5	.254	.420

Stanley Walter Pawloski, *Middle Infielder*

A service ball sensation who never made the grade in the majors, Pawloski led his Fort Lee team to a 24-game winning streak. A deft defender, Stan was adept at turning the double play. An article in the *Petersburg Progress-Index* claimed that "Pawloski's ability to get rid of the ball reminds one of Phil Rizzuto's sleight-of-hand feats in delivering a ball to first." After he was discharged from the army, the Indians brought him right along to Cleveland because they had middle infielders Bobby Avila and Sam Dente on the mend.

G	R	H	2B	3B	HR	RBI	BB	SO	SB	AVG	Slug
2	0	1	0	0	0	0	0	2	0	.125	.125

Charles Peete, *Outfield*

Peete played only half a season in the Negro Leagues when it was no longer considered a strong circuit. He quickly made the jump to the minor leagues and spent a year in the military during the Korean War. After his discharge from the service, Peete put up some good numbers in the Cardinals' minor league chain and earned a promotion at the end of the 1956 season. Considered a quality prospect with the Redbirds, Charlie's life ended tragically when he died on a plane crash while he was on his way to play winter ball.

G	R	H	2B	3B	HR	RBI	BB	SO	SB	AVG	Slug
23	3	10	2	2	0	6	6	10	0	.192	.308

Paul Eugene Penson, *Pitcher*

Accuracy was always an issue for Penson. His major league career consisted of sixteen innings with the 1954 Phillies directly after his military stint. No one could deny that the Phillies had a talented arm in Penson. While he served in the Air Force during the Korean War, Paul looked every inch like a Bob Feller. Stationed at Pensacola, Penson is credited with striking out more than 700 batters while he served his military hitch. After his discharge, wildness got the best of Penson, who found out that pro players are a bit more selective than soldiers at the plate.

W	L	PCT	G	GS	CG	IP	H	BB	SO	SHO	ERA
1	1	.500	5	3	0	16	14	14	3	0	4.50

Melvin Gray Perry, *Outfield*

Sometimes credited as "Bob" Perry, Mel played two years with the Los Angeles Angels during the 1960s. The outfielder missed the 1954 and 1955 seasons in the minors to military service.

G	R	H	2B	3B	HR	RBI	BB	SO	SB	AVG	Slug
131	35	103	17	1	6	30	23	83	2	.266	.362

John Melvin "Bubba" Phillips, *Third Base/Outfield*

Phillips missed some minor league action to military service during the Korean War. But his stint in the armed forces served as a showcase for Bubba. The Tigers liked what they saw out of him and shortly after his discharge traded veteran ace Virgil Trucks to acquire him. Bubba, who attended school at the University of Southern Mississippi, was employed as a third baseman by the White Sox who could play the outfield in a pinch.

G	R	H	2B	3B	HR	RBI	BB	SO	SB	AVG	Slug
1,062	348	835	153	8	62	356	182	314	25	.255	.358

Joseph Benjamin Pignatano, *Catcher*

A reserve catcher throughout much of his major league career, Pignatano played for his hometown team the last year they were in Brooklyn. Joe spent the 1951 and 1952 seasons in the military, and after his discharge he had one of his finest seasons at Asheville in 1953. Called up by the Brooklyn Dodgers in 1957, he was with the team when the Dodgers relocated to Los Angeles. Later in his career, when Alvin Dark acquired him, Dark said, "I'm told Pignatano will be one of the best defensive catchers in the league."

G	R	H	2B	3B	HR	RBI	BB	SO	SB	AVG	Slug
307	81	161	25	4	16	62	94	116	8	.234	.351

Alfred James Pilarcik, *Outfield*

A regular in the Baltimore Orioles outfield in the late 1950s, Pilarcik was regarded as a swift ballhawk in the pasture. The left-handed outfielder from Whiting, Indiana, missed two seasons in the minors to service in the military during the Korean War.

G	R	H	2B	3B	HR	RBI	BB	SO	SB	AVG	Slug
668	205	413	66	7	22	143	185	150	41	.256	.346

James Pete Pisoni, *Outfield*

A compactly built outfielder with decent power, Pisoni had five years at the major league level but never received substantial playing time. Jim was inducted into the armed forces in the early spring of 1951 and missed the next two seasons to the military. After his discharge, he made it up to the majors with the 1953 Browns.

G	R	H	2B	3B	HR	RBI	BB	SO	SB	AVG	Slug
103	26	40	3	3	6	20	16	47	0	.212	.354

Donald Joseph Plarski, *Reserve*

Plarski probably made more money writing about baseball than he did playing it. The diminutive ballplayer became a sportswriter after he hung up his spikes. Before Don was inducted into the army for the Korean War, he led his minor league circuit with a .997 fielding percentage. The mite from Chicago was inducted into the army in February of 1951 and served at Camp Breckinridge, Kentucky. Assigned to the 101st Airborne Screaming Eagles, Plarski earned his airborne wings while working for Uncle Sam. After his discharge, he had a cup of coffee with the 1955 Kansas City A's.

G	R	H	2B	3B	HR	RBI	BB	SO	SB	AVG	Slug
8	0	1	0	0	0	0	0	2	1	.091	.091

Herbert Eugene Plews, *Utility Infielder*

A decent infielder for the Senators who spent the bulk of his time at second and third base, Plews was considered a cat-like defender. Quick on his feet, Herb was smart on the double-play pivot. Drafted into military service during the Korean War, Plews was stationed at Camp Stoneman before he was given orders overseas. Shipped out to Camp Drake, an army replacement depot that processed soldiers for assignments to Korea and Japan, Herb was able to play some service ball at the Japanese camp. He teamed with Cubs first baseman-outfielder Bob Speake to give Camp Drake two fine major league prospects. During the 1952 season, Herb led Camp Drake with an astounding .467 batting average.

G	R	H	2B	3B	HR	RBI	BB	SO	SB	AVG	Slug
346	125	266	42	17	4	82	74	133	3	.262	.348

John Joseph Podres, *Pitcher*

A swell southpaw pitcher — the cat's pajamas in the 1955 World Series — Podres also enjoyed a stellar career as a respected pitching coach. In his third full major league season, Podres guided the Brooklyn Dodgers to the World Series in 1955 and proceeded to stand the mighty Yankees on their ears. He posted a 1.00 ERA for the Fall Classic and won the deciding Game Seven. However, shortly thereafter, Podres was inducted into the armed forces and lost the 1956 baseball campaign. Picking up right where he left off, Johnny returned in 1957 and paced the National League in shutouts and ERA. When the Dodgers moved to Los Angeles, Podres was their winningest pitcher their first year in sunny L.A before the dynamic duo of Koufax and Drysdale forced him into a supporting role.

W	L	PCT	G	GS	CG	IP	H	BB	SO	SHO	ERA
148	116	.561	440	340	77	2,265	2,239	743	1,435	24	3.67

Thomas George Poholsky, *Pitcher*

Poholsky made his major league debut as a 20-year-old with the 1950 St. Louis Cardinals. In his first full major league season, Tom led the Redbirds in strikeouts and tied with Gerry Staley for the team lead in complete games. He appeared to be on the right track when Uncle Sam beckoned his services after the 1951 baseball season. He missed the entire 1952 and 1953 baseball campaigns, as he served at Fort Myer in the army. While serving at Fort Myer, Tom started a quarterfinal game of the National Baseball Congress Tournament for the Military District of Washington held at Wichita, Kansas. He was discharged from the army on October 27, 1953, and played two more years with the Cardinals.

W	L	PCT	G	GS	CG	IP	H	BB	SO	SHO	ERA
31	52	.373	159	104	30	754	791	192	316	5	3.93

Daniel Edward Porter, *Outfield*

Porter's major league career consisted of thirteen games with the 1951 Washington Senators. The lanky outfielder tallied only nineteen career at-bats but missed the 1952 and 1953 baseball campaigns to service in the armed forces.

G	R	H	2B	3B	HR	RBI	BB	SO	SB	AVG	Slug
13	2	4	0	0	0	0	2	4	0	.211	.211

J.W. Porter, *Catcher*

A standout while he played American Legion ball at Oakland during high school, Porter was a highly sought-after commodity upon graduation. His entire life as a kid revolved around baseball. When his family moved from Oklahoma to California during the Dust Bowl days, they set up camp close to the Oakland ballpark, and J.W. took to the stadium. Porter said, "I grew up in Oakland when it was a minor league town. In fact, I grew up in the ballpark. I lived just a couple blocks from the old Oakland minor league park. I just lived there and had every job that a kid could possibly have at a stadium."

After shining shoes for such notables as Gene Bearden and Ferris Fain, Porter signed his first pro contract and started out in the minor league ranks. Sent to the Three-I League, Porter had a good showing and quickly made the majors as a 19-year-old with the 1952 St. Louis Browns. The top prospect made a quick run to the majors, but once he got there, he was taken away. Drafted into service for the Korean War, Porter left the Browns and spent the next two years in the military. Porter said, "When I was nineteen I was in the big leagues with the Browns. What a terrible time to lose a couple years. Even though I played a lot of ball while I was in the service, it just wasn't the same."

Inducted into the army at Fort Ord, Porter was sent to basic training but got removed from boot camp by major league fireman Plowboy Morgan. J.W. said of the removal from boot camp, "I wasn't in basic training a day when Morgan looked me up. He said, 'Do what you're told, keep your nose clean, and as soon as the orders can be cut, you'll be on the baseball team.' I was in the army for a week to ten days and then I was pulled over to Special Services, and all I did that year was play baseball."

Porter would later have to finish boot camp, but he returned to the Fort Ord baseball team. After Morgan, who was acting manager at the camp, was discharged from the army, the managerial duties fell upon J.W. He took control of the Fort Ord baseball team and led them to a stunning record. He said, "I spent the winter writing letters all over the states of California, Arizona, Nevada and Oregon, scheduling games. We wound up playing just over one hundred games. Our record was 100 and 4."

In order to achieve such a lofty record, the team had a terrific roster that outclassed the opposition. His Fort Ord connections enabled him to build a powerhouse at the California installation. Porter explained the process of building a service team, saying, "Fort Ord was the induction center for all the twelve western states, so I got names of ballplayers well in advance. I'd find out that, say, Dick Stuart was going to be drafted in February or Bob Lillis was going to be drafted in March, so I'd meet these guys at the gate and tell them that I was manager of the team and in a week or two you'll be playing ball for me. With that going for us, we pretty well dominated army baseball."

This system failed Porter once, with New York Yankees legend Billy Martin. Martin was the talk of baseball after he won the World Series MVP in 1953, but during that winter he was drafted for military service and destined for Fort Ord. Eager to claim Martin, skipper Porter knew that Billy would make his Fort Ord squad that much better. But when Martin took it upon himself to report to Fort Ord in excessive style, his orders were cut and he was shipped out to Fort Carson. Rather than take the military bus with the other reporting soldiers, Martin drove his brand-new World Series MVP convertible to the front gates and boisterously announced to Fort Ord that he had arrived. His behavior perturbed the commanding officer at the installation, and he told J.W. that Martin wouldn't play ball on his team. When Porter led his Fort Ord Warriors to the Sixth Army Championship, held at Fort Carson no less, Martin watched from the stands while Porter's squad won the tournament.

G	R	H	2B	3B	HR	RBI	BB	SO	SB	AVG	Slug
229	58	124	22	1	8	62	53	96	4	.228	.316

Arnold Mario Portocarrero, *Pitcher*

A big right-hander from New York, Portocarrero was a serviceable starting pitcher for the Kansas City A's in the 1950s. Arnie was drafted in January of 1952 and missed some valuable minor league seasoning time to service in the military.

W	L	PCT	G	GS	CG	IP	H	BB	SO	SHO	ERA
38	57	.400	166	117	33	818	778	320	338	5	4.31

Robert Leroy Powell, *Pinch Runner*

Powell appeared in two games over the course of two seasons in the major leagues. He played in a single game each campaign. His first action came in 1955 with the White Sox, and after a year in the military, he returned to the Windy City for one game in 1957.

G	R	H	2B	3B	HR	RBI	BB	SO	SB	AVG	Slug
2	1	0	0	0	0	0	0	0	0	—	—

John Calvin Powers, *Outfield*

A minor league power-hitting star, Powers never was given much of a shot in the majors. He was up and down with the Pirates in the mid 1950s and then had brief trials with the Reds, Angels and Indians afterwards. John missed the 1952 and 1953 seasons to military service during the Korean War.

G	R	H	2B	3B	HR	RBI	BB	SO	SB	AVG	Slug
151	26	42	7	2	6	14	22	48	0	.195	.330

Charles Henry Rabe, *Pitcher*

Rabe had no luck at the major league level. He posted a career 0–4 record in his short major league career despite decent peripheral stats. Before he made his debut at the highest level, Charlie served in the U.S. Army during the Korean War. Stationed at Fort Knox, Rabe was able to play plenty of service ball. During the Second Army's baseball tournament held at Fort Eustis, Charlie tossed a three-hit shutout against the Army Chemical Center of Edgewood, Maryland.

W	L	PCT	G	GS	CG	IP	H	BB	SO	SHO	ERA
0	4	.000	11	2	0	27	30	9	16	0	3.67

Lawrence Glenn Hope Raines, *Utilityman*

A valuable player for his teams, Raines could fill in just about anywhere on the field. As a rookie on the 1957 Indians, Raines played every infield position except first base and also toiled eight games in the outfield. A journeyed ballplayer, Larry began his pro career in the Negro Leagues before he was inducted into service and played ball in the army. After his discharge, Larry played some ball in Japan before the Indians gave him a trial in the late 1950s.

G	R	H	2B	3B	HR	RBI	BB	SO	SB	AVG	Slug
103	39	64	14	0	2	16	19	45	5	.253	.332

John Burwell "Jack" Reed, *Outfield*

Reed played with the Yankees from 1961 to 1963 when they captured the AL pennant each season. Although Jack was used quite often as a reserve outfielder, he was never asked to play in a World Series game. A collegiate football star at the University of Mississippi, Reed did get to participate in the Rose Bowl. Before he joined the Yankees, Jack served in the military during the Korean War.

G	R	H	2B	3B	HR	RBI	BB	SO	SB	AVG	Slug
222	39	30	5	2	1	6	14	22	7	.233	.326

Marshall Daniel Renfroe, *Pitcher*

Renfroe made one start at the major league level and was knocked out of the box early. He pitched his only game with the 1959 Giants. Before his one-game trial, Marshall served in the military during the Korean War.

W	L	PCT	G	GS	CG	IP	H	BB	SO	SHO	ERA
0	0	—	1	1	0	2	3	3	3	0	27.00

Peter Gerard Richert, *Pitcher*

A diminutive pitcher, Richert once cited fellow mighty mite Bobby Shantz as a ball diamond inspiration. The little southpaw with a crackling fastball began his major league career with the Los Angeles Dodgers of 1962. He was a member of the world champion Dodgers of 1963 and played briefly for the same outfit in 1964. Richert enjoyed his breakout year in 1965 with the Washington Senators when he paced the team in nearly every pitching category. He was just as good in 1966 when he finished third in the American League with 195 strikeouts.

Pete got off to a rough start in 1967 and was dealt to Baltimore where he finished out the season. The next year, Richert moved to the bullpen and also saw action with Uncle Sam's outfit. He served with a National Guard unit based out of Washington, D.C., which was federalized due to riots held in the nation's capital. Pete was on duty shortly after the assassination of Senator Robert Kennedy.

W	L	PCT	G	GS	CG	IP	H	BB	SO	SHO	ERA
80	73	.523	429	122	22	1,166	959	424	925	3	3.19

John Milton "Mickey" Rivers, *Outfield*

A colorful character who seemed at home offering bizarre statements in the vein of Berra and Stengel, Rivers was a fleet-footed outfielder for the Angels, Yankees and Rangers. Nicknamed "Mick the Quick"—for obvious reasons—he constantly bumped heads with teammate Reggie Jackson while they played together in New York. However, Mickey never looked for a confrontation, stating, "My mama told me to take people like they are and that's what I do." Rivers initially served with the United States Army and joined the Air Force Reserves later on.

G	R	H	2B	3B	HR	RBI	BB	SO	SB	AVG	Slug
1,468	785	1,660	237	71	61	499	266	471	267	.295	.397

Melvin Earl Roach, *Second Base*

A reserve infielder, Roach saw action in the major leagues with the Braves while they were stationed in Milwaukee as well as the Cubs and Phillies. Never a regular player, Roach backed up Hall of Famer Red Schoendienst in Milwaukee and suffered from chronic knee pain. Roach missed the 1955 and 1956 seasons to service in the navy. A standout collegiate quarterback at Virginia where he was a member of the Naval Reserves Officer Training Corps, Roach played service ball for a team based out of Little Creek, Virginia.

G	R	H	2B	3B	HR	RBI	BB	SO	SB	AVG	Slug
227	42	119	25	0	7	43	24	75	1	.238	.331

Michael Thomas Roarke, *Catcher*

Roarke was the captain of his football team at Boston College but opted to play professional baseball instead. The stout backstop served in the military during the Korean War. The year after his discharge, he was considered one of the two best prospects in the Sally League along with Hall of Famer Frank Robinson.

G	R	H	2B	3B	HR	RBI	BB	SO	SB	AVG	Slug
194	41	113	11	2	6	44	45	61	0	.230	.297

Donald Alexander Robertson, *Reserve*

Robertson's major league career consisted of a cup of coffee with the 1954 Cubs. Prior to his major league debut, Don had served in the armed forces during the Korean War.

G	R	H	2B	3B	HR	RBI	BB	SO	SB	AVG	Slug
14	2	0	0	0	0	0	0	2	0	.000	.000

John Romonosky, *Pitcher*

Prior to his debut with the 1953 Cardinals, Romonosky served in the military during the Korean War. The big right-hander played plenty of service ball while employed by Uncle Sam. Back home on furlough just before his discharge, he and his brother, Dick, a catcher, gave their hometown folks a show when they played an American Legion game while home on break. During the Korean War, John's brother served overseas in Egypt.

W	L	PCT	G	GS	CG	IP	H	BB	SO	SHO	ERA
3	4	.429	32	9	1	101	97	51	63	0	5.17

John Junior Roseboro, *Catcher*

Roseboro is best known for his part in one of baseball's ugliest incidents. When Johnny and Sandy Koufax felt that Giants pitcher Juan Marichal was low-bridging some of their Dodger mates, they began to low-bridge Marichal when he came up to bat. Koufax would pitch inside and when Roseboro would send the ball back to Sandy, he'd try to whistle it just past Marichal's ear. Juan promptly got upset and instead of issuing some choice words, he used his baseball bat as a club and Slugged Roseboro in the skull. A real donnybrook ensued, and this act kept Marichal out of the Baseball Hall of Fame for a while until Roseboro leant his support.

Before Roseboro was pulverized by Marichal, he served in the military during the Korean War. Johnny took basic training and afterwards was shipped out to the European Theatre. Attached to the 9th SP Division, Roseboro was able to don the mask and chest protector on occasion. He played some service ball in the USAREUR League and played some of his games at Vaihingen. After his discharge, Johnny joined the Brooklyn Dodgers for their last year in New York and spent many seasons with the Los Angeles-based Dodgers. He ended his career with the 1970 Washington Senators managed by the legendary Ted Williams.

G	R	H	2B	3B	HR	RBI	BB	SO	SB	AVG	Slug
1,585	512	1,206	190	44	104	548	547	677	67	.249	.371

Robert Edward Roselli, *Catcher*

A reserve catcher for a couple of years in the majors with the Braves and White Sox, Roselli never did see regular duty at the highest level. The backstop from San Francisco was drafted into the army during the Korean War and was sent to Fort Ord, California. While stationed there, Bob was able to play service ball under player-manager J.W. Porter.

G	R	H	2B	3B	HR	RBI	BB	SO	SB	AVG	Slug
68	8	25	7	1	2	10	12	31	1	.219	.351

Clifford Davis Ross, *Pitcher*

A live-armed southpaw, Ross was a terror for minor league batters. Before he was inducted into service for the Korean War, Cliff tossed two no-hitters for his Ogden team. But the nightmares batters had regarding Ross concerned his live arm coupled with his absence of accuracy. When Ross was inducted into service, batters around the Ogden area breathed a little easier. Ross served overseas during the war in the Pacific Theatre. He was stationed at times in Japan and Korea. After his discharge, Cliff returned to baseball but had only a cup of coffee at the major league level with the 1954 Reds.

W	L	PCT	G	GS	CG	IP	H	BB	SO	SHO	ERA
0	0	—	4	0	0	3	0	0	1	0	0.00

Floyd Robert Ross, *Pitcher*

Ross is another player whose major league career was rather brief, as he appeared in twenty games over the course of three seasons. His first action came in 1950 with the Senators, and Bob was used slightly more the following year. He missed the entirety of the 1952 and 1953 seasons to service under Uncle Sam at Fort Ord and didn't return to the majors until 1956 with the Phillies.

W	L	PCT	G	GS	CG	IP	H	BB	SO	SHO	ERA
0	2	.000	20	3	0	48	55	38	29	0	7.13

Frederick Donald Rudolph, *Pitcher*

A pretty fair major league pitcher with above-average control, Rudolph served in the military during the Korean War before he made his major league debut ... and before he met his wife. His bride, a showgirl named Patti Waggin, may win the title for the most unusual ballplayer's bride of all-time. Patti was a burlesque dancer/stripper, and sportswriters of the day had plenty of fun with Don and his wife's relationship. An article in the *Van Wert Times* showed a photograph of Don on the ball diamond with his lovely bride standing beside him, and the newspaper printed the caption, "Patti tries to influence Don to throw more curves. Don, however, will go with the slider and leave the curves to Patti."

Another crude article was printed across the nation by the Associated Press that showed the ample-chested Patti Waggin leaning over a railing at the ballpark and talking with her husband before his warm-up. The writer made the joke that during the off-season Don serves as Patti's catcher, retrieving her clothes as she throws them off during her routine. But their romance ended tragically when Don died in an automobile accident in 1968. The unusual love affair spurred writer Bob Brill to pen a biographical novel about Patti, Don and burlesque in general in 2009.

W	L	PCT	G	GS	CG	IP	H	BB	SO	SHO	ERA
18	32	.360	124	57	10	450	485	102	182	2	4.00

Frank Field Saucier, *Outfield/Catcher*

Every man leaves behind a legacy, no matter how small, and Saucier is best remembered for being the injured player that midget Eddie Gaedel pinch-hit for in 1951. Upon completion of high school, at the age of 16, he quickly enlisted in the navy. Saucier was commissioned an officer in the navy as an 18-year-old as part of the V-12 Program during World War II, which made him one of the youngest deck officers ever commissioned by the United States Navy. During the Second World War, Saucier was initially assigned as the skipper of Beach Party Team No. 76 of the Amphibious Forces. This assignment took him to the Philippines and Japan. He later served in China as a deck watch officer and second division officer on the flagship *USS Mt. Olympus*.

A legend in the minor league circuits, Saucier batted .446 to lead Organized Baseball when he played for Wichita Falls, which was the highest batting average ever to win the Louisville Slugger Silver Bat trophy. He was summoned to the major leagues by the St. Louis Browns but was recalled into the navy shortly thereafter. He served as a battalion commander at the Naval Air Station in Pensacola, Florida, during the Korean War. Upon his discharge from the navy, Saucier retired from baseball to become the CEO of Chemical Industries Inc.

G	R	H	2B	3B	HR	RBI	BB	SO	SB	AVG	Slug
18	4	1	1	0	0	1	3	4	0	.071	.143

Carl Ernest Sawatski, *Catcher*

Short and chunky, Swats possessed the stereotypical image of a catcher. A portside-swinging backstop, Sawatski made it to the major leagues for the first time with the 1948 Chicago Cubs. At the age of 23, Carl was drafted into the United States Army and was stationed at Fort Chaffee, Arkansas. While serving in the army, he married Little Rock singer Dorothy Lusk, and the avid golfer took part in the Fourth Army Golf Tournament held at Fort Sam Houston. Carl's stint in the army took him overseas to Japan. Upon his discharge from the army, Carl said that he planned to "get readjusted to civilian life and play a little golf."

G	R	H	2B	3B	HR	RBI	BB	SO	SB	AVG	Slug
633	133	351	46	5	58	213	191	251	2	.242	.401

Robert Benjamin Schmidt, *Catcher*

Before Schmidt made his major league debut, he served in

the armed forces during the Korean War. He missed the 1953 and 1954 seasons to military service. A big, strong catcher, Schmidt was the Giants' regular catcher his rookie year in 1958 — their first year in San Francisco. He finished second that year for the most home runs by an NL catcher. The Giants then platooned him with Hobie Landrith. He would later catch in the American League with the Senators and Yankees before retiring.

G	R	H	2B	3B	HR	RBI	BB	SO	SB	AVG	Slug
454	133	317	55	4	39	150	100	199	0	.243	.381

David Lee Schneck, *Outfield*

A compactly built outfielder for the Mets in the early 1970s, Dave was a member of their 1973 National League championship team. His road to the majors was an unlikely one. It began with his being taken as the 669th player in the draft — not the position elite prospects go. He started out with limited expectations, but when he showed signs of exceeding those expectations, he was inducted into the military during the Vietnam War. Schneck said, "I'll always remember the day I got my induction notice. I was married March 7, 1969, got the notice March 8, and was supposed to report for minor league camp in Florida March 9. My wife, Suzie, and I had one day to ourselves without tension."

The war presented a hardship for Schneck. Attached to Uncle Sam's fighting forces, Dave served with the 199th Light Infantry Brigade and thus saw combat action. He set foot on the Vietnam terrain in September of 1969 when the baseball season had reached its climax. Although his old baseball mates were nearing the end of their year, Dave's was just beginning. His unit was engaged in combat maneuvers in the jungle, and Schneck served several months in hostile fighting areas. But the fighting was an enlightening experience for Dave. After his discharge he said, "The experience in Vietnam helped me to mature. I learned how other people live. Our problems are minor compared to how they live."

G	R	H	2B	3B	HR	RBI	BB	SO	SB	AVG	Slug
143	31	82	14	4	8	35	27	73	4	.199	.310

Jerald Lee Schoonmaker, *Outfield*

A "bonus baby" from the University of Missouri, Schoonmaker was a career .130 hitter at the major league level. He initially reached the majors in 1955 with the Washington Senators and then missed all of the 1956 baseball season to service in the United States Army. Jerry was ordered to report to Fort Sill the day after the opening game of the 1956 season. He served as an artillery lieutenant in the Army Reserve. The reserve outfielder played briefly for the 1957 Senators — his last major league action — and once cited Mike "Big Bear" Garcia as the toughest pitcher he ever faced.

G	R	H	2B	3B	HR	RBI	BB	SO	SB	AVG	Slug
50	10	9	1	1	1	4	7	22	1	.130	.217

Paul Edward Schramka, *Reserve*

Schramka played two games with the 1953 Cubs but didn't record a time at bat. Just before his brief trial with the Cubs, Paul served in the army during the Korean War. Right when the Cubs officially placed him on their roster, he was inducted into the army and sent to boot camp. After basic training Paul was shipped overseas to the European Theatre where he was assigned to the 8th Infantry. Able to play service ball in Europe, Paul's 8th Infantry team was nicknamed the Bullets. During one game at Bamburg, Paul broke up a no-hitter and ended the game with two hits — the only two safeties the Bullets tallied in the contest.

G	R	H	2B	3B	HR	RBI	BB	SO	SB	AVG	Slug
2	0	0	0	0	0	0	0	0	0	—	—

Ralph Robert "Mickey" Scott, *Pitcher*

During the Vietnam War Scott was a member of the National Guard. His guard unit was activated in 1967 and he missed an entire season in the minors to active military duty. The southpaw would make his major league debut with the 1972 Orioles, the same year the team called up Vietnam vet Al Bumbry.

W	L	PCT	G	GS	CG	IP	H	BB	SO	SHO	ERA
8	7	.533	133	0	0	172	177	50	70	0	3.71

Richard Allen Severson, *Utility Infielder*

A member of the Kansas City Royals in 1970 and 1971, Rich served as a backup to the Royals' solid infield of Cookie Rojas, Freddie Patek and Paul Schaal. Before Severson made his major league debut he missed two seasons in the bushes to service in the military during the Vietnam War.

G	R	H	2B	3B	HR	RBI	BB	SO	SB	AVG	Slug
93	26	69	11	3	1	23	19	38	0	.256	.330

Walter Charles Shannon, *Second Base/Shortstop*

It is always nice to have relatives in high places. When Wally, who was property of the Cardinals, was inducted into the military for the Korean War, the Cardinals hired his father as their director of minor league operations. Shannon spent time in the service and made the Redbirds' roster in 1959 after his discharge.

G	R	H	2B	3B	HR	RBI	BB	SO	SB	AVG	Slug
65	7	31	5	0	0	6	3	18	0	.263	.305

Donald Wellington Shaw, *Pitcher*

A southpaw who was never able to master his control, Shaw played in the major leagues for pieces of five seasons with four different ballclubs. He made his debut with the last-place Mets of 1967; he posted a 4–5, 3.00 record. Shaw also made a brief stint with the armed forces. He pitched briefly for the Mets in 1968 and then became a member of the expansion Montreal Expos in 1969. His final major league action came with the world champion Oakland Athletics in 1972.

W	L	PCT	G	GS	CG	IP	H	BB	SO	SHO	ERA
13	14	.489	138	1	0	188	166	101	123	0	4.02

Norman Burt Sherry, *Catcher*

An intelligent catcher, Norm Sherry is often credited with assisting Sandy Koufax in his transformation from thrower to pitcher.

Norm, whose brother, Larry, enjoyed some success in the majors, served in the U.S. Army during the Korean War before his major league debut. He served with the 4th Division SP Troops in the European Theatre and was able to play service ball at such locales as Bad Kreuznach.

G	R	H	2B	3B	HR	RBI	BB	SO	SB	AVG	Slug
194	45	107	9	1	18	69	37	102	1	.215	.346

Ronald Lee Shoop, Catcher

Shoop's major league career consisted of a cup of coffee with the 1959 Detroit Tigers. Not given much of a chance in the majors, Ron was an all-star in the service ranks. During the Korean War, Shoop served in the European Theatre with the 1st Division. Stationed at Leighton Barracks, he was able to play service ball while in the army. He took part in a service all-star game held at Wuerzberg during his last year in service.

G	R	H	2B	3B	HR	RBI	BB	SO	SB	AVG	Slug
3	1	1	0	0	0	1	0	1	0	.143	.143

Norman Leroy Siebern, Outfield/First Base

An underrated ballplayer with decent power and an exceptional batting eye, Siebern made his debut with the Yankees in 1956. Norm was their regular left fielder for a few years until he was used to acquire Roger Maris. He then had a few good years in relative obscurity in Kansas City before the Orioles acquired him in 1964. Norm missed some minor league action when he was drafted into the army during the Korean War. He served at Fort McPherson and played some service ball with Vinegar Bend Mizell.

G	R	H	2B	3B	HR	RBI	BB	SO	SB	AVG	Slug
1,406	662	1,217	206	38	132	636	708	749	18	.272	.423

Curtis Thomas Simmons, Pitcher

The Philadelphia Phillies proved to be the first to fight. The club was the first team to lose a player to World War II, Hugh Mulcahy, and Curt Simmons was the first player drafted for the Korean War. Simmons' military summons couldn't have come at a worse time for the Phillies, as he was whisked away with one month left in the 1950 baseball season. That year, the Phillies captured the imagination of the nation with their youthful roster that was dubbed "The Whiz Kids." His National Guard unit was activated on September 10 and Curt was lost for the stretch drive. Despite Simmons' departure, the Phillies still won the NL flag but were swept by the Yankees in the World Series. The loss of Simmons forced skipper Eddie Sawyer to thrust reliever Jim Konstanty into the rotation and work the MVP tirelessly in the Fall Classic.

Simmons was on pass from Camp Atterbury when the World Series started, and speculation swirled as to whether or not the young southpaw was going to take part in the Fall Classic. Curt was eager to suit up with his teammates, stating, "I can get ready for the fifth, sixth or seventh World Series games." Despite his willingness to help out his club, manager Eddie Sawyer made this comment: "We will not ask to make Simmons eligible for the Series." He feared that a month worth of army training had built rust on Simmons' wing. Although Simmons was anxious to take part in the World Series, he didn't have the support of management but did have the backing of Commissioner Happy Chandler, who said, "On at least two other occasions in the past men were given leave from the army and played in the Series."

Through the eyes of a spectator is how Curt Simmons watched the 1950 World Series. He was eager to do his part but was relegated to moral support for the series. Before Game 1 of the World Series, Curt tossed batting practice to his teammates and ran with them in the outfield. After he watched his teammates lose the World Series, Simmons returned to his unit, where he served as a private first class in the 28th Division of the Pennsylvania National Guard. He was sent overseas to Europe late in 1951 after his promotion to sergeant. Early in 1952, Curt returned stateside to receive his discharge from the army, and when asked about baseball, said, "When you've laid off as long as I have, the old control ain't what it used to be."

Simmons picked up where he left off in 1952 and paced the National League with six shutouts on a 2.82 ERA. He posted a .600 winning percentage in 1956 with a fifth-place Phillies club and was dealt to the Cardinals early in 1960. In 1963, Simmons fashioned a 15–9 record and led the Redbirds with a 2.47 ERA. The following year, Curt was instrumental in the Cardinals' NL championship, and was finally able to participate in a World Series after missing his opportunity fifteen years prior. In the 1964 World Series, Curt posted a 2.51 ERA against the Yankees, but the Bronx Bombers were victorious in seven games. A veteran of twenty major league seasons, Simmons came close to 200 career victories but missed out on many due to playing with a poor Phillies club. Longtime teammate Robin Roberts once said of Simmons, "[He] may not have been the fastest pitcher of all time, but he surely was amongst them."

W	L	PCT	G	GS	CG	IP	H	BB	SO	SHO	ERA
193	183	.513	569	462	163	3,349	3,313	1,063	1,697	36	3.54

Ted Lyle Simmons, Catcher

The greatest catcher currently left out of the Baseball Hall of Fame, Simmons missed a small portion (three weeks to be exact) to service in the army during the 1970 baseball season. At the time of his three-week hitch, Ted had replaced Tim McCarver as the Redbirds' regular catcher. He enjoyed his breakout season the following year when he hit .304 and finished second on the club in RBIs.

G	R	H	2B	3B	HR	RBI	BB	SO	SB	AVG	Slug
2,456	1,074	2,472	483	47	248	1,389	855	694	21	.285	.437

David Michael Sisler, Pitcher

Dave was the son of Hall of Famer George Sisler, and Fort Meade milked his heritage while he was stationed there during the Korean War. Local papers in the Fort Meade area would entice people to come out to the camp and see the "son of George Sisler" pitch for the soldiers. A bonus baby, the Fort Meade publicity team also took full advantage of this information as well, with headlines telling readers that the "$42,000 Bonus Hurler" was pitching for the fort today. After his discharge from the army, the Red Sox brought Dave up in 1956. His last major league action came with the 1962 Reds.

W	L	PCT	G	GS	CG	IP	H	BB	SO	SHO	ERA
38	44	.463	247	59	12	655	622	368	355	1	4.34

Robert Ralph Skinner, *Outfield*

The star left fielder for the 1960 world champion Pittsburgh Pirates, Skinner enjoyed a fine career in baseball. Before he began in the majors, Bob served a brief hitch with Uncle Sam's fighting forces during the Korean War. Shortly after his discharge, the Pirates gave him his first look. When Bob was called up, he was used as a reserve that filled in occasionally at first base. He then took over left field from the all-hit, no-field Frank Thomas. Since World War II the Pirates had always had good power but limited defense in left with Ralph Kiner and then Thomas, but Skinner was a better all-around player despite his lack of punch. Bob retired after the 1966 season and watched as his son, Joel, played major league ball as a catcher.

G	R	H	2B	3B	HR	RBI	BB	SO	SB	AVG	Slug
1,381	642	1,198	197	58	103	531	485	646	67	.277	.421

Louis Peter Skizas, *Outfield/Third Base*

Nicknamed "The Nervous Greek," Skizas showcased solid power in his two years with the Kansas City A's. When Lou wasn't on the A's roster, his playing time was limited. A corner outfielder who could fill in at third base, Lou had solid power. Before he made his major league debut, Skizas served in the U.S. Army during the Korean War. Stationed in Germany with the 28th Division Artillery, Lou was able to play plenty of service ball. The hero in a contest at Goeppingen, Lou scored from third base on an infield popup that cemented their berth in the USAREUR quarterfinals.

G	R	H	2B	3B	HR	RBI	BB	SO	SB	AVG	Slug
239	80	196	27	4	30	86	50	37	8	.270	.443

Harold Raymond Smith, *Catcher*

Not to be confused with the Hal Smith who played for the champion Pirates in 1960, Hal Raymond Smith, known as "Cura," was also a catcher. Cura served in the military during the Korean War while in the minor leagues, which interrupted valuable seasoning time. After his discharge, he played with the Cardinals from 1956 through 1961.

G	R	H	2B	3B	HR	RBI	BB	SO	SB	AVG	Slug
570	126	437	63	8	23	172	102	128	6	.258	.345

Paul Leslie Smith, *Outfield*

Standing 5'8" and weighing slightly over 160 pounds, the diminutive Smith made for a less-than-frightening presence in the batter's box. Despite his small stature, he hit for a career .270 batting average. Paul's first major league action came in 1953 with the Pirates before he lost the 1955 and 1956 seasons to service in the armed forces. He returned to play two more years at the highest level.

G	R	H	2B	3B	HR	RBI	BB	SO	SB	AVG	Slug
223	54	152	16	7	7	56	42	44	3	.270	.361

Albert Donald Spangler, *Outfield*

Before Spangler made his major league debut with the Braves, he served in the U.S. Army during the Korean War. The outfielder played service ball at Fort McPherson with Senators catcher Steve Korcheck. After his army discharge, Spangler knocked around the minors for a time until the Braves called him up in 1959. A serviceable major league outfielder, Al would end his career in the late 1960s with the Cubs.

G	R	H	2B	3B	HR	RBI	BB	SO	SB	AVG	Slug
912	307	594	87	26	21	175	295	234	37	.262	.351

Robert Charles Speake, *Outfield/First Base*

Playing ball in the service had its benefits. Bob Speake, a natural first baseman, was able to experiment in the outfield while he served in the military. Had he been in organized ball, he wouldn't have been able to dabble in a position change on his own; instead, he would have been forced to hold a powwow with management to discuss possibilities. While he served in the U.S. Army at Camp Drake in Japan, Speake shagged flyballs in the outfield and patrolled the pasture after the call of the bugle.

Speake, who Milt Richman referred to as a "meat cutter under the GI Bill of Rights," played service ball in Japan with Herb Plews. They played some of their games in the Lou Gehrig Stadium at Yokohama. In between his duties at Camp Drake processing troops in transport to Korea, Speake played baseball and worked in the outfield. After his discharge, Speake saw that Dee Fondy was entrenched at first base in Chicago and he took it upon himself to shag fly balls in the outfield. Manager Stan Hack saw how well Bob did out there and decided to bench the struggling veteran Hank Sauer and give Speake a look. Hack said, "I noticed him out there and I saw that he caught the ball real well. When he came back to the bench, I asked him if he ever played the outfield before. He told me he had played about 70 games in the outfield while in the army, so I decided to give him a shot at it."

G	R	H	2B	3B	HR	RBI	BB	SO	SB	AVG	Slug
305	110	170	26	10	31	104	80	158	8	.223	.406

Daryl Dean Spencer, *Shortstop*

Although Cal Ripken Jr. is given credit for redefining the shortstop position by bringing size to the post, Big Dee, at 6'2" and 200 pounds, arrived long before Mr. Oriole. Spencer made his debut in 1952 with the New York Giants, and he split time between shortstop and third base that year. Spencer was groomed to replace Alvin Dark, but he was drafted into the armed forces in 1954, which put the Giants' plans for him on hold.

He was inducted into the army on February 15, 1954, at Kansas City and was assigned to Fort Sill, Oklahoma. While stationed at Fort Sill, Big Dee was able to play a reasonable amount of baseball. There was speculation as to whether or not he would take part in the National Baseball Congress Championship held in Milwaukee since he was due for a reassignment. Daryl had this to say regarding the issue: "Whether I'll play at Milwaukee will depend upon whether I can get my furlough at that time and how far we go in the All-Army Tournament at Fort Belvoir."

Spencer received his discharge in time for the 1956 baseball season, as his presence made the trade of Alvin Dark to the Cardinals for Red Schoendienst feasible. He came into his own in 1957 when he led the Giants with 31 doubles and excelled when the Giants relocated to San Francisco in 1958. Daryl played his last four seasons with three different clubs—the Cardinals, Dodgers and Reds.

G	R	H	2B	3B	HR	RBI	BB	SO	SB	AVG	Slug
1,098	457	901	145	20	105	428	449	516	13	.244	.380

Frederick Blair Stanley, *Utility Infielder*

Regarded as an all-field, no-hit infielder, Stanley had a long tenure with the New York Yankees. Fred spent a lot of time backing up such players as Bucky Dent and Willie Randolph. The wiry infielder missed one season in the minor leagues to military service during the Vietnam War.

G	R	H	2B	3B	HR	RBI	BB	SO	SB	AVG	Slug
815	197	356	38	5	10	120	196	243	11	.216	.263

Leroy Bobby Stanton, *Outfielder*

A powerfully built outfielder capable of socking fifteen or so home runs a year, Stanton is best remembered as part of one of baseball's most lopsided trades. The Angels sent veteran Jim Fregosi, who was near the end of his career, to the Mets for Stanton and some kid named Nolan Ryan. The Angels clearly won that deal as Nolan became a legend and Stanton led the Angels in home runs in 1975. Before Leroy played at the major league level, he served in the army during the Vietnam War. Stationed in the European Theatre, Stanton served with the Third Support Brigade and played some service ball at Stuttgart.

G	R	H	2B	3B	HR	RBI	BB	SO	SB	AVG	Slug
829	294	628	114	13	77	358	236	636	36	.244	.388

Robert Lloyd Stephenson, *Shortstop*

Regarded as an all-field, no-hit shortstop in the minor leagues, Bobby missed the 1953 and 1954 seasons to military service. He was given a trial the following year with the Cardinals but never played in the majors afterwards.

G	R	H	2B	3B	HR	RBI	BB	SO	SB	AVG	Slug
67	19	27	3	0	0	6	5	18	2	.243	.270

Chester Earl Stephenson, *Pitcher*

A left-handed relief pitcher, Stephenson was a minor league journeyman who spaced out his stints in the majors. He made his debut with the 1971 Cubs and then played for the Brewers in 1972. After several years back in the bushes, the Orioles called him up in 1977, and he played for them in 1978 as well. While still in the minors, before his debut in the majors, Earl missed a season to military service during the Vietnam War.

W	L	PCT	G	GS	CG	IP	H	BB	SO	SHO	ERA
4	5	.444	54	8	1	113	118	49	50	0	3.58

James Michael Strickland, *Pitcher*

A southpaw reliever for the Twins in the early 1970s, Jim was good at tallying strikeouts and missing bats, but in the process he would often miss the strike zone. Strickland, a wild fireman, missed some minor league action during the Vietnam War when he served as an aircraft mechanic in the military.

W	L	PCT	G	GS	CG	IP	H	BB	SO	SHO	ERA
4	2	.667	60	0	0	77	63	44	60	0	2.69

Richard Lee "Dick" Stuart, *First Base*

Nicknamed "Dr. Strangeglove" because of his poor defensive work at first base, Dick took the jokes in stride. To show that the unflattering moniker didn't bother him, Stuart had his license plate changed to "E 3" on his car. A big, raw-boned power hitter from the West Coast, Stuart belted home runs for Uncle Sam before he ever hit one for a major league squad. Dick served in the U.S. Army and was stationed at Fort Lewis, Washington, where he played service ball with catcher Charley Lau. After his discharge, the Pirates called him up in 1958 and he was a key ingredient in their turnaround from doormat to world champs in 1960. He led the team in home runs and RBIs that season, edging out Hall of Fame teammate Roberto Clemente in both departments.

G	R	H	2B	3B	HR	RBI	BB	SO	SB	AVG	Slug
1,112	506	1,055	157	30	228	743	301	957	2	.264	.489

Thomas Virgil Sturdivant, *Pitcher*

When Uncle Sam drafted Sturdivant for duty during the Korean War, the Kansas lad was being groomed for work in the infield. After two years in the service, Tom was discharged and promptly converted from an infielder into a pitcher. He made the Yankees in 1955 and had a solid career as a long relief man and spot starter.

W	L	PCT	G	GS	CG	IP	H	BB	SO	SHO	ERA
59	51	.536	335	101	22	1,136	1,029	449	704	7	3.75

Franklin Leal Sullivan, *Pitcher*

A two-time all-star, Sullivan was called up by the Red Sox less than a year after his army discharge. Frank spent the 1951 and 1952 seasons in the military, but Boston summoned his presence in 1953 when they needed arms.

W	L	PCT	G	GS	CG	IP	H	BB	SO	SHO	ERA
97	100	.492	351	219	73	1,732	1,702	559	959	15	3.60

John Junior "Champ" Summers, *Outfield/First Base/DH*

A decent power hitter when he was called upon to play, Champ was usually employed as a power-hitting pinch-hitter. A favorite of skipper Sparky Anderson, Summers played under Sparky when he piloted the Reds and then joined the Tigers as a designated hitter when Sparky was hired there. Champ's last action at the highest level came with the 1984 San Diego Padres—led by Tony Gwynn and Steve Garvey—that captured the National League pennant.

The story of how Champ Summers made the majors is an unusual one. He signed his first pro contract as a 25-year-old former combat veteran of Vietnam. During the war, Champ was a paratrooper in Uncle Sam's fighting forces. After his discharge, he attended college on a basketball scholarship but walked on the baseball team and impressed on the diamond. However, when the baseball draft began, teams passed on Champ because the ex-paratrooper was in his mid-twenties.

G	R	H	2B	3B	HR	RBI	BB	SO	SB	AVG	Slug
698	199	350	63	4	54	218	188	244	15	.255	.425

George Daniel Susce, *Pitcher*

His father, also named George, was a major league ballplayer as well. Before the younger George made his major league debut with the Red Sox, he served in the military during the Korean War. During his stint in the army, he played service ball with Don Newcombe at the Brooke Army Medical Center.

W	L	PCT	G	GS	CG	IP	H	BB	SO	SHO	ERA
22	17	.564	117	36	8	410	407	170	177	1	4.41

William Michael Taylor, *Outfield*

Used almost exclusively as a power bat off the bench, "Moose" missed the 1951 and 1952 seasons to service in the military during the Korean War. Given his first look in the majors during the 1954 season, Taylor was a preferred pinch-hitter of Leo Durocher.

G	R	H	2B	3B	HR	RBI	BB	SO	SB	AVG	Slug
149	17	41	8	0	7	26	5	39	0	.237	.405

Samuel Douglas Taylor, *Catcher*

The Cubs' regular catcher in the late 1950s until an injury in 1960 limited his mobility, Taylor had a good bat for a backstop. Sammy, a Korean War veteran before his major league debut, was traded by the Cubs in 1962 to the expansion Mets and thus has the stigma of playing for the worst team in modern times.

G	R	H	2B	3B	HR	RBI	BB	SO	SB	AVG	Slug
473	127	309	47	9	33	147	122	181	3	.245	.375

Charles Sherman Templeton, *Pitcher*

A big southpaw, Templeton served overseas with the 1st Division Artillery during the Korean War. Chuck, who struggled with command issues at the major league level, spent two years with the Brooklyn Dodgers just before they relocated to Los Angeles.

W	L	PCT	G	GS	CG	IP	H	BB	SO	SHO	ERA
0	2	.000	10	2	0	21	25	15	11	0	7.71

Jerry Wayne Terrell, *Utilityman*

A valuable man on a roster, Terrell could fill in just about anywhere. The versatile player spent time in the majors during the 1970s with the Twins and Royals. His last action came with the American League champion Royals of 1980. During the Vietnam War, Jerry served with the Army Reserves and was one of the lucky ones who didn't miss any baseball action to military service.

G	R	H	2B	3B	HR	RBI	BB	SO	SB	AVG	Slug
657	218	412	48	11	4	125	76	160	50	.253	.304

Maynard Faye Throneberry, *Outfield*

Not quite as famous as his brother Marv (who gained notoriety for ineptitude) Faye played a total of eight seasons in the major leagues, with two lost to the Korean War. Faye was initially called up in 1952 by the Red Sox and hit .258 as a fill in for Ted Williams. The following year, he joined Williams in the armed forces and served at Fort Jackson. While serving in the army, Throneberry played in the All-Army World Series held at Fort Sam Houston. He missed the entirety of the 1953 and 1954 Baseball seasons and returned to play sparingly with the Red Sox, Senators and Angels.

G	R	H	2B	3B	HR	RBI	BB	SO	SB	AVG	Slug
521	152	307	48	12	29	137	127	284	23	.236	.358

Gary Dale Timberlake, *Pitcher*

Timberlake's major league career consisted of two starts for the Seattle Pilots in 1969. During his lone year at the highest level, Gary also served in the armed forces.

W	L	PCT	G	GS	CG	IP	H	BB	SO	SHO	ERA
0	0	—	2	2	0	6	7	9	4	0	7.50

Frank Joseph Torre, *First Base*

Brother of former all-star catcher and future Hall of Fame manager Joe Torre, Frank was a first baseman/pinch-hitter at the major league level. A good batsman, Torre didn't have the power that most teams want out of their first baseman, which meant he would often platoon with or back up power hitters like Joe Adcock or Roy Sievers. Before Torre made his major league debut, he served in the U.S. Army at Fort Dix. He was able to play some service ball there with pitcher Erv Palica.

G	R	H	2B	3B	HR	RBI	BB	SO	SB	AVG	Slug
714	150	404	78	15	13	179	155	64	4	.273	.372

Gus Triandos, *Catcher*

One of the top power-hitting catchers of all time, Triandos was often among the leaders in home runs. He led Baltimore in home runs every year from 1956 to 1959. In 1958, Gus socked 30 home runs— the only catcher to do so. A three-time All-Star, Triandos was the face of the Orioles in the late 1950s. During the Korean War, Gus served at the baseball hotbed Brooke Army Medical Center.

G	R	H	2B	3B	HR	RBI	BB	SO	SB	AVG	Slug
1,206	389	954	147	6	167	608	440	636	1	.244	.413

Joseph Gerard Trimble, *Pitcher*

Trimble pitched briefly at the major league level with the 1955 Red Sox and 1957 Pirates. Before he made his debut he served in the armed forces during the Korean War.

W	L	PCT	G	GS	CG	IP	H	BB	SO	SHO	ERA
0	2	.000	7	4	0	22	23	16	10	0	7.36

Robert Trowbridge, *Pitcher*

A solid relief pitcher for the Braves in the late 1950s, Trowbridge was a member of the world champion Braves of 1957. Before he threw his first pitch for the Braves, Bob owned servicemen during the Korean War. Stationed at Nellis Army Airbase in Las Vegas, Bob was the sporting sensation on the installation. During one eight-game stretch at the base, Trowbridge averaged 22 strikeouts per game. In awe of Trowbridge's pitching accomplishments, Sergeant Kenny Braden, who served at Nellis, said, "If Trow goes as well for the Braves when he gets out of the service two years from now, Boston will really have something."

W	L	PCT	G	GS	CG	IP	H	BB	SO	SHO	ERA
13	13	.500	116	25	4	330	324	156	201	1	3.95

Robert Lee "Bullet Bob" Turley, *Pitcher*

Nicknamed "Bullet Bob" because he could toss the apple with unrivalled speed, Turley was a pitching prodigy who enjoyed a couple of great seasons but many more erratic ones. Although he could throw hard, the strike zone seemed to him the bull's eye on a dart board. A longtime Yankees hurler, Bullet Bob gained notoriety in 1954 when he paced the American League with 185 strikeouts as a member of Jimmy Dykes' Orioles. The following year he was shipped off to the AL champion New York Yankees and won the Cy Young Award in 1958 as the American League's lone 20-game winner.

The humble Bob Turley missed the entire 1952 baseball season as well as a portion of the 1953 season to service in the armed forces, where he served at the Brooke Army Medical Center. As a young twirler with a brilliant arm, Bullet Bob often heard his name spoken in the same breath with such legends as Big Train Walter Johnson. When Turley visited Washington—Johnson's old stomping grounds—he viewed accolades the Senators displayed at their stadium concerning the Big Train's career. Aghast, Bullet Bob said, "He won 414 games—113 of them shutouts—one out of every four. How can anybody mention me in the same breath with him? He must have been a superman."

W	L	PCT	G	GS	CG	IP	H	BB	SO	SHO	ERA
101	85	.543	310	237	78	1,711	1,366	1,068	1,265	24	3.65

William Ray Upton, *Pitcher*

Brother of infielder Tom Upton, Bill had a cup of coffee with the 1954 Athletics. The right-hander was one of the first ballplayers to be plucked by Uncle Sam for duty during the Korean War as he missed the 1950 and 1951 seasons to the conflict.

W	L	PCT	G	GS	CG	IP	H	BB	SO	SHO	ERA
0	0	—	2	0	0	5	6	1	2	0	1.80

Jack Elmer Urban, *Pitcher*

A long arm and spot starter for the Kansas City A's in the late 1950s, Urban finished his major league career with an even .500 winning percentage. Jack missed some minor league action to service in the military during the Korean War.

W	L	PCT	G	GS	CG	IP	H	BB	SO	SHO	ERA
15	15	.500	69	37	8	272	279	103	113	1	4.83

Vito John Valentinetti, *Pitcher*

While Vito was playing minor league ball for Colorado Springs in 1951, he was expecting his draft notice at any moment. Given that he knew Uncle Sam was certain to call, he sat out the early part of the season and prepared for his army induction. When the army failed to call when Vito expected, he returned to Colorado Springs and kept pitching. Finally, his draft board summoned him, and he was inducted well after his initial speculations. Valentinetti made the majors with the 1954 White Sox and pitched his last with the 1959 Senators.

W	L	PCT	G	GS	CG	IP	H	BB	SO	SHO	ERA
13	14	.481	108	15	3	257	266	122	94	0	4.73

Glen Gann "Buck" Varner, *Reserve*

During the Korean War, Varner served with the U.S. Marine Corps. He was reinstated from the Senators' service list in the summer of 1952, and Washington called him up late that year for his only trial at the highest level.

G	R	H	2B	3B	HR	RBI	BB	SO	SB	AVG	Slug
2	0	0	0	0	0	0	1	1	0	.000	.000

Osvaldo Jose Virgil, *Utilityman*

A peacetime soldier, Virgil joined the U.S. Marine Corps shortly after immigrating to the United States. Not familiar with baseball at the time, Ozzie learned how to play the game with the Marines. Virgil was still in the corps when the Korean War began but received his discharge and was able to put his newly acquired skills to work professionally. The Giants called him up in 1956 and he played ball in the majors and minors until 1970.

G	R	H	2B	3B	HR	RBI	BB	SO	SB	AVG	Slug
324	75	174	19	7	14	73	34	91	6	.231	.331

James "Bo" Wallace, *Catcher*

Bo Wallace's baseball career ended during the Korean War. While in the army, the catching prospect suffered a severe injury to his left hand when a grenade exploded, which permanently mangled his hand. Wallace had to give up baseball and took a job as a bartender.

(1948–1949): Newark Eagles and Houston Eagles

Kenneth Rogers Walters, *Outfield*

During the Korean War, Walters played service ball at Fort Ord under J.W. Porter. The outfielder from Fresno spent some time in the minors after his army discharge before he made the majors in 1960. He was the Phillies' everyday right fielder as a rookie that year but would play sparingly the remainder of his career.

G	R	H	2B	3B	HR	RBI	BB	SO	SB	AVG	Slug
259	71	157	20	2	11	58	25	89	6	.231	.314

Preston Meyer Ward, *Outfield*

Ward enjoyed an adequate major league career, which spanned nine seasons, and saw two slates interrupted by the Korean War. His first taste of baseball's highest level came in 1948 with the Brooklyn Dodgers; he appeared in 42 games as a 20-year-old rookie. He spent the entire 1949 season back in the bushes and returned to the majors in 1950 with the Cubs. He lost the 1951 and 1952 campaigns to service in the armed forces and returned to play out his career with the Cubs, Pirates, Indians and Kansas City Athletics.

G	R	H	2B	3B	HR	RBI	BB	SO	SB	AVG	Slug
744	219	522	83	15	50	262	231	315	7	.253	.380

Richard Henry Weik, *Pitcher*

Tall and lean, Dick Weik was as unassociated with the strike zone as a fish is with dry land. He is one of the few pitchers in the history of baseball to issue more walks than innings pitched. Be that as it may, Dick was able to pitch in the major leagues for five seasons, first with the Senators and then with the Indians and Tigers. He missed two full seasons, 1951 and 1952, to service in the U.S. Army. During his time in khaki, Dick was stationed at Fort Leonard Wood, Missouri, and was discharged from the service on November 10, 1952.

W	L	PCT	G	GS	CG	IP	H	BB	SO	SHO	ERA
6	22	.214	76	26	3	213	203	237	123	2	5.92

Leroy William Wheat, *Pitcher*

A member of the last Philadelphia A's team and the original Kansas City A's squad, Wheat was a big right-hander with decent control. Originally signed by the Cleveland Indians, Lee's high school coach was a birddog for the Tribe. The Indians assigned him to the Pacific Coast League in 1951 but Uncle Sam had other ideas. Inducted into the army, Wheat ventured off to Fort Riley for basic training. After he completed boot camp he was transferred to Fort Bliss for eight weeks of AIT. Lee's military occupation was in anti-aircraft gunning. He served as an instructor in the anti-aircraft school before he was transferred to a mess hall.

Like most ballplayers who served during the Korean War, Wheat was able to play the game. Recreation came second in the army, but the boys were still able to toil on the ball diamond after the sound of the bugle. Wheat said, "We worked a full day at our regular jobs then went out and practiced on our free time." Near the end of his military hitch, Lee was married to his sweetheart and asked his lieutenant to serve as best man. He used his accrued leave for a honeymoon and then reported to Fort Sill, where he was mustered out of service. Wheat pitched at the major league level in 1954 and 1955.

W	L	PCT	G	GS	CG	IP	H	BB	SO	SHO	ERA
0	2	.000	11	1	0	30	46	12	8	0	6.90

Thomas Peter Whisenant, *Outfield*

A journeyman outfielder with a decent speed and power combination, Whisenant made his major league debut with the 1952 Boston Braves. He enjoyed a sporadic and nomadic career with calls up to the majors and papers confirming trips back to the minors. Often seen in transaction sheets, Pete was traded a few times over the course of his career. During the Korean War, Pete was stationed at the San Diego Naval Training Station where he played service ball with a young prodigy named Eddie Mathews.

G	R	H	2B	3B	HR	RBI	BB	SO	SB	AVG	Slug
475	140	221	46	8	37	134	86	196	17	.224	.399

William DeKova White, *First Base*

A star first baseman during his playing days and listed as one of the Top 10 best defensive first basemen of all-time in the book *The Best of Baseball*, White spent 21 months in the service of Uncle Sam. During his stint in the military, White was stationed at Fort Knox, where he spent one year in the Special Service and another as a supply clerk. The slick fielding first sacker was already established at the major league level — he posted a solid line of 22 homers, 59 RBIs and a .256 batting average the year before he was drafted into the army — but returned to the Giants late in 1958 without a job. While White was serving his country, a power hitter named Orlando Cepeda took his role as the first baseman and Bill was dealt to the Cardinals the following year. However, it was in St. Louis where Bill White earned his status as an elite first baseman.

G	R	H	2B	3B	HR	RBI	BB	SO	SB	AVG	Slug
1,673	843	1,706	278	65	202	870	596	927	103	.286	.455

Floyd Euliss Wicker, *Outfielder*

A member of the first-year Milwaukee Brewers after their shift from Seattle, Wicker played pieces of five seasons at the major league level but never did stick. He also saw action with the Cardinals, Expos and Giants. Before he made his major league debut, Wicker served in the army during the Vietnam War. A military policeman, Wicker joined the army in December 1963 and took his basic training and AIT at Fort Gordon. While serving his country, Floyd married the former Francine Coble.

G	R	H	2B	3B	HR	RBI	BB	SO	SB	AVG	Slug
81	10	18	1	0	1	6	7	33	0	.159	.195

Robert George Wiesler, *Pitcher*

A switch-hitting southpaw pitcher, Wiesler was regarded as one of the Yankees' top pitching prospects at the time he was summoned for the Korean War. As a 20-year-old, Bob appeared in four games — three starts — with the Yankees in 1951 as a rookie. However, he served with a National Guard unit that was activated during his initial major league campaign. Wiesler lost the entire 1952 season and didn't return to the majors until the Yankees beckoned him back in 1954. After his tour with the Bronx Bombers, Bob spent pieces of three seasons with the Washington Senators.

W	L	PCT	G	GS	CG	IP	H	BB	SO	SHO	ERA
7	19	.269	70	38	4	240	250	218	113	0	5.78

Carlton Francis Willey, *Pitcher*

Before Willey made his major league debut, he served in the military during the Korean War. The right-hander from Maine made the majors in 1958 with the Braves, who were the defending champions. After the 1962 season, he was sent to the Mets, where he played under Hall of Fame skipper Casey Stengel. Carl invited Stengel to Maine for his first lobster bake.

W	L	PCT	G	GS	CG	IP	H	BB	SO	SHO	ERA
38	58	.396	199	117	28	876	830	326	493	11	3.76

Donald Fred Williams, *Pitcher*

Williams pitched three years in the major leagues but amassed only eleven games. He missed the 1954 and 1955 seasons to military service before he made his major league debut with the Pirates in 1958.

W	L	PCT	G	GS	CG	IP	H	BB	SO	SHO	ERA
0	0	—	11	0	0	20	29	4	7	0	7.20

James Francis Williams, *Utility Infielder*

Williams' playing career consisted of thirteen major league at-bats over the course of two seasons with the Cardinals. The middle infielder missed the majority of the 1966 season to service in the armed forces and returned to play in one game for the National League champion Cardinals in 1967. Williams is best remembered as a major league manager and coach. He served as a lieutenant to Bobby Cox in Atlanta, but helmed the Blue Jays, Red Sox and Astros during his managing career.

G	R	H	2B	3B	HR	RBI	BB	SO	SB	AVG	Slug
14	1	3	0	0	0	1	1	6	0	.231	.231

Theodore Samuel Williams, *Outfield*

Arguably the greatest hitter of all time, Williams spent his entire playing career with the Boston Red Sox but missed close to five full seasons to military duty. The Splendid Splinter spent three years during World War II training to be a pilot. With his background in flying, Uncle Sam called Ted's number again during the Korean War and Williams was shipped overseas, where he was engaged in combat flying with the Third Marine Wing. On one mission, Williams was suffering from flu-like symptoms but went in the air regardless. They were set to bomb a large enemy troop encampment but Ted got his plane down too low and was hit by fire.

In his autobiography, *My Turn at Bat*, Williams recalls the scary ordeal. He writes, "I was a target for I don't know how many thousands of enemy soldiers in that encampment, and sure as hell I got hit with small arms fire. When I pulled up out of my run, all the red lights were on in the plane and the damn thing started to shake.... I knew I had a hydraulic leak. Fuel warning light, fire warning light, there are so many lights on a jet that when anything serious goes wrong the lights almost blind you. I was in serious trouble."

Williams, with the assistance of his fellow flyers, was able to make it back to base and land the charred wreckage of what used to be his plane. Of course, Ted didn't land the plane but crashed the damaged vessel. He returned to the crash site and saw his plane's skid marks that ran 2,000 feet down the runway. Shortly thereafter, the sickness he was battling got the better of him and he was shipped off to Pohang, where he was diagnosed with pneumonia. He flew 39 missions before he was shipped back to the States to take care of his illness.

Although Ted Williams had a reputation for arrogance and his personality could be abrasive and off-putting at times, he was a class act. One of the greatest American celebrities, he earned his celebrity status through hard work and a firm sense of patriotism. He did possess much bravado on the baseball diamond, but when it came to serving his country, he was modest. Williams said, "Everybody tries to make a hero out of me over the Korean thing. I was no hero. There were maybe seventy-five pilots in our two squadrons and 99 percent of them did a better job than I did."

G	R	H	2B	3B	HR	RBI	BB	SO	SB	AVG	Slug
2,292	1,798	2,654	525	71	521	1,839	2,021	709	24	.344	.634

William Donald Wilson, *Outfield*

A stout man with major league power, Wilson showcased his pop at the highest level on an inconsistent basis. He made his major league debut in 1950 with the White Sox and missed the next two seasons to service in the armed forces. Wilson returned to Chicago in 1953, and played sparingly as a 24-year-old before he was dealt to the Athletics early in 1954. Under skipper Eddie Joost, Wilson paced the A's in long balls while he filled in for injured Slugger Gus Zernial. When the Athletics moved to Kansas City, Wilson went with them and played his final major league season under Hall of Fame skipper Lou Boudreau.

G	R	H	2B	3B	HR	RBI	BB	SO	SB	AVG	Slug
224	87	145	23	1	32	77	72	136	2	.222	.407

Edward Joseph Winceniak, *Utility Infielder*

Regarded as a good-field, no-hit infielder, Winceniak played parts of two seasons with his hometown Cubs. Before he made his major league debut, he served in the European Theatre during the Korean War with the 14th RCT.

G	R	H	2B	3B	HR	RBI	BB	SO	SB	AVG	Slug
32	6	14	3	0	1	8	3	12	0	.209	.299

George Adrian Witt, *Pitcher*

Witt, a strapping right-hander from Long Beach, served during the Korean War on the West Coast. Stationed at the San Diego Naval Training Station, "Red" played service ball with Hall of Famer Eddie Mathews and outfielder Pete Whisenant. After his discharge, Witt joined the Pirates and was a member of their World Series champion team of 1960. He was the only pitcher used by the Pirates in the Series that didn't surrender an earned run.

W	L	PCT	G	GS	CG	IP	H	BB	SO	SHO	ERA
11	16	.407	66	38	5	229	225	127	156	3	4.32

Harold Joseph Woodeshick, *Pitcher*

One of the top left-handed firemen of the 1960s, Woodeshick served in the military during the Korean War before his major league debut. In Hal's first two years at the highest level, he pitched with three different teams. He pitched a couple of years with the Senators before he settled in with the expansion Houston Colt .45s. A star relief pitcher in Houston, he ended his career by pitching a perfect inning in the World Series for the champion Cardinals in 1967. Offered to pitch in 1968, Hal said, "I could have gone to camp and hung on perhaps all season and made the same money, but you have to have some pride. I just wouldn't take their money knowing I couldn't help a big league club."

W	L	PCT	G	GS	CG	IP	H	BB	SO	SHO	ERA
44	62	.415	427	62	7	847	816	389	484	1	3.56

Roy Earl Wright, *Pitcher*

Wright made one start with the 1956 Giants—the extent of his major league career. Before his debut, Roy served in the armed forces during the Korean War. Stationed at Landstuhl, Germany, Wright was a supply clerk in the Air Force when he wasn't playing ball for the Landstuhl Raiders.

W	L	PCT	G	GS	CG	IP	H	BB	SO	SHO	ERA
0	1	.000	1	1	0	3	8	2	0	0	18.00

Norbert Henry "Norm" Zauchin, *First Base*

Standing 6'5" and tipping the scales at 220 pounds, Zauchin made for quite the intimidating presence in the batter's box. He made his big league debut in 1951 with the Red Sox and missed the next two seasons to service in the armed forces. After a year in the bushes, Norm returned to Boston in 1955 and finished one home run behind teammate Ted Williams for the highest mark on the team. Zauchin spoke highly of the Splendid Splinter and gave Ted credit for his 10-RBI game in 1955 in which Norm swatted three homers and smacked a double. After his dream game, Norm said, "It's great to have (Ted) Williams around. While he's been working out (from a layoff) I've talked to him about hitting — little things, but they've helped." When Norm closed his baseball career, he became a professional bowler.

G	R	H	2B	3B	HR	RBI	BB	SO	SB	AVG	Slug
346	134	242	28	2	50	159	137	226	5	.233	.408

George William Zeber, *Utility Infielder*

Each year Zeber played in the majors he was with a pennant-winning team. The Yankees gave him trials in 1977 and 1978, but with Willie Randolph playing his natural position, George wasn't needed. The switch-hitting infielder spent two years in the army as a young man.

G	R	H	2B	3B	HR	RBI	BB	SO	SB	AVG	Slug
28	8	21	3	0	3	10	9	11	0	.296	.465

Calling on Cooperstown

Cooperstown is the home of the National Baseball Hall of Fame Museum and Library. A person can travel the halls of this wondrous establishment and be taken back in time when Ed Walsh was baffling baseball with his spitball offerings and when Philadelphia was still home to two teams. There are hundreds of awe-inspiring relics displayed of the greatest of all games, from Taylor "Ballhawk" Douthit's dusty old glove to Anaheim's fabled Rally Monkey. Patrons can learn about the long since disbanded All-American Girls Professional Baseball League and the Negro Leagues. This building, holiest of all chapels for the baseball acolyte, serves as a gateway to the past. However great this building may be, like all things, it has its flaws.

Racing that wicked harpy we all know as Mother Nature, I journeyed from Randolph, New Hampshire, the home of former Philadelphia Athletics pitcher Bob Savage, south to Cooperstown, New York. The day prior to my trip to Cooperstown, I was snowed in at the rustic Mt. Madison Motel, but the snow had subsided, which allowed me a chance to trek south to baseball's Mecca. I was a moth attracted to a flame — my flame being the Baseball Hall of Fame — as I longed to visit this storied locale for many years. With my current project the only item on my mind, I desired to see how Cooperstown paid tribute to the ballplayers who served their country. I had visions of Joe and Dom DiMaggio in military fatigues and of Cecil Travis rewarded for his bravery for fighting at the Battle of the Bulge. In my mind's eye, I conjured images of Warren Spahn in complete battle dress and saw a showcase of Mickey Rivers and Bobby Murcer with their baseball uniforms placed beside their military fatigues. However, the mind can conjure many fictitious images, and when I arrived at Cooperstown, I saw none of the visions that had been created through fancy. Homage is paid to the military veteran in Cooperstown by a simple plaque that lists the Hall of Fame members who served during time of war. The names we all remember, such as Ted Williams, Bob Feller and Ernie Banks, are found on this plaque, but the names of the men with inferior statistics but equal valor remain shrouded in the shadows.

Where can Elmer Gedeon be found, I ask? The one-time Washington Senator made the ultimate sacrifice for his country, yet his name is banished to the regions of baseball's forgotten lore. Heroism can be found in spikes and a baseball uniform, but it is the man who achieves the status of hero and not the lofty statistics. I ask the Hall of Fame not to enshrine all the men found is this volume but to simply pay homage to their sacrifice. These men didn't ask for a war, they had reached their dream of playing in the major leagues only to have that dream dashed. George Yankowski, a catcher who appeared only in eighteen major league games but served his country for four years, said it best when he stated, "Serving your country dwarfs playing baseball."

In this, the final chapter, I plan to make a case for two men I believe should have a plaque in Cooperstown. These two men deserve to have their names and accomplishments displayed in bronze in the halls of our beloved Hall of Fame. Their career statistics, as good as they are, could have been added upon had they not missed three prime years to World War II. One of the men played for the hapless Washington Senators, a terrific shortstop whose star wasn't quite bright enough to be spotted by writers outside of the D.C. area. When he was taken away by Uncle Sam, only Honus Wagner — the greatest of all shortstops—could equal his batting average. Notice that I used the word *equal*, since not even the Flying Dutchman could excel the lofty batting mark of the great Cecil Travis. Travis missed the better part of four years to service in the army, where he took part in combat action in the European Theatre and suffered severe frostbite that greatly reduced his effectiveness when he returned to Washington.

The other man spent his entire career in the spotlight of his more charismatic and publicized older brother. Dominic DiMaggio would have easily been the best center fielder of his time had he not played in the same era as his older brother, Joe. Dom DiMaggio fought his way into the military — initially rejected on account of his poor eyesight — as his uncommon patriotism allowed him the chance to serve his country. As DiMaggio told this writer, "I wasn't about to play the war on the baseball field."

Although I only plan on making a case for Cecil Travis and Dominic DiMaggio in this chapter, know that there are others I would be inclined to put in the Baseball Hall of Fame. I find it rather difficult to reject Mickey Vernon, the great Senator first baseman who won two batting titles—one of which came the year after he missed time to the military. Pitcher Urban Shocker, who saw combat action in Europe during World War I, notched a lot of victories with the lowly St. Louis Browns in his career. Bob Shawkey, who served on a battleship during World War I, was a terrific pitcher who was at his best with the Yankees when the team was not at its best. "The Walking Man" Eddie Yost scored more runs than any fellow third baseman enshrined in Cooperstown that played before him.

Johnny Pesky led the American League in base hits his rookie year, then lost the next three years to World War II. When Pesky returned to the diamond, he led the AL in hits again, after a three-year hiatus. Ted Simmons, who just missed a short time due to military service, is the best catcher currently left out of the Baseball Hall of Fame — without question. Tommy Bridges was widely regarded as one of the top pitchers of his time and arguably the best in the American League before Bob Feller. Buck O'Neil, the Negro League great, won a batting title the season after his multi-year military tenure, just like Mickey Vernon. Sam Chapman, Muddy Ruel, Buddy Lewis, Johnny Sain, Larry French, Don Newcombe, Gil Hodges, Dick Bartell, Schoolboy Rowe, Curt Simmons, Dick Groat, Lonny Frey and such Negro Leaguers as Dick Redding, Dave Malarcher and Spot Poles all deserve words on their behalf. However, this chapter is dedicated to the two men that *belong* in the Baseball Hall of Fame: the sweet-swinging Senator Cecil Travis and the multi-talented Red Sox center fielder Dom DiMaggio.

Cecil Travis

It is commonly written that Cecil Travis is the third-best hitting shortstop in baseball history with a career .314 batting average. His career mark rests behind Arky Vaughan's .318 and Honus Wagner's .327 batting averages. However, when Travis left baseball for the military after the 1941 season, he was in a virtual tie with Wagner as the greatest hitting shortstop in baseball history. He lost the better portion of four years to the military, during which he suffered a severe case of frostbite while fighting at the Battle of the Bulge. Afterwards, Travis returned to baseball a mere fraction of the stellar player he was before the Great War.

Cecil Travis made a splash at the major league level like few have before or since. In his debut, he collected five hits, stroking a handful of hard-hit line drives in between the shortstop and third baseman — a hit that Tony Gwynn made fashionable many decades later. His offensive output did not shock his most ardent followers. Tubby Walton, who coached Cecil as an amateur with Kid Elberfeld, said, "When he started massaging that tomato with all the grace and skill of a finished product, I knew we had found a real embryonic star."

Joe Cronin, the manager of the Senators when Travis first came up, gave Cecil the starting third-base assignment in 1934. In his first full year in the majors, Travis hit .319, a mark that eclipsed every hot corner man in the game except the great Bill Werber and Pinky Higgins. After the 1934 season, Senators owner Clark Griffith sold Cronin to the Red Sox and named Bucky Harris the manager for the 1935 campaign. Harris' appointment spelled doom for all the youngsters in Washington, as Bucky had little patience and enjoyed juggling the lineup. It was because of Bucky Harris that such young players under his management weren't allowed to develop defensively, which led to some negative articles written about young charges like Travis and Buddy Lewis. Cecil hit .318 in 1935 under Harris, but he came under fire due to his lack of desire to pull the ball to right field. Pulling the ball equates to a greater chance of hitting the sphere over the wall, but the Senators' home field, Griffith Stadium, was a spacious lot that would make the argument for Travis to turn on pitches obsolete. Only one Senators player hit more than five home runs in 1935 — Jake Powell, with an even six.

With Buddy Lewis on the roster, Travis switched to shortstop in 1936 to accommodate his roommate. Travis hit .317 in 1936, which proved he possessed remarkable consistency at the plate. During his first full three years at the major league level, Travis hit for averages of .319 in 1934, .318 in 1935 and .317 in 1936. If he had gone unnoticed in those three seasons, he was certain to be seen in 1937. He hit .344 in 1937 — Luke Appling finished second among AL shortstops with a .317 mark — which was good for fifth place in the American League. It took such notable Sluggers as Charlie Gehringer, Lou Gehrig and Joe DiMaggio to top Travis' .344 mark. Cecil finished one point behind masher Zeke Bonura, who took the fourth slot in the standings.

Writer Richard McCann noticed Travis in 1937 when he wrote, "This season he's been harder to put out than an oil field fire." His defensive abilities were also lauded by McCann, who claimed, "He has one of the best arms in the game and a sure pair of hands. Once he gets hold of a ball there's no sense you running it out." As an encore for his breakout season of 1937, Cecil hit .335 in 1938 — a good 32 points higher than Hall of Famer Luke Appling that year. Although Travis was able to out-hit Gehrig (.295), Gehringer (.308) and DiMaggio (.324), he finished behind Jimmie Foxx and teammate Buddy Myer for the batting title.

Among Cecil Travis' career stats, the year 1939 seems out of place with the standards he attained earlier in his career. His batting average plummeted to a un-Travis like .292 in 1939 — however, only Hall of Famers Appling, Arky Vaughan and Cronin could top that mark among shortstops. Although Cecil Travis was never a man to offer excuses for poor play, he battled through a severe bout of influenza during the season. Of Travis' 1939 season, Paul Scheffels wrote, "His normal weight hovers around the 180-pound mark but that year influenza germs made his 6-foot-2-inch frame decidedly gaunt. Nevertheless, he registered a batting mark of .292 that several of the circuit's top-flight infielding stars would be hard put to match."

Putting a subpar 1939 season behind him, Travis returned to form in 1940. He raised his batting average to .322 — 22 points higher than position peer and Hall of Famer Arky Vaughan. His .445 Slugging average was better than every American League infielder on the left side of the diamond except for Hall of Famer Joe Cronin and big bat Harlond Clift. His Slugging average was better than Hall of Fame infielders Appling, Lou Boudreau, Pee Wee Reese and Billy Herman. But as good as Travis was in 1940, he was only beginning to warm up.

The year of 1941 is famous for two offensive milestones in the American League: Joe DiMaggio's 56-game hitting streak and Ted Williams' road to .400. However, it may come as a surprise to many readers that neither Joltin' Joe nor the Splendid Splinter paced the American League in hits that year. The leader was that fellow from Georgia, Cecil Howell Travis. Travis closed out the year with 218 base hits, far more than DiMaggio's 193 or Williams' 185. Had Williams been out of the picture, Cecil would have copped the batting crown as well. Nevertheless, Cecil finished second in the batting race with a .359 average, two points higher than Joe DiMaggio's mark. Of his shortstop peers, Arky Vaughan's .316 batting average came in second to Cecil's superior ledger. Despite his amazing season, Travis still went unnoticed. A sportswriter known simply as "Pap" offered this explanation: "Everyone seems engrossed in Joe DiMaggio's batting streak and Ted Williams' Slugging for the Red Sox. The explanation must be that Travis fails to catch the eye because he goes about his chores without fuss or fanfare."

Cecil Travis was only 28 years old when he entered the armed forces in 1942. At that age, most players are entering their prime. However, Travis' prime years were spent in the military, as he took his American League-best 218 hits and remarkable .359 batting average and played service ball under Uncle Sam. One can only speculate as to how Travis would have performed in the majors during the years he lost to the war. It seems reasonable to account for batting averages near .320, but then again, that could be short-changing Travis given his astounding 1941 season.

Take a look at a handful of Hall of Fame infielders who were able to play out their careers uninterrupted. Randomly, I have chosen Travis Jackson, Pie Traynor and Nellie Fox. For this exercise, I will remove the years played of the aforementioned trio when they were of the ages 28 through 31—the years Travis lost to World War II. The statistical line on the left shows the players' career stats while the right side shows their stats after the alteration.

Travis Jackson's Stats

G	R	H	AB	AVG	G	R	H	AB	AVG
1,656	833	1,768	6,086	.291	1,286	650	1,394	4,735	.294

Pie Traynor's Stats

G	R	H	AB	AVG	G	R	H	AB	AVG
1,941	1,183	2,416	7,559	.320	1,382	827	1,667	5,338	.312

Nellie Fox' Stats

G	R	H	AB	AVG	G	R	H	AB	AVG
2,367	1,279	2,663	9,232	.288	1,747	894	1,897	6,717	.260

The above figure shows how losing prime years affects a player's stats. In the case of Travis Jackson, who began his career young before fading early, removing his "prime years" actually benefited him. However, it greatly hinders most players—note the drastic effect it had on Nellie Fox. When his prime years are removed, Nellie becomes a rather typical ballplayer. His solid .288 batting average fell 28 points when I took away the seasons in which he was 28 through 31 years of age. Cecil Travis missed out on his prime years, as he was awarded a Bronze Star and three Battle Stars, yet still posted enviable career statistics.

Due to playing three years after the war with legs that still suffered from his severe case of frostbite, Travis' career batting average plummeted from .327, alongside Honus Wagner, to .314, just above Hughie Jennings and Joe Sewell. Can anyone imagine the third-best hitting second baseman, Eddie Collins, not having a place in the Baseball Hall of Fame? Or perhaps the third-best hitting right fielder—Babe Ruth? Picture the Baseball Hall of Fame without the third greatest hitting first baseman, George Sisler, or the third-best hitting third baseman, Pie Traynor. As far as career batting averages are concerned, Travis ranks 63rd all-time, third among shortstops, with a number that eclipses many Hall of Fame players. Had Travis not played his entire career with that ominous "W" stenciled on his cap, he would have received better press and his name would be immortalized with the stars at Cooperstown.

Dom DiMaggio

"Everything in life is comparison, and by every comparison I can make, Dominic stacks up awfully well."—Ted Williams

Imagine being an aspiring screenwriter with a world of talent, possessing a brilliant mind, capable of creating scripts that are both clever and unique. You have found your calling in life. Now, imagine that you have an older brother in the same field. This brother has won numerous awards, a handful of Oscars and such, and is lauded as the best screenwriter in the movie business. Despite the sheer brilliance of your scripts, they are seen as inferior to your more popular and already established older brother. Regardless of the material you write, you will be seen as nothing more than the kid brother of a legendary screenwriter. This was the life of Dominic DiMaggio. He was forever stuck in the vast shadow cast by his charismatic and celebrated older brother Joe.

When Dominic DiMaggio made his debut in the major leagues, his brother, Joe, had led the American League with a .381 batting average the year prior. With the same last name as the best player in the league, Dominic wasn't allowed to come to the majors in obscurity. With veteran Doc Cramer entrenched in center field at Fenway, Dom became the Red Sox's right fielder in 1940, his rookie campaign. He had a solid initial season, hitting the apple at a .301 clip, however, that mark was 51 points behind Joltin' Joe. With Cramer gone in 1941, Dominic settled in at center field, the position he would hold throughout the rest of his career. He hit .283 while drawing 90 walks, a total that eclipsed all other AL center fielders.

In 1942, his last year before his military induction, Dominic hit .286 and posted more doubles than any center fielder in baseball. His all-around game was lauded by skipper Joe Cronin, who said, "He can field, he can run the bases and he can throw. They don't come any better." Joe also sang his praises, in a forlorn tone, by saying, "That little sonuvagun has robbed me of more base hits than any five outfielders in the league. Maybe there are some better outfielders around but I've never seen any."

The next three years Dom DiMaggio served in the navy and missed out on three important seasons when he was 26, 27 and 28 years of age. Many players begin to settle in during those years, even achieving their top production, but Dom DiMaggio wasn't so fortunate. However, after a three-year wartime layoff, Dom returned to Fenway and led all regular center fielders with a .316 batting average. With his return, as well as the return from the military of Ted Williams, Johnny Pesky and Bobby Doerr, the Red Sox handily won the American League, finishing twelve games ahead of second-place Detroit. In his only World Series appearance, Dom stroked three doubles—tops among Red Sox players—but suffered a sprained ankle that forced him out of Game Seven which set the stage for Enos Slaughter's "Mad Dash" home.

Dom DiMaggio went into 1947, his fifth year at the major league level, as a thirty-year-old man. Writer Oscar Fraley felt that the "Little Professor," as Dominic was known, was destined for greater things. Fraley wrote, "Naturally he has been in the shadow of his highly publicized brother ever since he came into the Majors, but he is coming into his own and yet may overshadow the Bronx Bombers' big man." The Little Professor led the American League with 648 at-bats in 1948 while also drawing 101 free passes. Among outfielders, only teammate Ted Williams, who led the league with 126 walks, drew more than Dominic. His 40 doubles were tops among baseball's center pasture guardians, as Hoot Evers finished second with 33 and Joe DiMaggio a distant third with just 26 two-baggers.

In 1949, Dominic hit .307, tops among American League center fielders with at least 275 at-bats. Once again showcasing his remarkable batting eye, Dom led all center fielders with 96 bases on balls. The Red Sox, who boasted two men with 159 RBIs—Ted Williams and Vern Stephens—finished a game behind the first-place Yankees. That year was the last time Dom DiMaggio came close to another World Series appearance. Despite the Red Sox slowly descending in the standings, the Little Professor was still productive. Dominic led the American League in runs scored and stolen bases in 1950 and tied for the league lead in triples with eleven. His batting average reached an all-time high of .328 as the 33-year-old Little Professor guided the Red Sox to a third-place finish.

He led the league in consecutive years in the runs scored department, as Dom crossed the plate 113 times in 1951. His 34 doubles also eclipsed the totals tallied by his position peers, and his 189 base hits finished two behind league leader George Kell. He retired early in the 1953 season, bowing out of the game while he was still a productive player.

A complete package, Dominic DiMaggio was a gifted defender as well as a reliable offensive force. He was a doubles machine who knew how to get on base, either by slapping a base hit or drawing a walk. Of Dom's defensive game, catcher Sammy White said, "Squatting behind the plate I see everything that happens on the field. I've watched Dom make impossible catches as casually as you light a cigarette."

Ted Williams stated that Dom "stacks up awfully well" when comparing him to Hall of Famers. The sensible way to compare players is with position peers—meaning ballplayers that played in roughly the same era and at the same position. A sensible individual would never compare Babe Ruth with Joe Morgan—the Babe played in the outfield during the 1920s while Morgan was a little second baseman in the 1970s. The chart below shows the career stats of Dom DiMaggio compared with those of fellow outfielders who played in roughly the same era.

Name	R	H	2B	3B	HR	RBI	BB	SO	AVG
Dom DiMaggio	1,046	1,680	308	57	87	618	750	571	.298
Hack Wilson	884	1,461	266	67	244	1,063	674	713	.307
Chick Hafey	777	1,466	341	67	164	833	372	477	.317
Lloyd Waner	1,201	2,459	281	118	27	598	420	173	.316
Joe DiMaggio	1,390	2,214	389	131	361	1,537	790	369	.325
Ralph Kiner	971	1,451	216	39	369	1,015	1,011	749	.279

Despite Dom and Waner's lack of power, Dom DiMaggio compares favorably with his peers. I should mention that his only *true* peer that is enshrined is his brother, Joe DiMaggio, meaning they played in the same era and also manned the same position. Of Dominic's other *true* peers, none have made the Baseball Hall of Fame, and none can hold a candle to the Little Professor. His *true* peers are a list of such players as Joe DiMaggio, Hoot Evers, Walt Judnich, Barney McCosky, Terry Moore and Pistol Pete Reiser. The chart below proves the DiMaggio brothers, Dominic and Joe, were in a class all to themselves.

Name	R	H	2B	3B	HR	RBI	BB	SO	AVG
Dom DiMaggio	1,046	1,680	308	57	87	618	750	571	.298
Joe DiMaggio	1,390	2,214	389	131	361	1,537	790	369	.325
Hoot Evers	556	1,055	187	41	98	565	415	420	.278
Walt Judnich	424	782	150	29	90	420	385	298	.281
Barney McCosky	664	1,301	214	71	24	397	497	261	.312
Terry Moore	719	1,318	263	28	80	513	406	368	.280
Pete Reiser	473	786	155	41	58	368	343	369	.295

Clearly, the DiMaggio Brothers separate themselves quite substantially from the rest of the pack. They are the only two to tally at least 1,000 career runs scored and 1,500 base hits. Joe, obviously, is in a class all to himself, but if a peer were to join him, it would be brother Dominic.

Now, let us revisit the chart that showcased the stats of his Hall of Fame peers. I will modify their career stats in the same fashion I did while conducting the same exercise with Cecil Travis. Dom DiMaggio missed the baseball seasons when he would have been 26, 27 and 28 years of age, so I shall alter the career stats of the Hall of Fame group to align them with the Little Professor, discarding the stats they produced when they were of the ages that Dominic lost to the war.

Hack Wilson's Stats

G	R	H	AB	AVG	G	R	H	AB	AVG
1,348	884	1,461	4,760	.307	915	579	953	3,160	.302

Chick Hafey's Stats

G	R	H	AB	AVG	G	R	H	AB	AVG
1,283	777	1,466	4,625	.317	907	474	984	3,212	.306

Ralph Kiner's Stats

G	R	H	AB	AVG	G	R	H	AB	AVG
1,472	971	1,451	5,205	.279	1,019	619	968	3,578	271

Now, compare the modified stats of the Hall of Fame gentlemen with the stats of Dominic DiMaggio. The modification removes three prime years from the men who did not miss these years to the military, which, in turn, makes them more comparable to the Little Professor.

Name	G	R	H	AB	AVG
Dom DiMaggio	1,399	1,046	1,680	5,640	.298
Chick Hafey	907	474	984	3,212	.306
Ralph Kiner	1,018	619	968	3,578	.271
Hack Wilson	915	579	953	3,160	.302

Maybe Ted Williams was selling Dom DiMaggio short when he said Dom "stacks up awfully well" when compared to Hall of Famers. The above figure proves that Dom is the one who casts the shadow that his enshrined peers reside in.

Appendix: Service Lists

During the two World Wars, there were only sixteen teams in the major leagues. The American League and National League had eight teams each at their command. While the wars were underway, teams kept "service lists" in order to keep track of their players in the military. These service lists weren't as all-encompassing as they would probably be nowadays. For instance, teams labeled only their major league players on their service lists, while each minor league team had its own service lists. So, Yogi Berra, who entered the military before his major league debut, was not on the Yankees service list, but his minor league club's list.

Listed below are the service lists of the sixteen major league clubs for both World Wars.

World War I

Boston Braves: Fred Bailey, Hugh Canavan, Rip Conway, Sam Covington, Dana Fillingim, Ed Fitzpatrick, Hank Gowdy, Bill James, Joe Kelly, Rabbit Maranville, Ray Powell, Wally Rehg, Art Rico, Hank Schreiber, Zeb Terry, Walt Tragesser

Boston Red Sox: Jack Barry, Jimmy Cooney, Del Gainer, Dick Hoblitzell, Hal Janvrin, Dutch Leonard, Duffy Lewis, Wally Mayer, Stuffy McInnis, Mike McNally, Paul Musser, Herb Pennock, Chick Shorten, Fred Thomas, Jimmy Walsh

Brooklyn Dodgers: Leon Cadore, Burleigh Grimes, Harry Heitmann, Jim Hickman, Ernie Krueger, Duster Mails, Lew Malone, Al Mamaux, Rube Marquard, Johnny Miljus, Clarence Mitchell, Jeff Pfeffer, Jack Russell, Ray Schmandt, Red Sheridan, Sherry Smith, Chuck Ward

Chicago Cubs: Vic Aldridge, Grover Alexander, Paddy Driscoll, Rowdy Elliott, Pete Kilduff, Bill Killefer, Fred Lear, Bill Marriott, Morrie Schick, Harry Weaver

Chicago White Sox: Eddie Collins, Red Faber, Pat Hardgrove, Joe Jenkins, Ted Jourdan, Tom McGuire, Fred McMullin, Swede Risberg, Jim Scott

Cincinnati Reds: Nick Allen, Rube Bressler, Pat Duncan, Morrie Rath, Dutch Ruether

Cleveland Indians: Josh Billings, Hank DeBerry, Joe Evans, Lou Guisto, Joe Harris, Ed Klepfer, Otis Lambeth, Guy Morton, Elmer Smith, Tris Speaker, Red Torkelson, Bill Wambsganss

Detroit Tigers: Joe Cobb, Ty Cobb, Johnny Couch, Ben Dyer, Howard Ehmke, Bert Ellison, Eric Erickson, Ira Flagstead, Harry Heilmann, Bill James, Willie Mitchell, Fred Nicholson

New York Giants: Fred Anderson, Al Baird, Jesse Barnes, Rube Benton, Waite Hoyt, Benny Kauff, George Kelly, Eddie Sicking

New York Yankees: Neal Brady, Howie Camp, Alex Ferguson, Ray Fisher, Bill Lamar, Bob McGraw, Ed Monroe, Wally Pipp, Muddy Ruel, Bob Shawkey, Ernie Shore, Walt Smallwood, Sammy Vick, Aaron Ward

Philadelphia A's: Walt Anderson, Gene Bailey, Ray Bates, Jimmy Dykes, Bob Geary, Pat Haley, Jing Johnson, Dave Keefe, Merlin Kopp, Otis Lawry, Elmer Myers, Rollie Naylor, Win Noyes, Socks Seibold, Whitey Witt, Tom Zachary

Philadelphia Phillies: Claude Cooper, Dixie Davis, Pickles Dillhoefer, Pat McGaffigan, Eppa Rixey, Ben Tincup, Possum Whitted, Frank Woodward

Pittsburgh Pirates: Fred Blackwell, Tony Boeckel, Hal Carlson, Buster Caton, Adam Debus, Bill Evans, Earl Hamilton, Charlie Jackson, Lee King, Ray Miller, Elmer Ponder, Ben Shaw, Casey Stengel, Hooks Warner, Billy Webb

St. Louis Browns: Wally Gerber, Baby Doll Jacobson, Ernie Koob, Les Nunamaker, Bill Rumler, Hank Severeid, Urban Shocker, George Sisler, Tod Sloan, Ken Williams

St. Louis Cardinals: Doug Baird, Tony Brottem, Walton Cruise, Marv Goodwin, Bruce Hitt, Oscar Horstmann, Jakie May, Dots Miller, Lou North, Jack Smith, Frank Snyder

Washington Senators: Eddie Ainsmith, Molly Craft, Doc Lavan, Joe Leonard, Mike Menosky, Horace Milan, Val Picinich, Sam Rice, Earl Yingling

World War II

Boston Braves: Chet Clemens, Ducky Detweiler, Bill Donovan, John Dudra, Tom Earley, Nanny Fernandez, Sam Gentile, Buddy Gremp, Jim Hickey, Art Johnson, Max Macon, Frank LaManna, Ray Martin, Johnny McCarthy, Frank McElyea, Gene Patton, Damon Phillips, Hugh Poland, Bill Posedel, Woody Rich, Skippy Roberge, Chet Ross, Bama Rowell, Connie Ryan, Johnny Sain, Sibby Sisti, Warren Spahn, Lou Tost, Lefty Wallace, Max West, Ace Williams, Tom York

Boston Red Sox: Mace Brown, Bill Butland, Paul Campbell, Tom Carey, Bill Conroy, Emerson Dickman, Dom DiMaggio, Joe Dobson, Bobby Doerr, Danny Doyle, Clem Dreiseward, Al Flair, Andy Gilbert, Mickey Harris, Tex Hughson, Earl Johnson, Roy Partee, John Pesky, Frank Pytlak, Jim Tabor, Charlie Wagner, Hal Wagner, Ted Williams

Brooklyn Dodgers: Rex Barney, Boyd Bartley, Jack Bolling, Bob Bragan, Al Campanis, Hugh Casey, Cliff Dapper, Dutch Dietz, Herm Franks, Larry French, Joe Gallagher, Chris Haughey, Ed

Head, Billy Herman, Gene Hermanski, Kirby Higbe, Gil Hodges, Roy Jarvis, Chet Kehn, Cookie Lavagetto, Gene Mauch, Cal McLish, Rube Melton, Eddie Miksis, Don Padgett, Pee Wee Reese, Pete Reiser, Lew Riggs, Johnny Rizzo, Lou Rochelli, Stan Rojek, Bill Sayles, Tommy Tatum

Chicago Cubs: Dale Alderson, Hi Bithorn, Cy Block, Zeke Bonura, Dom Dallessandro, Marv Felderman, Bill Fleming, Charlie Gilbert, Al Glossop, Emil Kush, Walt Lanfranconi, Mickey Livingston, Peanuts Lowrey, Red Lynn, Clyde McCullough, Russ Meers, Lou Novikoff, Vern Olsen, Whitey Platt, Marv Rickert, Bob Scheffing, John Schmitz, Joe Stephenson, Lou Stringer, Bob Sturgeon, Eddie Waitkus, Lon Warneke, Ben Warren

Chicago White Sox: Luke Appling, George Dickey, Ed Fernandes, Stan Goletz, Don Hanski, Val Heim, Myril Hoag, Ralph Hodgin, Jake Jones, Frank Kalin, Bob Kennedy, Don Kolloway, Dario Lodigiani, Ted Lyons, Gordon Maltzberger, Bill Metzig, Bill Mueller, Len Perme, Dave Philley, John Rigney, Roy Schalk, Dave Short, Ed Smith, Thurman Tucker, Ed Weiland, Leo Wells, Sammy West, Taft Wright

Cincinnati Reds: Joe Beggs, Ewell Blackwell, Lonny Frey, Lonnie Goldstein, Harry Gumbert, Bert Haas, Frank Kelleher, Jim Konstanty, Ray Lamanno, Ed Lukon, Bob Malloy, Max Marshall, Mike McCormick, Ray Mueller, Jack Niemes, Kent Peterson, Hank Sauer, Ed Shokes, Clyde Shoun, Junior Thompson, Johnny Vander Meer, Clyde Vollmer, Dick West, Ben Zientara

Cleveland Indians: Soup Campbell, Eddie Carnett, Pete Center, Jack Conway, Chubby Dean, Gene Desautels, Cal Dorsett, Hank Edwards, Harry Eisenstat, Red Embree, Bob Feller, Tom Ferrick, Jim Hegan, Ken Keltner, Joe Krakauskas, Bob Lemon, Ray Mack, Buster Mills, Rusty Peters, Eddie Robinson, Hank Ruszkowski, Ted Sepkowski, Gene Woodling

Detroit Tigers: Al Benton, Jim Bloodworth, Tom Bridges, Hoot Evers, Murray Franklin, Charlie Gehringer, John Gorsica, Hank Greenberg, Ned Harris, Pinky Higgins, Billy Hitchcock, Fred Hutchinson, John Lipon, Barney McCosky, Dutch Meyer, Les Mueller, Pat Mullin, Bob Patrick, Rip Radcliff, Hank Riebe, Birdie Tebbetts, Virgil Trucks, Dick Wakefield, Hub Walker, Hal White, Joe Wood

New York Giants: Jack Aragon, Morrie Arnovich, Dick Bartell, Buddy Blattner, Vic Bradford, Bob Carpenter, Harry Danning, John Davis, Hugh East, Charlie Fox, Sid Gordon, Andy Hansen, Dave Koslo, Whitey Lockman, Hugh Luby, Willard Marshall, Buster Maynard, Johnny Mize, Hal Schumacher, Ken Trinkle, Mickey Witek, John Wittig, Babe Young

New York Yankees: Norm Branch, Tommy Byrne, Spud Chandler, Bill Dickey, Joe DiMaggio, Joe Gordon, Randy Gumpert, Bud Hassett, Rollie Hemsley, Tom Henrich, Billy Johnson, John Lindell, Al Lyons, Hank Majeski, Steve Peek, Mel Queen, Phil Rizzuto, Aaron Robinson, Red Ruffing, Marius Russo, Ken Sears, George Selkirk, Ken Silvestri, Charlie Stanceau, John Sturm, Jake Wade, Roy Weatherly, Butch Wensloff

Philadelphia A's: Vern Benson, Herm Besse, Bud Blair, Charlie Bowles, Al Brancato, Norm Brown, Fred Caligiuri, Jim Castiglia, Sam Chapman, Lou Ciola, Tom Clyde, Joe Coleman, Eddie Collins, Crash Davis, Hal Epps, Everett Fagan, Dick Fowler, Ford Garrison, Bob Harris, Lum Harris, Rankin Johnson, Jack Knott, Bruce Konopka, Bert Kuczynski, Sam Lowry, Phil Marchildon, Ben McCoy, Ray Poole, Don Richmond, Bob Savage, Carl Scheib, George Staller, Pete Suder, Porter Vaughan, Elmer Valo, Jack Wallaesa, Johnny Welaj, George Yankowski

Philadelphia Phillies: Roy Bruner, Bill Burich, Jim Carlin, Dick Conger, Ben Culp, George Eyrich, Ed Freed, Lee Grissom, Granny Hamner, Ray Hamrick, Bill Harman, Frank Hoerst, Tom Hughes, Si Johnson, Dale Jones, Ernie Koy, Tex Kraus, Gene Lambert, Andy Lapihuska, Charlie Letchas, Tony Lupien, Hal Marnie, Joe Marty, Pinky May, Rogers McKee, Dee Moore, Emmett Mueller, Hugh Mulcahy, Moon Mullen, Dick Mulligan, Ed Murphy, Danny Murtaugh, Sam Nahem, Ron Northey, Ike Pearson, Bill Peterman, Ken Raffensberger, Schoolboy Rowe

Pittsburgh Pirates: Ed Albosta, Bill Baker, Russ Bauers, Bill Brandt, Bill Clemensen, Billy Cox, Elbie Fletcher, Huck Geary, Hank Gornicki, Jack Hallett, Ken Heintzelman, Roy Jarvis, Bob Klinger, John Lanning, Ed Leip, Fritz Ostermueller, Culley Rikard, Vin Smith, Bud Stewart, Billy Sullivan, Oad Swigart, Maurice Van Robays, Burgess Whitehead, Lefty Wilkie

St. Louis Browns: Pete Appleton, George Archie, John Berardino, Frank Biscan, Denny Galehouse, Joe Grace, Hank Helf, Hooks Iott, Walt Judnich, Chet Laabs, John Lucadello, Glenn McQuillen, Al Milnar, Maury Newlin, Fred Sanford, Hank Schmulbach, Chuck Stevens, Steve Sundra, Tom Turner, Al Zarilla

St. Louis Cardinals: John Beazley, Al Brazle, Jimmy Brown, Walker Cooper, Creepy Crespi, Jeff Cross, Murry Dickson, Erv Dusak, John Grodzicki, Lou Klein, Howie Krist, Max Lanier, Dan Litwhiler, Terry Moore, Whitey Moore, George Munger, Stan Musial, Earl Naylor, Howie Pollet, Fred Schmidt, Walt Sessi, Enos Slaughter, Harry Walker, Ernie White, Johnny Wyrostek

Washington Senators: Red Anderson, Lou Bevil, Bruce Campbell, Milo Candini, Frank Croucher, Vern Curtis, Jake Early, Al Evans, Stan Galle, Sid Hudson, Alex Kampouris, Bill Kennedy, Al Kvasnak, Hillis Layne, Bill Lefebvre, Buddy Lewis, Jim Mallory, Walt Masterson, Phil McCullough, Jim Mertz, Ron Miller, Jerry Priddy, Sherry Robertson, Jack Sanford, Ray Scarborough, Stan Spence, John Sullivan, Lou Thuman, Cecil Travis, Mickey Vernon, Max Wilson, Early Wynn, Ed Yost

Bibliography

Books

Adomites, Paul, and Saul Wisnia. *The Best of Baseball.* Lincolnwood, IL: Publications International, 1996.

Adomites, Paul, et al. *Hall of Fame Players: Cooperstown.* Lincolnwood, IL: Publications International, 2005.

Bruce, Janet. *The Kansas City Monarchs: Champions of Black Baseball.* Lawrence: University Press of Kansas, 1985.

Cobb, Ty, and Al Stump. *Ty Cobb: My Life in Baseball.* New York: Doubleday, 1961.

Cohen, Richard M., David S. Neft, and Michael L. Neft. *The Sports Encyclopedia Baseball 2006.* New York: St. Martin's, 2006.

Dawidoff, Nicholas. *The Catcher Was a Spy: The Mysterious Life of Moe Berg.* New York: Pantheon, 1994.

Heaphy, Leslie A. *The Negro Leagues: 1869–1960.* Jefferson, NC: McFarland, 2003.

James, Bill. *Whatever Happened to the Hall of Fame?: Baseball, Cooperstown, and the Politics of Glory.* New York: Fireside, 1995.

Kirkpatrick, Rob. *Cecil Travis of the Washington Senators.* Jefferson, NC: McFarland, 2005.

Kirsch, George B. *Baseball in Blue and Gray: The National Pastime During the Civil War.* Princeton, NJ: Princeton University Press, 2003.

Lanctot, Neil. *Negro League Baseball: The Rise and Ruin of a Black Institution.* Philadelphia: University of Pennsylvania Press, 2004.

O'Neil, Buck, David Conrads, and Steve Wulf. *I Was Right on Time: My Journey from the Negro Leagues to the Majors.* New York: Simon & Schuster, 1996.

Purdy, Dennis. *The Team by Team Encyclopedia of Major League Baseball.* New York: Workman, 2006.

Ribowsky, Mark. *A Complete History of the Negro Leagues: 1884 to 1955.* New York: Citadel Press, 1995.

Riley, James A. *The Biographical Encyclopedia of the Negro Leagues.* New York: Carroll and Graf, 1994.

Terwilliger, Wayne. *Terwilliger Bunts One.* Guilford, CT: Globe Pequot, 2001.

Williams, Ted, and John Underwood. *My Turn at Bat.* New York: Simon & Schuster, 1988.

Online Sources

Baseball-Reference.com (http://www.baseball-reference.com)

New York Division of Military and Naval Affairs (http://dmna.state.ny.us/index.php)

Pa-Roots (http://www.pa-roots.com)

Society for American Baseball Research (http://sabr.org)

Periodicals

The Anniston (AL) Star
Bennington (VT) Banner
Bridgeport (CT) Standard Telegram
Des Moines News
The Frederick (MD) Post
Gettysburg (PA) Times
Lima (OH) Daily News
The Lowell (MA) Sun
Oakland Tribune
The Ogden (UT) Standard
Oil City (PA) Blizzard
Olean (NY) Evening Herald
Racine (WI) Journal News
The San Antonio Light
The Sheboygan (WI) Press
Stars and Stripes
Syracuse Herald
The Washington Post
Waterloo (IA) Evening Courier
Yank, the Army Weekly
Zanesville (OH) Signal

Interviews

Bartirome, Tony. Telephone Interview. April 2007.
Brancato, Al. Telephone Interview. June 2007.
Carnett, Eddie. Personal Interview. February 2007.
Chaney, Darrel. Telephone Interview. January 2011.
Dapper, Cliff. Telephone Interview. August 2007.
DiMaggio, Dominic. Telephone Interview. February 2007.
Doerr, Bobby. Telephone Interview. July 2007.
Durham, Joe. Telephone Interview. August 2007.
Gorin, Charles. Telephone Interview. January 2011.
Heim, Val. Personal Interview. March 2007.
Herbert, Ray. Telephone Interview. April 2007.
Hudson, Sid. Telephone Interview. March 2007.
Knowles, Darold. Telephone Interview. March 2007.
Korcheck, Steve. Telephone Interview. March 2007.
Layne, Hillis. Telephone Interview. February 2007.
Lodigiani, Dario. Telephone Interview. July 2007.
Massa, Gordon. Telephone Interview. June 2007.
Perme, Len. Telephone Interview. July 2007.
Porter, J.W. Telephone Interview. September 2007.
Savage, Bob. Personal Interview. March 2007.
Stevens, Chuck. Telephone Interview. April 2007.
Yankowski, George. Telephone Interview. May 2007.

Index

Aber, Al 218
Abernathy, Ted 218
Aberson, Cliff 60
Abrams, Cal 60
Acker, Tom 218
Adams, Bobby 60
Adams, Dick 60
Adams, Herb 218
Addis, Bob 60
Agganis, Harry 218
Ainsmith, Eddie 12
Akers, Bill 60
Alabama, USS 102
Alameda Station 235
Albosta, Ed 61
Albright, Jack 61
Albury, Vic 218
Alderson, Dale 61
Aldridge, Vic 12
Alexander, Bob 61
Alexander, Grover C. 12–13
Alexander, Matt 218
Algiers 114
All-American Girls Baseball League 56, 262
Allen, Ham 3
Allen, Nick 12
Allen, Tom 13
Allentown, Pennsylvania 116
Allison, Doug 3
Alston, Tom 61
Altizer, Dave 3
Amarillo Airfield 172
Ambler, Wayne 61
Anderson, Andy 61
Anderson, Ferrell 61
Anderson, Fred 13
Anderson, Red 62
Anderson, Sparky 256
Anderson, Walter 13
Andre, John 62
Andrus, Bill 62
Annapolis 105, 107, 132
Anniston, Alabama 10
Anson, Cap 5
Antietam 6, 8
Antonelli, Johnny 218, 230
Antonello, Bill 62
Anzio 185–186
Appenine Mountains 76
Appleton, Pete 62
Appling, Luke 62, 150, 263
Appomattox 8–9
Aragon, Jack 62
Archie, George 62
Ardennes 87
Ardizoia, Rugger 63
Ardmore Airfield 109
Arft, Hank 63, 149
Argonne Forest 16, 25–26, 43, 47

Arkansas, USS 51
Arlen, Richard 165
Arlington National Cemetery 5, 14, 46, 175
Arlington Pond 1, 9
Arnovich, Morrie 63, 176
Asheville, North Carolina 83
Aspromonte, Ken 219
Atkins, Jim 63
Atlanta Air Station 170
Atwell, Toby 64
Atwood, Bill 64
Augsburg 71
Austin, Henry 3
Australia 179
Avrea, Jay 64
Awkard, Russell 64
Aylward, Dick 64

Bad Kreuznach 254
Bahr, Edson 64
Bailey, Ed 219
Bailey, Fred 13
Bailey, Gene 13
Bailey, Sweetbreads 13
Baird, Al 13
Baird, Doug 13
Baker, Bill 64
Baker, Del 14, 49
Baker, Frank 219
Bamberger, Hal 64
Bamburg 253
Bankhead, Dan 64
Banks, Ernie 167, 219, 224, 262
Barber, Sam 65
Barclay, Curt 219
Barker, Alfred 3
Barkley, Red 65
Barnes, Jesse 14
Barnes, William 65
Barney, Rex 65, 88
Barnhart, Vic 65
Barnicle, George 147
Barrow, Ed 14
Barry, Jack 14, 95
Bartell, Dick 65, 189, 263
Bartirome, Tony 219
Bartley, Boyd 66
Bartosch, Dave 66
Basgall, Monty 66, 73
Bastogne 125
Bates, Ray 14
Battle Creek Reception Center 232
Battle of Bull Run 3, 7
Battle of the Bulge 71, 102, 125, 129, 136, 151, 154, 176, 192, 199, 201–202, 211, 262
Batts, Matt 66
Bauer, Hank 66, 222

Bauers, Russ 66
Baumann, Frank 220
Baumholtz, Frankie 67
Baxes, Mike 220
Bay, Harry 5
Beach Party Team No. 76 185, 252
Beard, Ted 67
Bearden, Gene 67, 250
Beaumont, Ginger 19
Beazley, Johnny 67
Beck, Rich 220
Becker, Charlie 14
Becker, Joe 68
Beggs, Joe 68
Behney, Mel 220
Behrman, Hank 68
Belanger, Mark 24
Bell, Bill 220
Bell, Jute 68
Bella, Zeke 220
Belleau Wood 43
Bengough, Benny 98
Bennett, Joe 14, 68
Bennett Airfield 214
Benson, Vern 68
Benswanger, William 143
Bentley, Jack 14
Benton, Al 68, 179
Benton, Rube 15
Berardino, Johnny 68
Berg, Moe 69
Berkenstock, Nate 4
Bernhard, Bill 7
Bernhardt, Walter 15
Berra, Yogi 69, 108, 125, 165, 233, 240
Berry, Neil 69
Berry, Tom 4
Berry Field 67
Berthrong, Harry 4
Bescher, Bob 53
Besse, Herman 69
Beverly, Fireball 220
Bevil, Lou 70
Bezdek, Hugo 15, 44
Bibby, Jim 220
Bickford, Vern 70
Bielaski, Oscar 4
Biittner, Larry 221
Bilbrey, Jim 70
Billings, Josh 15
Biot, Charlie 70, 212
Birdsall, David 4
Biscan, Frank 70
Bishop, Charlie 70
Bishop, Max 161
Bithorn, Hiram 70
Black, Bill 221
Black, Joan Lorraine 162
Black, Joe 70

Black, Lloyd 166
Blackburn, Jim 71
Blackburn, Ron 221
Blackwell, Ewell 71, 110, 136, 218
Blackwell, Fred 15
Blair, Buddy 72
Blair, Garnett 72
Blake, Ed 72
Blanchard, Johnny 221
Blatnik, Johnny 72
Blattner, Buddy 72, 121
Block, Cy 72
Bloodworth, Jimmy 72
Blue, Lu 15
Bluege, Ossie 81, 158, 200, 202
Blytheville Airbase 168
Blyzka, Mike 221
Bocek, Milt 72
Bockman, Eddie 73
Boeckel, Tony 15
Bois Frehaut 16
Bolden, Ed 49
Bolling, Frank 221
Bolling, Jack 73
Bollweg, Don 73
Bongiovanni, Nino 73
Bonura, Zeke 26, 73, 216
Boone, Ray 73
Bosser, Mel 74
Bostock, Lyman 74
Boston, USS 75
Bottarini, John 74
Bouchee, Ed 221
Boudreau, Lou 222, 263
Bougainville Theatre 193
Bowers, Billy 74
Bowers, Stew 74
Bowles, Charlie 74
Boxer Rebellion 3
Boyd, Ray 15
Boyer, Cloyd 74, 221
Boyer, Ken 134, 221
Brabender, Gene 222
Bracken, Doc 74
Braden, Kenny 258
Bradford, Bill 75
Bradford, Vic 75
Bradley, George 75
Bradshaw, George 75
Brady, Neal 15
Bragan, Bobby 75
Branca, Ralph 64
Brancato, Al 75, 135
Branch, Norm 75
Brandt, Bill 76, 135
Brandt, Jackie 222
Brantford, Ontario 105
Brazle, Al 76
Breadon, Sam 138
Brecheen, Harry 231, 247

Breckenridge, Bill 76
Bremer, Annie 6
Bremerhaven 220
Bresnahan, Roger 29, 39
Bressler, Rube 15
Bressoud, Eddie 222
Brest 132
Brett, George 1, 238
Brewer, Tom 222
Brideweser, Jim 76
Bridges, Tommy 76, 195, 202, 263
Bridwell, Al 35
Briggs, Otto 16
Brill, Bob 252
Brinkopf, Leon 222
Brissie, Lou 76
Bristow, George 4
Brittin, Johnnie 77
Brodowski, Dick 222
Bronson Field 202
Bronze Arrowhead 87
Brooke Army Medical Center 225–226, 236, 240, 246, 257–258
Brooks Field 132
Broskie, Sig 77
Brosnan, Jim 222
Brottem, Tony 16
Brouthers, Dan 11
Brovia, Joe 77
Brown, Alton 77
Brown, Barney 77
Brown, Bobby 222
Brown, Hal 77
Brown, Jimmy 78
Brown, Mace 72, 78, 104
Brown, Mordecai 32, 34
Brown, Norm 78
Brown, Willard 78
Brubaker, Wilbur Dr. 76
Bruce, Janet 21
Brucker, Junior 78
Bruner, Roy 78
Bruton, Bill 78
Bryant, Lefty 79
Bucha, Johnny 79
Buckley Field 132
Buddin, Don 222
Budge, Donald 131
Buffalo Arms Corporation 108
Buhl, Bob 223
Bull Durham 91
Bumbry, Al 1, 223
Bunker Hill Training Station 171
Burbrink, Nels 79
Burdette, Lew 79
Burgess, Smoky 79, 148, 247
Burich, Bill 79

271

Index

Burk, Mack 223
Burma 144
Burnside, Pete 223
Burpo, George 79
Burr, Alex 16
Burris, Paul 79
Burrus, Dick 16
Burtschy, Moe 79
Busby, Jim 80
Bush, Bullet Joe 55
Bush, Pres. George, Sr. 152
Butland, Bill 80
Butler, Kid 16
Byrne, Tommy 80

Cadore, Leon 16
Caffyn, Ben 4, 16
Cain, Bob 80
Calderone, Sammy 224
Caligiuri, Fred 80
Cambria, Joe 147
Camp, Howie 16
Camp Adair 136
Camp AP Hill 230
Camp Atterbury 222, 227, 238, 254
Camp Battle 216
Camp Beale 63, 81, 99, 123
Camp Berkeley 134
Camp Blanding 158
Camp Bowie 31, 70
Camp Breckinridge 229, 235, 249
Camp Butler 138, 165
Camp Callan 168
Camp Croft 138, 197
Camp Crowder 76, 183, 195, 204
Camp Custer 33, 42, 72, 114
Camp Davis 120
Camp Devens 31, 55, 97, 143, 177, 179–180, 229, 239
Camp Drake 226, 230, 249, 255
Camp Edwards 136, 162, 206
Camp Elliott 96
Camp Forest 68
Camp Grant 41, 67, 120, 136, 156, 160, 181, 204
Camp Greenleaf 21
Camp Kearns 113, 140, 191, 195
Camp Kilmer 147
Camp Lejeune 231
Camp Livingston 61, 123, 177
Camp Maxey 139
Camp McCoy 72, 141, 151, 153, 176, 234
Camp McIntire 129
Camp Merritt 20, 55, 57
Camp Patrick Henry 196
Camp Pendleton 247
Camp Phillips 131
Camp Pike 22, 44, 50
Camp Reynolds 180
Camp Ritchie 141
Camp Roberts 96, 208, 212, 231
Camp Robinson 193
Camp Sendal 238
Camp Shelby 39, 73
Camp Shelton 68, 188
Camp Sheridan 51, 63, 98, 117, 156
Camp Sherman 20, 24, 32, 52

Camp Sibert 182
Camp Stoneman 233, 249
Camp Taylor 54, 56, 58
Camp Travis 36, 54
Camp Tyson 115
Camp Upton 26, 113
Camp Wheeler 95, 103, 175, 193, 201
Camp White 109
Campanis, Al 80
Campbell, Bruce 80, 126
Campbell, Paul 80
Campbell Soup 81
Canavan, Hugh 17
Candini, Milo 81
Cantillon, Joe 3
Cardines Field 165
Carey, Tom F.A. 81
Carey, Tom J. 5
Carlin, Jim 81
Carlisle, Lick 81
Carlsen, Don 81
Carlson, Hal 17
Carnett, Eddie 81
Carpenter, Bob 82
Carroll, Tommy 224
Carswell, Frank 82
Carter, Marlin 82
Cartwright, Alexander J. 6
Casablanca 207
Casale, Jerry 224
Cascade Mountains 119
Case, George 144–145, 179, 208
Casey, Hugh 82, 141
Cassini, Jack 82
Castiglia, Jim 82
Castiglione, Pete 82
Castleman, Foster 224
Castro, Fidel 124
Cathey, Hardin 83
Caton, Buster 17, 228
Cebu Island 9
Ceccarelli, Art 224
Cedar Creek 9
Center, Pete 83
Chambers, Cliff 83
Chandler, Happy 105, 149, 254
Chandler, Spud 83
Chaney, Darrel 1, 224
Chapel Hill 88, 119, 170, 184, 188
Chaplin, Bert 17
Chapman, Ben 123
Chapman, Harry 17
Chapman, Ray 5
Chapman, Sam 83, 137, 263
Chappell, Larry 17
Charles, Ed 224
Charleston, Oscar 17, 207
Cheney, Tom 224
Chesnes, Bob 83
Chiti, Harry 225–226, 246
Christensen, Bruce 225
Chu Lai 239
Church, Bubba 83
Churn, Clarence 225, 243
Cicotte, Eddie 22, 47
Cieslak, Ted 83
Cihocki, Al 84
Ciola, Lou 84
Cisar, George 84
Civil War 3–11
Clark, Allie 84
Clark, Edmund 5
Clark, Mel 84
Clark, Mike 84

Clark, Phil 225
Clark Field 201
Clarke, Fred 19
Clarke, Stu 84
Clarkson, Bus 84
Clemens, Chet 85
Clemensen, Bill 85
Clemente, Roberto 256
Clemons, Verne 17
Clift, Harlond 148, 263
Clyde, Tommy 85
Cobb, Joe 18
Cobb, Ty 1, 18, 22, 28, 39, 41, 46
Cobbledick, Gordon 176
Coble, David 85
Coble, Francine 259
Cochrane, Mickey 67, 76, 85, 154, 169, 172, 182, 202, 214
Cochrane, Mickey, Jr. 85
Cohen, Hy 225
Cohen, Jim 85
Cold Harbor 5
Cole, Dick 85
Coleman, Gordy 225
Coleman, Jerry 86, 225, 242
Coleman, Joe 86, 157
Coleman, Percy 5
Coleman, Ray 86
Coles, Chuck 225
Collins, Eddie 18, 86
Collins, Eddie, Jr. 86
Collins, Joe 86
Collum, Jackie 86
Colzie, Jim 86
Combs, Merrill 86
Comiskey, Charles 17
Comiskey, Dorothy 178
Congalton, Bunk 5
Conger, Dick 86
Conlan, Jocko 18
Connolly, Bud 87
Connolly, Ed 87
Connors, John W. 10
Connors, Merv 87
Conroy, Bill 87
Conway, Jack 87
Conway, Rip 18
Conyers, Herb 87
Cook, Rollin 18, 88
Cooke, Dusty 88
Coombs, Danny 225
Cooney, Bob 88
Cooney, Jimmy 18
Cooper, Bill 88
Cooper, Cal 88
Cooper, Claude 18
Cooper, Walker 88
Corbitt, Claude 88
Corpus Christi Air Station 83, 137, 157
Corvette Brisk 216
Cotter, Ed 88
Couch, Johnny 19
Coughlin, Dennis 5
Courtney, Clint 88
Coveleski, Stan 44
Covington, Sam 19
Covington, Wes 225
Cox, Bill 89
Cox, Billy 89
Craft, Harry 89
Craft, Molly 19
Craghead, Howard 89
Craig, Roger 226
Craig Field 146
Crandall, Del 226

Crane, Sam 21
Craver, Bill 5
Creeden, Pat 89
Creighton, Jim 7
Cremins, Bob 89
Crespi, Creepy 89
Crimian, Jack 90
Cronin, Joe 78, 170, 201, 263
Crosby, Bob 172
Cross, Jeff 90
Cross, Lave 134
Croucher, Frank 90
Cruise, Walton 19
Crump, Buddy 90
Crutchfield, Jimmie 90
Cuddy, Jack 204
Cullenward, Nelson 165
Culp, Benny 90
Cunningham, Ed 144–145
Curtis, Gene 19
Curtis, Vern 90
Curtis Bay 185

Dagmar 217
Dahlen, Bill 26, 53
Dahlke, Jerry 226
Daily, Jack 105
Daley, Pete 226
Dallessandro, Dom 90
Daniel Field 83, 92, 150, 211
Daniels, Bennie 226
Danning, Harry 91
Dapper, Cliff 91
Dark, Alvin 91, 97, 249
Daubert, Jake 41
Davie, Jerry 226
Davis, Crash 91
Davis, Dixie 19
Davis, Glenn 1
Davis, John 91
Davis, Ross 91
Davis, Sam 84
Davis, Tod 91
Davison, Mike 226
Dawson, Joe 19
Day, Leon 1, 91, 145, 164, 168
Dean, Chubby 92, 214
Dean, Dizzy 10, 63, 72, 107, 133, 162, 190, 201, 239, 243
Deas, Yank 19
DeBerry, Hank 19
Debus, Adam 20
DeBusschere, Dave 226
Deitrick, Bill 92
Dejan, Mike 92
Delahanty, Ed 10
Del Monte Pre-Flight School 88
Del Savio, Garton 92
Delsing, Jim 92
DeMars, Billy 93
Dempsey, Con 93
Dente, Sam 93
Derr, Johnny 144
Desautels, Gene 92–93
Detweiler, Ducky 93
Devine, Joe 133
Devlin, Jim 5
Devore, Josh 20
Dickerson, Clark 20
Dickey, Bill 69, 93, 133, 142, 179
Dickey, George 93
Dickman, Emerson 93
Dickson, Murry 94
Diering, Chuck 94
Dierker, Larry 226

Dietz, Dutch 94
Dillhoefer, Pickles 20
Dillinger, Bob 94, 190
DiMaggio, Dom 71, 94, 96, 156, 262–266
DiMaggio, Joe 54, 60, 83, 95, 134, 194, 214, 262, 264
DiPietro, Bob 95
Dismukes, Dizzy 20
Ditmar, Art 227
Dixon, Sonny 95
Dobens, Ray 95
Dobson, Joe 95
Doby, Larry 96
Doerr, Bobby 18, 96, 127, 265
Donaldson, John 20
Donlin, Mike 20
Donovan, Bill 96
Dooin, Red 43
Dorish, Harry 96
Dorsett, Cal 96
Dotterer, Dutch 227
Doubleday, Abner 6
Douglas Airbase 174
Downs, Bunny 21
Doyle, Danny 96
Doyle, Jacob 6
Dreiseward, Clem 97
Dressen, Chuck 108, 132, 233
Drew Field 197
Dreyfuss, Barney 40
Driscoll, Paddy 21
Dropo, Walt 97
Dudra, John 97
Duffy, Hugh 14, 41
Dunbar, Lee 197
Duncan, Frank 97
Duncan, Junior 97
Duncan, Pat 21
Dunlap, Grant 97
Dunn, Jake 97
Durham, Joe 227
Durrett, Red 97
Dusak, Erv 98, 137
Duser, Carl 227
Dyck, Jim 98
Dyer, Ben 21
Dyer, Eddie 60, 115, 119
Dykes, Jimmy 21, 132, 150, 193

Earley, Arnie 227
Earley, Tom 98
Early, Jake 98, 155
Earnshaw, Moose 98
East, Hugh 99
Easterling, Howard 99
Ebbetts, Charlie 16, 53
Eccles, Harry 21
Edgewood Chemical Center 250
Edisto Island 9
Edwards, Bruce 99
Edwards, Foster 99
Edwards, Hank 99
Edwards, Henry P. 28, 36
Eggleston, Mack 21
Ehmke, Howard 21
Ehrhardt, Rube 22
Einstein, Albert 69
Eisenhardt, Jake 99
Eisenstat, Harry 99
Elberfeld, Kid 263
Elder, Heinie 22, 99
Ellington Airbase 88, 106
Elliott, Rowdy 22

Index

Ellison, Bert 22
El Toro Base 225, 228
Embree, Red 100
Engel, Joe 143
Ennis, Del 84, 100
Ennis, Russ 22, 100
Epperly, Al 100
Epps, Hal 100
Erautt, Eddie 99–100
Erautt, Joe 100
Erickson, Don 227
Erickson, Eric 22
Ermer, Cal 100
Erskine, Carl 101
Esposito, Sammy 227
Eta Jima 226
Etten, Nick 144
Evans, Al 101
Evans, Bill J. 22
Evans, Bill L. 101
Evans, Joe 22
Evers, Hoot 101, 126, 265
Evers, Johnny 23, 27, 31, 34
Eyrich, George 101

Faber, Red 22
Fagan, Everett 101
Fain, Ferris 101, 156, 250
Fair Oaks 4
Faircloth, Rags 23
Falk, Bibb 102
Farragut, Adm. David 11
Farragut Naval Station 65, 128, 214
Fast, Darcy 228
Fear, Vern 102
Federoff, Al 102
Feinberg, Eddie 102
Felderman, Marv 102
Feller, Bob 2, 63, 101–102, 109, 121, 154, 182, 263
Ferguson, Alex 23
Fernandes, Ed 103
Fernandez, Frank 228
Fernandez, Nanny 103
Ferrarese, Don 228
Ferrazzi, Bill 103
Ferrell, Wes 91
Ferrick, Tom 103
Ferriss, Boo 103
Fewster, Chick 23
Field of Dreams 62
Fields, Red 103
Figueroa, Eduardo 228
File, Sam 103
Fillingim, Dana 23
Filmore, Joe 103
Finigan, Jim 228
Fisher, Ray 23
Fitz Gerald, Ed 103
Fitzgerald, J.V. 14
Fitzpatrick, Ed 23
Flager, Wally 104
Flagstead, Ira 23
Flair, Al 104, 137
Flanders 43
Flanigan, Ray 104
Fleming, Bill 104
Fletcher, Elbie 104, 180
Fletcher, Van 104
Flick, Elmer 5, 10
Flowers, Wes 104
Fodge, Gene 228
Fohl, Lee 28, 44
Folkers, Rich 228
Fondy, Dee 104
Fonseca, Lew 102
Ford, Ted 228

Ford, Whitey 229
Fort Banks 143
Fort Belvoir 231, 255
Fort Benning 66, 71, 152, 173, 209, 217, 229, 236, 241
Fort Bliss 74, 168, 220, 244, 259
Fort Bragg 90, 104, 120, 141, 155, 210–211, 241
Fort Campbell 133, 141, 223–224
Fort Carson 231, 240, 243–244, 250
Fort Chaffee 187, 222, 252
Fort Corcoran 7
Fort Dix 22, 34, 48, 57, 81, 84, 118, 152, 204, 222, 224, 231–232, 248, 257
Fort Eustis 118, 225, 239, 241, 243–244, 250
Fort Gordon 55–56, 80, 104, 170, 259
Fort Hamilton 105
Fort Hood 220, 244
Fort Huachuca 28, 44, 49, 245
Fort Jackson 123, 178, 218–219, 223, 226–227, 233, 236, 243, 257
Fort Knox 115, 144, 219, 250, 259
Fort Leavenworth 69
Fort Lee 62, 85, 117, 120, 193, 204, 225–226, 246, 248
Fort Leonardwood 72, 116, 223, 228–229, 233, 259
Fort Lewis 49–50, 63, 91, 166, 176, 238, 256
Fort MacArthur 169
Fort McClellan 158–159, 208
Fort McPherson 144, 201, 223, 225, 236, 243–244, 247, 254–255
Fort Meade 23, 160, 222, 238, 254
Fort Monmouth 219
Fort Myer 175, 219, 236, 246, 248
Fort Myers Gunnery School 178
Fort Niagara 116
Fort Oglethorpe 67, 135, 190
Fort Ord 226, 234, 237–238, 240–242, 244, 247, 250, 252, 258
Fort Pickett 221, 245
Fort Polk 230
Fort Richardson 229, 237
Fort Riley 89, 121, 141, 177, 206, 259
Fort Sam Houston 90, 125, 137, 221, 252, 257
Fort Sill 84, 171, 224, 253, 255, 259
Fort Slocum 23
Fort Sumter 3, 6
Fort Thomas 109
Fort Totten 164

Foster, Rube 39
Four Rivers Plant 40
Fournier, Jacques 37
Fowler, Dick 105
Fox, Charlie 105
Fox, Nellie 264
Foxx, Jimmie 80, 100, 104, 198
Fraley, Oscar 98, 125, 172, 265
Francona, Tito 229
Frankhouse, Fred 105
Franklin, Murray 105
Franks, Herman 105
Frazee, Harry 39
Frazier, Joe 105
Fredericksburg 6–7
Freed, Ed 105
Freitas, Tony 105
French, Larry 106, 229, 263
French War Cross 46
Frey, Carolyn 67
Frey, Lonny 106, 263
Fricano, Marion 106
Frick, Ford 106, 196, 206
Fridley, Jim 106
Friend, Owen 225, 229, 235
Frill, John 23
Frink, Fred 107
Frisch, Frankie 35
Froats, Bill 229
Frye, Charlie 107
Fullerton, Hugh 94
Fulmer, Washington 6
Furillo, Carl 107

Gabler, Frank 107
Gables, Ken 107
Gaedel, Eddie 80, 185, 252
Gainer, Dellos 23
Gaines, Jonas 107
Gaines, Nemo 107
Gaiser, Fred 24
Galan, Augie 106
Galehouse, Denny 107
Gallagher, Gil 24
Gallagher, Joe 107
Galle, Stan 108
Galloway, Bad News 24
Gamble, Lee 108
Gandil, Chick 32
Gans, Jude 24
Garagiola, Joe 108
Garber, Bob 229
Garcia, Mike 108, 218, 253
Gardner, Larry 22
Garrett, Wayne 229
Garrison, Ford 108
Garrity, Hank 108
Garver, Ned 108
Gautreaux, Sid 137
Geary, Bob 24
Geary, Huck 108
Gedeon, Elmer 109, 262
Gehrig, Lou 46, 181
Gehringer, Charlie 93, 101, 109, 140, 188, 209
Gehrman, Paul 109
Geislinger, Germany 212
Genewich, Joe 24, 109
Genovese, George 109
Gentile, Sam 109
Georgia, USS 48
Gerber, Wally 24
Gessner, Charlie 6
Gettysburg 5–6, 8
GI Had Fun 63
Gibson, Josh 49, 78
Giebell, Floyd 109
Giel, Paul 229
Gilbert, Andy 110
Gilbert, Charlie 110
Giles, Warren 205
Gill, Ed 24

Ginsburg, Joe 110
Gionfriddo, Al 110
Gladd, Jim 110
Gladu, Roland 110
Glaviano, Tom 110
Gleason, Billy 24
Gleason, Roy 229
Gleeson, Jim 110
Gleich, Frank 24
Glenn, Harry 25
Glossop, Al 110, 172
Goeppingen 255
Goggin, Chuck 230
Goldstein, Izzy 111
Goldstein, Lonnie 111
Goletz, Stan 111, 133
Goltz, David 230
Gonzales, Joe 111
Goodman, Billy 111
Goodwin, Clyde 25
Goodwin, Marv 25
Goolsby, Ray 111
Gordon, Joe 111
Gordon, Sid 112
Gorin, Charlie 1, 112, 230
Gorman, Herb 112
Gorman, Tom A. 112
Gorman, Tom D. 112
Gornicki, Hank 113
Gorsica, Johnny 113
Goulait, Ted 25
Gowdy, Hank 25, 55, 154
Graber, Rod 230
Grace, Joe 113
Graff, Milt 230
Graham, Jack 113
Grand Island Airfield 81
Grant, Eddie 1, 25
Grant, Leroy 26
Grasso, Mickey 113
Gray, Dick 230
Gray, Milt 113
Gray, Pete 84
Gray, Ted 113
Grayson, Harry 20, 119, 158, 166, 237
Greason, Bill 114, 231
Great Lakes Security Watch 182
Green, Lenny 231, 244
Greenberg, Hank 60, 114, 206, 213
Greene, Joe 114
Greengrass, Jim 114, 242
Greenig, John 6
Greenland 141
Greensboro ORD 82, 108
Gregory, Howie 26
Gremp, Buddy 115, 184
Griffin, Doug 231, 235
Griffith, Bob 115
Griffith, Clark 24, 36, 48, 190, 201, 263
Grim, Bob 231
Grimes, Burleigh 26
Grimes, John 6, 26
Grimm, Charlie 87, 156
Grissom, Lee 115
Groat, Dick 231, 263
Grob, Conrad 231, 238
Grodzicki, Johnny 115
Groskloss, Howdy 115
Grove, Lefty 115
Guadalcanal 97, 198
Guam 103, 143, 147, 157, 178, 181, 194, 208
Guenther, Jack 102
Guintini, Ben 115

Guisto, Lou 26
Gulfport Training Center 121
Gumbert, Harry 116
Gumpert, Randy 116
Gwynn, Tony 1, 256

Haas, Bert 116
Haas, Bruno 26
Habenicht, Bob 116
Hack, Stan 62, 134, 155, 255
Haddix, Harvey 231
Hadley, Bump 85
Hafey, Chick 265, 266
Hahn, Dick 116
Hajduk, Chet 116, 181
Halas, George 27
Haley, Pat 27
Halifax Bomber 153
Hall, Bob 116
Hall, John 116
Hallahan, Wild Bill 116
Hallett, Jack 117
Halliday, Newt 27
Hamby, Jim 117
Hamilton, Earl 27
Hamner, Granny 117
Hampton Roads Station 102
Hamrick, Ray 117
Hancken, Buddy 117
Hand, Jack 103, 128
Hanebrink, Harry 117
Hanlon, Ned 9, 11
Hannah, Truck 49
Hanning, Loy 117
Hansen, Doug 232
Hanski, Don 117
Hanson, Earl 27
Hanson, Harry 27
Harder, Mel 228
Hardgrove, Pat 27
Hardy, Paul 117
Harman, Bill 117
Harpers Ferry 9
Harrington, Billy 232
Harrington Dog Track 137
Harris, Bob 118
Harris, Bucky 263
Harris, Herb 118
Harris, Joe 27, 43
Harris, Lum 118
Harris, Mickey 118, 161
Harris, Ned 118
Harshany, Sam 118
Hartje, Christian 118
Hartnett, Gabby 74
Hartsfield, Roy 119
Hartung, Clint 119
Haslin, Mickey 119
Hassett, Buddy 119
Hasson, Gene 119
Hastings, Scott 6
Hatcher's Run 5
Hatfield, Fred 120
Hatton, Grady 108, 120
Hauger, Art 120
Haughey, Chris 120
Haugstad, Phil 120
Hawkins, Lemuel 28, 199
Head, Ed 120
Heaphy, Leslie A. 20, 70
Heard, Jay 120
Hearn, Ed 28
Hearn, Jim 120
Hegan, Jim 120
Hegan, Mike 232
Heidelberg, Germany 192
Heilmann, Harry 28, 98

Index

Heim, Val 121, 139
Heintzelman, Ken 121, 232
Heintzelman, Tom 232
Heisenberg, Werner 69
Heitmann, Harry 28
Helena, USS 67
Helf, Hank 121
Hemsley, Rollie 121
Hennigan, Phil 232
Henrich, Tommy 122, 191
Henry, Preacher 122
Herbert, Ray 232
Herman, Babe 23
Herman, Billy 100, 119, 122, 174, 263
Hermanski, Gene 122
Herriage, Troy 232
Herrmann, August 21
Herzog, Whitey 233
Hess, Otto 6, 28
Hesselbacher, George 28
Hetki, Johnny 122
Hickey, Gen. Edward 236
Hickey, Jim 122
Hickey, Ruth 170
Hickman, Jim 28
Hicks, Buddy 122
Hicks, Joe 233
Hicks, Nat 7
Higbe, Kirby 108, 122
Higdon, Wild Bill 123
Higgins, Pinky 123, 223
High, Andy 29, 219
Hilcher, Whitey 123
Hill, Jesse 123
Hiroshima 91, 199
Hitchcock, Billy 123
Hitt, Bruce 29
Hittle, Lloyd 123
Hoag, Myril 123
Hoak, Don 124
Hobbs, Bill 29
Hoblitzell, Dick 29
Hock, Eddie 29
Hoderlein, Mel 124
Hodges, Gil 124, 263
Hodgin, Ralph 124
Hoerst, Frank 124
Hofman, Bobby 124
Hofmann, Bootnose 229
Hogue, Bobby 124
Holbrook, Sammy 124
Holland, Mul 124
Holloman, Bobo 125
Hollywood, Florida 183
Holt, Jim 233
Holtzman, Ken 233
Honiton, England 164
Hooks, Alex 125
Hooper, Bob 125
Hoover, Dick 125
Hopp, Johnny 89
Hopper, Bill 29
Horne, Billy 125
Hornsby, Rogers 19, 37, 201
Horstmann, Oscar 29
Houk, Ralph 125, 235
House, Frank 233
Houtteman, Art 233
Howard, Elston 167, 233
Howe, Cal 125
Howell, Dixie 126
Howell, Dixie E. 125
Howell, Roland 29
Howlett, George 4
Howser, Dick 240
Hoyle, Tex 126

Hoyt, Waite 29
Hrabosky, Al 234
Hubbard, Jess 30
Hubbell, Carl 115, 208
Hubbert, Jim 192
Huber, Clarence 30
Huber, Otto 126
Hudson, Dick 77, 103
Hudson, Sid 126, 198
Huenke, Al 30
Huggins, Miller 25
Hughes, Jim 126
Hughes, Long Tom 47
Hughes, Sammy T. 126
Hughes, Tommy 127
Hughson, Tex 127
Hulihan, Harry 30
Hunter, Herb 30
Huston, T.L. 43
Hutchinson, Fred 127
Hyde, Dick 234

India 64, 81, 83, 114
Indiantown Gap 187, 236
Iott, Hooks 127
Iran 205
Irvin, Monte 1, 127
Irwin, Walt 30
Isbell, Frank 44
Itzoe, Phil 65
Iwo Jima 84, 92, 128, 167, 178, 181, 216

Jackson, Charlie 30
Jackson, Joe 18, 48, 55–56
Jackson, Mike 234
Jackson, Travis 263–264
Jacksonville Training Center 107, 109
Jacobs, Tony 127
Jacobson, Baby Doll 30, 52
Jakucki, Sig 127
James, Bill 30
James, Seattle Bill 31
Janvrin, Hal 31
Jarvis, Ray 234
Jarvis, Roy 128
Jefferson, Willie 128
Jefferson Barracks 76, 89, 121, 135, 162, 177, 195
Jenkins, Joe 31
Jennings, Bill 128
Jennings, Hughie 22, 263
Jensen, Jackie 128
Jessee, Dan 128
Jewett, Nat 7
Johnson, Art 128
Johnson, Ban 51
Johnson, Bill 31
Johnson, Billy 128
Johnson, Bob 234
Johnson, Byron 128
Johnson, Caleb 7
Johnson, Connie 128
Johnson, Don 129
Johnson, Earl 129
Johnson, Ernie 129
Johnson, Footer 234
Johnson, Fred 31
Johnson, Heavy 31
Johnson, Jing 31
Johnson, Josh 129
Johnson, Ken 129
Johnson, Paul 31
Johnson, Rankin 129
Johnson, Silas 129
Johnson, Tom 31
Johnson, Walt 32

Johnson, Walter 10, 47, 102, 258
Johnson's Island 8
Joiner, Roy 130
Jok, Stan 130
Jolly, Dave 130
Jones, Art 130
Jones, Bobby 234
Jones, Dale 130
Jones, Gordon 234
Jones, Jake 130
Jones, Nippy 130
Jones, Percy 32
Jones, Sheldon 130
Jordan, Milt 130
Jordan, Niles 131
Jordan, Slats 7
Jourdan, Ted 32
Judnich, Walt 131, 147, 190, 265
Judson, Howie 131
Juelich, Red 131
Jumonville, George 131
Jungels, Ken 131
Juul, Herb 32

Kaefertal 237
Kahle, Bob 131
Kahn, Owen 132
Kalin, Frank 132
Kamm, Willie 174
Kampouris, Alex 132
Kane, Frank 32
Kaneohe Air Station 242
Karow, Marty 132
Karpel, Herb 132
Karr, Benn 32
Karst, Gene 244
Kauff, Benny 18, 32
Kavanagh, Charlie 32
Kazak, Eddie 132
Keane, Johnnie 220
Kearse, Eddie 133
Keefe, Dave 32
Keegan, Bob 133
Keeler, Willie 11
Keene, Jack 25
Keesler Field 60, 142
Kehn, Chet 133
Kelleher, Frankie 133
Kelleher, John 32
Keller, Charlie 95, 97, 107
Keller, Ron 235
Kellert, Frank 133
Kellner, Alex 134
Kelly, Big Bill 134
Kelly, George 33
Kelly, Joe 33
Kelly, Pat 235
Kelly Field 10, 12, 33, 138, 143
Keltner, Kenny 134, 181
Kenna, Ed 33
Kennedy, Bill 134, 137
Kennedy, Bob 134
Kenney, Art 134
Kenney, Jerry 235
Kenney, John 149
Kerksieck, Wayman 134
Kern, Jim 235
Kerns, Russ 134
Kibbie, Horace 134
Kibble, Happy Jack 33
Kiefer, Joe 33
Kiel 153
Kiely, Leo 235
Kilduff, Pete 33
Killefer, Bill 33

Killy, Dick 172
Kimbro, Arthur 34
Kimbrough, Larry 135
Kimmick, Wally 34
Kinder, Ellis 135
Kindle, Bill 34
Kiner, Ralph 135, 239, 265, 266
King, Lee 34
King, Lynn 135
King, Nellie 235
Kingman, Harry 34
Kirby, LaRue 34
Kirrene, Joe 235
Kirksey, George 207
Kirtland Field 74
Kish, Ernie 135
Klein, Lou 135
Kleinhans, Ted 34, 135
Klepfer, Ed 27, 35
Kline, Ron 235
Kling, Johnny 35
Klinger, Bob 135
Klippstein, Johnny 136
Knaupp, Cotton 35
Knickerbocker, Austin 136
Knickerbocker, Bill 136
Knott, Jack 136
Knowles, Darold 235
Kokos, Dick 1, 214, 236
Kolloway, Don 71, 136
Konikowski, Alex 236
Konopka, Bruce 136
Konstanty, Jim 136, 254
Koob, Ernie 35
Koosman, Jerry 236
Kopf, Wally 35
Kopp, Merlin 35
Korcheck, Steve 223, 236, 247
Korean War 218–261
Koshorek, Clem 136
Koski, Bill 237
Koslo, Dave 137
Kosman, Mike 137
Koy, Ernie 137
Kozar, Al 137
Kracher, Joe 137
Krakauskas, Joe 137
Kramer, Jack 137
Kraus, Tex 138
Krausse, Lew 138
Kravitz, Danny 237
Kreitner, Mickey 138
Kremer, Ray 12
Kress, Chuck 138
Kretlow, Lou 138
Krieger, Kurt 138
Krist, Howie 138
Kroh, Floyd 35
Krueger, Ernie 35
Kryhoski, Dick 138
Kubiak, Ted 237
Kucab, Johnny 139
Kucks, Johnny 237
Kuczek, Steve 139
Kuczynski, Bert 139
Kuhel, Joe 73
Kuhn, Red 36
Kush, Emil 121, 139
Kuzava, Bob 139
Kvasnak, Al 139

Labine, Clem 139
Lackland Airbase 227
Lade, Doyle 139
Lafata, Joe 139
Lafitte, Ed 36

Lajeskie, Dick 140
Lajoie, Nap 35
Lake, Fred 22
LaMacchia, Art 140
Lamanna, Frank 140
Lamanno, Ray 140, 197
Lamar, Bill 36, 140
Lambert, Clayton 140
Lambert, Gene 140
Lambert Air Station 139, 187–188
Lambeth, Otis 36
Lamline, Fred 36
Lamotte, Bobby 36
Lanctot, Neil 209
Land, Grover 37
Land, Harry 109
Landis, Bill 237
Landis, Jim 237
Landis, Judge K.M. 21, 32, 41, 73, 87, 168, 178
Landstuhl 261
Lane, Jerry 140
Lanfranconi, Walt 141
Lang, Don 141
Lange, Bill 11
Lanier, Max 141
Lanning, John 141
LaPalme, Paul 141
Lapan, Pete 37
Lapihuska, Andy 141
LaPointe, Ralph 141
Larkin, Ed 37
Larkin, Steve 141
Larsen, Don 237
Lary, Frank 237
Lasorda, Tommy 141
Latham, Arlie 37
Lathers, Chick 37
Latimer, Carter 193
Latimer, Scoop 77
Lau, Charley 238, 256
Lavagetto, Cookie 141, 233
Lavan, Doc 37, 142
Law, Vern 238
Lawing, Garland 142
Lawrence, Brooks 142
Lawrence, Frank 120
Lawry, Otis 38
Lawson, Bob 38
Lawson, Roxie 142
Lawson General Hospital 62
Layden, Gene 38
Layden, Pete 142
Layne, Hillis 1, 142
Layton, Les 143
Lazzeri, Tony 56
Lear, Fred 38
Leary, John 38
LeBourveau, Bevo 38
Lee, Bill 238
Lee, Billy 38
Lee, Robert E. 9
Lee, Scrip 38
Lefebvre, Bill 143
Lefler, Wade 38
Leggett, Joe 7
Le Havre, France 201
Lehman, Ken 238
Lehner, Paul 143, 211
Leighton Barracks 254
Leip, Ed 143
Leipheim 220
Lemon, Bob 143, 240
Lemon, Jim 238
Lenhardt, Don 143
Lennon, Bob 238

Index

Leon Springs, Texas 50
Leonard, Dutch 39
Leonard, Joe 39
Leovich, John 143
Lerchen, George 144
Letchas, Charlie 144
Levan, Jesse 144, 157
Leverenz, Walt 39
Levy, Ed 144
Lewis, Buddy 142, 144, 263
Lewis, Duffy 39
Lewis, Rufus 145
Leyte Invasion 102
Liddle, Don 145
Lido Beach 204
Lieber, Dutch 145
Lillard, Bill 145
Lillard, Gene 145
Lillis, Bob 237–238, 250
Limesy 201
Limmer, Lou 145
Lincoln, Abraham 4
Linde, Lyman 145
Lindell, Johnny 145
Linden, Walt 146
Lint, Royce 146
Lint, Wilma 146
Lipon, Johnny 80, 146
Litwhiler, Danny 146
Lively, Buddy 146
Livengood, Wes 147
Livermore Air Station 140
Liverpool 45
Livingston, Mickey 147
Lloyd, Pop 54
Loane, Bob 147
Locklin, Stu 239
Lockman, Whitey 147
Lodigiani, Dario 131, 147
Loes, Billy 239
Logan, Johnny 147
Lohrke, Jack 147
Lombardi, Vic 148
Long Beach Ferrying Command 91
Lonnett, Joe 239, 243
Lopata, Stan 148
Lopatka, Art 148
Lopez, Arturo 239
Lost Battalion 26
Lou Gehrig Stadium 255
Loudenslager, Charlie 39
Lowdermilk, Lou 39
Lowenstein, John 239
Lown, Turk 148
Lowrey Peanuts 148
Lowry, Sam 148
Lowry Field 211
Lubbock Flying School 144
Luby, Hugh 148
Lucadello, Johnny 148
Lucey, Joe 149
Lukon, Eddie 149
Lupien, Tony 149, 166
Lusk, Dorothy 252
Lutz, Joe 149
Lutz, Red 149
Luzon 123, 156
Lynn, Red 149
Lyons, Al 150, 182
Lyons, Ed 150
Lyons, Herschel 150
Lyons, Jimmie 39
Lyons, Ted 150, 169, 178

Maas, Duke 239
Macdonald, Bill 239
Mack, Connie 7, 16, 21, 27–28, 31, 44, 58, 75–77, 83, 103, 105, 136, 139, 145, 153, 185
Mack, Ray 150
Mackinson, John 150
Macon, Max 151
MacPhail, Larry 87
Maddern, Clarence 151
Maddox, Garry 239
Maddox, Nick 83
Madison, Dave 151, 239
Magee, Sherry 10
Magner, Stubby 39
Magnuson, Jim 240
Maguire, Jack 151
Mahoney, Tony 40
Mails, Duster 40
Main, Woody 151
Majeski, Hank 151
Malarcher, Dave 40, 263
Malinosky, Tony 151
Malis, Cy 151
Malkmus, Bobby 240
Mallory, Jim 151
Malloy, Bob 152
Malmberg, Harry 152
Malone, Ed 152
Malone, Fergy 7
Malone, Lew 40
Maltzberger, Gordon 152
Malzone, Frank 240
Mamaux, Al 40
Mancuso, Frank 152
Mangan, Jim 240
Manila 98, 108, 123, 140
Manning, Max 145, 152
Mantle, Mickey 221, 232, 244
Manville, Dick 152
Mapes, Cliff 152
Maple, Howie 153
Maranville, Rabbit 40, 228
Marchildon, Phil 105, 153
Mare Island 39
Margoneri, Joe 225, 240
Mariana Islands 111, 157
Maris, Roger 125
Markland, Gene 153
Markle, Cliff 40
Marnie, Hal 153, 170
Marolewski, Fred 240
Marquard, Rube 26, 41
Marquis, Bob 153
Marriott, Bill 41
Marsh, Freddie 153
Marshall, Chip 154
Marshall, Cuddles 240
Marshall, Max 154
Marshall, Willard 154
Martin, Barney 154
Martin, Billy 240, 250
Martin, Gene 241
Martin, Morrie 154
Martin, Pepper 84
Martin, Phonney 8
Martin, Ray 154
Martin, Whitney 69
Martinez, Buck 241
Martini, Carolyn 232
Marty, Joe 154
Martyn, Bob 241
Massa, Gordon 241
Masterson, Walt 75, 154
Mathews, Eddie 241, 259
Mathews, Fran 155
Mathewson, Christy 18, 41
Matthews, Denny 72
Mauch, Gene 155, 191

Maxwell Field 88, 146, 155
May, Jakie 41
May, Pinky 155
Mayer, Wally 41
Maynard, Buster 155
Mays, Willie 145, 219, 239, 241
McAleer, Jimmy 16
McBride, Dick 8
McCahan, Bill 155
McCall, Dutch 155
McCann, Richard 263
McCardell, Roger 242
McCarthy, Jerry 155
McCarthy, Joe 32, 93
McCarthy, Johnny 155
McClellan Field 156, 190
McCord, Butch 155
McCormick, Frank 149
McCormick, Henry J. 87
McCormick, Mike 155
McCosky, Barney 82, 156, 265
McCoy, Benny 94, 156
McCullough, Clyde 156
McCullough, Phil 156
McDevitt, Danny 235, 242
McElyea, Frank 156
McGaffigan, Patsy 41
McGlothin, Pat 156
McGraw, Bob 41
McGraw, John 7, 9, 13–15, 20–21, 26, 29–31, 34, 41, 51
McGuire, Tom 42
McInnis, Stuffy 42
McKechnie, Bill 74, 187, 203
McKee, Rogers 157
McKennan, Art 57
McLean, Al 157
McLeland, Wayne 157
McLeod, Ralph 157
McLish, Calvin 157
McMahon, Don 242
McMullin, Fred 42
McNabb, Carl 157
McNally, Mike 42
McNeely, Earl 42
McQuillen, Glenn 157
Meeks, Sammy 144, 157
Meers, Russ 157
Meine, Heinie 158
Mekong Delta 232
Melton, Dave 242
Melton, Rube 158
Memphis Ferrying Command 78, 178
Menosky, Mike 42
Merkle, Fred 35, 38
Merriman, Lloyd 158, 242
Merritt, Lloyd 242
Merson, Jack 158
Mertz, Jim 158
Metz, France 202
Metzig, Bill 158
Meusel, Bob 15
Meyer, Dutch 158
Meyer, Russ 158
Miami Beach 198, 201, 211, 215
Micelotta, Mickey 243
Middlebury, Vermont 29
Middleton, John 42
Miksis, Eddie 158
Milan 114
Milan, Horace 42
Miljus, Johnny 42
Miller, Bob 159

Miller, Dots 43
Miller, Hughie 43
Miller, Larry 243
Miller, Norm 243
Miller, Ray 43
Miller, Ronnie 159
Mills, Buster 159
Milnar, Al 159, 208
Minarcin, Rudy 225, 243
Mine Run 5, 8
Minner, Paul 159
Minnick, Don 243
Mississippi, USS 37
Mitchell, Clarence 43
Mitchell, Fred 24
Mitchell, Willie 44
Mitterwald, George 243
Mize, Johnny 100, 111, 135, 159
Mizell, Vinegar Bend 236, 243, 254
Modak, Mike 160
Mohardt, John 160
Moisan, Bill 160
Monchak, Alex 160
Monroe, Ed 44
Monroe, Marilyn 217
Monroe, Zach 231, 244
Monroe, Louisiana 72
Moore, Anse 160
Moore, Dee 160
Moore, Dobie 44
Moore, Euel 160
Moore, Ferdie 160
Moore, Red 160
Moore, Scrappy 44
Moore, Terry 118, 161, 177, 265
Moore, Whitey 161
Moran, Billy 244
Morgan, Bobby 161
Morgan, Tom 244, 250
Morgan, Vern 244
Morrell, Bill 161
Morris Field 81
Morse, Newell 161
Morton, Guy 44
Moschitto, Ross 244
Moser, Arnold 161
Moss, Howie 161
Moss, Mal 161
Motton, Curt 244
Mt. Olympus, USS 185
Mueller, Bill 161
Mueller, Emmett 162
Mueller, Gordy 162
Mueller, Les 162
Mueller, Ray 162
Muffett, Billy 244
Muir, Joe 162
Mulcahy, Hugh 78, 80, 104, 114, 137, 162, 254
Mullen, Moon 163
Mulligan, Dick 163
Mullin, Pat 163
Munger, George 163
Munson, Thurman 244
Munson's Hill 6
Murcer, Bobby 244, 262
Murmansk 67, 124
Murphy, Dick 245
Murphy, Ed 163
Murray, Jim 177, 211
Murray, Joe 163
Murray, Ray 163
Murtaugh, Danny 163
Musial, Stan 1, 127, 140, 161, 164, 203, 244

Musser, Paul 44
Mussolini, Benito 114
Myer, Buddy 72, 263
Myers, Elmer 44
Myers, Hy 33

Nagy, Steve 164
Nahem, Subway Sam 164
Naples 76
Naragon, Hal 245
Naton, Pete 245
Naylor, Earl 164
Naylor, Rollie 44
Necciai, Ron 245
Nehf, Art 25
Neighbors, Bob 164, 245
Nellis Airbase 257
Nelson, Rocky 164
Nevers, Ernie 165
New Guinea 104, 123, 126, 159, 163, 206
New York, USS 106
Newcombe, Don 231, 245, 263
Newfoundland 164
Newhan, Ross 72
Newkirk, Floyd 165
Newland, Russ 165
Newlin, Maury 165
Newman, Ray 246
Newport News Naval Station 55
Niarhos, Gus 165
Nichols, Chet 246
Nicholson, Bill 60
Nicholson, Fred 44
Nielsen, Milt 165
Niemes, Jack 165
Niemiec, Al 166
Nimitz, Chester W. 99
Norfolk Air Station 82, 91, 176, 190
Norman Naval Center 68, 179, 207, 213
Normandy 69, 78, 106, 136, 142, 170, 179, 188
North, Lou 45
Northey, Ron 146, 166, 246
Northey, Scott 246
Novotney, Rube 166
Noyes, Win 45
Nunamaker, Les 45, 53
Nuremberg 121
Nuxhall, Joe 170

Oak Ridge Military Institute 13, 16, 101
O'Brien, Eddie 246
O'Brien, Johnny 246
Ockey, Walter 166
O'Connell, Danny 246
O'Dell, Billy 236, 246
Odom, Dave 166
Oertel, Chuck 247
Oeschger, Joe 16
Offutt Airbase 222
Okinawa 77, 92, 109, 146, 175–176
Okrie, Len 166
Oliver, Tom 166
Olsen, Barney 166
Olsen, Vern 167
Olson, Karl 247
Omaha Beach 81, 154
O'Neil, Buck 1, 20, 167, 200, 263
O'Neill, Harry 167
O'Neill, Steve 15, 146

Onis, Manuel 167
Oravetz, Ernie 247
Oro Bay 63
Osteen, Darrell 247
Ostermueller, Fritz 167
Ostrowski, Joe 168
Ott, Mel 64, 104, 127, 238
Outlaw, Edith 165
Owens, Jim 247

Paddock, Del 45
Padgett, Don 94, 168
Page, Joe 195
Pagliaroni, Jim 247
Paige, Satchel 47, 84, 174, 194, 201
Paine, Phil 247
Palica, Erv 248, 257
Palm, Mike 168
Palys, Stan 248
Panama 118, 161, 173, 181
Panther jet 242
Papai, Al 168
Parisen, Otto 8
Parker, Harry 248
Parker, Salty 168
Parker, Tom 168
Parks, Bill 8
Parks, Charlie 168
Parnell, Mel 168, 220
Parris Island 43, 93, 139, 172
Partee, Roy 169
Patrick, Bob 169
Patterson, Daryl 248
Patterson, Pat 169
Patterson, Tom 8
Patton, Gene 169
Patton, Gen. George 65
Pavletich, Don 248
Pawelek, Ted 169
Pawloski, Stan 248
Payne, George 45
Pearson, Ike 169
Peek, Steve 169
Peel, Homer 176
Peete, Charlie 248
Peking 3
Pellagrini, Eddie 169
Pennock, Herb 45, 86
Pensacola Pre-Flight School 27, 105, 112, 202, 212, 230, 248
Penson, Paul 248
Perkins, Cy 169
Perkowski, Harry 170
Perme, Len 170
Perry, Mel 248
Perryville 3
Pershing, Gen. John 12, 38
Pertica, Bill 170
Pesky, Johnny 170, 193, 263, 265
Petacci, Clara 114
Peterman, Bill 153, 170
Peters, Rusty 170
Petersburg 8–9
Peterson, Kent 170
Petit Maujoy 55
Petty, Jesse 45
Pfeffer, Jeff 45
Philley, Dave 171
Phillips, Bubba 249
Phillips, Jack 171
Phlegar, Ben 223
Picinich, Val 46
Pickering, Urbane 171
Piechota, Al 171

Pierro, Wild Bill 171
Pigg, Leonard 171
Pignatano, Joe 249
Pilarcik, Al 249
Pilney, Andy 171
Pinkham, Ed 8
Pipp, Wally 46
Pippen, Cotton 171
Pisoni, Jim 249
Plank, Eddie 28
Plarski, Don 249
Platt, Whitey 172
Plews, Herb 226, 249
Podbielan, Bud 172
Podres, Johnny 249
Poffenberger, Boots 172, 216
Pohang 260
Poholsky, Tom 249
Poland, Hugh 172
Poles, Spot 46, 263
Polivka, Ken 172
Pollard, Nat 172
Pollet, Howie 172, 211
Ponder, Elmer 46
Pool, Harlin 173
Poole, Ray 173
Pope, Dave 173
Porter, Dan 249
Porter, J.W. 1, 233, 237, 250
Portocarrero, Arnie 250
Posedel, Bill 173
Posey, Cum 47, 99
Possehl, Lou 173
Post, Wally 242
Potter, Nelson 128
Povich, Shirley 202
POW Camp 71, 113, 125–126, 153, 190, 196
Powell, Bill 173
Powell, Bob 250
Powell, Ray 46
Powers, John 250
Pramesa, Johnny 173
Pratt, Al 9
Prendergast, Jim 173
Presidio 5, 50
Price, Jackie 173
Priddy, Jerry 173
Prothro, Doc 75, 193
Pullen, Neal 46
Pytlak, Frankie 174

Quantico 169
Queen, Mel 174
Quick, Hal 174
Quigley, E.C. 21
Quinlan, Finners 46
Quinn, Bob 98
Quinn, Wimpy 174
Quisenberry, Dan 234
Quonset Airbase 62, 165

Rabe, Charlie 250
Radcliff, Rip 174
Radcliffe, Double Duty 174
Raffensberger, Ken 175
Raines, Larry 250
Ramazzotti, Bob 175
Randolph Field 85, 102, 152
Raney, Ribs 175
Rapp, Earl 175
Rappahannock Station 5, 8
Raschi, Vic 175
Rath, Morrie 47
Reach, Bob 9
Redding, Dick 1, 47, 263
Reder, Johnny 175
Reed, Billy 175

Reed, Jack 251
Reeder, Bill 175
Reese, Jimmie 176
Reese, Pee Wee 176, 192, 263
Regan, Bill 47
Rego, Tony 47
Rehg, Wally 47
Reich, Herm 176
Reis, Tommy 176
Reiser, Pete 176, 203, 211, 265
Renfroe, Marshall 251
Repass, Bob 177
Republic Aircraft 183
Restelli, Dino 177
Reulbach, Ed 25
Rhine River 36
Rhona, HMS 133
Ribowsky, Mark 16, 92, 96
Rice, Hal 177
Rice, Sam 48
Rich, Woody 177
Richert, Pete 251
Richland Airfield 152
Richman, Milt 255
Richmond, Don 177
Richter, Allen 178
Rickert, Marv 143, 178
Rickey, Branch 18, 48, 180–181, 245
Rico, Art 48
Riddell, Nancy Jane 79
Riebe, Hank 178
Riggs, Lew 178
Rigney, Bill 178, 211
Rigney, Johnny 100, 178
Rikard, Culley 178
Riker's Island 5
Riley, James A. 78
Ripken, Cal, Jr. 24, 255
Risberg, Swede 22, 48
Ritchey, John 179
Rivers, Mickey 251, 262
Riviere, Tink 179
Rixey, Eppa 48
Rizal Stadium 206
Rizzo, Johnny 179
Rizzuto, Phil 174, 179, 248
Roach, Mel 251
Roanoke 8
Roarke, Mike 251
Robello, Tony 179
Roberge, Skippy 179
Roberts, Robin 180, 254
Roberts, Roy 48
Robertson, Charlie 48
Robertson, Don 251
Robertson, Sherry 111, 180
Robinson, Aaron 180
Robinson, Eddie 180
Robinson, Frazier 180
Robinson, Jackie 96, 127, 180
Robinson, Wilbert 20, 22, 34
Robinson Barracks 227
Rochelli, Lou 180
Rock, Les 181
Rock Island, Illinois 4
Rockefeller, Nelson 69
Roe, Preacher 64
Rogalski, Joe 181
Rogan, Bullet 49
Rogers, Lee 181
Rogers, Packy 181
Rojek, Stan 181
Romby, Bob 181
Rome 116, 186

Romonosky, John 251
Roseboro, Johnny 251
Roselli, Bob 252
Rosen, Al 181
Rosenthal, Si 181
Ross, Chet 182
Ross, Cliff 252
Ross, Floyd R. 252
Rosso, Frank 182
Rowe, Schoolboy 135, 172, 182, 263
Rowell, Bama 176, 182
Rozek, Dick 182
Rudolph, Don 252
Ruel, Muddy 22, 33, 49, 143, 263
Ruether, Dutch 49
Ruffin, Leon 183
Ruffing, Red 183, 209
Rumler, Bill 49
Runnels, Pete 183
Russ, William E. 240
Russell, Branch 49
Russell, Jack 49
Russell, Lloyd 183
Russo, Marius 144, 183
Ruszkowski, Hank 183
Ruth, Babe 27, 32, 49, 89, 143, 264
Ryan, Blondy 183
Ryan, Connie 183
Ryan, Jimmy 11
Ryan, Nolan 1, 256

Sacka, Frank 184
Sacramento Airbase 131
Saffell, Tom 184
Sailor's Creek 9
Sain, Johnny 184, 263
St. Augustine 135
St. Claire, Ebba 184
St. Davids, Wales 164
St. Die Sector 16
St. Mary's Pre-Flight School 109, 123, 166, 178, 186, 211
St. Mihiel 12
Salem, USS 39
Salvo, Manny 184
Salzburg, Austria 169, 240
Sampson Training Station 100, 136, 182–183, 202, 204, 216
San Antonio Cadet Center 90, 143, 159, 163, 191, 211
San Diego Marine Depot 228
San Diego Naval Station 112, 241, 259–260
Sandlock, Mike 184
Sanford, Fred 184
Sanford, Jack 184
Sanicki, Ed 184
San Juan Air Station 70
San Pedro 73
Santa Ana Airbase 60, 95, 172
Santo, Ron 134
Santop, Lou 49
Sarni, Bill 185
Saucier, Frank 80, 185, 252
Sauer, Hank 185
Saunders, Rusty 185
Savage, Bob 169, 185, 204, 262
Sawatski, Carl 252
Sawyer, Eddie 254
Sayles, Bill 186

Scarborough, Ray 186
Schacht, Al 50, 63, 69, 186
Schacht, Sid 186
Schacker, Hal 186
Schaeffer, Harry 186
Schalk, Ray 36
Schalk, Roy 186
Schallock, Art 186
Scheffels, Paul 263
Scheffing, Bob 187
Scheib, Carl 187
Schelle, Jim 187
Schenz, Hank 187
Scherbarth, Bob 187
Schick, Morrie 50
Schlei, Admiral 9
Schmandt, Ray 50
Schmidt, Bob 252
Schmidt, Freddy 187
Schmitz, Johnny 187
Schmulbach, Hank 187
Schneck, Dave 253
Schoendienst, Red 187
Schofield Barracks 31
Schoonmaker, Jerry 253
Schrader, Gus 160
Schramka, Paul 253
Schreiber, Hank 50
Schulmerich, Wes 187
Schulte, Johnny 50
Schultz, Bob 188
Schumacher, Hal 121, 188
Schwaebisch-Gmuend 222
Schwamb, Blackie 28, 188
Scott, Jim 50
Scott, Joe 188
Scott, Mickey 253
Scully, Vin 72
Sears, Ken 188
Seay, Dick 188
Sebring, Jimmy 19
Sehorn, Jay 42
Seibold, Socks 50
Selfridge Field 35
Selkirk, George 189
Seminick, Andy 132, 148
Sepkowksi, Ted 189
Serena, Bill 189
Sessi, Walter 189
Severeid, Hank 22, 50
Severson, Rich 253
Sewell, Joe 35, 51, 263
Sewell, Luke 167
Seymour, Cy 20
Shaner, Wally 189
Shannon, Wally 253
Shantz, Billy 189
Shantz, Bobby 189
Sharman, Ralph 51
Sharpe, Bob 189
Shaw, Ben 51
Shaw, Don 253
Shaw Field 203
Shawkey, Bob 51, 262
Sheely, Bud 189
Sheepshead Bay 143
Sheffield, Alabama 29
Shenandoah Valley 9
Shepard, Bert 189
Sheppard Field 65, 164, 245
Sheridan, Red 51
Sherman Field 197
Sherry, Norm 253
Shocker, Urban 51, 262
Shokes, Eddie 190
Shoop, Ron 254
Shore, Ernie 52
Short, Dave 164, 190

Index

Short, Phil 163
Shorten, Chick 52
Shoun, Clyde 181, 190
Shudt, Roy 202
Sick, Emil 166
Sicking, Eddie 52
Siebern, Norm 236, 254
Sievers, Roy 190
Silva, Danny 52
Silvera, Charlie 190
Silvestri, Ken 190
Sima, Al 191
Simmons, Curt 199, 254, 263
Simmons, Ted 254, 263
Simpson, Harry 191
Sioux Falls Airfield 66, 73
Sioux Indian Campaign 6
Sisler, Dave 254
Sisler, Dick 150, 191
Sisler, George 38, 52, 254, 263
Sisti, Sibby 143, 191
Skinner, Bob 255
Skinner, Edna 182
Skizas, Lou 222, 255
Slaughter, Enos 143, 191, 206
Sloan, Tod 52
Sloat, Dwain 191
Smalley, Roy 191
Smallwood, Walt 52
Smaza, Joe 191
Smith, Earl 52
Smith, Eddie 191
Smith, Elmer 52
Smith, Gene 192
Smith, Hal 255
Smith, Jack 52
Smith, John Ford 192
Smith, Paul 255
Smith, Sherry 53
Smith, Vinnie 192
Smyrna Airfield 146
Snider, Duke 192
Snider, Steve 61
Snyder, Frank 53
Sodd, Bill 192
Solomon Islands 123, 166
Sommers, Bill 192
Souchock, Steve 192
South Mills 8
Spahn, Warren 71, 96, 192, 262
Spangler, Al 223, 236, 255
Spanish-American War 3–11
Speake, Bob 226, 249, 255
Speaker, Tris 27, 45, 53
Spence, Stan 192
Spencer, Daryl 255
Spicer, Bob 193
Spragins, Homer 193
Squire, Hank 79
Squirrel Level Road 9
Stack, Kenneth 114
Stahl, Jake 3
Stalag III 113
Staley, Gerry 193
Stallcup, Virgil 193
Staller, George 193
Stallings, George 7, 13, 46
Stanceau, Charley 193
Stanley, Fred 256
Stanton, Leroy 256
Starr, Dick 193
Staunton Military Academy 17, 185
Stearns, Bill 9

Steinbacher, Hank 193
Stengel, Casey 28, 44, 53, 73, 125, 139, 179, 192, 259
Stephens, Vern 24, 84, 265
Stephenson, Bobby 256
Stephenson, Earl 256
Stephenson, Joe 193
Stevens, Chuck 194
Stevens, USS 112
Stewart, Bud 194
Stewart, Stuffy 53
Stine, Lee 194
Stirnweiss, Snuffy 146
Stock, Milt 37
Stockton Airbase 211
Stone, Eric 188
Stone, Tige 194
Stone's River 3
Stovall, Firebrand 58
Strang, Sammy 10
Street, Gabby 10, 53
Strickland, George 194
Strickland, Jim 256
Stringer, Lou 133, 194
Strong, Ted 194
Stuart, Dick 238, 256
Stuart, Gloria 165
Stuart, Marlin 195
Studley, Seem 10
Stuffel, Paul 195
Sturdivant, Tom 256
Sturgeon, Bobby 195
Sturm, Johnny 195
Stuttgart, Germany 221, 227, 256
SubPac Goldpanners 218
Suche, Charley 195
Suder, Pete 68, 195
Sullivan, Alex 26
Sullivan, Billy 195
Sullivan, Denny 54
Sullivan, Frank 256
Sullivan, John 196
Sullivan, Tom 54
Sulphur Springs, West Virginia 157
Summers, Champ 256
Summers, Lonnie 196
Sundra, Steve 196
Surkont, Max 196
Susce, George 257
Sutcliffe, Butch 196
Sutherland, Dizzy 196
Sweatt, George 54
Swigart, Oad 196
Szekely, Joe 197

Tabor, Jim 197
Tamulis, Vito 197
Tatum, Tommy 197
Tauby, Fred 197
Taylor, Bill 257
Taylor, C.I. 10, 20
Taylor, Harry 197
Taylor, Jelly 197
Taylor, Johnnie 197
Taylor, Sammy 257
Tebbetts, Birdie 65, 80, 126, 159, 191, 198, 218
Tekulve, Kent 234
Temple, Johnny 198
Templeton, Chuck 257
Tepsic, Joe 198
Terrell, Jerry 257
Terry, Zebulon 54
Terwilliger, Wayne 198
Tesreau, Jeff 30
Third Coal Exchange 4

Thomas, Claude 54
Thomas, Clint 54
Thomas, Fred 54
Thomas, Kite 199
Thomas, Leo 199
Thomas, Ray 199
Thomas, Roy 10
Thompson, Hank 199
Thompson, Jocko 199
Thompson, Junior 199
Thompson, Lee 54
Thompson, Tim 200
Thomson, Bobby 200
Thorpe, Ben 200
Thorpe, Jim 200
Throneberry, Faye 257
Thuman, Lou 200
Thurman, Bob 200
Ticonderoga, USS 79
Tierney, Cotton 54
Timberlake, Gary 257
Tincup, Ben 55
Tipton, Joe 200
Titus, John 10
Toenes, Hal 200
Tokyo Bay 91
Toledo Training Station 142
Tomasic, Andy 201
Torgeson, Earl 201
Torkelson, Red 27, 55
Torrance, Torchy 201
Torre, Frank 257
Tost, Lou 201
Totter, Audrey 69
Tragesser, Walt 55
Tramback, Red 201
Travis, Cecil 63, 71–72, 107, 142, 151, 174, 201, 262–265
Traynor, Pie 78, 263–264
Treadway, George 10
Treasure Island 65–66, 94, 101, 173, 189
Tremark, Nick 202
Trenton Airbase 153
Triandos, Gus 257
Trice, Bob 202
Trimble, Joe 257
Trinkle, Ken 202
Tripler Army Hospital 228
Trosky, Hal 81
Trowbridge, Bob 257
Troy, Bun 55
Troy, Phil 95
Trucks, Virgil 85, 202, 233
Truk 99
Truman, Pres. Harry 81, 91
Tucker, Thurman 203
Tunisia 113
Tunney, Gene 102
Tunney Program 83
Turbeville, George 203
Turley, Bob 258
Turner, Earl 203
Turner, Terry 35
Turner, Tom 203
Tutwiler, Elmer 203
Tyler, Clancy 55
Tyler, Johnnie 203

U-Boat 35
Upton, Bill 258
Urban, Jack 258
Usher, Bob 203
Utah Beach 91, 104

Vaihingen 252
Valentinetti, Vito 258

Valo, Elmer 93, 156, 177, 203
Vance, Dazzy 45
Van Cuyk, Johnny 204
Vander Meer, Johnny 204
Varner, Buck 258
Van Robays, Maurice 204
Vaughan, Arky 264
Vaughan, Porter 204
Veeck, Bill 173
Verdel, Al 204
Vernon, Mickey 179, 201, 204, 263
Vick, Sammy 55
Vico, George 205
Vierzy 43
Vietnam War 218–261
Vietnamese Cross of Gallantry 230
Villa, Pancho 38
Virgil, Ozzie 258
Vitelli, Joe 205
Vollmer, Clyde 205
Von Kolnitz, Fritz 55
Voyles, Phil 56, 205

Waco Airfield 80, 101, 126, 159, 191, 198
Waddell, Rube 40, 102
Wade, Jake 205
Waggin, Patti 252
Wagner, Charlie 118, 205
Wagner, Hal 205
Wagner, Honus 26, 56, 201, 262
Wahl, Kermit 205
Waitkus, Eddie 206
Wakefield, Dick 206
Wakeman, Ruth 164
Walczak, Ed 206
Walden, Fred 56
Walker, Harry 63, 206
Walker, Hub 142, 206
Wallace, Bo 258
Wallace, Lefty 206
Wallaesa, Jack 207
Walsh, Jimmy 56
Walsh, Junior 207
Walter Reed Hospital 40, 186
Walters, Ken 258
Walton, Tubby 263
Wambsganss, Bill 56
Waner, Lloyd 90, 265
Ward, Aaron 56
Ward, Chuck 56
Ward, Preston 258
Ward Island 132
Warneke, Lon 100, 207
Warner, Hooks 56
Warnock, Hal 207
Warren, Bennie 207
Warren, Tommy 207
Washington, John 207
Washington Monument 10
Watson, Johnny 208
Watts, Andy 208
Weatherly, Roy 159, 208
Weaver, Harry 57
Weaver, Monte 208
Webb, Billy 57
Webb, Melville, Jr. 17
Webster, Speck 57
Wehrmachters 63
Weigel, Ralph 208
Weik, Dick 259
Weiland, Ed 208
Welaj, Johnny 208

Wellman, Bob 208
Wells, Leo 208
Welmaker, Roy 209
Wensloff, Butch 209
Werle, Bill 209
Wertz, Vic 145, 209
West, Dick 209
West, Max 209
West, Sammy 209
Westlake, Wally 210
Westrum, Wes 210
Wheat, Lee 259
Wheat, Zach 41
Whinery, Gail 17
Whisenant, Pete 241, 259
White, Bill 259
White, Deacon 11
White, Ernie 210
White, Fuzz 210
White, Hal 210
White, Sammy 265
White, Warren 11
White, Will 11
White Oak Swamp 5
Whitehead, Burgess 210
Whitehouse, Charlie 57, 211
Whitman, Dick 211
Whitted, Possum 57
Wicker, Floyd 259
Wickware, Frank 57
Wiedemeyer, Charlie 211
Wiesler, Bob 259
Wight, Bill 211
Wilber, Del 211
The Wilderness 5, 8
Wiley, Doc 57
Wilhelm, Hoyt 211
Wilhelm, Kaiser 57
Wilkie, Lefty 212
Wilkinson, J.L. 20, 49
Willey, Carl 259
Williams, Ace 212
Williams, Almon 212
Williams, Bobby 57
Williams, Cy 16
Williams, Don 259
Williams, Earl 212
Williams, Jimy 260
Williams, Ken 58
Williams, Smokey Joe 47
Williams, Ted 1, 18, 76, 80, 94, 126, 145, 150, 154, 170, 191, 198, 204, 212, 236, 242, 260–265
Williamsburg 4
Wilmore, Al 212
Wilson, Archie 212
Wilson, Bill 260
Wilson, Eddie 212
Wilson, Emmett 212
Wilson, George 213
Wilson, Hack 265, 266
Wilson, John N. 58
Wilson, John S. 213
Wilson, Jud 58
Wilson, Maxie 213
Wilson, Mike 58
Wilson, Mutt 58
Wiltse, Hooks 30
Winceniak, Ed 260
Winford, Cowboy 213
Wingo, Ivy 13
Winsett, Tom 213
Wise, Archie 213
Wistert, Whitey 213
Witek, Mickey 213
Witt, George 260

Index

Witt, Whitey 58
Witte, Jerry 213
Wittig, John 213
Witzel 115
Wood, Joe 214
Wood, Ken 214
Wood, Smoky Joe 35
Woodeshick, Hal 260
Woodling, Gene 214
Woodward, Frank 58
World War I 12–59
World War II 60–217
Worthington, Red 214
Wright, Glenn 65, 214
Wright, Harry 4, 6
Wright, Johnny 214
Wright, Roy 260
Wright, Taft 108, 214
Wright, Tom 215
Wuerzberg 254
Wynn, Early 215
Wyrostek, Johnny 215
Yankowski, George 177, 215, 262
Yarnall, Rusty 215
Yellow River Gunnery School 146
Yingling, Earl 58
Yochim, Ray 216
York, Tony 216
Yorktown 4, 7
Yost, Eddie 216, 262
Young, Babe 216
Young, Dick 216
Young, W.B. 106
Youngblood, Al 58, 216
Yount, Eddie 216
Yuhas, Eddie 216
Yvars, Sal 216

Zachary, Tom 59
Zapp, Jim 217
Zarilla, Al 217
Zauchin, Norm 261
Zeber, George 261
Zernial, Gus 217
Zettlein, George 1, 11
Zientara, Benny 217
Zinser, Bill 217
Zouaves 5, 8
Zuverink, George 217
Zwickau 176